The Traveler's Atlas

A READER'S DIGEST BOOK

First published in Australia in 1998
Reprinted 1999
by Reader's Digest (Australia) Pty Limited
26-32 Waterloo Street, Surry Hills, NSW 2010

Project editor: Gilly Cameron Cooper
Copy editors: Gilly Cameron Cooper, Nigel Rodgers, Maggi McCormick
Design: Steve McCurdy
Cartographer: Julian Baker
Indexer: Dorothy Frame
Picture Research: Gill Metcalfe
Art Editor: Elizabeth Healey

A Quarto Book

National Library of Australia Cataloguing-in-Publication data
The traveler's atlas: a global guide to the places you must see in a lifetime.
Includes index.
ISBN 0 86449 349 5.
1. Travel—Guidebooks. I. Man, John.

910.202

Color separation by Universal Graphics Pte. Ltd., Singapore
Printed and bound by Star Standard Industries (Pte.) Ltd., Singapore

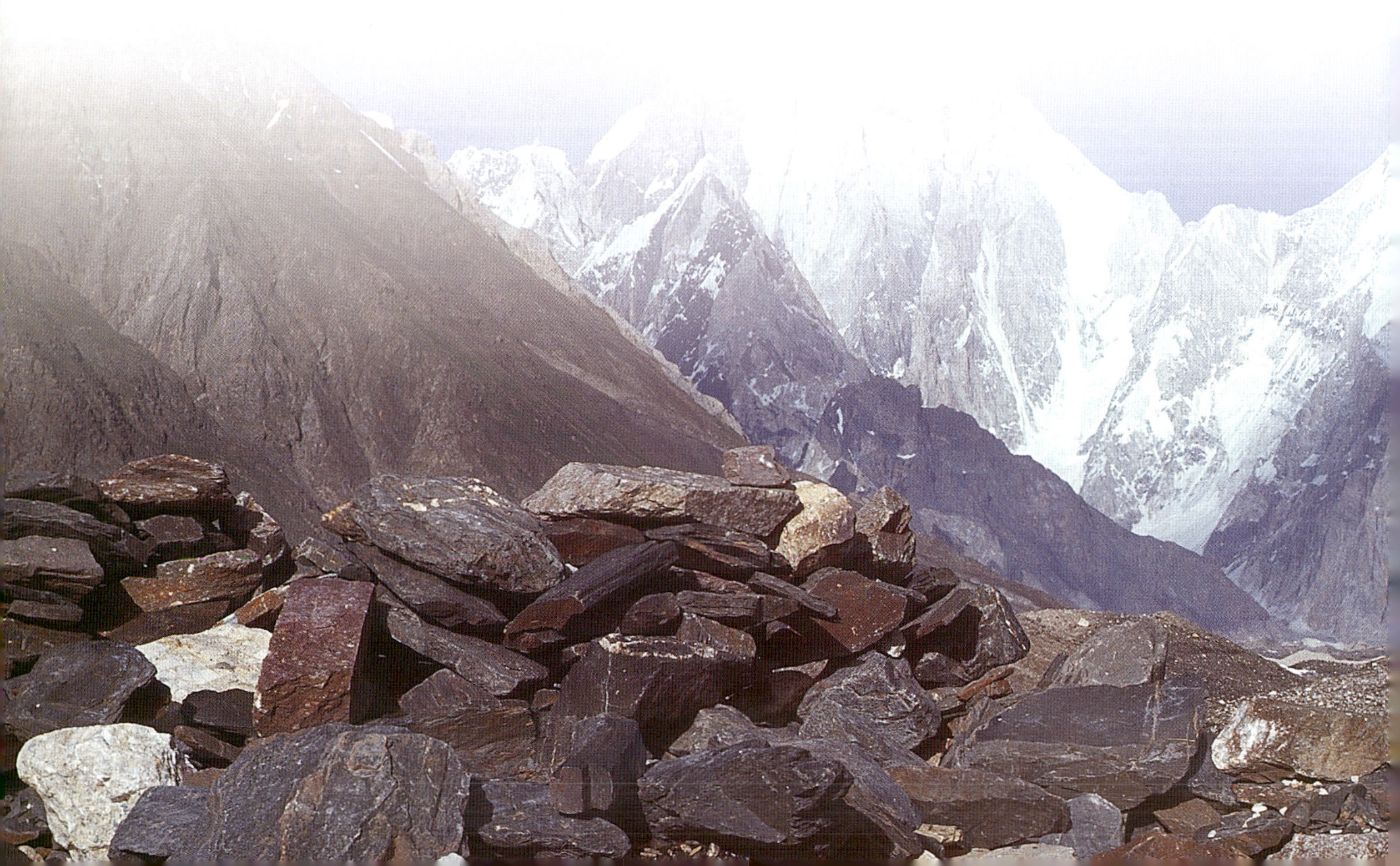

The Traveler's Atlas

A global guide to the places you must see in a lifetime

JOHN MAN • CHRIS SCHÜLER
GEOFFREY ROY • NIGEL RODGERS

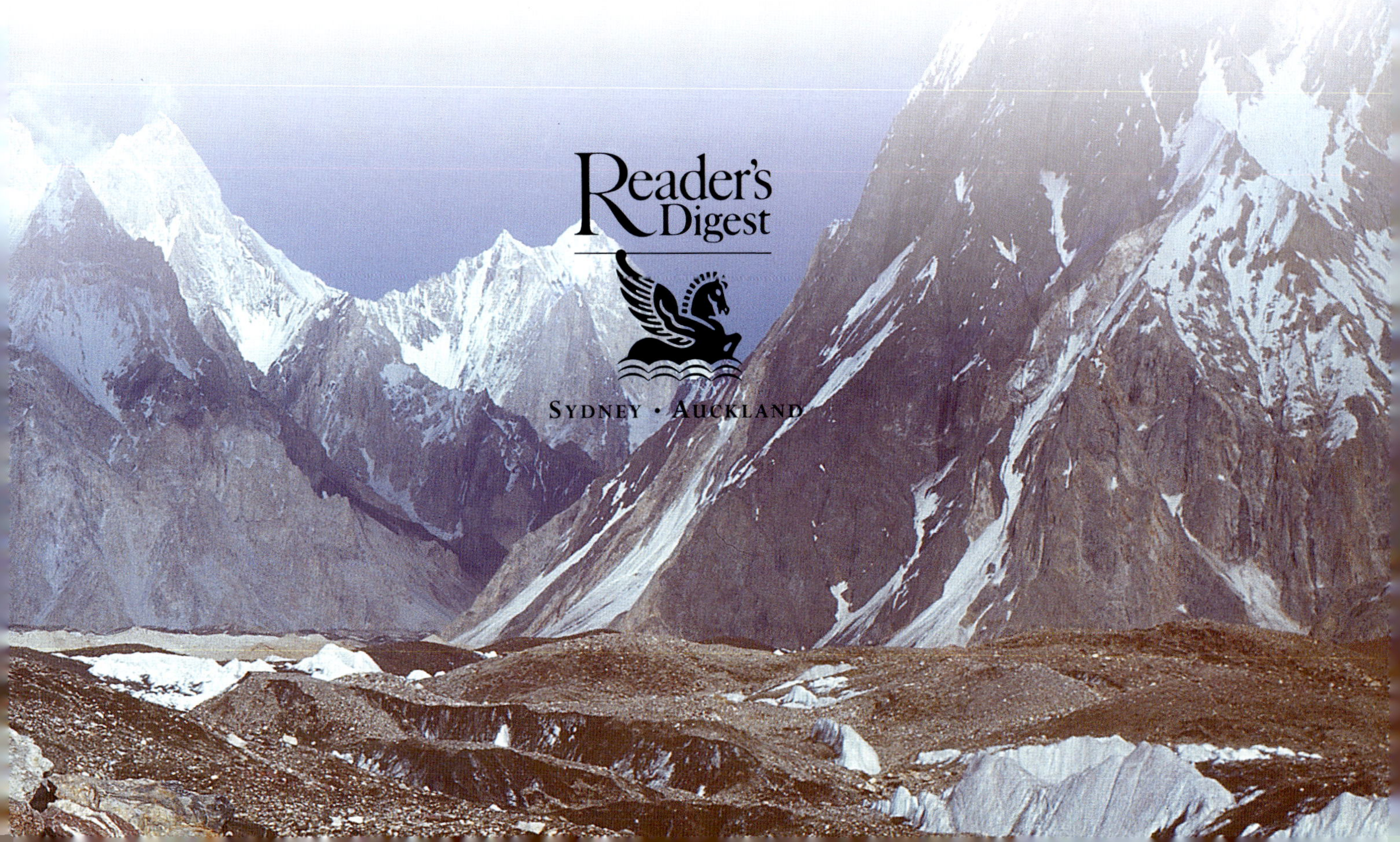

Reader's Digest
SYDNEY • AUCKLAND

Contents

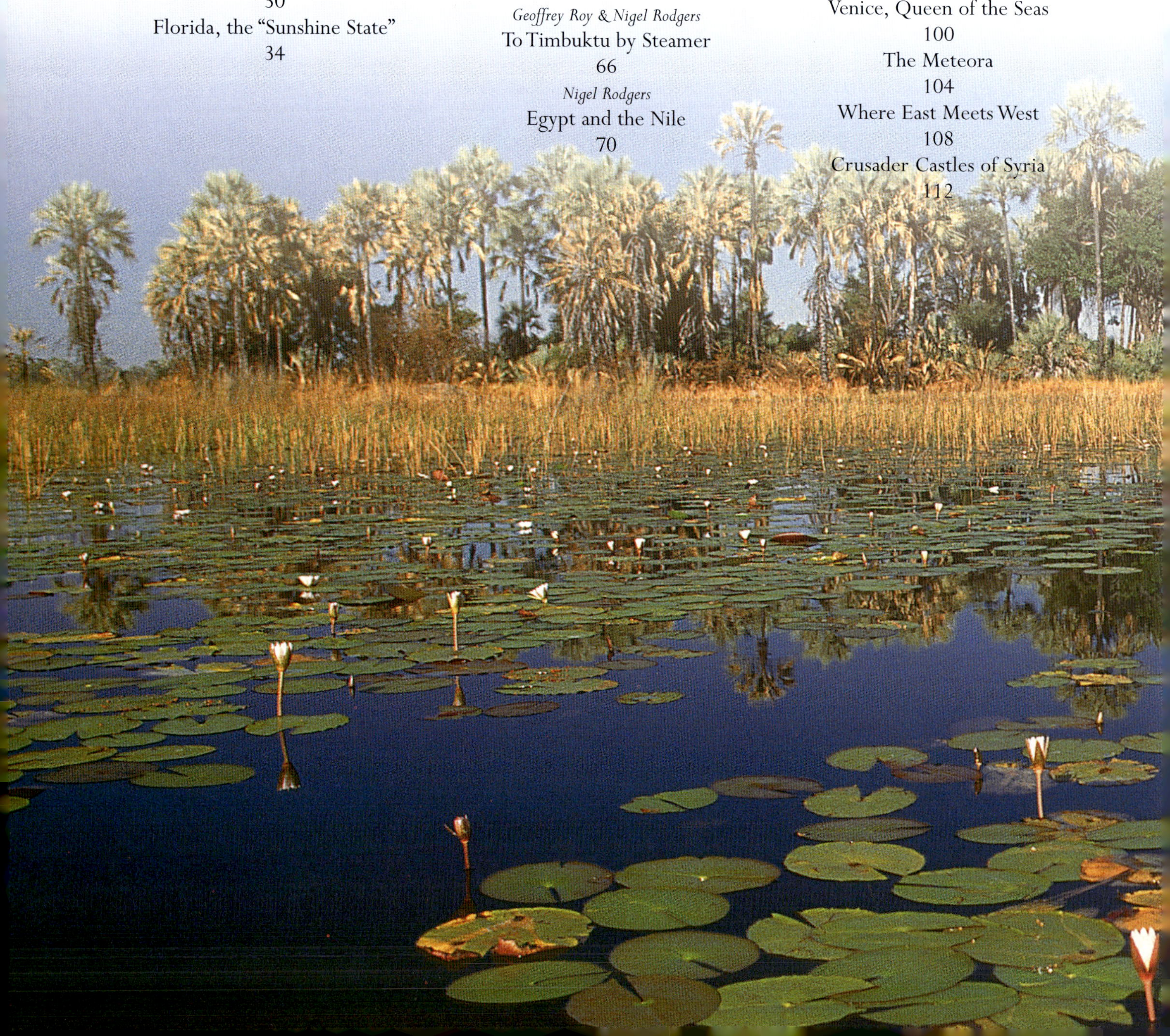

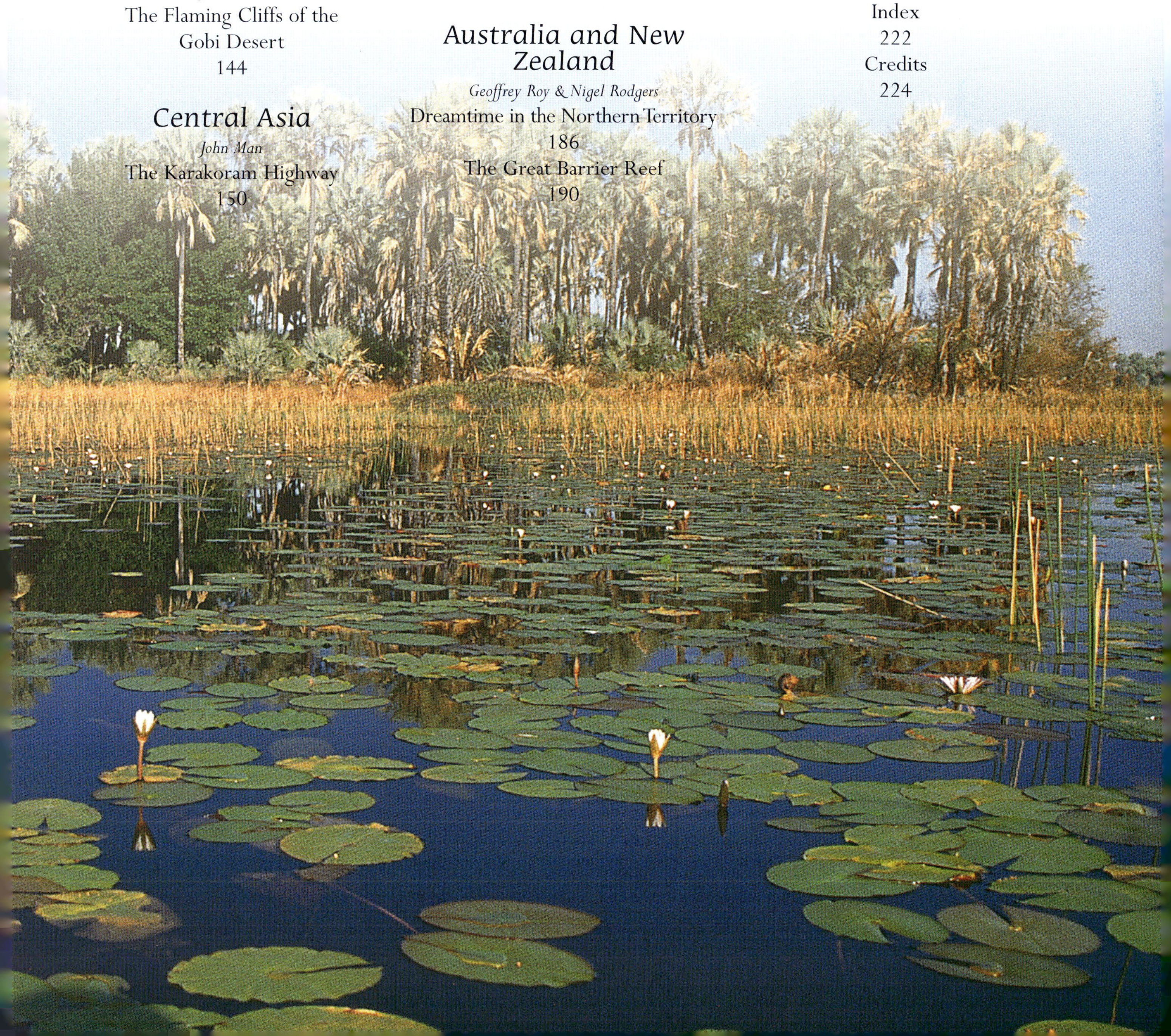

Introduction

"Travel, in the younger sort, is part of education; in the elder, a part of experience."
—Francis Bacon.

THE LONGEST JOURNEY EVER MADE was to a place already known, researched, and intimately described. Yet that journey, which might have done nothing but confirm established views, provided all mankind with a revelation. The journey was, of course, to the moon. And the most striking discovery of the first lunar journey in 1969 was an insight into what had been left behind—that image of a marbled dot standing in an infinite void. It was a strange irony of that voyage to travel for three days to the moon, and rediscover the earth.

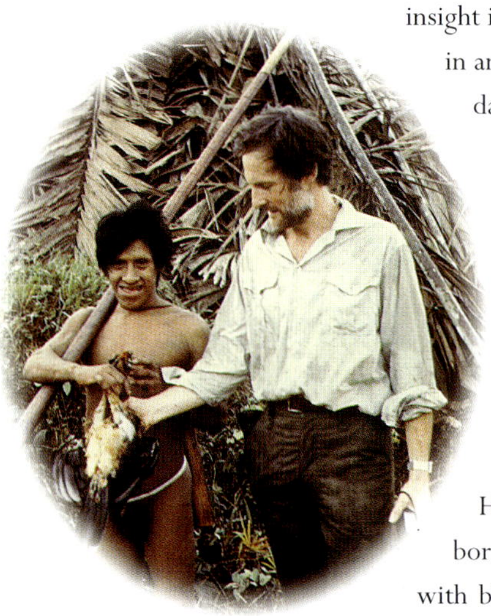

It should not have been all that surprising, for that has always been the true purpose of travel: to see, experience, feel, and understand distant places, but then find another reward to gain a deeper knowledge of home, of one's culture, of oneself.

The first time I traveled, I mean really traveled, I found myself beside a small airstrip in the Amazon jungle in eastern Ecuador. I had come to write about a tribe that had been contacted not much more than 20 years previously, the Waorani (now usually spelled Huaorani). The adults of the small group I was to live with had been born into the Stone Age, without metal tools of their own. They hunted with blowguns and spears, were renowned for their ferocity, and had no clothing. I arrived with tape-recorder, camera, and notebooks. The shock of the first meeting was one of the most intense of my life. To have naked men and women, their earlobes vastly extended to accommodate plugs of balsawood, crowding around, pulling my shirt up to examine my skin, touching me everywhere, fingering my precious possessions, it all made me very, very nervous. I had no idea what was happening, or what to expect. I had never felt so helpless.

Tasmania, the only island state of Australia, is a land of high rainfall, but great unspoiled wildernesses of mountains, lakes, and waterfalls (right).

The author, John Man (above), on the trip to the Waurani Indians which changed his perception of his own life and culture.

My worries faded, my interest grew. I was accompanied by one of the few guides who spoke the language. The group was peaceable. I learned names, and a few words of the language. What surprised me later was how quickly I became used to my new surroundings. It would have taken years to absorb the culture, but within days I felt at ease enough to go naked myself (except for shoes—feet take six months or so to harden). The simple body decoration and the dangling earlobes seemed quite natural. It made other tribes, my own included, seem wildly eccentric.

Within two weeks—a timespan which will be applied to many of the journeys in this book—my sense of what was normal acquired new dimensions. I came to see several things in my own culture differently. For instance, I had uncritically assumed that Freud was right, that sex was the fundamental drive. But here it

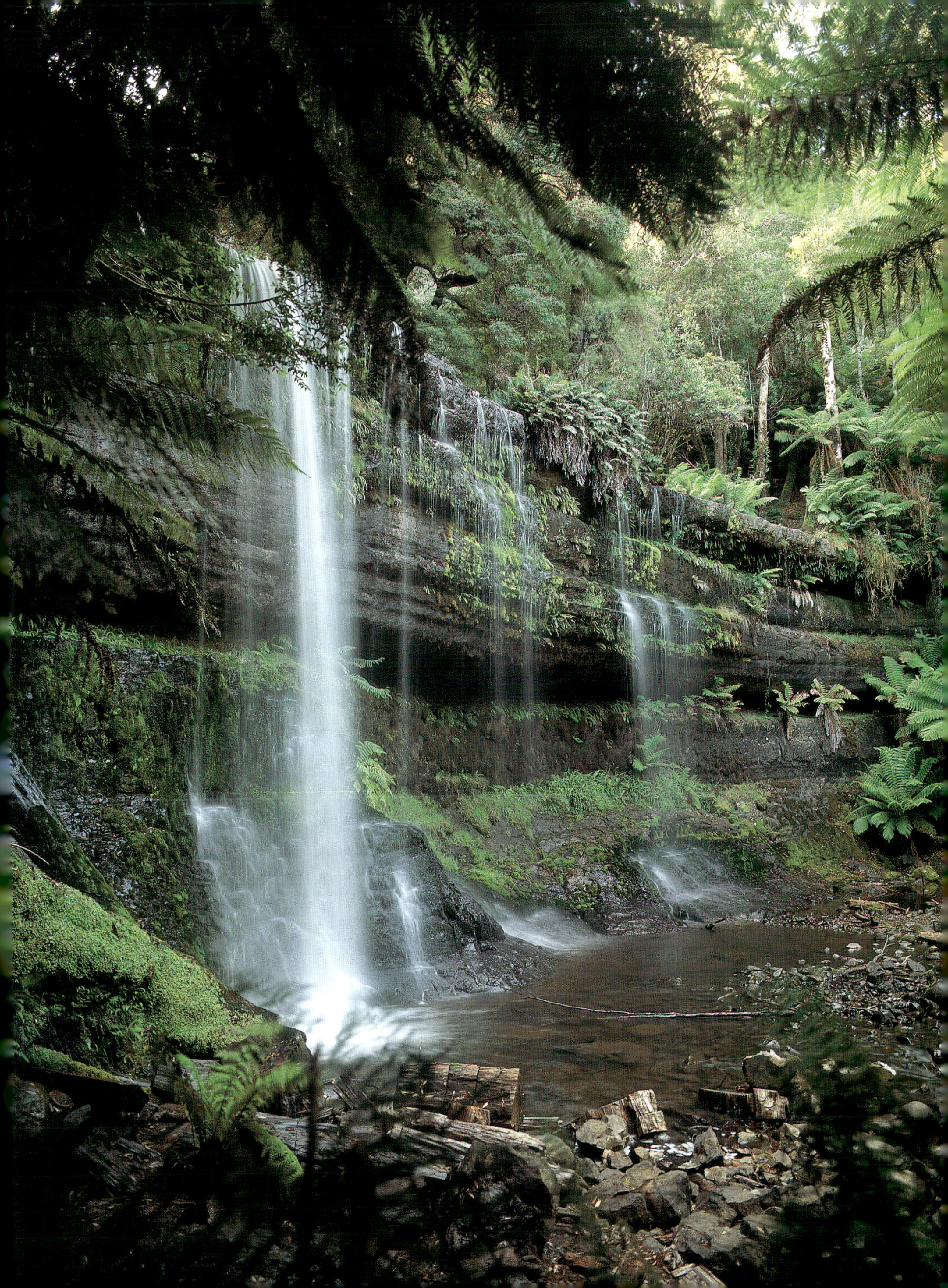

The Global Village
The places visited in this book are plotted on a map of the world's climatic zones.

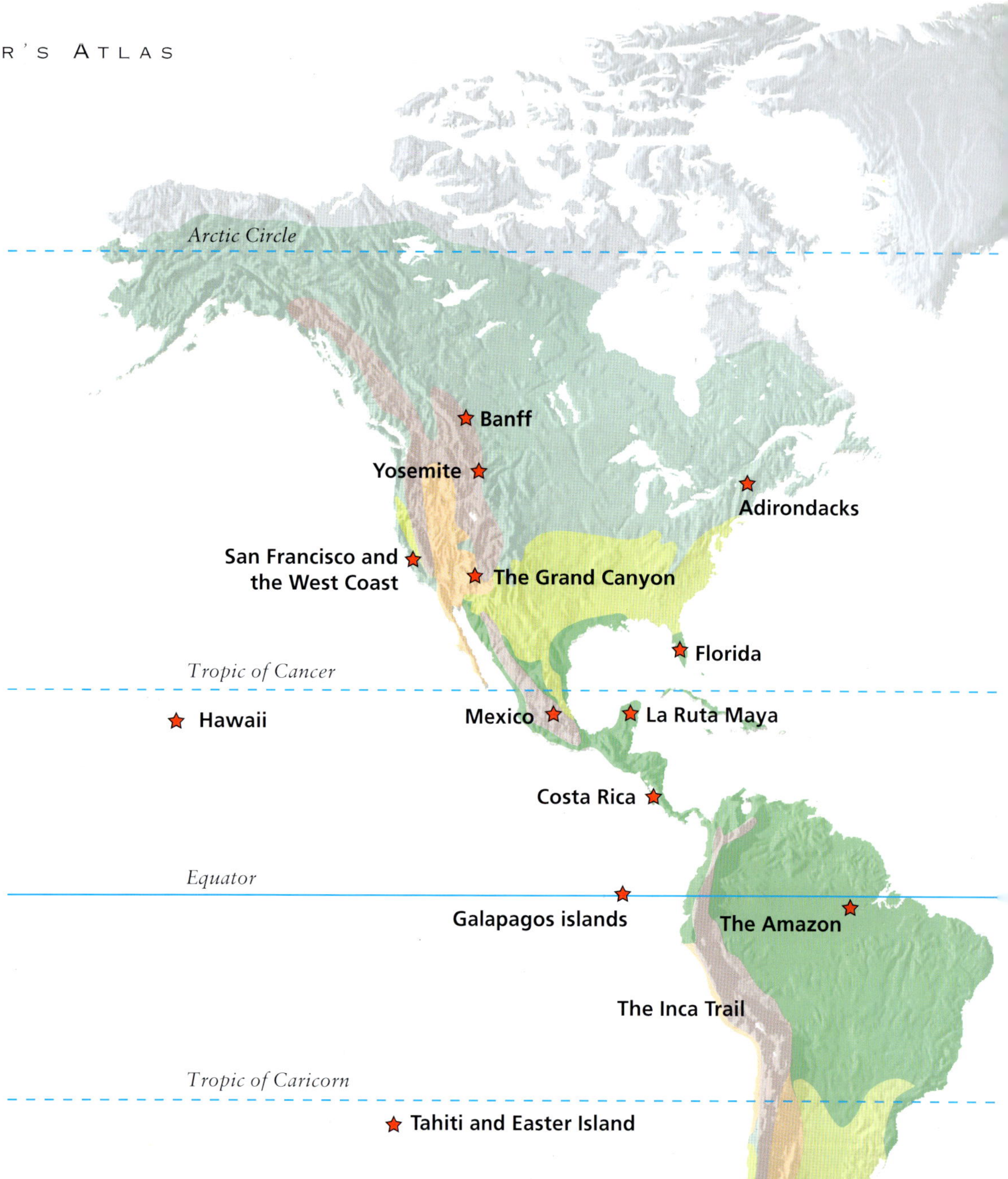

took a backseat to survival. Marriage was dictated by the overwhelming need for a joint economy: a man to hunt, a woman to grow manioc. I marched briefly to the rhythm of a different drum. I came back changed.

A WORLD TO SHARE

Why not simply read? Why travel at all? Couldn't we all be happy stay-at-homes, and simply read, or zap or surf our way through the world's wonders, and absorb them that way? No. Books, videos, and the Internet are never substitutes for life-changing experiences. Like me, you will find, if you haven't already, that there are sights and experiences and feelings that change lives, and you cannot know what they will be in advance. The joy of travel is the surprise, the tingle factor. For a while, perhaps no more than a few minutes, you feel again the rush of joy and astonishment that comes from the onset of youthful love. Oh, my God, you say, I had no idea this mountain or that temple would be so small, or big, or beautiful.

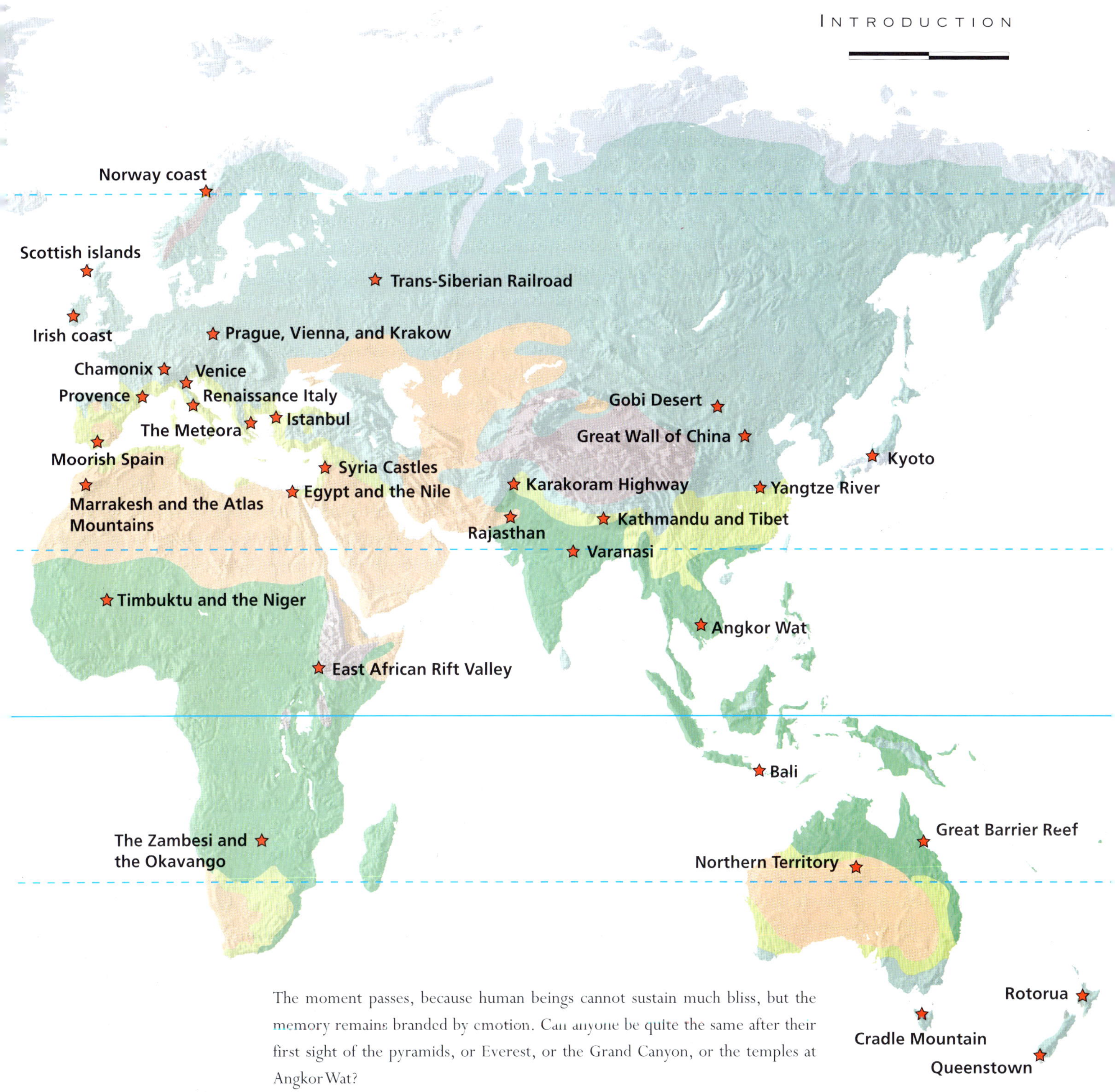

The moment passes, because human beings cannot sustain much bliss, but the memory remains branded by emotion. Can anyone be quite the same after their first sight of the pyramids, or Everest, or the Grand Canyon, or the temples at Angkor Wat?

Don't think the experience will change the world directly. Its effect is utterly private, and if it is not private, it can easily be as tedious as a vacation shot bliss recycled as cliché. Thousands see such visions every year, and the world remains unimproved by their reactions. If and when something tremendous happens, it is only to you. There is no sure way, unless you are a poet or artist, that you can transfer the feeling into the mind of another. Best not to try, but to hug it to yourself, and know that you have gained something ineffable.

But, even through us non-poets, the experience has an effect indirectly. Look at it the other way around. These things are part of a common heritage. It is not simply that you are enriched by the experience of travel to exotic places, but that

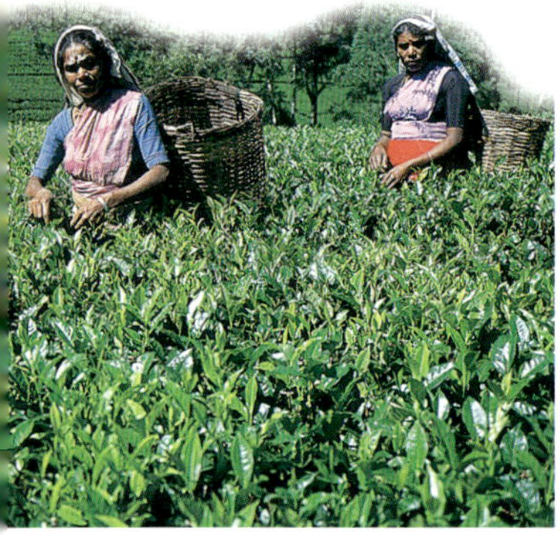

Leave your cup of tea behind at home, to journey to the source of tea, the plantations of Camellia sinensis, a native plant of the mild, moist mountain region between India and China.

if you do not seek them out, you remain impoverished, cut off from what should be truly yours as an inhabitant of the world on the brink of a new millennium.

Once humans were limited to the speed and distance they could cover on their feet, on a horse, in a canoe, or on a ship. It took weeks, or years, to seek out and experience new worlds. The Grand Tour of Europe, undertaken by the wealthy in the 1700s, took many months. One of the greatest of medieval travelers, Ibn Battuta, ranged across northern and eastern Africa, to the Middle East, to the Volga, to India, to China, but it took him 30 years of solid travel. Now we can all see what he saw, or at least the modern equivalents. Travel at its best allows us to share our world, and our heritage. As inhabitants of the global village, we had better be aware of what we should inherit, and what we should pass on.

THE RIGHT TIME

Never was there a better time to go. Today, a traveler can be in Miami in the morning and with the Waorani the same night (though they are not as they were when I first saw them). All of Ibn Battuta's destinations could be visited inside a few months. It is not just the difference between them and us, between here and there, that would have astonished Ibn Battuta or our traveling 19th-century ancestors, but the speed of the transposition.

Such experiences are yours for the asking. Of all the places in this book, almost all can be visited within 24 hours, from anywhere in the world. You can, if you wish, chug for days up the Amazon to the rubber-boom town of Manuas; but you can also fly in straight from Rio. A Londoner or New Yorker can be in the world's remotest habitable spot, Easter Island, within a day and a night. A rich and dedicated traveler could taste every place and journey mentioned in this book in the space of a single year.

But don't even think of trying it. Travel, or rather arrival, may indeed broaden the mind, but only if it is done with discrimination. One purpose of this book is to show you how to slow down to experience in depth, to absorb, for the flip side of ready access is overload and superficiality, the curse of instant travel. "If this is

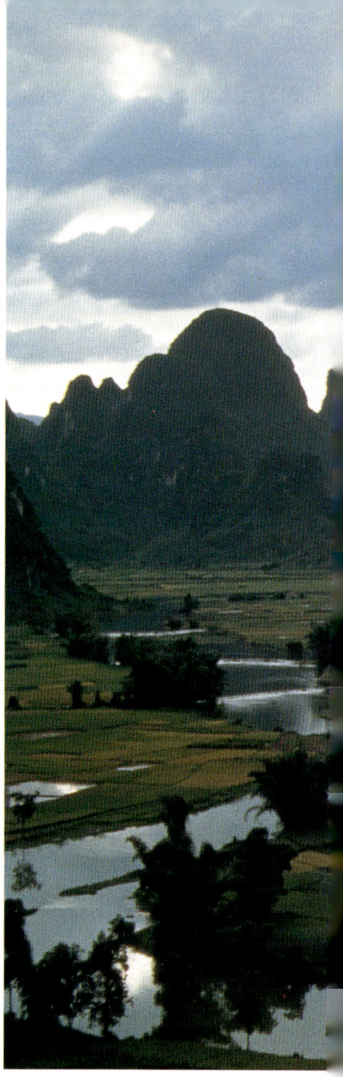

A CHECKLIST OF TIPS

Focus first on what suits you: wilderness or city; a new culture or your own; near or far. See what you can accomplish in the time available. Compare costs: There's almost always a cheaper way, and it may be better.

Health: *Check out the risks.*

Equipment: *Usually best bought in advance, but sometimes it's better to buy locally on arrival.*

Insurance: *Get it well in advance. Check the small print. Can you be sure of reparation and/or treatment locally? Will it get you home?*

Emergencies: *Have a back-up plan in case of trouble. Know your contacts. Check alternative travel possibilities.*

Language: *In an unfamiliar culture, a good local English-speaking guide is the key to enjoyment. A bad one is a nightmare. Be warned: there are no guarantees.*

Communications: *Consider taking a mobile cell phone with international dialing. In an emergency it can save time, money, the lives of professional rescuers, even your own life.*

Numbers: *One is scary. A group is often bland. Between two and four offers a good balance.*

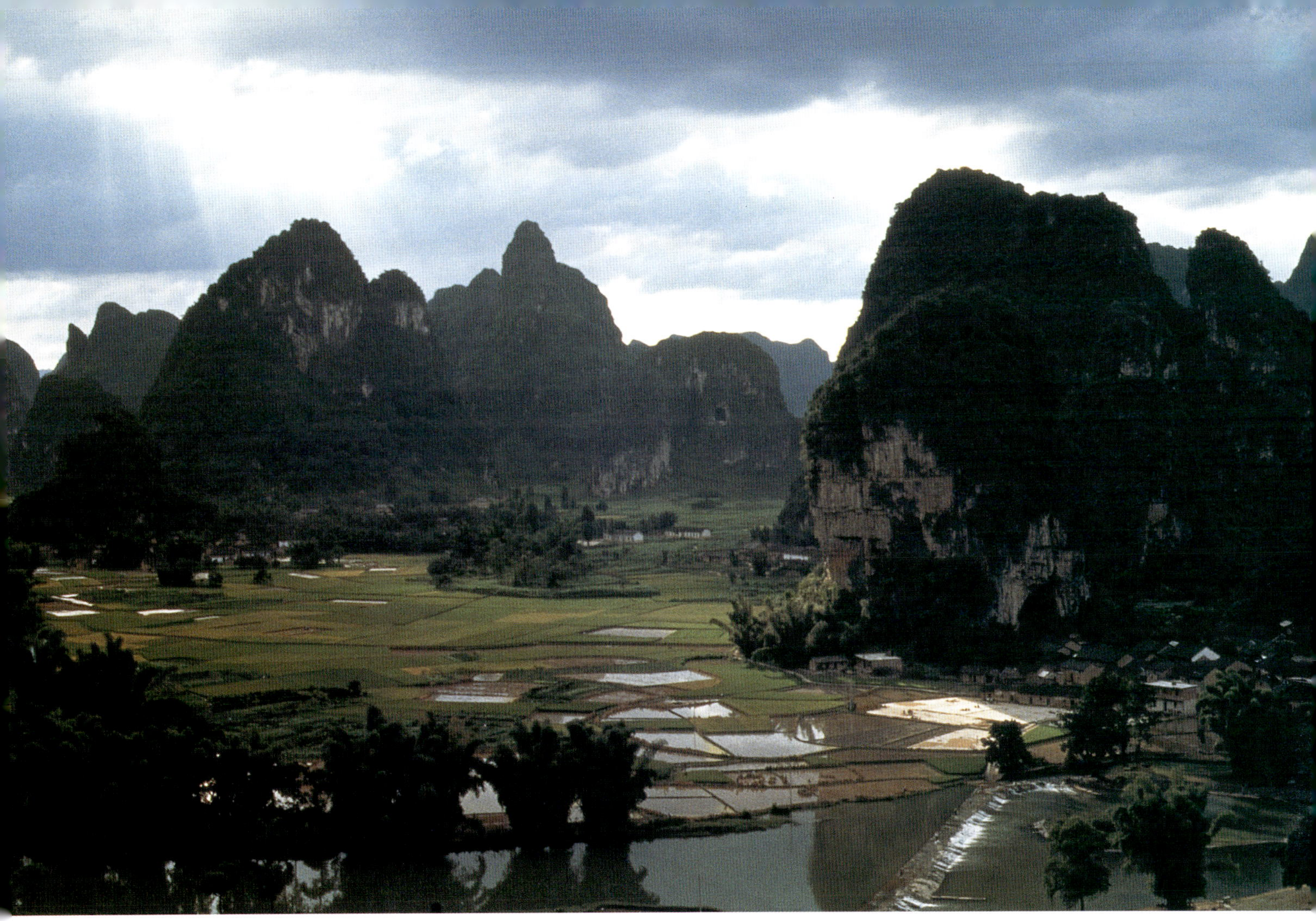

Travelers can take a riverboat journey along the Li Jiang river in southwest China, to where the extraordinary geological formations of the Guilin Hills erupt from a sea of flooded paddy fields.

Tuesday, it must be Rome" is not just a joke on mass-tourism—it's a sad truth.

So another purpose of this book is to broaden the mind by narrowing the vision. Every destination and journey offers something of significance, something that should take time to savor, something that rewards commitment. Of course, few have world enough and time, let alone money, for detailed study. Most, though, can steal a week or two from a busy life. This book strikes a balance between expertise and instant access. To know Kyoto, one would have at least to live with the language and culture for years; wildlife experts and geologists make careers out of studying the Grand Canyon or Yosemite; but two weeks in these places is enough to gain a sense of them, thanks to modern transportation. A vacation spent in relative safety traveling across the Karakorams into China can provide insights as deep (though different) as those acquired by walkers or riders obsessed by concerns about whether they and their horse can make it over the next ridge.

Narrowing the vision fulfills another purpose—it provides an objective. To fulfill an ambition is itself a satisfaction, whatever the nature of the experience when you arrive. One final thought: you can choose to fine-tune that satisfaction by not always taking the easiest option. Modern travel allows room for you to take a path slightly less traveled: the ramshackle rather than the air-conditioned, the slower rather than the faster. A little suffering helps. To venture by bus into Tibet's chilly and barren highlands is a risky business, but it makes the arrival in Lhasa all the more rewarding.

John Man

North America

"...travel is more than the seeing of sights; it is a change that goes on, deep and permanent, in the ideas of living."

MIRIAM BEARD, B. 1901, AMERICAN WRITER

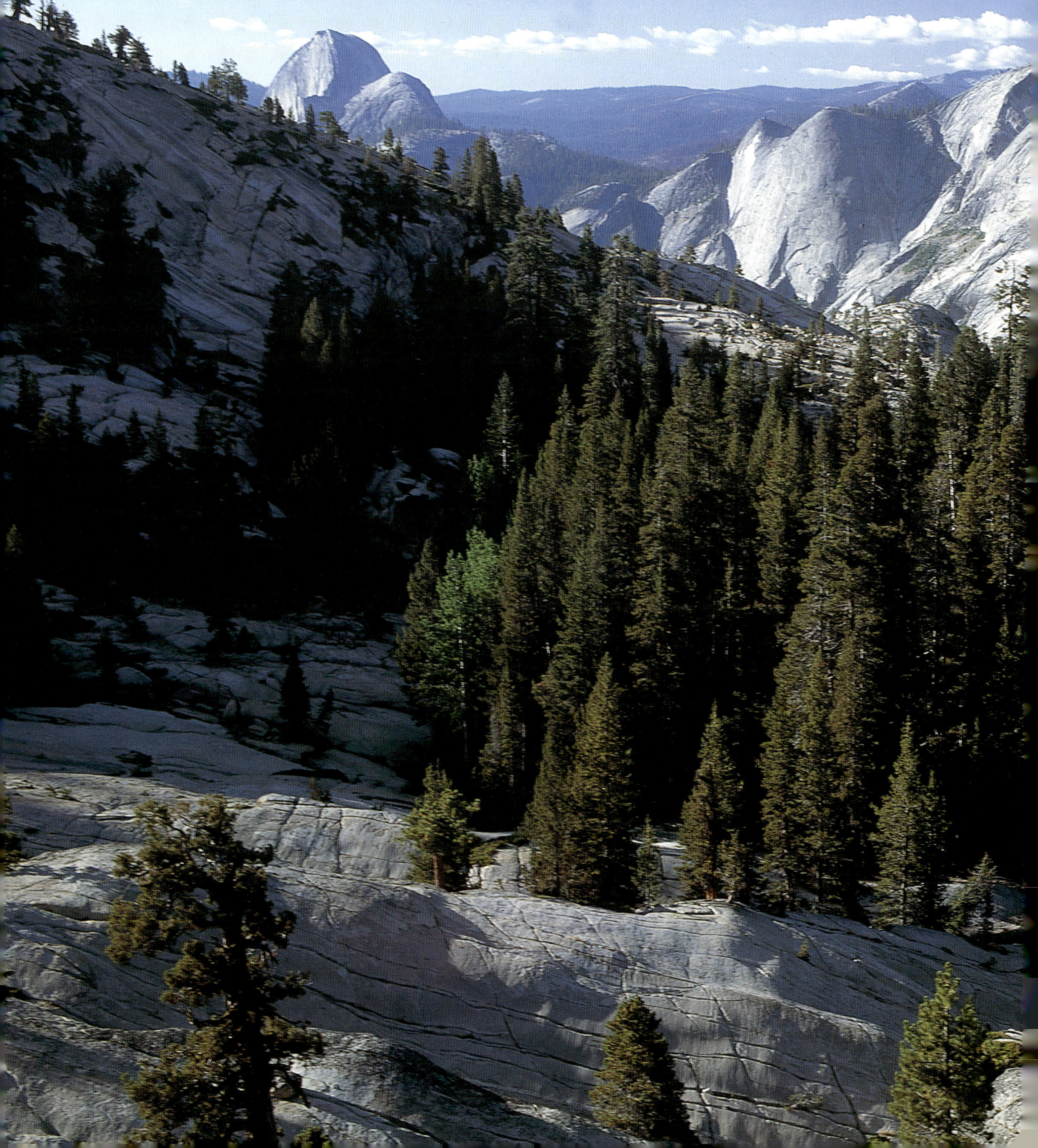

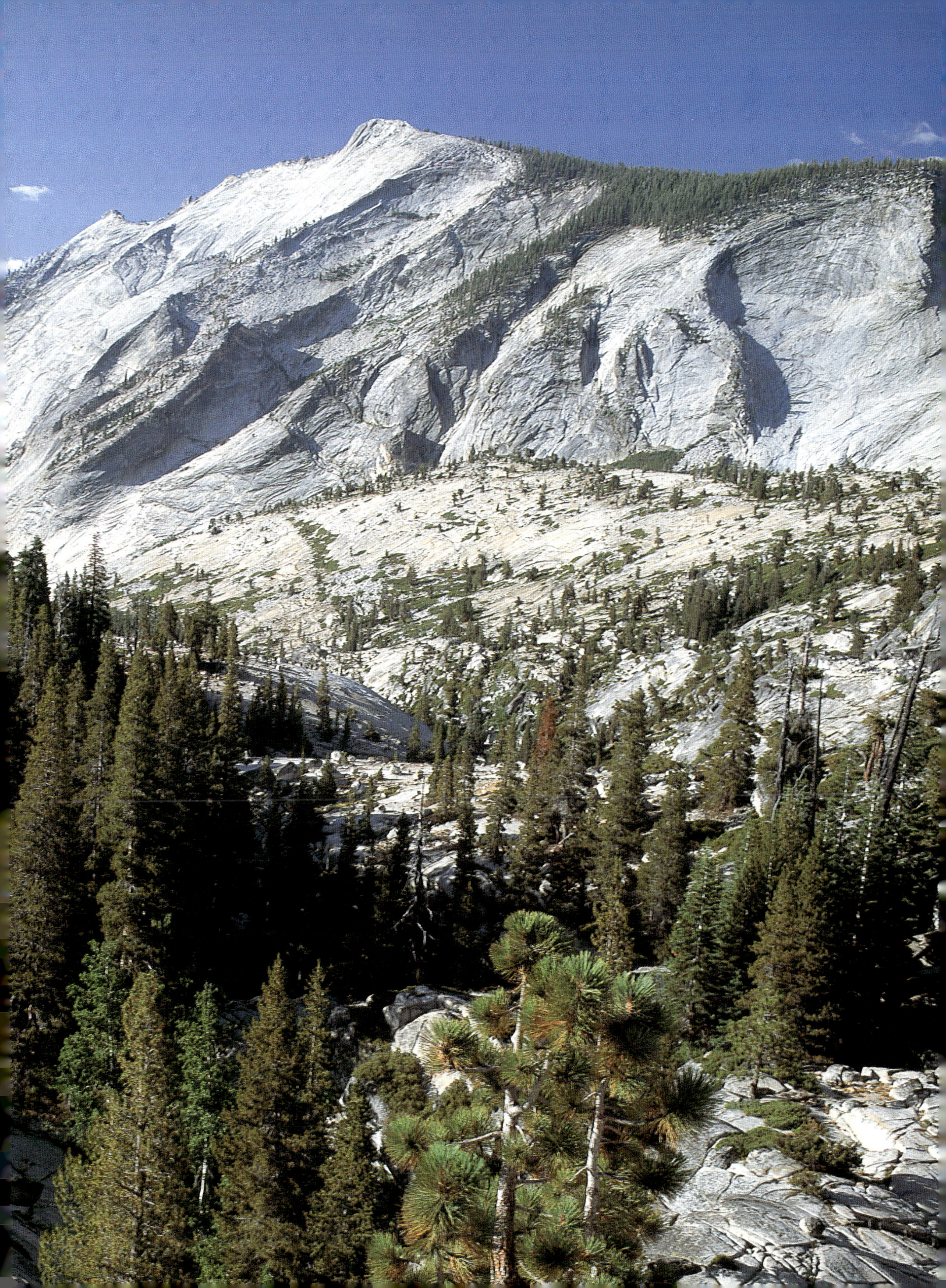

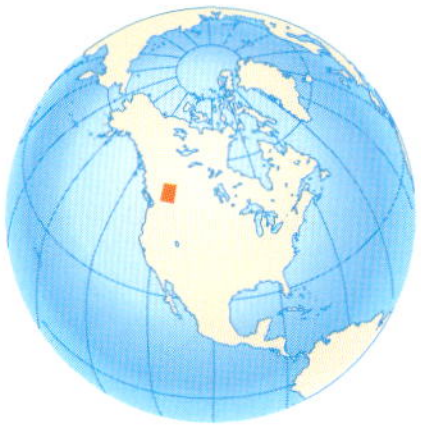

Banff National Park

"I never, in all my explorations of these five chains of mountains throughout western Canada, saw such a matchless scene.... I felt puny in body, but glorified in spirit and soul"—Explorer Tom Wilson, 1882.

FACT FILE

Airports: Calgary, Edmonton.

Winter sports high season: March.

Columbia Icefields Center: Mid-May— mid-September.

Average snowfall: 100 inches (251 cm).

Banff Infocenter: (403) 762-1550.

Lake Louise Information Center: (403) 522-3833.

Permits: Needed by motorists and motorcyclists in all Rockies parks (other visitors enter free). Permits, valid for all the parks, range from one day ($5.00) to annual ($30).

Bears: Black bears and grizzlies are dangerous, though rarely encountered. Follow the guidelines in local literature. In brief: don't approach, don't feed, don't run. Back away slowly.

THE CANADIAN ROCKIES run 1,000 miles (1,600 km), right up the western edge of the country and on into Alaska, but its heart—and their most accessible region—is the area around Banff. Every summer, every winter, millions of hikers, climbers, and skiers come here. Despite the crowds, anyone can feel as puny and as glorified as Tom Wilson, for the wilderness is as matchless as ever.

These are young mountains, formed as part of the crumple zone when the two American continental plates rammed into the Pacific plate 70 million years ago. Youthfulness in mountains, as in body sculpting, leads to great definition. Ice, snow, wind, frost, and rain have chiseled out peaks and sheer cliffs, leaving edges unblunted by time. From high icefields, glaciers grind down, turning rock to powder that clouds the icy lakes. Thick forests of aspen, pine, fir, and spruce flow over the lower slopes and lap the lakesides. Higher up, alpine meadows splashed with bluebells and heather give way to bare and wind-blasted heights. This varied wilderness, once the domain of moose, black bear, and grizzlies, was opened up little more than a century ago. In 1858, Dr. James Hector, exploring the Bow River valley, was kicked unconscious by his pack horse. His Indian guides, thinking him dead, prepared to bury him, but he opened his eyes, and survived to see Kicking Horse Pass named for him. Soon afterward, pioneers discovered that the cold above ground is matched by the heat below ground. Subterranean furnaces warm the meltwaters and percolate them back to the surface. Sulfur springs turned Banff into a spa renowned for its surrounding glories, and the area became Canada's first national park in 1885—a mere 10 square miles (26 sq km).

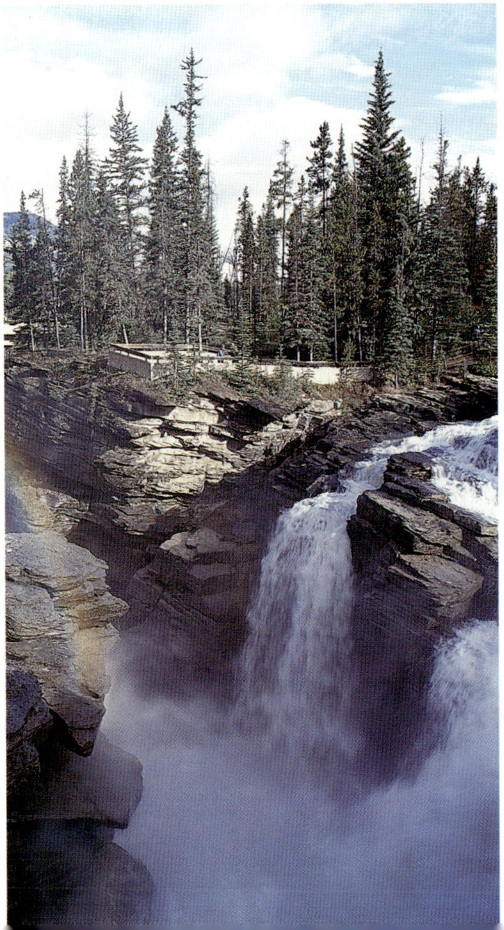

Glaciers and waterfalls (right) wash out silt, giving the waters of Lake Moraine (far right) its particular pearly radiance.

Now the heart of this heartland is Banff National Park, 2,580 square miles (6,680 square km) of peaks, meadows, lakes, and glaciers running for 150 miles (240 km) along the borders of British Columbia and Alberta. It is only one of three other parks—Jasper, Yoho, Kootenay—that form an even vaster wilderness, all loosely laced with trails. Banff National Park alone has 1,000 miles (1,600 km) of them.

Once, the Canadian Pacific Railroad brought in most visitors. Today, the railroad is for freight only (except for a luxury weekly service running between Vancouver and Calgary, via Banff). Visitors mostly drive or bus in from Calgary, 90 minutes away, arriving in one of the two main centers, Banff and Lake Louise. Be warned: both places are packed out in high season, both winter and summer.

A VICTORIAN MONSTER

Banff's hot springs, once the town's equivalent of a gold mine, are as crowded as ever, especially the Upper Hot Springs near the base of the cable cars (known as gondolas) which shoot up the 7,440 foot (2,263 m) Sulfur Mountain. The town is still dominated by one of its original resorts, a 578- room monster of Victorian gothic, the Banff Springs Hotel, the world's largest hotel when it was built in the 1890s. About 11 miles (18 km) south, another gondola combines with a chair lift to reach the Continental Divide.

Banff hosts an annual arts festival but most people come not for the town but for its surroundings. While day hikers can head up the Spray River and Sulfur Mountain from the Banff Springs Hotel, more serious

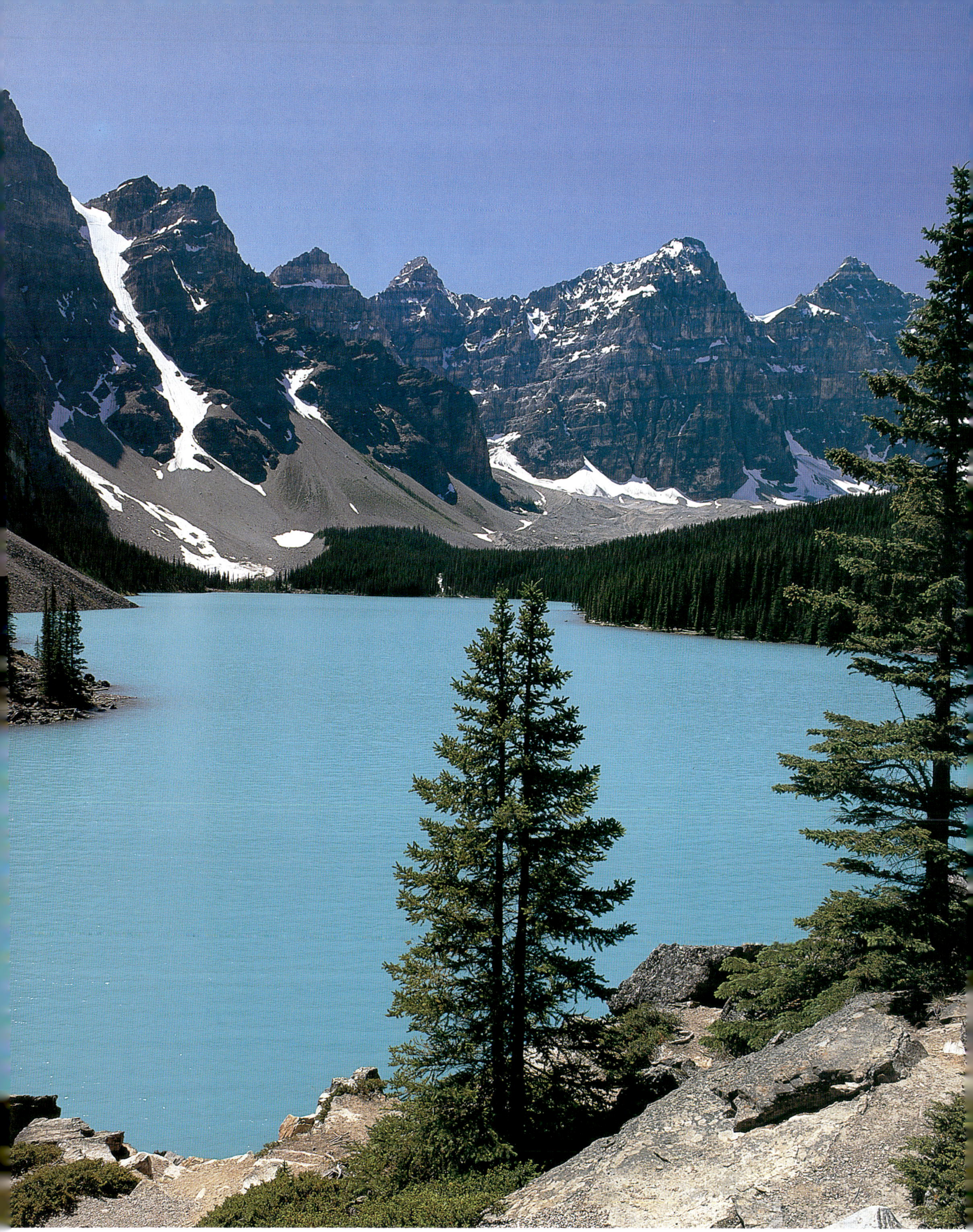

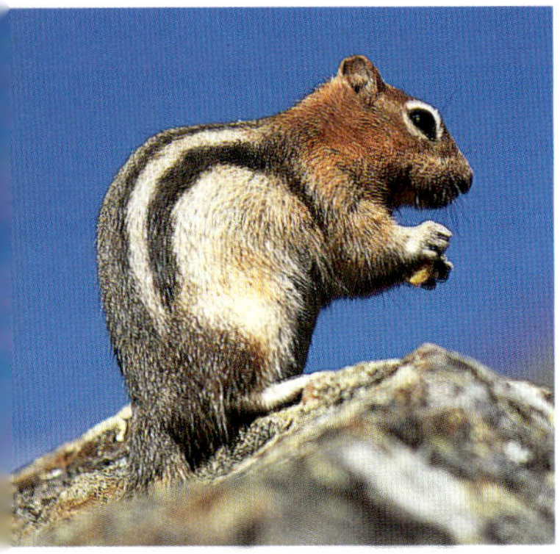

A gold-mantled ground squirrel is among the denizens of Banff's untouched forests.

backpackers start outside the town, and higher up. Two highways follow the railroad north along the Bow River, whose emerald waters come crashing down from Kicking Horse through a wilderness that still retains its pristine grandeur. From the faster Highway 1 and the new, scenic Bow River Parkway, five trails—from 3 miles (5 km) to 17 miles (28 km) long—lead up past waterfalls and lakes to stupendous outlooks.

Some of these interlink with the trails surrounding Lake Louise, 37 miles (59 km) from Banff. The resort is both a village and the lake itself, which is three miles (4.8 km) away. It is the lake that is the draw. Known as the "gem of the Rockies," its waters are made pearly by "rock flour," the powder ground out of the mountains by glaciers. The result—despite the intrusive presence of a 1920's hotel—is an image of postcard perfection, which at sunset and sunrise reflects the surrounding snowcapped peaks and forested slopes in colors "distilled from peacocks' tails," in the words of one awed writer.

Naturally, in summer the lakeside trails are crowded. The trail around Lake Agnes, less than a mile from Lake Louise, is said to be the most heavily used path in the Rockies. But for the more ambitious, the wilderness is within easy reach. Just 8 miles (13 km) away is Lake Moraine, a sight so beautiful, with its vivid turquoise waters and backdrop of ten peaks, that it was used on old Canadian $20 bills. Of several trails leading away

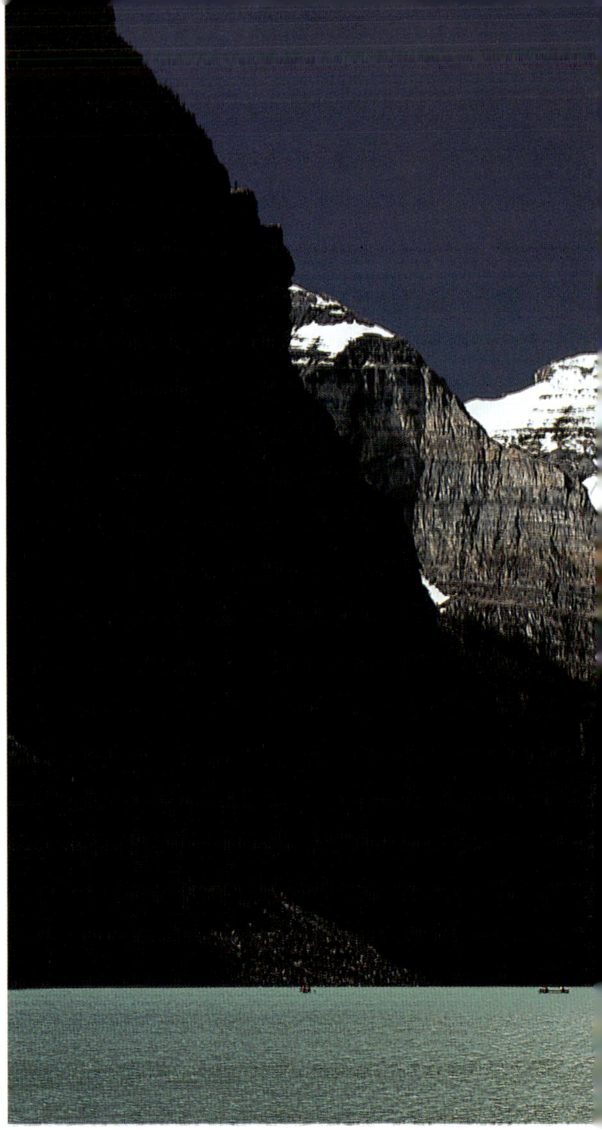

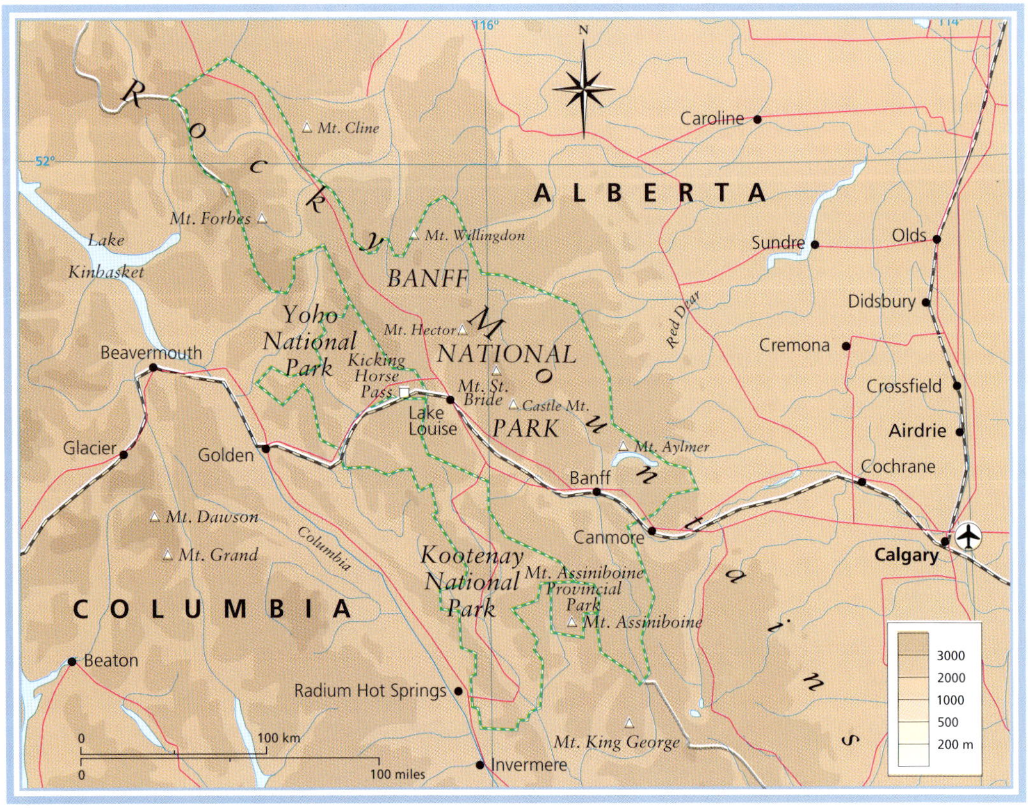

Lake Louise (above right) beneath the bastion of Mount Victoria, is one of Canada's most visited sights, while the heights above Bow River (below right) attract only the intrepid.

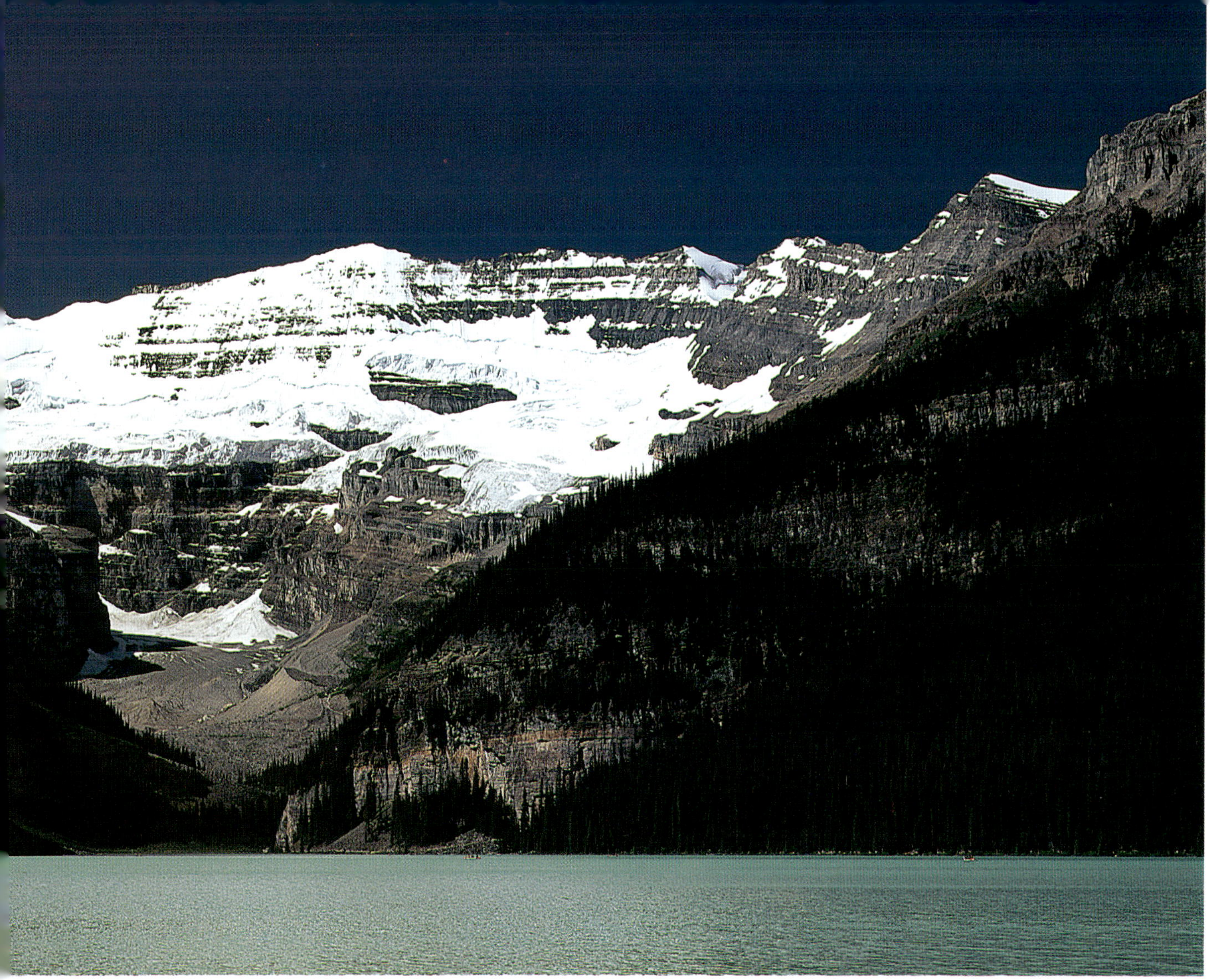

from the lake, one leads up to 8,600 feet (2,605 m), the highest point reached by a major trail in the Canadian Rockies. This is also Canada's prime winter playground, with six major winter resorts, two near Banff and one near Lake Louise (the others are Nakiska, Fortress Mountain, and Jasper). Between them these places offer downhill and cross country skiing, dog sledding, ice climbing, skating, snowmobiling, snowshoeing, canyon crawling, and fishing. Mount Norquay, just north of Banff, is popular with advanced downhill skiers and also offers the area's only night skiing.

GIANT ICEFIELD

Those seeking wilderness of a different sort can head north toward Jasper along Highway 93—the Icefields Parkway. Though a million people a year make the journey, it is still surprisingly underdeveloped. In 143 miles (230 km) there are only two service stations, and snow often closes the road between October and May.

Some 75 miles (120 km) north of Lake Louise is the Columbia Icefield, 120 square miles (325 sq km) of ice and snow that is the largest glacial area south of the Arctic Circle and north of the equator. It is the source of six major glaciers, three of which can be seen from the parkway. An Icefield Center offers views and information about ice walks, which for those with the right equipment—good boots, and clothing to ward off the bitter winds, for the temperature plummets beside the icefields—provide a dramatic insight into the forces that are still carving these wild peaks.

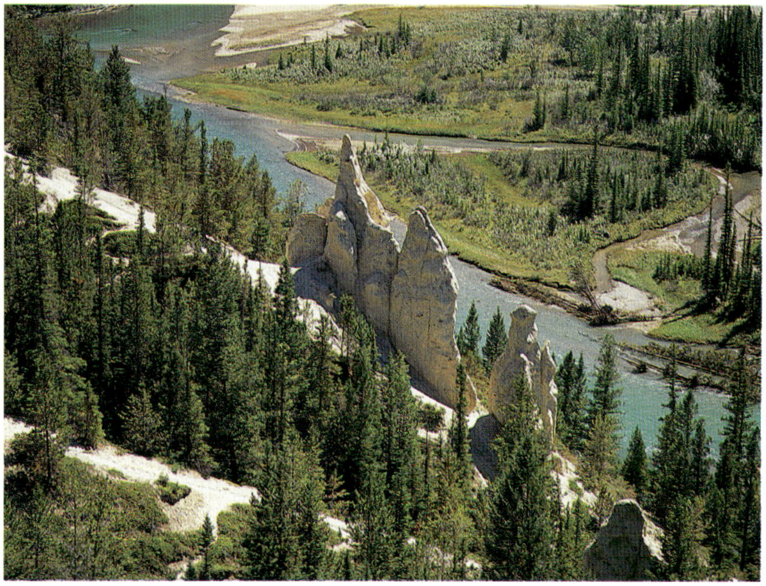

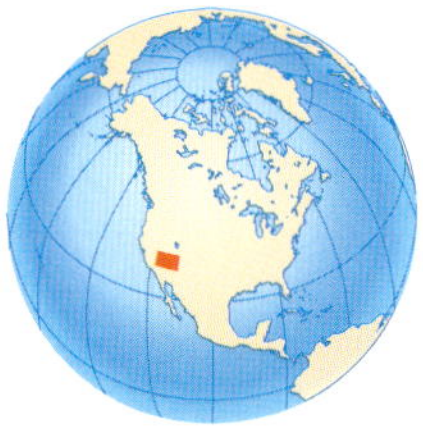

The Grand Canyon

"Whoever stands upon the brink of the Grand Canyon beholds a spectacle unrivaled on this earth."—Geologist François E. Matthes.

The Grand Canyon (below) is a cross section of the uppermost level of the earth's crust. If you were to cut a slice out of an African, Asian, or Australian plateau, the visual effect would be much the same.

IT HAS BECOME A CLICHÉ OF TRAVEL WRITING that all descriptions of the Grand Canyon become clichés—that mere words cannot prepare the mind for the immensity that opens in Arizona's northern plateau.

The area of the gorge is astonishing enough; the canyon would swallow 64 Manhattans before its floor was covered. But it is the third dimension, its depth, that staggers belief. It would take another three layers of Manhattans—some 250 in all—for the topmost skyscrapers to show above the surface of the surrounding ground.

Ever since a 56-mile (90 km) stretch was made a national park in 1919, the canyon's changing moods when seen from the rim have been legendary. The rocks are predominantly red. But dawn sun splashes the far walls with gold and silver, while sunsets turn exposed ledges to flame. On spring mornings, mist fills the chasms. In moonlight, flanks stand out white against indigo shadows. Snows blanket the forested approaches

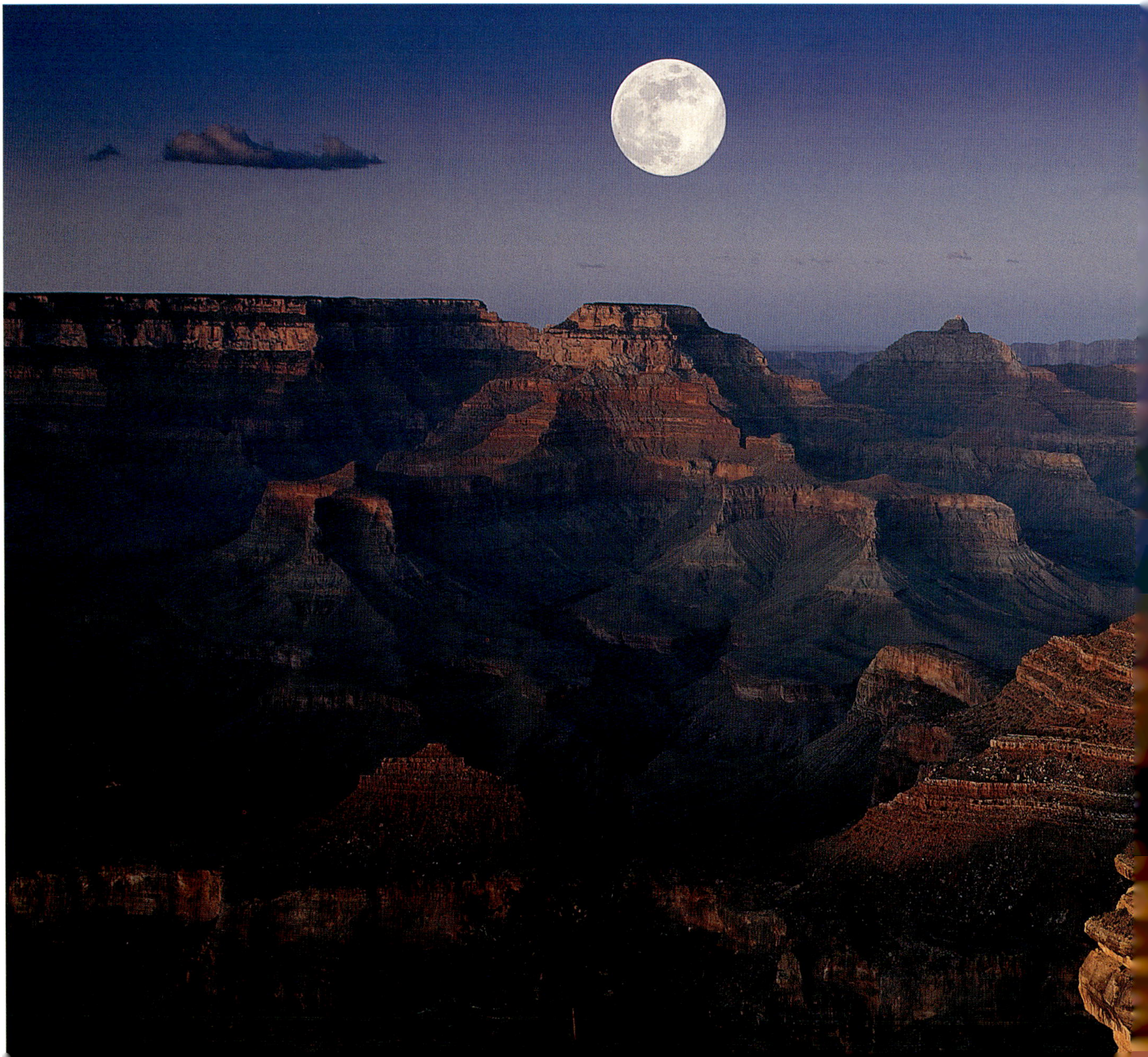

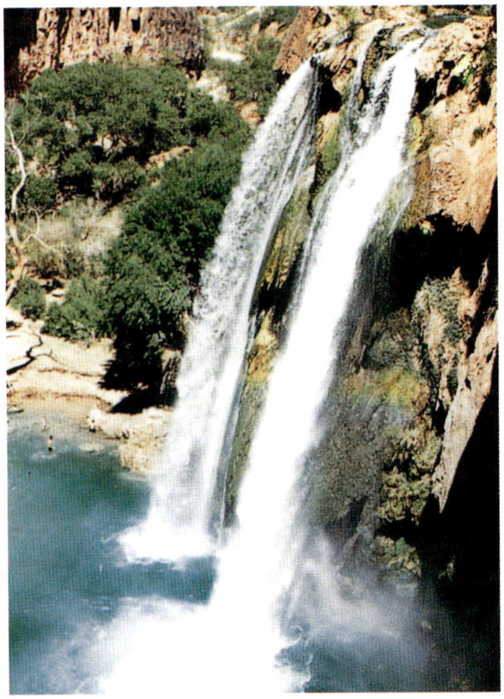

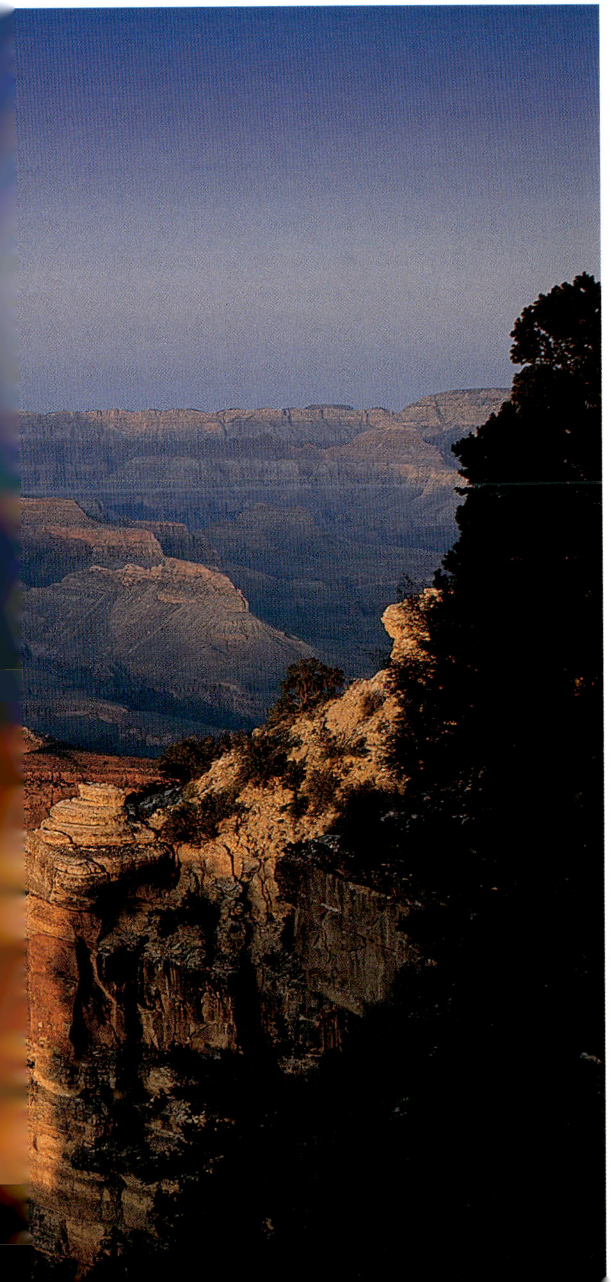

until well into May. It is, of course, one of the top tourist attractions in the United States, with several million visitors a year, and there is an entrance fee for cars, walkers, bikers, or bus passengers. The National Park has its own airport, buses cover the 70 miles (112 km) from Flagstaff to Grand Canyon Village with its visitor center several times a day. Campsites are crowded, and though there are many hotels, they are expensive and impossible to get into without a reservation, which must usually be made a year in advance. The vintage Grand Canyon Railroad, which ceased service in 1953, is now restored and runs from Williams, west of Flagstaff, to the South Rim.

But the crowds make little impact on the real wilderness into which the intrepid and the fit can escape. From the more accessible and crowded South Rim, two maintained trails, the Bright Angel and the South Kaibab, lead downward away from the touristy East and West Rim Drives. Both trails have rest stops. But it takes 4 to 5 hours to cover the 8-mile (13 km) 4,620-foot (1,408 m) descent and 8 to 9 hours to climb back up, a hike that can turn legs to rubber and induce heat prostration. Other trails like the Boucher are not maintained and are suitable only for the experienced. Hikers are advised to plan on taking 1-1.5 gallons (4.5-7 liters) of water for a day's walk. Those who book well in advance can take a mule—though brochures warn "Those who are disturbed by heights or large animals should reconsider"—or stay in Phantom Ranch on the canyon floor. Overnight campers require a permit.

The North Rim—1,000 feet (305 m) higher—is harder to get to, and closed during the winter, but its

FACT FILE

Length: 277 miles (443 km).

Depth: 1 mile (1.6km).

Width: c. 4-18 miles (6-28 km).

Best time to go: Mid-May through mid-June, to avoid the worst crowds and heat.

Best time to view: Morning and evening, when it's cool and the sun casts a slanting light.

Climate: Summer high over 100°F (38°C); winter low down to 0°F (-18°C)

What to take: Good boots, water bottles.

Information: Grand Canyon National Park Visitor Center ((520)638-7888).

Cascades in the Havasu Indian Reserve (above left) where "the people of the blue-green water" live in a remote and verdant outpost of the Grand Canyon.

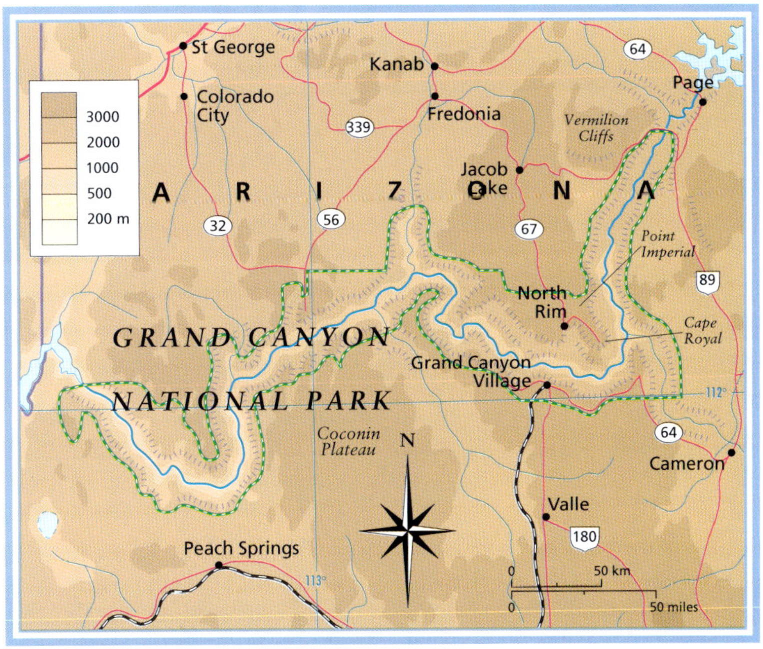

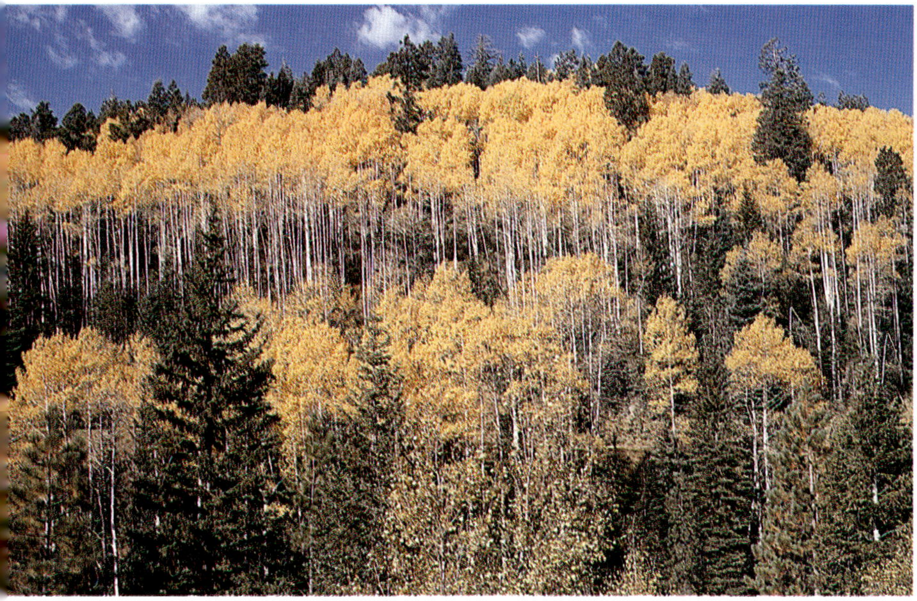

The secluded forests of the North Rim's Kaibab Plateau contrast with the bare, crowded South Rim.

forested heights give on to awe-inspiring lookout points, including the canyon's highest, Point Imperial at 8,803 feet (2,683 m). A single trail the North Kaibab leads down into the canyon connecting to the South Kaibab, allowing a 13-mile (20 km) rim-to-rim hike; by road it's 235 miles (377 km).

Once inside the canyon, visitors enter other worlds. Like a mountain range in reverse, ecologies change with altitude, every 1,000 feet (300 m) being the equivalent of 300 miles (480 km) of travel southward. Mountain creatures like bighorn sheep live close to desert species like rattlesnakes, while animals living on the North Rim are entirely cut off from those to the south—each side has its own variety of squirrel.

A CHAINSAW RIVER

Standing on the rim it seems incredible that water, scarcely visible from above, could have been responsible for this gigantic wound. Close up though, the Colorado reveals itself as a raging chainsaw of a river, bearing away a daily half-million tons of abrasive sediment which in the local phrase makes it "too thick to drink, too thin to plow."

In a sense the river, which seems the most volatile element in this static panorama, is the most stable for it predates the landscape it sculpted. Six million years ago the Colorado began to scour this route. Then, at the rate of just one-hundredth of an inch (2.5 mm) a year, the land rose slowly enough to allow time for the river to grind away the rising surface and producing a paradoxical landscape—a river flowing from east to west, a plateau sloping from north to south. The result is a cross section through the pages of the earth's history. In the Inner Gorge, where the river now runs, strata half the age of the earth reveal that they were once part of a mountain-range. A billion years later, the mountains lay beneath a sea that left a fossil record of plankton dating from the earliest eons of life. Higher up, later strata hint at a succession of mountains, plains, coral seas, and volcanoes.

Perhaps the most exhilarating way of seeing the canyon is to take a rafting trip. Once this was a life-and-death venture. But in 1963 the Glen Canyon dam tamed the river (to the continuing fury of environmentalists). Information about rafting companies is available at the National Park headquarters. Trips range from smooth-water day-trips to white-water ventures lasting several days. Newcomers often find the rapids frankly terrifying—one drop, the Sockdolager, measures 19 feet (5.7 m)—but afterward most assert the ride ranks as one of life's most exhilarating experiences.

HAVASU CANYON: A WORLD APART

It's a long haul but Havasu Canyon, traditional home of the Havasupai Indians, is a jewel set in a rocky clasp protected from the ravages of mass tourism. The Indians rejected a planned highway to their village, Supai, and there is a 60-mile (96 km) drive from Highway 66 through forest and high plateau to Hualapai Hilltop, then an 8-mile (12.8 km) walk (or mule ride) into the canyon to Supai itself—the only place in the U.S. to receive its mail by horseback. In addition to its houses and tribal arts museum, Supai has a campground and a 24-room lodge—but book well in advance for both. With an Indian as a guide, you can take a trail on downwards past three waterfalls that tumble over the red rocks to a turquoise pool, Havasu Creek. The Indians, named "People of the Blue-Green Water" after this spot, still grow corn, beans, squash, and sunflowers on the canyon floor.

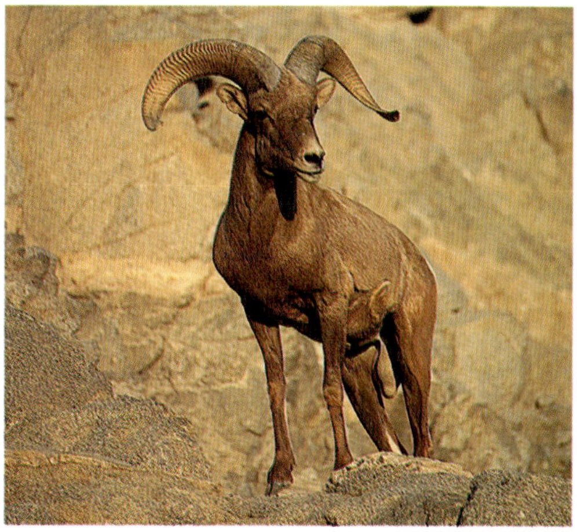

Bighorn sheep (right) can be seen in less accessible parts of the Canyon.

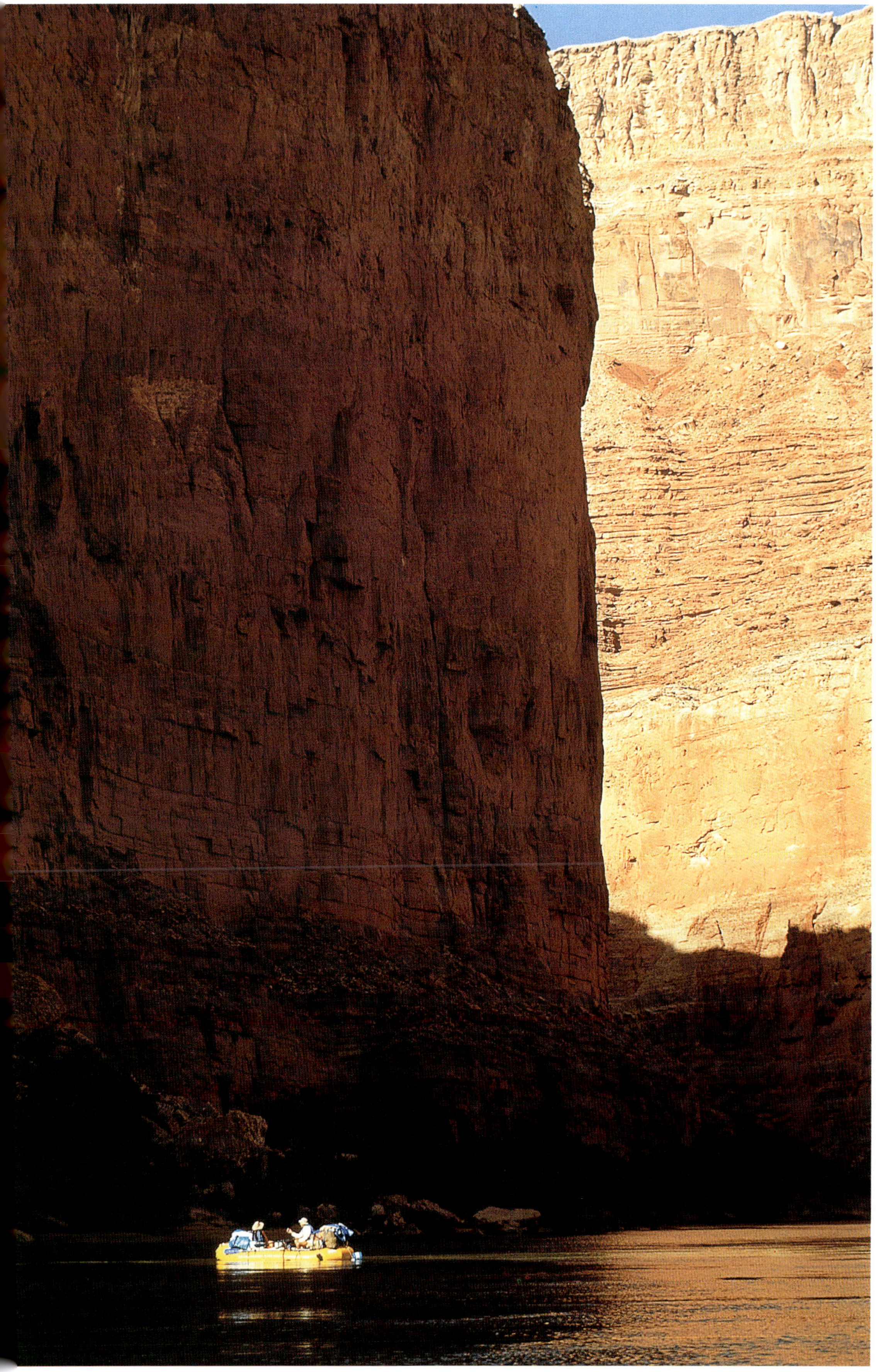

White-water rafters make stately progress past the sheer cliffs of Marble Canyon, but elsewhere the Colorado River displays its cutting edge.

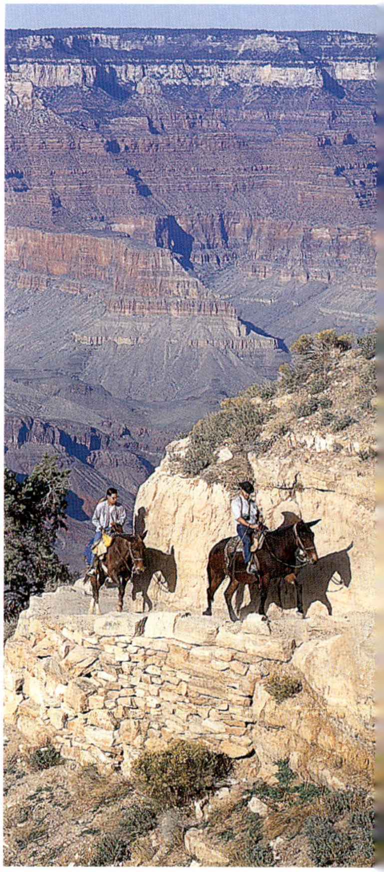

Those who book well in advance can ride mules down the vertiginous trail from the South Rim to the Canyon floor.

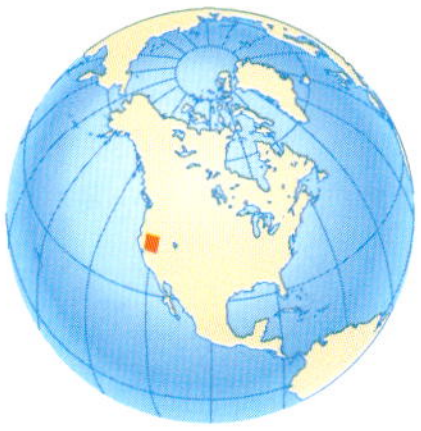

Towering Cliffs of Yosemite

John Muir, Yosemite's founding father, wrote that the valley was like a mountain mansion into which "Nature had gathered her choicest treasures."

FACT FILE

Dimensions of valley: 7 miles (11.2 km) long, and up to 1 mile (1.6 km) wide.

Size of national park: 1,200 square miles (3,108 sq km).

Information: From the Visitors Center, Yosemite Village (372-0229), and Wilderness Center, PO Box 577, Yosemite National Park 95389.

Best climbing seasons: April—May; September. In winter it is snowed under.

IN 1851, a troop of California Volunteers deep in the Sierra Nevada Mountains chased some Native Americans into a hidden refuge on the Merced River, and found themselves in a wonderland of granite monoliths, giant trees, and foaming waterfalls. One of the troop, a young physician named Lafayette Bunnell, learned that the local tribes called the place after their word for "grizzly bear"—Yo-sem-it-y. Its fame spread, and in 1864 it became State property. In 1890 the 750,000-acre (303,000-ha) valley with its surrounding area became one of the first three U.S. national parks.

Some 10 million years ago, the Sierra Nevada arose. Then two other forces—the flowing waters of the Merced and the scouring action of ice-age glaciers—succeeded each other, several times. The glaciers, which once filled this valley to a depth of around 3,000 feet (almost 1,000 m), scooped out bowls, or cirques, below the peaks, and sliced vertiginous cliffs like the

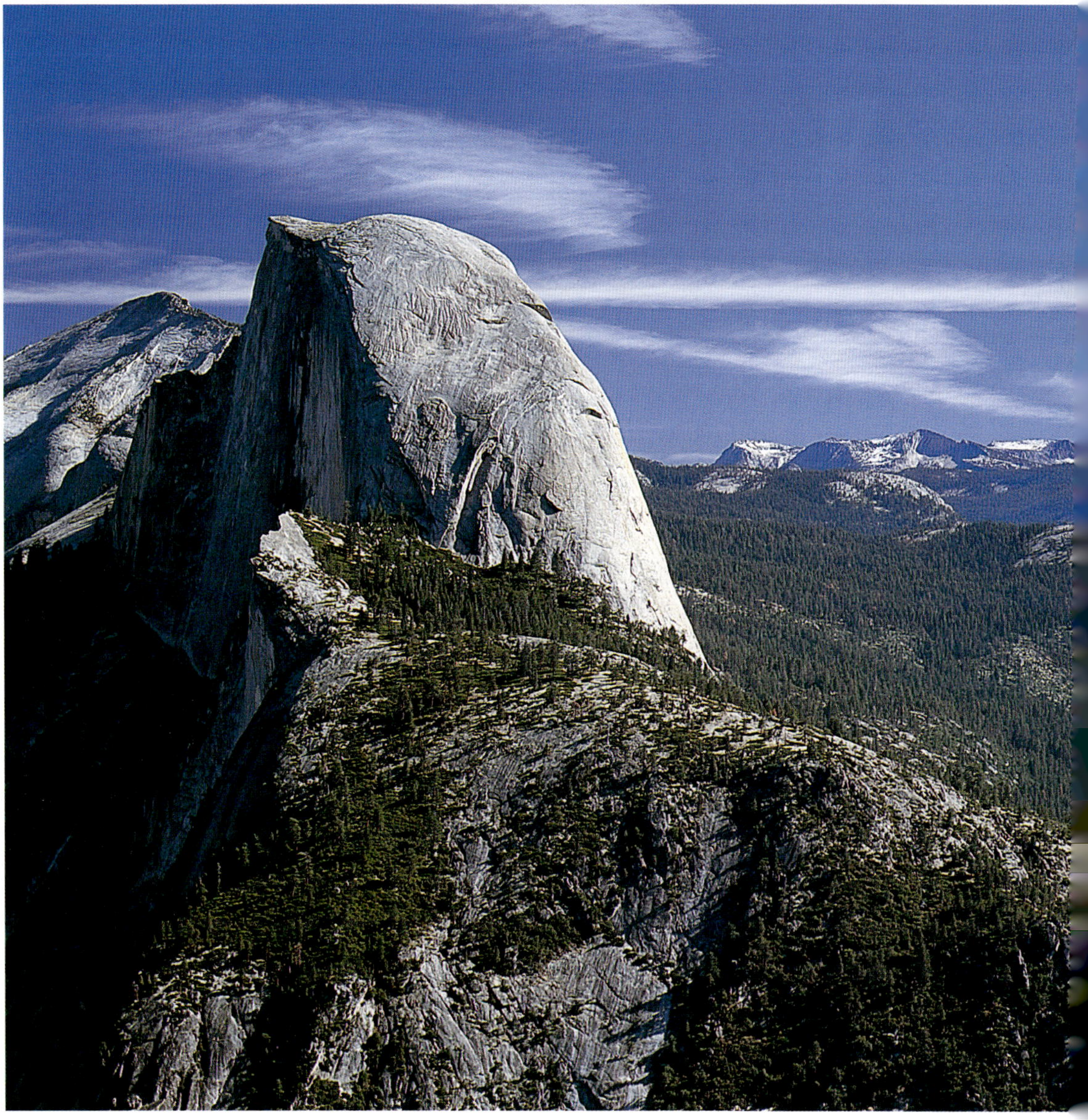

The vertical cliff of Half Dome (right) was formed when a glacier moving through the valley undermined the mountain, causing it to split.

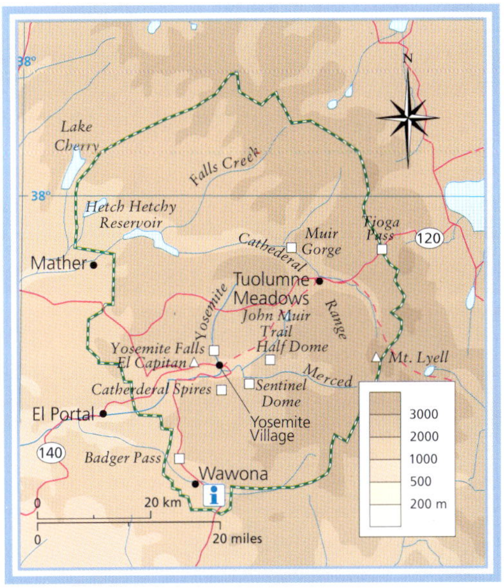

Cathedral Spires (right) are among the Yosemite peaks that have been exposed after glaciers and rivers eroded surrounding softer rock.

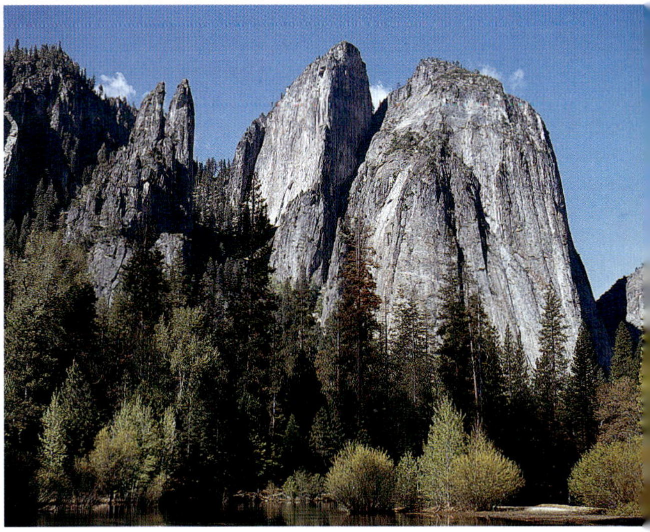

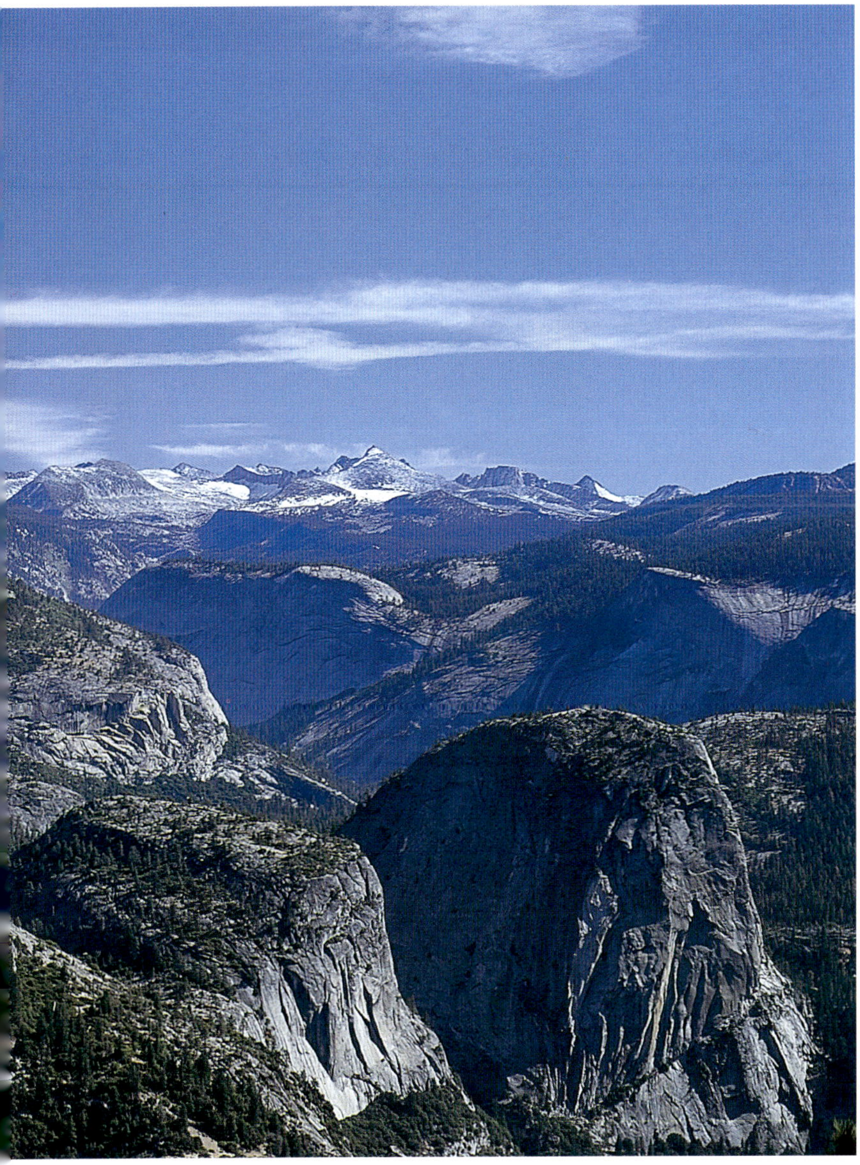

drop of Half Dome and the sturdy prow of El Capitan—at 3,500 feet (1,066 m) the world's biggest slab of exposed granite. When the ice vanished the last time, meltwater lakes silted up to form fertile valleys.

Milder forces of erosion are still at work, as shown by glories like the 620-foot (189 m) Bridalveil Falls and the double waterfall, the Upper and Lower Yosemite, which together form the highest falls in North America at 2,425 feet (739 m).

The soil's fertility is reflected in the 1,000 species of wildflowers and the variety of trees—black oak, incense cedar, ponderosa pine, and giant sequoias. Though not as tall as the related coastal redwoods, the sequoia is bulkier, making it the largest living thing on earth. In three separate groves, the sequoias soar over 200 feet (60 m). In the largest, the Mariposa Grove, a veteran known as the Grizzly Giant is an estimated 2,700 years old.

Most of the 4 million visitors a year, stick to Yosemite Village with its visitor center, shuttle buses, and campgrounds, and the scenic drive along Tioga Road, once a wagon route to mines on the far side of the Sierra Nevada. Strollers have ready access to Yosemite Falls, Mirror Lake, and Half Dome. Walkers prefer the hiking trails northeast to the alpine slopes of Tuolumne Meadows, or to the south through Mariposa Grove to see the Grizzly Giant and a "tunnel tree" with a road through it (there were two until one fell in 1969). But these trails,too, can be extremely crowded.

FAR FROM THE MILLING CROWDS

Intrepid visitors prepared for longer stays can head away from the roads and popular trails. There are climbing classes for beginners, and the experienced can choose from thousands of feet of granite cliff. Half

The Bridalveil Falls (right) were known as the "spirit of the puffing wind" to local Indians.

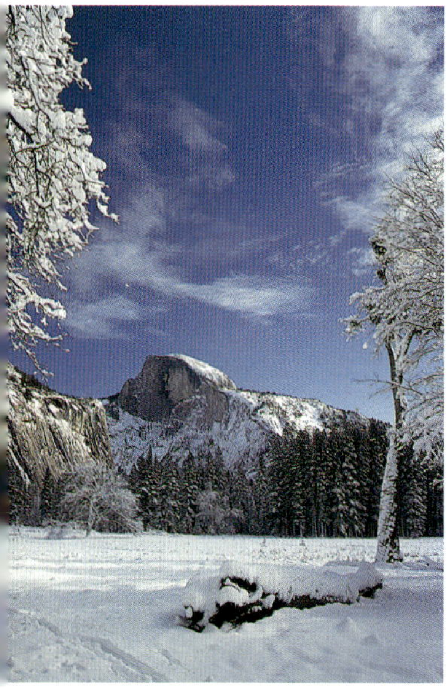

With a mantle of snow, Half Dome stands guard over the valley floor.

Dome claims the continent's sheerest cliff—only seven degrees from vertical—and Glacier Point, at 3,200 feet (969 m), less than a mile from Half Dome, offers stupendous views. Hiking permits are limited: half are issued in advance on application to the Wilderness Center, the rest issued daily from ranger stations. Hikers then have access to rough mountain campgrounds and more than 700 miles (1,120 km) of trails. They will discover a staggering range of ecologies reflecting very different environments. From dry foothills with pines and oaks, trails climb along streams and through meadows to forests of maple, dogwood, and Douglas fir. Higher up, white bark pines thin out as they approach the timber line, above which the crest of the Sierra Nevada rears, with two peaks (Lyell and Dana) reaching over 13,000 feet (almost 4,000 m).

Hikers share the backcountry with coyote, fox, skunk, and racoon. The grizzlies for which the valley and park are named have long since vanished, but in the backcountry hikers may see mule deer—so-called from their long ears—grazing in meadows. Occasionally, visitors stumble on a black bear scavenging for anything to eat, from berries to discarded candy. Black bears—which are in fact mainly brown—are rather aggressive and may attack if alarmed. Hikers should make plenty of noise and campers should store food safely out of bears' reach. Never feed them!

One trail that strikes a balance between the excessively rigorous and overly popular is the 17-mile (27 km) ascent of Half Dome. A steep path along the Little Yosemite Valley leads up nearly 2,000 feet (600 m) past the Vernal and Nevada Falls, on behind Half Dome, then upward over the rock's vast humped back with the aid of steps and fixed cables to the near-vertical, 4,800-foot (1,450 m) drop. It is possible to do this in a day, but you do need to be fit and start early.

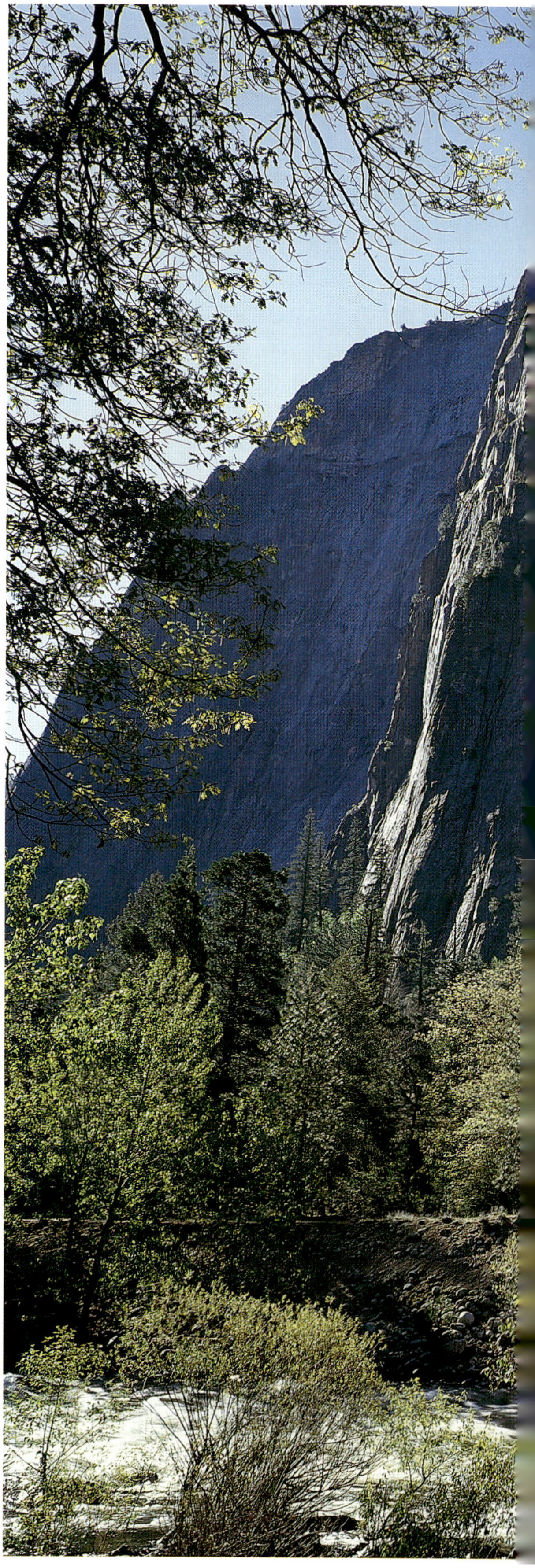

JOHN MUIR, THE FIRST KING OF CONSERVATION

Yosemite was made a national park largely at the instigation of John Muir (1838-1914), the Scottish -born father of American conservation. When he arrived in San Francisco in 1868, he asked directions to "anywhere that's wild" and learned of the Yosemite Valley. It was he who realized the valley was the product of glacial erosion. His visits there and to other pristine western landscapes inspired him to take a lead in protecting the Sierra range. This in effect established both the conservation movement and a pressure group to inspire federal action which, in 1890, gave birth to the first national parks. In 1892 he was the cofounder and secretary of the Sierra Club, whose members still work to keep the wilderness unspoiled and accessible. The club's members soon established regular summer camps in Yosemite's Tuolumne Meadows, and John Muir is memorialized in the trail named for him, part of the Pacific Crest which leads from Yosemite Village through the Meadows and southward to Mount Witney, 120 miles (192 km) away.

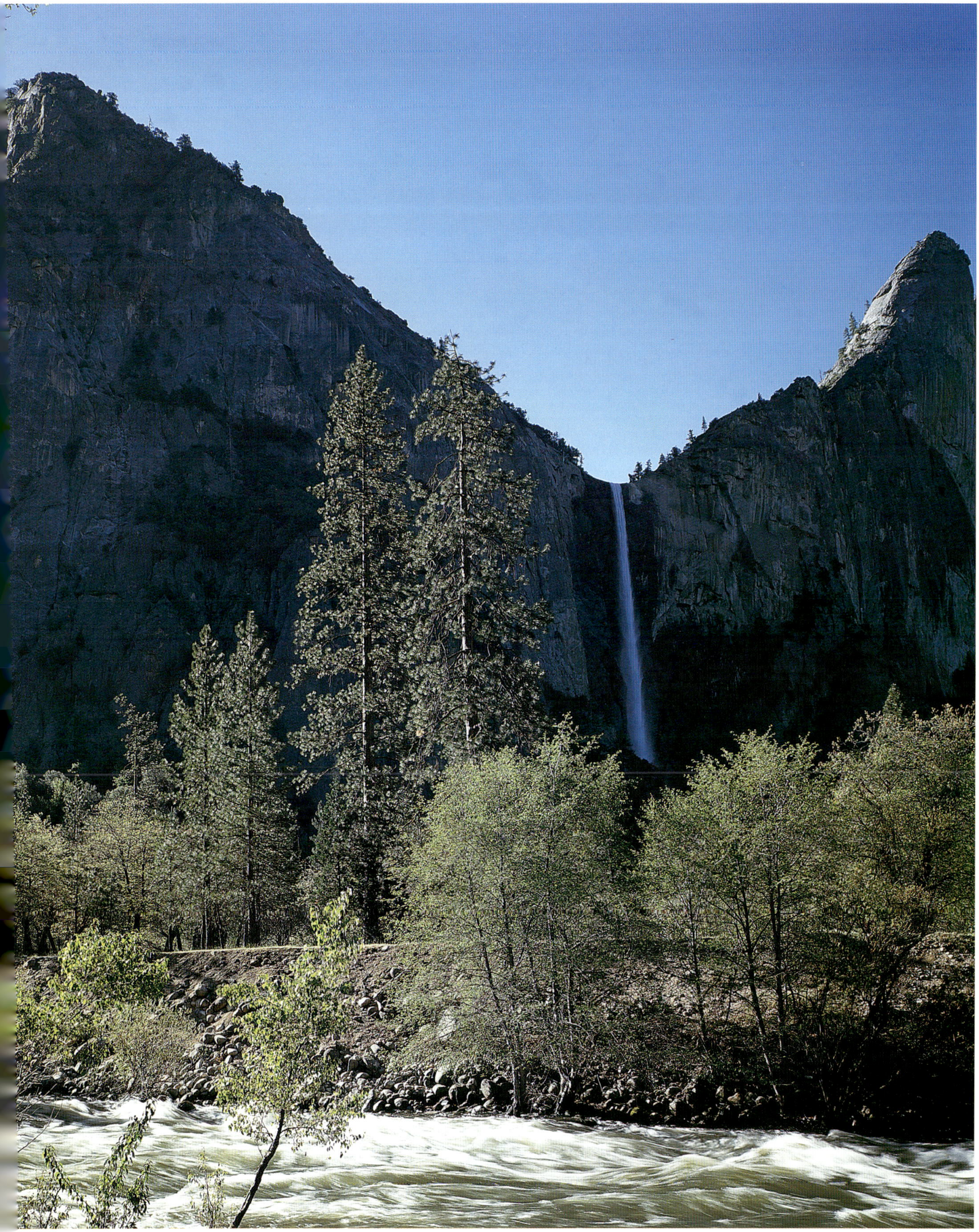

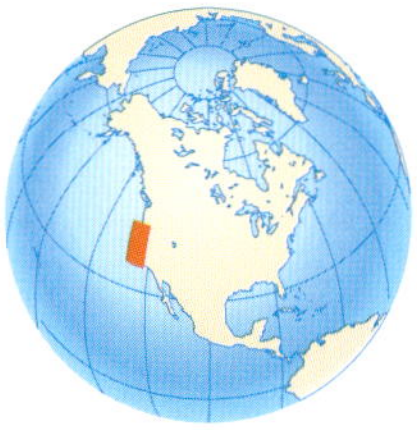

San Francisco and the West Coast

In 100 miles (160 km), from San Francisco Bay to the Big Sur, city life at its most sophisticated turns to nature in the raw.

IT WAS THE DISCOVERY OF GOLD in the Sierra Nevada that stimulated the growth of San Francisco in the mid-1800s. That, combined with its superb setting overlooking a natural harbor, has produced a city that to its inhabitants and millions of visitors often seems golden. Its strait—the Golden Gate—between California's largest bay and the Pacific Ocean, is bridged by one of the world's engineering glories. Its climate—cold waters and warm lands combining to create quick changes in the weather—architecture, culture, and setting all match its golden origins. With a population of 750,000 and an area of just 46 square miles (116 sq km), it combines small-town charm with a big-town zest, all shot through with a unique liberalism. Here beatniks, hippies, and gays have all found a congenial home.

Part of the city's charm comes from its accessibility. Although on the edge of one of the country's largest metropolitan areas (the Bay area), it is constrained by the rugged peninsula on which it lies. It is one of the few American cities that does not demand a car. In good walking shoes or trainers, the city is yours, if you carry a jacket to counter the sudden chill of fogs and are prepared to tackle hills—there are more than 40 of

Night lights show off San Francisco's unique combination of bayside and hill, lowrise and highrise.

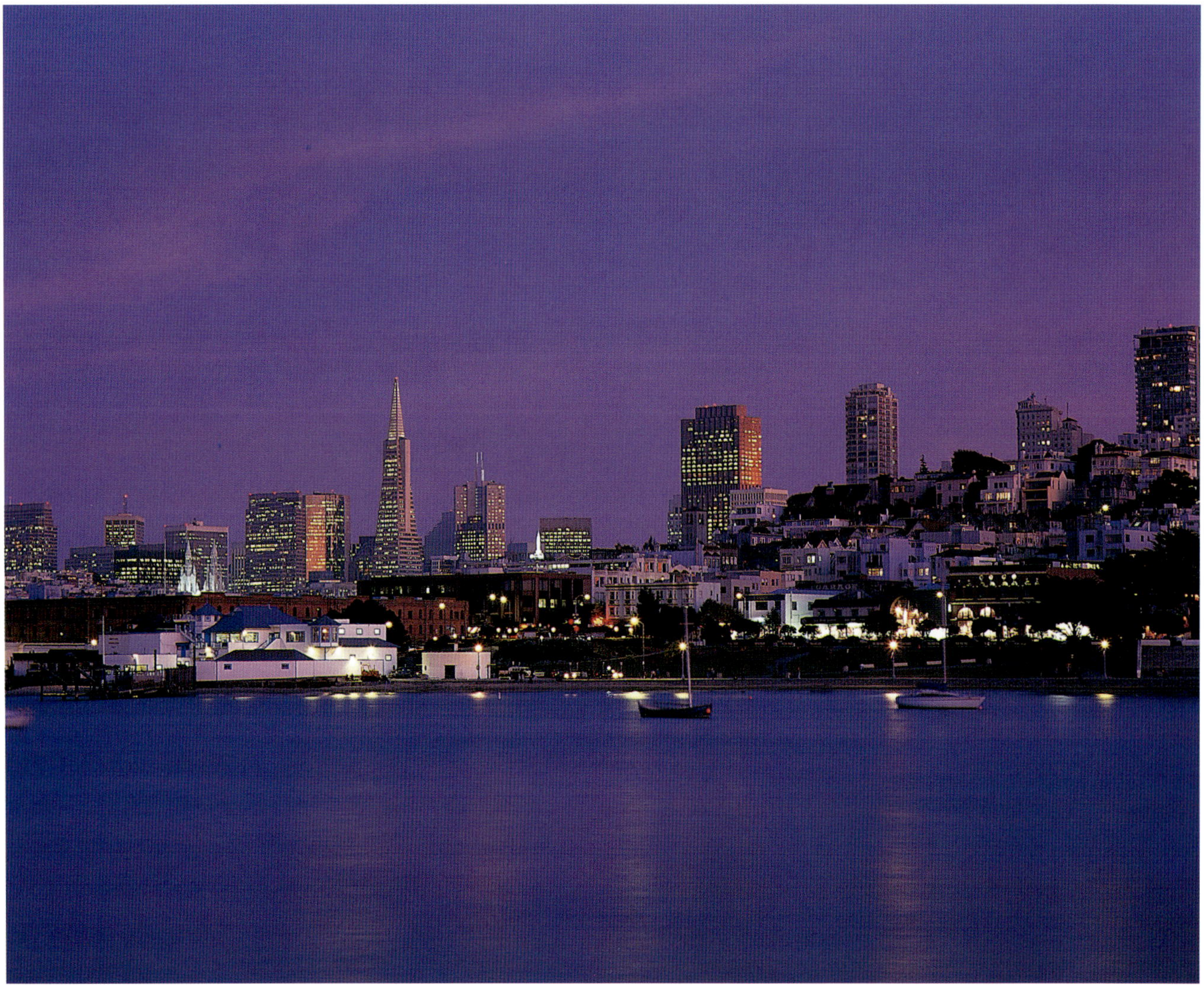

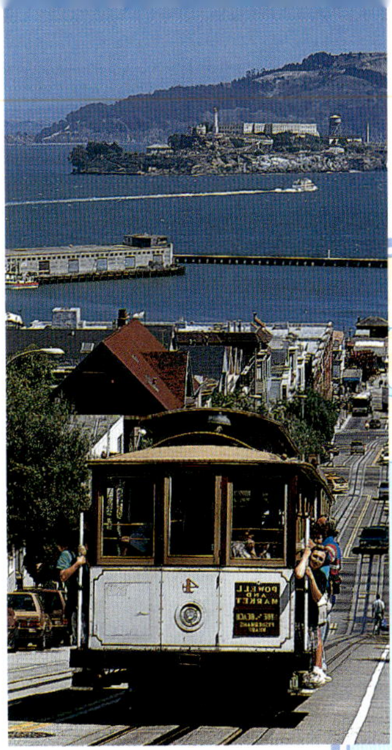

★ *Two of the city's most characteristic sights in one image (above): cable cars and the former island prison of Alcatraz.*

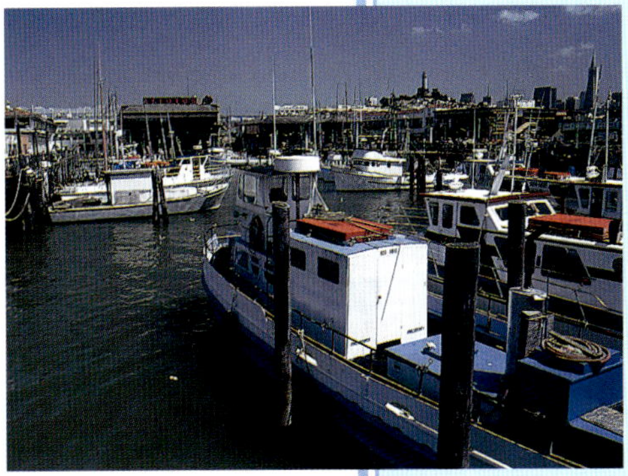

★ *Fisherman's Wharf, once a working harbor, is now a place of restaurants and tourist stores.*

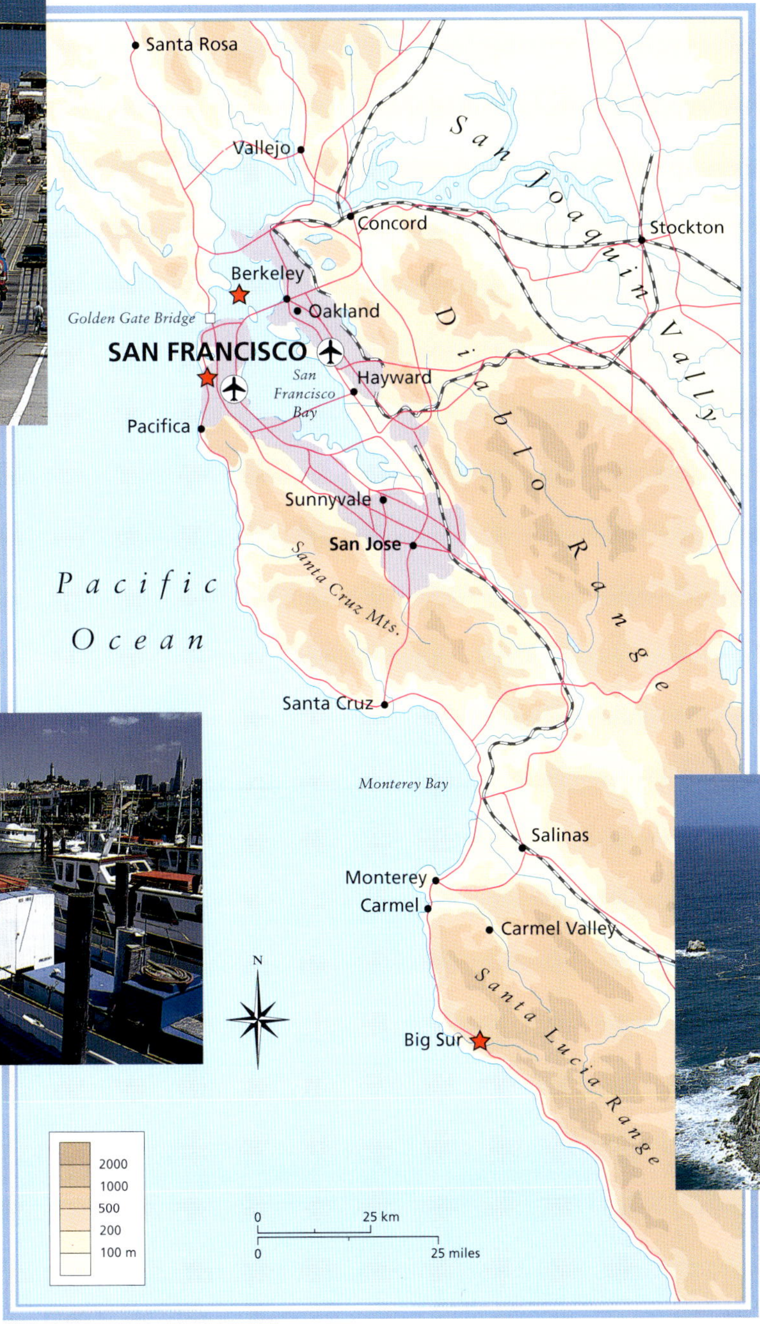

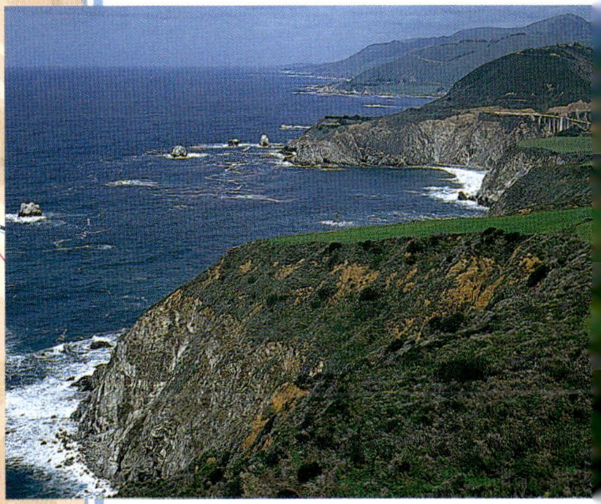

★ *South of San Francisco, Big Sur (above) is a spectacular stop along the cliff-hugging Coast Highway 1.*

FACT FILE

Best time: October, for Halloween's gay parades in The Castro, and with fewer people and less fog along the coast.

City driving: On the many steep hills, park with the wheels turned into the curb.

City accomodation: Seldom a problem. Tourism is the city's greatest business, and you'll never be stuck for a room.

Big Sur travel: Public transportation is poor. Best to use a car, and then walk.

them—that rise like flights of stairs. If exhaustion threatens, the city's three ancient and revered cable car lines are standbys, carrying commuters and tourists up and down from the Bayside.

The starting point, historically and geographically, should be the docks. A triangle of land to the south, its 6-mile (9.6 km) perimeter marked by Van Ness Avenue, Market Street, and the Bay-side Embarcadero is the city's heart or downtown. Fisherman's Wharf, with its touristic shops and restaurants, backs onto North Beach which still retains the bohemian feel that made it famous as the base of the "Beat generation" in the 1950s. A short climb brings you to Telegraph Hill topped by Coit Tower, a monument to the city's firemen decorated by fine murals.

Or from Fisherman's Wharf visitors can take a cable car up to Union Square, where tourists gawp at the sumptuous Art Deco lobby of the Westin St. Francis Hotel. Nob Hill, as its name suggests, like neighboring Russian Hill, has the mansions and grand hotels that catered to the rich who made their fortunes in the skyscrapers of the Financial District below. To the south lies Chinatown, a seething neon-lit world of its own, served by its own schools, banks, temples, and newspapers, as well as more than 100 restaurants. Southwest lie the disconcerting slums of the Tenderloin

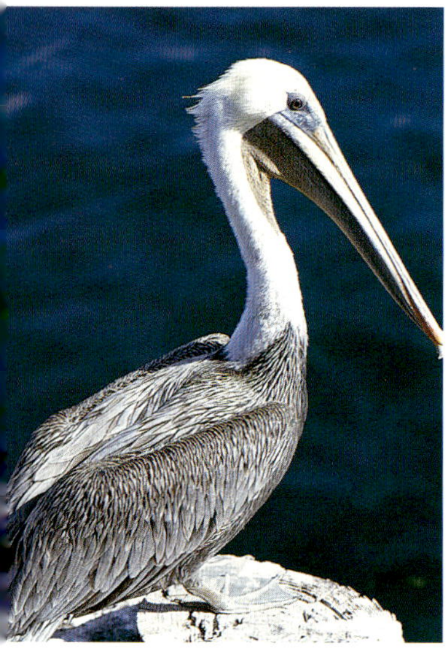

Pelicans fly with slow, heavy deliberation, like prehistoric birds, over the beaches of Monterey and Carmel.

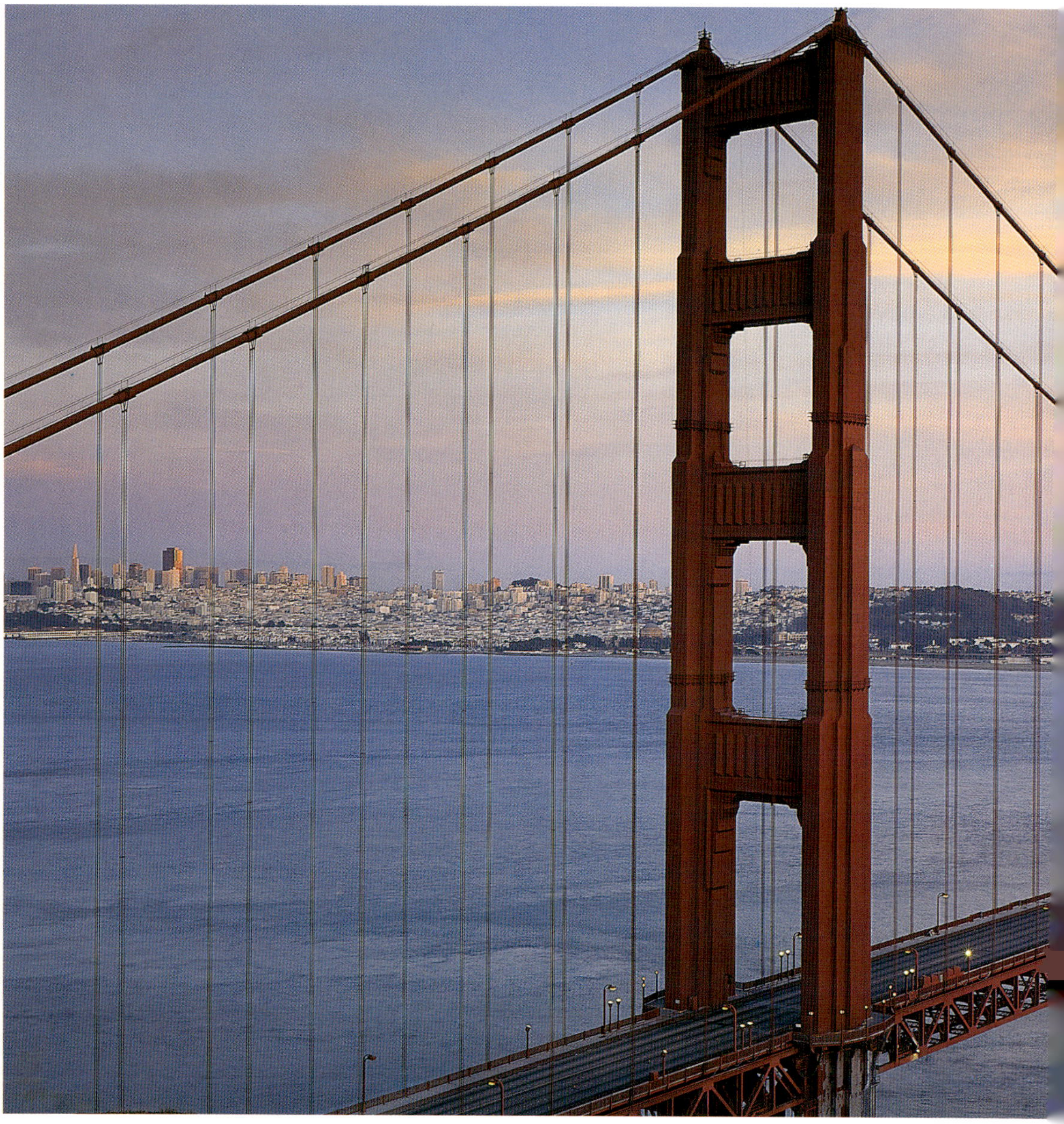

Turn-of-the-century domestic architecture (below) is as much part of San Francisco's identity as its scintillating highrises.

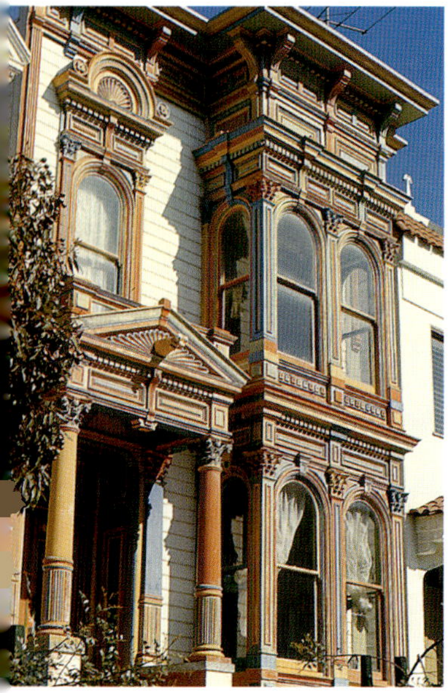

district, which contrasts with the grandeur of the neighboring Civic Center. But there is more to San Francisco than can be revealed in one day's walking. Westward from Fisherman's Wharf is Golden Gate Bridge, the world's first great suspension bridge, with a span of three-quarters of a mile (1.2 km). Though completed back in 1937, it still holds its own as an arresting piece of architecture, one that becomes magical when fog blankets its base. Its lure is occasionally fatal as well: every month, half a dozen people jump from the midway point to their deaths in the water 260 feet (80 m) below.

A mile south is Golden Gate Park, designed by Frederick Olmsted, creator of New York's Central Park. This is a glorious 1,000-acre (404 ha) playground, with meadows, lakes, and gardens, numerous museums, a buffalo paddock, and the tallest artificial waterfall in the West, overlooking the massive—but forbiddingly cold—Pacific surf.

SURF, WHALES, AND WILDERNESS

The city has contrasts enough for a lifetime, let alone two weeks, but many visitors seek out greater privacy and peace by driving south along the dramatic coastal road, Highway 1. Some 75 miles (120 km) south lies Santa Cruz, a city founded by a Spanish missionary in 1791. There is little sign of Spanish Catholicism now, apart from a replica 1792 mission. The Pacific waves rolling into Monterey Bay, and a giant rollercoaster, make it a sensational beach playground.

Monterey itself arose as a sardine and canning town, but Cannery Row—immortalized in the title of John Steinbeck's novel—and Fisherman's Wharf are now

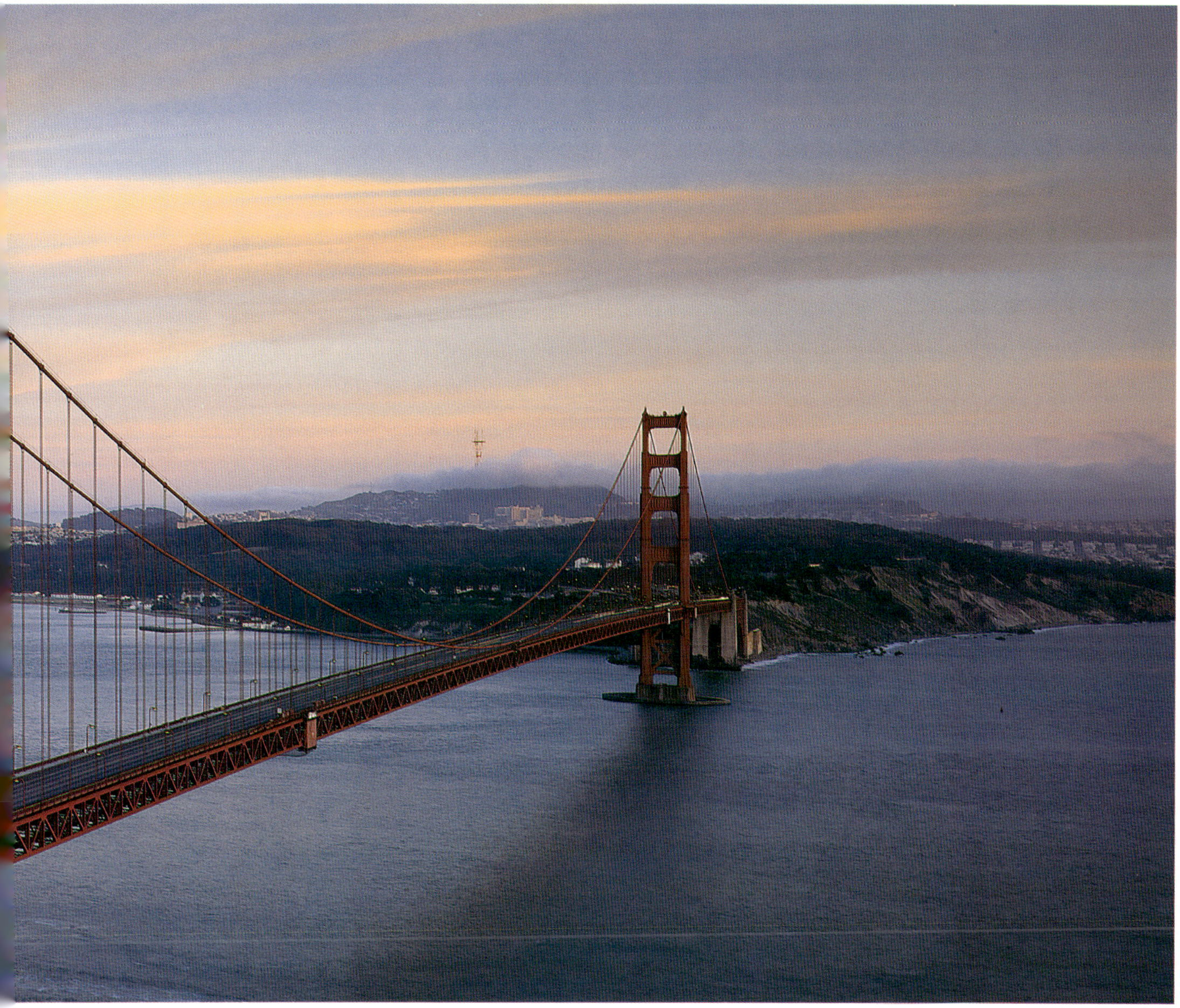

glitzy shopping arcades, bars, and discos. The city's best-known sight is the Monterey Bay Aquarium, with its kelp forest, a pool where visitors can stroke rays, and a vast window, claimed to be the world's largest, which provides an underwater view of the Pacific environment, complete with turtles, sunfish, sharks, and man o' war jellyfish. The 17-mile-drive (27 km) around the Monterey Peninsula, which swings through forests of Monterey cypresses, offers a chance to see seals basking, then skirts the shopping mecca and artists' colony of Carmel where music is banned in public places.

The true glory of the coast, and the ultimate contrast with the urban areas to the north, lies south of Monterey along the stretch known as Big Sur. Here a line of surf-battered cliffs marks the border between the Los Padres National Forest and the Santa Lucia range. It is one of the world's great unspoiled coastlines along which Route 1 snakes past rocky coves and through canyons. One of the few places you can reach the shore is Pfeiffer Beach where a seacut arch stands out at the foot of massive cliffs and visitors can spy pelicans fishing beyond the icy breakers.

Here, camping is virtually a way of life. There are half a dozen major campgrounds, while a mile inland from Pfeiffer Beach on the Big Sur River is a campground that acts as a gateway into the Pfeiffer Big Sur State Park. Dozens of trails lead away into the Big Sur and Los Padres hinterland, where deer and bobcats roam. A tough two-hour climb up the tortuous Buzzard's Roost Trail leads to a panoramic view over the whole region. In spring the wildflowers are glorious, but October through November offers glimpses of sea otters and gray whales, with fewer foggy days.

The 1,400 yard (1,272 m)-long Golden Gate Bridge spans the entrance of San Francisco Bay to the Pacific Ocean.

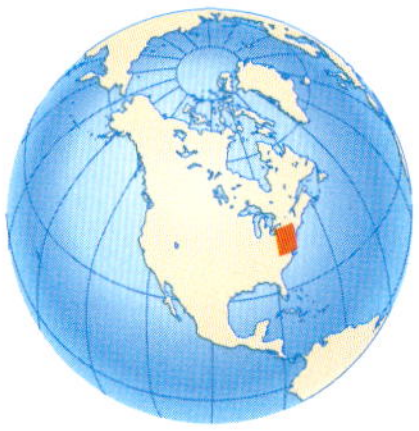

America's Largest Wilderness

"Stanley had found Livingstone in darkest Africa before most New Yorkers knew much about the wilderness at their back door."—Nature writer Lincoln Barnett.

FACT FILE

Time to avoid: Blackfly season (early June to mid-July).

Information on hiking and camping: The Adirondack Mountain Club on Lake George (Tel: 1-518-668-4447) or Lake Placid (1-518-523-3441). High Peaks Information Center, three miles south of Lake Placid.

Transportation: Buses run from Albany to lakes Placid, Tupper, and George.

THIS WILDERNESS IS SOMETHING OF A PARADOX. It is larger than several states, larger than some countries, being almost the size of Belgium. Yet it lies close to the most densely populated part of the U.S.—the Adirondack State Park is just 200 miles (320 km) from New York City.

The area's 5,000 square miles (12,950 sq km) of lakes, forests, rivers and low, rounded hills were virtually unknown until the 1830's. Lake Champlain on its northeast borders had been fought over between French, British and Indians for almost two centuries, for it was a fine water route between Canada and the Hudson River. But the wilderness itself was not even named until 1838, when geologist Ebenezer Emmons proposed it as an anglicized form of a name given to a tribe of Algonquin Indians. Supposedly, the name arose from their habit of living on tree buds and bark during the harsh winters, for which they were known as "ratirontak"—eaters of trees—by their Iroquois enemies. The region became one of the nation's first state parks when in 1894 New York State declared that "this forest preserve shall be forever kept as wild forest land."

Until the 1980s, it was the largest park in the U.S. (now Wrangell-St. Elias in Alaska is larger). It incorporates land in a range of categories, from the 1,500 square mile (3,885 sq km) wilderness areas kept entirely undeveloped, and where access is only on foot or horseback, to areas with many well-maintaind state campgrounds, ski centers, public beaches, and boating facilities.

ANCIENT FORMATION

The Adirondacks are part of one of the most ancient mountain systems on earth. There are no fossils—the rocks were formed 700 million years before life emerged on earth. Back then, the area's foundations were a seabed that became gorged with lava and sediments. Later, a primeval continental collision

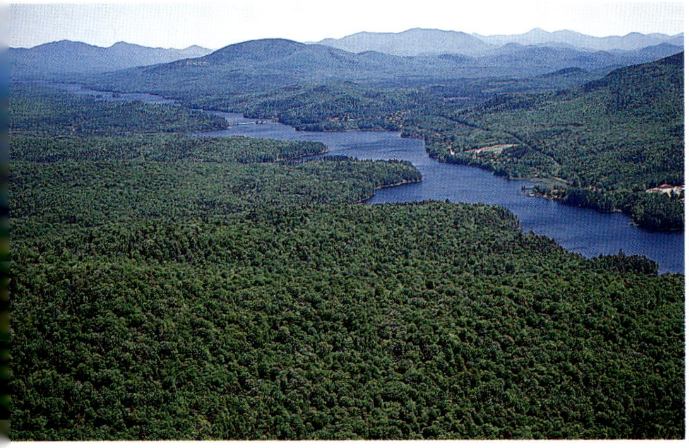

The ribbon of Long Lake (above) stretches for 13 miles (21 km) through the center of the National Park, but is in parts only 100 yards (91 m) wide.

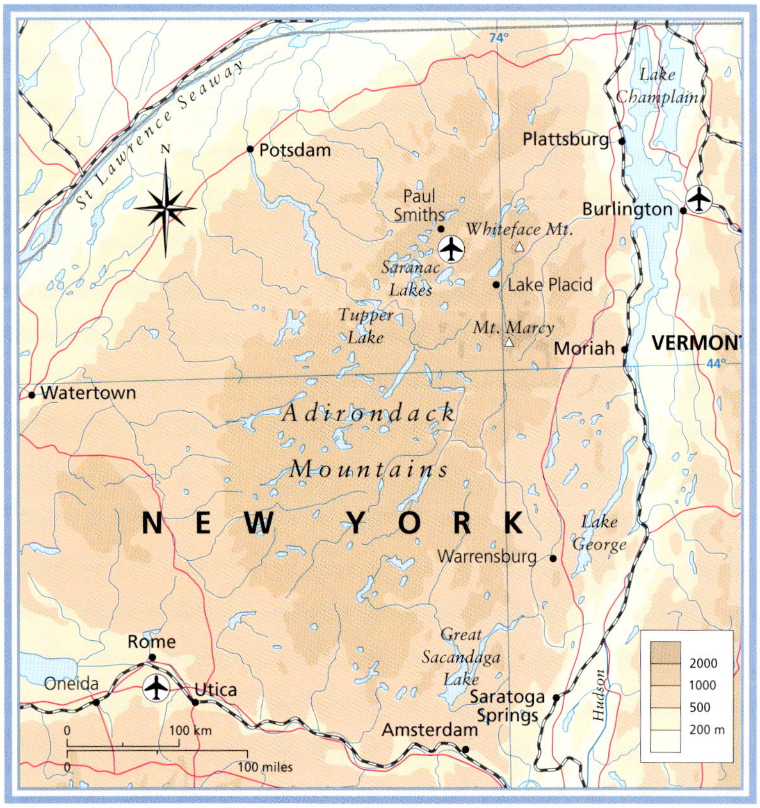

The heartland of this huge region (right) is dominated by the ancient eroded stumps of once-high mountains and hundreds of small lakes.

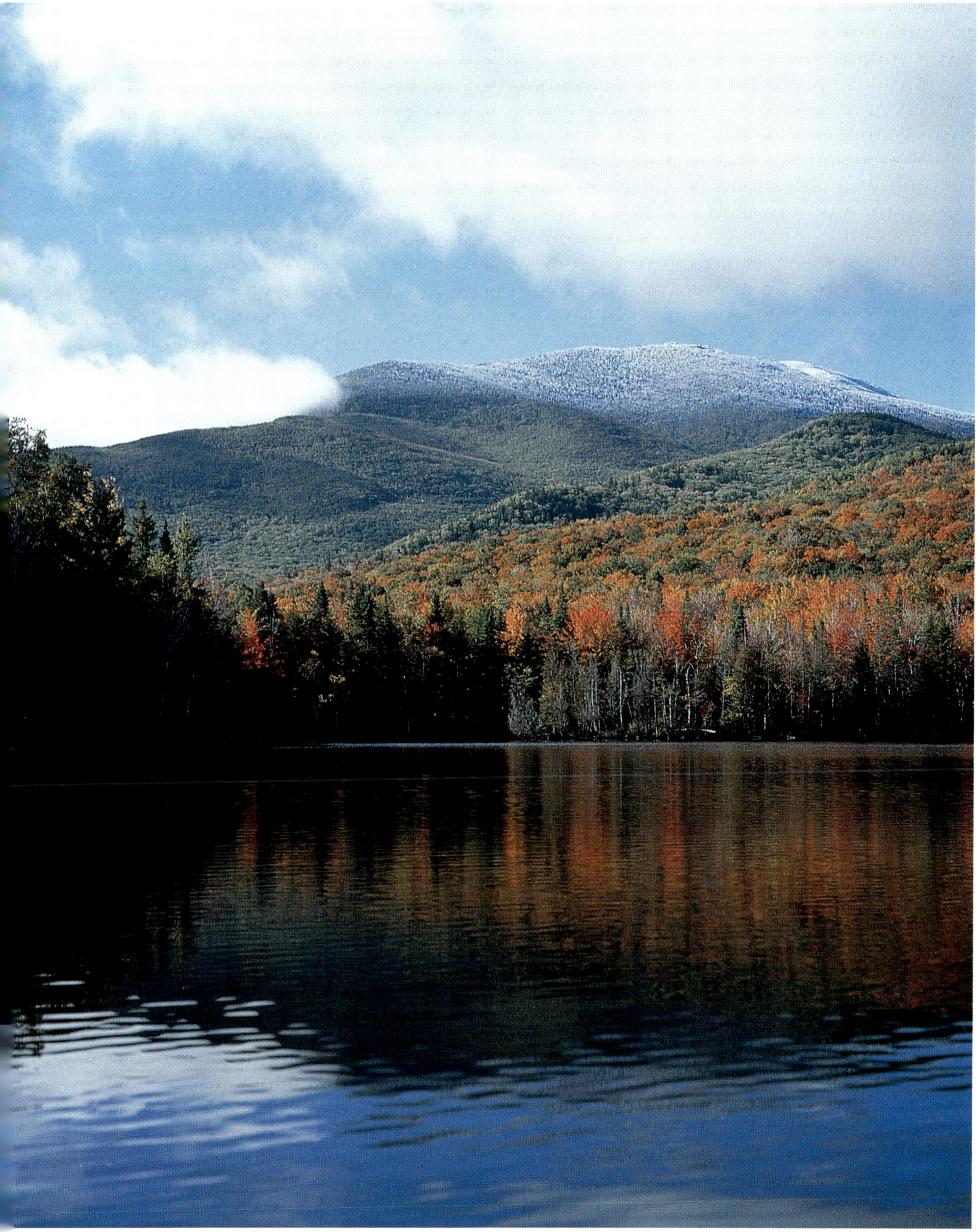

Lake Placid's wooded shores and central island (right) are sheltered by the broad shoulders of Whiteface Mountain.

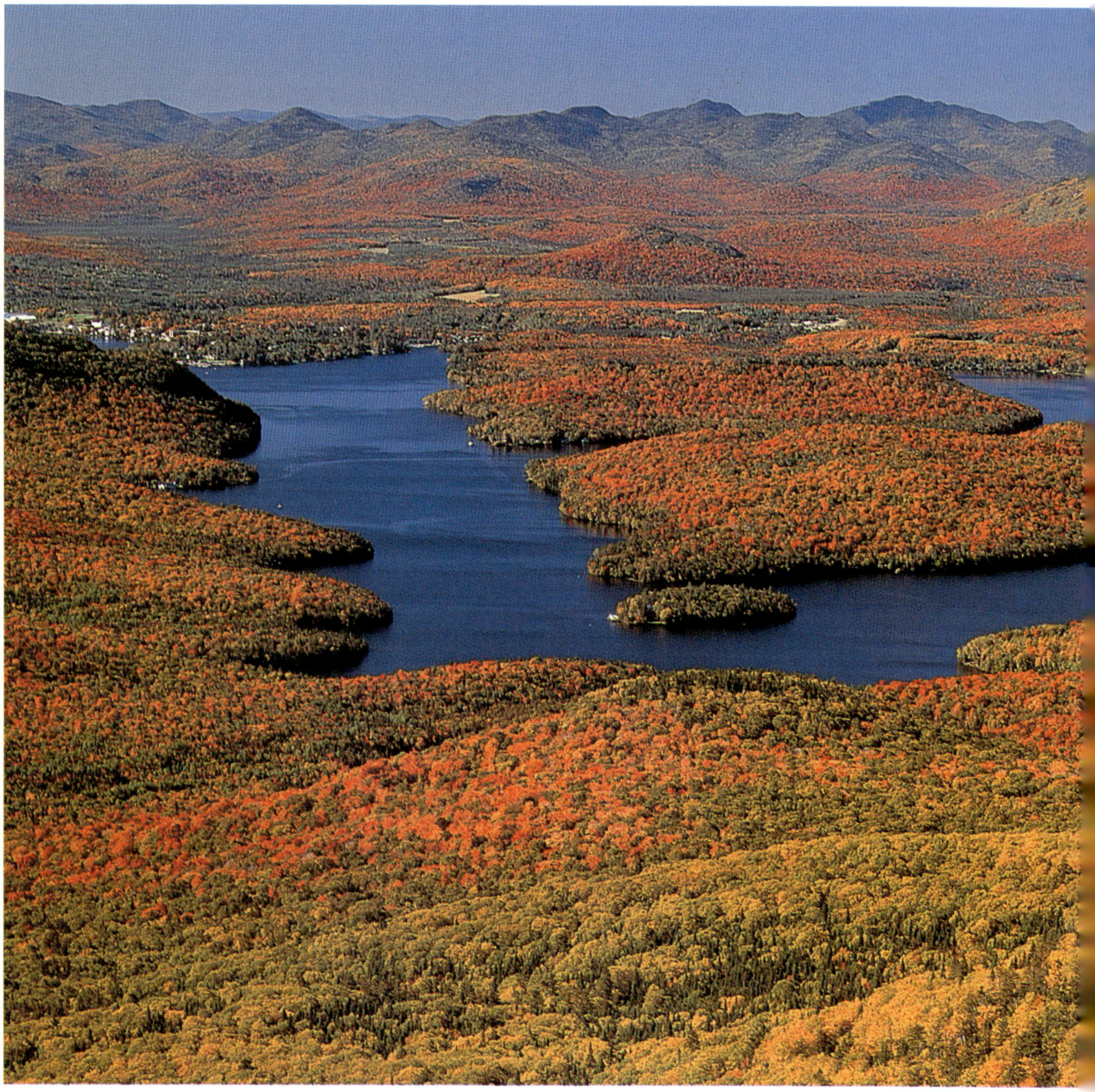

A hotel on Lake Placid's secluded banks (below) provides a haven from which to walk and fish.

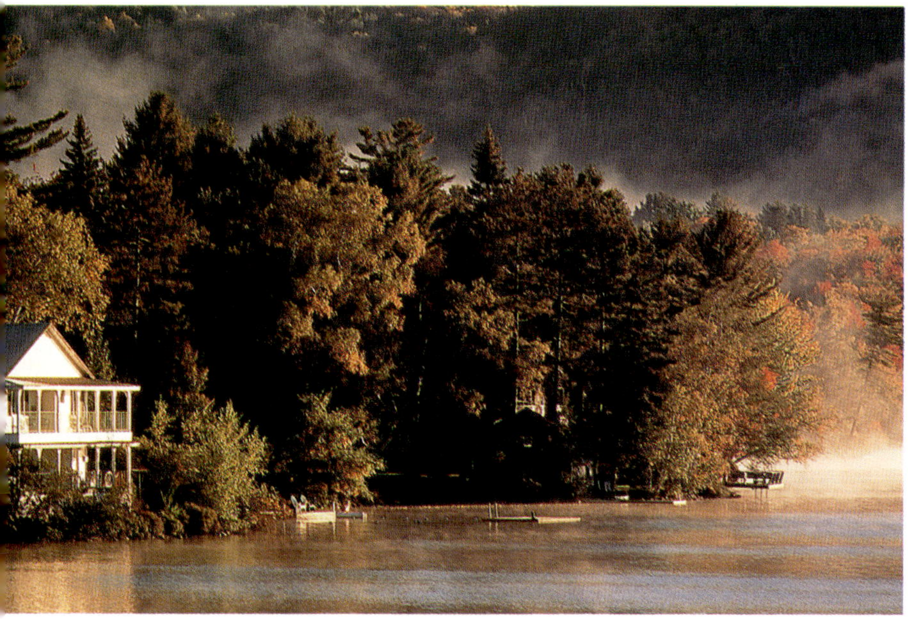

buckled these rocks upward into 20,000-foot (6,095 m) peaks, in five ranges running northeast-southwest—lines that can still be traced today.

By roughly 500 million years ago, as the drifting continents parted again, erosion had worn the mountains to stubs. About 425 million years ago, North America collided again with Europe, throwing up the Appalachians, building a new edge to the American continent, and shielding the Adirondacks. For hundreds of millions of years the area seems to have been tranquil. Then came the last climactic chapter in the region's formation. Over a period of a million years, four great ice sheets blanketed North America, grinding off the surface, gouging out valleys. As the ice retreated for the last time 10,000 years ago, valleys and depressions filled with water, creating river systems and the Adirondacks' 2,000 lakes.

So the soil is thin and the mountains low, but the forests are varied, from softwoods like spruce and

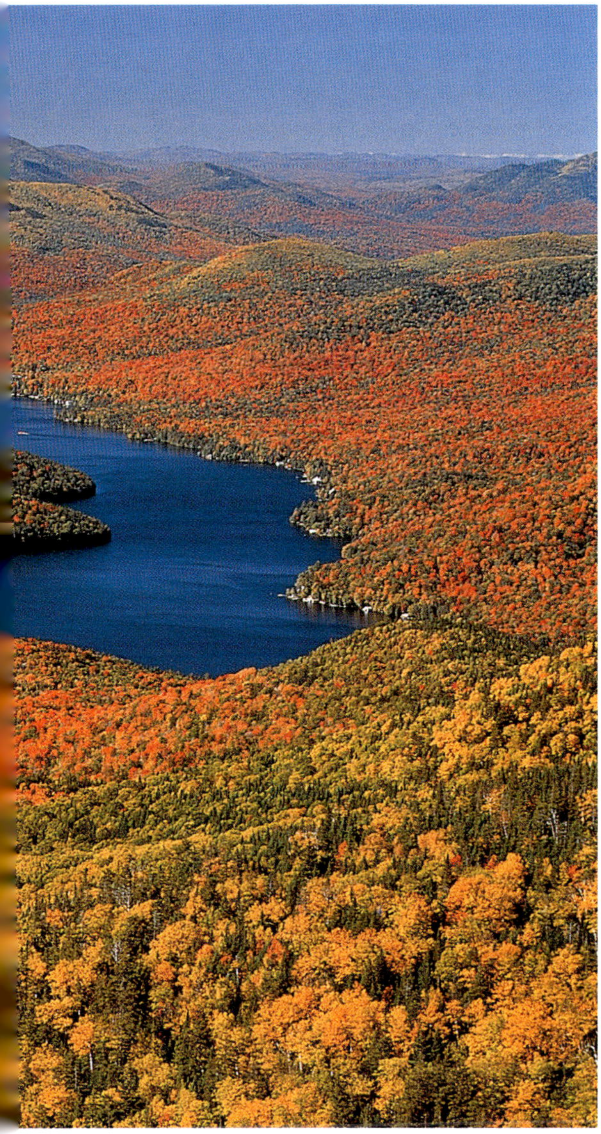

balsam fir in wetlands to hardwoods on the valley sides, to the alpine plants and naked rocks above the 4,900-foot (1,493 m) timberline. Trailwalkers favor the northeast, the High Peaks area, where 46 summits of around 4,000 feet (1,219 m) cluster around the highest point in New York State, Mount Marcy at 5,334 feet (1,625 m). From here the view is spectacular—as its first conqueror, John Cheney described in 1837: "Old Champlain, though 50 miles off, glistens below you like a strip of white birch bark when slicked up by the moon on a frosty night; and the Green Mountains of Vermont beyond it fade and fade away, till they disappear as gradually as a cold scent when the dew rises."

LAND OF THE DEERHUNTER

Though there are black bears in the mountains, they are seldom seen round campgrounds because garbage is no longer left out in the open, but lone campers should heed the guidlelines about food storage. The most common creatures are white-tailed deer, which live off grass, ferns, and goldenrod in the summer, and hemlock, ash, and maple in the bitter winters. Since their predators—chiefly wolves—vanished long ago, the deer population would boom, destroying their winter food sources, if they were not controlled by humans: this is prime deer-hunting country.

The population is sparse—some 125,000—but every year about 9 million come in to ski, fish, camp, hunt, and climb (there is a club for those who have climbed Mount Marcy and its 45 neighbors: the Fortysixers). Most of them come in summer, after mid-July (before then, for about six weeks mornings and evenings can be made a torture by biting blackflies).

Lake George is a popular and ever expanding resort. But with 2,000 miles (3,200 km) of trail, hikers can spend days without seeing anyone, and campers can pitch tents freely as long as they are 150 feet (45 m) away from a trail, road, water source, or campground, and no higher than 4,000 feet (1,219m). Canoers can use a 170-mile (275 km) network of lakes and streams, for which Lake Saranac is a good starting point. There are a dozen skiing centers—Lake Placid, with a speed skating oval in the middle of town, hosted the 1980 Winter Olympics. Cross country skiers have 60 miles (96 km) of groomed trails, and for downhill skiers Whiteface Mountain has 65 runs and 10 lifts.

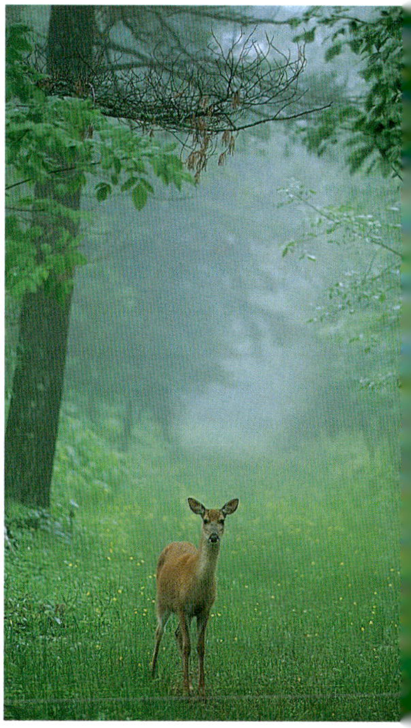

White-tailed deer are common in the forests, feeding on grass, ferns, and trees, and in summer often splashing through lake shallows seeking out aquatic plants.

THE HUDSON'S SECRET SOURCE

Of the Adirondacks' countless rivers, the best known is the Hudson—by name, at least, for this section of the river is known to very few. At its mouth 306 miles (490 km) away along the New York-New Jersey border, it sustains the world's largest seaport. But here the Hudson is a stream that flows from Henderson Lake—or so it was believed when the first maps were made. In fact, the river's headwaters originate 6 miles (9.6km) up from Henderson, in a little pool first seen only in 1872 by the state surveyor Verplanck Colvin. It was, he reported, a "minute, unpretending tear of the clouds, a lovely pool shivering in the breezes of the mountains." The phrase appealed to his bosses, and they named it accordingly: Lake Tear. Like most of the region's ponds, the lake is silting up as plant debris and silt washes from the slopes of Mount Marcy. But in other ways the area remains much as Colvin found it.

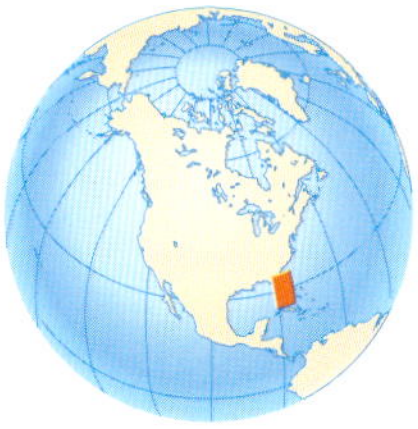

Florida, the "Sunshine State"

This is a land of extremes—the best (and worst) of tourism, the most diverse of populations, the finest examples of Art Deco architecture and the most advanced space technology, the longest beaches and the wettest wetlands.

FACT FILE

Insect repellent: Away from cities, take it.

Miami's crime: Falling. In 1980, the murder rate was five times Manhattan's. In 1996, it was two and half times that of Manhattan. itself falling.

When to go: Winter—temperatures average 59-75°F (15-24°C), and Walt Disney World is less crowded, except during the Christmas break.

Average surf temperature: 74°F (24°C).

Everglades information: Everglades National Park 40001 State Rd 9336, Homestead, FL 33034-6733. (Tel:305-242-7700).

Walt Disney World information: 1-407-824-4500.

THE CENTER OF FLORIDA'S UNIVERSE is Miami; and the center of the center is South Beach. Once this was the epitome of urban decay. Then came the weekly television cop show *Miami Vice*, causing an inrush of publicity and cash. Now, with its miles of glorious white sands, impossibly blue skies, and quirky 1930s architecture, South Beach (or "SoBe") explodes with life and high fashion. Scantily dressed rollerbladers swish down Ocean Drive. Models of centerfold beauty pose in the dazzling light. In one square mile (2.6 sq km), 900 buildings in pastel, cream-cake shades define an Art Deco National Historic District, with its own Welcome Center. Lincoln Road is home to a symphony orchestra, a ballet and numerous galleries. Many visitors find so much to see and do on SoBe, they never go outside it.

That's a mistake. Miami is a collection of different worlds, each having its own special appeal (more so since strict policing has brought Miami's notorious criminals under control). The driverless Metromover offers a cheap (25 cents), quick (50 minutes) bird's-eye view of downtown's skyscrapers, shops, and bay front parks. Coral Gables, 12 square miles (31 sq km) of fountains, plazas, gateways, and Mediterranean architecture, is one of the first planned districts in the U.S. The Biltmore Hotel has the largest swimming pool

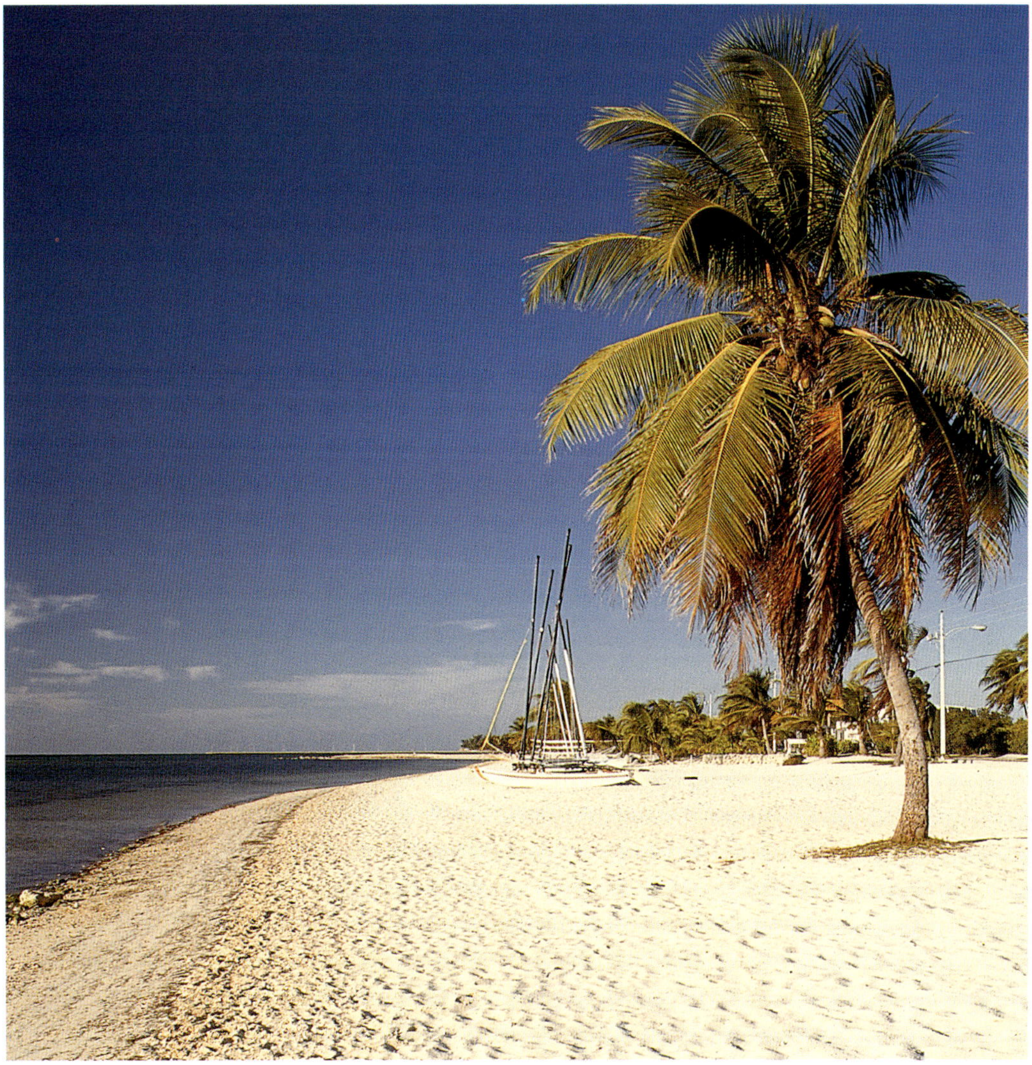

At the end of a 100-mile (160 km) causeway of islands, Key West is a Caribbean playground of palm-fringed beaches.

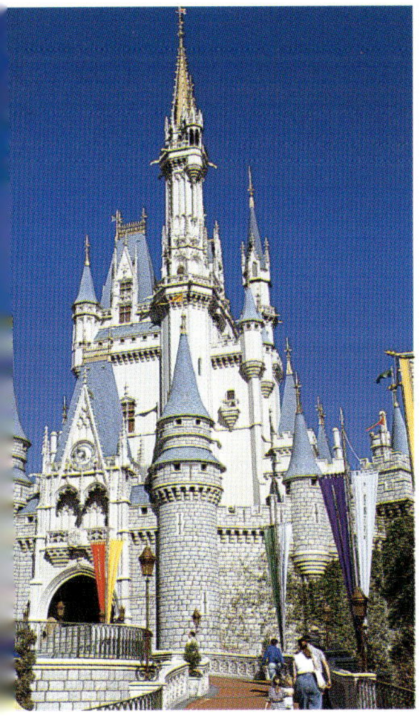

★ ***Disneyworld's castle (above) is part of a fairytale universe so huge that few experience it all. The Everglades (below) in the south offer the contrast of an accessible wilderness with many rare animals.***

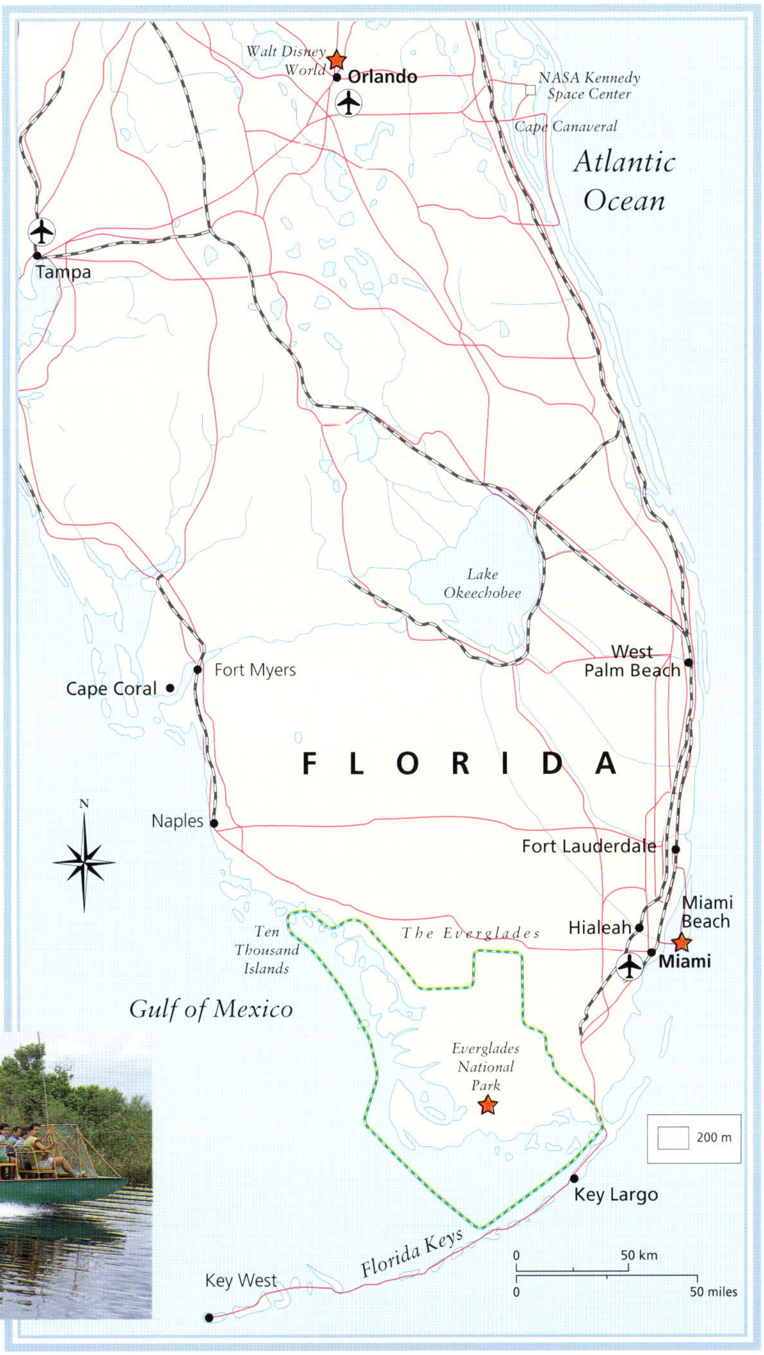

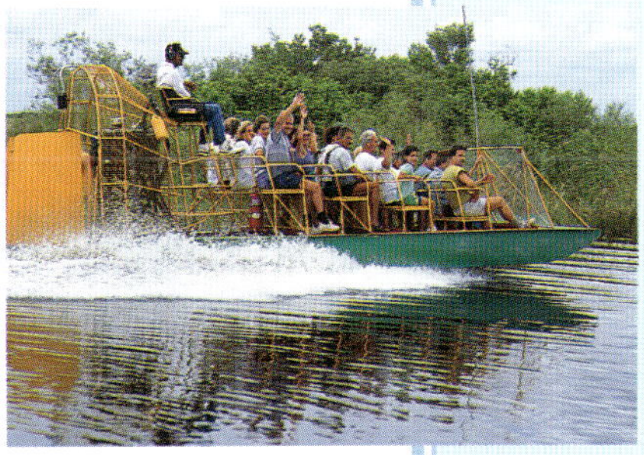

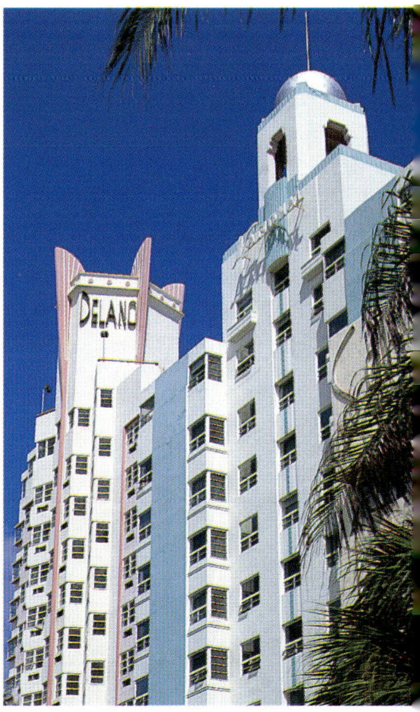

★ ***Miami's Art Deco hotels (above) are distinguished by their sugarcandy colors.***

in North America. The Fairchild Tropical Garden is a treasure, for its atmosphere and diversity of plants. Coconut Grove, base for Miami's first 300 settlers when they cut roads through marshland a century ago, retains its prickly nonconformity.

These areas, like almost all of Miami and its businesses, are shot through with Latin-American culture, which is reflected in the food, and dynamic music and dance. English is the second language in many areas, especially in Little Havana, where there is a large community of Cubans. Half of Miami's residents are from Cuba, Guatemala, Nicaragua, and Haiti. If Miami palls, nature both tamed and raw is a mere two hours away in the Everglades, the largest area of subtropical wilderness in North America. This watery region occupying the bottom 80 miles (150 km) of the state is formed by the Okeechobee River puddling outwards to form a vast, plant-choked lake never more than some 3 feet (about 1 m) deep. It is also a huge reservoir, vital for six million people and their industries. Much of the area is a national park, one that is so special in its plants and animals that it is the only national park in the world under United Nations protection. Though large animals are threatened—

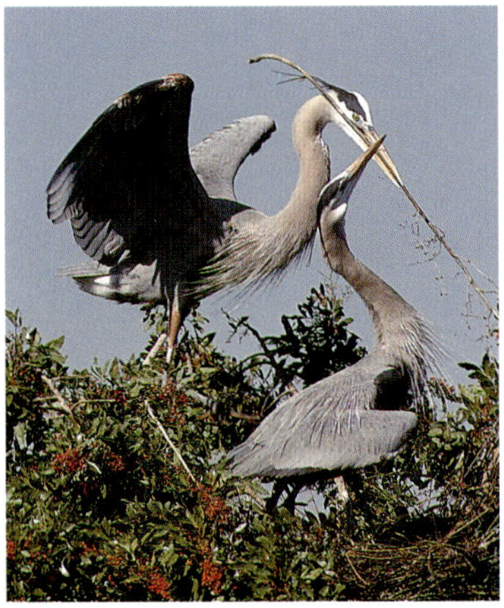

Great blue herons are part of the rich ecology of the Everglades.

there are now thought to be only about 10 panthers, and black bears are seldom seen—it remains the only place on earth where alligators and crocodiles live together. Expanses of sawgrass are dotted with mangroves and "hammocks," as the low-lying islands are called.

It is best to go in the dry season, November through May, to avoid the rains and mosquitoes. In the north, Shark Valley lies 25 miles (40 km) west of the Florida Turnpike. Airboat rides provide exhilarating trips through the sawgrass, while a 13-mile (21 km) road leads to the heart of the Everglades. Alligators often drowse on the road, and although they are wary of human beings, they can turn nasty if you get too close.

Farther west, in Ten Thousand Islands, where the Everglades mingle with the waters of the Gulf of Mexico, you can see some of the endangered manatees, or sea cows. These massive, gentle creatures are easily injured by boats, and there are only some 1,200 left. A southern approach leads, via the Main Visitor Center, to the Flamingo Visitor Center, with walking and canoe trails through mangrove forests.

Farther south, you can drive the 113 miles (180 km), connecting the 45 small low Key islands in a viaduct to Key West, an island more Caribbean than American, with pretty 19th-century houses and intimate alleys. Northward from Miami, the Cuban influx and the growth of crime inspired a "white flight" into burgeoning suburbs like Palm Beach and Boca Raton. Now these areas have evolved distinctive characters of their own. Fort Lauderdale has a much publicized gay community, and Palm Beach is legendary for its wealth, stars, and scandals.

Another world is within reach (literally, until 1972): Kennedy Space Center. Once this area around Cape

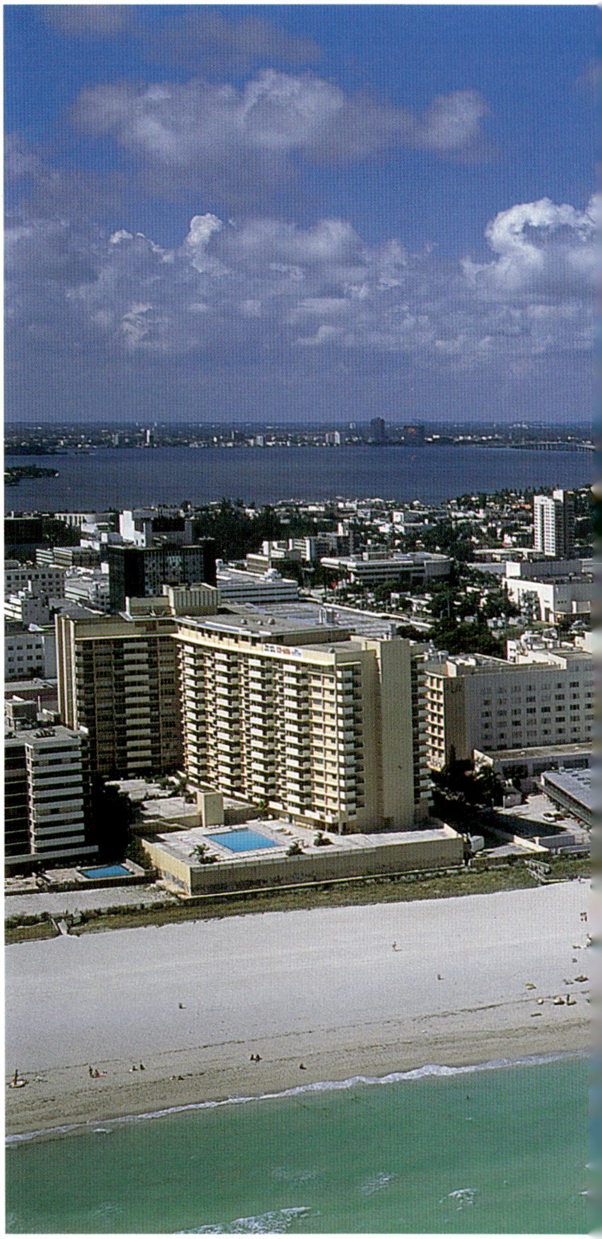

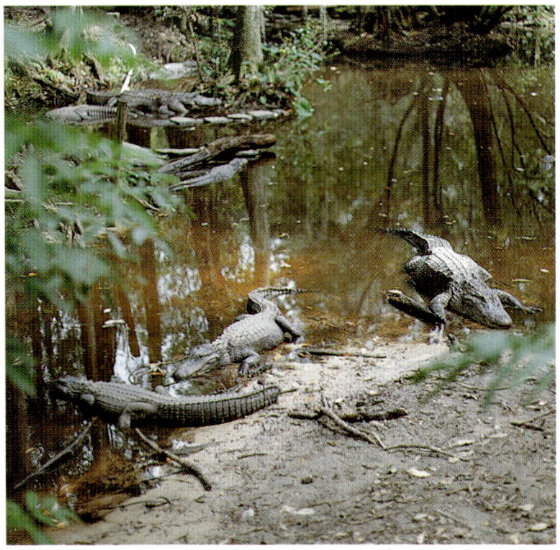

Everglades alligators are a common sight. But visitors ar warned that familiarity should breed nothing but respect.

Canaveral was a wasteland of marsh and mosquitoes. Then, in the 1960s, the "new frontier" opened with the Apollo Moon shots (1969-72). Now that's history, and the complex is the base for the Space Shuttle. You can feel the gut-wrenching thunder of a launch from the beaches and highways (though the public is not allowed closer than 3.5 miles (5.6 km), or by proxy with a close-up look at a Saturn rocket. Combine this with the experience of seeing one of the space films shown on the Center's five-story IMAX screen. For a complete contrast, the Cape's unspoilt seashore is where giant loggerhead turtles lay their eggs in summer. Or carry on another 100 miles (160 km) up the coast to St. Augustine, a beautiful, relaxed , historic town.

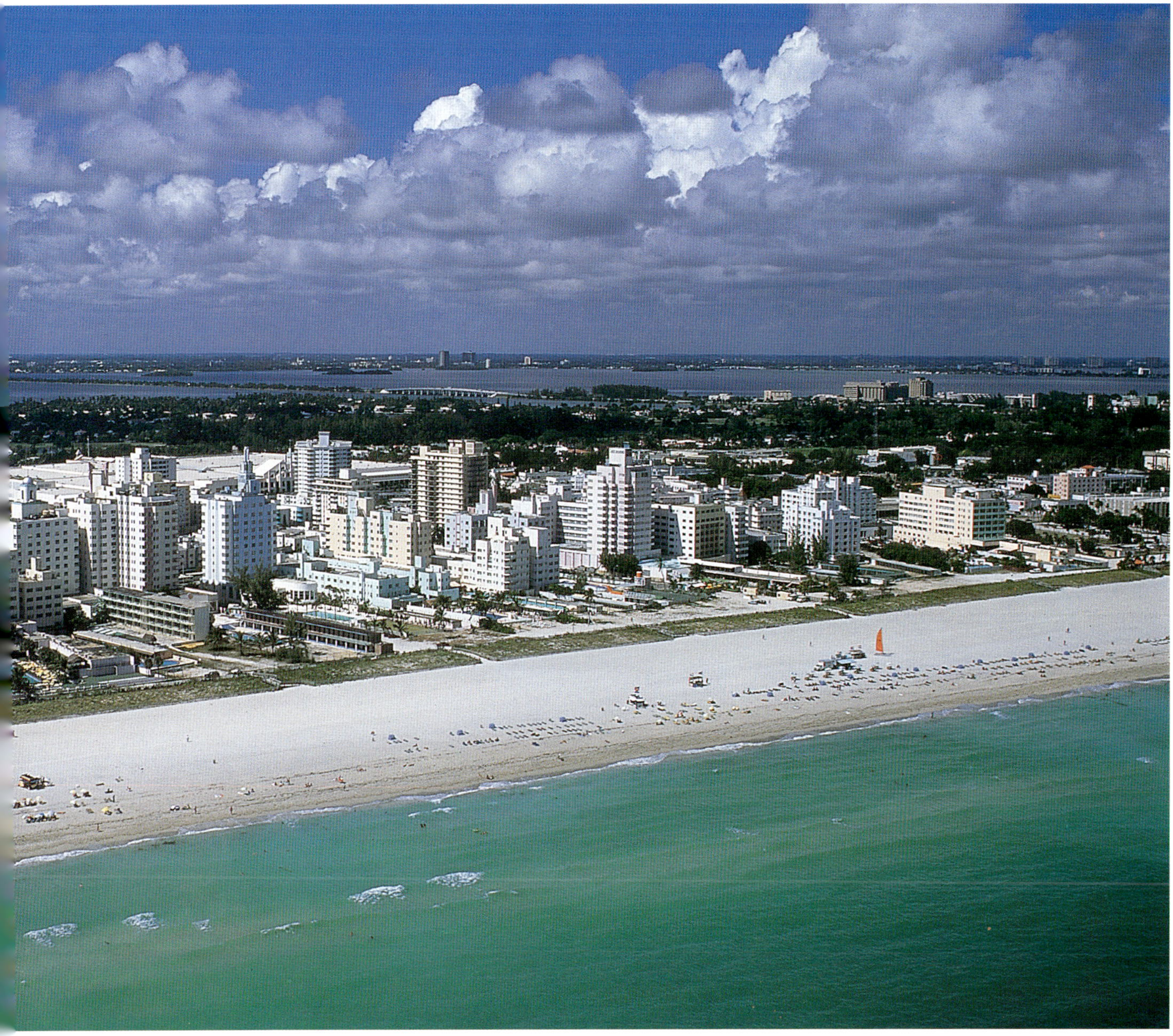

Miami's white beaches and blue skies draw a frenetic mix of young and old, high fashion and tackiness, tourists and residents.

WALT DISNEY WORLD

Orlando was once famous for little more than oranges. Then, in 1971, Walt Disney World opened. Now Orlando has 86,000 hotel rooms, 36 million visitors every year, and a vibrant, not to say lurid, lifestyle. And Walt Disney World is its own 43-square-mile (111 sq km) universe, complete with its own smalltown community: Celebration.

It could easily take a week to see—let alone experience—the three theme parks, water parks (such as Blizzard Beach that soaks guests in a snow-capped tropical paradise), night complex, and a newly opened Animal Kingdom. Every statistic makes the mind reel: 21,000 hotel rooms, 800 campsites, five golf courses. There is a lot for all. Kids of all ages go for Magic Kingdom, where the Space Mountain rollercoaster and the ExtraTERRORestrial Alien Encounter leave you boggled by shock and delight. There's a same-but-different reaction to the Twilight Zone Tower of Terror at Disney-MGM Studios. Epcot ("Experimental Prototype Community of Tomorrow") is an evolving, thought-provoking duo (Future World and World Showcase) of special-effect "infotainment" based on science and the attractions of different nations.

North of Orlando, there is calm to be found among the orange groves, wineries, gentle hills, and 1,000 lakes of Lake County.

Central and South America

"Too often... I would hear men boast only of the miles covered that day, rarely of what they had seen."

Louis L'Amour, American writer, 1908-1988.

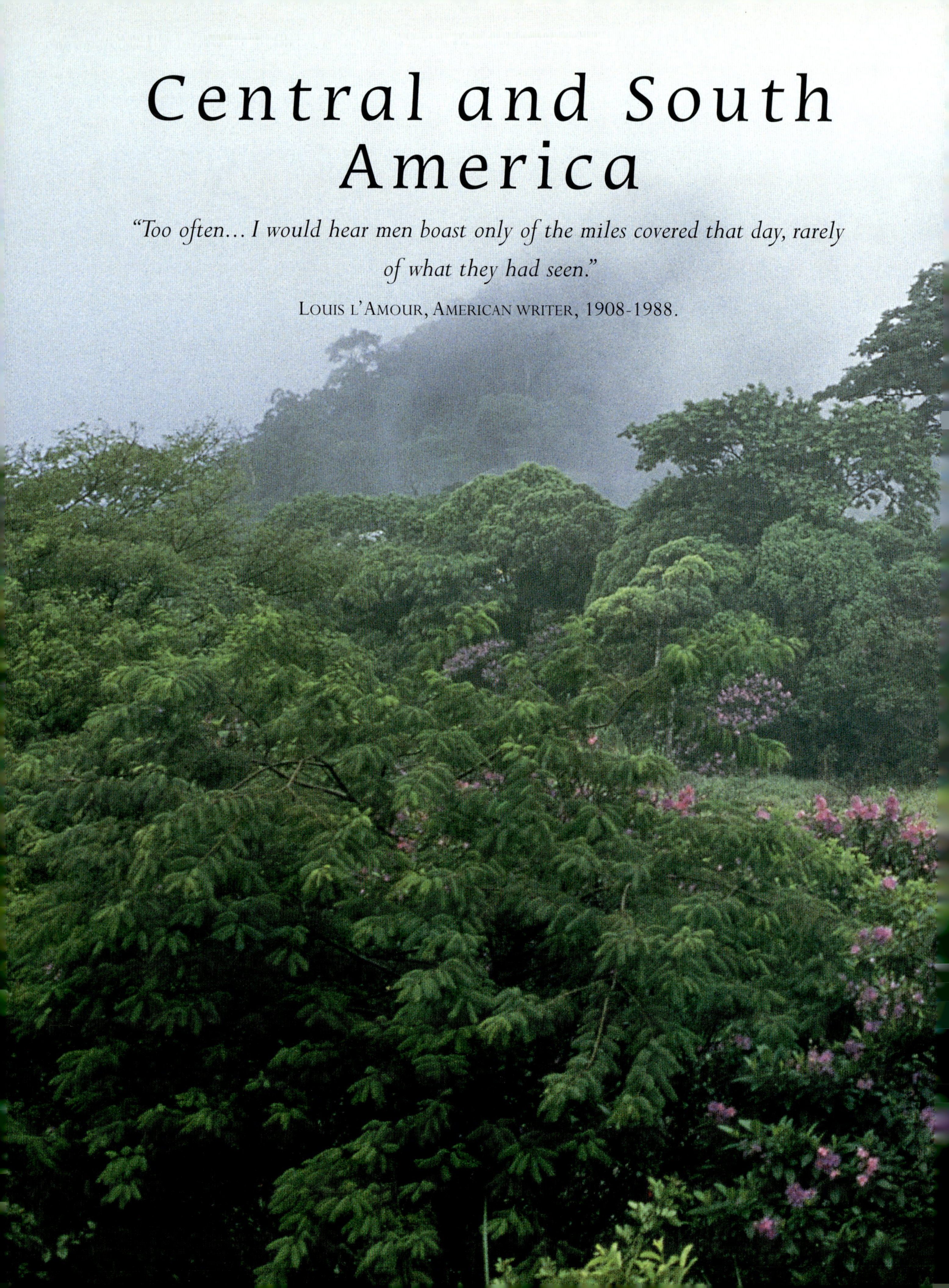

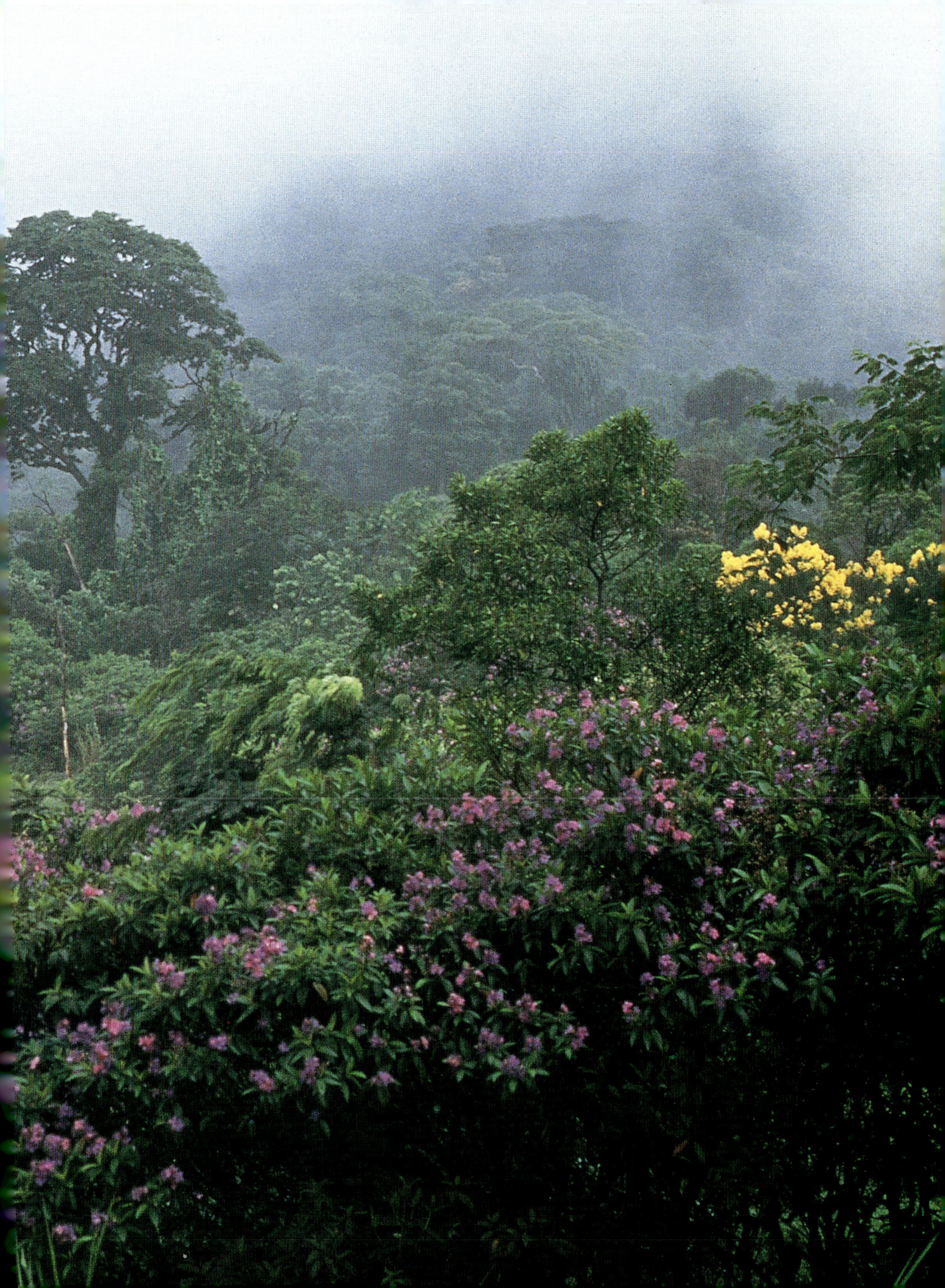

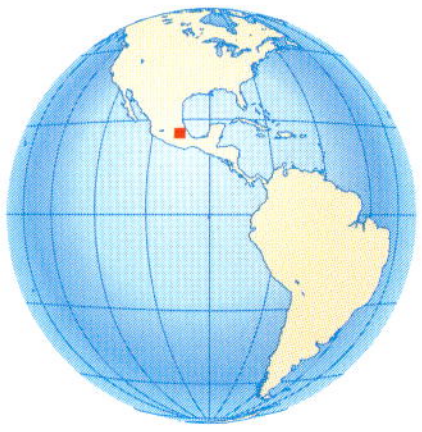

The Heart of Mexico

Beneath Mexico's modern, dynamic capital lie the temples and palaces of the Aztecs, and just beyond it stands the ancient city of Teotihuacán.

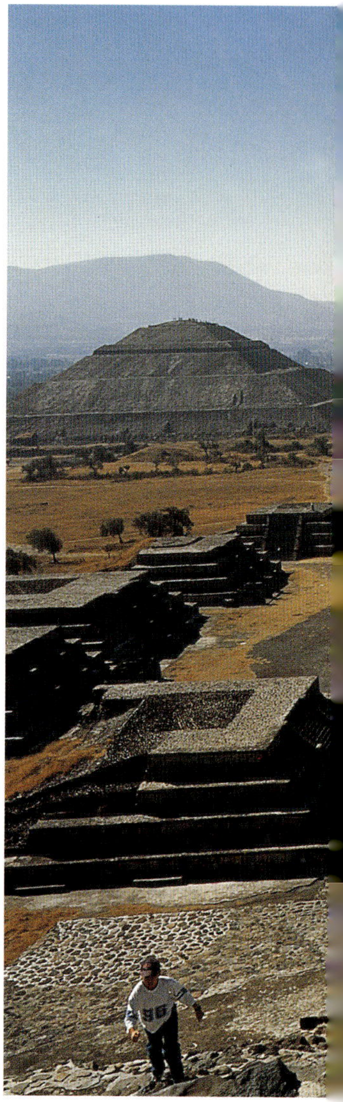

IN 1519, SPANISH TROOPS LED BY HERNÁN CORTÉS marched through the pass between the twin volcanoes Popocatéptl and Ixaccihautl, and looked down into the high valley of central Mexico. What they saw astounded them. Below them, built on artificial islands in a lake, lay the Aztec capital Tenochtitlán, with its countless temples and pyramids. "When we saw all those cities and villages built on the water," wrote the expedition's chronicler Bernal Díaz, "some of our soldiers asked whether or not it was all a dream."

Lake Texcoco has long since been filled in, and most of the Aztec city was razed during its capture in 1521. Yet, scattered through the modern city, haunting remnants survive. Around the capital, in the high mountain valley that still forms the heart of Mexico, are ancient temples and cities, mysterious witnesses to the vision and skill of the Aztecs and the civilizations that preceded them. Their legacy lives on in the modern nation, which is of mixed Spanish and Amerindian descent—in the passion for living and awareness of death that surface everywhere—in lurid TV soaps, in the savage, vibrant murals of Diego Rivera, and in the annual *Día de los Muertos* (see p.42).

Mexico City is not to everyone's taste—the highest, second largest, and maybe the most polluted metropolis in the world. Just breathing its air, they say, has the same effect as smoking two packs of cigarettes a day. Its core of elegant colonial mansions and gleaming skyscrapers around the broad, palm-lined Paseo de la Reforma is ringed by ever tattier suburbs that crumble at the edges into rambling shanty towns.

But if you like hard-edged, fast-paced urban life, lived with grit, grace and flair, Mexico City is intensely invigorating, a perpetual fiesta of car horns and street hassle. There is high life and night life, especially in the Zona Rosa, the lively district of cafés, restaurants, and classy shops in the streets—picturesquely named after the great cities and rivers of the world—that lead off Reforma. There are the *mariachi* bands who gather every evening in the Plaza Garibaldi to play their mournful yet festive music of guitars, violins, and trumpets. They're looking for work—weddings, parties, anything.

There are bars and eateries of every description. Eat an enchilada in one of Mexico City's respectable, mid-range restaurants and the chances are it will taste like minced cardboard wrapped in parchment; buy the same dish from a street vendor and the succulent little parcel will explode with flavor, stunning the taste buds. Mexican beer is a good way to restore them back to life afterwards.

IN THE HEART OF THE CITY

Right in the middle of town is the Plaza de la Constitución, known (like all main squares in Mexico) as the Zócalo, a vast paved square once the heart of the Aztec city. From here, the Aztecs would have looked out on the smoking cone of Popecatéptl, but nowadays the volcano can seldom be seen through the smog. Religious and temporal power occupy the same ground they did in Aztec times: the massive, gloomy Baroque cathedral stands where priests once piled the skulls of their sacrificial victims, while the presidential office (Palacio Nacional) stands on the site of Montezuma's palace. Inside, the desperate historical struggle is depicted in Diego Rivera's huge colorful murals.

The Templo Mayor, the Aztecs' main temple, was long believed to have been completely destroyed in the siege, but in 1978, during the construction of the Metro (subway), workers unearthed an eight-ton stone

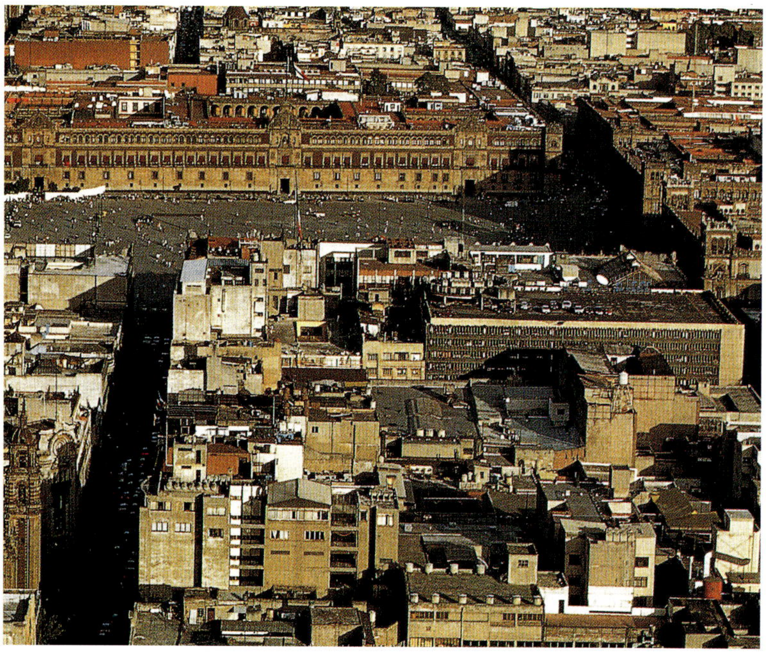

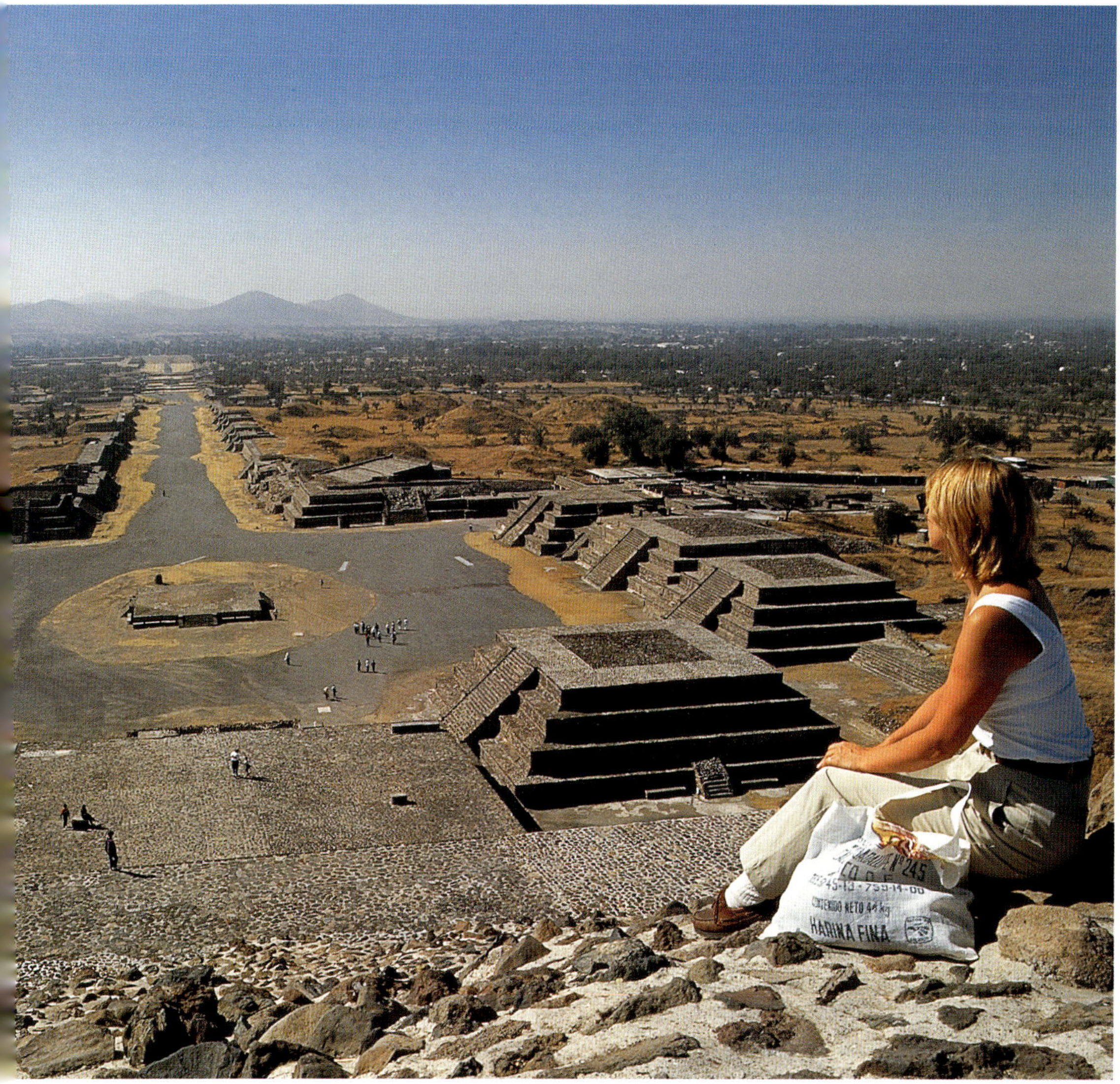

FACT FILE

Mexico City Population: 20 million.

Currency: Nuevo Peso. The peso can devalue dramatically, so do not change your dollars all at once.

Climate: Summer temperatures in Mexico City reach about 75°F (24°C), and it remains dry and fairly warm October—May; temperatures can fall to freezing December—February.

Time to go: October—May.

Nearest airport: Mexico City.

What to take: Pills for altitude sickness, which affects some people in Mexico City when combined with the air pollution; insect repellent, sunglasses; diarrhea pills.

What to buy: Silverware, pottery and ceramic tiles, rugs, embroidery.

Health: Vaccinations against typhoid, cholera, hepatitis A, and polio recommended. Outside of major cities, beware of tap water or ice made from it.

Food and drink: Mexican cuisine, now known the world over, reflects the country's past influences: Amerindian, Spanish, French (from the 1800s). Turkey mole is a popular sauce, containing chilies, tomatoes, peanuts, chocolate, and garlic. Guacamole is made from the same ingredients but with avocados replacing chocolate. Tacos (maize pancakes) and tamales come from Mexico, as does tequila, made from the maguey cactus.

The ancient city of Teotíhuacán (above) was one of the world's greatest metropolises between the 4th and 7th centuries A.D. By the time the Aztecs arrived, it was already a ruin.

The Zócalo, Mexico City's central square (left) is dominated by the façade of the Palacio National, now the seat of Mexico's Government.

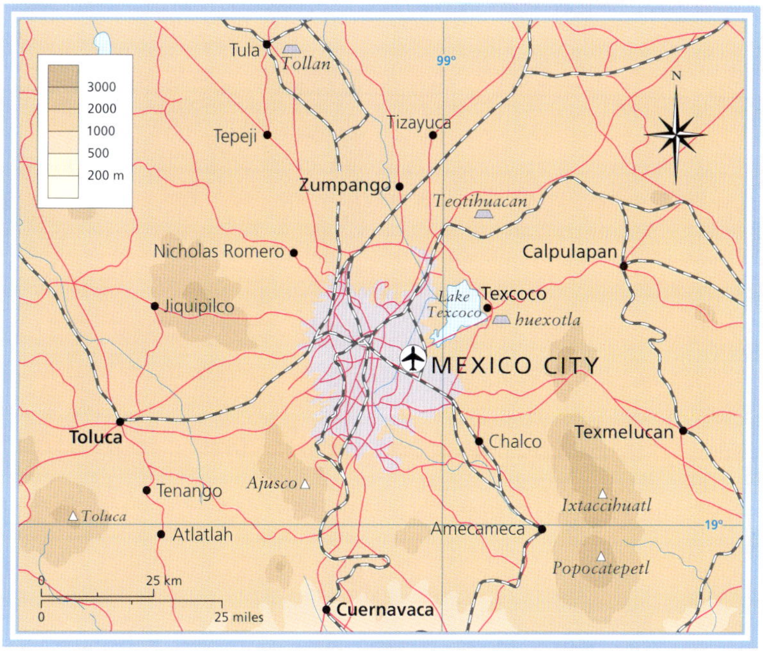

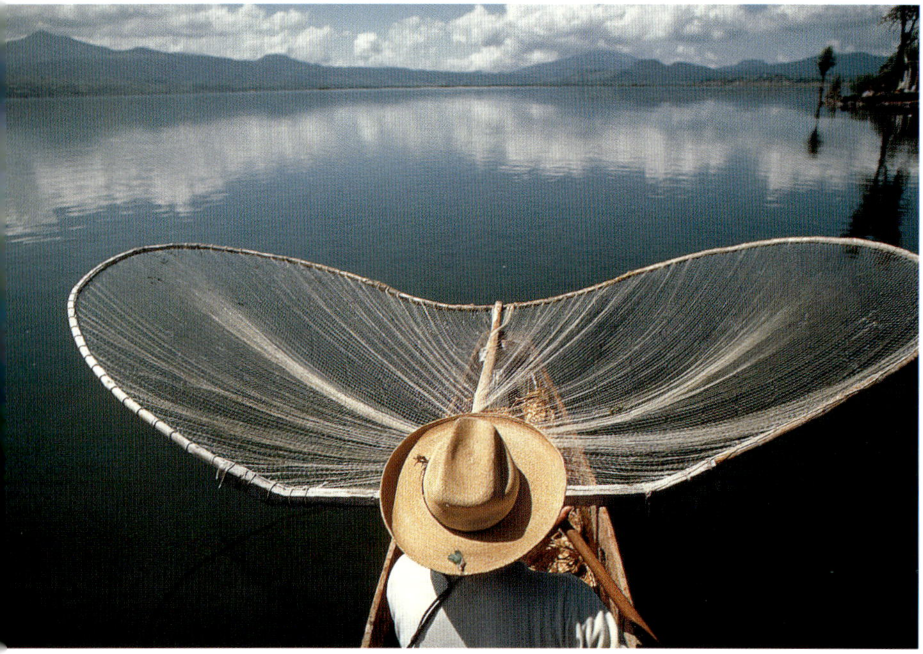

The old town of Patzcuaro is a center for the Tarascan Indians who still fish on the lake with their distinctive "butterfly" nets (above).

disk carved with the image of the moon goddess Coyolxauhqui. The site, just east of the cathedral, was then excavated, and you can now see the remains of several successive temples where prisoners had the hearts torn from their living bodies to give the sun god the strength to rise the next day. It is unsettling to stand in the middle of a modern city looking at the carvings of serpents and skulls powerfully evoking the implacable Aztec gods.

The Aztecs were relative latecomers, building their empire in less than two centuries before the Spanish arrived to demolish it. Just 30 miles (48 km) northeast of the city center stand the ruins of Mexico's first great civilization, Teotihuacán, dating back 2,000 years.

PLACE OF THE GODS

The local bus from Mexico City winds through wooded valleys that are still astonishingly rural, despite their proximity to the capital. Suddenly, through the trees, a pyramid can be glimpsed. Then the bus veers off in the opposite direction, and you think you've missed the stop. You haven't—there's another half an hour to go yet as the bus makes its circuitous way through dusty villages where chickens scratch in the road and men sleep in the shadow of adobe walls.

At its peak in the 500s A.D.. Teotihuacán probably had 200,000 inhabitants, more than any contemporary city in Western Europe; by the time the Aztecs came, it was already archaeology. They named it Teotihuacán, "the Place of the Gods." The massive, stepped Pyramid of the Sun stands 230 feet (70 m) high, the third largest pyramid in the world. The view from its flat summit, across wooded valleys to the far mountains, is astounding. Beside the smaller Pyramid of the Moon stands the finest of the houses and palaces that flank the broad, central Avenue of the Dead—the Palace of the Quetzal Butterfly. It produces an eerie feeling of opening a door into an ancient world; columns, built round a courtyard and carved with butterflies and quetzal birds, still support a roof, and the murals, showing priests dressed as butterflies, are still bright.

THE DAY OF THE DEAD

Mexico's most distinctive fiesta is the Day of the Dead (Día de los Muertos), when the souls of the dead are believed to return to earth, held through the night of November 1-2 each year. To northern sensibilities, accustomed to muffling the reality of death in euphemisms, it is a bizarre, even morbid affair, but far from gloomy, as somber thoughts blend with friendship and celebration. Excited children crowd the markets to buy cardboard caskets bearing the names of the living, papier maché skeletons, and candy skulls that eerily recall the carvings of the Aztecs. On the evening of November 1, people bring offerings of fruit and flowers to the cemetery, where they hold a candlelight vigil through the night, chanting over the graves of their dead. Much of this undoubtedly goes back to pre-Hispanic times, but has been grafted on the Catholic feast of All Souls.

The Day of the Dead is celebrated throughout Mexico, but perhaps the best place to witness it is at Pátzcuaro in the state of Michoacán, about 180 miles (300 km) west of Mexico City. It is a beautiful old town on a lake, full of 16th-century Spanish churches, winding streets of peeling stuccoed buildings, and old-fashioned hotels in Spanish colonial mansions.

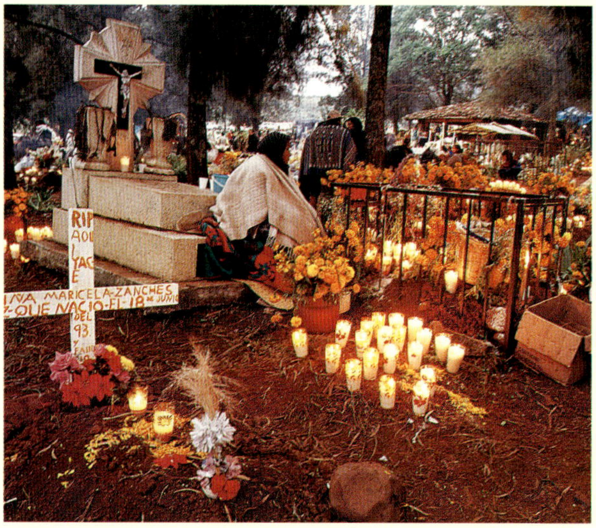

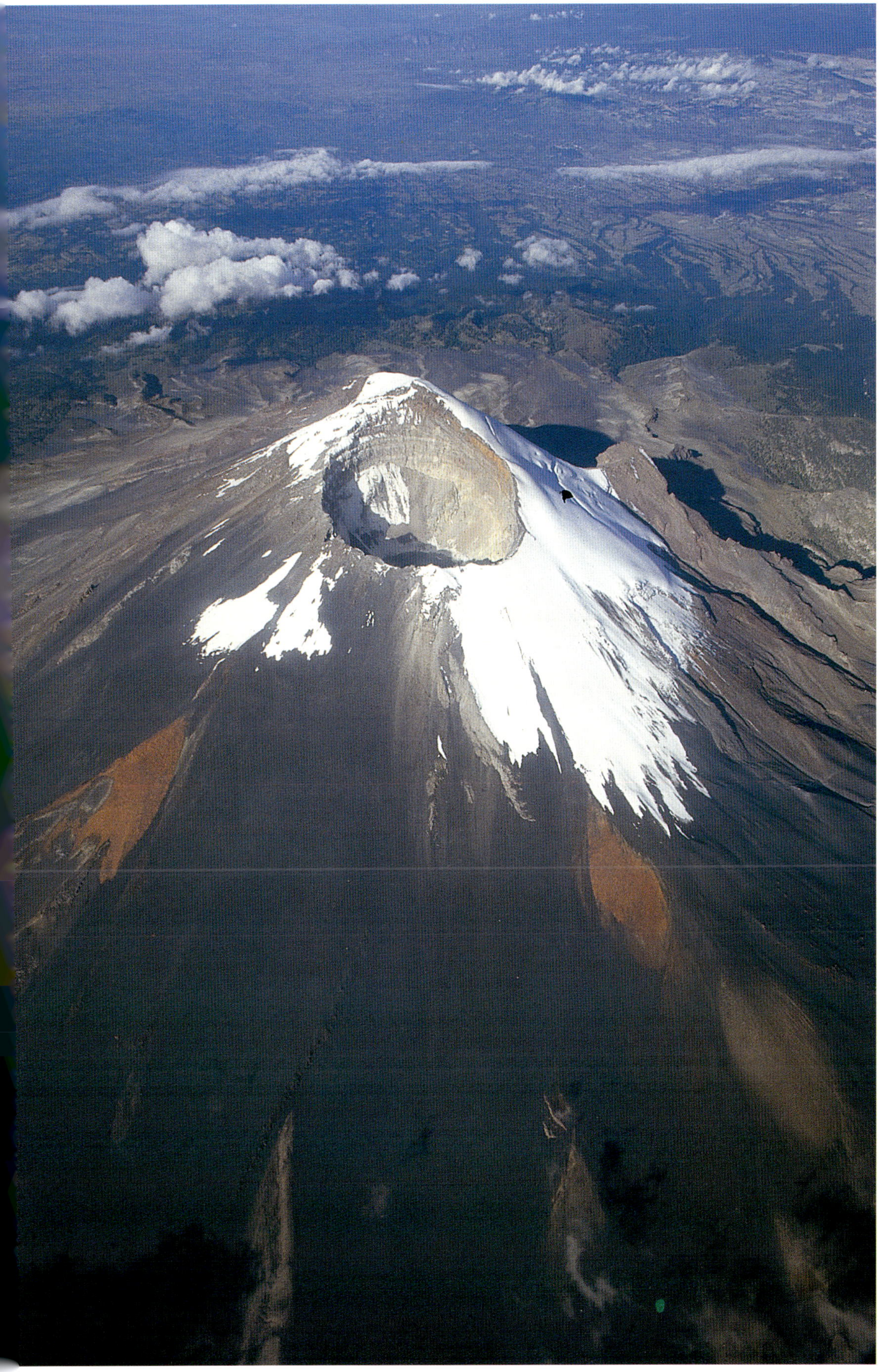

The volcano Popocatépetl (left) southeast of Mexico City, has not erupted since 1802, but still emits the odd cloud of smoke; its name means "smoking mountain."

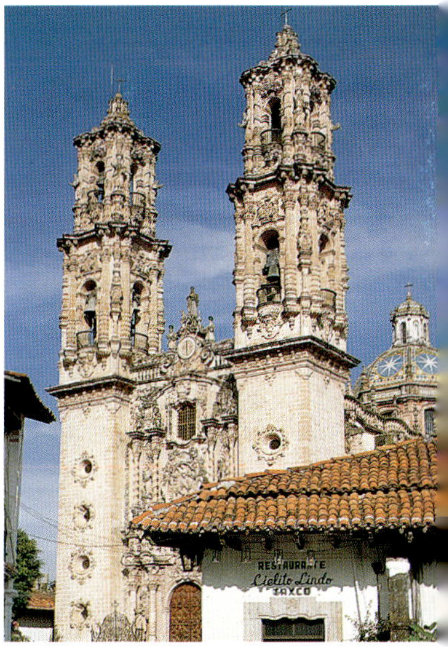

Florid, colonial Spanish Baroque architecture is a feature of many towns in the area; the one (above) in Taxco, 60 miles (100 km) southwest of Mexico City was built with the wealth from nearby silver mines.

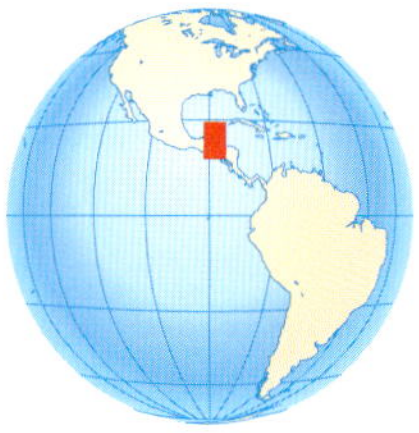

La Ruta Maya

Trace the marvels of a once great civilization by following the Mayan Route via stepped pyramids deep in the rainforest and dramatic ruins on the edge of the blue Caribbean Sea.

LONG BEFORE THE AZTECS ARRIVED, a brilliant civilization flourished for many centuries in what is now southern Mexico, Guatemala, and Belize. The Mayas constructed massive cities and temples of stone without metal tools, pack animals, or the wheel. Most were mysteriously abandoned before the Spanish arrived in the 1500s, but in their heyday the Mayas had a hieroglyphic writing still not completely deciphered and, thanks to their remarkable astronomy, a highly accurate calendar.

To see all of the Maya cities—there are hundreds—would take years, but it is possible to visit the main sites by following the 1,500-mile (2,400-km) Ruta Maya (Mayan Route), by bus or jeep, in two to three

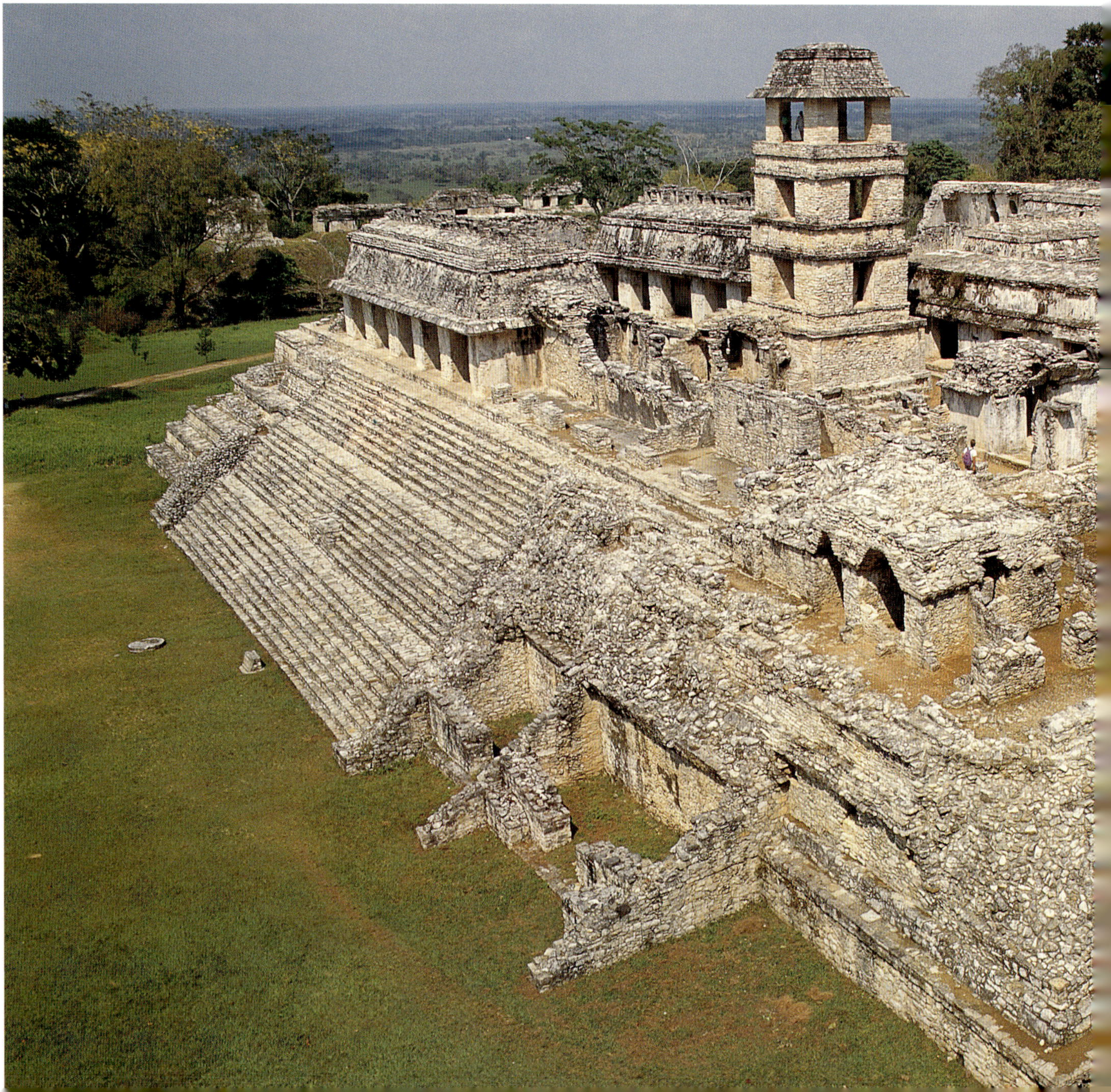

weeks. The journey—a modern, not an ancient route—goes through still remote areas, where old Spanish churches molder in quiet squares, the descendants of the Mayas follow their traditional way of life, and many—especially women—still wear traditional costume such as the *huipile* (a decorated cotton blouse). Many travelers, once bitten by the Maya bug, return venturing farther off the beaten track to visit temples lost deep in the rainforest.

The best base is the fine old Spanish colonial town of Mérida in the north of the Yucatan peninsula. With an air of faded grandeur, it is noted for excellent hammocks. Near Pisté, a small town 60 miles (100 km) on the road east, stands the most famous, most visited Mayan city, Chichén Itzá. Too many visitors can destroy its atmosphere, but fortunately there are hotels in old houses and haciendas nearby, so it is possible to arrive the previous evening and see the ruins early before the bus parties.

Chichén Itzá is unlike any other Mayan site. Its architecture and sculpture reveal the influence of the warlike Toltecs of central Mexico, who occupied the city in the 900s A.D. Everything is aligned with mathematical and astronomical precision; if you add up all the steps of the huge Pyramid of Kukulkán that dominates the site, they total 365. At the spring and autumn equinoxes, the parapet at the top casts long, zigzag shadows down the side of the pyramid to meet the stone serpents' heads at the bottom, creating the effect of giant snakes descending. Inside the pyramid, a

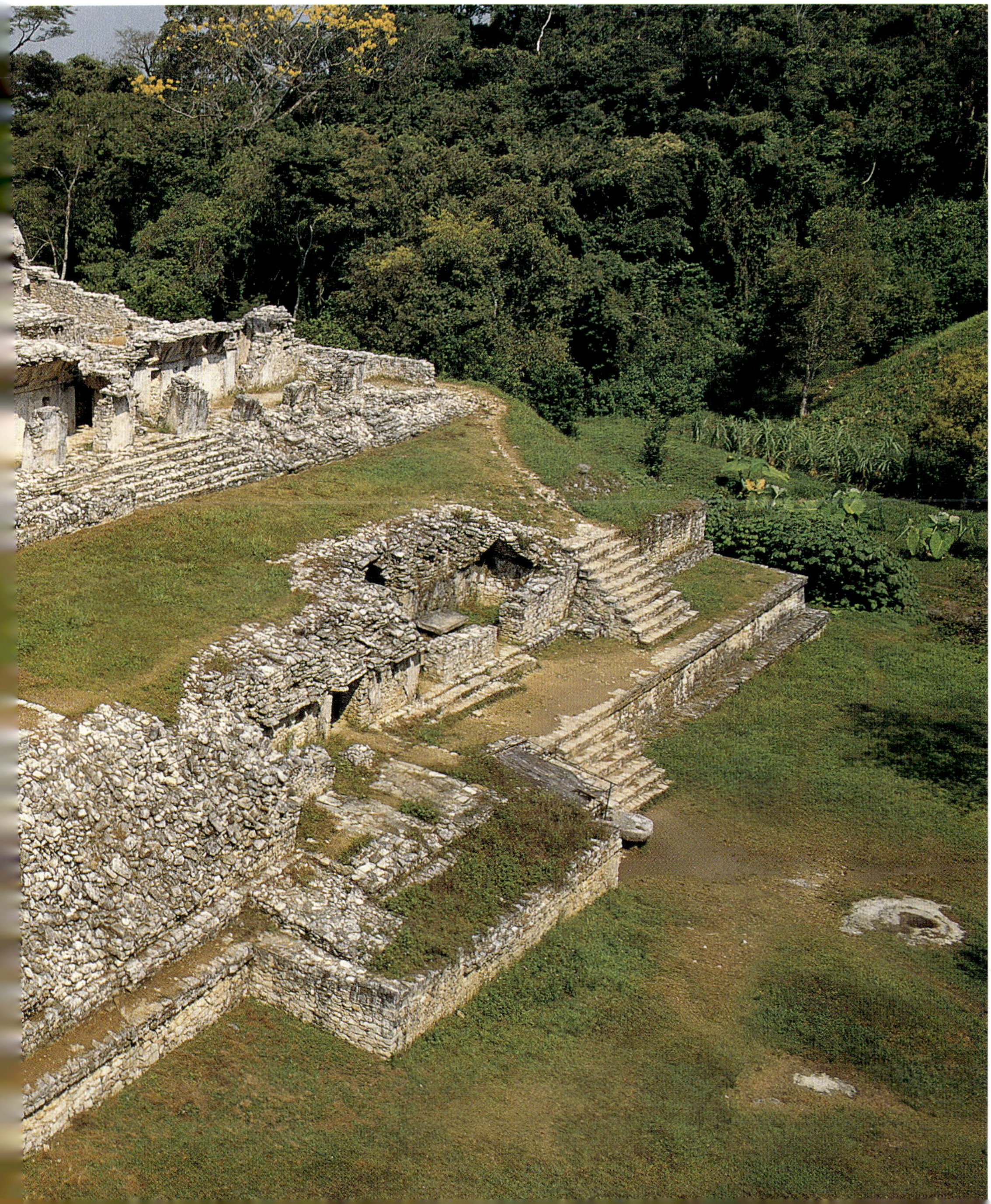

FACT FILE

Currencies: Peso, Mexico; Quetzal, Guatemala; Lempira, Honduras; Belize dollar, Belize. All can devalue suddenly; take U.S. dollar traveler checks.

Languages: Spanish is the official language except in Belize, but many Indians still speak Maya-related tongues. English is widely understood.

Climate: Summer temperatures can easily reach 90°F (32°C) and above, and the climate is intensely humid. It rains May—October.

Time to go: October—March.

Nearest international airports: Cancún, Mérida, Belize City.

What to take: Snorkeling gear; water purifier; insect repellent; sun block; sunglasses; good hiking boots; waterproof clothing; binoculars.

What to buy: Hammocks, Panama hats, silverware.

Health: Vaccinations against typhoid, polio and hepatitis A recommended. Malaria is a problem. Avoid tap water, uncooked vegetables, and salads.

Palenque (left) is one of the most graceful of all Maya sites, a 7th-century enssemble of palaces and temples crowned by a tower for astronomical observations.

Uxmal's Pyramid of the Sorcerer (right) soars with tremendous verve above the elegant Nunnery Quadrangle.

long, slippery staircase climbs to the temple at the top, where the red-painted jaguar throne has jade eyes and flint fangs. Beneath the pyramid, Chac Mool—the Toltec rain god—reclines in the courtyard, holding a cup to receive the heart of the sacrificial victim.

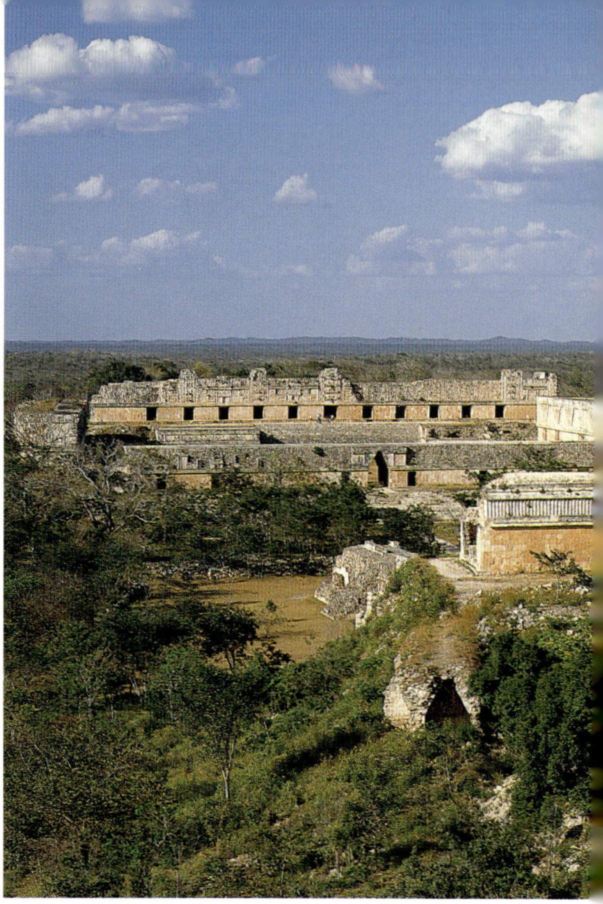

THE SORCERER'S PYRAMID

Some 45 miles (72 km) south of Mérida stand the awesome ruins of Uxmal, a city that flourished between 600 and 900 A.D. The place is dominated by the astonishing pyramid known as El Advino—the sorcerer. Unlike other Maya buildings, it appears almost modern: its smooth, round cornered slopes soar at an alarming gradient to its 100-foot (30 m) summit, where a squat temple looks out over the Puuc Hills nearby. Climbing the almost vertical stairs to the top is a dizzying experience, closer to rock climbing than climbing a staircase. The so-called Nunnery Quadrangle, on a small rise just to the north, shows the power and sophistication of the Mayan architects in a different way. The lower half of its long facade is plain honey-colored limestone, punctuated by square openings; the upper half is completely covered with an intricately carved geometric frieze.

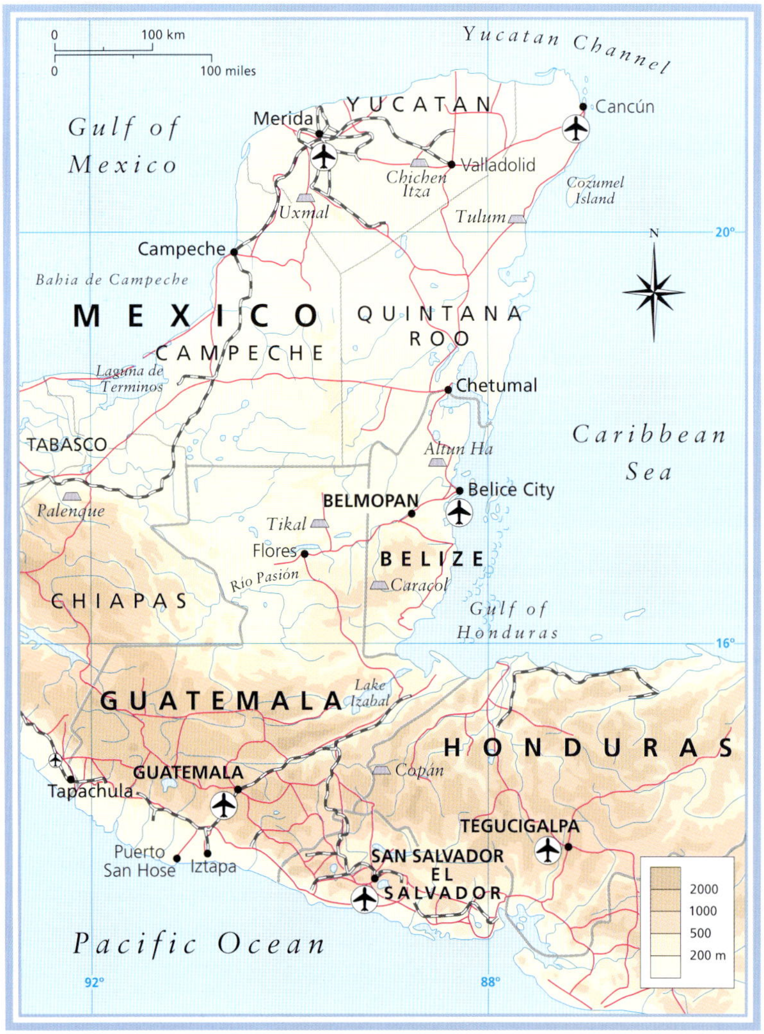

Moving south through the state of Tabasco and into Chiapas, it becomes increasingly hot and steamy, and the landscape is more densely wooded. Chiapas has the largest Indian population of any Mexican state. Since 1994, Zapatista rebels have been fighting Mexican government forces in the region, demanding rights for the campesinos (peasants). Except for occasional security checks, this is unlikely to affect visitors along the Ruta Maya, but check for news of the situation before setting out.

Just where the highlands of Chiapas begin stands Palenque. The natural setting is superb—the ruins rise from a clearing in the emerald jungle amid the constant chirrup of insects and the screech of howler monkeys. This is a hot, humid place, so stay in the new village 4 miles (7 km) up the road and visit the archeological zone in the early morning; not only is it cooler, but the sight of the temples emerging from the morning mist is marvelously atmospheric.

Three broad tiers of steps lead up to the long, porticoed facade of the palace complex, to one side of which stands the four-story astronomical tower, looking like a Chinese pagoda transported to the Central American rainforest. The decoration throughout the site is exquisite, especially on the Temple of Inscriptions pyramid, to the right of the palace complex. A dank and eerie tunnel leads into the heart of the 80-foot (25 m) stepped pyramid, to a crypt

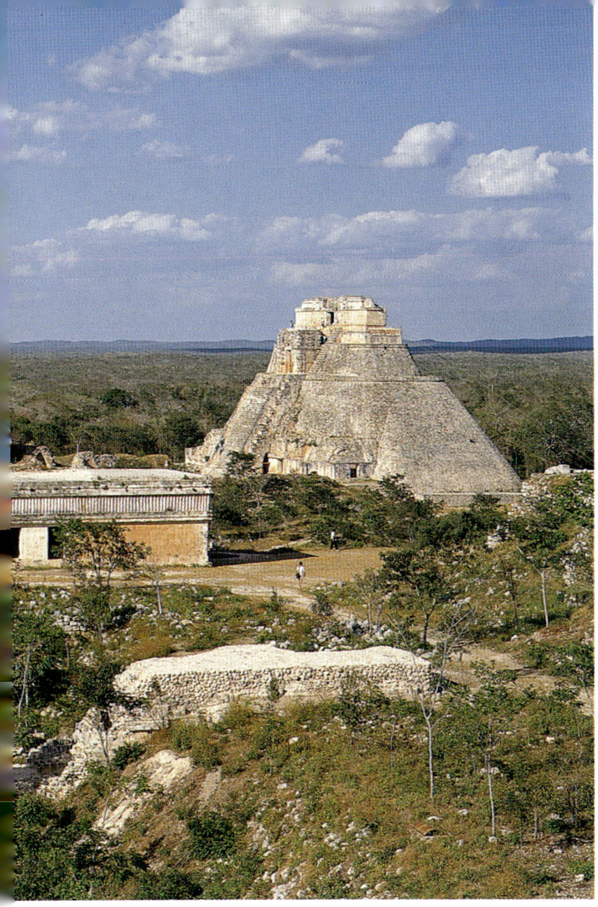

north of Belize City, you feel like an explorer as you come upon the great pyramid of Caracol deep in the rainforest of western Belize—at 140 feet (42 m), still the tallest building in the country.

From Belize City, you can return to Mexico through Quintana Roo, the easternmost state of the Yucatan peninsula, stopping at Tulum. It is not the biggest of Mayan cities, but it is the only one on the coast, and the location is dramatic. The place was still occupied when Spanish first came this way, and as you walk along the beach watching the great waves crashing against the limestone cliff beneath the towers, there is little to spoil the illusion that you have chanced upon an outpost of a still-powerful state, whose officials might emerge from the ramparts to check your credentials.

From here, it is about 80 miles (130 km) north to Cancún, with its international airport. The highway runs along the coast beside white sand beaches, but if you prefer not to end your Mayan odyssey in a brash new development, return to Belize City and fly from there.

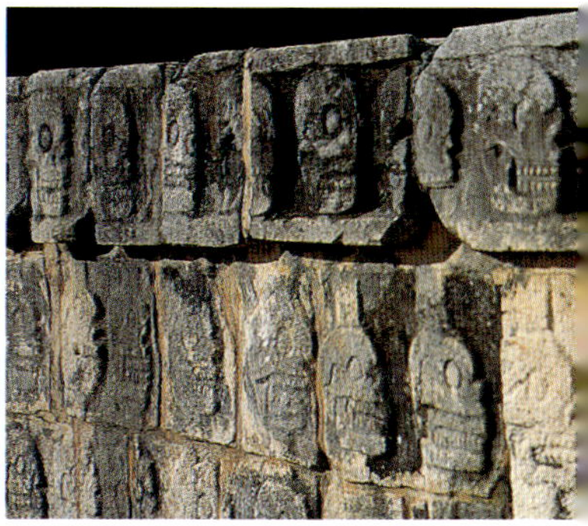

Chichen Itza's forceful pyramid (below) was probably built by Maya architects for the Toltecs, a warlike nation from Central Mexico, whose ceremonies are recalled in the carving (above) of a skull storage rack.

that houses the stone sarcophagus of the Mayan King Pacal. He ruled Palenque during the 7th century A.D, when the main buildings were constructed.

Mayan highrises

There is a bus connection from Palenque, via the border town of La Palma, to Flores in the remote, densely forested Petán region of Guatemala, near the Mayan ruins of Tikal. A more enticing way to arrive, however, is by boat along the Usumacinta and Pasion Rivers. A path leads beneath the canopy of trees; suddenly, improbably, a tall, steep-sided pyramid of blackened limestone soars up. Then another, and another: the pyramids of Tikal are the skyscrapers of the Maya world, 20-story temples with almost impossibly sheer stairways to their summits. Only a fraction of the site has been excavated, and it's thrilling to look out over the treetops from a pyramid and contemplate the undiscovered temples still beneath the dense foliage all around.

From here, make the short excursion across the Honduran border to another classic Mayan site, Copán, or continue to the former British colony of Belize. With its Afro-Caribbean population, this small, laid-back, English-speaking nation feels more like the West Indies than Central America. Just off the coast is the largest coral reef in the western hemisphere, ideal for snorkeling and scuba diving in blue Caribbean waters as schools of exotic fish swim past you. Despite these advantages, Belize attracts surprisingly few visitors. Visiting the impressive Mayan ruins of Altun Ha, just

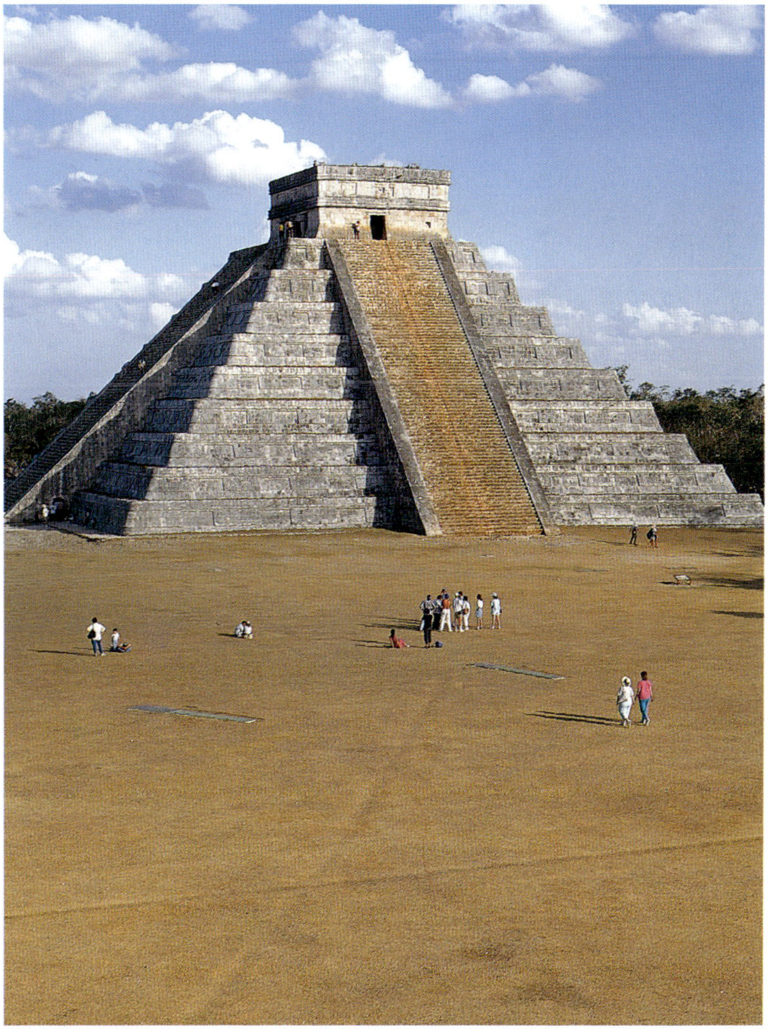

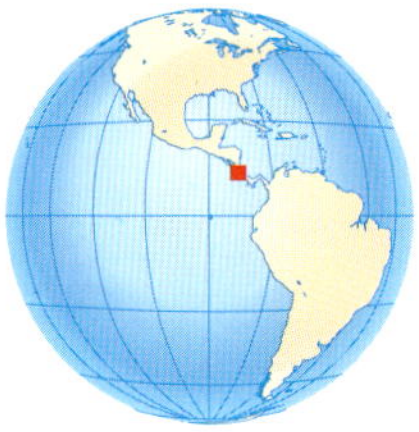

Wildlife Watching in Costa Rica

See the world in its primordial state in Costa Rica, a land of smoldering volcanoes and pristine forests that teem with exotic wildlife.

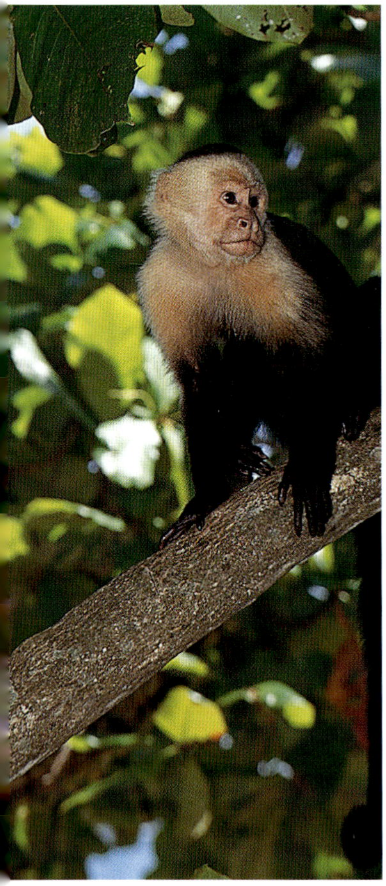

DEEP IN THE CAVERNOUS GREEN STILLNESS of a mist-shrouded forest, a shaft of sunlight falls on the bright splash of an orchid or butterfly. A scarlet macaw bursts from the foliage in a sudden explosion of color and sound. Fantastic bromeliad plants cling to trees, drawing nourishment from the air itself. This is Costa Rica.

This small, peaceful country that has escaped many of the troubles afflicting its Central American neighbors, thanks mainly to its lack of an army. The capital, San José is a spruce little city of 400,000 people, remarkable for its orderliness and lack of obvious squalor:

"If San Salvador or Guatemala City were hosed down," wrote travel writer Paul Theroux, "all the shacks cleared and the people rehoused in tidy bungalows… those cities would, I think, begin to look a little like San José." It is an agreeable place to relax and to use as a base for exploring the beautiful Meseta Central region. There are hotels to suit all budgets, lively cafés steeped in the rich aroma of roasting Costa Rican coffee beans, an attractive blend of colonial and modern Spanish architecture. There are countless restaurants, most of them serving simple Central American fare such as *gallo pinto* (rice and beans with grilled meat or chicken).

ALONG THE SPINE OF THE CONTINENT

From San José it is a five-hour journey to Corcovado National Park in the southeast of the country, through scenery of epic grandeur, and taking you through Alajuela, Costa Rica's dignified second city nestling under the awesome, smoking cone of Volcán Poás. The Pan American Highway then climbs up into the Cordillera Talámanca, following the 1,000 foot (300 m) ridge of mountains over steep-sided canyons and forested slopes. The views are unbelievable; perched on the spine of the continent, you can see both the Pacific Ocean and the Caribbean when the weather's clear.

Eventually the road winds down through cane fields to the decaying port of Golfito, looking out onto the Golfo Dulce. Beyond the clear, glassy waters of the gulf, the Osa Peninsula juts into the Pacific. This clump of rolling hills and deep canyons, cloud forests and

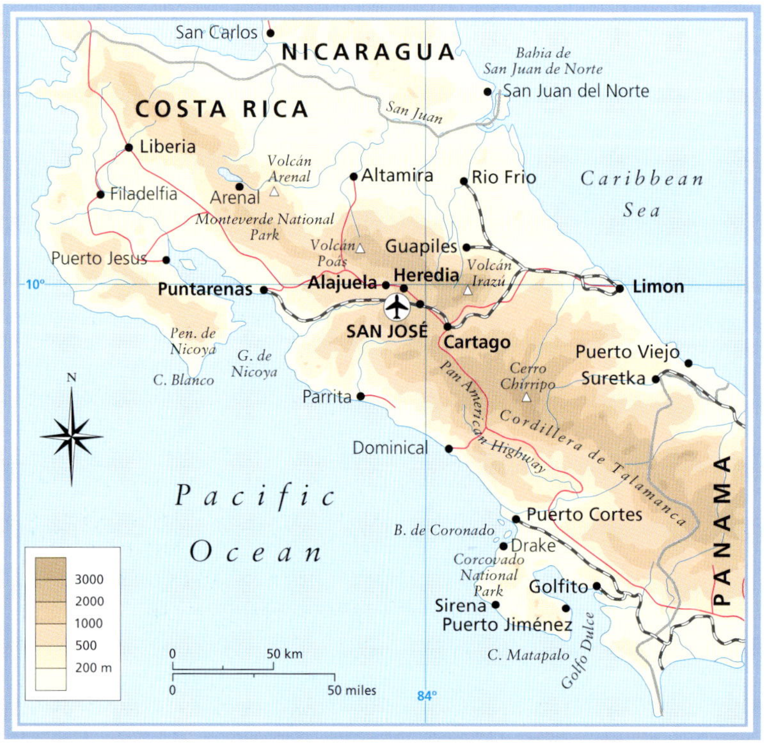

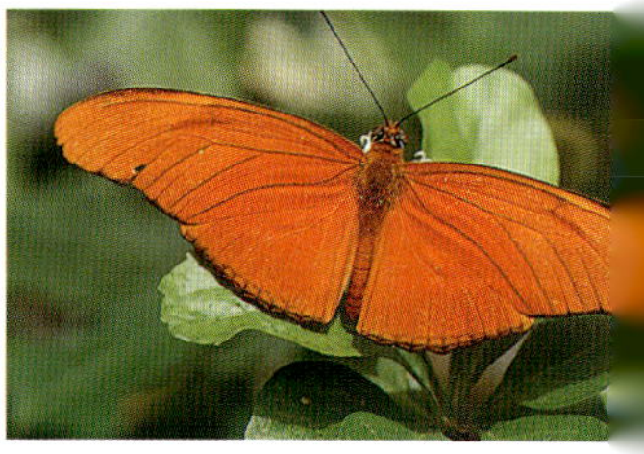

The white-faced capuchin monkey (left) lives in the understory to midstory levels in the forests of Costa Rica and eats ripe fruit and insects. The cloudforest of Monteverde, in particular, is home to an extraordinary variety of insect and bird life (above and right).

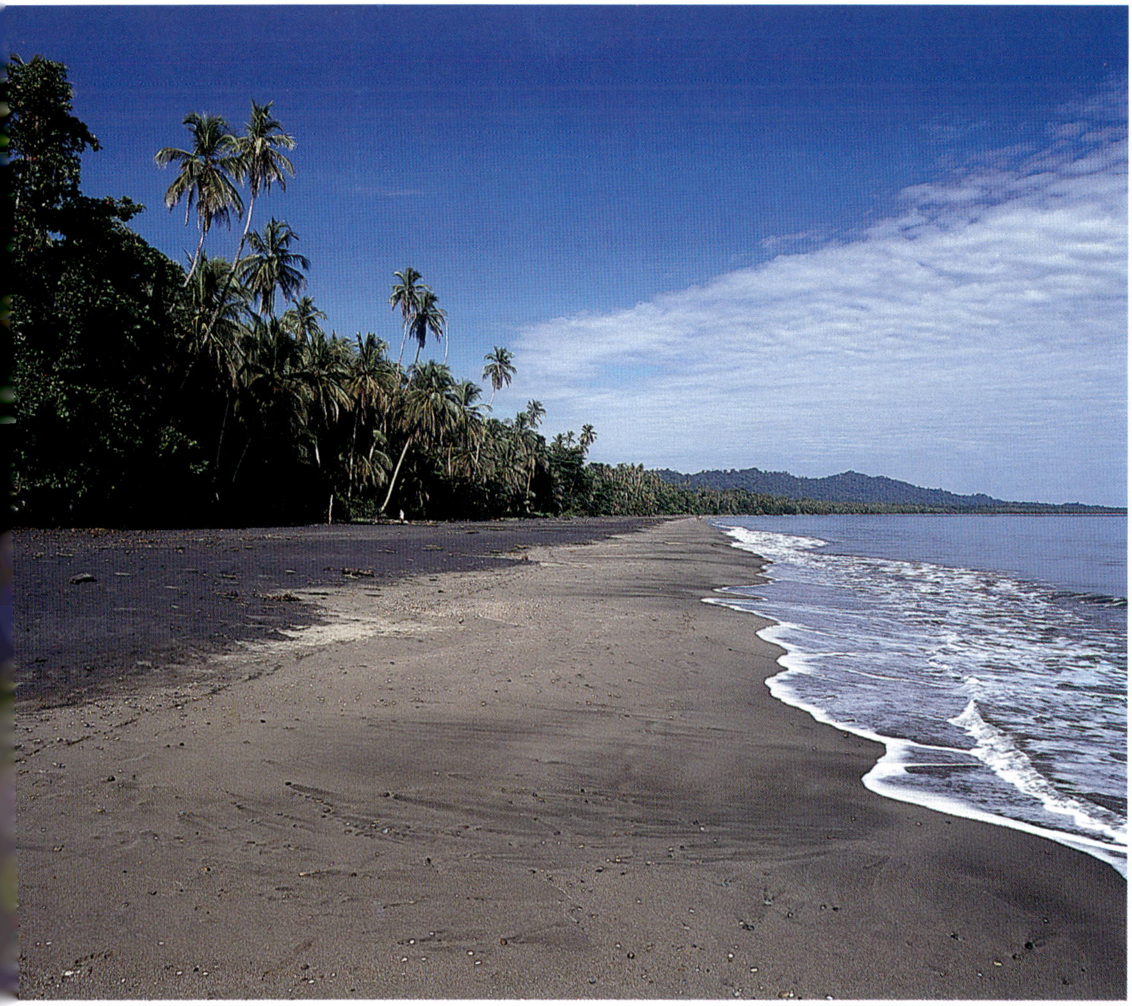

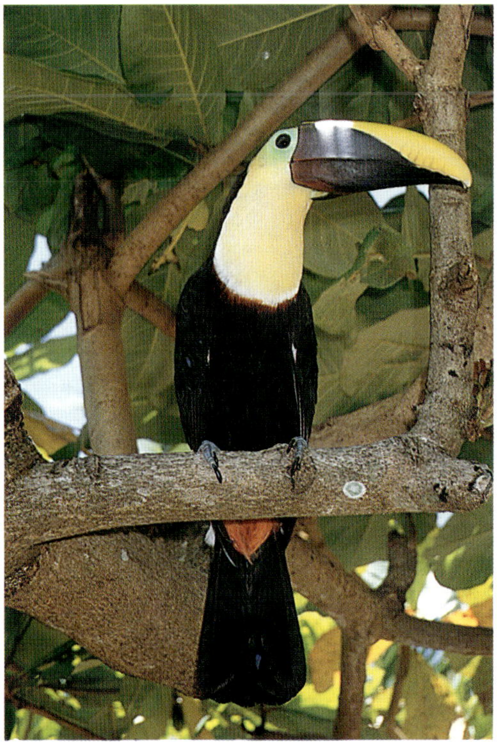

Puerto Vieja (above) is one of the many beaches and ports on the Caribbean coast worth visiting.

mangrove swamps, is still a remote, inaccessible region fought over by gold miners and conservationists. Fortunately, a third of it—some 200 square miles (51,800 hectares)—has been set aside as the Corcovado National Park. Its huge coastal tracts and pristine forests are home to most of the country's endangered species, including jaguars, tapirs, and monkeys; caymans and crocodiles swim in its waters; turtles drag themselves onto the long, white beaches to lay their eggs, while the world's largest bird of prey, the harpy eagle, can sometimes be seen wheeling in the skies above.

There is plenty of accommodation in Puerto Jímenez, the main town on the peninsula, which can be reached by boat from Golfito, but it is still several hours' journey by bus and on foot to the park, and better, therefore to stay in the park itself, at one of the ranger stations at Los Patos or Sirena; camping is also available. The rangers will give advice about self-guided

FACT FILE

Population: 3,500,000.

Currency: Costa Rican Colón. Dollars are also useful, as the Colón devalues frequently.

Languages: Spanish is the official language, but English is widely spoken.

Climate: Cloud forest regions are very humid; rainfall may average as much as 190 inches (500 333cm) a year. Temperatures seldom fall below 72°F (22°C) in San José, and then only in December and January. The coast is even hotter.

Time to go: December through March is the least rainy period, also the coolest and the best for birdwatching.

Main airport: San José.

What to take: insect repellent, flashlight, goodhiking boots, waterproof clothing, binoculars.

What to buy: Coffee; Costa Rican artesania including leather goods and painted woodwork.

Health: Malaria is prevalent in areas below 2,400 feet (730 m), but otherwise there are no special health problems.

Food and drink: Among popular dishes are sopa negra (made with black beans and a poached egg), casado (rice, beans, stewed bee,f and cabbage), and tortas (tortillas with meat and vegetables). Coffee is excellent.

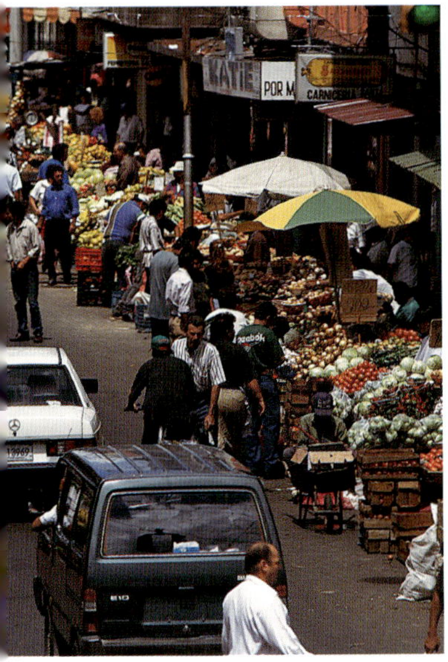

The fruit market in San José, Costa Rica's capital city (above).

tours through the park. In the stations biologists and ecologists mingle with hikers and nature lovers, discussing the animals and habitats of the area. But once you are hiking through the reserve, staying at the strategically placed lodges, your only companion will be the sights and sounds of nature in the echoing forest and along the endless, deserted beaches.

THE CLOUDFOREST OF MONTEVERDE

Some 50 miles (80 km) north of San José, on the crest of the Cordillera Tilarán, is another reserve remarkable not only for its astounding cloud forest but also for a unique social and environmental experiment. The Monteverde Cloud Forest Reserve was first created by 40 Quakers who left Fairhope, Alabama, in 1950 in search of political and religious freedom—many of them had recently served jail sentences for refusing to be drafted, and Costa Rica had just disbanded its army. They bought land from local Costa Ricans and developed a dairy farm on the steep slopes. Environmentalists before their time, they set aside an area of virgin cloud forest to protect the watershed.

The reserve now protects some 40 square miles (10,360 hectares) of forest, though it is not an isolated pocket of conservation. Despite sporadic conflicts of interest, the Quaker project—and the visitors it has attracted—have inspired other local landowners to set aside forest and create nature trails. Even on the farmland outside of the reserve, you can walk from banana and coffee fields and moist, flower-filled cow pastures into dark, mysterious woods.

The reserve is approached via the ramshackle town of Santa Elena, 112 miles (182 km) northwest of San José (four and a half hours by bus) and just 22 miles (35 km) north of the Pan American Highway. A narrow, unpaved road leads from Santa Elena, through the village of Monteverde, and up the mountain slope to the reserve entrance. It is only a few miles, but the road is often made difficult by dust in summer and mud slides during winter.

The forest itself is home to an astounding variety of wildlife, including the brilliant red quetzal bird, toucans, bellbirds, the bare-necked umbrella bird, the endangered tapir, monkeys, armadillos, coatimundis, and the brilliantly colored, two-inch golden toad. Orchids and bromeliads festoon the towering, ancient rain forest trees, while more than 200 species of fern provide a moist, rich-smelling undergrowth.

The Quakers remain determined not to sacrifice this unique environment to mass tourism, though they have developed a wide range of amenities for visitors, all very discreetly arranged so as not to compromise the area's natural beauty. In Monteverde village, there are several simple but comfortable hotels, cozy pubs and restaurants (vegetarians are catered for), camping facilities, handicraft and book stores. On the reserve, the visitor center provides maps of the trails, and details of the birds and mammals you may see in the forest; and two simple but comfortable lodges allow you to hike for days without leaving this enchanted world.

It is even possible to rent a horse and ride to the nearby Río Negro reserve, from where you can see the lowering cone of Volcán Arenal, billowing gray plumes of lava smoke, which at night, turn an infernal orange, shot though with sparks. The volcano is no more than 10 miles (16 km) away; to get there you must skirt Lake Arenal, a trip of some 30 miles (48 km). You can rent a four-wheel drive in nearby Fortuna to take you up the western slope. Looking down from the rim into the crater of bubbling lava gives an awe-inspiring sense of the raw power of nature, but don't do it without an experienced guide—Arenal is active volcano, and you definitely do not want to be up there when she blows.

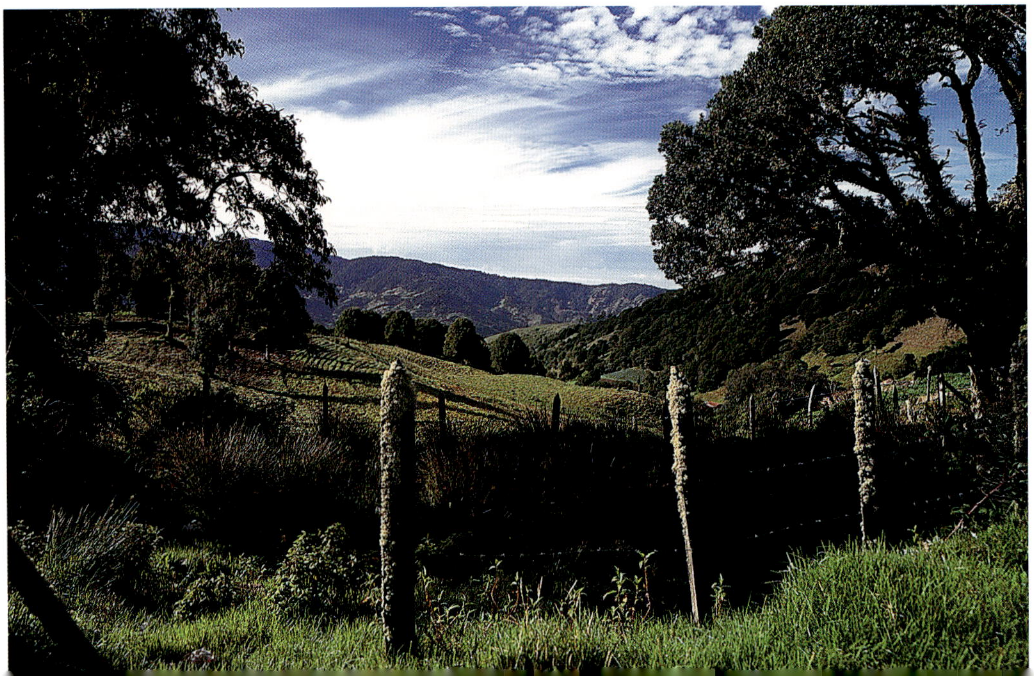

The rolling hills of central Costa Rica (left), are banded by lowlands along the Caribbean and Pacific coasts, while to the south are mountains of volcanic origin.

Follow the trails through Corcovado National Park's virgin forest (right), the home of the country's highest tree, a 230 foot (70 m) ceibo.

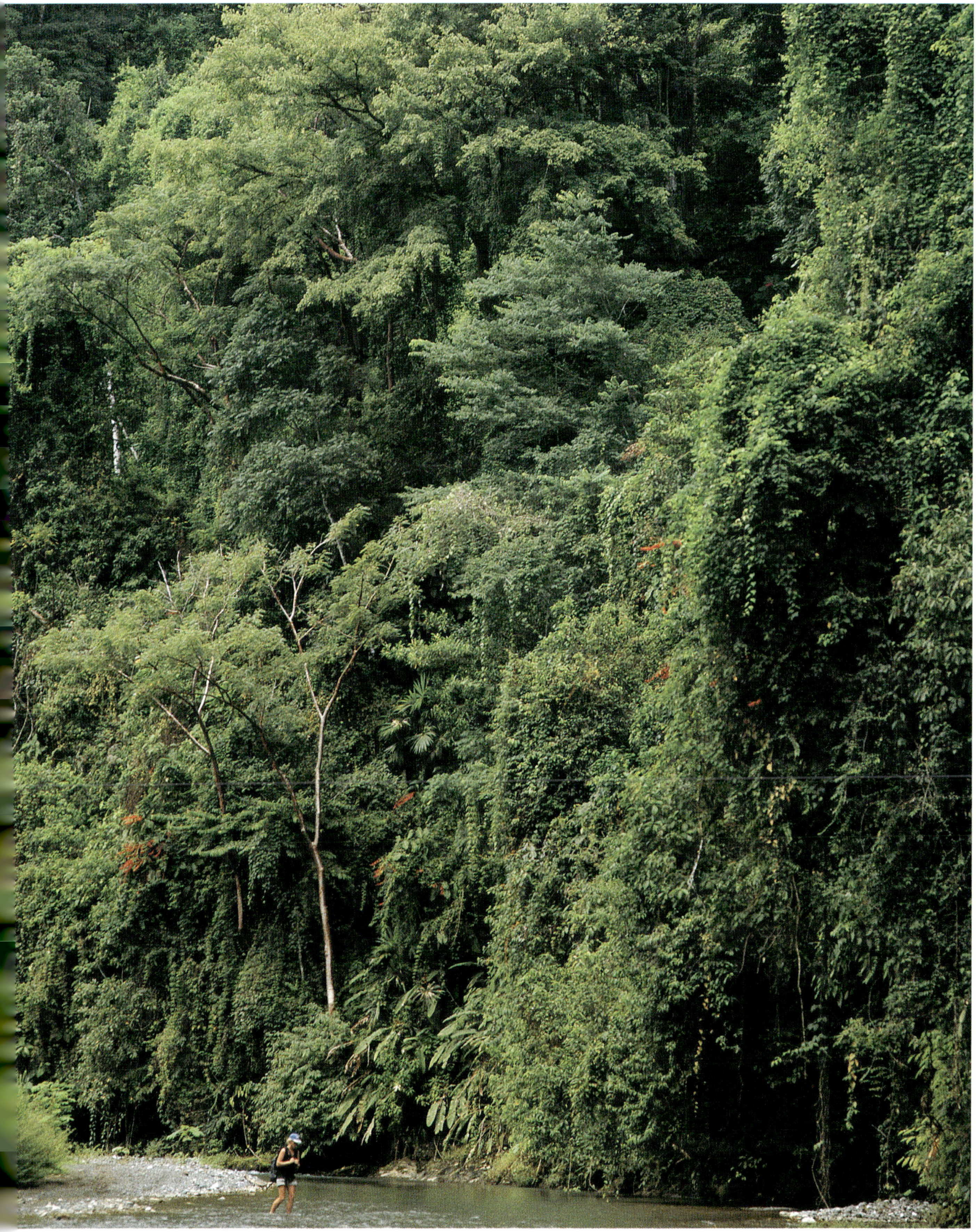

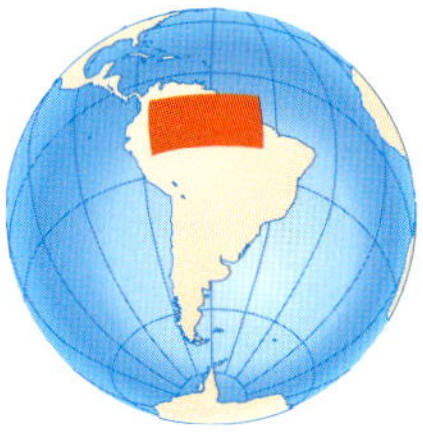

Riverboat on the Amazon

A thousand miles upriver from the Amazon's mouth, in the heart of the rainforests, lies the exuberant city of Manaus, once the world's rubber capital. Even farther beyond is the faded glory of Iquitos in Peru.

TO MANY CHILDREN who open a battered school atlas at the map of South America and point a finger at the dot labeled Manaus, it looks unspeakably remote in the middle of the continent's green heart on the long ribbon of the Amazon. Later, seeing television wildlife documentaries or perhaps the image of the demented conquistador floating downstream on a raft in Werner Herzog's film *Aguirre: The Wrath of God*, confirms the impression, and the Amazon becomes an unmissable destination.

There are basically two ways to see it. One is to book a tour, flying into Manaus or Iquitos, from where comfortable boats chug through the backwaters to one of the ecolodges built in the rainforest. These are usually constructed in traditional local style of tropical hardwood and thatched with palm leaves, and may float on the river or be perched on stilts amid the treetops. From their observation platforms there are panoramic views across the rainforest; accommodation is in comfortable chalets (huts) with private bathrooms, and most lodges have a restaurant offering local and international cuisine. Take a canoe along the rivers to spot alligators, piranha fish, and animals along the riverbank or one of the organized walking tours in the jungle. The disadvantage is that you travel in a hermetically sealed bubble, seeing the natural environment, but detached from local human life.

The old riverboats (below) that ply the Amazon provide a picturesque, if slow (and often uncomfortable) means of traveling from the river mouth at Belém to the river's upper reaches in Peru .

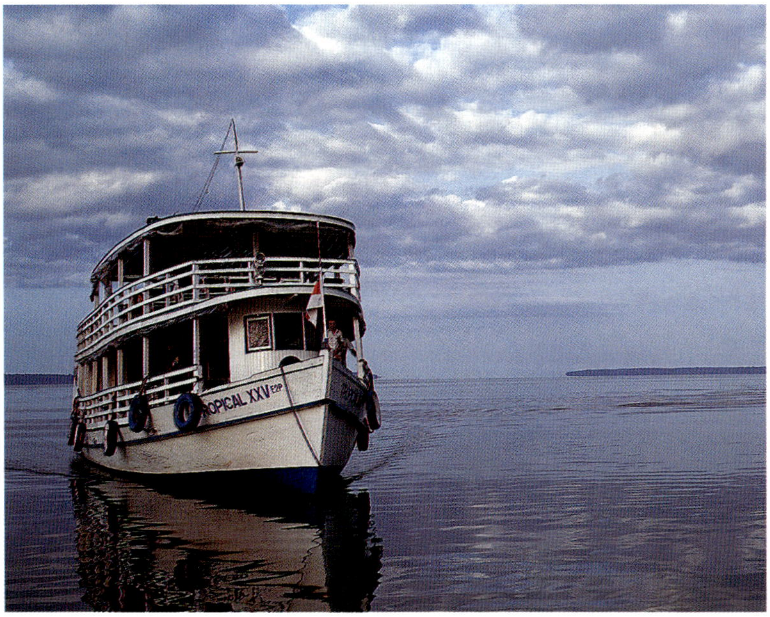

BY RUSTING RIVERBOAT

The other way is to go down to the ocean port of Belém, a vibrant city with a splendid market where old Portuguese colonial buildings are framed by a Manhattan skyline of sleek towers, and ask around for one of the passenger boats that ply the river. There's no doubt that this is the hard way to travel. The rusty old riverboats are packed with passengers, livestock, and freight. Accommodation consists of a sweltering shared cabin or a hammock on deck, and often the only source of water is a standpipe that comes straight up from the river. The food served on board seldom varies—fish with rice and yuca, a sweet potato-like vegetable, with the occasional piece of chicken. But its quality varies alarmingly; the fish that was deliciously fresh when it was first taken on board may be served up, rotten and slimy, three days later. Remember these are lawless

The Amazon rainforest (right) has the largest number of plant species in the world, dominated by trees that rear 200 feet (60 m) above the forest floor.

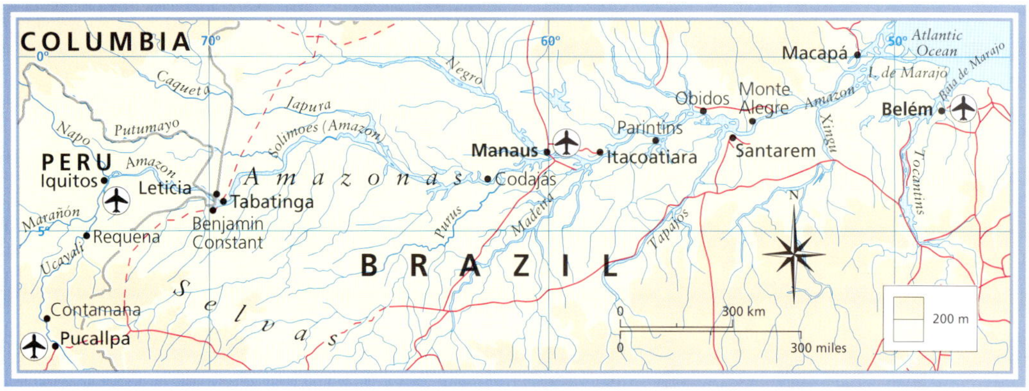

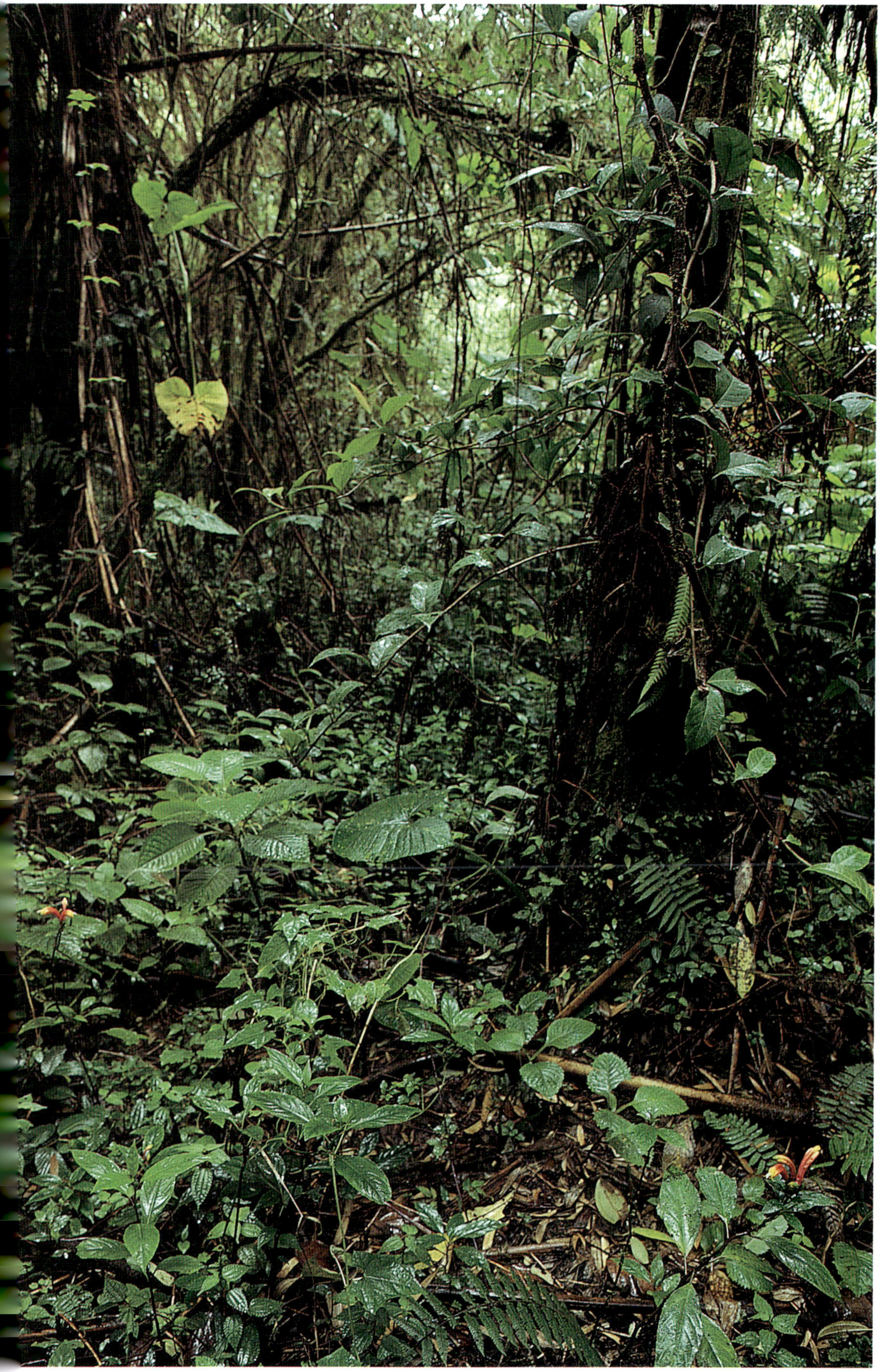

FACT FILE

Currency: Brazilian Real; Peruvian Inti. Both currencies have a history of frequent devaluations, so travel with U.S. dollar traveler checks.

Climate: Equatorial; expect temperatures of around 90°F (32°C) or higher and heavy rains January—May, especially in eastern Amazonia; central Amazonia, around Manaus, is dryer.

Time to go: July— October.

Nearest international airports: Manaus, Iquitos.

What to take: Sunglasses; water purifying pills; hammock; insect repellent; flashlight; good hiking boots; waterproof clothing; binoculars.

What to buy: Duty-free electronic goods (in Manaus); and local craftworks, including bongo drums and terracotta figurines.

Health: Vaccinations against typhoid, yellow fever, and polio strongly advised. Malaria resistant to drugs is a major problem; mefloquine is recommended. Do not drink water unless bottled or sterilized; avoid salads, uncooked vegetables, unpeeled fruits, and undercooked meat, especially from street sellers.

Languages: In Brazil Portuguese is the official language, but English and Spanish are widely spoken. In Peru, Spanish is the official language but English is understood in some tourist areas.

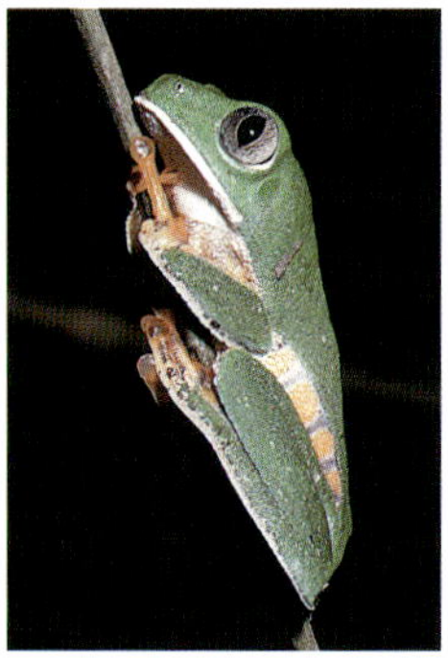

Many of the creatures of the rainforest are masters of camouflage, such as the leaf frog (above).

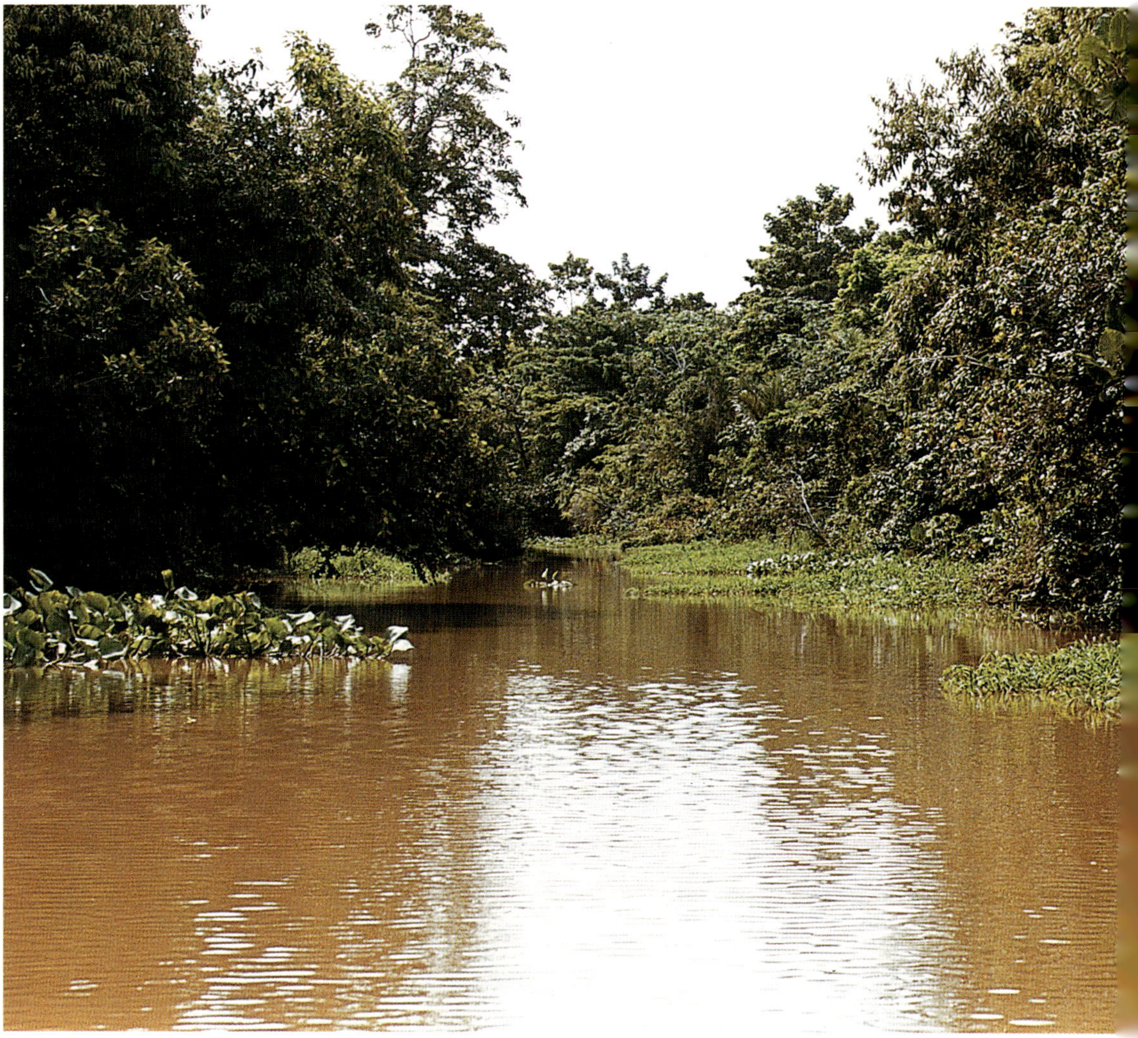

The backwaters and tributaries of the Amazon (above right) are home to the giant waterlily, Victoria amazonica (below), whose leaves are strong enough to support the weight of a child.

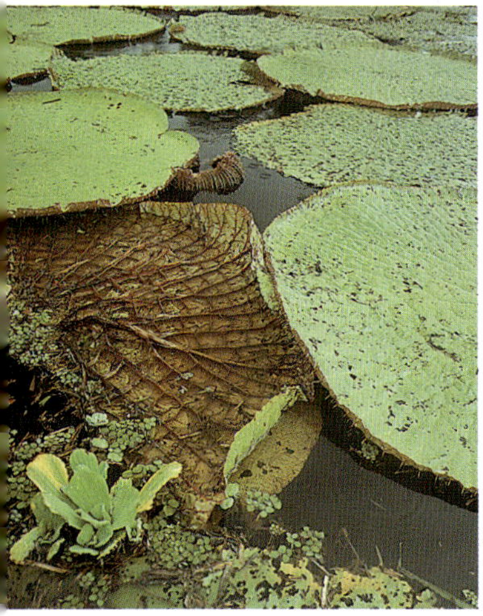

parts. When the monotony of the journey is relieved by the occasional stop at a riverside village—often little more than a landing stage with a scruffy bar—a lot of alcohol gets drunk and tempers flare. Although most passengers will be scrupulously honest, there's nowhere secure to store valuables, so it is wise to leave them at home.

Another disadvantage is that the riverboats stay close to the main channel of the river—which is often 6 miles (9..5 km) wide—and far from the banks, so you won't see so much wildlife. But for the intrepid, travel by local boat has advantages. First, it is astonishingly cheap; as probably the only gringos (westerners) on the boat, you'll learn basic Portuguese and/or Spanish fast; and what you lose in wildlife watching, you'll make up for in human drama.

Time passes slowly as the endless curtain of green jungle slides past the boat. When the boat stops at a riverside settlement, it is a major event. There's a flurry of activity as members of the crew trade staples such as toothpaste and cigarettes for local produce, and passengers get on and off: a farmer bringing home a new tractor part, a woman and her daughters taking chickens to sell in the market, a young man returning crestfallen from the big city where his grand plans have failed. Then it's back to the slow rhythm of the journey, lying on the baking tin roof of the boat watching birds wheel over the unbelievably wide expanse of muddy brown water. At night, fireflies follow the boat, and the eyes of a cayman glint from the water.

MEETING OF THE WATERS

Approaching Manaus, the river divides into two streams of distinctly different colors—to the left, a yellowish swirl, to the right, a wide band of dark water. This is what gives the Río Negro its name. The water darkens as the two great rivers join. On the banks of the Río Negro, 9 miles (14 km) north of the confluence, is Manaus. For travelers, the city is a culture shock: big, glamorous, and sleazy, the one metropolis of all of Amazonia, with a seedy dockland, bustling commercial center, and throbbing nightlife. The turn-of-the-century rubber boom left the town with a grand neoclassical opera house, where international megastars such as Sarah Bernhardt and the Ballet Russe once performed. Then the boom collapsed—rubber plants smuggled out to Malaya broke Brazil's lucrative monopoly—leaving the place almost impoverished. But massive tax concessions have restored the local economy, turning Manaus into the consumer capital of Amazonia; people fly in from as far afield as Colombia and Venezuela to buy refrigerators and dishwashers in its warehouse emporia.

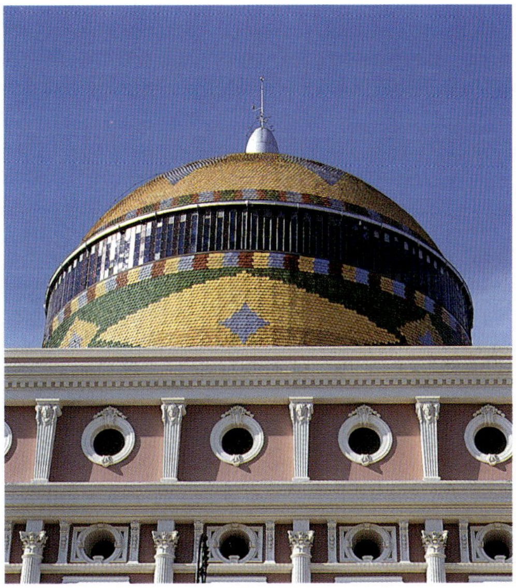

The opera house in Manaus (left) was built in 1896 at the height of the rubber boom.

Broad, Parisian-style boulevards (below)—a relic of the evanescent prosperity of the late 19th-century rubber boom—give Manaus an improbably European feel in the heart of Amazonia.

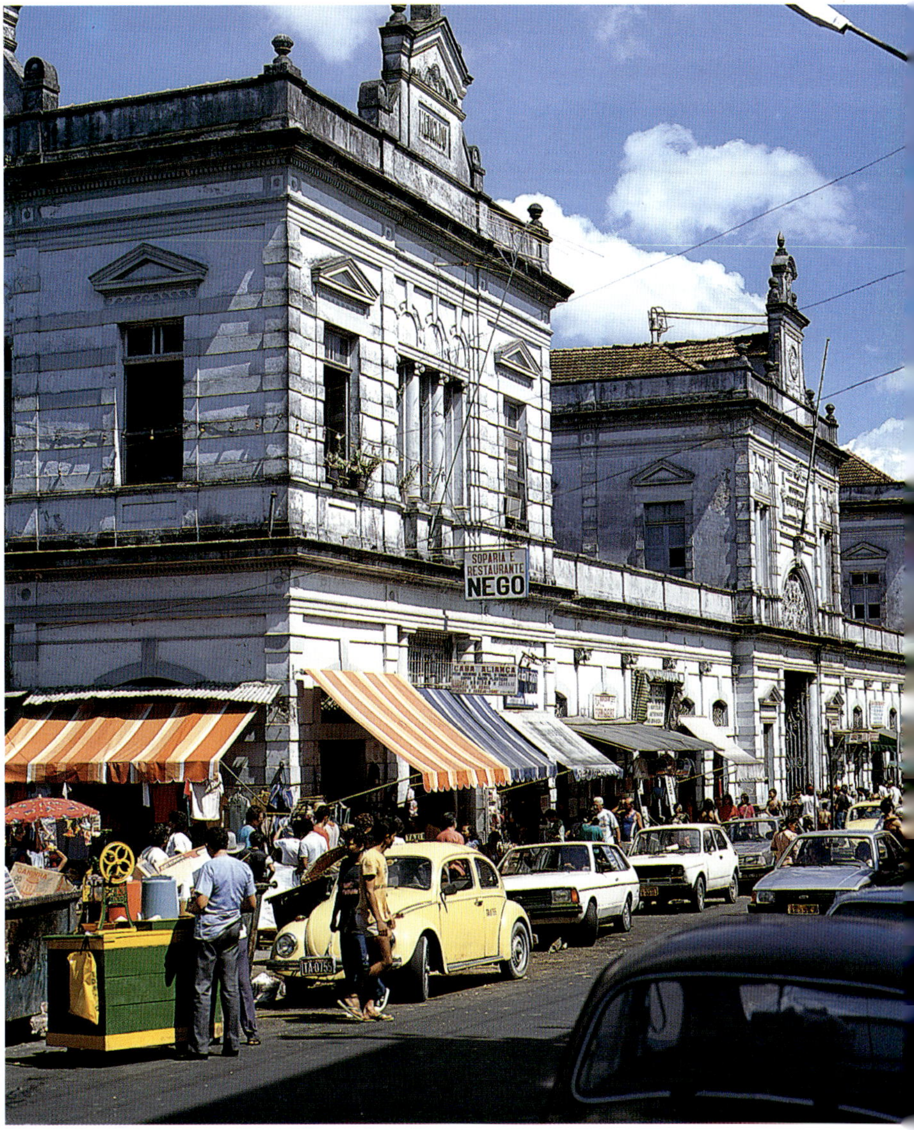

FADED ELEGANCE

The Amazon port of Iquitos, 1,200 miles (1,920 km) farther upstream, and cultural center of eastern Peru provides a better idea of how Manaus once looked. Above Manaus, Brazilians call the river the Solimoes, though it is still known to the rest of the world as the Amazon. At Tabatinga, on the three-way frontier between Brazil, Peru and Colombia, you'll probably have to change boats. This is a grim, gritty modern border town, but its old quarter has a faded elegance and some decent hotels.

Iquitos, the main city of the Peruvian Amazon, is a surreal outpost of European elegance of the 1800s surrounded by virgin rainforest; no roads connect it with the outside world, it can only be reached by plane or riverboat. The town has several improbable relics of the rubber boom, including some grand old hotels, the Tarapaca Pier, and the curious Iron House, designed by the French engineer Gustave Eiffel for the 1889 Paris World Fair and reassembled in Iquitos.

In the riverside quarter of the Puerto de Belen area, traditional thatched houses stand on stilts at the water's edge. Above Iquitos, the river divides, with the Marañon continuing west and the Ucayali turning abruptly south. Those travelers brave—or demented—enough can push on up the Ucayali to Pucallpa, a raffish port on the edge of the rainforest and the Peruvian highlands. Here is the end of the Amazon basin, within a day's bus ride of the Andean realm of the Incas.

RIVERBOAT JOURNEY TIMES

Brazil	*upstream*	*downstream*
Belém to Manaus:	5-6 days	4-5 days
Manaus to Tabatinga:	5-8 days	3-4 days
Peru		
Tabatinga to Iquitos:	4 days	2 days
Iquitos to Pucallpa:	5 days	3 days

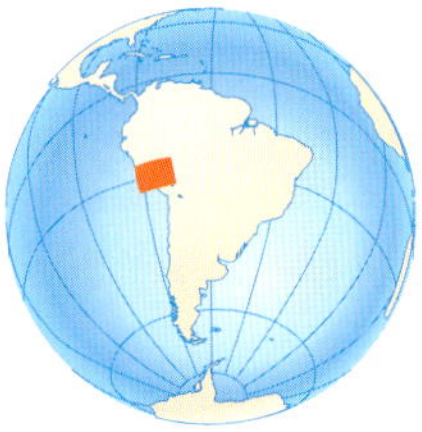

The Inca Trail

Follow paved roads built centuries ago by the people of the Inca Empire, through jungles and spectacular mountain passes, to reach the "lost city" of a once-great civilization.

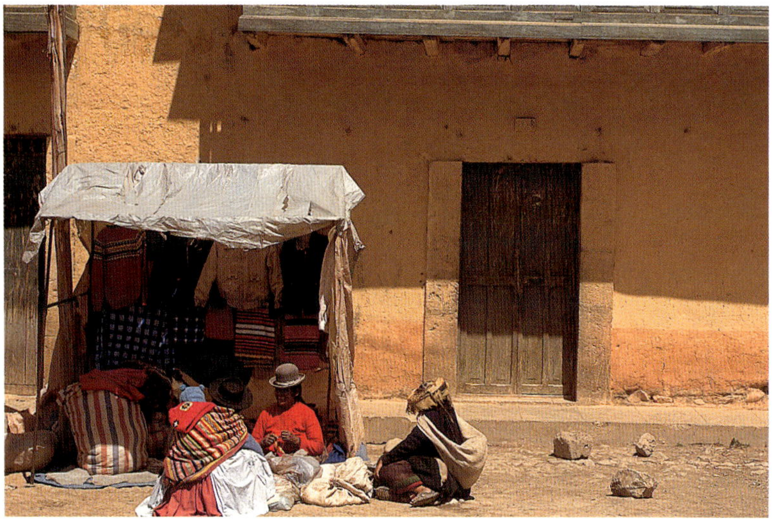

Descendants of the Inca people (above) in Ollantaytambo form a large percentage of the town's population and Quechua, the main Inca language, is still widely spoken.

IN 1533 THE INCA EMPIRE FELL to Spanish conquistadors led by Francisco Pizzaro, and the complex Inca civilization was totally destroyed. Since the rediscovery of many Inca monuments in the early 1900s, the magnificent and melancholy remains of this lost empire have lured visitors from around the world. Traveling from the old Inca capital of Cuzco through the "Sacred Valley" of the Río Urabamba to the ruined Inca city of Machu Picchu on its mountain peak, you discover the Inca world still survives in the high mountains: in the Quechua language spoken by some 10 million people (half the population), in the traditional costumes of the Andean *campesinos* (peasants), and in the Catholic saints' days, often a thinly veiled homage to the old gods.

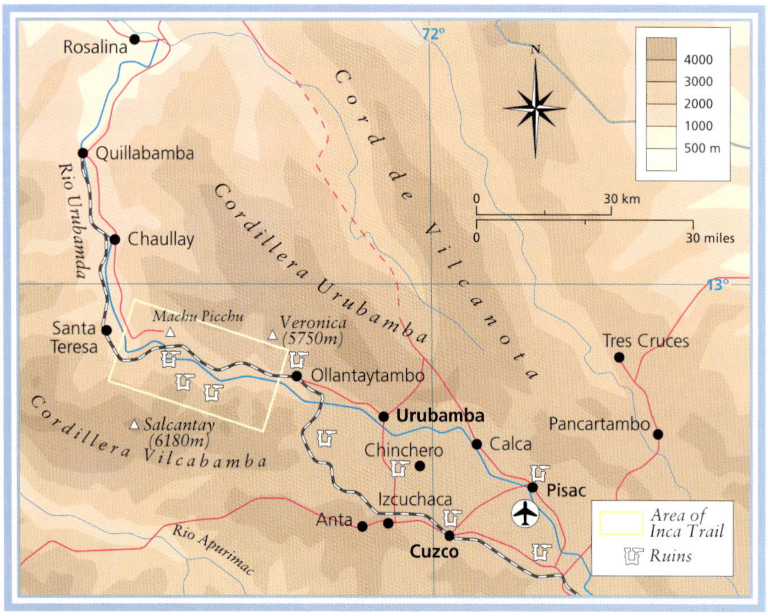

ACCLIMATIZATION IN CUZCO

Cuzco is a graceful colonial town in a valley 11,024 feet (3,360m) high, ringed by snow-capped mountains. The oldest continuously inhabited city in the Americas, it was half destroyed when the Incas rose against the Spanish in 1536. The amazingly neat Inca masonry has since been incorporated into later buildings, and many—including the ornate Baroque cathedral—rest on the foundations of Inca palaces. The main square, the broad Plaza de Armas, was once the ceremonial center of the Inca capital; stop for a meal or a coffee beneath its arcades, and you'll probably find a chunk of Inca masonry beside you.

Arriving by plane from Lima, altitude sickness symptoms may strike: breathlessness, dizzy spells, and nausea, and it is worth spending a few days of acclimatization in Cuzco before climbing to greater heights. There is no shortage of hotels—many of them are old and charming—and Cuzco has delightful cobbled streets with wooden-balconied colonial buildings and mysterious courtyards. In the street market by the station, fruit and vegetables are sold alongside traditional crafts—fabrics made from alpaca (llama wool) dyed with natural colors such as cochineal. Sample a plastic cup of *chicha*, a weak and cloudy beer made from (prechewed) fermented maize, or buy a bag of coca leaves to chew.

On a ridge above the town stand the remains of the Inca fortress Sachsayhuaman. The Inca city was planned in the shape of a puma, and the fortress formed the animal's head. Though damaged during the 1536 uprising, its tiers of zigzag granite ramparts, with characteristic trapezoid doorways, still look powerfully impressive. There were originally three towers at the summit; the circular foundations of one give a good idea of its immense size. From here there are marvelous views of the surrounding mountains and over the tiled roofs and church towers of Cuzco.

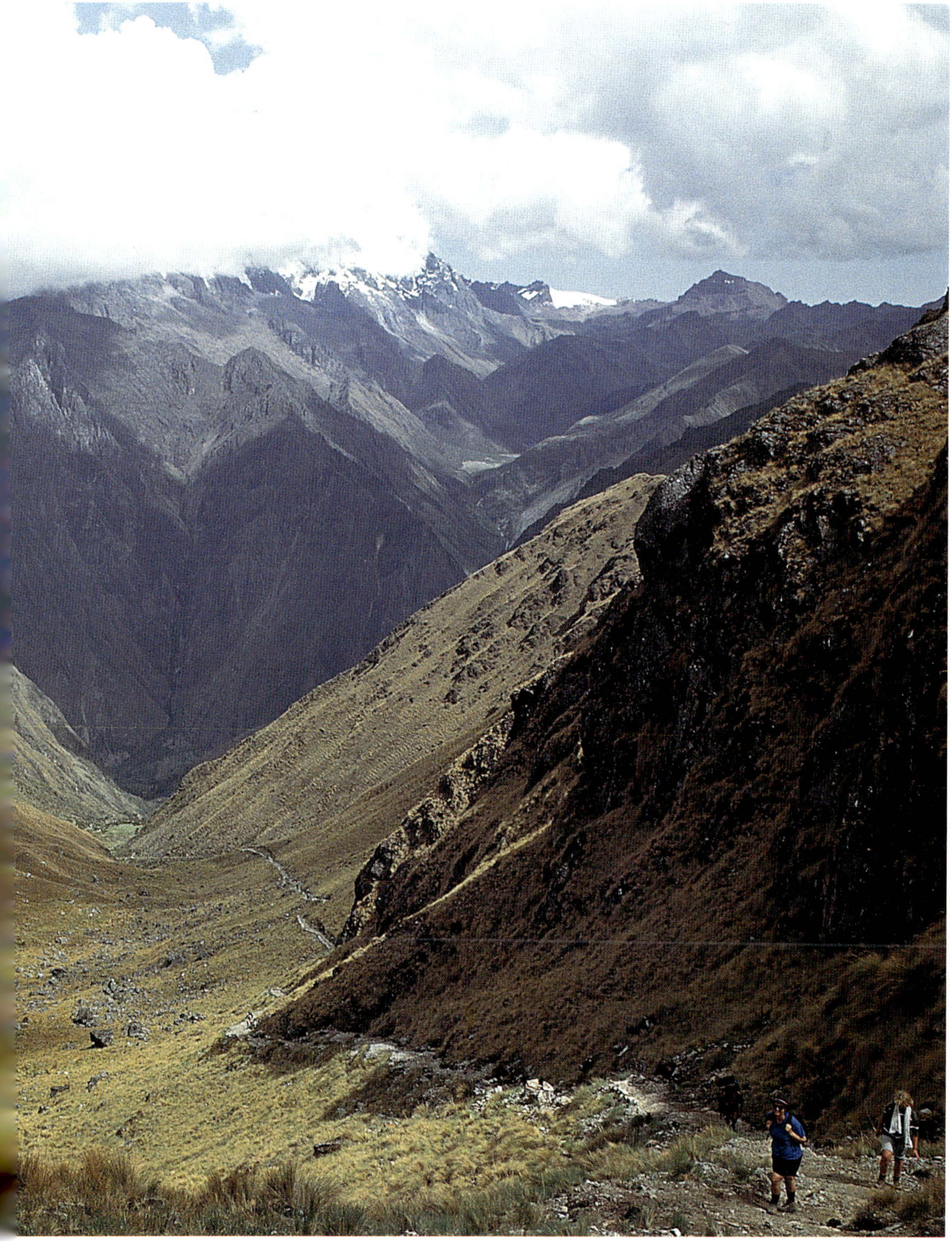

FACT FILE

Currency: New Sol. U.S. dollars welcomed.

Visas: Required by all nationalities.

Health: Yellow fever, typhoid, and polio vaccinations strongly recommended. Drink only bottled or boiled water, avoid salads, uncooked vegetables, and peeled fruits. Rest, and/or head for lower altitudes if you have severe symptoms of altitude sickness.

Language: Spanish is the official language, but Quecha is widely spoken. English is understood in the main centers.

Climate: Subtropical but varies dramatically with altitude. It can be very cold high up; heavy rains December— April.

Time to go: April— November.

Nearest airport: Cuzco.

What to take: Pills for malaria; insect repellent; sunscreen, sunglasses, sunhat; hiking boots; windproof ,warm clothing; binoculars; flashlight.

Food and drink: Pisco sour a potent brandy, is the national drink, *Aji* and *ajo* (pepper and garlic) form the basis of most dishes, along with rice and about 2,000 types of native potato. *Aji de gallina* (chicken in a spicy cream sauce) is popular. Avocados and tropical fruit are abundant.

What to buy: Handicrafts, alpaca rugs and blankets, ceramics, carved gourds.

The view from the highest pass on the Inca Trail (above).

ON THE INCA TRAIL

To control their empire, which stretched into modern Ecuador and Chile, the Incas built an elaborate network of trails, running more than 2,500 miles (4,000 km) through highlands, Amazon valleys, and coastal deserts. The trail of some 30 miles (48 km) in the Urabamba valley to Machu Picchu takes four days to walk as there are some big gradients. There are campsites and shelters along the way, but take your own food.

Crossing the fast-flowing river on a small suspension bridge, the trail starts amid dense, subtropical vegetation before climbing into the bleak highlands; far below, the silver ribbon of the Urabamba runs along the bottom of its gorge, while snow-capped Andean peaks tower above. On the way are Indian villages and

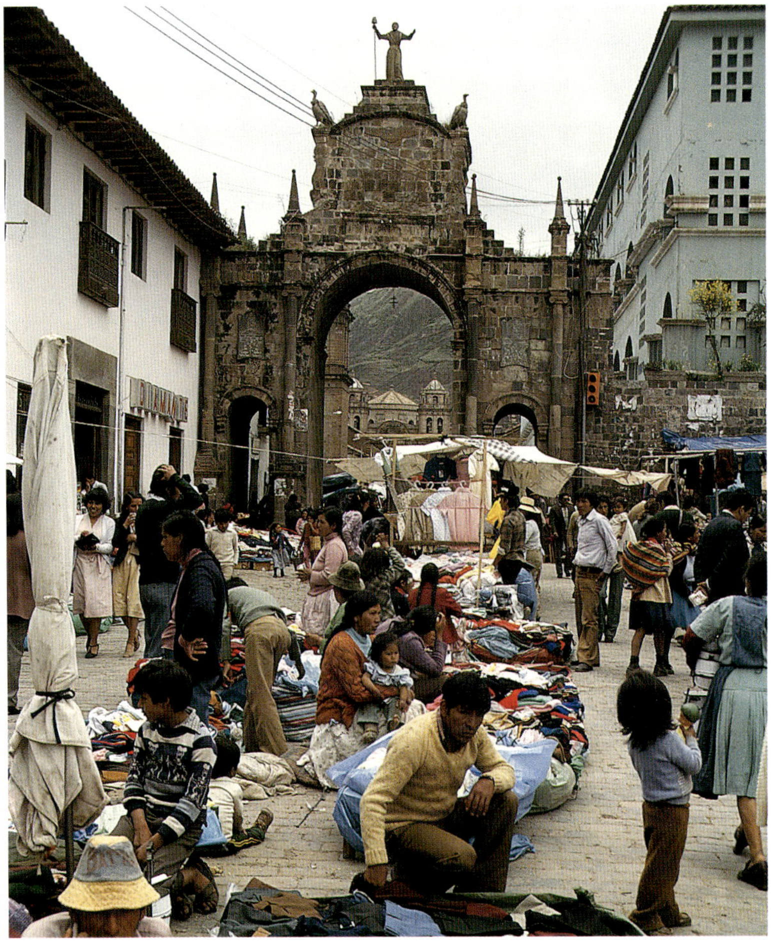

In Cuzco's main market, in front of a Spanish colonial archway, Indians from the surrounding countryside sell herbs and traditional crafts alongside domestic goods.

abandoned Inca towns, which were sited to control the route. At first, the trail is just a dirt track, but on the third day, after crossing a cold, windy mountain pass, the Abra de Runkuracay, the trail changes to a narrow roadway, paved with close-fitting Inca stones.

Farther on, the roofless and overgrown Inca town of Sayacmarca ("Dominant Town") clings to a rock above the trail, accessible only by a narrow stairway cut into the stone between an overhanging rock wall and a sheer precipice. Nearby is an ancient stone aqueduct. More evidence of Inca engineering skills appears beyond the next valley, where a 26-foot (8 m) tunnel—wide enough to allow laden beasts to pass through—has been cut into the rock.

The ruined Inca city of Machu Picchu (right) clings to steep, cloudforested slopes high above the Urambamba river.

The "Lost City"

You emerge from the next pass to an awe-inspiring view of the Urabamba Valley and the glistening glaciers of the 19,000-foot (5,787m) Nevada Verónica. Just below, the Inca ruins of Phuyupatamarca ("Cloud Level Town") cling to the slope, surrounded by the terraced fields that fed its population. A steep granite stairway cuts down into the forested slopes of the Urabamba Gorge toward another Inca town, Huinay Huayna ("Forever Young"), with a campsite and a visitor center nearby. From here, a broad level path leads through scrub and light woodland to narrow stone steps. These lead into a small structure, Intipunku, Gateway to the Sun. Through the rectangular stone doorway, the "lost city" of Machu Picchu appears on its mountain ridge, walls and thatched huts often wreathed in clouds, and you feel as if you were its first discoverer. From Intipunku, a path leads directly to Machu Picchu itself.

An alternative to the four-day hike is by train from Cuzco to Las Ruinas, the station immediately below Machu Picchu. If you disembark at the station before, where the village of Aguas Calientes nestles in its cloud-filled valley beneath densely wooded slopes, you can spend a peaceful night in one of the small hotels, listening to the rushing river and strange animal cries from the cloud forest. Then, set off early next morning to walk the mile along a steep valley, through which the Río Urabamba gurgles it way to Machu Picchu.

Hewn from a Sacred Mountain

Clinging to the flanks of a steep ridge, tier upon tier of defensive walls, gardens, palaces, and temples rise. Fountains gurgle down through stepped basins. Walls of many-sided stones, so finely worked that you couldn't slip a scalpel between them, loom above. Massive, sloping stone doorways lead onto wide plazas filled with swaying grass and poppies. At the highest point is an altar, from which a mysterious square pillar known as the "Hitching Post of the Sun" projects. Altar, post, and the steps that lead up to them are all hewn from mountain rock, which the Incas held sacred.

The whole site is overlooked by a towering granite pinnacle, Huayna Picchu. The original Inca stairway leads through cloud forest festooned with orchids and air plants to the summit, where bright butterflies flutter about your head. From the top, you can see the entire site amid its setting: the cloud-capped peaks, the forested valleys, and the river far below. The ruins are especially impressive at dawn or sunset but many buildings are currently being restored.

Hiram Bingham, the American archaeologist who discovered the city in 1911, thought that he had found Vilcabamba, where the last Incas held out against the Spanish until 1572. But the Machu Picchu dates from the mid-1400s, and the less impressive ruins of the Incas' last capital were later discovered 100 miles (160 km) west at Espiritu Pampa. Machu Picchu may have been a religious center abandoned before the Spanish arrived, possibly as a result of the civil war and smallpox epidemic around 1527. But such theories remain speculation. The purpose and fate of Machu Picchu are shrouded in mystery.

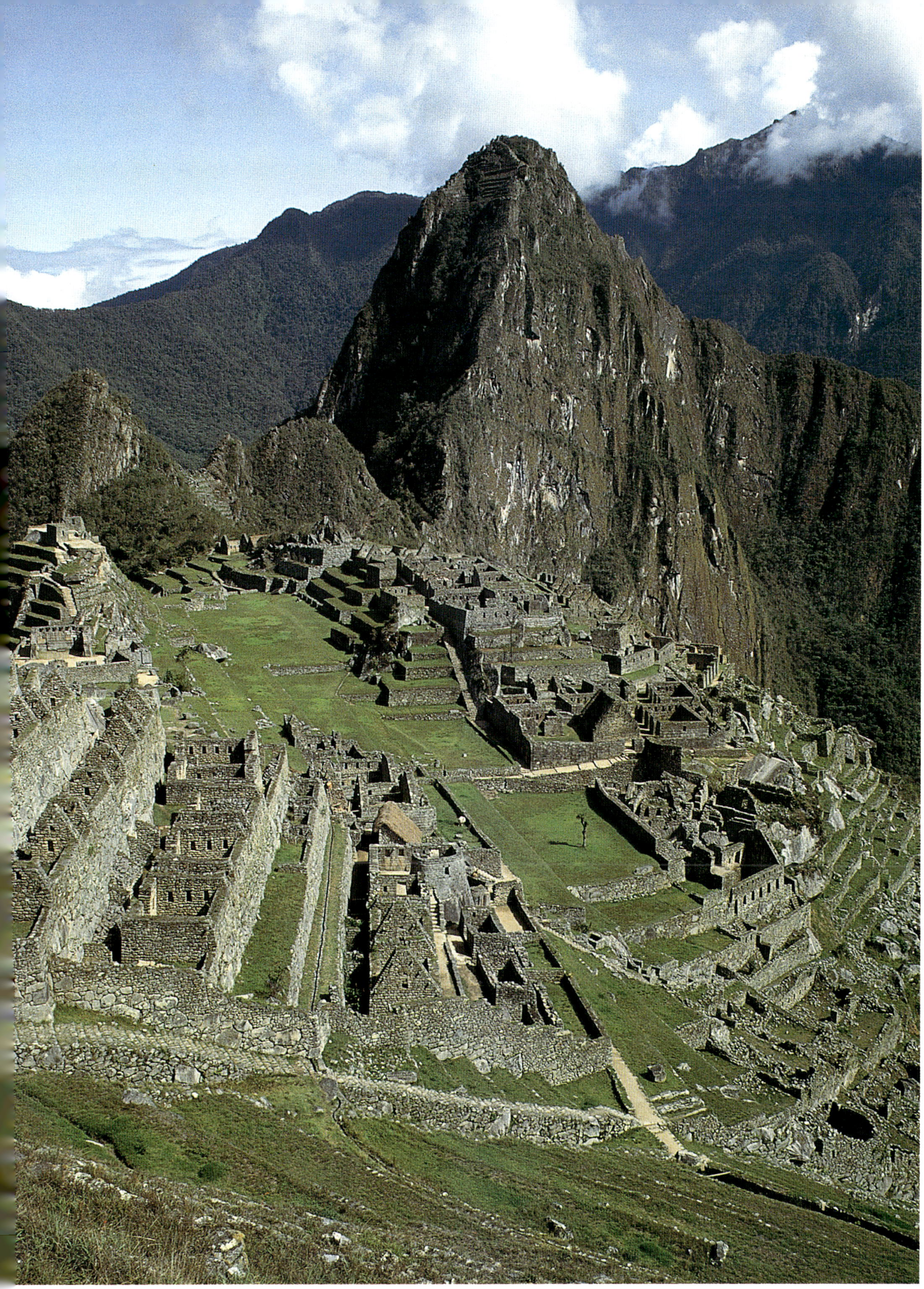

Africa

"Going up that river was like traveling back to the earliest beginnings of the world, when vegetation rioted on the earth and the big trees were king."

Joseph Conrad, Russian-born English writer, 1857-1924

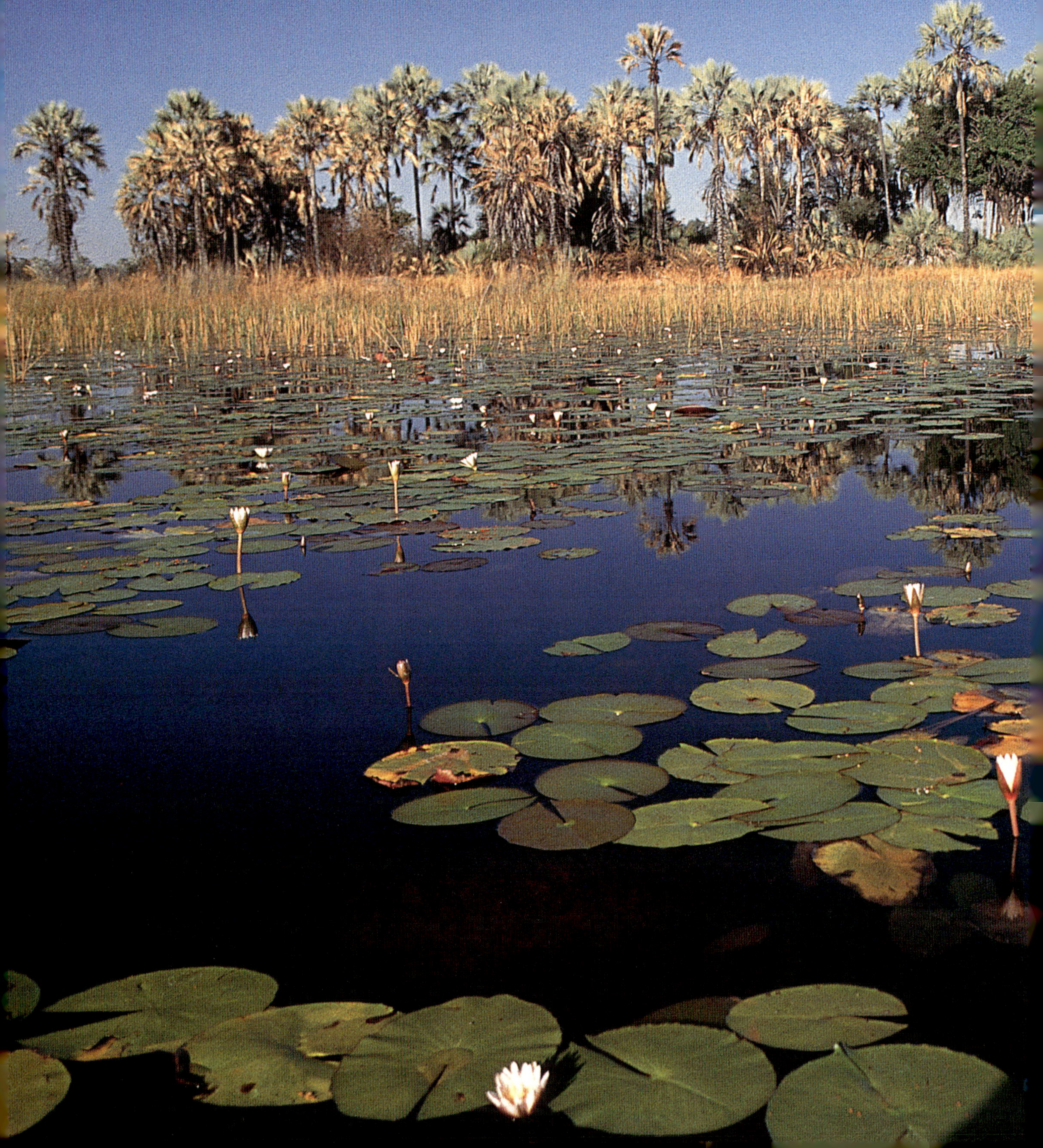

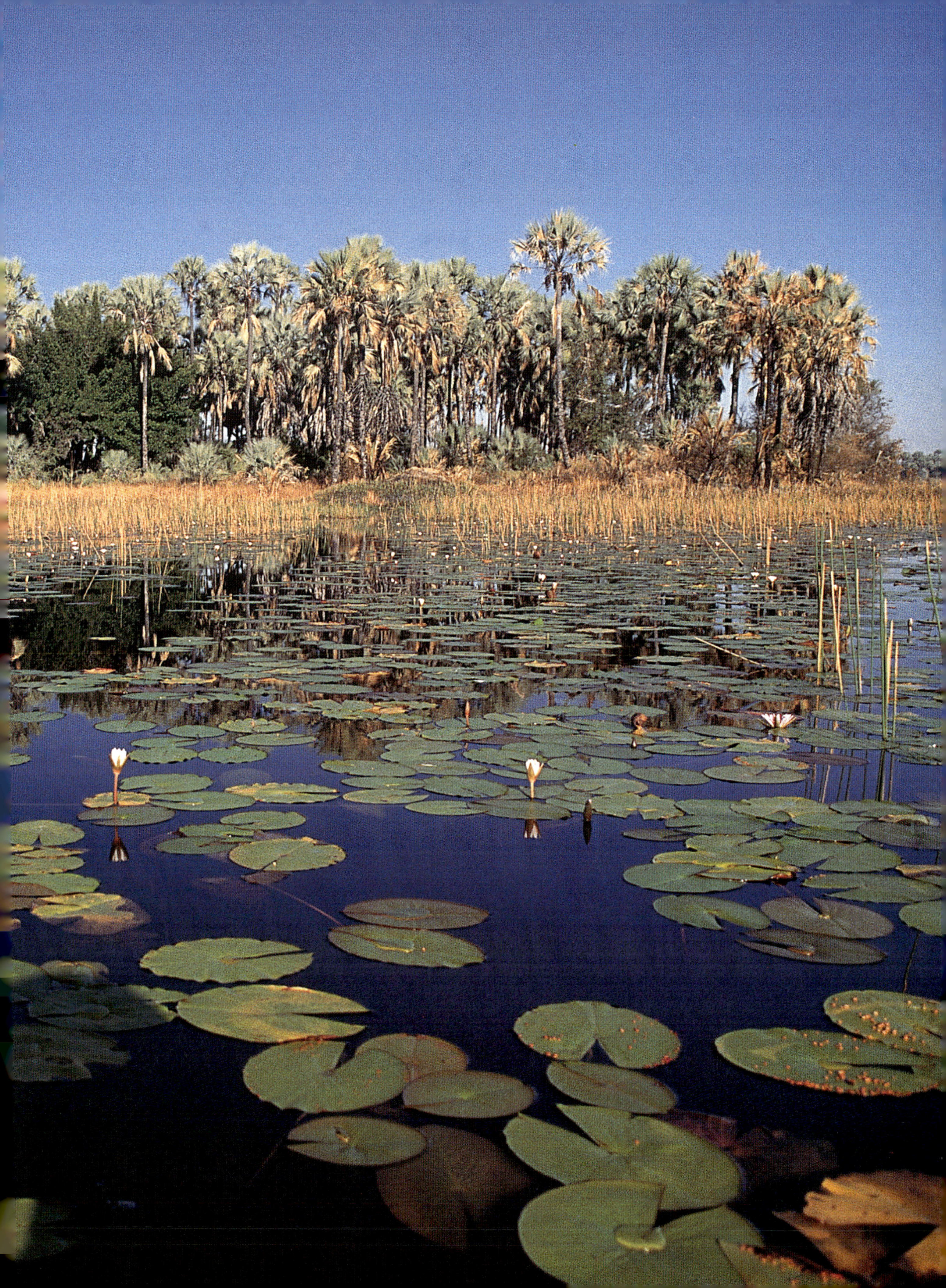

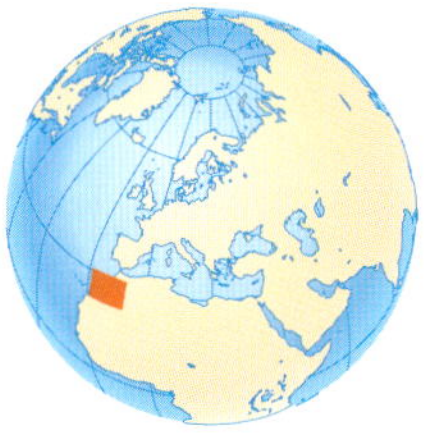

Marrakesh and the Atlas Mountains

A city seething with life, and snow-fed mountain slopes keep the desert at bay.

CLIMB TO THE FLAT ROOF of any of the small hotels in the heart of old Marrakesh, and you will see a panorama of mosques, minarets, and towers, with palm trees rising above hidden courtyards. Beyond, seeming very close in the clear air, the peaks of the High Atlas Mountains, snow-capped most of the year, flash white against deep blue skies. Over everything lies a reddish pall, the dust which gives Marrakesh its name, "the Red City", reminding you that, though green with gardens, this city is an oasis amid a desert. But don't spend too long admiring the panorama. Just beneath, throbbing with cacophonous life, is the Djema el Fna, which means Place of the Dead—though nowhere could be livelier than Marrakesh's greatest square. The acrobats, musicians, dancers, snake charmers, fortunetellers, and storytellers filling the dusty expanse might have stepped from the pages of *The Arabian Nights*. The square, an oblong surrounded by low buildings, is a stage for their daily performances, but it is at night that the unscripted free show is at its most brilliant—and not just for tourists, for the stories related are all in Arabic or Berber, not French or English. Rows of open-air food stalls are set up where you can eat typical Moroccan food—try *harira*, a thick soup—and sip mint tea, the standard Moroccan drink served with quantities of sugar. Beware, however, of the touts who will hassle you nonstop, trying to sell you their services as guides or almost anything else. Don't imagine that pretending ignorance of French, English, or any other language will save you from their attentions: they seem to speak every tongue under the sun.

Marrakesh (right), which by day can seem drab and dusty, hums with life far into a night lit by thousands of lamps.

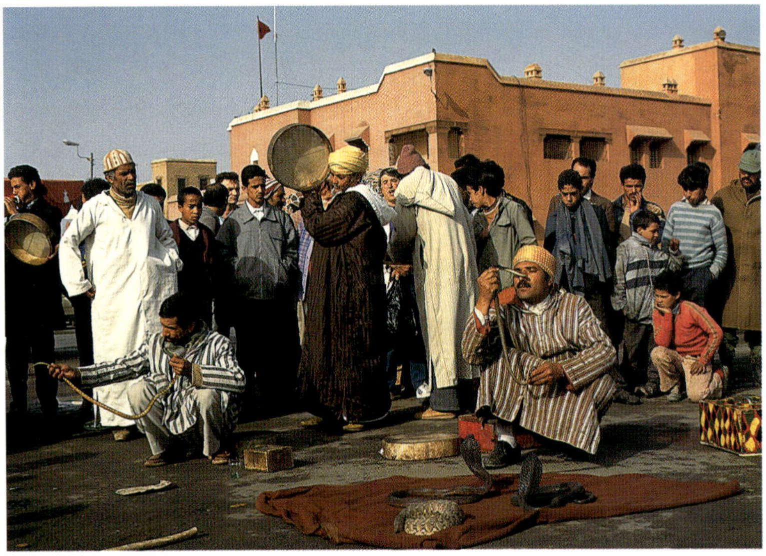

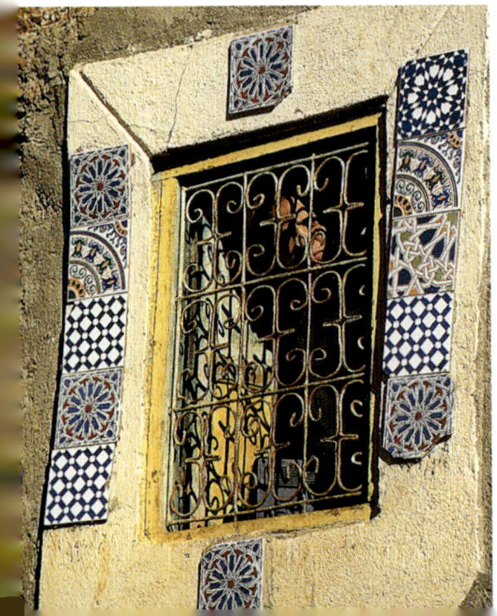

Windows in exterior walls (left) are rare in reclusive Marrakesh, but the few visible often have elaborate iron grills and colorful tilework, reflecting the influence of Mozarabic craftsmen from Granada in Spain.

Snake charmers (above), usually Berbers, perform daily in the main square of Marrakesh, the Djema el Fna. The charmers control the reptiles as much by their own body movements as by their music.

GUIDE TO BARTERING

Unless traveling with an organized tour, it is helpful for first-timers to hire a guide, either from the Tourist Office or, almost as good, from among the more agreeable individuals in Djema el Fna; they cost little. Once with your chosen guide, you are safe from all others as he zealously leads you around. You will undoubtedly end up in a shop in the souks, the maze of tiny covered alleys crammed with stands selling leatherware, silver, silk, wool and cotton clothes, carpets, spices, ornate daggers, and much plastic trash. The shop chosen will probably be run by someone the guide just happens to know, who will—such is your astounding luck—generously offer you an "extra special price." Haggling is not only expected, it is almost obligatory: express utter disbelief at the price first demanded and doubts over whether the item is really what you want. It should be a leisurely process, marked by the consumption of endless mint teas. Once a price is agreed, most shopkeepers prove surprisingly knowledgable about credit cards and air freight home if the item is too large to carry.

ENDURING GLORIES

But Marrakesh is not just an emporium, it is a former imperial city, with some of the greatest architecture in the Islamic world, reflecting its glorious if turbulent past. Founded in 1062 by the Almoravid dynasty, who

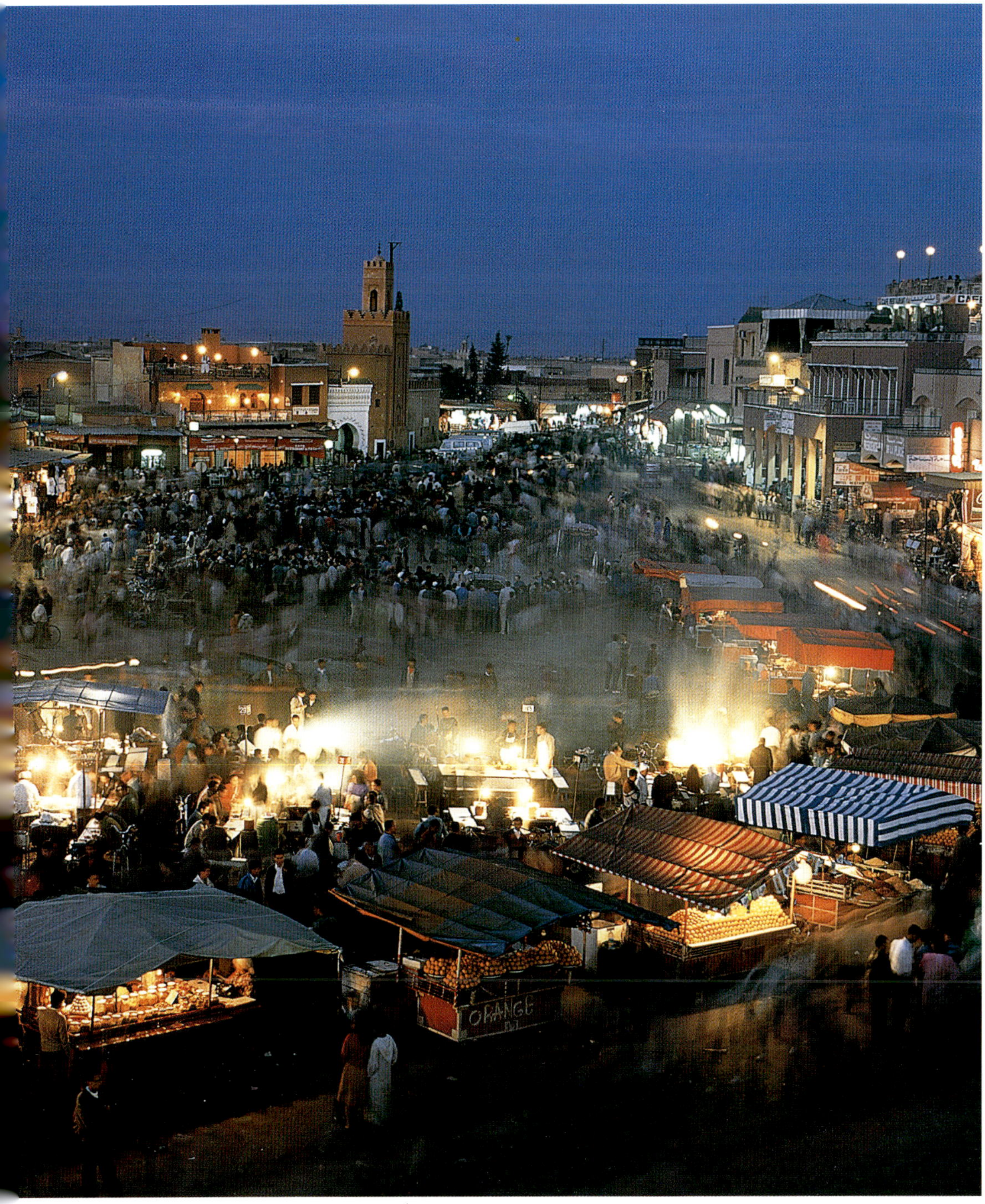

ruled an empire from Toledo, Spain, to Senegal, the city has since been deserted, ruined, and rebuilt many times. Its golden age was the 1100s, when Moorish craftsmen came from Spain to build mosques and palaces. Unfortunately, non-Muslims are strictly barred from entering mosques, but you can admire the outside of the Koutoubia Mosque tower, a classic of Moorish Andalucian architecture, and actually go inside the Medersa Ben Yousef, a *madrasa* (theological college) of the 1500s, with intricate stucco ceilings. More romantic are the Saadian Tombs, also dating from the 1500s, where among slender cypresses and rosebeds lie the graves of the Saadi Sultans. Inside the gloomy but stunningly opulent Hall of Twelve Columns is a dome covered in what looks like gilded lace, another example of Moroccan stucco.

Outside of the city walls stretches the still elegant Ville Nouvelle (new town), built under the French protectorate (1912-56), with French restaurants and cafés lining busy boulevards planted with flowering orange trees. Here, too, are luxury hotels set in verdant gardens around swimming pools, where the former

FACT FILE

Currency: Moroccan Dirhams.

Languages: Arabic and Berber (spoken by 40% of the popultion), with French and some English. Take a phrase book.

Climate: Mediterranean/ Saharan. Very hot in summer, over 100°F (38°C) in Marrakesh, but often cold in the mountains. It can rain heavily in winter.

When to go: October through April to avoid the heat, but take warm clothing.

Two don'ts: don't drink the tap water and don't go around half-naked, especially if you are young and female. Although some tourists do, it upsets Moroccans.

Airports: Marrakesh, Ouazazarte, Agadir

Getting around: Reasonable bus services along the main routes but for freedom rent a car.

What to buy: Carpets, leatherware, pottery, silver and copper, spices.

Food and drink: The great national dish is tajine, made with fish, or spiced meat balls, young lamb or chicken and prunes, infused with lemon and olive and cooked slowly in a clay dish. Most Moroccans, being Muslim, do not touch alcohol, but go go for mint tea or fresh fruit juice, but good potent local wine can be found in restaurants for westerners. Try Cabernet President among the reds and Oustalet Rosé for a refreshing pink. The whites are not recommended.

British Prime Minister Winston Churchill used to stay and paint. Unless you really love the hubbub of the old city, this is the best area to stay, only half an hour on foot from Djema el Fna, less by bus or fiacre (horse-drawn carriage).

MOUNTAIN AND DESERT

Beyond Marrakesh lie the mountains and desert of what the French called *le Grand Sud* (the Deep South), now accessible by bus or rental car, provided you stick to the main asphalted routes—the lesser roads can be just tracks over naked rock. Some 30 miles (50 km) beyond the city, the road climbs through green oak woods toward the peaks of the High Atlas. These are the greatest mountains of North Africa, rising over 13,000 feet (3,900m), and in spring are covered with wildflowers. The village of Telouet, 12 miles (20 km) east of the highway, is worth a detour; stone houses with unglazed windows and flat earth roofs surround a grim looking kasbah (fort). Telouet was once the headquarters of the Glaoui tribe, who governed most of southern Morocco for the French with medieval ferocity until the 1940s, hanging their enemies' heads on the walls of Marrakesh. The highway snakes up to the Tizi n'Tichka Pass, at 7,467 feet (2,275m) the highest in Morocco and snowbound in winter, and then descends into a barren, rocky landscape.

Ouarzazarte, about 90 miles (144 km) from Marrakesh, was once a vital frontier fort on the edge of the world's greatest desert. From first sight its red cubes of houses and palm trees look like a movie set for an oasis, and movies have been indeed shot here. There are now several hotels and even a golf course, thanks to the Dra River. The river, fed by Atlas snows, cuts a gorge through a range of the Anti-Atlas Mountains, then heads south into the desert where it finally expires. En route, it creates green, intensively cultivated oases with mudbuilt villages surrounded by palm trees, just like a miniature Nile Valley. The road follows the river, and it is worth stopping at the village of Agdz to admire the carpets for which it is famous.

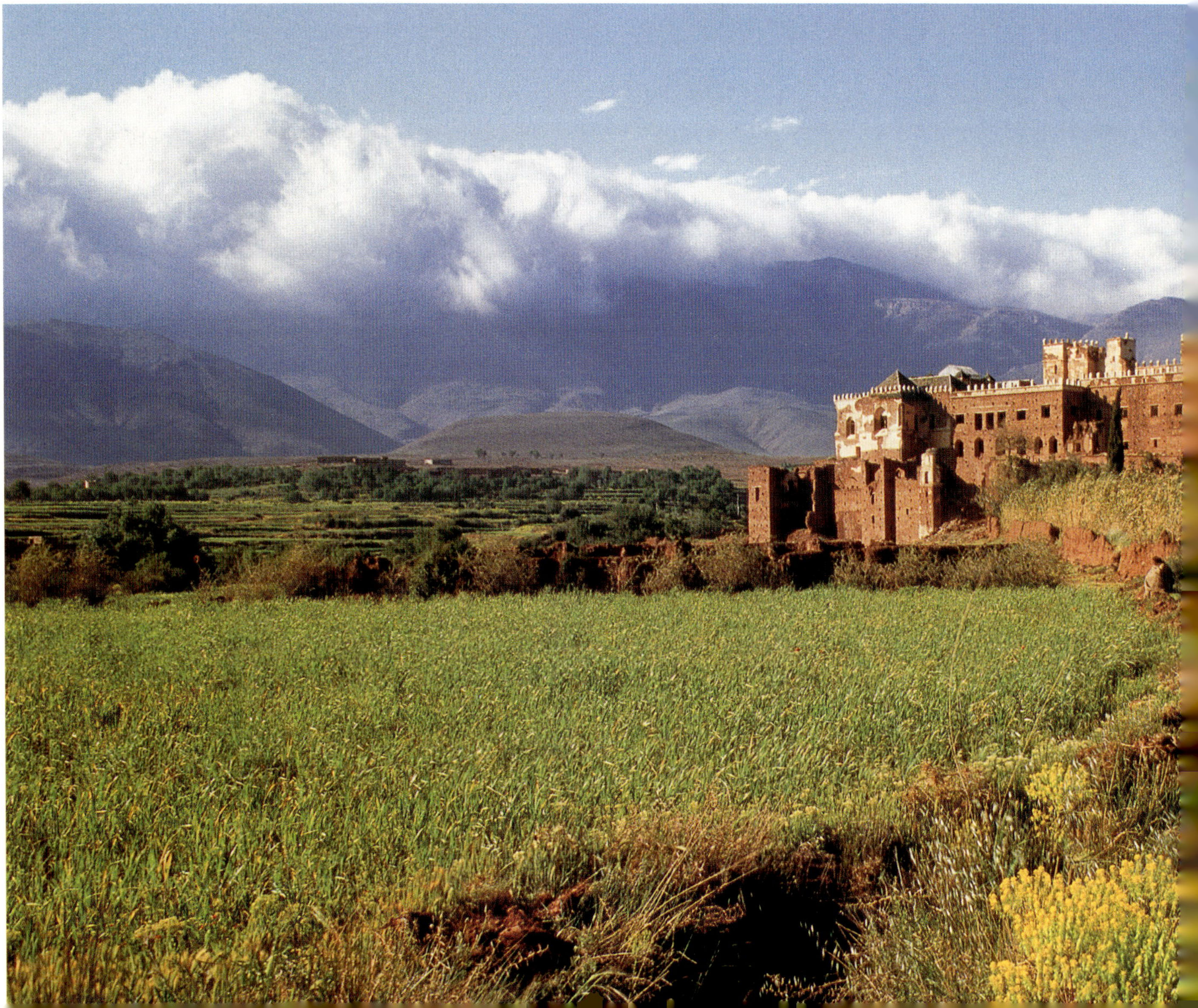

The half-ruined kasbah (fort) of Telouet rises above fertile cropland (below) irrigated by waters from the Atlas Mountains. The views from its flat roof are spectacular.

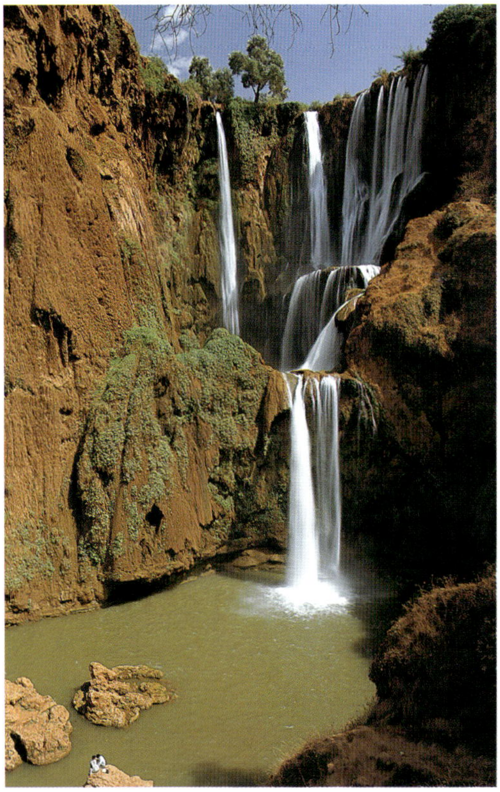

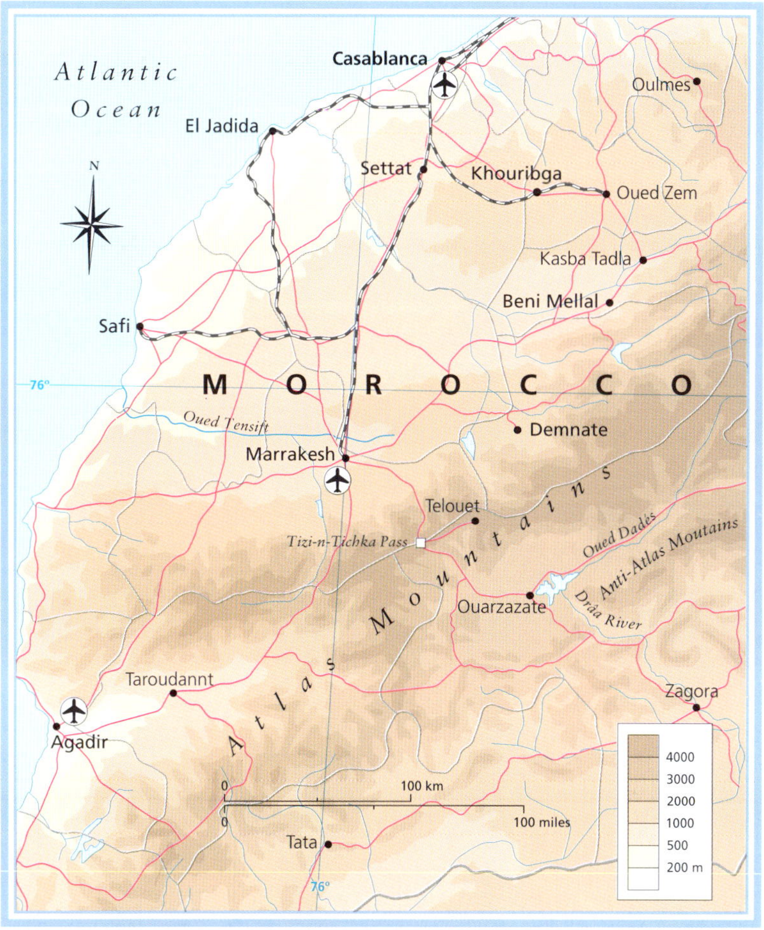

Hidden within the folds of the Atlas, waterfalls such as the one at Ouzand (above) seldom cease their flow, even in midsummer, thanks to the slow-melting mountain snows.

Zagora, 104 miles (168 km) southeast of Ouarzazarte, and another former frontier fort, is rather drab compared to the surrounding scenery, but useful as a base for exploring the desert and especially for renting camels. If you can ride these strangely lurching beasts in comfort—some people get seasick—you can arrange desert expeditions here for up to a week, complete with guides and tents. You sleep under canvas and can see the stars rise with stunning clarity above the desert, which spreads south and east for thousands of empty miles.

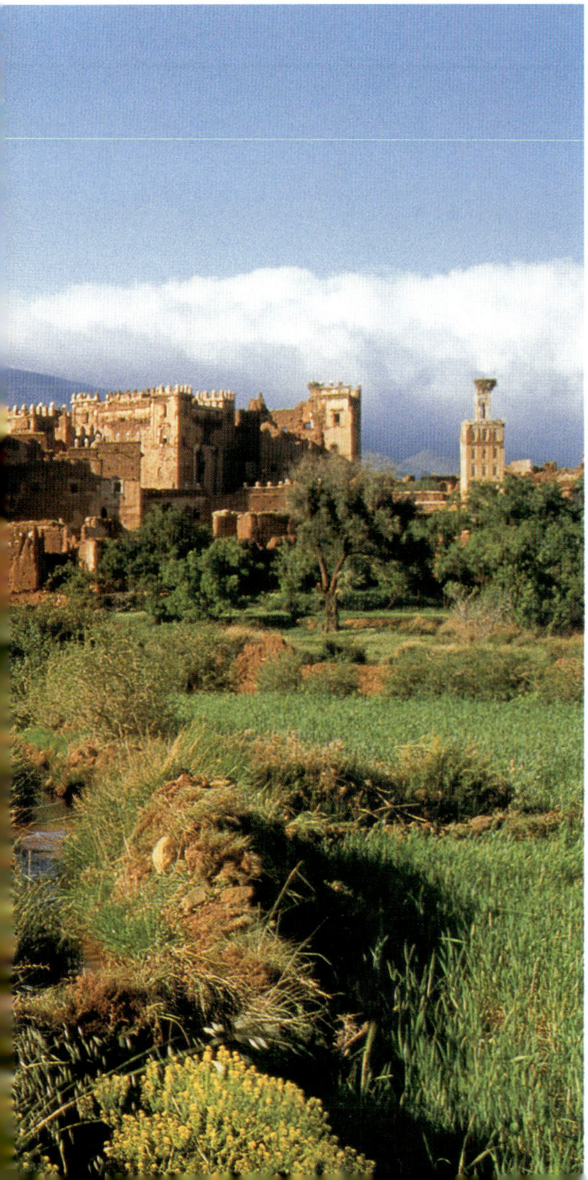

Ouarzazate once was nothing but the lonely frontier fort of Taouirt (right) on the desert's edge, but now has dozens of hotels, an airport, and a zoo.

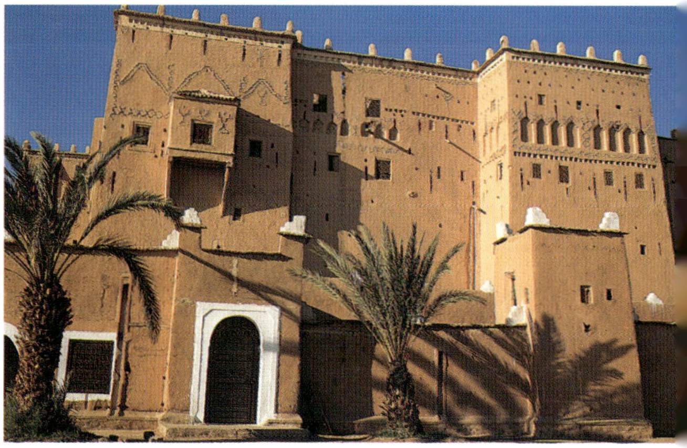

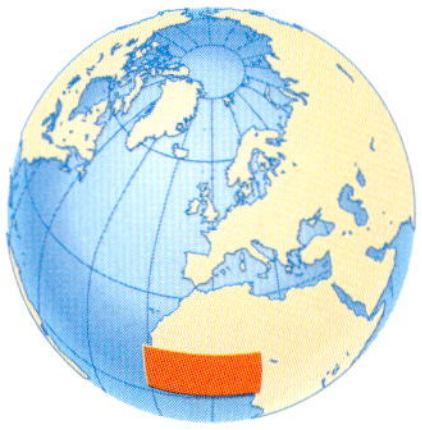

To Timbuktu by Steamer

The legendary "city of gold," may no longer quite live up to its former reputation, but the river journey to it cuts through the Republic of Mali, the throbbing pulse of West Africa.

FACT FILE

Language: French is the official language, but there are several local languages.

Currency: West African CFA Franc.

Climate: Rainy season June—September. Hottest March—May 104° F (40° C) The *harmattana*, a dry, hot, dusty wind, blows from the Sahara December—February.

When to go: The boats run August—November when the river is high enough.

What to buy: Woodcarvings, masks, woolen goods, copperware.

Health Warning: Take precautions against malaria, yellow fever, hepatitis and rabies. Avoid unboiled milk, unbottled or unsterilized water, and uncooked fruit and vegetables.

THE RIVER NIGER is the main artery of life in the heart of West Africa; a source of food, the home of around 200 species of fish, and along the navigable section from Koulikoro downstream and eastward to the fabled city of Timbuktu, where the vast majority of the population is focused. For the visitor, a passage along one of its navigable sections provides a remarkable insight into aspects of rural Africa. Timbuktu's former glories may have faded, but taking the one of the Compagnie Malienne de Navigation (CMN) boats, along the Niger from Koulikoro to Korioum, Timbuktu's river port, provides a panorama of life sliding by along the river's banks. Small towns and mudhut villages, punctuated by the spiked towers of the distinctive local mosques, cling to the main source of life amid a barren landscape.

The Niger, the largest river in West Africa, begins its long journey in the highlands of Guinea and then wanders deep into the ever-expanding Sahara Desert. At Timbuktu it turns south into Nigeria and flows toward the Atlantic Ocean. Most of the river's flow is dependent on rains in the distant Guinea highlands, supplying it both with water and the fertile silt so vital to farming along the only green land in the desert. The

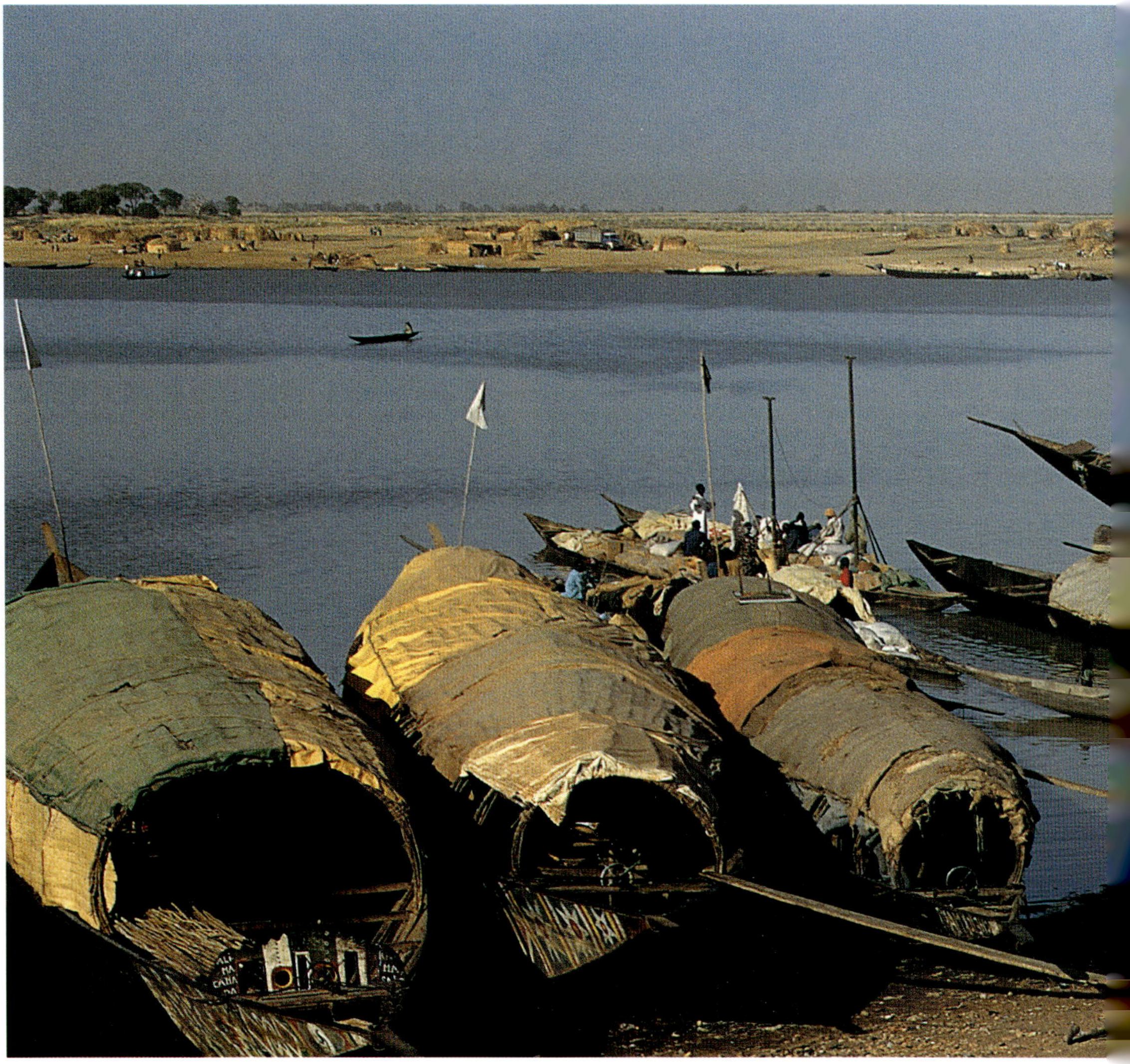

Canvas-covered pinasses and canoe-like pirogues (right) at Mopti, at the confluence of the Niger and the Bani rivers.

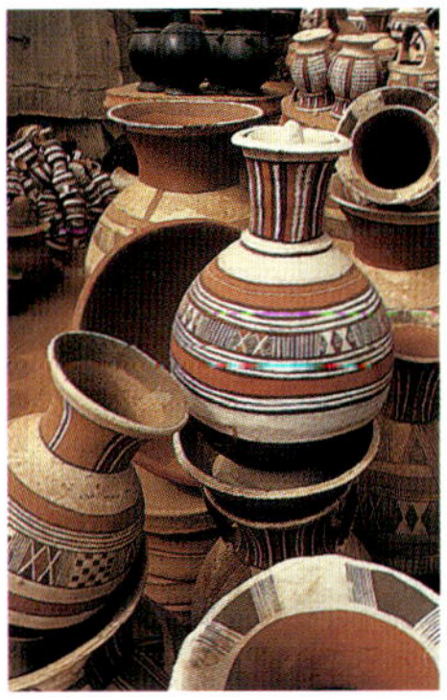

Unglazed earthenware pots (above) can be bought at Mopti.

Djenné's Grande Mosquée (right) has to be resurfaced each year after the rainy season.

steamers themselves resemble floating villages with sweltering cabins, loud music in the bars, and cargo spread everywhere with people piled on top. Accommodation varies from luxe—luxury cabins with air conditioning—and two levels of first class with beds or bunks, to the very hot and dirty if very lively, fourth class, which shares the lower deck with the cargo. Food is included in first and second, and sometimes third classes, but it is usually uninteresting. Bottled water can be purchased on board or before you travel and is available in all the towns along the way. Otherwise drinking water is simply water drawn from the river—so don't ever drink it!

Ségou is the first sizable town you come to heading downstream toward Timbuktu. Quieter than Bamako and less touristy than Djenné or Mopti farther down, it is a thriving, unspoiled African market town. Since it is off the beaten track, harassment by beggars or touts is still minimal. The market is open all week and is especially good on Mondays selling fine examples of Bambara pottery, rugs, and blankets.

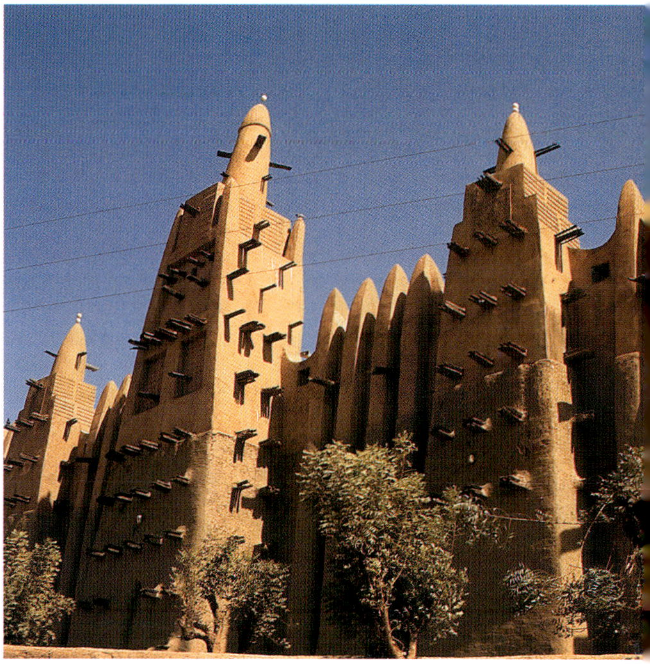

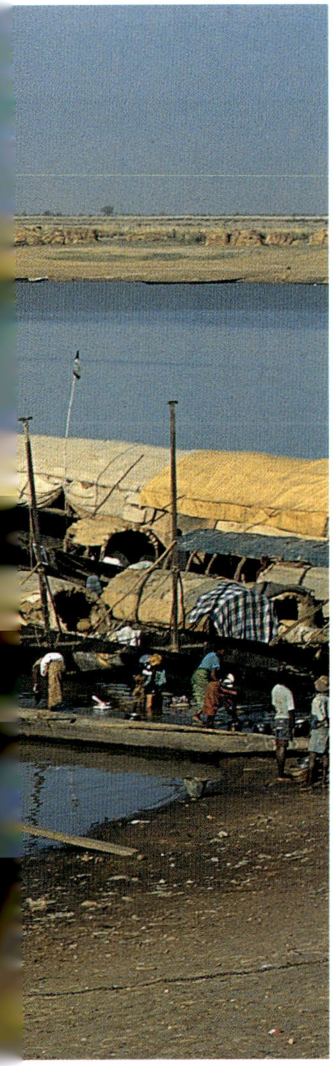

The Dogons

The boat's next stop is Mopti. Until the French colonial period, Mopti was a small riverside village. Then, situated midway between the two administrative centers of Bamako and Gao and with commerce expanding along the river, Mopti began to grow. More importantly, Dogon country is only a day away, in the Bandigara Escarpment. The Dogons are animists, believing that natural objects have souls. Their religion impregnates everything they do, influencing even the design of their villages and homes. Villages are built to resemble the human body, with houses representing arteries and veins. Their art is considered among the finest in Africa, particularly the intricate masks. Their architecture is also distinctive, with multistory houses clinging precariously to rock faces.

Partly because of the Dogon traditions, Mopti has become Mali's premier tourist destination, as well as the most vibrant port on the Niger River, lying at the junction of the Niger and Bani rivers in a vast inland delta. The *Grand Marché* (Great Market) is in the old town about 10 blocks from the port. Market day is Thursday with Bozo fisherman converging on the city

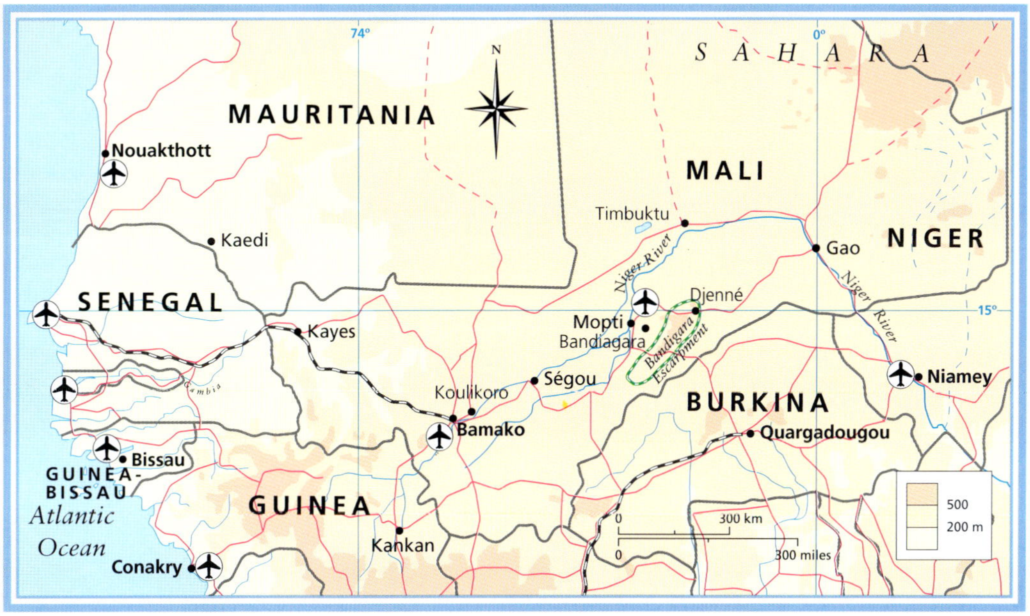

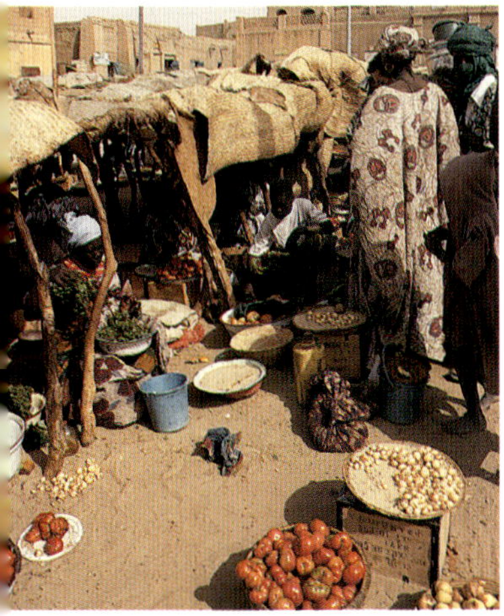

to sell white slabs of salt from the camel caravans from northern Mali. Mopti is also famous for blankets: wool or wool-cotton mix blankets; camel hair blankets; and the ornate (and expensive) Fulani wedding blankets. The town's mosque is of typical Sudanese mud architecture found throughout Sahalien Africa. Each year the gray mud coating is washed off by the rains and has to be replaced during the dry season. The protruding beams are not merely decorative; they make the refacing task easier.

The grand market at Timbuktu sells mainly vegetables, but there is a smaller artisan's market nearby.

Elegance in a Desert

Djenné, standing amid the flood plains of the Niger farther downstream, has a similar task on a grander scale. Its elegant mosque, built in 1905, was based on designs of its predecessor which dated from the 11th century. This sleepy, attractive town, founded in the 9th century, reached the height of its importance at the same time as Timbuktu in the 1300s, when it profited from the trans-Saharan caravan trade, Morocco being 55 days by camel train to the north. Today the whole town comes alive on market day (Monday) when the Grand Marché is held in front of the Grande Mosquée.

Timbuktu lies about 7 miles (11 km) north of the Niger. It was once spread along the river's banks but the river has since changed course. Time has not been kind to the city, with its low, gray mud-bricked houses lining narrow, sandy streets. But along the alleyways are the ghosts of a time when this was an important center of Islam. There are many mosques, and some fine limestone houses—which recall the architecture of Egyptian temples—built by wealthy Moorish merchants of the 16th century. Many of the grand monuments of a prouder past have gone with the drifting sands of the Sahara, but the magic of its name and its past still give the town a unique atmosphere.

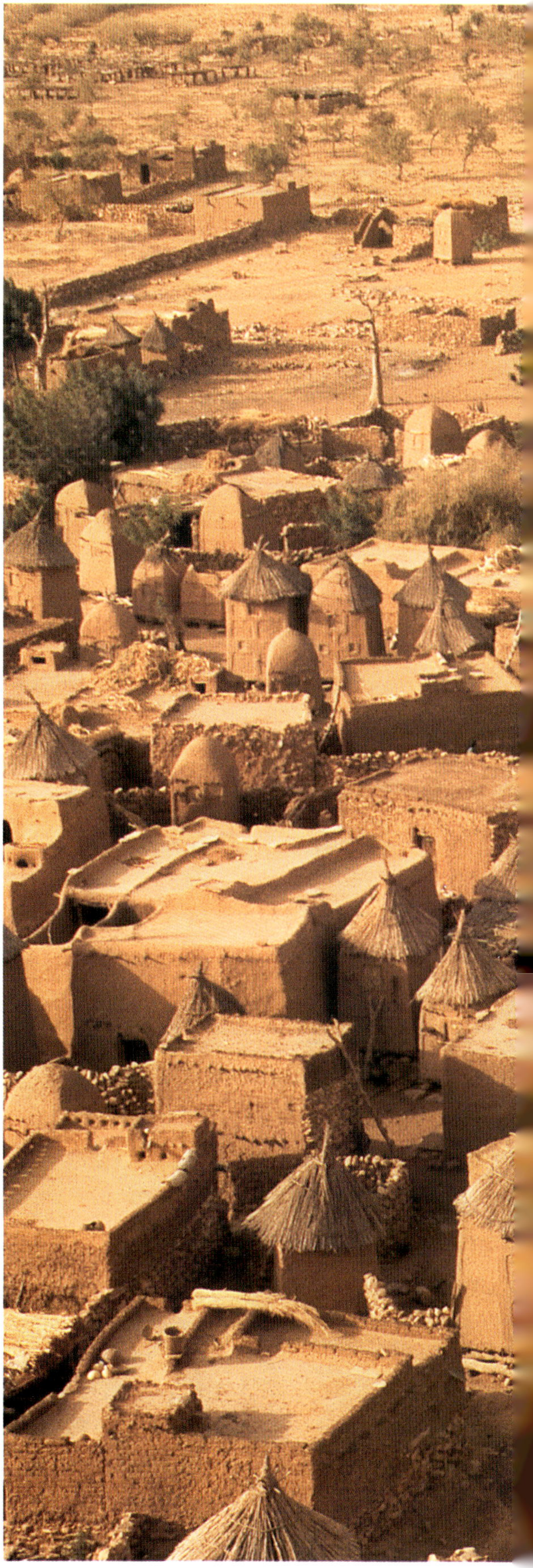

The village of Songo (right), around 50 miles (84 km) southwest of Mopti, presents a fine example of the mud and stone Dogon architecture.

René Caillié, Discoverer of Timbuktu

In 1824 the Geographical Society of Paris offered a 10,000-franc prize for proof that Timbuktu really existed. The winner had to survive the journey and bring back firm proof. Inspired by the name, René Caillié, a self-educated man with little money, set out for Africa to seek Timbuktu—the forbidden "Golden City." Starting in April 1827 he traveled disguised as an Arab. His notes were kept inside his copy of the Koran, and he recorded his journey by pretending to study the scriptures. On reaching Timbuktu in April 1828 he "experienced an indescribable satisfaction" but was disappointed at finding the city of gold as "ill looking houses built of mud" and no gold roofs or pavements. He returned to Europe by traveling 1,000 miles (1,600 km) across the Sahara via Morocco in a desert caravan. His "proof" that Timbuktu existed was a sketch of the town and his meticulous notes.

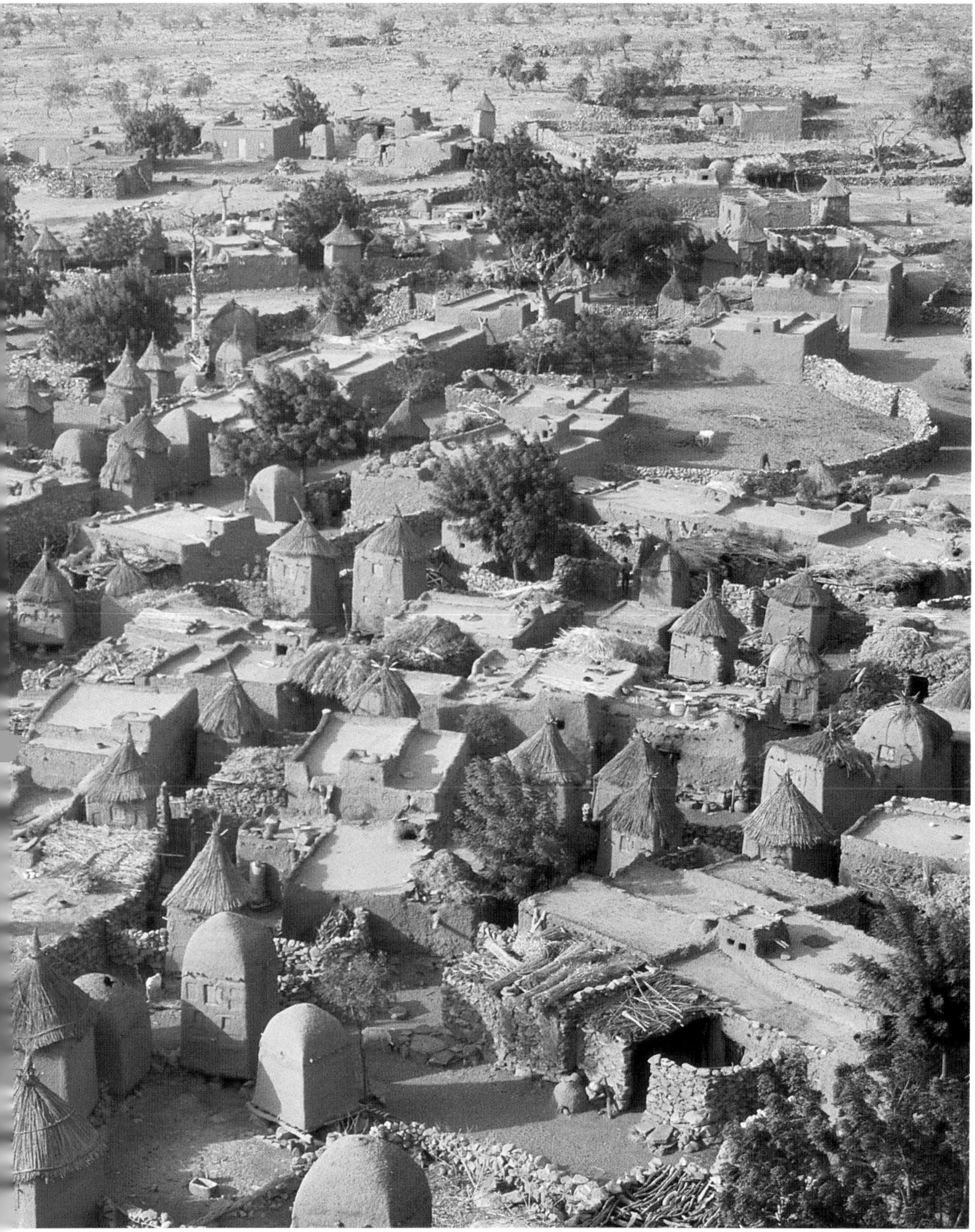

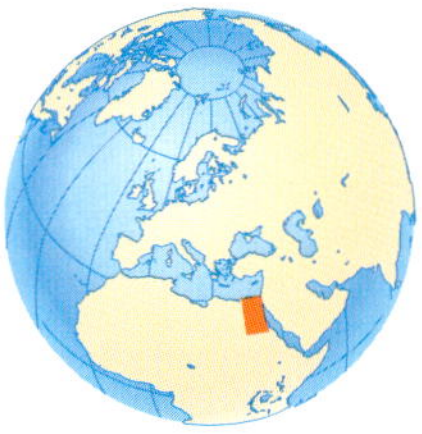

Egypt and the Nile

Egypt, kingdom of the pharaohs, is a land of pitiless desert and cool oases, where extraordinary wealth and sophistication exist side by side with primitive lifestyles—and some of the oldest buildings on earth.

FACT FILE

Language: Arabic (official) Berber, English is widely spoken

Best time to Go: November through March

Climate: Hot and dry year round. Summer: Cairo 97 °F (36°C), Aswan 108 °F (42°C) Dust storms in April. Very little rain except on the coast

Major airports: Cairo and Luxor

Bargaining: Part of everyday life in Egypt and applies to everything. It's expected!

What to Buy: Gold and silver jewelry (seek advice when buying), papyrus paintings, leather goods, carpets, perfumes, spices, and alabaster (best in Luxor)

What to take: Insect repellent and high-factor sun cream.

EGYPT WAS DESCRIBED by the ancient Greek historian Herodotus as being "the gift of the Nile." Even today, both urban and rural life are dependent upon the fertile strip of river which divides the Egyptian desert into two. The Nile, the world's longest river, travels 4,160 miles (6,695 km) from its beginnings in Uganda and Ethiopia north to where the delta meets the Mediterranean Sea, and knits the country together: around 96 percent of Egypt's population lives in the lands of the delta and along the fertile, narrow strip. Rainfall is negligible and until the construction of the Aswan Dam (opened 1970) regulated its flow, Egypt depended totally on the Nile's annual flooding for its continued existence. As a desert country climatic swings are extreme, with daytime temperatures ranging from 60°F (15°C) in January to 108°F (42°C) at the height of summer. At night in winter the temperature may drop to freezing. Sandstorms are common March through May when the khamsin, a dry, hot, dusty wind blows in from the Western Desert. Winter is generally the best time to visit, particularly if you want to wander around the

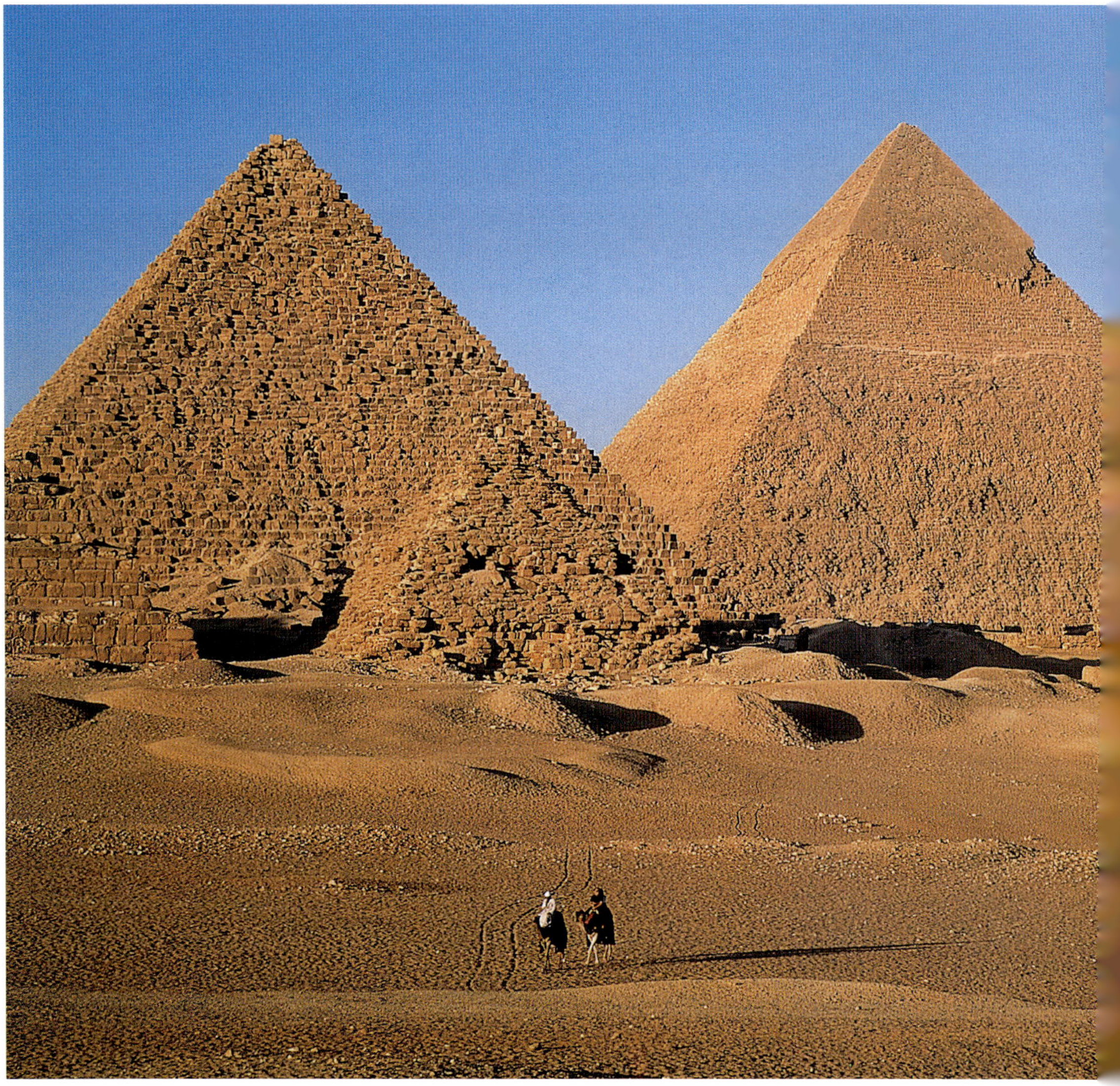

Approach the pyramids of Giza from the desert to the west (left), preferably by mule or on horseback. They say you can hear them whisper at dawn: certainly you will escape the burning heat of the midday sun, and the worst of the tourist coaches.

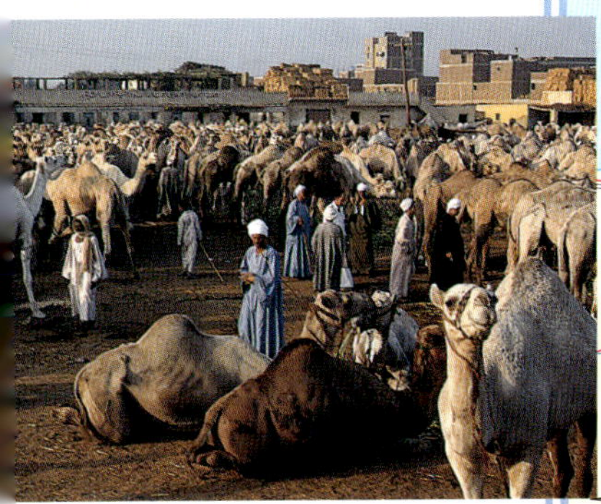

The camel market is one of the many souks, or markets, in old Cairo, a world away from the highrise offices and hotels of the new city.

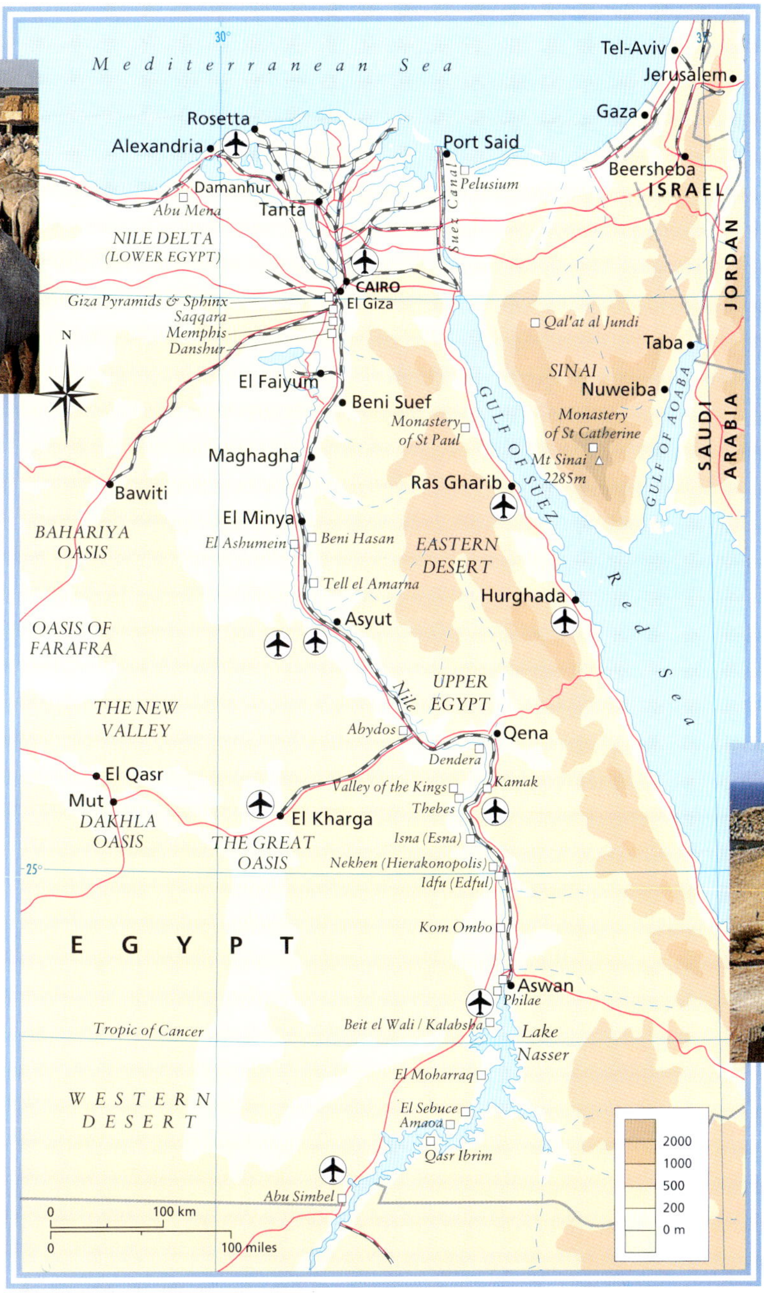

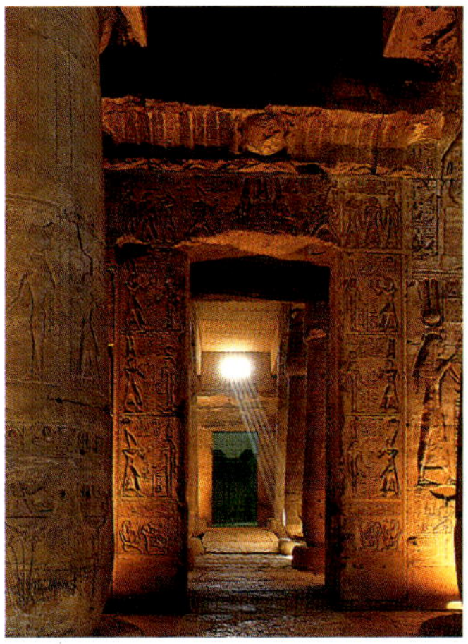

The mortuary temple of Seti I at Abydos, is unique in the delicacy of its reliefs, and in its seven sanctuaries dedicated to Osiris and six other deities.

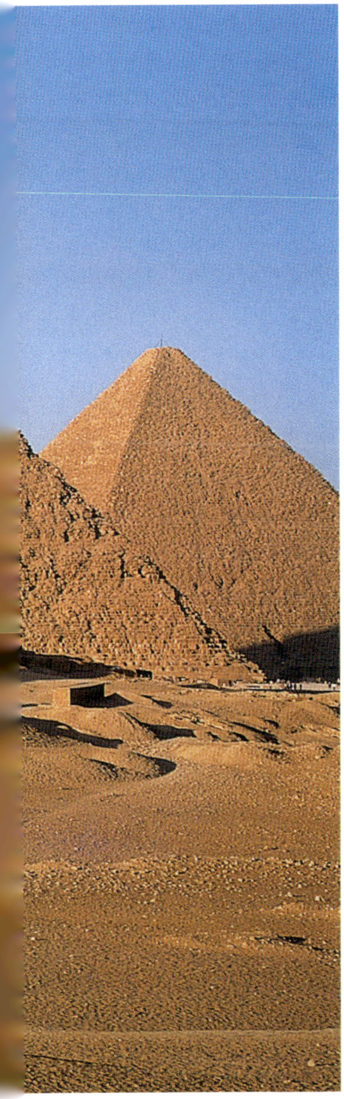

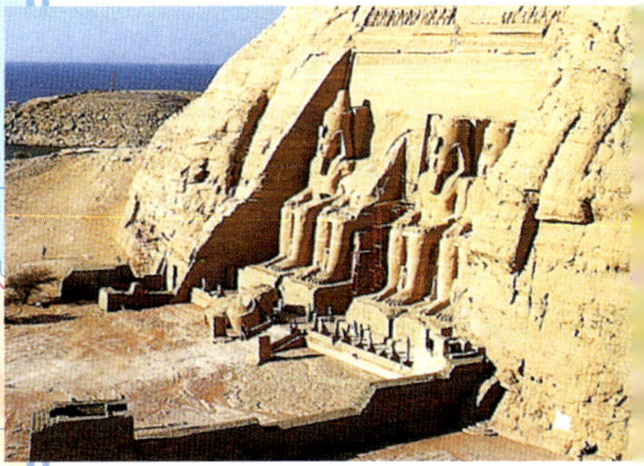

The temples at Abu Simbel were raised 210 feet (64 m) to save them from the waters of Lake Nasser when the Aswan Dam was built.

ancient sights of Upper Egypt at Aswan and Luxor. In summer these places are unbearably hot. This also applies to visiting some of the desert oases. Cairo is also at its most pleasant in the spring and autumn.

No matter how many clichés have been used to describe them, the pyramids remain unique, the only one of the Seven Wonders of the Ancient World still intact today. There are other pyramids on the west bank of the Nile, but the three at Giza are the largest and finest of them all. They were built as royal tombs over 4,500 years ago, overlooking the river northwest of the ancient capital of Memphis, whose mud bricks have now all disappeared back into the Nile or are buried yards deep beneath modern Cairo. Today the site is an easy 30-minute taxi ride from the center of Cairo, but such an approach misses their awe-inspiring sense of scale and mystery, as there is no real desert left between the Cairo suburb of Giza and the ancient site. Instead, hire a horse or a camel for a couple of hours from the nearby village of Nazlat Al Samman and ride across the desert sands from the far side. Negotiate the fare in advance (haggle!) and pay only on completing your trip. From this direction you can appreciate the perfect geometry of the pyramids set against the desert landscape, and imagine how they once looked, for part of their original coating of smooth, white ashlar remains on their western sides.

There are three main pyramids, each of which can be

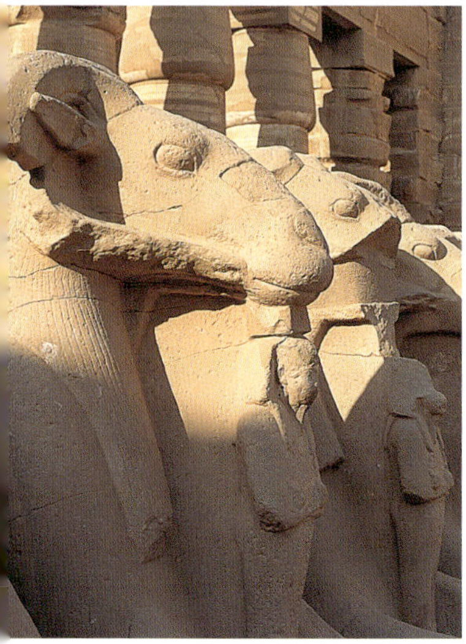

entered, but only the Great Pyramid, the tomb of the Pharaoh Khufu (known as Cheops by the Greeks), who died in 2567 B.C, holds anything of interest. Visitors can clamber through its claustrophobic passageways to reach three chambers within, including the King's Chamber with its impressive granite sarcophagus. The museum behind the Great Pyramid is worth a visit to see the Solar Boat of the Pharaoh, unearthed from a nearby vault. It is the breathtaking scale of these monuments that makes them so dramatic. Cheops is the largest pyramid ever built, incorporating more than 2,250,000 blocks of stone, weighing on average more than $2^{1}/_{2}$ tons each.

The vast temple at Karnak, of Amun, the "king of the gods," is approached by a row of ram-headed statues (above). Amun was often shown with a ram's head.

Cairo itself is a colorful, cosmopolitan city, where East meets West, North meets South in culture, religion, and lifestyles. Fine mosques and a skyline of minarets reflect Cairo's long history as one of the greatest of all Muslim cities, but the crowds beneath them are made up of Coptic Christians, Jews, Northern Europeans, and black Africans. Ever-increasing numbers of migrants arrive daily from the countryside, many of them sleeping in the cemeteries.

The old walled city to the south encloses 400 mosques, vibrant bazaars, whitewashed stone houses and narrow streets, and the relative quiet of the Coptic Christian quarter. To the north and west is the modern Cairo of broad avenues, designer shops, smart hotels, and international business, as befits Africa's largest city.

The Egyptian Museum houses Tutankhamen's treasures among one of the best collections of Pharaonica and Byzantine art and sculpture.

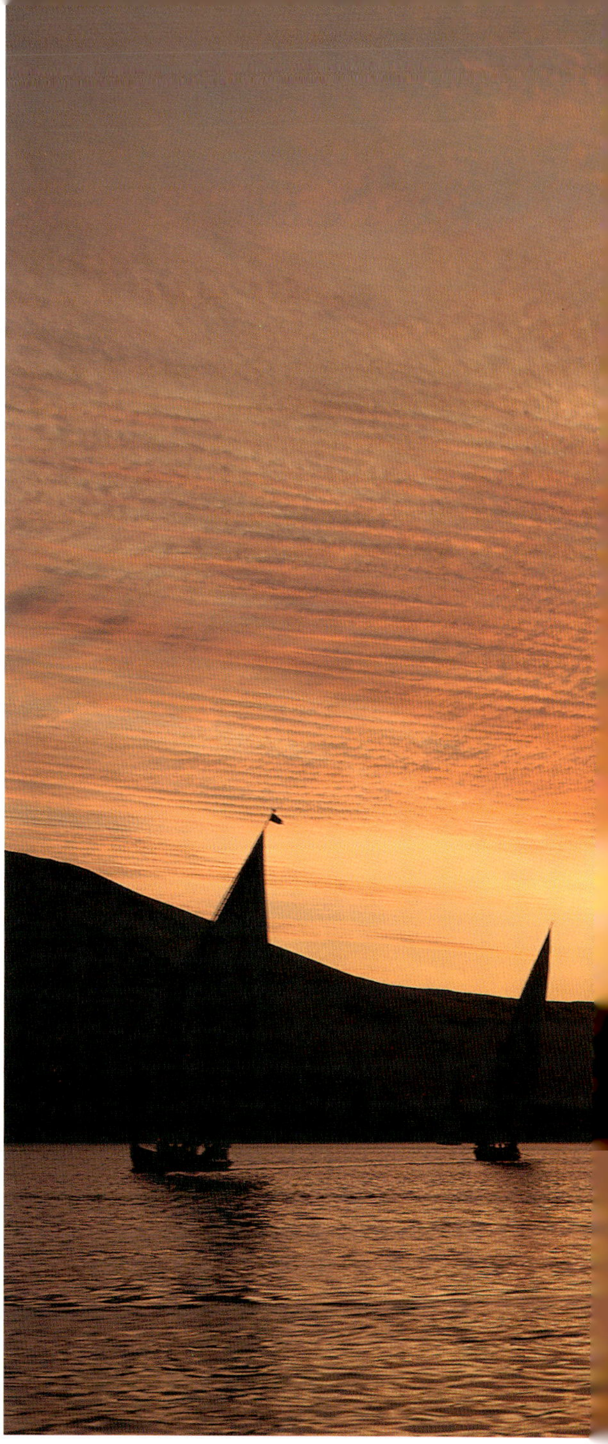

By felucca on the Nile

No journey to Egypt would be complete without sailing along the Nile from Aswan to Luxor in a felucca, a traditional sailboat. The Nile's current flows from south to north, but the prevailing wind blows the opposite way, up the Nile Valley from the Mediterranean, so boats can float effortlessly downstream with the current and use sail power to return easily and elegantly. You see life going on along and on the river as it has for millennia: fishermen with their nets, *fellahin* (peasant farmers) plowing with oxen, mud huts, waterwheels, and date palms. Feluccas can be chartered for groups of travelers, but cruising between Luxor and Cairo is discouraged because of the dangers of terrorism by Islamic Fundamentalists.

Most travelers fly or take the train down to Luxor, one of Egypt's premier attractions, and then spend a few days cruising on one of the many comfortable, often luxurious, Nile steamers. Luxor, built on and

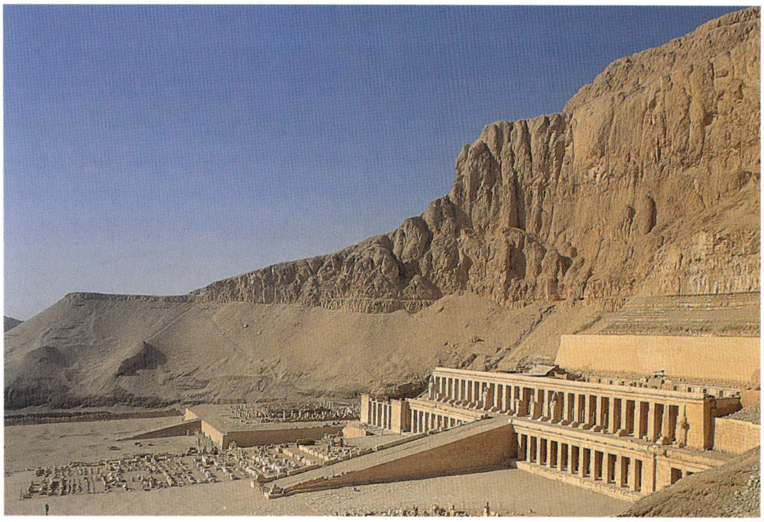

The tomb, at Luxor, of Queen Hatshepsut (above), who gained unprecedented power for a queen during her reign1503-1482 B.C.

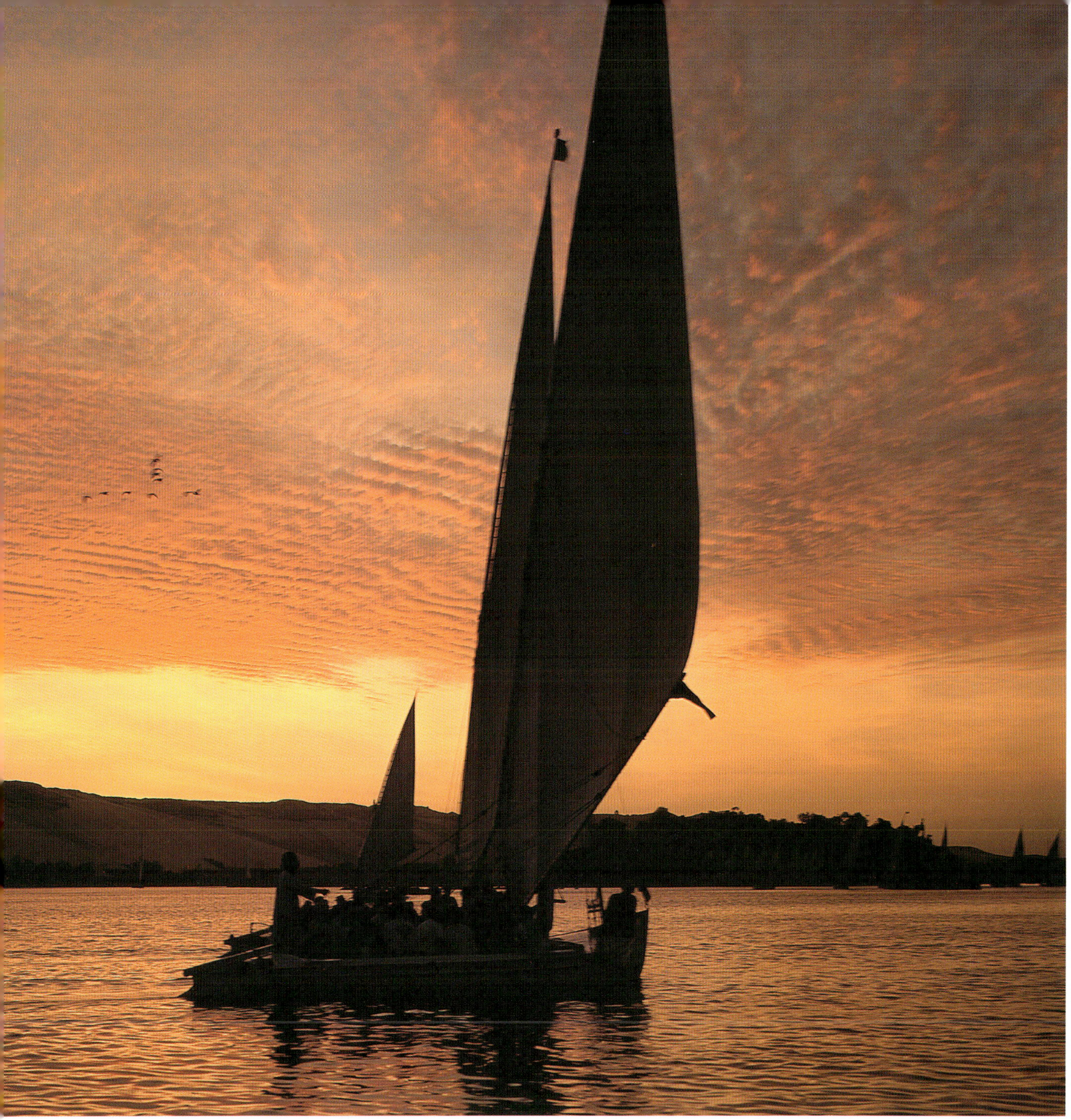

around the 4,000-year-old site of ancient Thebes, capital of Egypt under the New Kingdom (c.1700-1000 B.C.), is almost a huge open -air museum.

On the west bank of the Nile, some 300 miles (500 km) south of Cairo on the edge of the desert, lie the monuments and necropolis of ancient Thebes, including the staggering temple and tomb complexes of the Valley of the Kings and the Valley of the Queens—the sites of the tombs of Tutankhamen and Queen Hatshepsut, and giant images of 64 pharaohs carved into the rock.

On the east bank is the lively city of Luxor itself, with picturesque if decrepit balconied houses. In the nearby village of Karnak is the immense and well-preserved temple of Amun, whose obese columns make it the most grandiose in all Egypt, along with other ancient sites scattered among gardens and palm groves. Karnak is also a pleasant spot for eating out, though Egyptian food outside Cairo is too often a bland mingling of western influences. However, Egyptian brandy and beer are good.

A four or five day cruise from Luxor is Aswan, gateway to sub-Saharan Africa, a city with a delightful island of gardens in mid-river. There are relatively few antiquities here, and the Aswan dam is immense but dull, but it is a short flight to Abu Simbel, the Great Temple of Ramses II. The temple was moved by a Herculean UNESCO effort in 1964 from its original site, which now lies beneath the waters of Lake Nasser, to its present site 210 feet (64 m) above.

Traditional feluccas (above) can be chartered as more peaceful alternatives to steamers and motor cruisers.

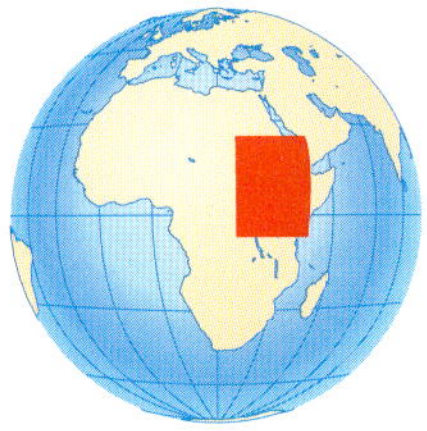

The East African Rift Valley

A vast depression of land which encompasses soda lakes and flamingos, volcanic craters and sulfur springs, and simmering plains that teem with wildlife.

FACT FILE

Best time to go: Tanzania: June—July and December—January; Kenya: August—September and October; Ethiopia: December—January.

Climate: East Africa has two rainy seasons: April—May; and late October and early November. Coolest June and July when average daytime temperature is 72°F (22°C).

Things to buy: Native handicrafts, Makonde carvings, batiks, soapstone carvings, and kiondos (woven sisal bags and baskets).

Airports: Nairobi and Mombasa in Kenya, Dar es Salaam in Tanzania.

Things to do: Wildlife safaris, camel safaris, mountain trekking, white-water rafting, scuba diving, dhow sailing, balloon and cycling "safaris."

Getting around: Generally easy with buses, trains, planes, and cars widely available.

Health: Malaria, cholera, and yellow fever are all prevalent, so take relevant precautions. Don't drink the water, or eat salads or uncooked vegetables.

TEN MILLION YEARS AGO, a huge wedge of land stretching over 4,000 miles (6,400 km) from Jordan and the Red Sea to southeast Africa, subsided to create a depression known as the Great Rift Valley. Plateau lands rise gradually toward the valley rim, and then drop up to 3,000 feet (900 m), at a series of fault lines in the rocky crust of the earth. In parts of the East African part of the Rift Valley, such as Tanzania, the forces of erosion have obscured the effects of this massive earth movement, but elsewhere there are e high cliffs bordering fantastic broad valleys, like lost worlds, between 30 and 40 miles (48 to 64 km) wide. Distinct ecosystems developed, the sheltered lands of the depression often providing conditions in which a wealth of wildlife could flourish. While tropical forests thrived to the west, the rainshadow area created by the rift valley cliffs evolved into dry grassland, the savannah plains and the heart of East Africa's safari land.

Much of the valley is made up of a series of troughs and swells along the fault lines. The troughs are around

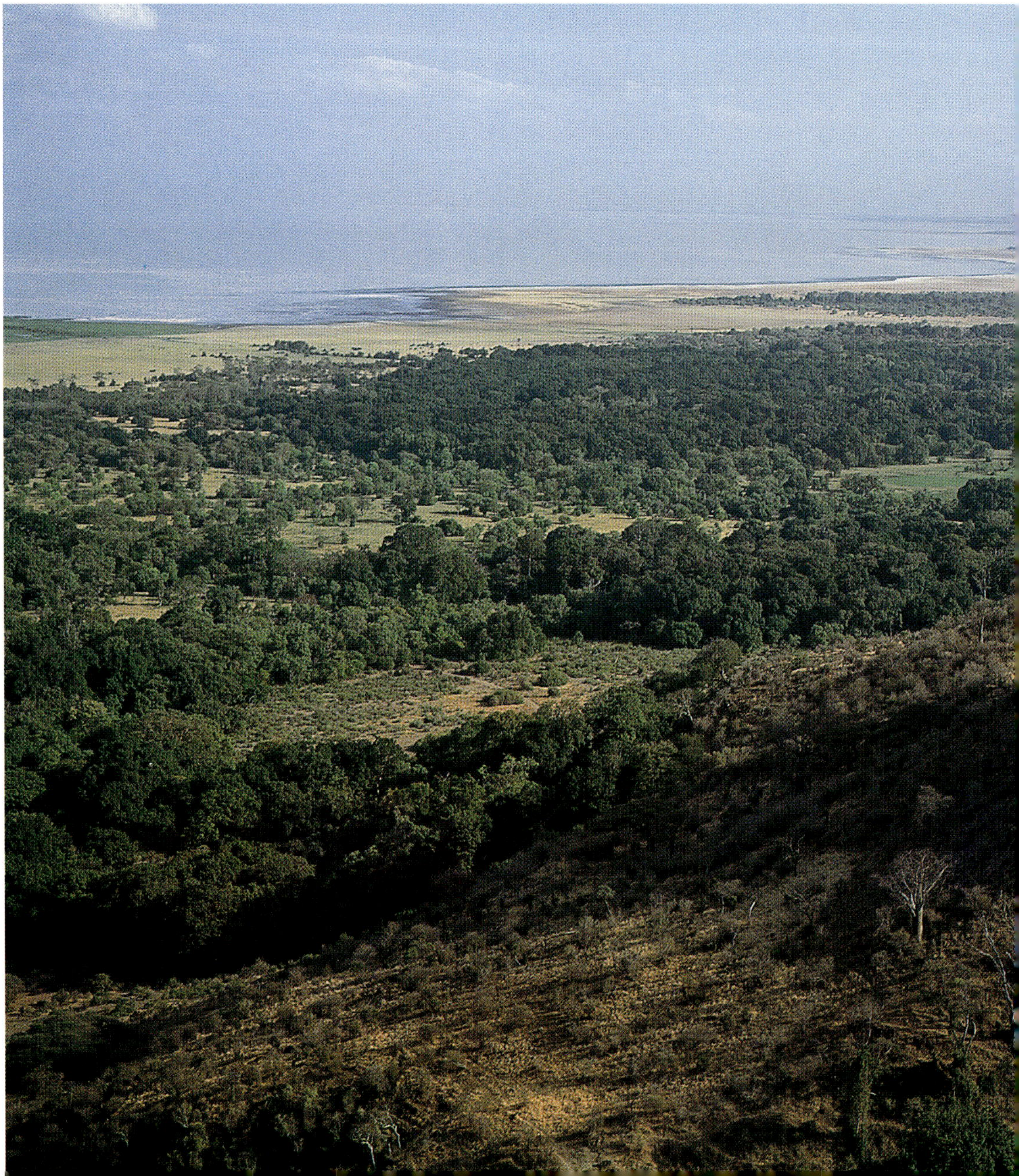

The full impact of the land that slid between two faults to create the Rift Valley is seen from the top of the escarpment rim at Lake Manyara in Tanzania.

25 miles (40 km) wide, and along the western branch of the rift have filled with fjord-like lakes, whose depths often plunge below sea-level. They include Lake Tanganyika—the second deepest freshwater lake in the world after Lake Baikal—which covers 12,700 miles (32,900 sq km). Along its shores are fine beaches and abundant wildlife.

In the eastern branch of the East African Rift Valley, which runs through Ethiopia, Kenya, and Tanzania, shallow soda lakes like Lake Natron have formed. Their alkaline waters are low in fish, but the algae and other tiny organisms attract gawky flamingos in their thousands, startlingly pink against mirror-dazzling water and relentless blue sky. Along this eastern branch too, are mighty volcanic uplifts where molten rock has burst through the thinned continental crust into volcanos such as Ol Doinyo Lengai—"Mountain of God" to the local Masai people—Mount Kilimanjaro,

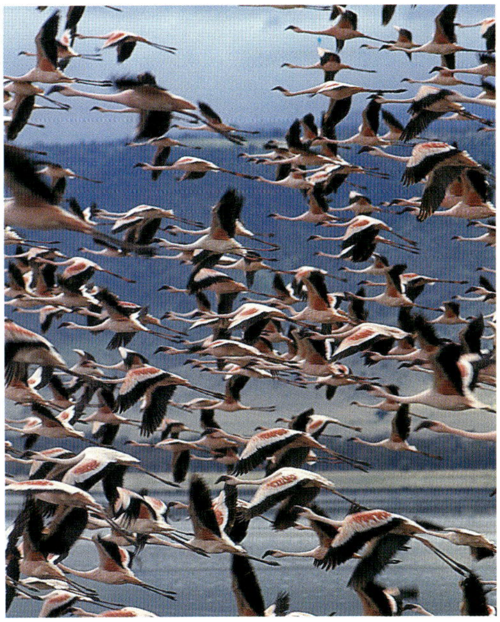

Flamingos feed on the algae and other minute organisms in the soda lakes of the eastern branch of the East African Rift Valley. Their pink coloring comes from the pigments in the algae.

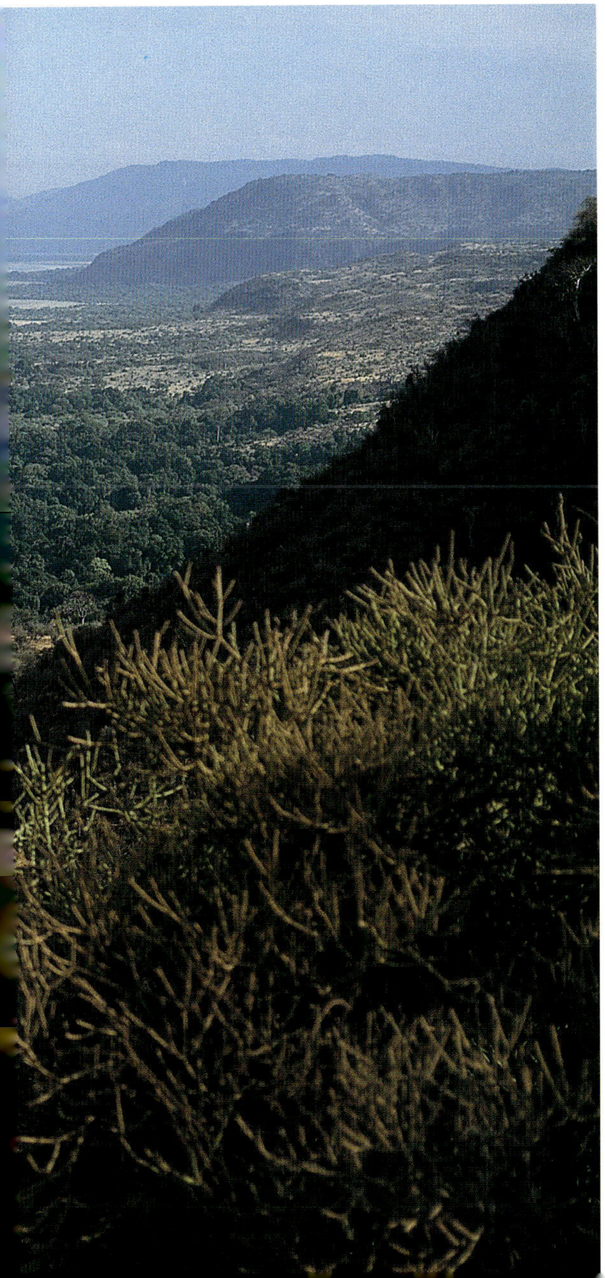

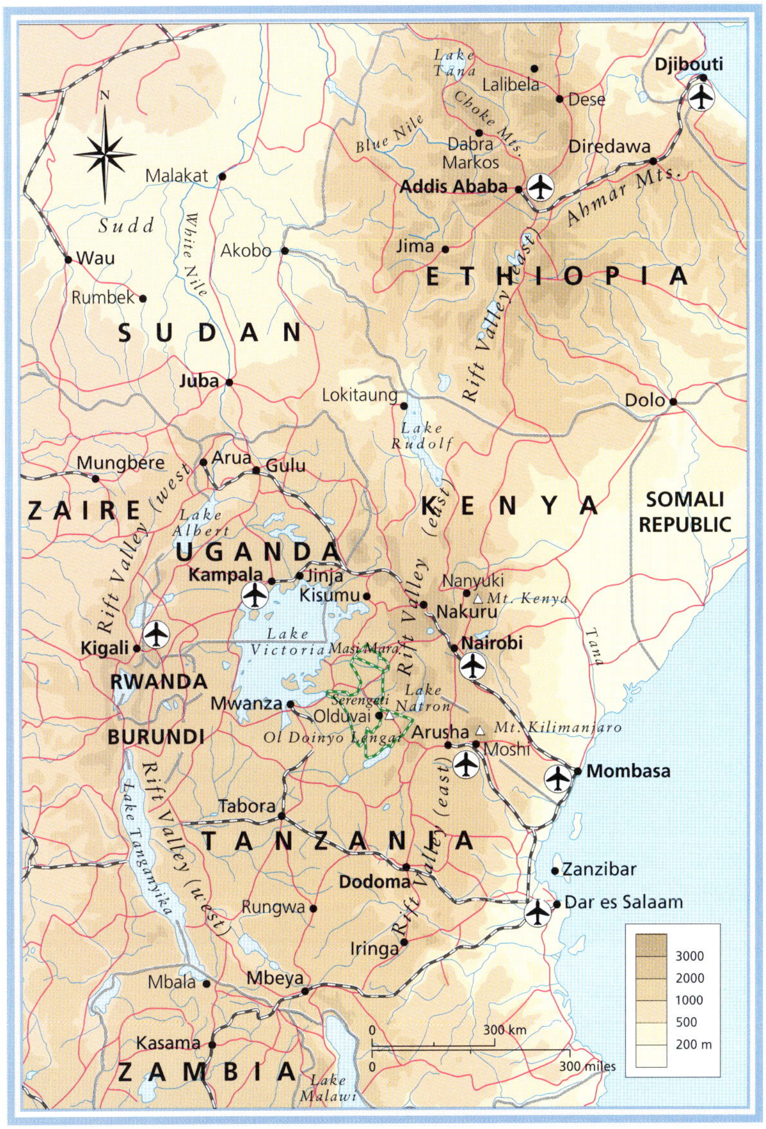

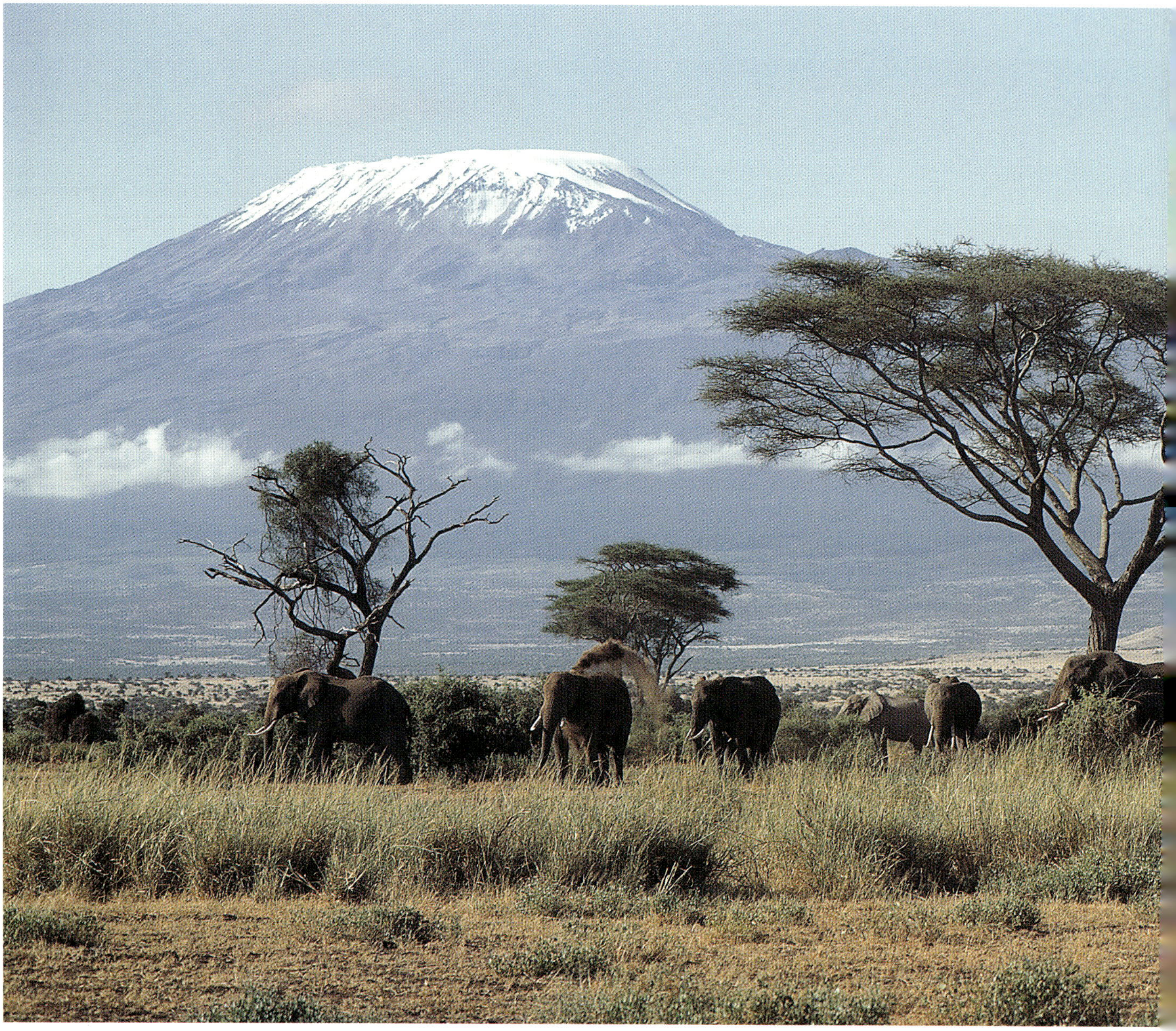

Although Mount Kilimanjaro (above) is only 3 degrees from the Equator, its summit is permanently covered in snow, while banana, coffee, and maize are grown on the fertile lower slopes.

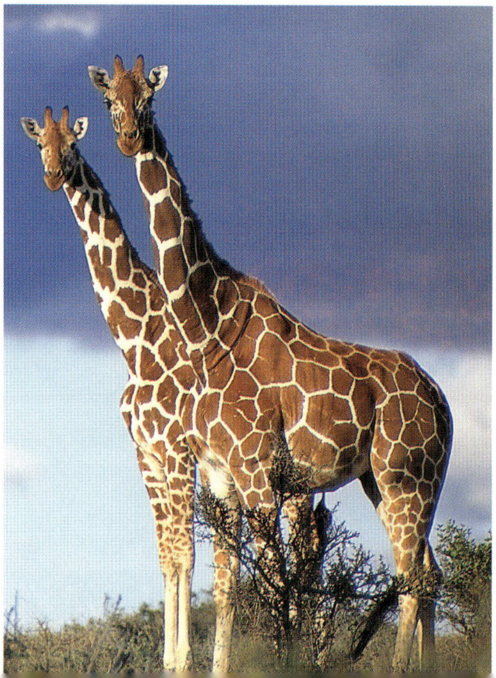

Giraffes are animals of the savannah, feeding mainly on acacia leaves. They are a protected species.

and Mount Kenya. As you climb Mount Kilimanjaro—at 19,340 feet (5,895 m) Africa's highest mountain—you pass through the world's vegetation zones, from desert through tropical forest, to permanent snows.

West of Ol Doinyho Lengai is the Serengeti Plain in Tanzania, whose dusty soils are probably a fallout of volcanic ash. The endless grasslands that flourish here are the home of the African elephant, and grazed by giraffe, zebra, wildebeest, and impala, eland, as well as their predators—lions, leopards, and hyenas. Every year, in July and August, more than a million wildebeest move north from Tanzania's Serengeti National Park across the Mara River and into Kenya In search of the fresh pastures created by the seasonal rains, the ungainly beasts, accompanied by the more graceful zebras, move en masse often at a gallop and in single

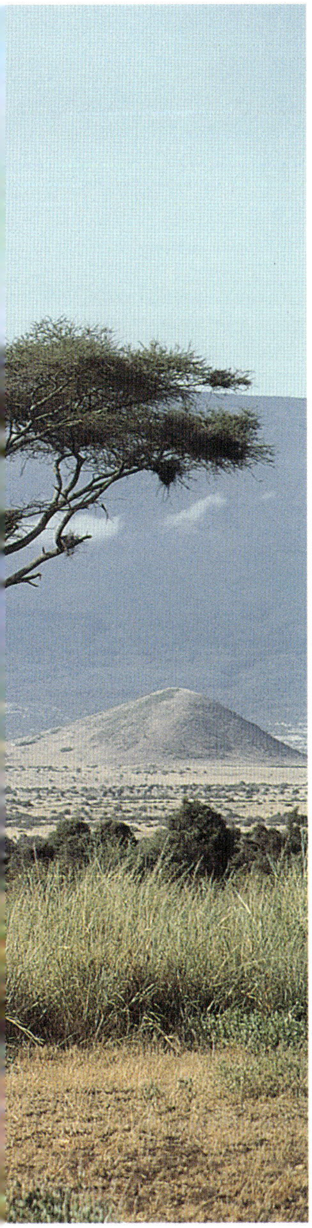

file. When the rains come again in November, they head back south to Tanzania and the cycle begins all over again. Although migrations occur in other parts of Africa, nowhere else are the numbers so prolific or the sight so easy to see. It is possible to rent a trip in a hot air ballon to view the spectacle.

HUMAN DEVELOPMENT

The grasslands that formed as a result of the earth's great rift also proved more suitable than the surrounding tropical forests for an upright, two-legged, sharp-eyed species to evolve. In a small place called Olduvai in northern Tanzania, not far from the town of Arusha, Dr. Louis B. Leakey and his wife Mary had been searching intermittently for the best part of 20 years when in 1959 they found part of a hominoid skull, which they called Zinjanthropus (*Australopithecus boisei*). The skull fragments were dated at 1.8 million years old, making it part of the oldest discovered hominoid at that time.

In 1979 Mary made another important discovery at Laetoli, some 40 miles (64 km) away, of footprints in a riverbed made by a man, woman, and child. Subsequent investigation dated these footprints at 3.5 million years. Since they were made by hominoids that walked upright, the discovery pushed the dawn of mankind much further back in time than previously thought. Today you can see where the Leakeys excavated in a hole, now roofed over with a pipe-like opening. Here the layers of soil and rock mark the journey back in time as you descend into the earth, a n awe-inspiring experiences. At the top of the gorge, there is a sense of overwhelming peace as you sit and reflect on the fact that you could be sitting on the very spot where Eve, the "mother" of all human beings, once sat admiring the same landscape several million years ago.

A LAND THAT TIME FORGOT

The geological complexity and pure, raw beauty of the East African Rift Valley is nowhere more obvious than in Ethiopia. The very nature of the landscape has kept invaders out and the inhabitants in, allowing the country to develop its own very distinctive culture and religion far removed from external influences and fashions. Ethiopia's style of Christianity—and much else about Ethiopian life—has changed little since Christianity was first introduced by Egyptian Coptic monks in the second century.

At Lalibela in the central highlands, there are 11 churches carved out of solid rock. But the real treasure of Ethiopia is found farther north at Axum, where lies the very basis of Ethiopian religion and culture. In the church of St. Mary's of Zion lies the Tabot. This is, according to local legend, the original "Ark of the Covenant"—the vessel holding the original Ten Commandments which was given to Moses by God on Mount Sinai and later stolen from King Solomon by Menelik I, Solomon's son by Makeda, Queen of Sheba.

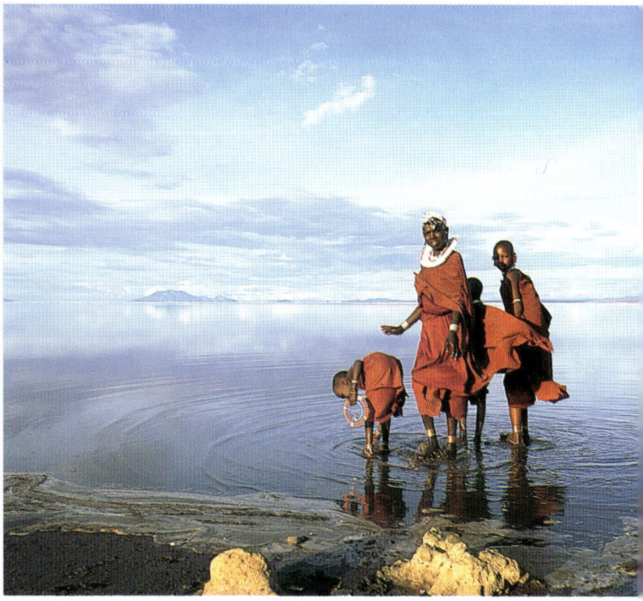

Children of the Masai (above right), a nomadic cattle-herding people of Tanzania and Kenya, on the shores of the soda lake, Natron.

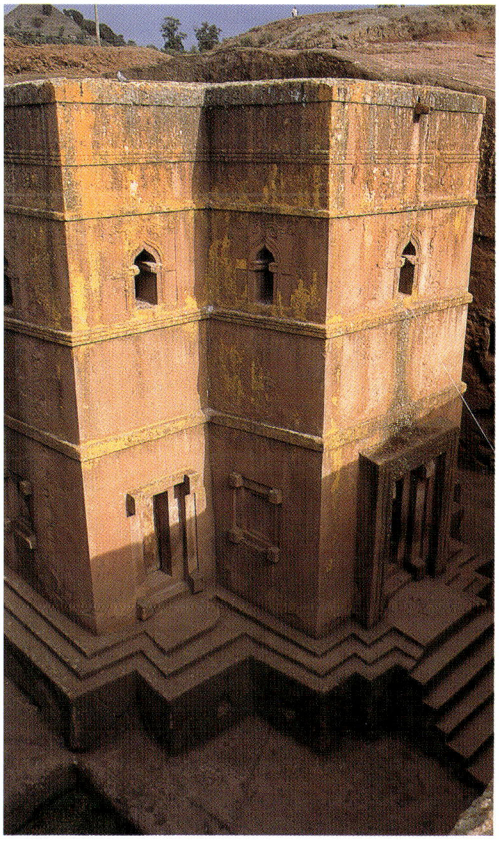

An Ethiopian rock church in Lalibela (right). The geographical seclusion created by the Rift Valley helped a distinctive culture to be preserved.

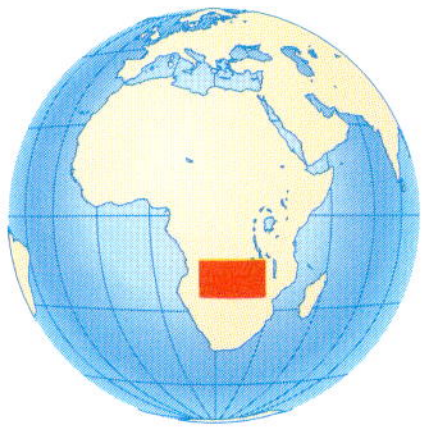

The Zambesi and the Okavango

From a raging river gorge and the world's largest waterfalls to a delta in a desert.

JUST A PLANE RIDE TRANSPORTS YOU from two dramatically contrasting faces of Africa—from where water falls with such force that its spray is visible from 25 miles (40 km) away, to the sluggish waters of a river and the world's largest inland delta. Both have unique and remarkable ecosystems:the microclimate of the Victoria Falls rainforest, and the swamps and reedbeds, rich in wildlife, of the Okavango Delta in the heart of the Botswana desert.

THE SMOKE THAT THUNDERS

Mosi oa Tunya—the "smoke that thunders"—is the resonantly poetic name the local Makololo people give the immense series of waterfalls which make up Victoria Falls. The whole area shakes perpetually as the Zambesi River, $1\frac{1}{2}$ miles (2.5 km) wide, cascades an average 1,200 million gallons (550 million liters) of water 330 feet (100 m) into the Zambesi Gorge every minute, creating the largest waterfalls on earth. The falls are divided between Zambia, and Zimbabwe (which has most of the best sites) but you can walk easily across the border.

The sheet of water which plummets suddenly from gently rolling grassland into the rocky canyon of the Zambesi Gorge, is split into three main sections by jutting rock islands on the lip of the Falls:the Main Falls, the Rainbow Falls, and the Eastern Cataract. The clouds of spray create an unusual and ecologically significant rainforest, particularly rich in great ferns found nowhere else in Zimbabwe or Zambia. You can walk through the rainforests in a perpetual—and very wet—mist, beneath arcs of spray.

"No one can imagine the beauty of the scene…scenes so lovely must have been gazed upon by angels in their flight," the British explorer Dr. David Livingstone wrote on seeing the Victoria Falls. His words live on today in the "Flight of Angels," a journey by plane, helicopter, or microlight over the gorge. The aircraft follow the zigzagging course of the river, seemingly only feet above the dense clouds of spray and rainbows created from them. The effect of light at different times of the day as it refracts through the ever-present mists is

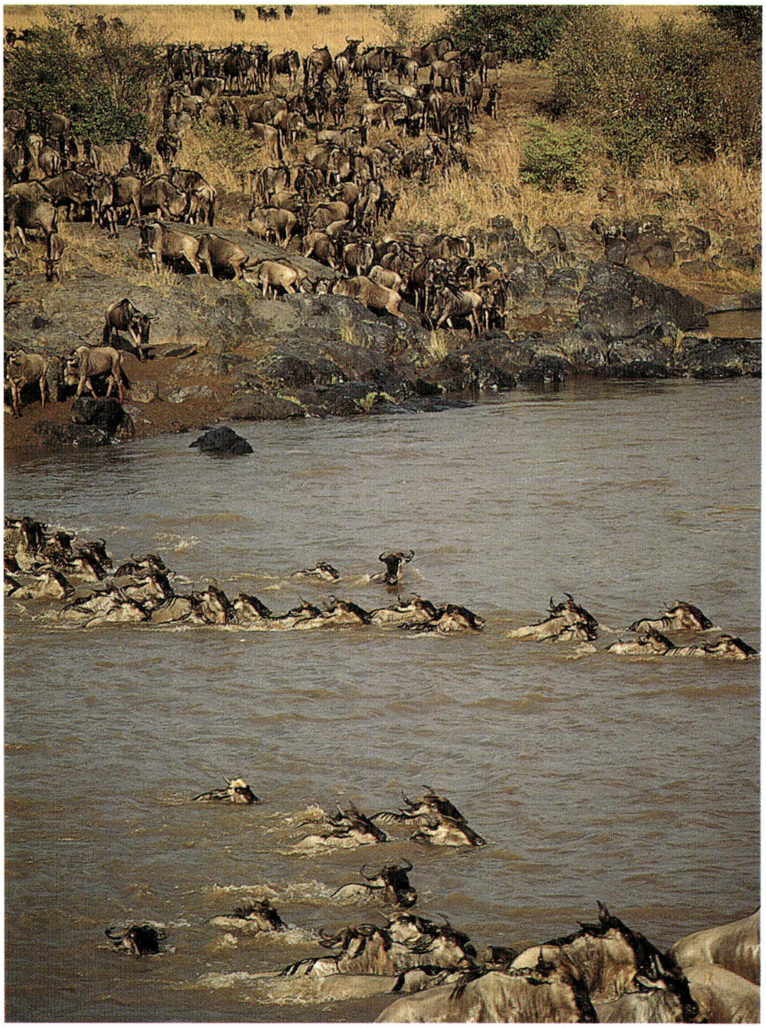

Each year millions of wildebeest (above) migrate across the plains of Africa, seeking water and fresh grazing.

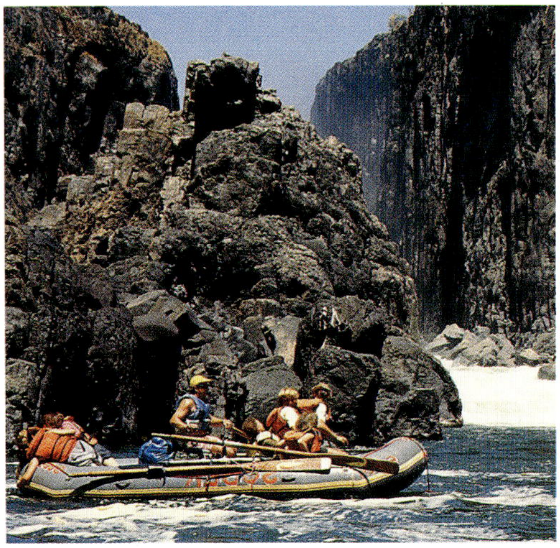

The Zambesi has attractions for geologists, wildlife watchers...and adventure seekers.

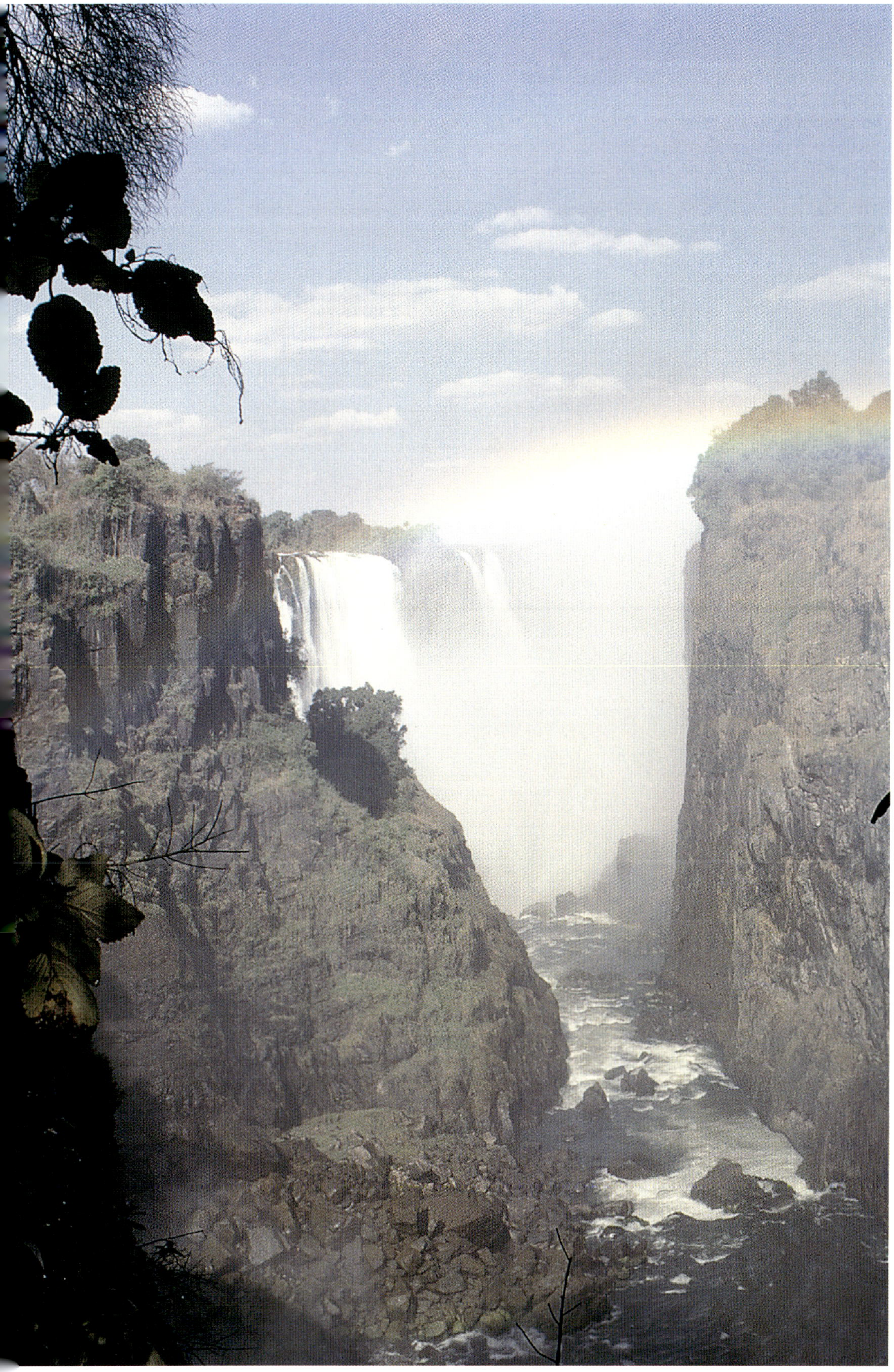

FACT FILE

Getting there Fly into Harare in Zimbabwe. The falls are only a few of hours away by bus, car, or train. For the Okavango Delta, Maun is the nearest town and the hub of the region, but Gabarone is Botswana's main airport.

Best time to go: Okavango Delta, July—September; Victoria Falls, all year.

Climate: Zimbabwe's location on a high plateau converts tropical temperatures to those of a Mediterranean summer. **Botswana** is predominately desert with searing daytime temperatures plunging to near-freezing at night. The delta, although hot in the day, is quite pleasant at night.

Health: Innoculations for cholera, typhoid and polio; and possibly rabies, recommended; malaria risk below1,200 feet November—June. Drink sterilized or bottled water only. Avoid swimming in fresh water due to risk of bilharzia.

What to take: Insect repellent, waterproofs, sunscreen.

Food and drink: International food at most main hotels and lodges. Zimbabwean beer is popular, as is the traditionl maize beer, *whawha.*

What to buy: African handicrafts.

The river cuts through vulnerable cracks in hard basaltic rock of the Zambian plateau (right), while the Victoria Falls cascade over crosswise fault lines.

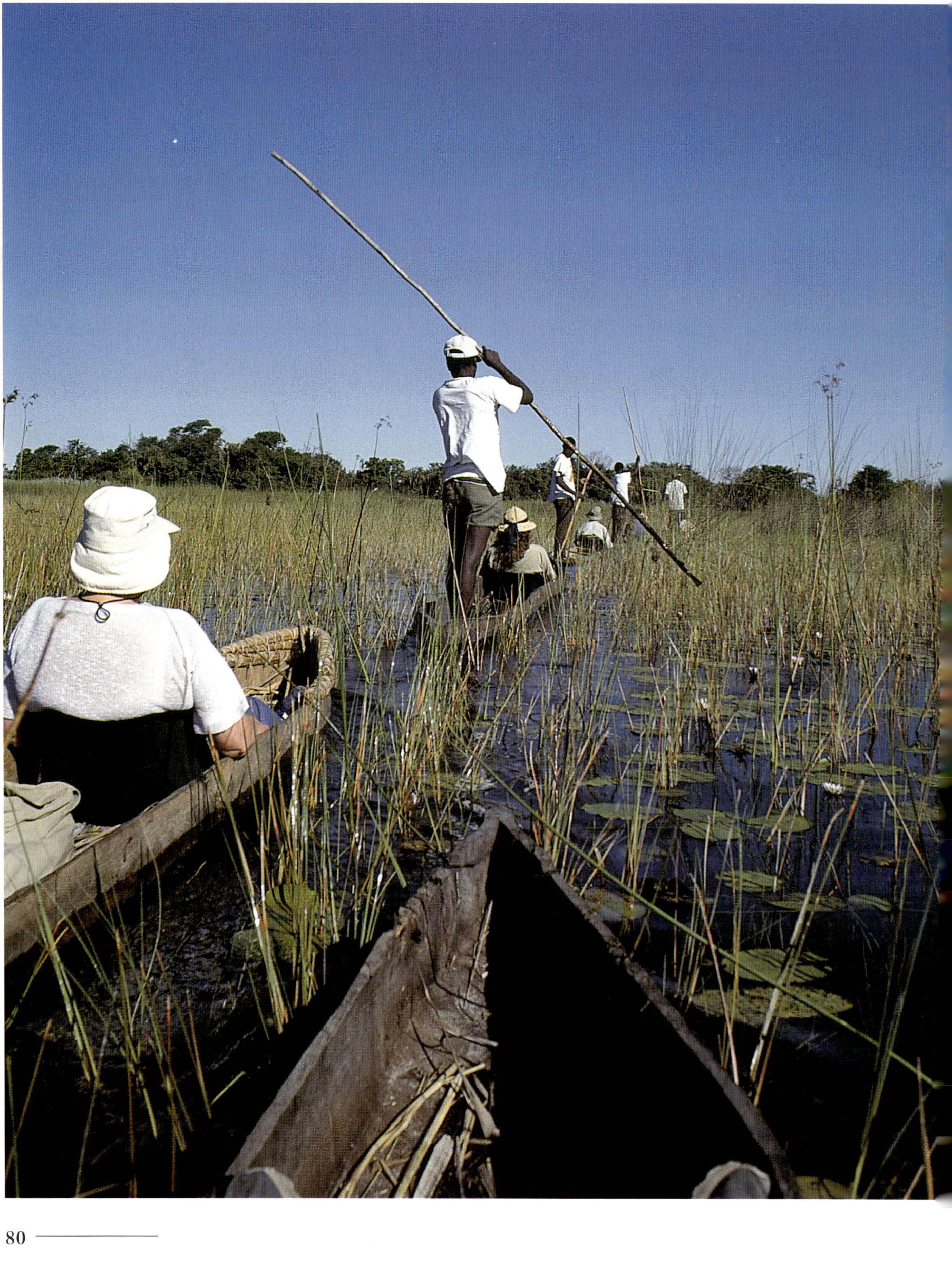

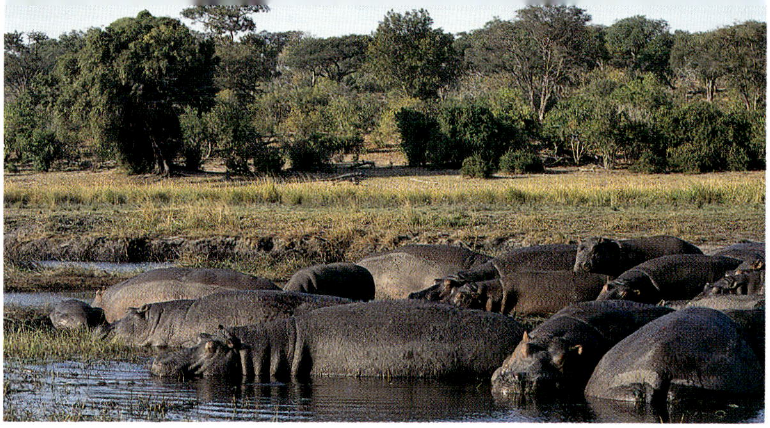

Hippopotamus help maintain the waterways of the Okavango as they trudge through them in their quest for food.

quite ethereal. Beneath a full moon, there is a delicate silver, ghostly glow, and even, maybe a lunar rainbow.

The chasm cut by the Zambesi has become a focus for adventure activities, including the world's highest commercial bungee jump from the Zambesi Bridge—two seconds of sheer terror strapped to a giant elastic band plummeting head first 330 feet (100 m) toward the river—or running the 23 sets of rapids that make up the lower Zambesi.

River rafting is graded from I to VI—from gentle rapid to impossible to run. The Zambesi rapids clenched between steep cliffs up to 700 feet (213 m) high, are mostly grades IV and V, making this a serious rollercoaster ride in a flimsy rubber boat. Trips downriver vary from a half day and 12 rapids to a full day and the whole river. There are opportunities for recuperative wildlife watching in the nearby Zambesi National Park, where sable, antelope, and other wild animals graze in a parkland setting.

The Jewel of the Kalahari

For the ultimate contrast to the roar of the Zambesi, take a short plane flight from Victoria Falls to the Okavango Delta in neighboring Botswana. Landing at one of the region's lodges or campsites provides an eagle-eye view of the world's largest delta which runs into a desert rather than the sea. The Okavango River flows from the highlands of Angola and ebbs into the northwestern Kalahari Desert. And there it runs its course; it doesn't flow out again but subdivides into smaller and smaller streams, channels, and lagoons before evaporating or soaking into the sand.

The 6,000 square miles (15,000 sq km) of delta is one huge oasis, a pristine habitat for many species of wildlife on the many islands created by the streams and channels, protected in the Moremi Wildlife Reserve. Among the 36 species of mammal are lion, elephant, giraffe, buffalo, wildebeest, zebra, and numerous species of gazelle. Hippo and crocodile, fish eagles, cormorants, and cranes are all permanent residents. There are no roads, only the occasional four-wheel drive vehicle, and no crowds.

To make the most of this tranquil habitat and its wildlife, explore the delta in a *mekoro* (dugout canoe) poled by a local fisherman and accompanied by a guide. You can spend days winding your way through 250 miles (400 km) of waterways, floating from island to island, camping wild under the stars, and eating fresh-caught fish. Alternatives include a tented camp at Xaxaba and luxury safari lodges.

The lilac-breasted roller (below) is just one of over 400 bird species that live in the delta lands of the Okavango.

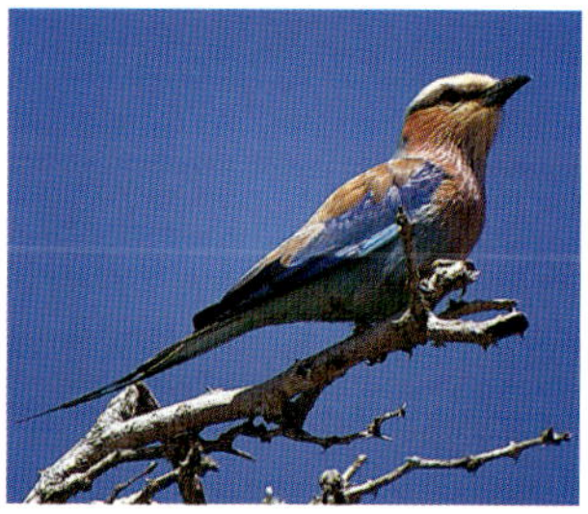

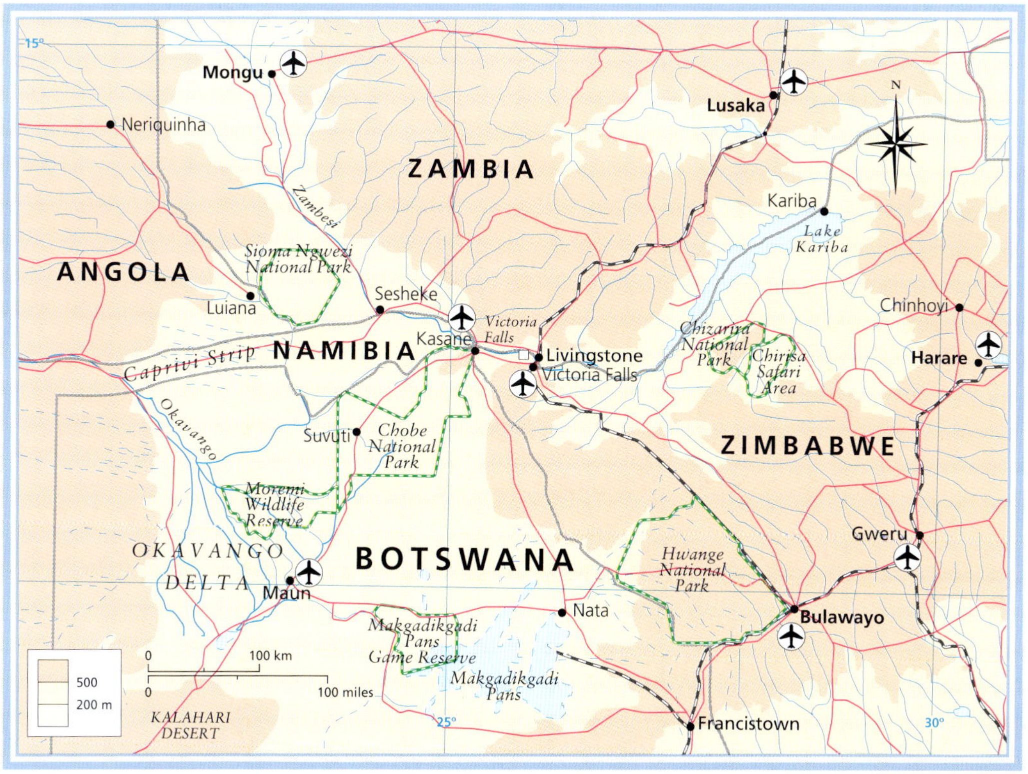

The waterways of the Okavango, with their extraordinary range of wildlife, can be explored in the mekoro, the dugout canoe of the native baYei, a tribe of aquatic hunters.

Mediterranean and the Near East

"The real voyage of discovery consists not in seeing new landscapes, but in having new eyes."

Marcel Proust, French writer, 1871-1922.

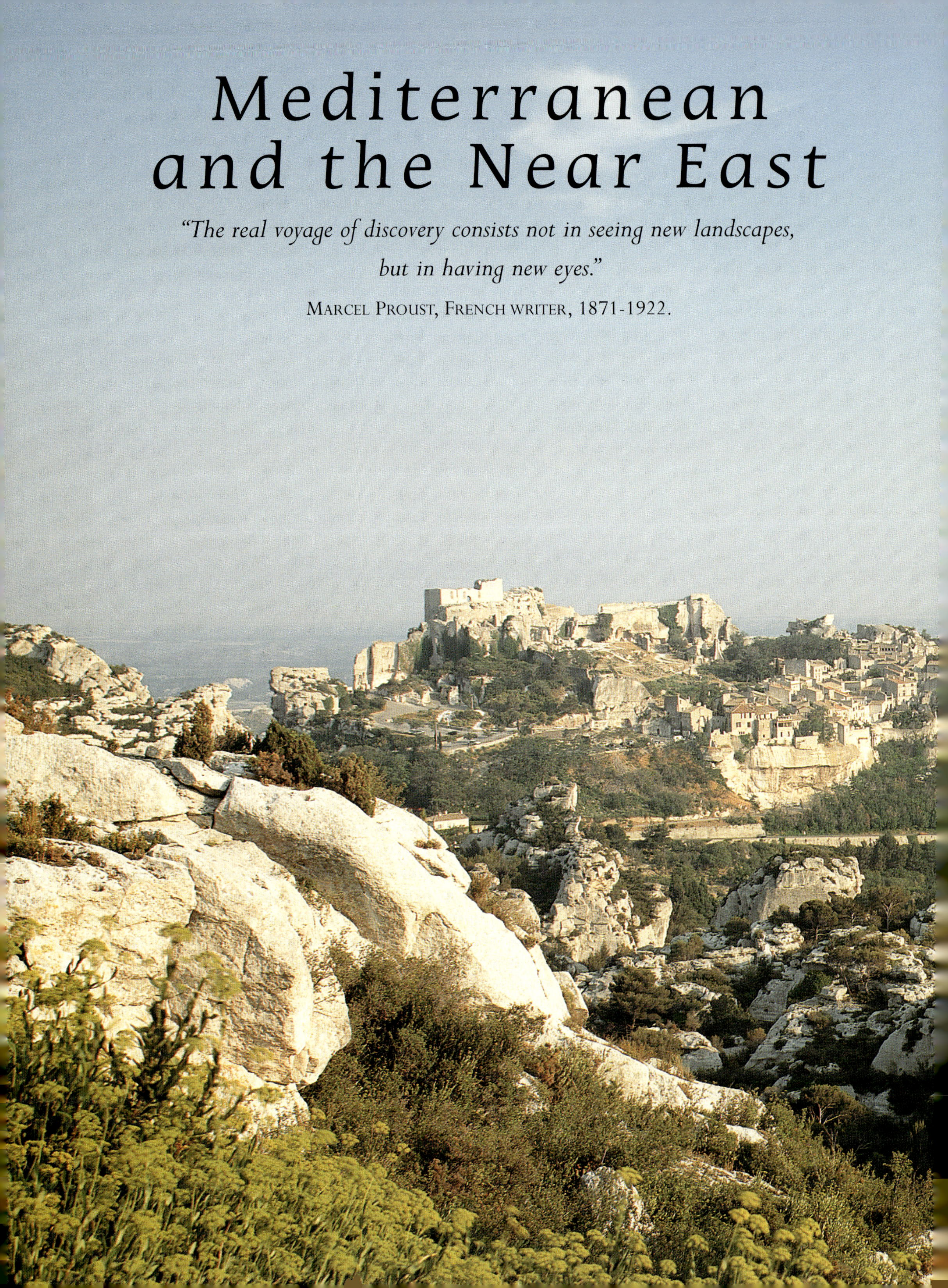

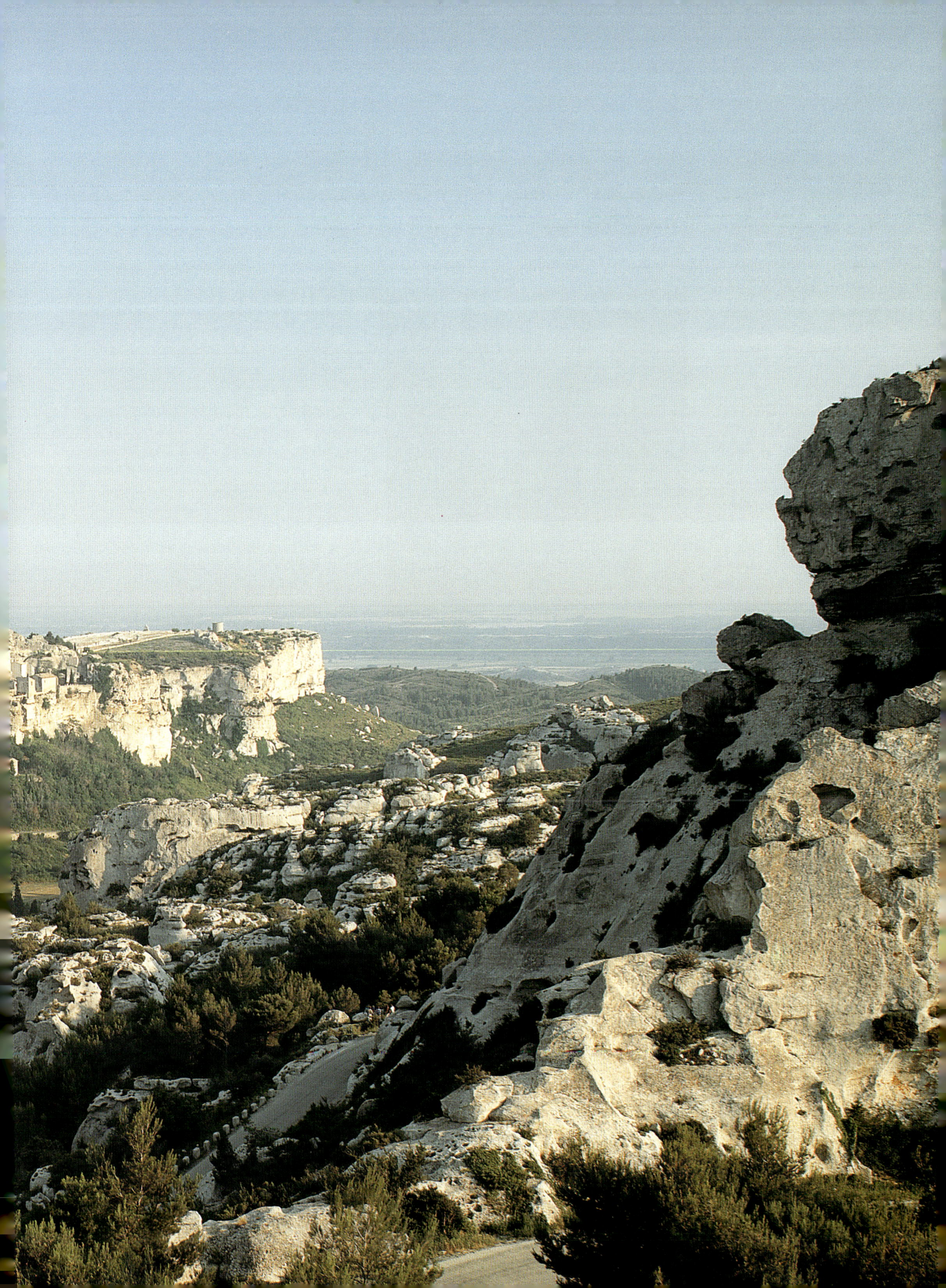

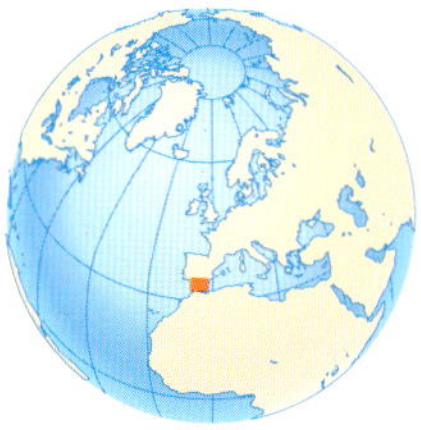

Moorish Spain

Amid the gardens and orange groves of southern Spain, the relics of the old Moorish civilization of Andalucia still survive almost magically.

FACT FILE

Population: 7 million (about 20% of Spain).

Area: 87,300 km sq (17.3 % of Spanish Territory).

Currency: Spanish peseta

Climate: Mediterranean; July–Aug 104° F (40° C), snow in winter.

Time to go: Winter and spring to avoid the crowds and see the snow on the Sierra's peaks.

Nearest airport: Seville, Malaga, Granada; Córdoba is connected to both by rail.

Food and drink: Sherry from Jerez , accompanied by olives and tapas (snack). Fish, including fresh anchovies; jabugo (ham); gazpacho (chilled vegetable soup).

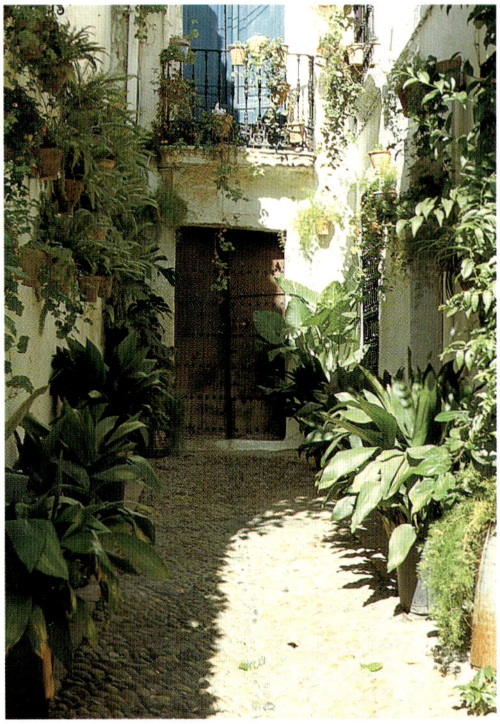

The old Moorish quarter of Cordoba (above) is still full of narrow streets with balconied houses set around quiet, leafy courtyards.

IT IS SOMETIMES SAID that old Moroccan families still keep the keys to their long-lost houses in Spain. At a time (A.D.800-1000) when most of Europe was still barbarous, a brilliant civilization flourished in the Muslim realm of *Al Andalus*—Andalucía. The Moors, a mixed race of Berbers and Arabs, crossed into Spain from Morocco in 711, and within four years had conquered most of the peninsula. Gradually, over almost eight centuries, the Spanish regained their lost territory. Though they tried to erase all traces of the Moors, much glorious architecture survives. The Moors also left a more subtle mark on Andalucia: in its proud independence (it now has its own regional government); in the landscape, which they lovingly irrigated; in the gardens and squares which decorate its cities; in the passionate Arabic cadences of the flamenco; and even in dishes such as lamb stewed with almonds, or *ajo blanco*, a soup made with garlic, grapes, and almonds which is directly descended from a medieval Moorish recipe.

At the heart of Moorish Spain is Córdoba, a modern city which has one of the best preserved medieval quarters in Europe. For three centuries the country was

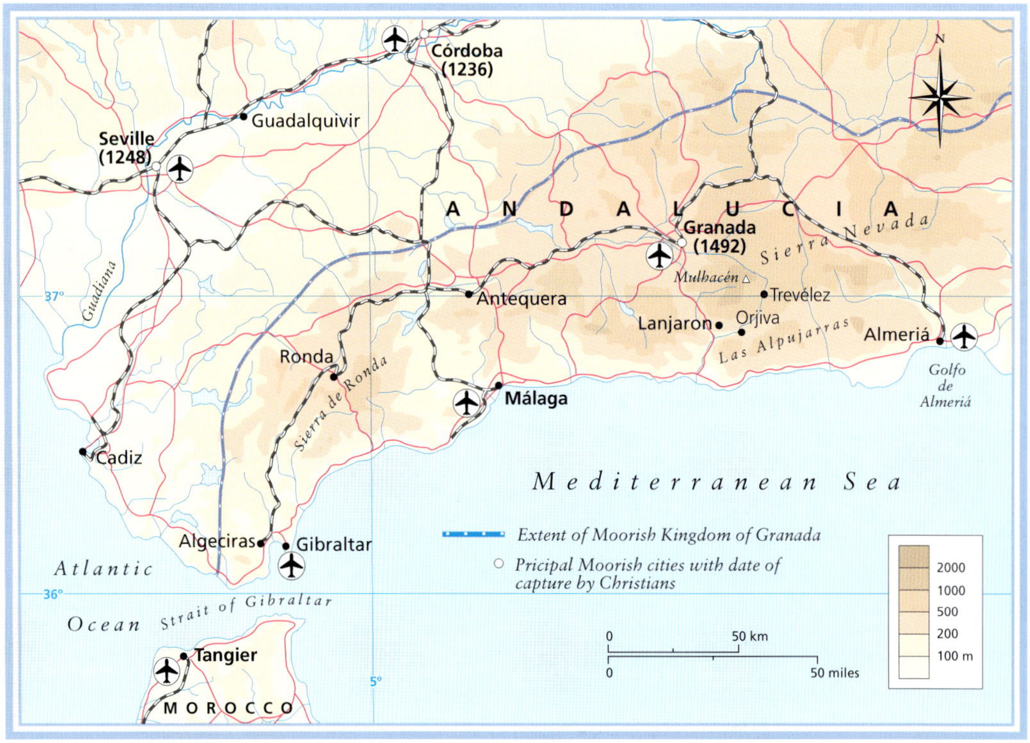

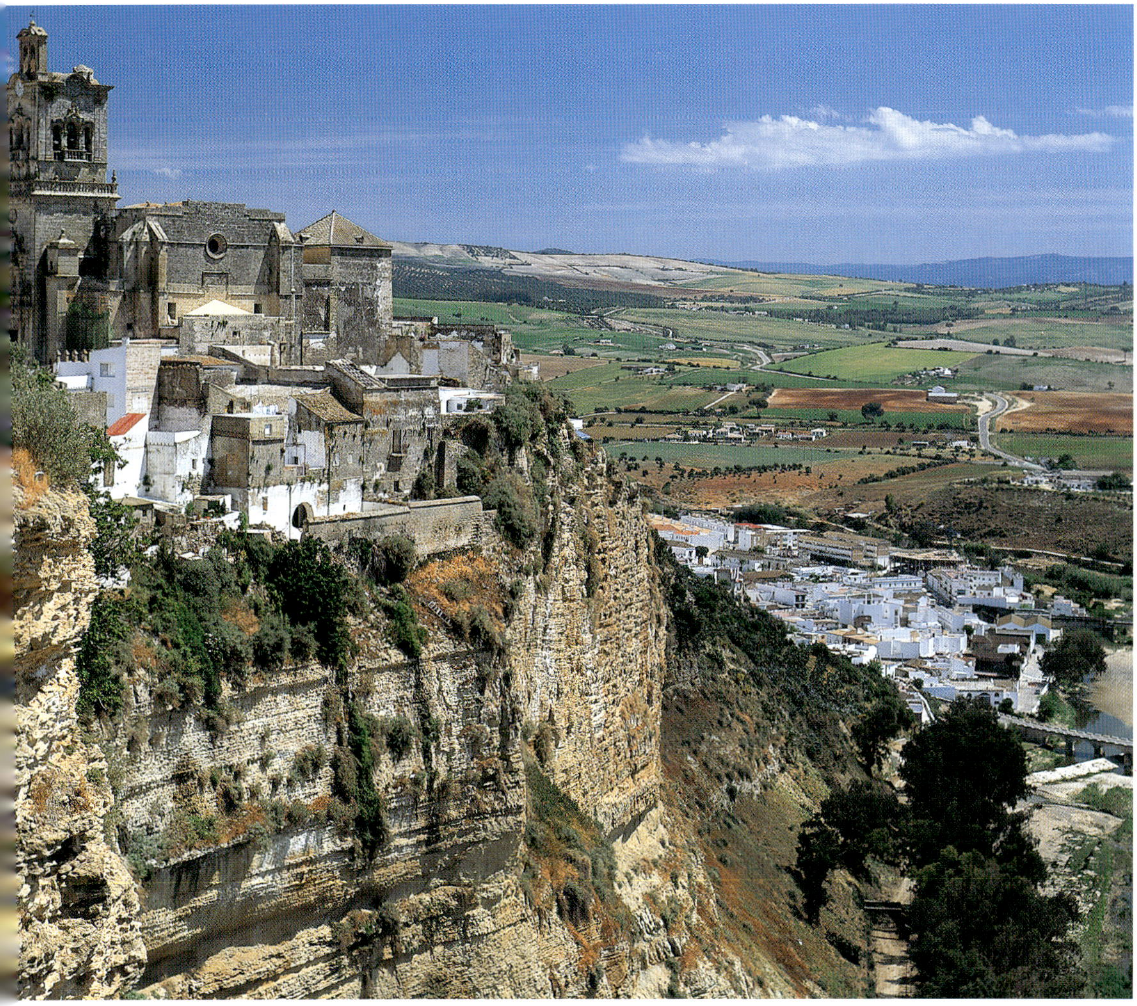

The Andalucian countryside is a harmonious blend of patterned agricultural land, whitewashed towns such as Arcos de la Frontera (left) and distant sierras.

Seville's Torre del Oro was built by the Moors in the 13th century to guard the city's river port.

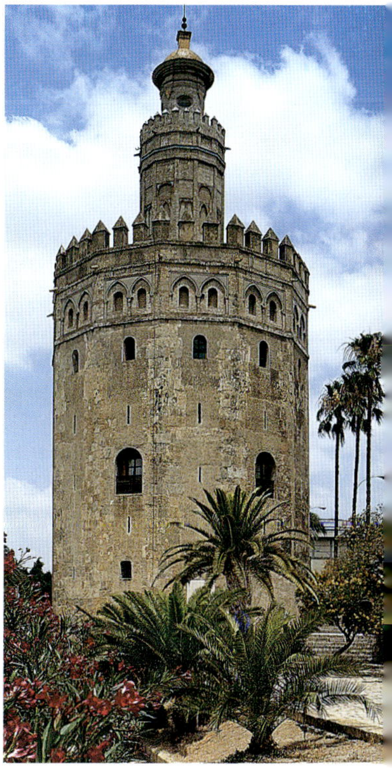

ruled from this great metropolis of commerce and learning. The Moors created a network of irrigation channels in the surrounding countryside which fed the city's gardens, and outlying vineyards and orchards. Vestiges of this horticultural luxuriance can be seen in the Patio de los Naranjos.(Court of Oranges) in the city and at Medina Azahara..

Other Moorish splendors can be glimpsed in the Great Mosque—"La Mezquita"—once the largest in the world after the Kaaba in Mecca. After the Christian Reconquest in 1236, it was converted into a cathedral. The minaret was left standing, but was later encased in a Baroque façade. Inside, a hypnotic succession of red and white marble arches is supported by 600 columns. Outside, rows of orange trees still grow in the courtyard, where worshippers once washed at the fountain before entering the mosque.

Under the tolerant Moors, always a minority in Spain, Córdoba became a great center of Jewish culture. North of the Mezquita is a labyrinth of narrow streets still known as the Judería (Jewish quarter); many of its old houses are now fashionable restaurants. At the heart of the Judería is a small, half ruined synagogue of 1315, one of the few to survive in Spain. Like much other Spanish architecture that looks Moorish, it is *mudéjar*—work done by Christians or Jews in a Moorish style.

CITY OF VITALITY

After the Caliphate of Córdoba collapsed in the 11th century, power shifted to Seville, 70 miles (110 km) down the Guadalquivir River. Seville—the largest city in southern Spain—throbs with life, its inhabitants packing its cafés and bars all day and night. Thanks to its gardens, all this urban excitement is accompanied by the scent of jasmine and the sound of birdsong. In spring comes the *Semana Santa* (Holy Week) procession, where hooded penitents are followed by floats bearing images of the Virgin or Christ, followed by the *Ferma de Abril*, a week-long party in which men parade on horses and women dance in gypsy dresses. It is possible to stay in hotels in restored old mansions around courtyards, but book early. Everywhere in Seville you will seldom be out of sight of a striking remnant of its Moorish past: the 320 foot (92 m) minaret La Giralda. It was built in

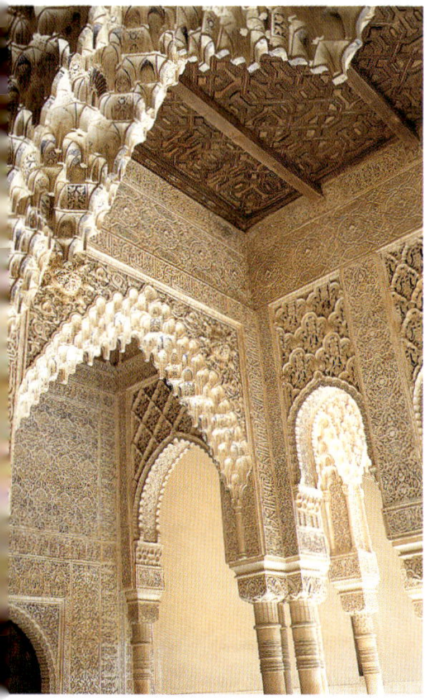

Moorish decoration is distinguished by its delicate symmetry as in these filigree arches at the Alhambra in Granada.

the late 1100s, just 50 years before the Reconquest, and now serves as a tower to the cathedral that supplanted the mosque. Adjacent to the cathedral is the Alcázar, the royal palace where Spain's Muslim and Christian traditions met in a brief but extraordinary fusion. Begun in the 9th century, but completed by Muslim craftsmen after the Reconquest, its elegant pavilions—decorated with arabesques and inscriptions in both Arabic and Gothic script—face onto courtyards and gardens planted with orange and lemon trees. And down along the river you can still see the huge cigarette factory where Carmen, the tragic gypsy heroine of Bizet's opera, supposedly once worked.

A FINAL FLOWERING

By 1275, the Moors had retreated to Granada 160 miles (250 km) southeast of Seville, in the fastness of the Sierra Nevada. Granada witnessed the extraordinary last flowering of Moorish culture. If the modern city lacks Seville's vitality, its Moorish monuments more than compensate. Two promontories extend from the Sierra foothills into the city itself, divided by the valley of the Río Darro. On one of these stands the Alhambra, whose red stone walls and towers glow in the evening sun. Within, the architecture encapsulates all the symmetry and grace of Islamic design. At the foot of the steep path to the imposing Gate of Justice, the entrance to the palace is a grove of elms planted by the Duke of Wellington during the Peninsular Wars. Archways lead through arcaded courtyards and pavilions of the *Casa Real* (Royal Palace), built almost entirely of wood and stucco and decorated with exquisite arabesque patterns and calligraphic inscriptions from the Koran. Symmetry, order, and water are the keynote themes: pools and fountains in enclosed paradise gardens offer relief from the dusty olive groves and dry Mediterranean landscape of the surrounding countryside. The complex is set amid terraced rose gardens looking out over plains toward the mountains. At the rocky tip of the promontory is the Alcazaba, a (now somewhat ruinous) fortress dating from the 11th to 13th centuries. From its ramparts, you can see one of the most unexpected cityscapes in Europe: the white, flat-roofed buildings, the palms and cypresses, and the tall minarets outlined against the sky, seem to have been transported from Morocco. This is the Albaicín, a settlement founded by Moors driven from Baeza in the 1200s. The western wall of the old Moorish citadel and the city gates with their horseshoe arches still exist. Most of the churches are built on the foundations of mosques, and besides many of the minarets—now bell towers—you can still see the cisterns at which the faithful would wash before entering.

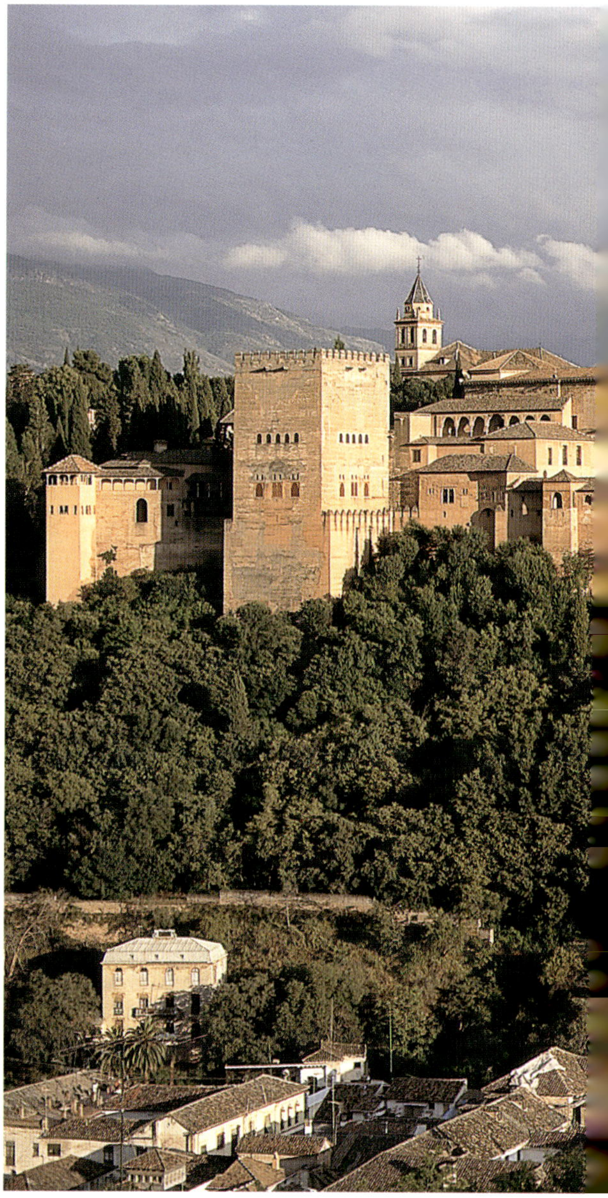

Cordoba Cathedral (below) was built around the main mosque of western Islam after the city was captured by the Christians in 1236.

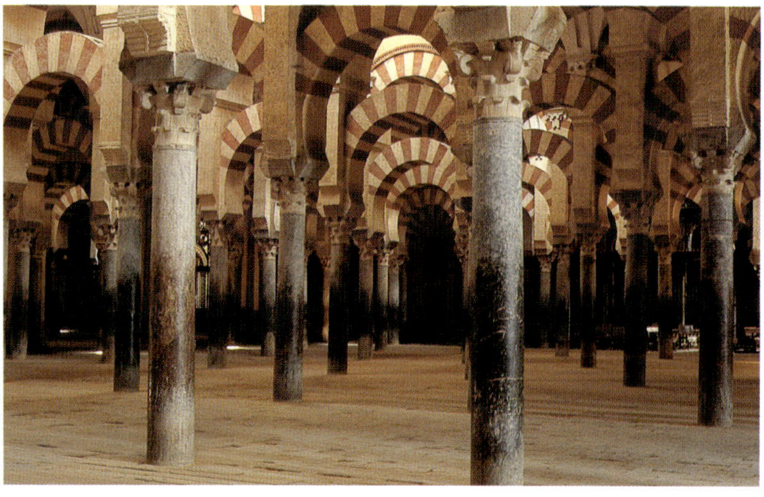

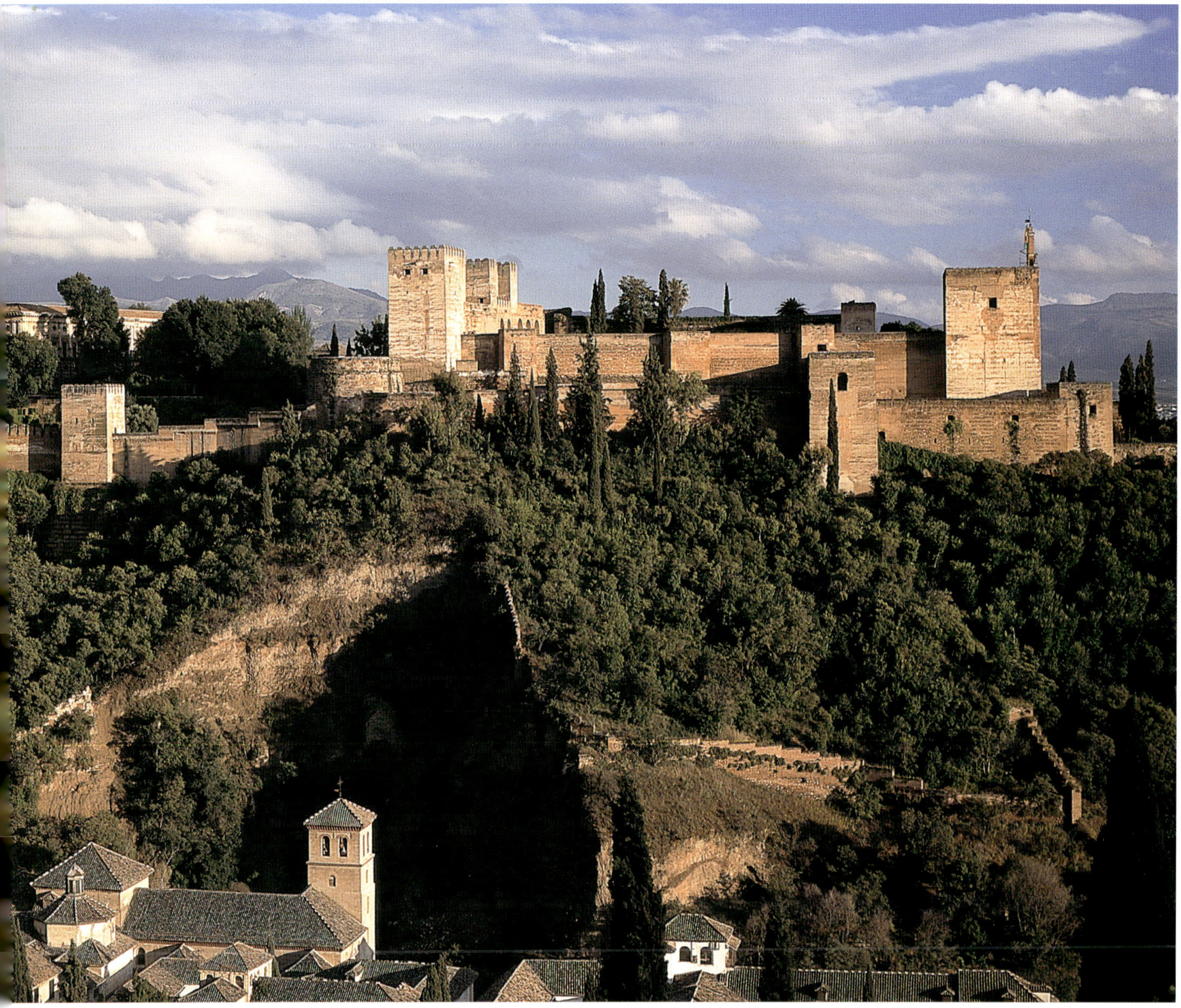

The Alhambra—the extraordinary culmination of Moorish architecture—sits atop a hill dominating the city of Granada. The name is from the Arabic for "red fort."

The Moor's Last Sigh

Heading southeast from Granada into the Sierras, you reach the pass known as El Ultimo Suspiro del Moro—the Moor's Last Sigh. Here Boabdil, last Emir of Granada, looked back over his lost kingdom after the city fell to Ferdinand and Isabella in 1492. Boabdil was allowed to retire to the Alpujarras, a mountain range just south of the Sierra Nevada whose valleys the Moors had transformed into a verdant landscape of olives, almonds, and orchards through elaborate irrigation channels (acequias) which still cut through the hills today. Many of Boabdil's subjects followed him, but the Christian monarchs soon broke their agreement and drove him out. With its lush valleys of poplars and willow, forests of holm oak and pine, rivers and rushing torrents, the Alpujarras is one of the most unspoilt corners of Spain. You can trek along ancient mule tracks from one whitewashed village (pueblo blanco) to another for much of the way from Bubion, on the brink of the Poqueria Gorge, to Trevélez, the highest village in Spain. Towering over it is Mulhacén, at 11,400 feet (3,482 m) the highest mountain in Spain; from its peak you can see Morocco on a clear day. From Bérchules, with views across the Guadalfeo valley to the almond- and olive-covered slopes of the Sierra de la Contraviesa, another acequia leads to the convergence of the Chico and Grande Rivers.

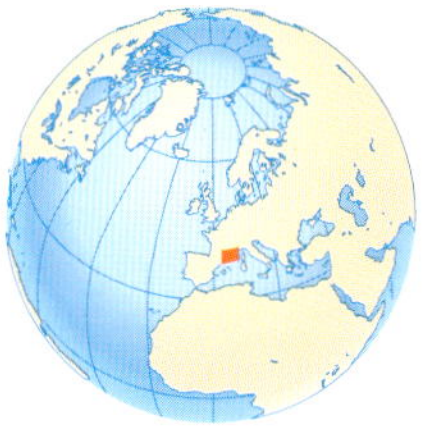

The Essence of Provence

Provence was once ancient Rome's favored "provincia," and has some of the most evocative remains of antiquity in western Europe, as well as two of its last wildernesses: the Camargue and the Gorge du Verdon.

Lapped by a sea of sunflowers, the little town of Mornas in the Rhône valley nestles at the foot of a massive limestone cliff, overlooked by a ruined castle.

PROVENCE IS A SENSUOUS LAND of strong colors, aromatic scents, and dramatic landscapes. It embraces the windswept flatness of the Camargue in the west and the rugged, limestone canyon of Verdon in the foothills of the Alps.

The quality of light exaggerates the region's rich ochers and dark greens, the fierce yellow of sunflowers, and the purple of cultivated lavender. The hills smell of *herbes de Provence* , and it is no accident that the center of France's perfume trade is the Provençal hill town of Grasse. Craggy hills and gnarled vines shelter medieval towns where old men play boules (bowls) and sip pastis beneath plane trees. Baked by the summer sun and often scoured by the ferocious Mistral wind roaring down the Rhône valley, Provence is a place for people who like their hedonism salted by an awareness of unforgiving nature. The region's wines are less *grands vins* than rich or fruity brews, its famous dishes—*bouillabaisse, ratatouille, salade niçoise*—not *haute cuisine* but earthy fare that tastes of the soil and the sea.

Amazingly, this pungently characterful region still survives relatively close to the great population centers

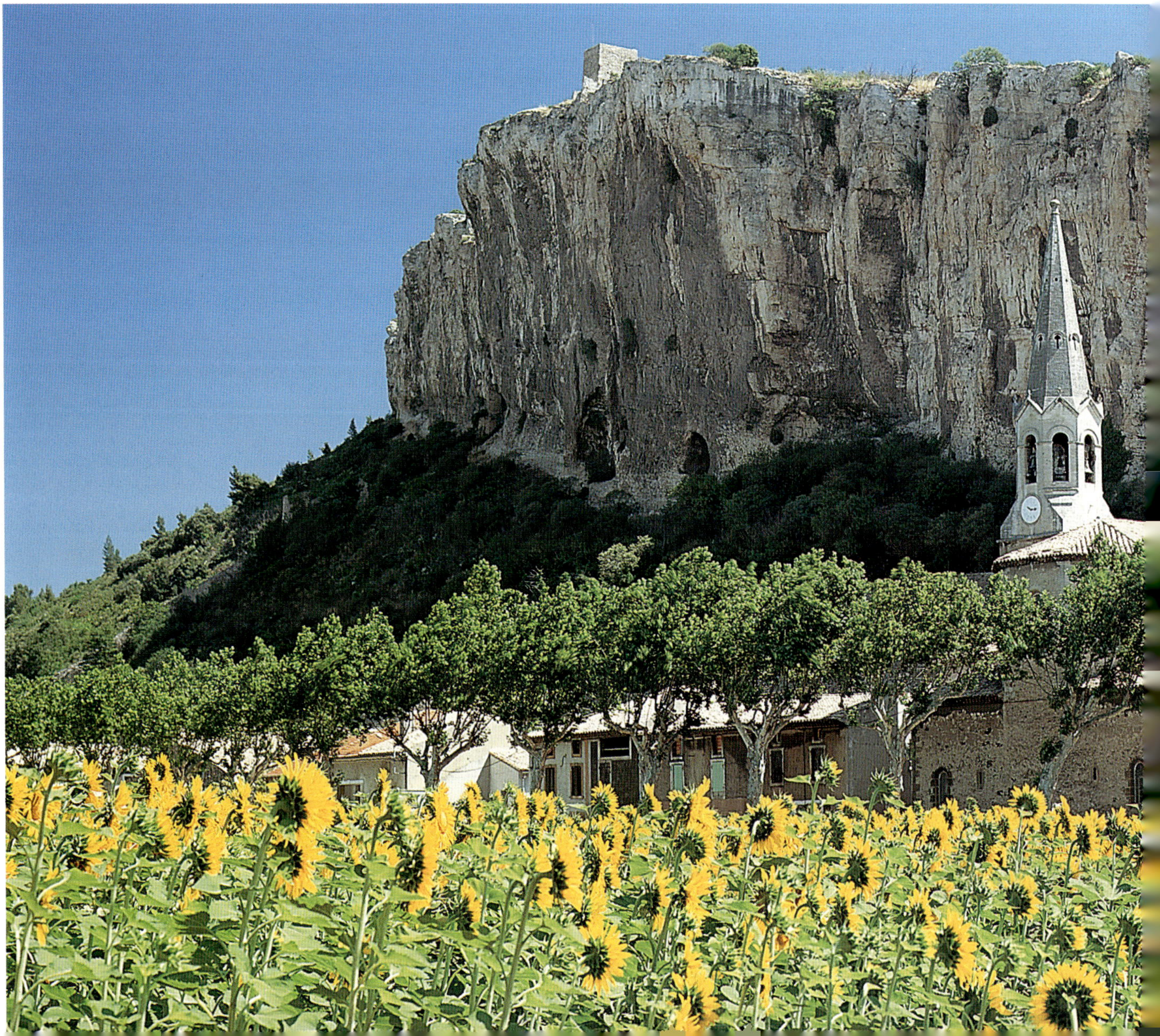

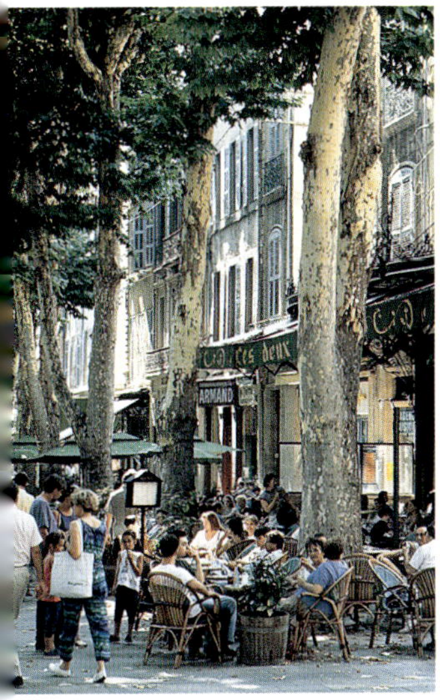

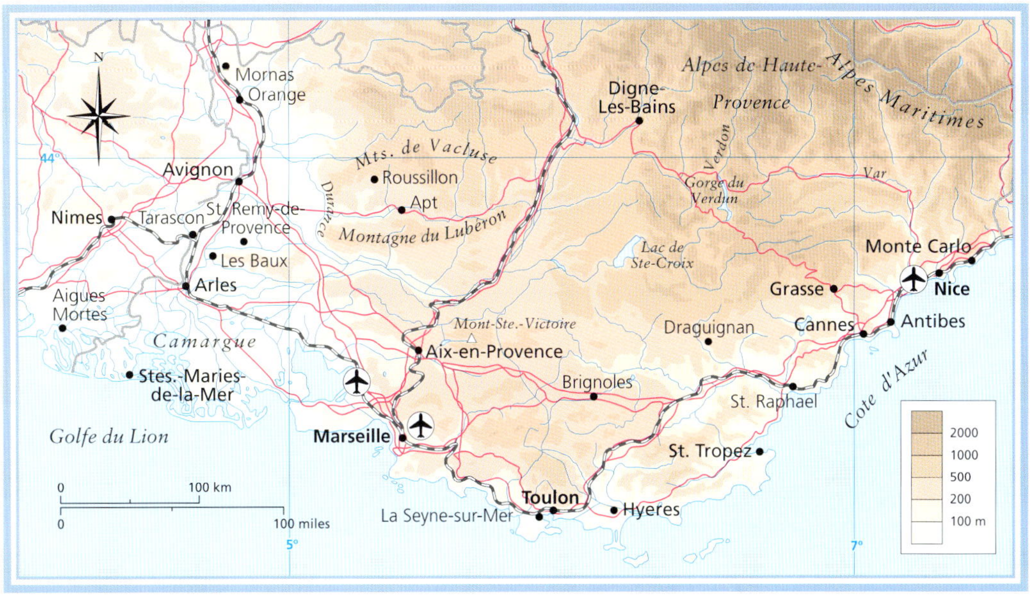

In the Cours Mirabeau, Aix en Provence, cafés spread onto the sidewalks beneath massive plane trees.

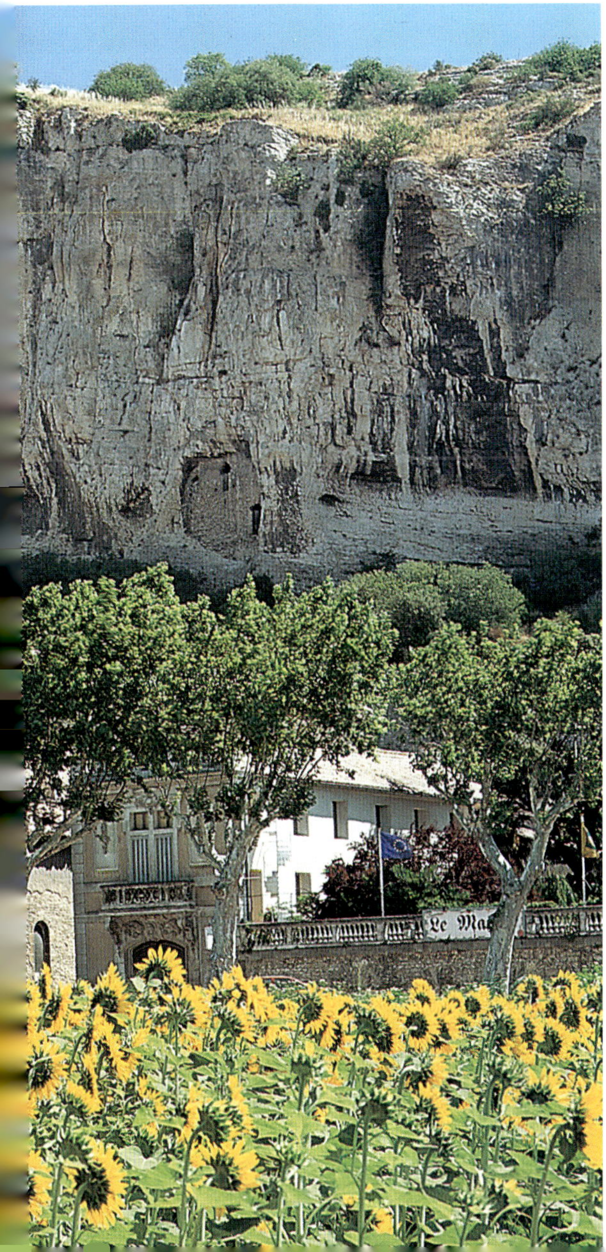

of northwest Europe. Inevitably, it has attracted a great deal of attention—not least from painters such as Vincent Van Gogh, Paul Cézanne, Henri Matisse, and Pablo Picasso—yet despite the books, films, and television programs, the region and its people have resisted being turned into touristic parodies of themselves.

The west of the province is bound by the 346,000 acres (140,000 ha) of lagoon, saltmarsh, dune, and pasture of the Camargue, where the Rhône moves slowly into the sea. It is an eerie landscape of massive skies, shivering waters, and windbent reeds. In summer the mud bakes into cracked, salt-crusted polygons; in winter it feels as though you've come to the bleak edge of the world. There are pink flamingos, and white horses ridden by the *gardians* (cowboys) who tend the black bulls unique to the area. The best way to discover the Camargue—the least damaging to the area's fragile ecology—is on horseback. Riding tours can be arranged through the Association du Tourisme at Saintes Maries de la Mer.

Classical and Medieval influences

On the westernmost edge of the Camargue, the medieval village of Aigues Mortes shelters inside astonishingly well-preserved walls built by King Louis IX (reigned 1226-70) to launch his doomed Crusade of 1248. In the inland towns of Arles and Avignon north of the Camargue, Classical Rome meets medieval Europe. Arles was once a Roman imperial capital; today remnants of that era—massive ruins, including an amphitheater (still used for bloodless bullfights in which matadors simply snatch rosettes from the beasts'

FACT FILE

Climate: Mediterranean; July–Aug 82°F (28°C); snow in inland areas in winter, heavy rains possible everywhere.

Time to go: October through June (to avoid the worst crowds)

Nearest airport: Marseille.

What to buy: Perfumes, wine, santons (Christmas figures), lavender products.

Transportation: The major towns are connected by rail, while buses ply the routes between the smaller centers. For more remote regions, rent a car. Beware local drivers who think nothing of taking mountain hairpins at 70 mph (110 kph).

horns)—loom above narrow medieval streets of old shuttered houses and traditional cafés. West of the town are the limestone hills of the Alpilles where white peaks rise starkly above slopes clad with oak and pine. At their northern edge is Saint-Remy de Provence, a gracious little town encircled by 14th-century walls, and full of pavement cafés and restaurants. Vincent Van Gogh stayed in an asylum near here after cutting off his ear. Rome is not far away: just outside the town is the ruined town of Glanum, with triumphal arch and mausoleum, a 60 foot (18 m) high limestone wedding cake commemorating Emperor Augustus's heirs Caius and Lucius, who died young.

Popes in exile from Rome held court at Avignon in the 1300s. Today, the town has a disproportionate metropolitan verve due to a large student population and vibrant arts scene. Its international music and theater festival draws performers and visitors from around the world every July and August. The medieval bridge immortalized by the song *Sur le pont, d'Avignon, on a dansé...*) has only three of its arches left after centuries of flooding. The city center—full of old churches and elegant 17th- and 18th-century houses—is still enclosed by medieval walls, and dominated by the huge, battlemented Palais des Papes (Papal Palace).

Medieval spirits dominate in Les Baux, a village which has given its name to bauxite (aluminum ore). The mineral lends a shimmering whiteness to the white crag on which the old village sits, enclosed by forbidding medieval walls. It is a brooding, unsettling place, a medieval ghost town where mullioned windows gape at a fierce cobalt sky. From 1000 to 1400 the lords of Les Baux ruled from here with mixed splendor and savagery, patronizing troubadours who sang of courtly love, and slinging enemies off the cliff. The present village clings to the lower slopes, among olive groves and scrub, leaving the old part deserted.

The modern town of Orange, 15 miles (24 km) north of Avignon, conceals a distinguished Roman past, complete with triumphal arch. The Roman theater is awe-inspiring, with curving banks of seats cut into a steep hill, and a stage backed by an enormous sandstone wall with a statue of the Emperor Augustus in a central niche. Battered by time it may be, but this is no mere ruin, for operas are regularly performed here.

THE HEART OF PROVENCE

The Lubéron, a 35-mile (56 km) range of beautiful, rugged hills, captures the essence of Provence. The lush plateau of the Petit Lubéron is separated from the rugged and higher Grand Lubéron—a superbly scenic national park—by a wooded valley, the Combe de Lourmarin. The northern face of the Lubéron is damp and alpine, while the vine-covered southern slopes bask in 300 days of sunshine a year—though the heights get bitterly cold in winter. Here are hiking and riding trails, rivers to canoe, *gîtes* (cottages) to rent, and lives of artists to trace.

Ocher for artists' paint is extracted from the rocks of Roussillon, a hilltop village north of the Lubéron. Everything about the place is red: sand, stone, stucco, tiles—all surmounted by a red church tower with a rusty wrought-iron belfry. The views are wonderful, though sadly the place has become too popular for its own good. The artist Paul Cézanne was born here in 1839, and his studio is preserved as it was when he died in 1906—complete with a wine glass by his easel—on the north side of town. The distinctive cone of the Montagne Sainte-Victoire, which Cézanne painted over

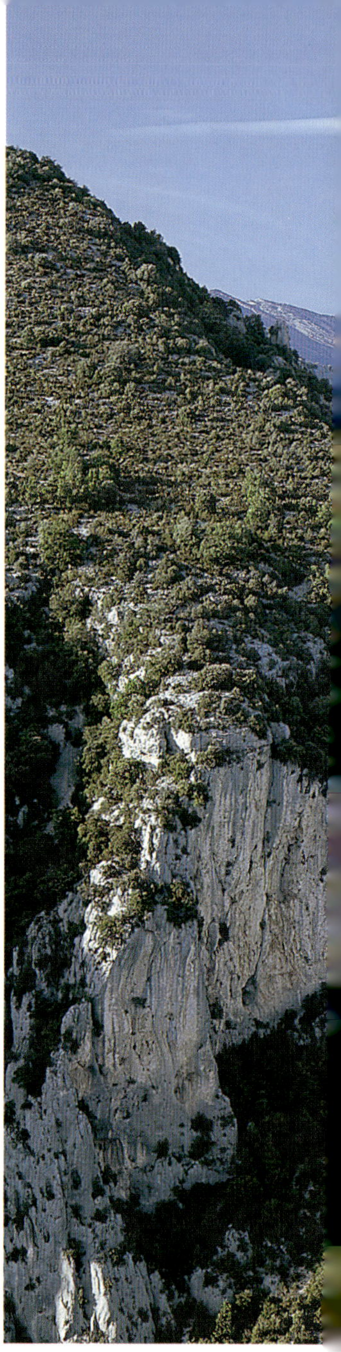

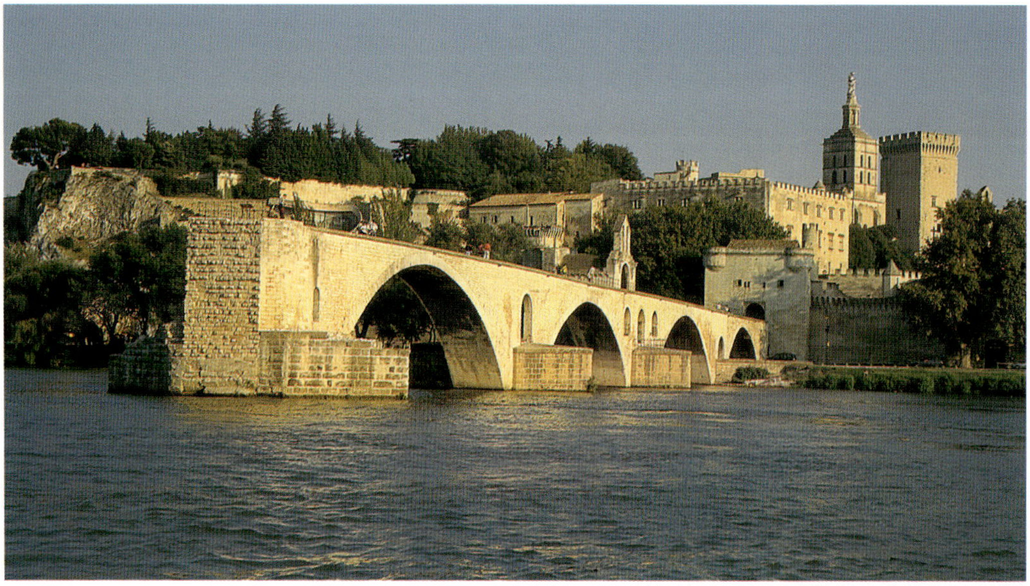

The vast palace built by the popes during their medieval exile in Avignon looms over the remaining spans of the Pont St. Bénézet, the "pont d'Avignon" of the French song.

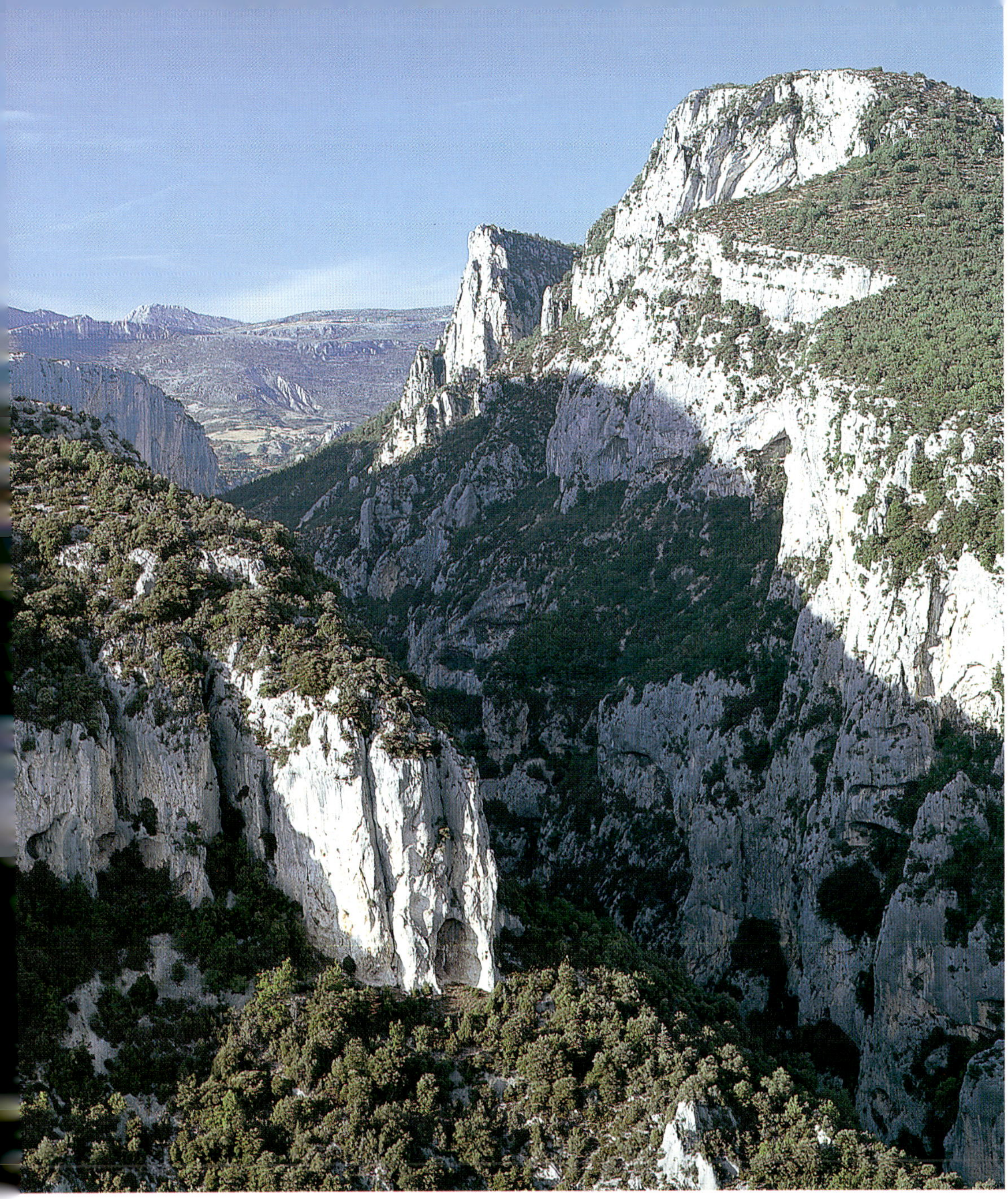

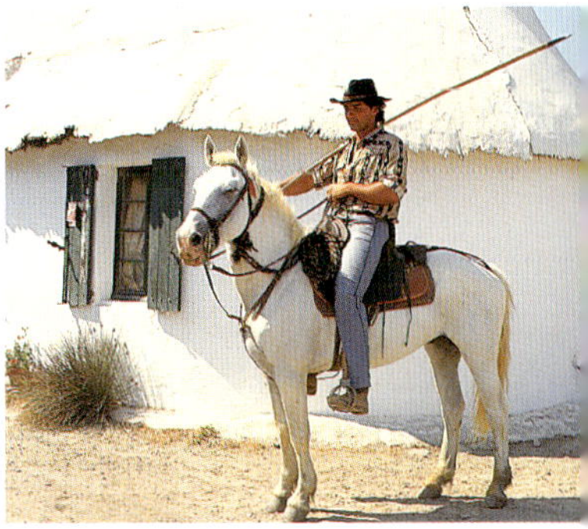

A gardian—a cowboy of the Camargue on one of the small white horses which are unique to the region.

A scenic road winds its way around dizzying hairpin bends at the brink of Europe's largest natural canyon, the wild and rugged Gorges du Verdon.

and over again, rises 9 miles (15 km) east of Aix. Today it is an elegant town of fountains, grand avenues lined with 17th- and 18th-century town houses, sculpted doorways, wrought-iron balconies, fine restaurants geared to leisurely lunches, and old cafés.

The Lubéron subsides into the rolling countryside of the Var, and the land rises toward the deeply scarred limestone plateau of upper Provence with stunning panoramas falling away, layer upon layer. Suddenly, the land falls away into the grand canyon of the Gorge du Verdon, a sheer 700 feet (200 m) to the Verdon River. The canyon is impassable by car, but can be negotiated on foot or by whitewater raft. But once entered at the Point Sublime, there's no way out until the river emerges some 15 miles (24 km) later into Lac de Sainte-Croix. It is possible to drive around the rim of the canyon; there are many hair raising bends and the 65 mile (103 km) loop takes the better part of a day.

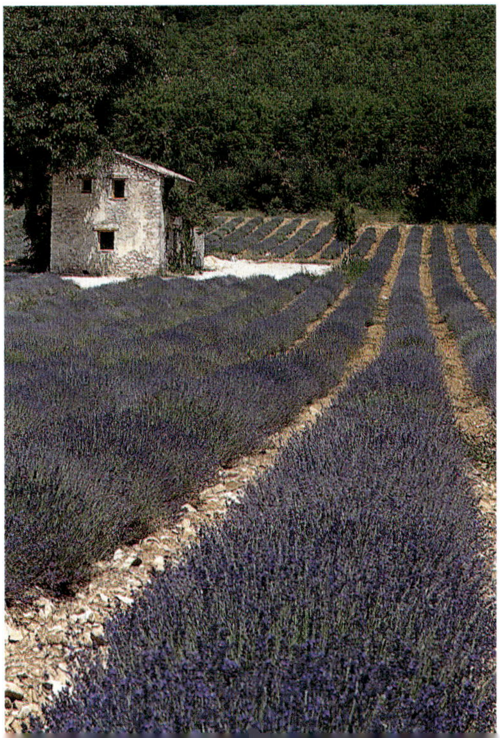

Lavender fields contribute to Provence's characteristic colors and scents; the distilled essence of the flowers is a vital ingredient in some of France's finest perfumes.

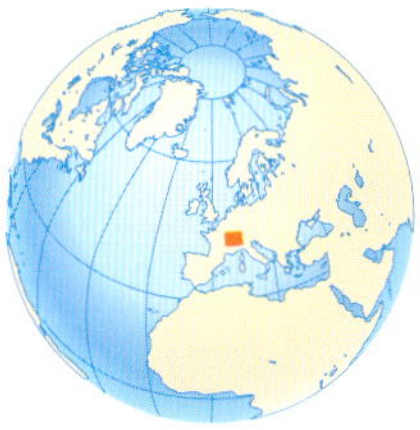

Téléférique from Chamonix

"One of the most grand and sweeping bits of granite I have ever seen . . . The Charmoz glacier on my left sank from the moraine in broken fragments, and swept back under the dark walls of the Charmoz, lost in cloud." John Ruskin, 1849.

FACT FILE

Currency: French franc, Italian lira.

Climate: Alpine; even in the summer, temperatures can fall below freezing on the peaks.

Time to go: December—March for skiing; May—September for hiking

Nearest airport: Lyons, Geneva, Turin.

What to take: Sunglasses, sunblock creams, good boots, warm windproof clothing, binoculars.

More information: Tourist Office, 45 place du Triangle-de-l'Amitié, Chamonix, France, tel: 04.50.53.00.24, fax: 04.50.53.58.90. Piazza Chanoux 8, Aosta, Italy, tel: 0165 74040.

WHERE THE BORDERS OF FRANCE, Italy, and Switzerland meet, the earth's surface crumples into a great jumble of splintered rocks thrown up by the cataclysmic impact of two continental plates some 200 million years ago. Rising above it all is the 15,760 foot (4,807 m) ice-capped summit of Europe's highest mountain, Mont Blanc, surrounded by lesser peaks and deeply crevassed glaciers, and ringed by fearsome spears of rock known as *aiguilles* (needles).

The nearest town to Mont Blanc, and the obvious base from which to explore this savage and exhilarating landscape, is Chamonix, nestling in the green valley of the River Arve, where the wooded hillsides and lush meadows—carpeted with wild flowers in summer—form a lyrical contrast to the sheer mountains that rise on either side. It is no longer the little mountain village from which Dr. Pacard and Jacques Balmat set out to climb Mont Blanc for the first time in 1786, and to which Ruskin returned year after year, but a large and lively town full of hotels, restaurants, and bars catering for tourists, climbers and skiers.

But the landscape, with its constantly shifting effects of light and weather, remains as magical as ever. Sometimes the aiguilles, struck by the rays of the setting sun, glow like fiery stalactites. Sometimes the mountains are completely obscured by cloud, and you look out onto a gentle landscape of green meadows and dark wood—until the mist evaporates and suddenly the mountains appear so close you could reach out and touch them, their glistening snow faces and dark screes picked out with unearthly clarity.

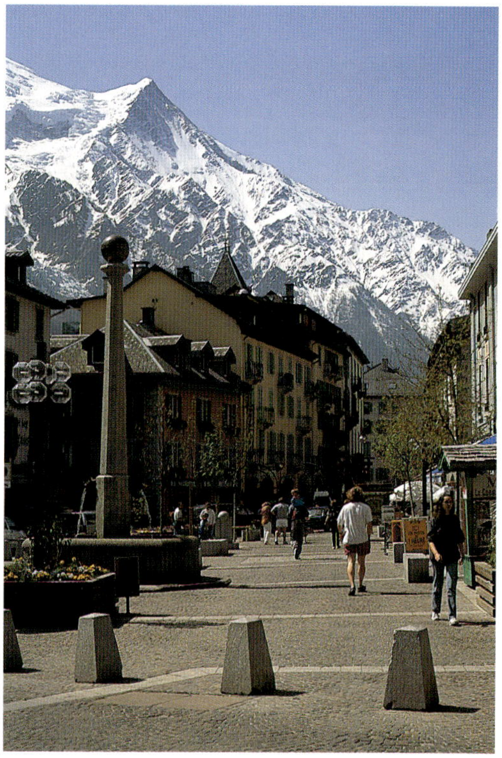

Chamonix (above) has been a mountaineering center since Paccard and Balmat first climbed Mont Blanc (right) in 1786. This view shows the sharp profiles of the appropriately named Aiguilles ("needles") du Midi in the middle distance.

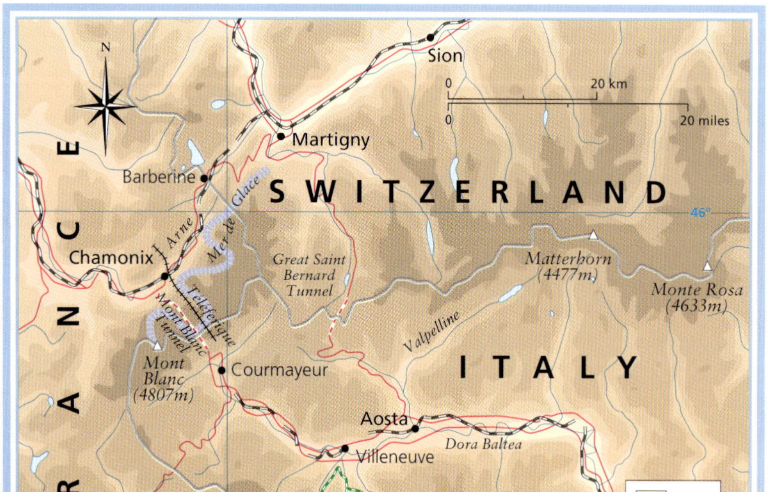

From Chamonix, you can take a rack and pinion railway up to the Mer de Glace, a vast tongue of ice 9 miles (14 km) long, 3/4 mile (1,200 m) wide, and up to 1,300 feet (400 m) deep in places. If you're feeling fit you can hike up—there are several trails. Close up, the glacier seems less beautiful and more powerful, no longer a white glimmering sheet but a threatening

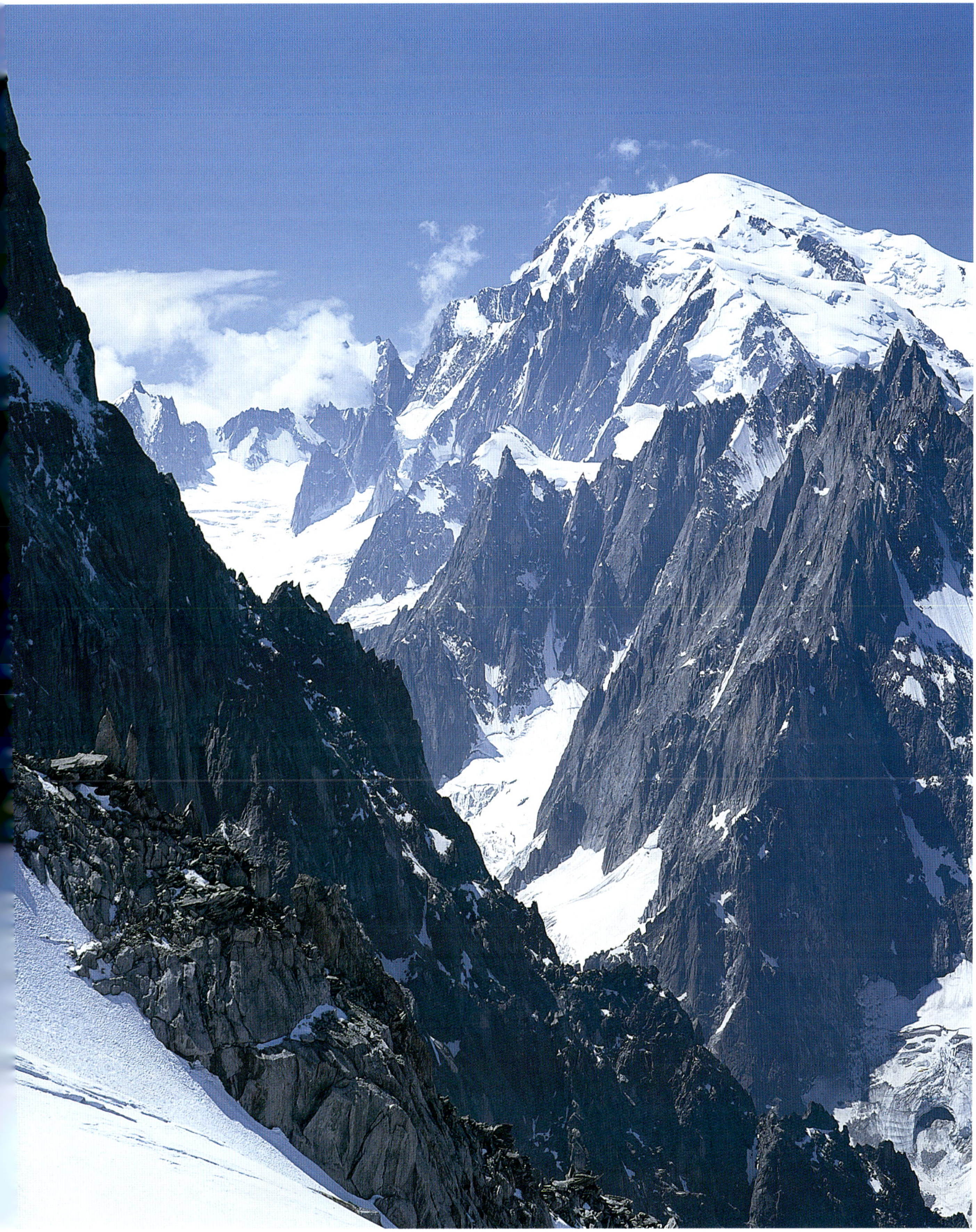

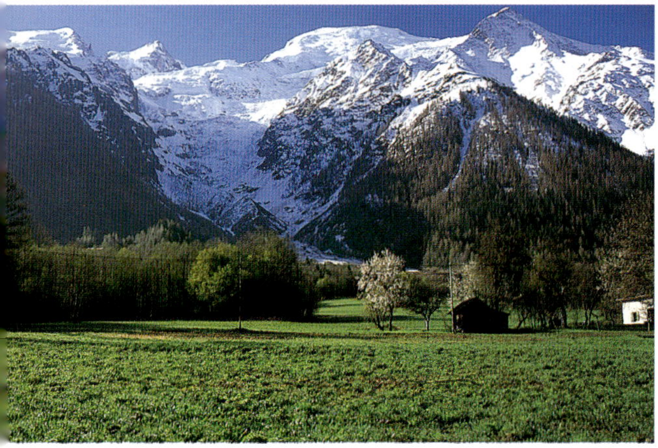

There is some fine walking among alpine meadows such as this one near Chamonix (above) in the summer months.

The Mer de Glace (right), one of the largest glaciers in the Alps, can be reached by cable car.

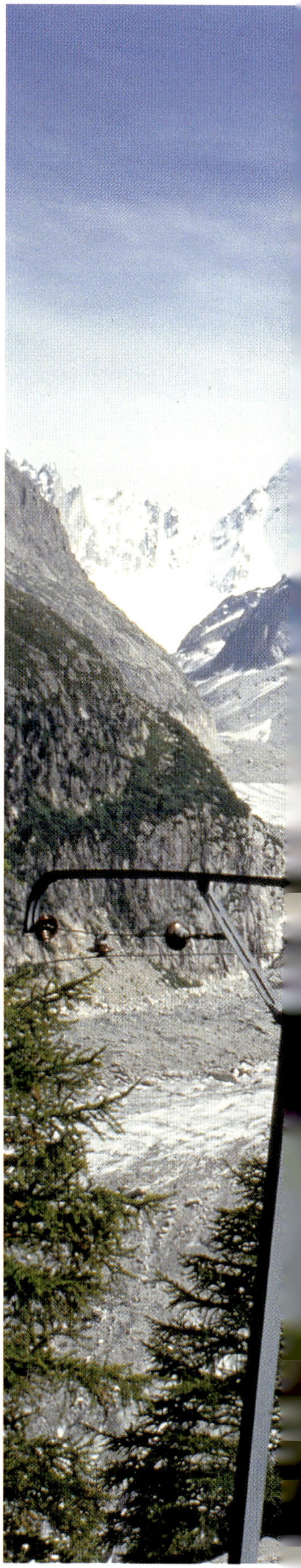

mass, striated into great folds and dirty with the rock it has scoured from its path. Once at the top, you look out across the ice and snow to the pyramid-shaped Grands Charmoz and the Aiguille du Dru—looking for all the world like a fearsome stake that has just this moment burst upward through the surface of the planet. Whatever you do, don't venture out onto the glacier without a guide—deep crevasses often lurk beneath a thin covering of snow and ice, ready to swallow the unwary walker. You can take a short cable car ride right down through a tunnel carved into the depths of the glacier. It is an eerie experience—the light gleams greenly though the ice, and you hear strange creaking and cracking noises as the glacier inches its way down the mountainside. Because of this movement, the tunnel has to be remade every spring.

A VERTIGINOUS ASCENT

One of the best views of Mont Blanc can be obtained by taking the téléférique from Chamonix to the top of the 12,600 foot (3,842 m) spike of granite known as the Aiguille du Midi. Set out early, by 9 A.M. at the latest, because it gets very crowded after then, and the summit is often clouded by midday. Be sure to dress warmly: even in summer it can be well below freezing at the top. The 2-mile (3 km) ascent is one of the highest and steepest in the world, and it must be said that swaying in a little cage of metal and glass over an awesome 1,800 foot (600 m) abyss is definitely not for vertigo sufferers. After a stop to change cars at Plan de l'Aiguille, the téléférique climbs to the lower of the Aiguille du Midi's twin peaks, the Piton Nord, where the cable car station and a restaurant perch precariously over the void.

From here, a bridge leads to the higher Piton Central, crowned by a telecommunications tower; there's an elevator to the top. The view across snow fields, glaciers, sheer rock faces and splintered crags to the summit of Mont Blanc is utterly awe-inspiring. Rank upon rank of snow-topped mountains recede into the distance; far away to the east—if the weather conditions are favorable—you can see Monte Rosa in Italy and the distinctive jagged barb of Switzerland's Matterhorn.

From the téléférique station on Piton du Nord, you can take a series of cable car rides over the snowy Vallée Blanche, via the Pointe Helbronner—right on the Italian border—and down the Italian face of the mountains to the village of La Palud. It is an unforgettable half-hour journey, crossing an international frontier by swinging from peak to peak through some of the wildest and most spectacular alpine scenery without setting foot on the ground. From La Palud, a bus will take you the 10 miles (16k m) back to Chamonix through the Mont Blanc tunnel.

A TASTE OF ITALY

It is well worth making a more extended foray into Italy; the tunnel—a terrific feat of engineering opened in 1965—takes you through into the Valle d'Aosta, one of Northern Italy's loveliest regions. Its main town, Aosta, is just 30 miles (48 km) by road from Chamonix. Now a busy town on the main route from France to Turin, Aosta—the name derives from "Augusta"—was once an alpine outpost of Rome. The town center is a lively and stylish place with a distinctly Italian feel, elegant tree-lined boulevards, and an impressive Roman triumphal arch, all framed by a wonderful backdrop of mountains.

Aosta is also the gateway to the Gran Paradiso 12 miles (20km) to the south. Dominated by the mountain of the same name, Italy's oldest national park encompasses 175,000 acres (70,000 ha) of glorious wilderness—high mountain valleys under perpetual snow, bleak hillsides to which a few, wind-twisted firs cling, sparkling brooks, mountain tarns, and lush lower valleys whose wooded slopes give way to meadows full of wild flowers. Once the hunting preserve of King Vittorio Emanuele II (ruled 1849-78), the park now provides a refuge for endangered species such as ibex and chamois. And if by now you've had enough of cable cars and the paraphernalia of skiing, these southern valleys are ideal hiking country, threaded by mountain trails, with refuges positioned at convenient spots.

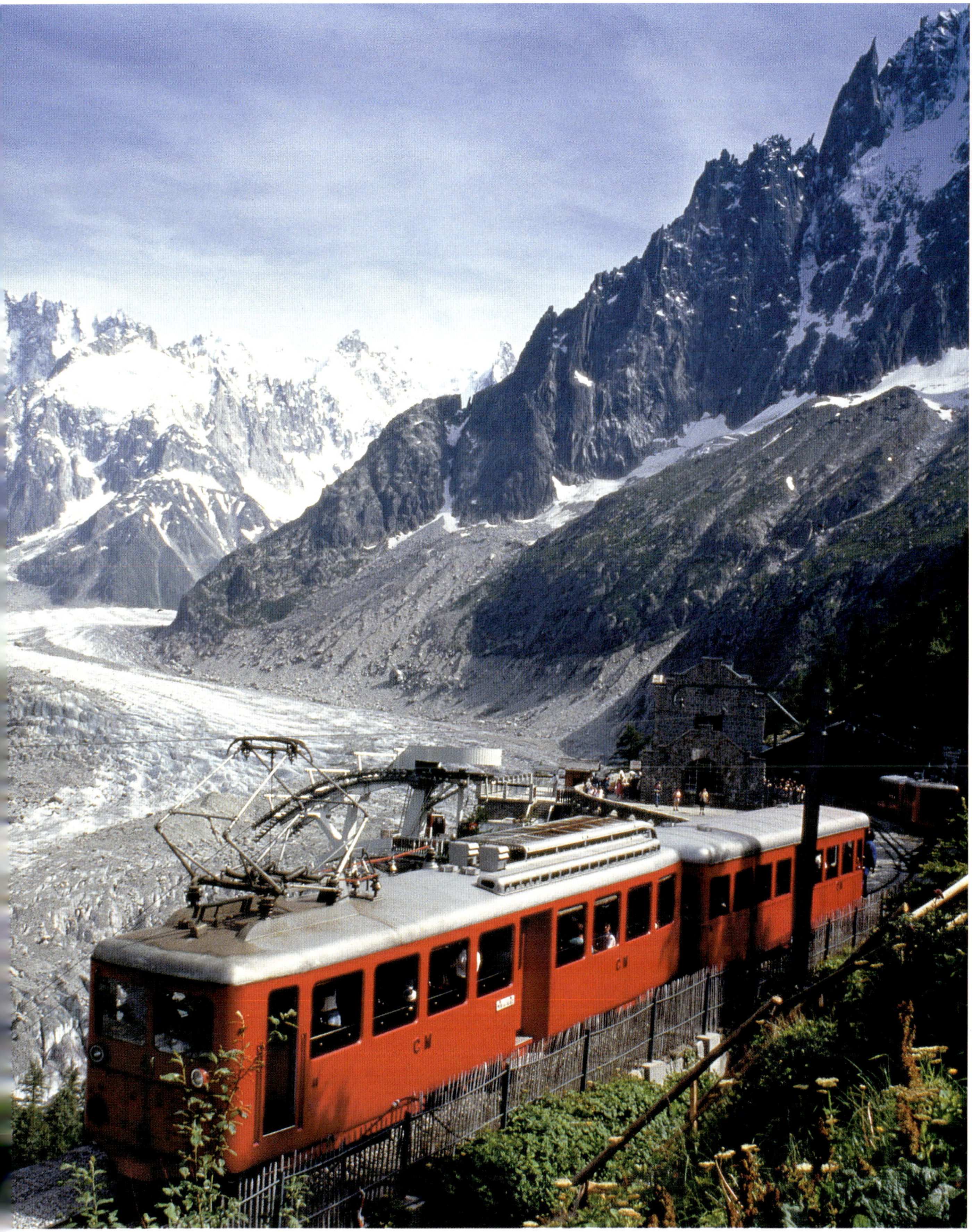

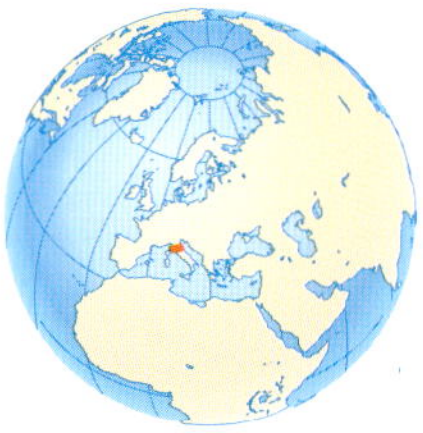

Renaissance Italy

A land of raw umber and burnt siena, of rolling meadows and the dark flames of cypress trees; an artist's paradise, a cultural heartland, and a gourmet's delight.

FACT FILE

Population: 340.000 in the metropolitan area; 79,000 in the historic center.

Currency: Italian lira.

Climate: Generally Mediterranean; very hotJuly—September; in winter frequently foggy, snows rarely, may be flooding.

What to take: Waterproof footwear and warm clothing in winter and umbrellas any time of the year.

Best time: October—March (to avoid the crowds) but beware the busy if picturesque Carnival season in the ten days before Lent (variable date).

Nearest airport: Marco Polo Airport is on the mainland, 8 miles (13 km) north of the historic center by water-taxi or take the bus to Piazzale Roma.

What to buy: antiques, jewelry, glass, lace, masks, and costumes.

City accommodation: Can be a problem; book well in advance.

Cypresses and parasol pines stand out dark against a sky baked eggshell blue. An old farm turned into a holiday villa rests calmly beneath its red-tiled roof in the curve of a valley, its swimming pool glinting a bright blue. In the distance the towers of a miniature city rise above vineyards and olive groves. The landscape of Tuscany and Umbria, patiently molded by thousands of years of human cooperation with nature, is so beautiful that it is easy to forget that the charming little hilltop or valley towns adorning it once buzzed with an urban dynamism which produced one of the greatest turning points, revolutions even, in human history: the Renaissance.

To grasp the full immensity of this revolution, go to the Uffizi Gallery in Florence and look at Gentile da Fabriano's *Adoration of the Magi* of 1423, with its stately, stiff figures, flat perspective and lavish use of gold leaf. Then cross the river to the church of Santa Maria del Carmine and contemplate Masaccio's *Expulsion from Paradise* fresco, with its emotive, startlingly modern-looking nudes of Adam and Eve, painted just four years later. This was not merely a change of artistic fashion,

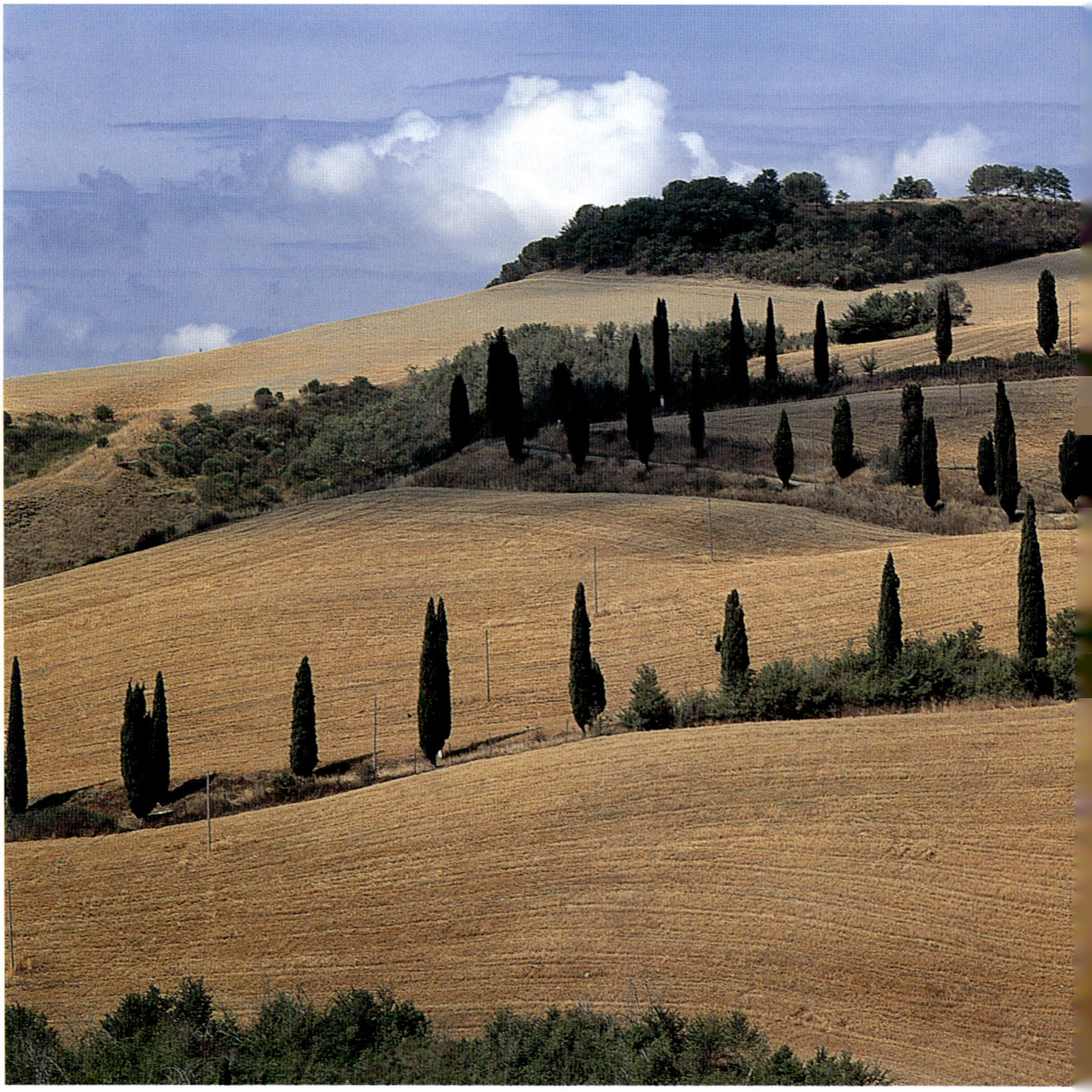

A typically idyllic Tuscan landscape of gently undulating hills punctuated by cypress trees in the Val d'Orcia near Bagno Vignoni, to the south of Siena.

but a radical shift in the way we look at the world and ourselves. It's no coincidence that "scientific perspective," so fundamental to the way we now see the world, was worked out by two Florentines: Leon Alberti (1404-72) and Filippo Brunelleschi (1377-1446), or that it was a Florentine philosopher, Niccolò Machiavelli (1469-1527), who formulated the principles of Realpolitik with such brutal elegance in his book *The Prince*. The modern world started here with the Florentine Renaissance.

Florence stands on the Arno River, between the Chianti hills to the south and those of Fiesole to the north. It began its rise in 1115, when it became a republic. Despite ferocious internal conflicts, it gradually became the region's preeminent city, ruling most of Tuscany. In 1434 the wealthy Medici family seized power, although at first they disguised their autocracy in republican trappings. What the Florentines lost in political liberty they gained in stability—and art. The Medicis were phenomenally enlightened patrons—perhaps the greatest ever—and soon the city's cultural achievements were such that it could boast of being new Athens. This was no idle boast, for the Medici commissioned works from the most adventurous artists and architects of the time, including Botticelli (1445-1510) and especially Michelangelo (1475-1564), who is buried in the church of Santa Croce.

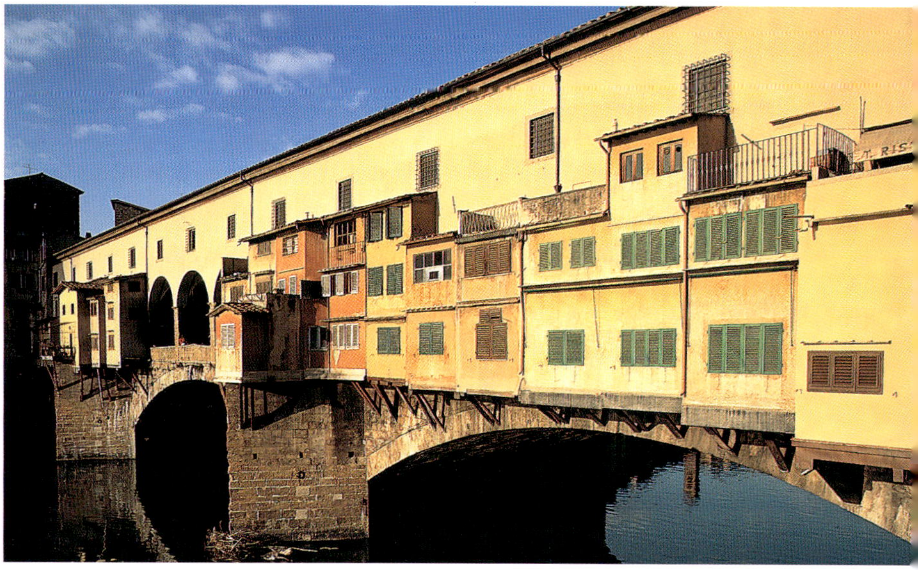

The Ponte Vecchio (above) spanning the River Arno at Florence, was built in 1345, although the jewelers' shops that crowd its arcades date from the 1500s. You can still cross the bridge via the secret passage constructed for the city's powerful Medici rulers.

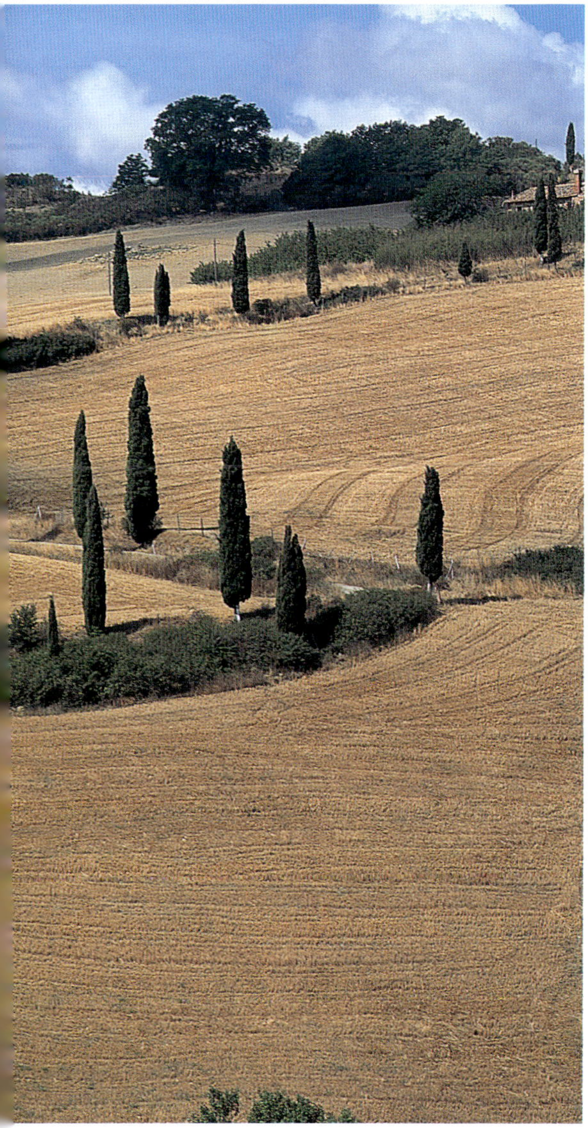

Stand on a hill overlooking Florence—at Fiesole with its graceful villas, or San Miniato with its Romanesque church—and you will see the city spread before you, looking much as it did 500 years ago to Leonardo da Vinci, another Florentine. The view is dominated by the vast red dome with which Brunelleschi crowned the city's green and white marble Gothic Duomo (cathedral) in the 15th century.

HEART OF THE RENAISSANCE

Florence is a compact city and all of its main sights can be reached on foot—fortunately, cars are now banned from the narrow streets of the medieval and Renaissance center. Within that small space lies probably the greatest concentration of artistic masterpieces on earth. A short walk south of the Duomo is the Piazza della Signoria, a square bounded on one side by the Gothic arcades of the Loggia housing the *Perseus* by Benvenuto Cellini (1500-71) and on the other by the Palazzo Vecchio, a brown stone medieval fortress with a 300 foot (91 m) tower. In front of this stands Michelangelo's heroic statue of David—or did, until the original was removed to the Accademia Gallery to escape pollution and this replica was

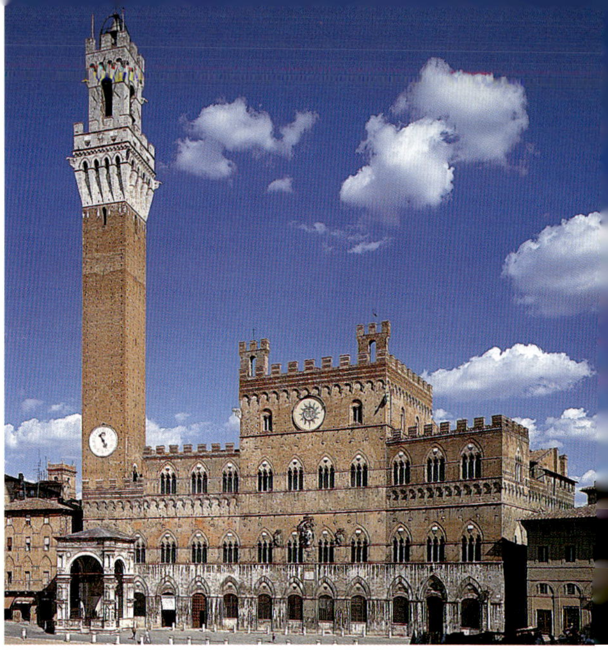

Siena's main square, the Campo (right), is dominated by the splendid 14th-century Gothic Palazzo Pubblico (town hall), with its vretiginous 320-foot (97 m) belltower.

Exploring the regional wines — including Chianti and Brunello di Montalcino (below)—and food such as the sweet panforte, is an esential part of the Italian experience.

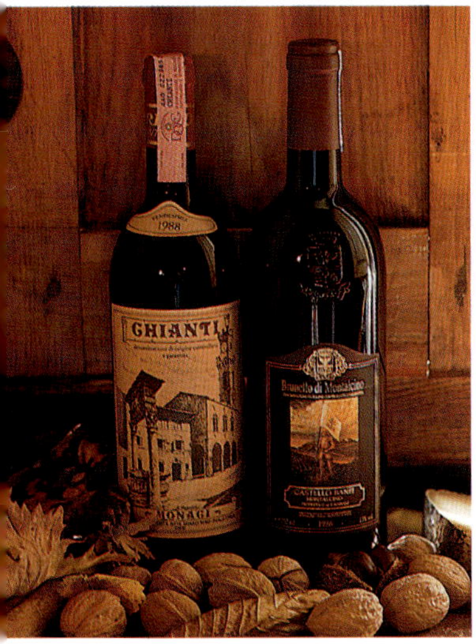

substituted. The adjoining Uffizi is one of the world's great art galleries, crammed with paintings—such as Botticelli's *Birth of Venus* or *Primavera*—so famous they seem images from your own subconscious. The Uffizi becomes very crowded in high season and advance tickets are now required.

A covered walkway runs from the Uffizi across the Ponte Vecchio—the 14th-century bridge that still has its galleries of shops. According to legend, the great poet Dante—another Florentine—glimpsed his beloved Beatrice on this bridge. Standing at dusk on the bridge, with the bats swooping over the waters of the Arno as it flows past the palaces and under the exquisite Renaissance arches of Ponte Santa Trinità—bombed in World WarII but lovingly reassembled—it seems a plausible story. Whatever happens, do not miss Michelangelo's statues in the Medici tombs in the Medici Chapel, which he also designed, adjoining the Church of San Lorenzo. These almost nude recumbent figures, symbolizing Morning, Evening, Day, and Night, seem too tragically noble just to commemorate minor Medici princelings. After so much high art, try one of the excellent pizzas outside. Florence is justly proud of its cuisine: Tuscan olive oil, greenish black and reputedly the world's best, fresh herbs, and vegetables create distinctive flavors for local dishes. The best local hams come from Tuscan wild boar while Pecorino, creamy sheep's cheese, is another treat. Light red Chianti is matched by heavy Vino Nobile di Montepulciano.

Florence's great rival, Siena, 35 miles (54 km) to the south is astonishingly well preserved in its traffic-free center. In Siena even today city life preserves its medieval form, for it is divided into 17 *contrade* (quarters). Every aspect of civic and social life—births, marriages, employment, deaths—takes place within an individual's *contrada*. Rivalry between them is intense, and erupts twice a year in the Palio, a horse race held on July 2 and August 16 in the town's main square.

Known as the Campo, this huge cobbled oval flanked by venerable brick buildings is dominated by the Gothic Palazzo Pubblico (town hall), built in the 14th century and surmounted by its vertiginous 300 foot (100 m) tower. Narrow streets radiate from the Campo. In the 14th century the city planned to double the size of its Duomo, bizarrely striped in white and dark green marble like licorice, by building a new nave. But before it could be completed, Siena's fortunes waned, and the unfinished arcades stand open to the sky like the skeleton of a beached whale.

HILTOP TOWNS OF UMBRIA

Although there is a slow train between Florence and Siena, it is easier to explore the countryside by car. Amid olive groves west of Siena, San Gimignano bristles with medieval towers. To the east lies Umbria, a region with even more rural beauty than Tuscany. To the

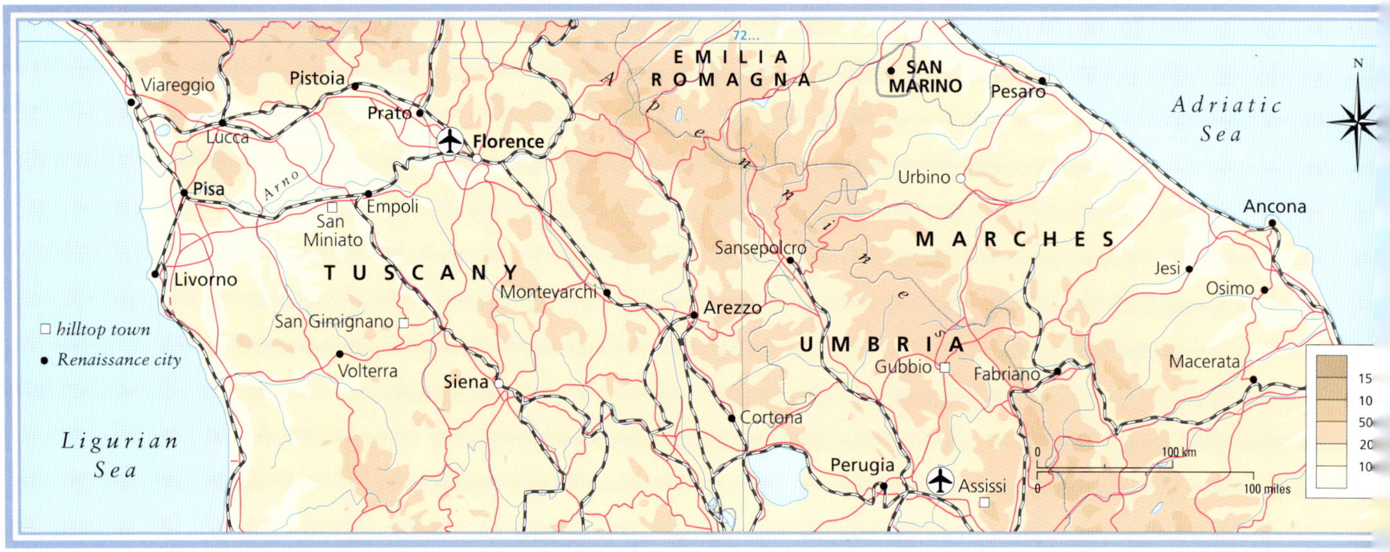

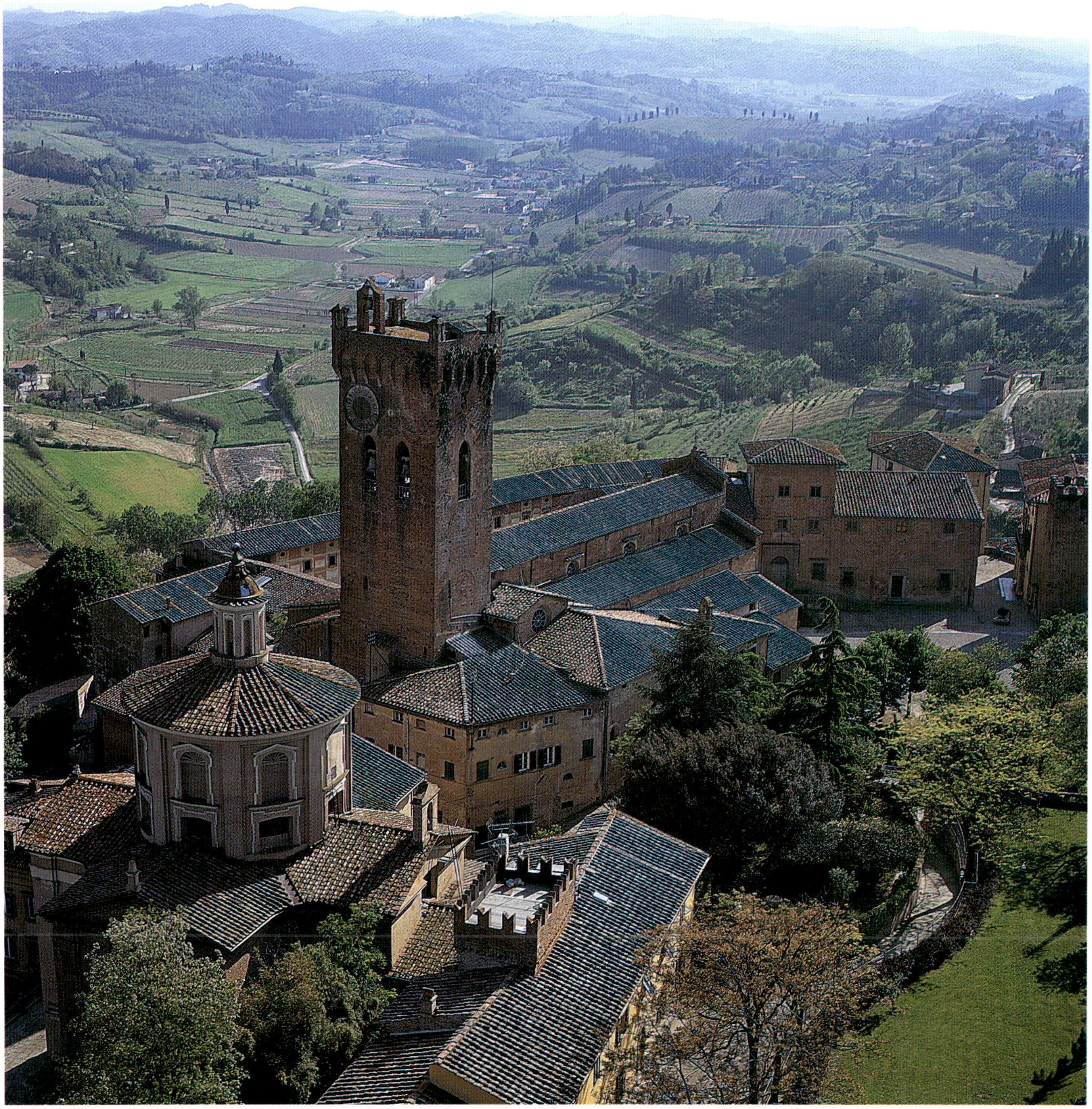

southwest is Assisi, home of St. Francis, recently devastated by an earthquake.

Traveling east, the landscape becomes more mountainous toward the Apennines, where wild boar still forage. Deep snows often make mountain villages inaccessible in winter; while heavy spring and autumn rains keep the tourists at bay. The town of Gubbio clings tenaciously to its windswept crag as it clung for centuries to its freedom. Narrow lanes climb steeply between somber palazzi to the main square where the 14th-century crenellated town hall juts out over a dizzying drop. Some 25 miles (40 km) north of Gubbio, the little town of Urbino crowns a hill. Above a cluster of magnificent Renaissance churches loom the twin towers of the Palazzo Ducale, seat of the Montefeltro dynasty, an untouched, early Renaissance gem, where the great painter Raphael (1483-1520) grew up. Here one of the most brilliant Renaissance courts flourished in the 15th century, and the town today retains much of its 16th-century character. Around 1476 Piero della Francesca painted the twin portraits of Duke Federigo da Montefeltro and his wife (which are now in the Uffizi in Florence). The tough, shrewd politician and his duchess contemplate each other through the picture frames; in the background, hills and plains stretch sublimely away.

Tuscany and Umbria are studded with fortified hilltop towns. San Miniato is crowned by the tower of the Rocca, built by the Emperor Frederick II in the 13th century when the town was an oupost of the Holy Roman Empire.

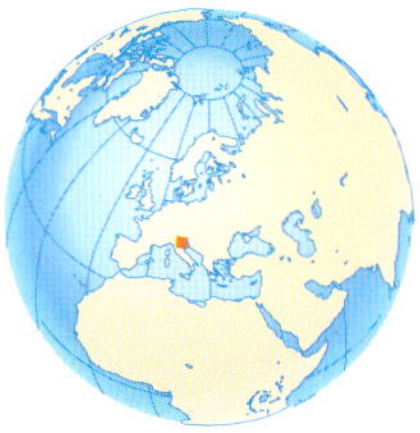

Venice, Queen of the Seas

See Venice, as Goethe suggested—"with artist's eyes"—to appreciate the translucency of light, the reflections and shadows of the waters, the colors and movement on canals and in the piazzas.

FACT FILE

Population: 340,000 in the metropolitan area; 79,000 in the historic center.

Currency: Italian lira.

Climate: Generally Mediterranean; very hot July—September; in winter frequently foggy, but it rarely snows, though it can flood.

What to take: Waterproof footwear and warm clothing in winter and umbrellas any time of the year.

Best time: October—March (to avoid the crowds) but beware the busy, if picturesque, Carnival season in the ten days before Lent (variable date).

Nearest airport: Marco Polo Airport is on the mainland, 8 miles (13 km) north of the historic center by watertaxi or take the bus to Piazzale Roma.

What to buy: Antiques, jewelry, glass, lace, masks, and costumes.

City accommodation: Can be a problem; book well in advance.

VENICE OWES ITS EXISTENCE TO THE SEA—to experience the full truth of this statement, take a boat out to the islands of the lagoon around it and watch the city recede into the wide expanse of water and sky, becoming a mirage of domes, pinnacles, towers, and palaces. Like many of the world's most evocative cities—Istanbul, St. Petersburg, New York—Venice is untypical of the country to which it belongs, but nowhere else is really like Venice at all. Whether sweltering beneath the summer sun or swathed in winter fogs, the city is literally unique.

Venice is built on a collection of islands, seahorse shaped, and crisscrossed by more than 150 canals and 400 bridges, which were settled in the 5th century by refugees from the mainland. The republic they established lasted more than a thousand years, growing fabulously rich on trade with the East, extending its rule over islands and cities. Such mixed eastern

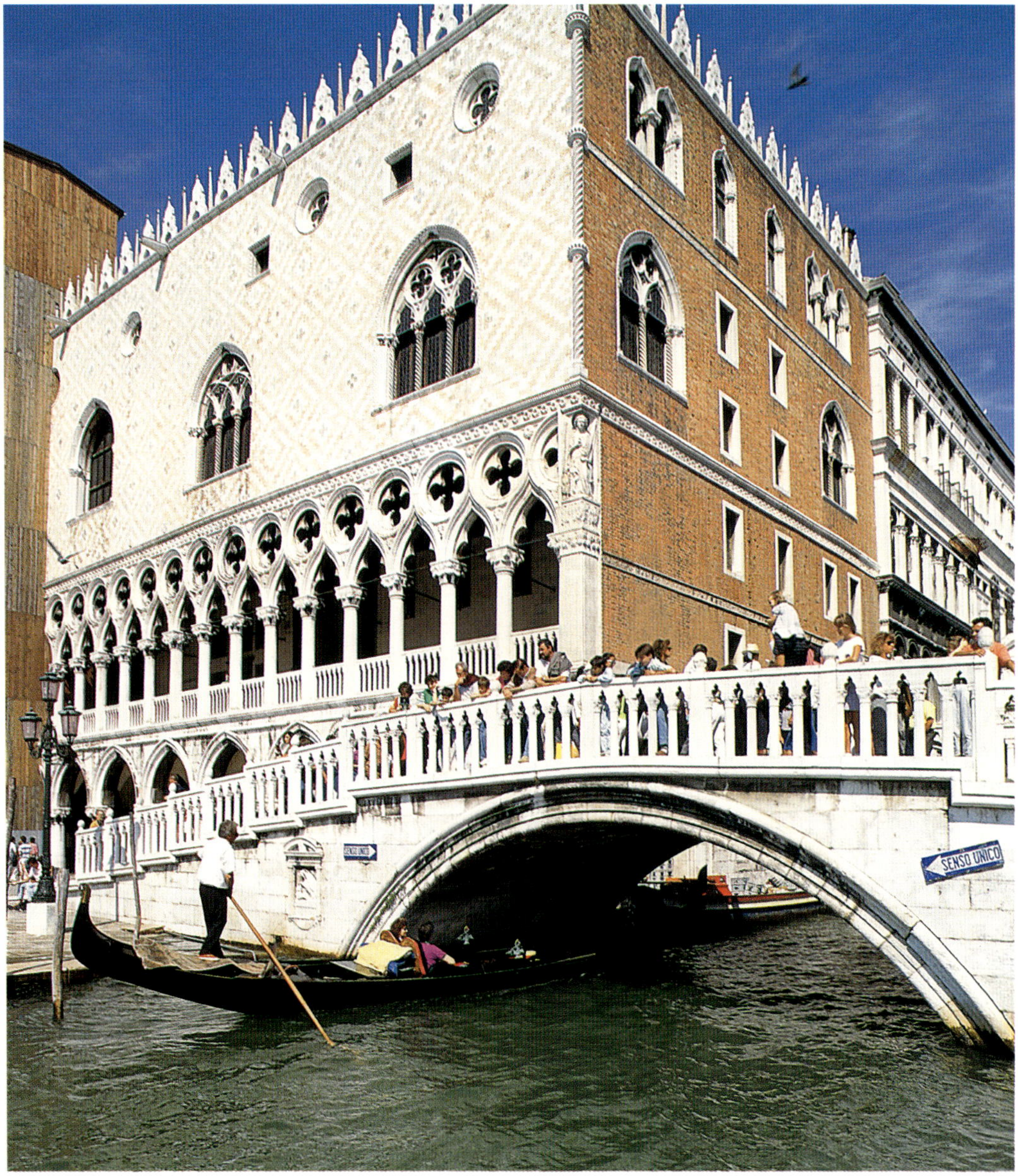

A gondola glides beneath the Ponte della Paglia in front of the 15th-century Palazzo Ducale, where the most secret machinations of the Venetian State were once conducted.

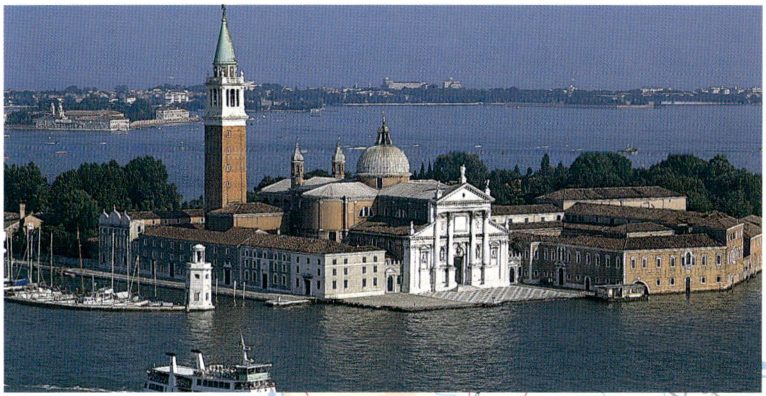

★ *The island of San Giorgio Maggiore (left), with its church by the Renaissance architect Palladio, lies just south of the city's core across the waters of the Bassino San Marco.*

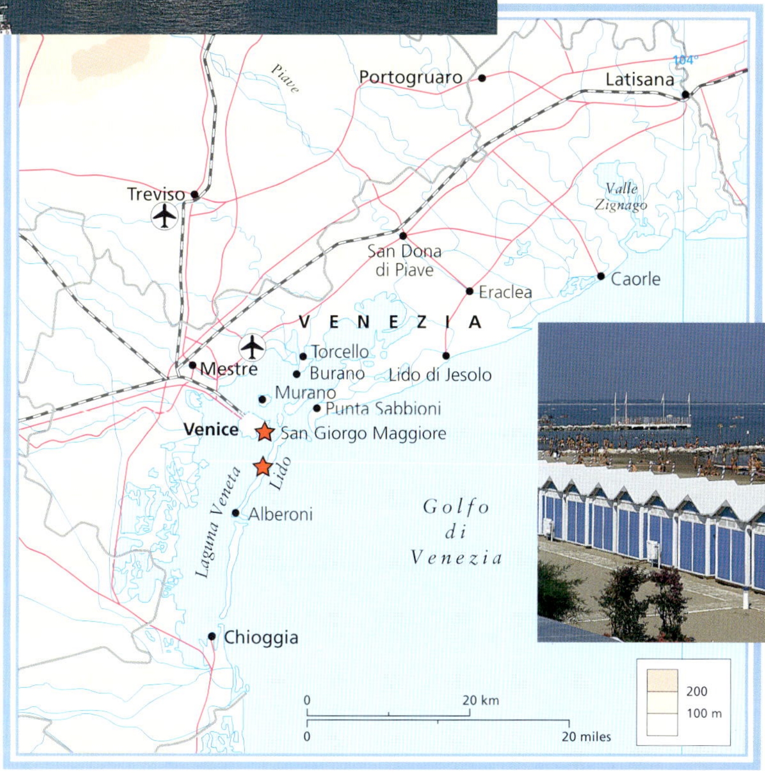

"STREETS COVERED WITH WATER. PLEASE ADVISE," an American writer once cabled his publisher. A gondola can take you through a labyrinth of canals.

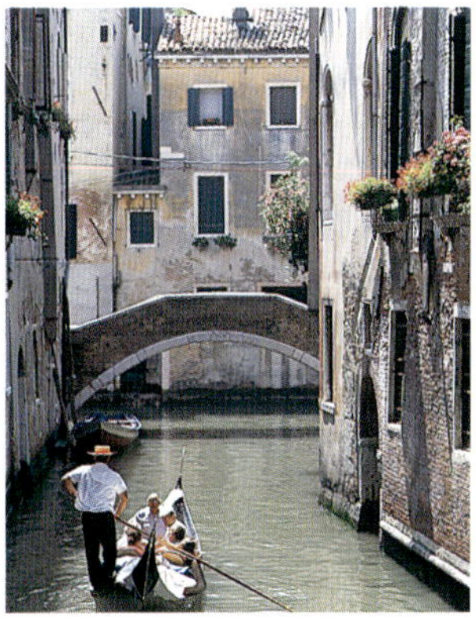

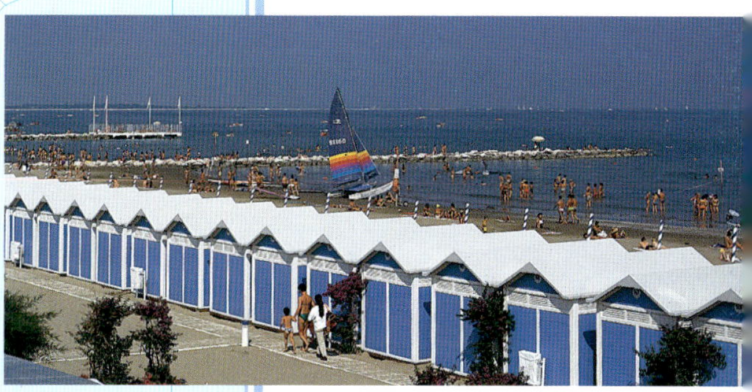

★ *The Lido—the long strip of sand that forms Venice's seaside playground—still basks in the faded elegance of a turn-of-the-century resort.*

influences, and especially such wealth, are reflected in Venetian art and architecture—often fantastically rich and ornate—but not noticeably in its food, where seafood is the chief allure. *Vongole* (small clams) are a local delicacy, caught in the lagoon and fried live in olive oil and garlic.

In Venice you either walk—or go by water. To see Venice the very first time (assuming you are not coming from the airport by water taxi), take a *vaporetto* (water bus) from the railroad station or the (only) parking lot in Piazzale Roma. On the slow journey down the Canal Grande, you see palace after palace rise from the waters, some Gothic in style such as the fanciful 15th century Ca' d'Oro, some Renaissance such as the massive somber Ca' Grande, but almost nothing seems to have changed in the two centuries since Canaletto painted it all.

After chugging under the bridge of the Rialto, once the city's commercial center, the vaporetto reaches the Piazza San Marco (St. Mark's Square). This immense square, though often crowded, remains the heart of Venice, with Renaissance arcades on three sides housing famous cafés such as Florian's or Quadri, once Richard Wagner's favorite. Napoleon called it the "finest drawing room in Europe," and orchestras still play here every evening. Be warned: these cafés are not cheap! On the Piazza's fourth side rises Venice's cathedral: St. Mark's Basilica, a five-domed Byzantine church overlaid by an extraordinary fantasy of pinnacles and gold stars on an azure ground. On its front stand four ancient Roman bronze horses looted from the Hippodrome at Byzantium (Istanbul)—but the ones you see now are reproductions, the originals being inside to protect them from pollution. The tall campanile (bell tower) beside the Basilica is also a replica, the original having collapsed with minimal damage to surrounding buildings in 1902. To the right is the Palazzo Ducale (Ducal Place) with its Gothic arcades and red and white

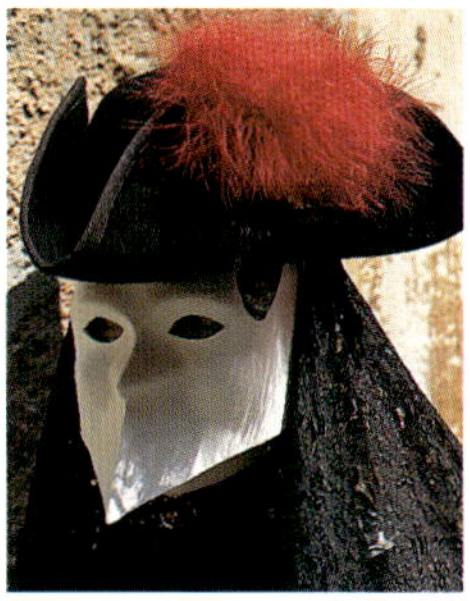

The Carnival at the end of Lent (above) is one of the city's oldest traditions; it was ruled by commedia dell' arte characters such as Harlequin.

Overlooked by the exotic splendor of St. Mark's Basilica, the Piazza San Marco (below) is one of the world's classic café locations.

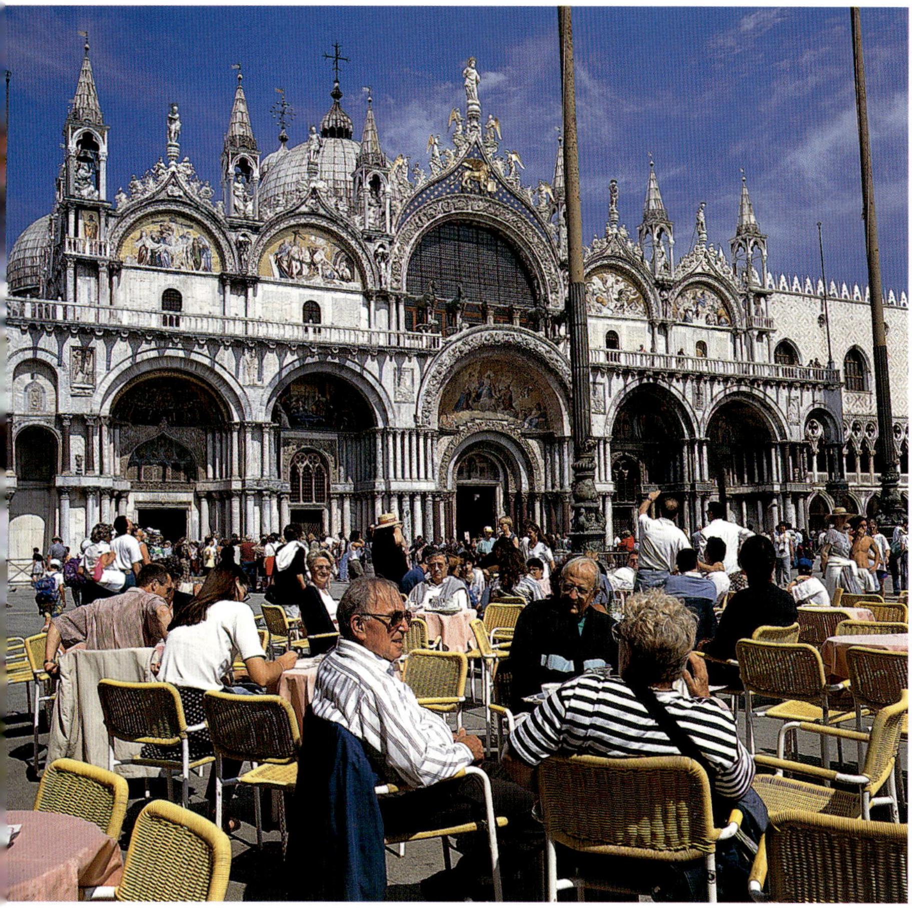

diamond-patterned façade. The Republic was ruled from here, and from here prisoners were led over the Bridge of Sighs to the prison. Casanova, most famous of its prisoners, escaped over the roof of the Palace, the only captive ever to do so.

Almost any turning in Venice will bring you face to face with some architectural marvel or a gallery full of world-class paintings. Among the many churches which give the Venetian skyline its air of elegant fantasy are the Renaissance Santa Maria dei Miracoli, the Baroque Santa Maria della Salute (with paintings by Titian and Tintoretto), and on the island of the same name, San Giorgio Maggiore by the Renaissance genius Palladio, whose pale dome is one of the city's landmarks. The Accademia Gallery houses masterpieces of Venetian art down the centuries but for a more modern note try the Peggy Guggenheim Foundation in the half-built Palazzo Venier, noted for its Surrealist art.

Sooner or later everyone gets lost in the labyrinth of canalside pathways that is Venice away from the crowds. Despite being one of the world's most touristed cities, you need only take a wrong turn to find yourself in a narrow alley beside walls punctated only by barred windows, before you emerge into some square basking in the afternoon sun. Then, footsore and hot, is the time to take to the water. Gondolas, the obvious first choice, are as fantastic as anything in Venice—fantastically impractical and expensive, but very romantic if you don't object to bobbing around in the wakes of the motorboats. If you want to gondola cheaply, take a *traghetto*—communal gondolas which cross the Canal Grande at various fixed points.

The Lagoon and Islands

When you tire of the city, take another *vaporetto* to the lagoon and islands. The *vaporetto* from Fondamente Nuove chugs along through the (normally) placid lagoon like an old train pulling up at wayside halts lying scarcely above the water. Murano, biggest of the lagoon islands, is crowded with glassmakers' workshops; the craft has been practiced here for centuries, and if the island's products—multicolored fish with arabesque fins, cute little dogs—are often kitsch, there's undeniable satisfaction in taking home something you have seen created with such skill. Burano, bright with colored houses, is famed for its fishing and lacemaking, and again you can watch its lacemakers practice their traditional calling. Torcello, the farthest of these scattered islands, was among the first to be settled; some of the houses on the Rialto were moved stone by stone from here when the island became malarial and was abandoned. Today it is a lonely, evocative place, with little besides its imposingly plain cathedral standing amid overgrown fields. If you enjoy solitude (like Ernest Hemingway who wrote *Across the River and Into the Trees* here) you can stay at Torcello's one small hotel, but you'll be stranded on the island after the last *vaporetto* leaves in the early evening.

Biggest by far of all these islands, the one which shelters the lagoon from the sea, is the 9-mile (14 km) long Lido. The poet Byron, when he lived in Venice in 1816-19, used to ride along the then-deserted beach under the pine trees, but for the last century it has been Venice's seaside resort. Grand hotels line the wide beach, and none is grander than the Grand Hotel des Bains, a luxurious *fin de siecle* building where the German novelist Thomas Mann wrote *Death in Venice* in 1911 and where, 60 years later Luchino Visconti made the movie of the book. But more typically Venetian in its ornate fantasy is the Moorish-style Hotel Excelsior. Even if you don't want to swim or sunbathe, the Lido is worth a visit.

The mouth of the Grand Canal (right) is dominated by the domes of Santa Maria della Salute. Begun in the 1630s in thanksgiving for the city's deliverance from the plague, the church took 50 years to complete.

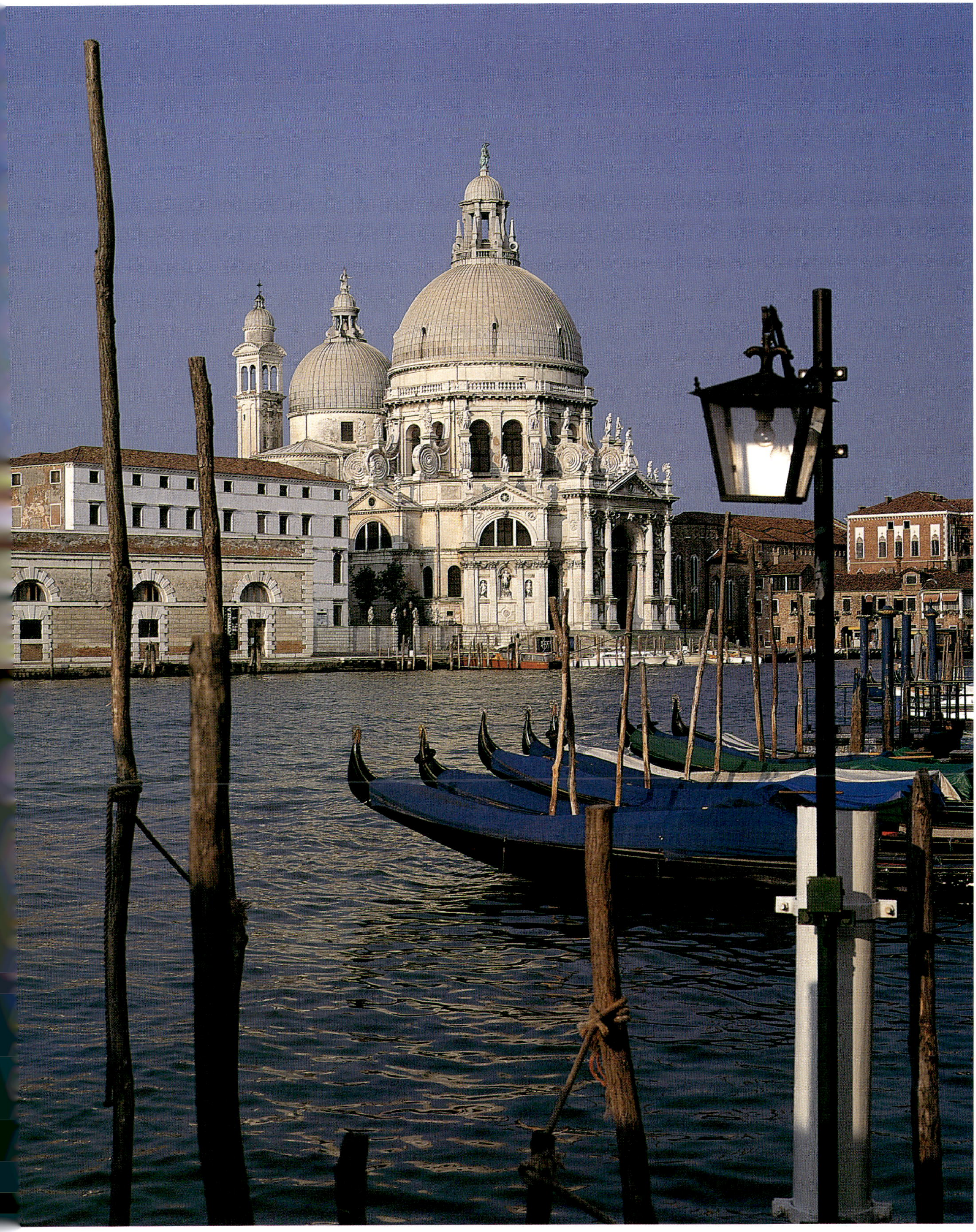

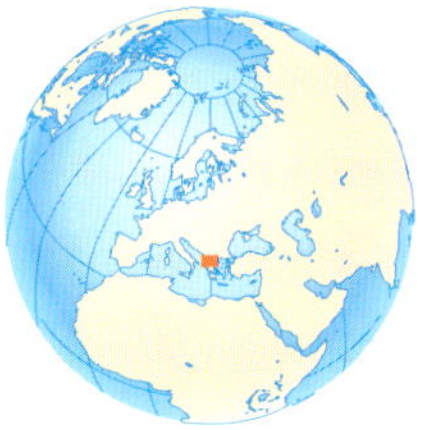

The Meteora

Pinnacles of rock with monasteries perched precariously on their summits form a dramatic gateway to the backbone of Greece.

THE GIANT, ELEPHANTINE STUMPS of the Meteora erupt suddenly and with dizzying verticality from the completely flat plain of Thessaly. They are an extraordinary and unexpected geological formation contained in a tiny 25 square miles (65 sq km) at the innermost point of the plain, standing like natural monoliths marking the gateway to the Pindhos mountains, the backbone of mainland Greece. The mountains beyond them stutter to a halt in these great splinters of blue-gray rock, soaring hundreds of feet into the air above the fertile valley floor, fissured and scarred by the prehistoric seas that once covered the region.

Such a landscape is surreal enough in itself, but stranger still are the Greek Orthodox monasteries that perch on its almost inaccessible peaks. Hermits first began to seek solitude in which to commune with God on these pinnacles in the 9th century. It is extraordinary to contemplate exactly how they scaled the sheer rock faces, which climbers rate among the toughest in Europe—St. Athanasios, who founded the Grand Meteoron in the 1300s, is said to have flown up on the back of an eagle. Until stairs were hewn into the rocks in the 1920s, all access was by means of ladders or a net winched up by rope. One traveler, asking how often the rope was replaced, was given the reassuring answer, "When the Good Lord permits it to break."

The area was long a lawless border country, part of the Serbian empire created by Stephan Dushan in the 14th century, later the refuge of Greek rebels against Ottoman rule, and then the stronghold of Greek partisans in the Second World War and communist fighters in the grim civil war that followed. At its peak in the 1500s, the Meteora—the name literally means "suspended in air"—included 13 monasteries and some 20 dependencies, drawing revenues from estates as far off as the Danube valley. Decline set in during the 1700s, when the least accessible monasteries began to be abandoned, and by the middle of the present century there was just a handful of monks and nuns struggling to maintain the disintegrating buildings. They were saved from complete ruin only by the construction of the road that made the monasteries accessible to tourism. If the Meteora's sense of solitude has diminished, at least the survival of the monasteries has been assured.

WORKING MONASTERIES

Many people "do" the Meteora in a day or a weekend. Better to explore on foot the high meadows with, in spring, the wild flowers for which Greece is justly famed, and the secret clefts and strange, turbulent rock formations between the monasteries. You will also discover abandoned troglodytic dwellings and monasteries, and trace the fly-on-the-wall progress of climbers up the awesome cliff faces. Five monasteries are still functioning. Perched at the top of a massive

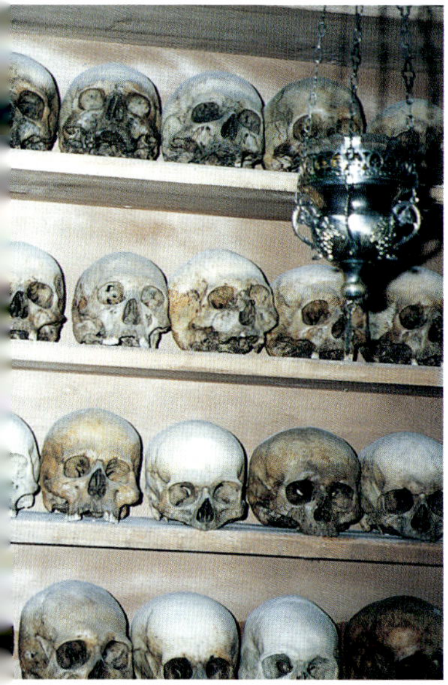

Skulls of former head monks (above) in the chantry of Great Meteoron greet today's tourists.

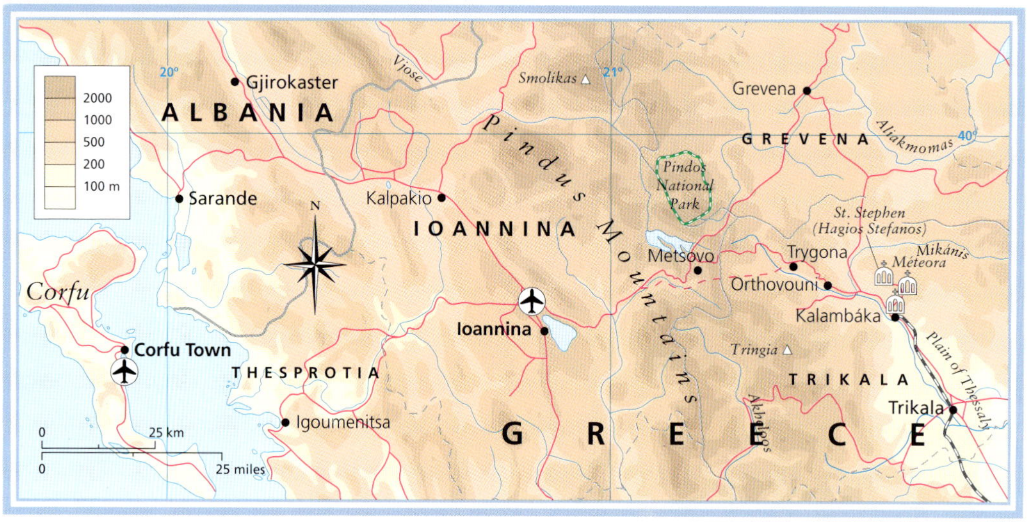

Materials to build the precariously positioned monasteries (right) were hauled to the summits by rope ladders and pulleys.

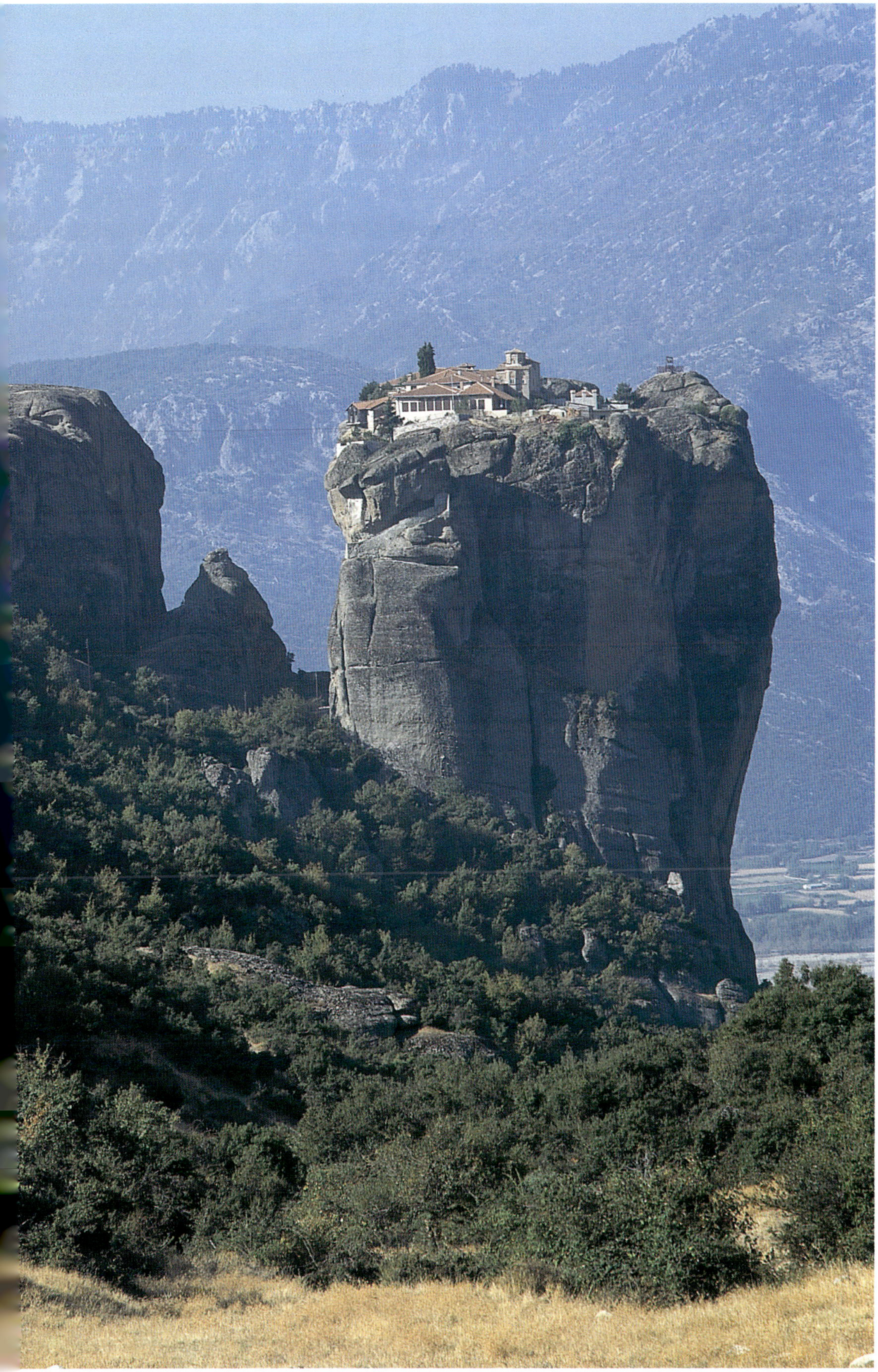

FACT FILE

Currency: Greek drachma.

Climate: Wet and cool November—March, hot in summer.

Time to go: Late January, early February for Greece's "halcyon days," a spell of fair weather in midwinter, and April, to avoid the crowds, catch spring sun, flowers, and Greek Easter.

What to take: Respectable clothes (skirts for women); walking gear.

Nearest airport: Thessaloniki, but Athens has far more flights.

Public transportation: There are regular buses to Kalambaka from Ioannina, Trikala, Thessaloniki, and Athens, and trains from Thessaloniki or Athens, changing at Stavros.

Accommodation: 2 camp sites in Kastraki, and various small hotels and tavernas.

The honeycombed rockfaces were once inhabited by troglodytes and made into chapels, the ruins of which remain.

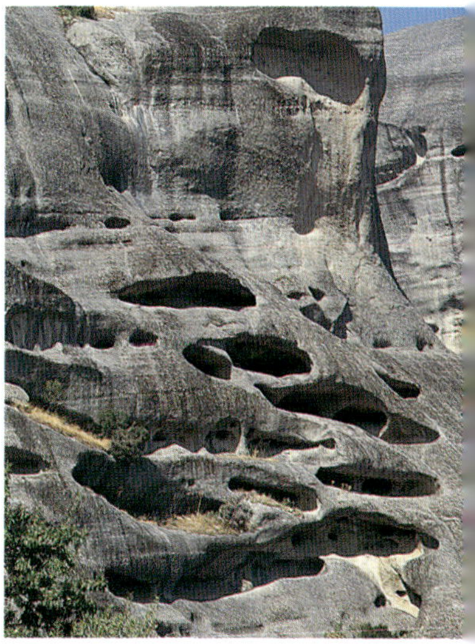

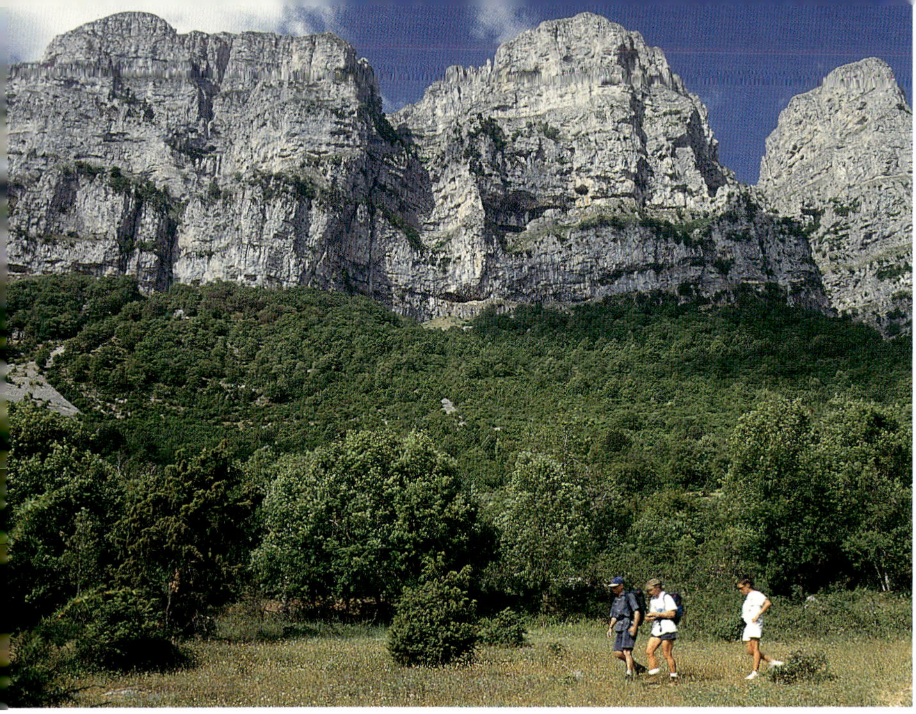

The mighty Pindhos mountains (left), the backbone of mainland Greece, provide unspoiled walking country.

From the hidden valleys and high meadows of the Meteora are breathtaking views of the Thessaly Plain and the Pindhos mountains (right).

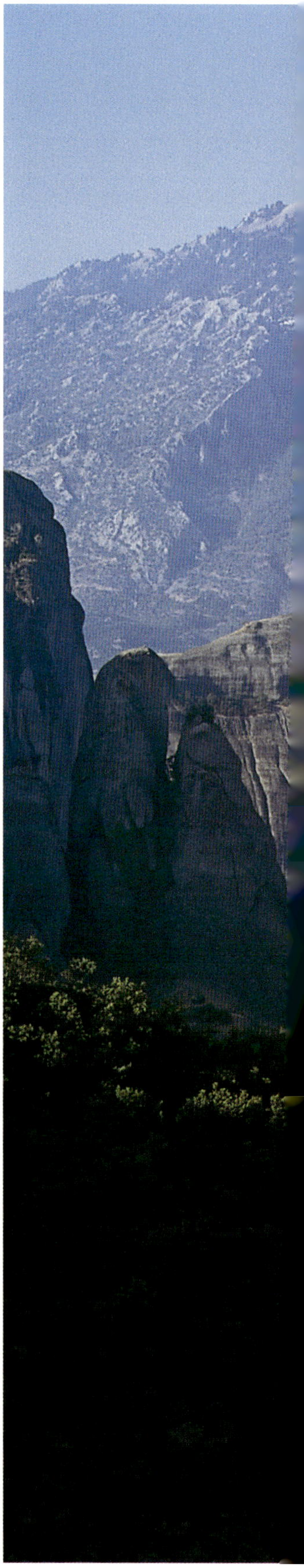

1,750- foot (533-m) spur known as the Platys Lithos (broad stone) is the highest of them, the Great Meteoron. Its high-domed Church of the Transfiguration was built in the 1500s on the traditional Byzantine square cross plan. The interior is surprisingly light and airy, displaying the well preserved frescos to advantage. The 1557 refectory, with its round stone table and vaulted roof supported by five pillars, was rescued from dereliction in 1960 and converted into a museum in which many fine icons and other monastic treasures are displayed. The views from the Great Meteoron across to the neighboring pinnacles and the tantalizing ring of mountains are an incentive to stay longer and explore the area at leisure.

The monastery of St. Stephen (Hagios Stefanos), though the farthest from Kalambaka by road, is the only monastery visible from the village. It is also the most accessible, since it can be reached from the main mass of Kuklioli hill by a drawbridge. A cobbled path climbs through a dark, vaulted entrance passage into the sunlit courtyard flanked by wooden galleries. There are two churches: the plain, late 18th-century Church of St. Charalambos, and the dark and somewhat somber St. Stephen's, built in the 1300s. Rousanou, also known as Hagia Varvara, is a small monastery now occupied by nuns. It sits tightly on a sharp spire of rock close to the main mountain face, to which it is now connected by an iron footbridge. There is scarcely an inch of ground to spare, and the wooden upper stories are built out over the vertiginous abyss.

Each of the inhabited monasteries at Meteora charges a small admission fee. Orthodox standards of dress are strictly enforced. Sleeveless clothing and shorts are prohibited, and women must wear skirts. Some monasteries provide shawls and skirts at the entrance, but don't rely on this. Monasteries may be visited all year round, but from July to October they are crowded, and in May every child in Greece seems to come here on a school trip. There are hotels in the village of Kastraki, from where the monasteries can be reached on foot, but there is more choice—and a fine 13th-century Byzantine cathedral—in Kalambaka, about a mile down the road. Both villages have become very tourist-orientated, but the old walled town of Trikkala—once the capital of Serbian emperors—just 13 miles (22 km) away is connected to Kalambaka by a regular bus service.

If you want to avoid the crowds, go from November through April. Though the weather will be cool and often damp, you may be rewarded by days of crystal-clear winter sunshine, the "Halcyon Days" between January and mid-February. Then you can look out across to long- abandoned inaccessible monasteries, unvisited for centuries except by the Egyptian vultures and red kites that nest there. And if you're really lucky you may even see a golden eagle, like the one that bore St. Athanasios to the peak of the Great Meteoron, riding a thermal far below you.

DEEP INTO THE BACKBONE OF GREECE

The main E92 road is one of the most spectacular mountain routes in a country full of them, and the only pass over the Pindhos that remains open all year. It takes you deep into virgin Greece, the source of five of t he country's major rivers, where deep limestone ravines are clad in forests of beech, oak, chestnut, and fir. Away from the main towns, the most aggressive sign of tourism is the occasional hiker, where physical isolation has preserved regional dialects and traditions from outside influences—including Turkish domination. Metsovo, some 37 miles (60 km) beyond the Meteora (and on the bus route), has bowed to the pressures of commercial tourism, but is perched on two sides of a ravine looking over splendid mountains to the south and east.

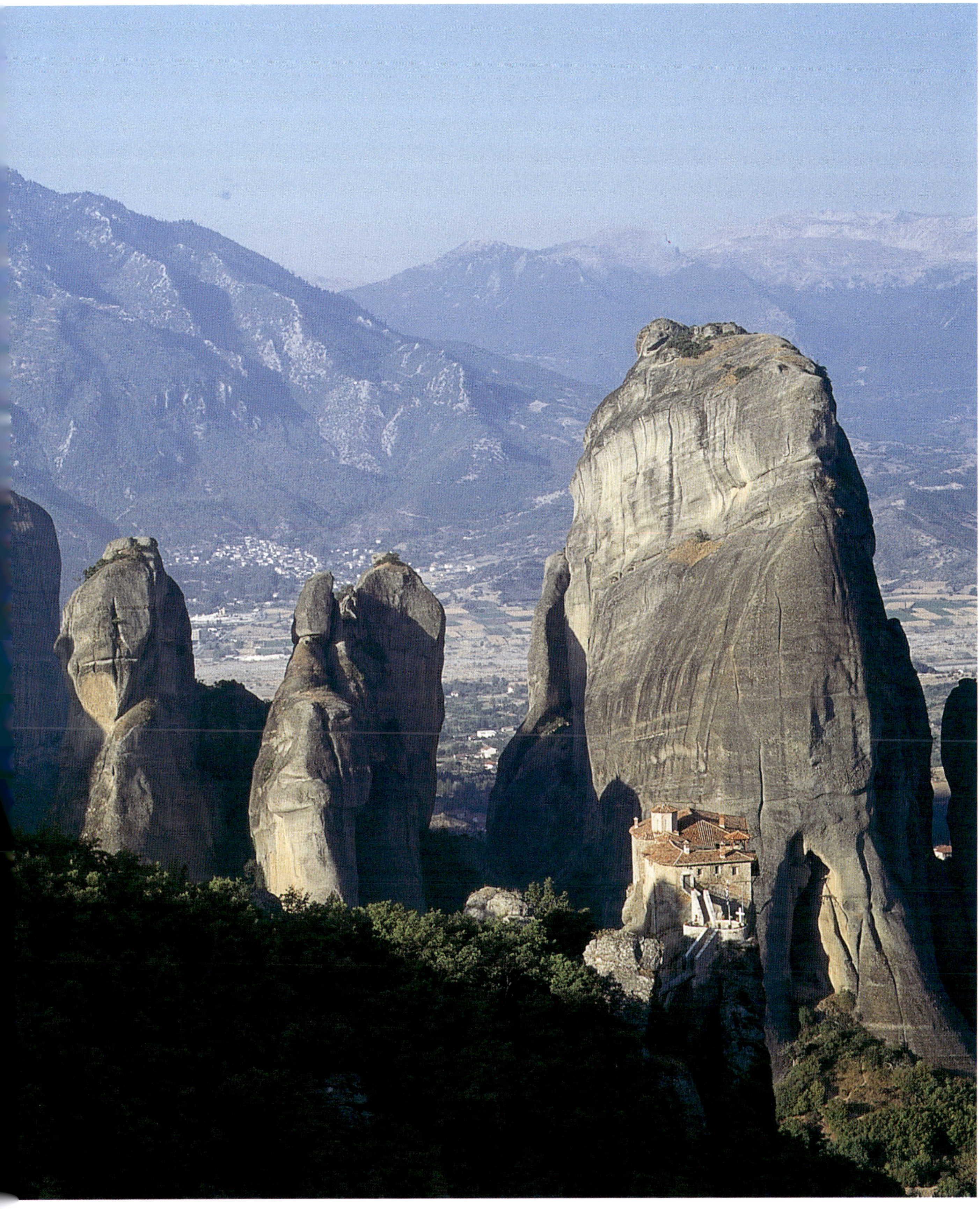

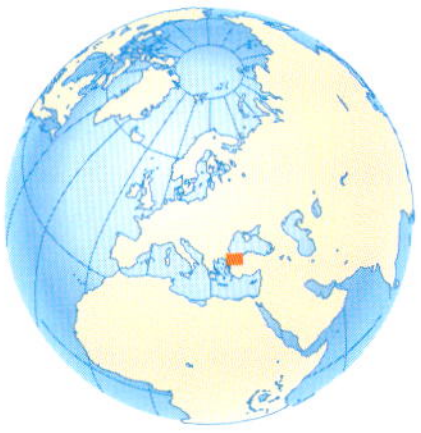

Where East Meets West

"It is more like some enchanted city out of 'The Thousand and One Nights' than like any real town built of bricks, stones, and mortar..."—Demetrius Coufopoulos, 1895.

FACT FILE

Population: 10 million.

Currency: Turkish lira.

Climate: Mixed maritime/continental; often hot June —August, it may snow in winter.

Time to go: Any time, but spring is most pleasant.

Nearest airport: Ataturk International Airport is 15 miles (24 km) from the city with a bus service into the center.

What to buy: Carpets, jewelry, leather goods.

What to take: A moneybelt to deter pickpockets, warm clothes in winter.

City accomodation: Normally plentiful, from the cheap, including the youth hostel situated right opposite Hagia Sophia, to the luxurious, including the faded splendor of the old Pera Palace Hotel, once a haven for travelers on the Orient Express.

THIS ANCIENT CITY AT THE MEETING POINT of Europe and Asia has had three names in its long history: Byzantium, Constantinople, and Istanbul. Today it is filled with the staggering legacy of the two empires that made it their capital: the Byzantine Greeks and Ottoman Turks. Still Turkey's greatest city, marvelously sited on a peninsula, it is among the most colorful, noisy, and fascinating places in the world, a mecca for shoppers, gourmets (Turkish cuisine is rightly renowned), and travelers.

The double Theodosian walls—named for the 5th century Byzantine emperor who had them built—stretch 4 miles (6.4 km) across the neck of the peninsula and are still wonderfully intact. With the area they enclose, they have been designated a UNESCO World Heritage Site. Modern Istanbul sprawls far

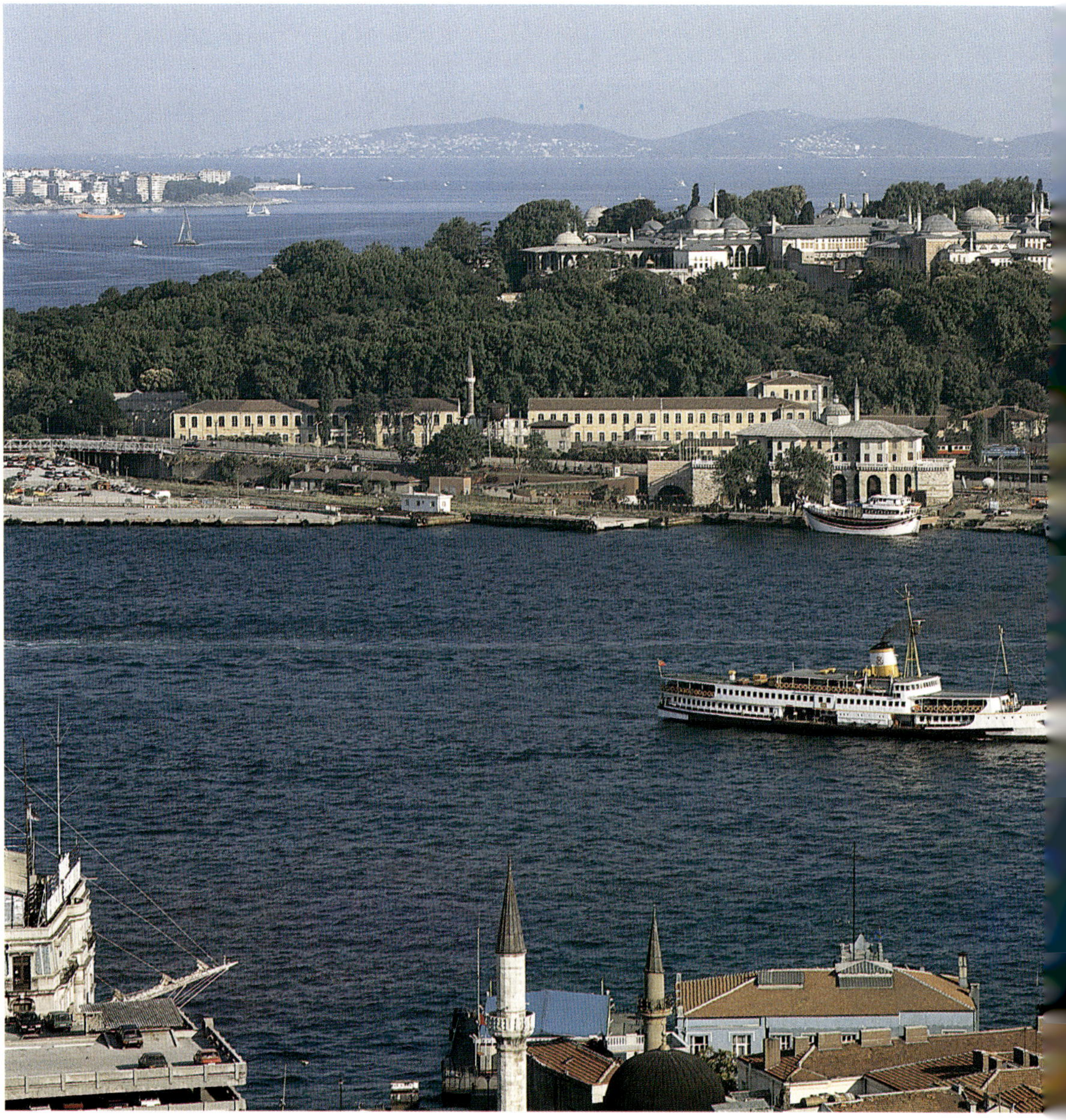

The Golden Horn (right) divides Istanbul in two, with the old imperial center on one side, and more recent cultural and business development on the other.

beyond the walls but within them old Istanbul forms a complete contrast to the manicured historic sites of western Europe. Here antiquity—just—survives cheek by jowl with the present: the homeless squat in the towers of Roman walls, antique capitals serve as bird baths in a muddy yard, an autorepair shop turns out to be part of an Ottoman building, and football is played in a filled-in Byzantine reservoir. As you admire thousand-year-old monuments, the modern city's traffic roars past inches away. Such chaotic intermingling of past and present reflects the city's mixed ancestry.

Looking for a new capital, Roman Emperor Constantine (reigned A.D. 306–337) chose the Greek city of Byzantium, defensibly sited, which then became Constantinople, city of Constantine. After the fall of the

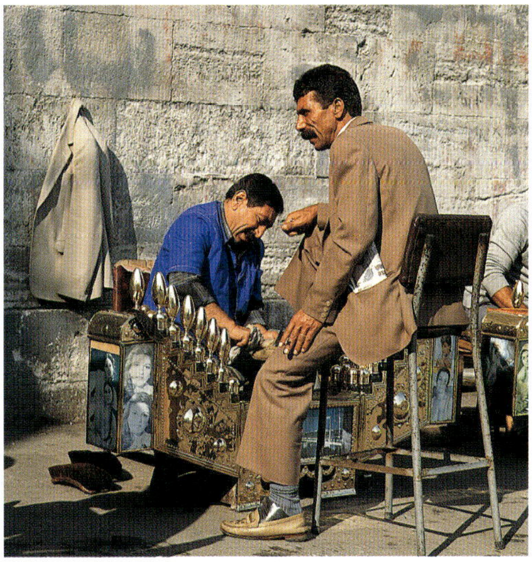

Shoe shine is just one of the many trades enacted throughout the old city.

West Roman Empire in 476, Constantinople continued to rule the slowly declining East Roman or Byzantine Empire for a thousand years until it fell to the Ottoman Turks in 1453. The city's conqueror Sultan Mehmet II (reigned 1451–81) made it capital of the Ottoman Empire, which it remained until Turkey became a republic in 1922 with its capital at Ankara.

Today, if you stand in the heart of the old city on the site of the former Byzantine hippodrome—now just a grassy park—your eye will be drawn to two majestic

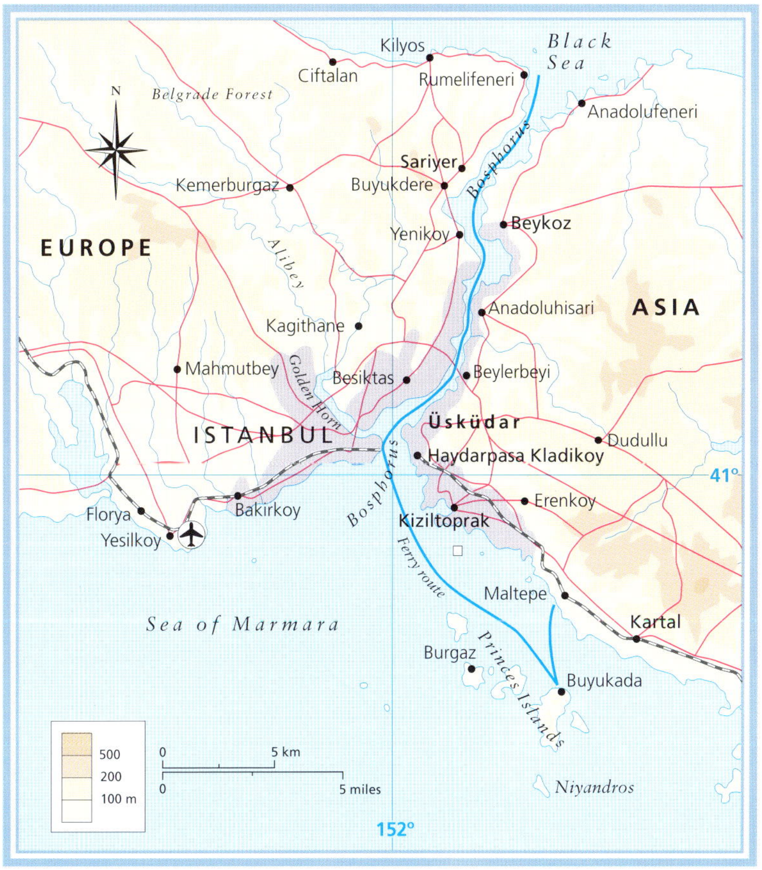

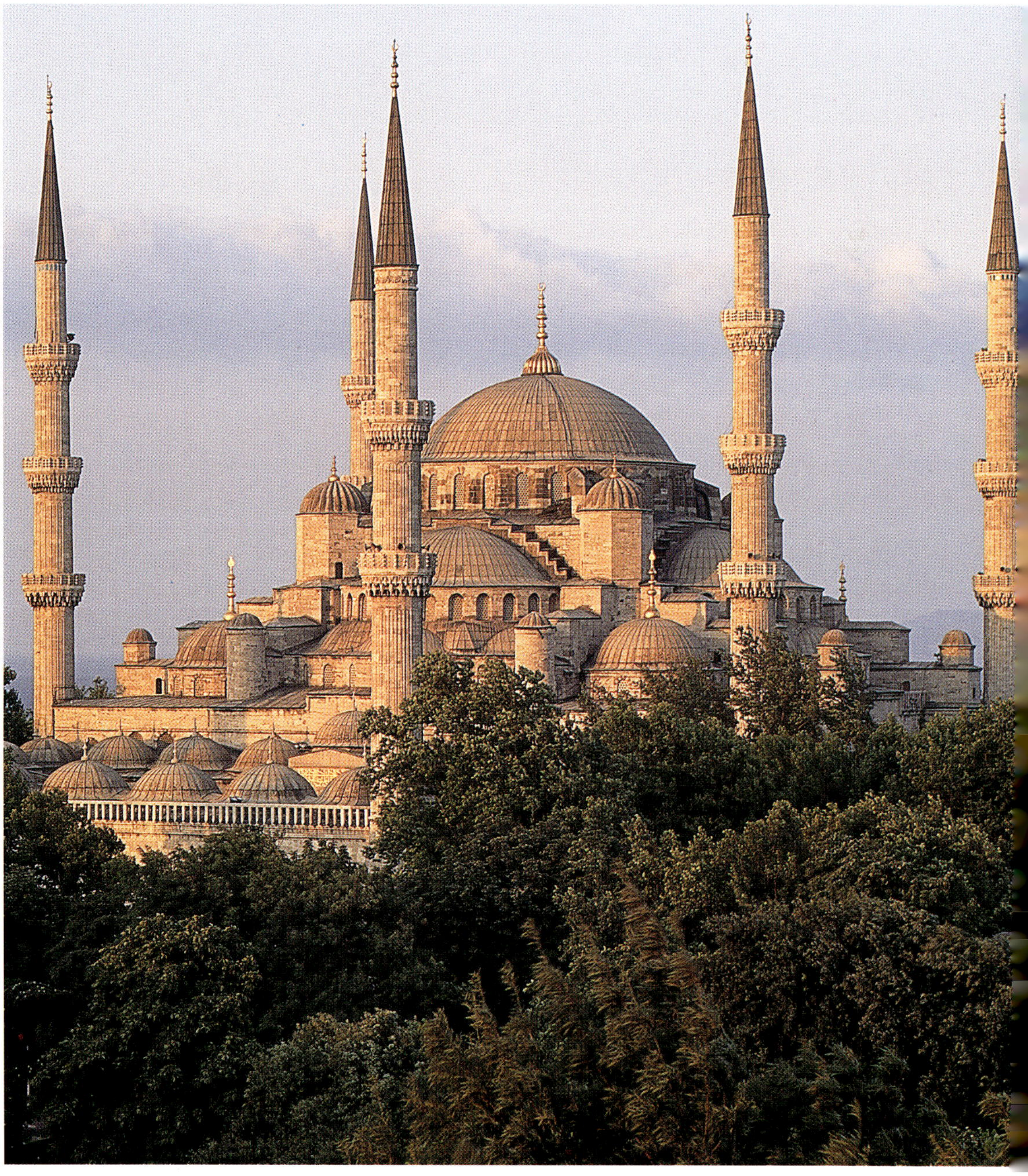

Over 20,000 Iznik ware tiles decorate the interior of the Blue Mosque (right), and gave it its name. On the outside, however, its dome and six minarets are the impressive features.

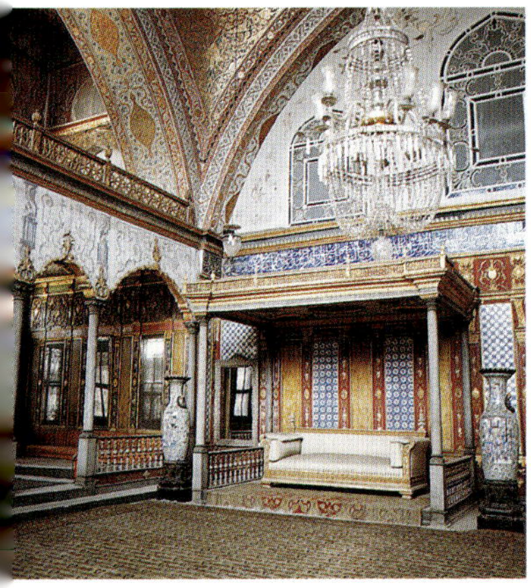

The imperial hall of the harem in the Topkapi Palace (above) where the man of the house lived with his wives. The word "harem" is Arabic for "forbidden," but increasing numbers of rooms are being opened to the public.

domes. The older and smaller is that of the great Byzantine cathedral of Hagia Sophia—the name means Holy Wisdom—which was built by Emperor Justinian in 533-39. Its shallow dome, rising 180 feet (55 m) above the ground and spanning 100 feet (31 m), is now flanked by four minarets added by the Ottomans after it was converted into a mosque but the interior preserves much of its original appearance, a vast, airy space with columned galleries, glittering mosaics, and multicolored marble brought from every part of the Empire. On the walls angels and other Byzantine icons can still just be seen. Hagia Sofia is now a museum.

The Byzantines themselves never surpassed Hagia Sophia and came to regard its construction as almost miraculous, but the Ottomans finally did so with the other great dome which dominates Istanbul's skyline: the six-minaret Sultan Ahmet Mosque. Built between 1609 and 1616 by the architect Mehmet, it is often known as the Blue Mosque on account of the blue and white Iznik tiles that give the interior its cool elegance. It is still a working mosque.

At the tip of the peninsula is Topkapi Palace, a graceful complex of courtyards, apartments, pavilions, and gardens overlooking the waters of the Golden Horn and Bosphorus. Construction started in 1466 and for centuries this was the residence of the sultans from which the vast Ottoman empire was governed; by the 1800s some 5,000 officials, courtiers, and servants lived within its walls. Opened to the public in 1924, it is now the world's largest palace museum, displaying 86,000 historic artifacts including costumes, jewelry, furniture, and a marvelous display of calligraphy. The gardens of Topkapi now make a welcome oasis of quiet in a city notably lacking green spaces—and you can look out across the busy maritime traffic of the Bosphorus to the shores of Asia.

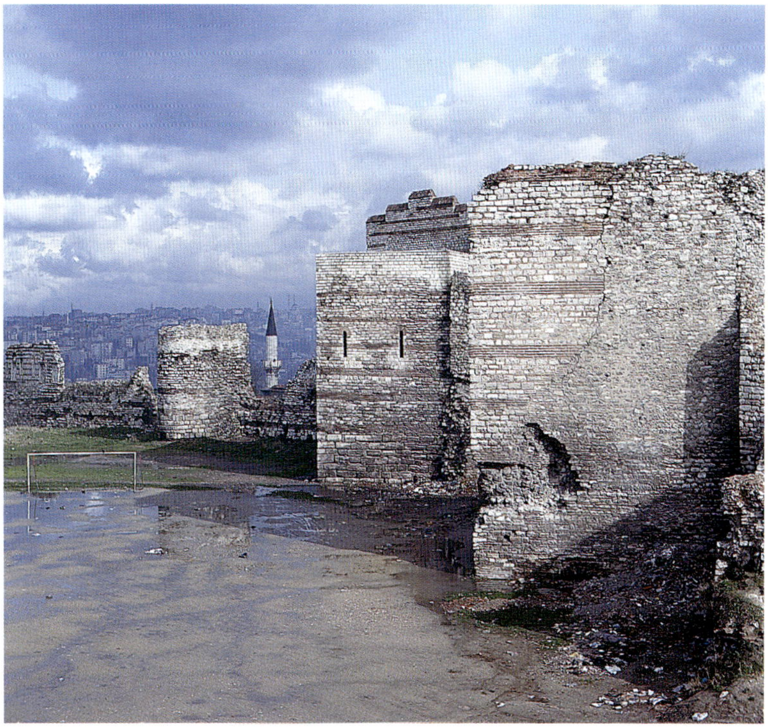

THE GRANDEST BAZAAR

Istanbul is an exciting city for shoppers, especially those who are good at haggling. The Kapali Carsi or Covered Bazaar, the world's largest, dates back to early Ottoman times. This labyrinth of streets and passages houses more than 4,000 shops selling Turkish crafts: carpets, hand-painted ceramics, gold jewelry, copper- and brass-ware, meerschaum pipes, and leather goods. Beware of buying anything that could be classed as an antique—in the unlikely event of it turning out to be genuine, you'd be liable to a prison sentence if you tried to take it out of the country without a license. Behind the Yeni Mosque at Eminönü is the Misir Carsisi (Egyptian or Spice Bazaar), where the air is laden with the scents of caraway, cinnamon, mint, saffron, and thyme.

Turkish food is considered one of the three great classic cuisines of the world—along with French and Chinese—though vegetarians should beware that many innocuous looking dishes of chickpeas, okra, or other vegetables are made with beef stock and may contain a small cube of meat for good measure. Fish in particular is excellent in Istanbul—the catch is landed directly on the waterfront from the teeming waters of the Bosphorus, where you can buy it freshly grilled over charcoal and served between slices of bread. For a more leisurely meal, there is a cluster of good fish restaurants around Kumkapi. Turkish beer, notably Efes, and wine are good, too.

The sea is never far away—as you turn down an alley between ramshackle wooden houses you may catch sight of its glittering waters, and at night you can hear the foghorns of the great tankers laboring through the Bosphorus. Some of the best excursions from the city are by boat. A two-hour ferry ride from Sırceki Pier will take you to the Princes Islands. Once a place of exile for out of favor Byzantine royalty, these islands in the Sea of Marmara are covered in pine forest and wild lilac, dotted with fine old wooden mansions and Greek Orthodox monasteries, and remain entirely free of motor traffic. From Eminönü you can take a two-hour boat trip up the Bosphorus to the Black Sea. Trees spill down to the water's edge as you pass the Dolmabahce Palace, once the residence of sultans, old villages such as Arnavutköy with their little Greek tavernas and excellent fish restaurants, and the Belgrade Forest with its elaborate system of Ottoman aqueducts.

One of the charms of Istanbul is the mingling of past and present, as in the football pitch lying beneath ancient city walls built to defend against Attila the Hun's forces.

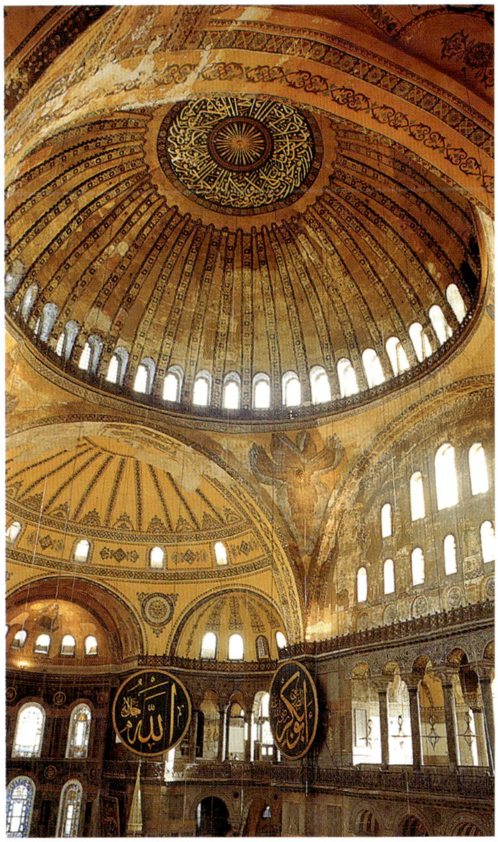

Hagia Sophia (left) originally a Christian church, then a mosque from 1453, and now a museum, is renowned for its beautiful mosaic decoration.

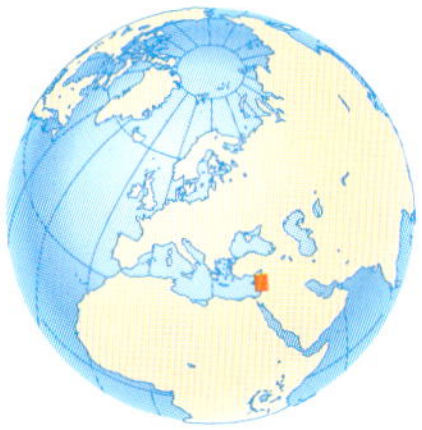

Crusader Castles of Syria

Built to withstand all enemies including time, the massive Crusader castles still dominate the valleys and mountains of western Syria seven centuries after they were abandoned.

FACT FILE

Languages: Arabic, French, and English.

Currency: Syrian pound.

Climate: Summer is very hot, 85°F (29°C); midwinter can be cool and wet 50°F (10°C).

Time to go: Spring, for the flowers, and autumn.

Nearest airport: Damascus.

What to buy: Carpets, jewelry, brass, and copper.

What to take: A flashlight (torch) for exploring ruins, and insect repellent.

Important note: Travelers with an Israeli visa in their passport will not be admitted to Syria. Those who intend to visit both countries usually arrange to carry two passports.

IN 1909, A YOUNG OXFORD STUDENT set out through Palestine and Syria to visit as many of the Crusaders' castles as he could. Fired with the romance of history, he traveled more than 1,000 miles (1,600 km) on foot in the heat of summer, enduring many hardships. His observations were eventually published in 1936 as *Crusader Castles*. By then, however, its author, T. E. Lawrence, had acquired a very different fame as Lawrence of Arabia.

Nowadays you can visit the main castles in much greater comfort, as specialist operators run tours with expert guides. Even if you want to forge your own path, you won't need to walk; buses and microbuses ply the routes from the main centers of Damascus, Homs, Hama, and Latakia. For maximum independence, your best option is to rent a car in the capital, Damascus. Though no castle is more than a day's round trip from a town with accommodation, each is sufficiently remote to make your journey an adventure and discovery.

GUARDIANS IN THE LANDSCAPE

The castles are situated on the edge of Syria's fertile plains between the Jebel al-Ansariye mountains and the Mediterranean coast. The countryside here is unexpectedly pretty, very different from the harsh desert of the interior. Provided you do not travel in midsummer, you pass through grassy hills covered

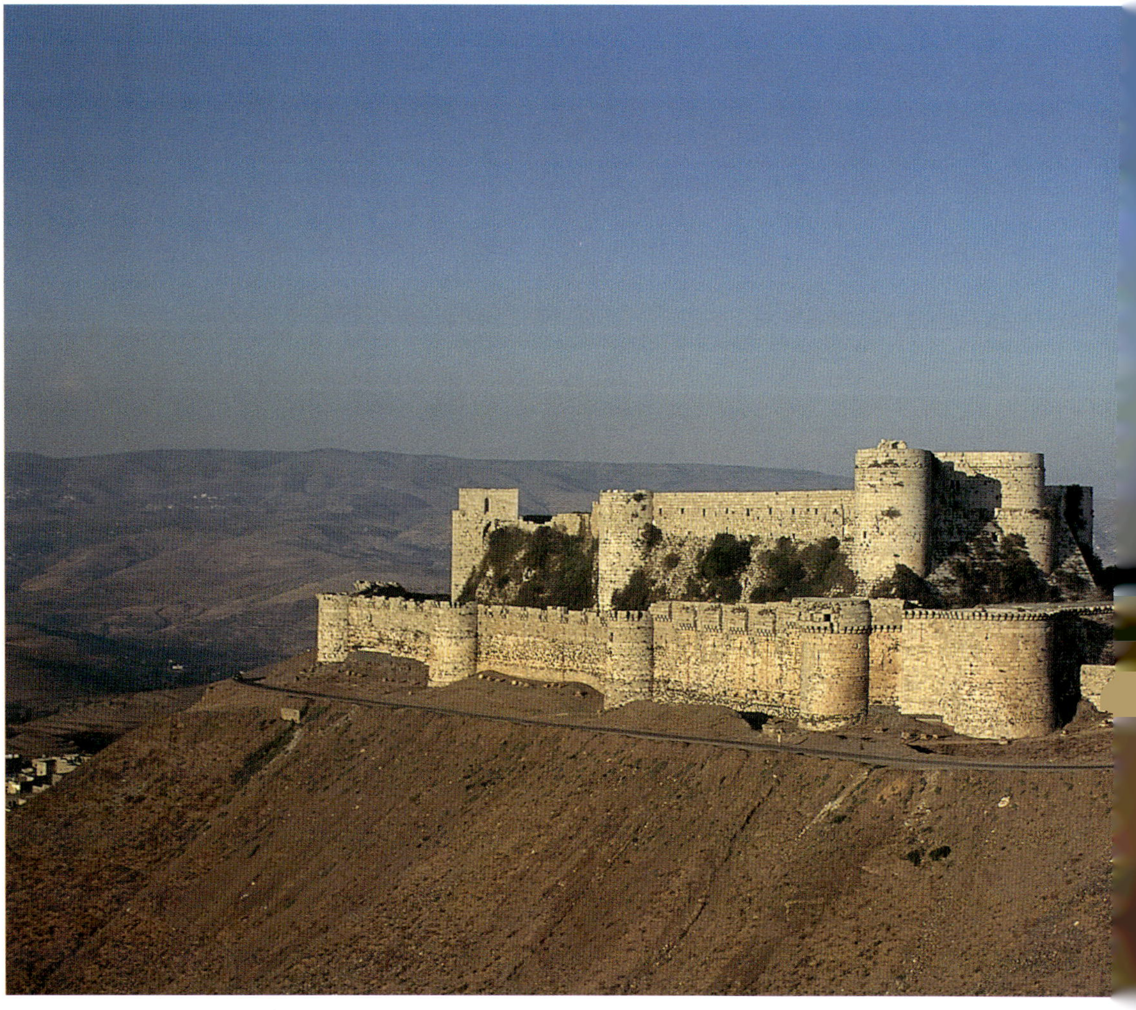

Krak des Chevaliers (right) is one of the best preserved medieval castles in the world, a testimony to the determination of the Crusader monks who built it.

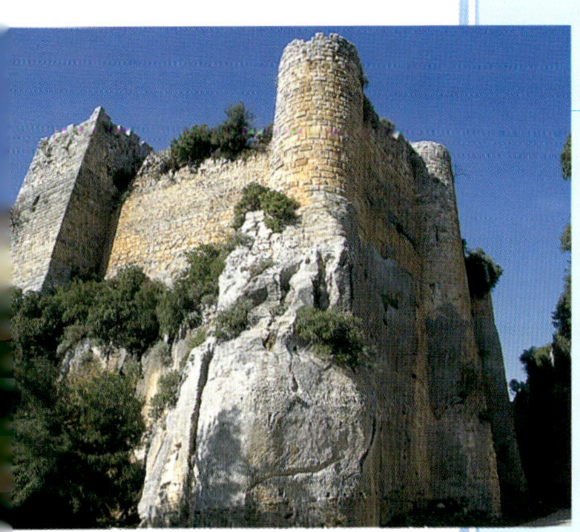

The height from the depths of the moat to the uppermost ramparts of the main keep at Qalaat Saladin (above) is an impressive deterrent to invaders.

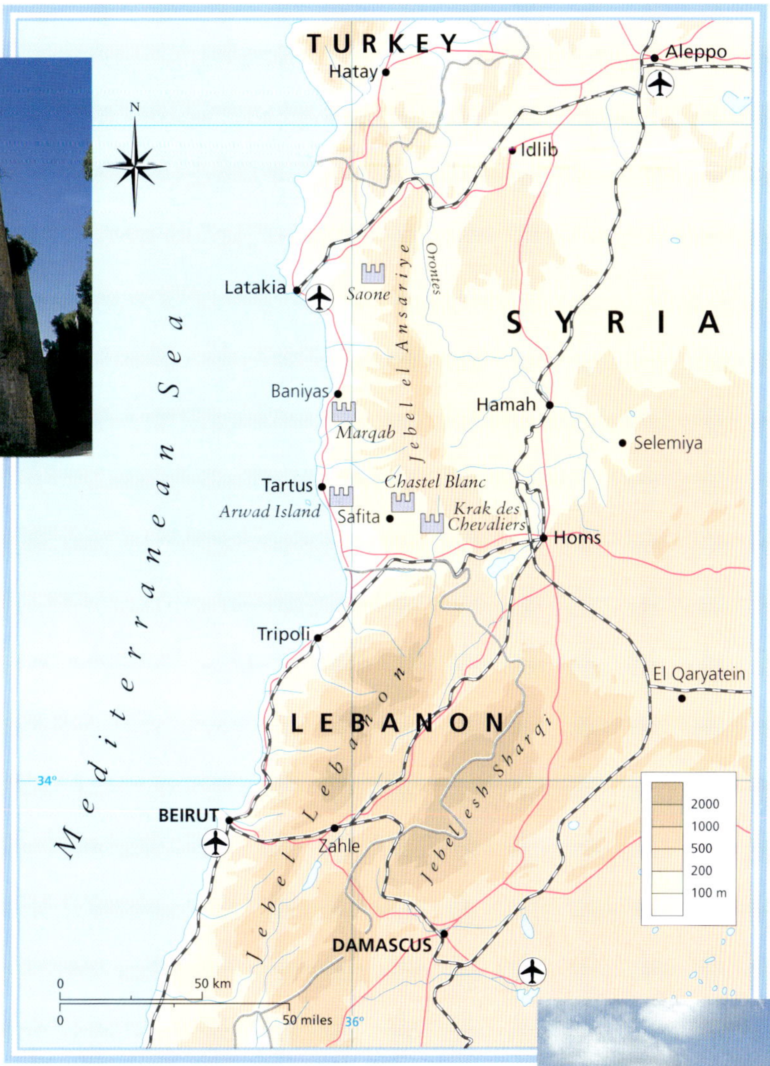

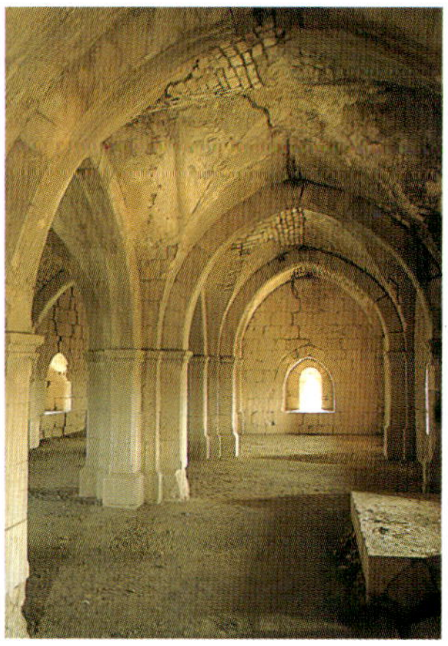

The fortress of Safita (above) reflects the infiltration of northern Europe's Gothic style in the Middle East.

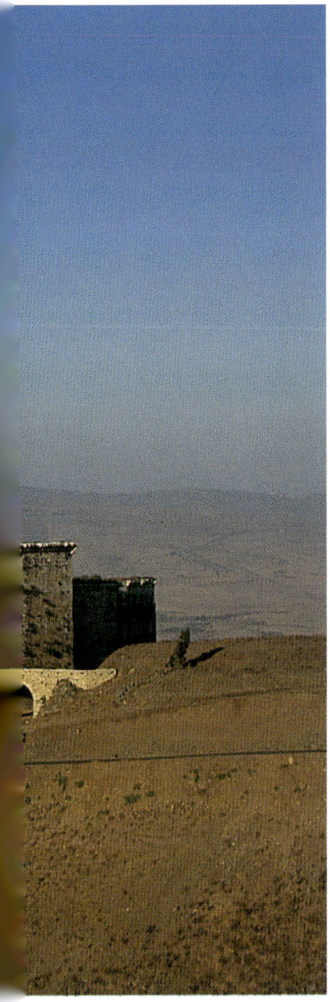

Marqab Castle (below) stands on a volcanic peak, from which the basalt of its walls was quarried.

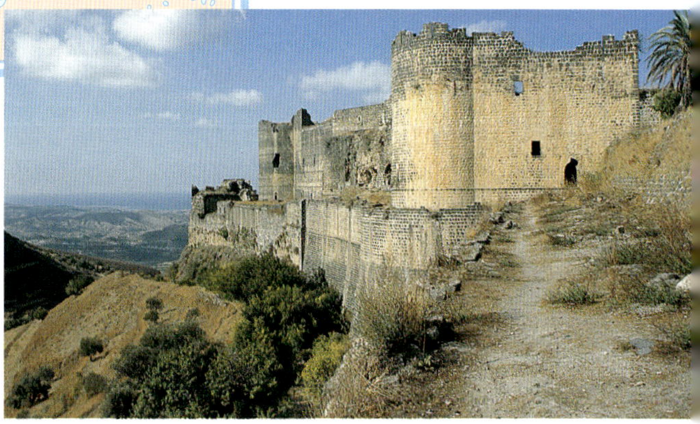

with wild anemones in spring, citrus orchards, olive groves, and stands of oak and pine, often with high mountains visible to the east and the Mediterranean Sea to the west.

Traveling 40 miles (65 km) east from the industrial city of Homs, is the greatest of all Crusader castles, Krak des Chevaliers (Qalaat al-Husn), incredibly well preserved. As you approach through rolling landscape, massive walls loom up ahead from a 2,200 foot (670 m) hill. Lawrence described it as "the finest castle in the world." However, this is no romantic ruin, but military architecture that means business, all smooth, sweeping planes designed to leave an attacker exposed to merciless defensive fire. First occupied by Crusaders in 1110, Krak des Chevaliers was given in 1142 to the Knights Hospitaller. An order of "fighting monks" that grew up during the Crusades, the Hospitallers were responsible for much of the existing fortifications. Protected by two concentric rings of walls and towers, with a rock-cut moat between, the castle resisted the great Sultan Saladin's attempt to capture it in 1188, only falling in 1271. Inside the inner ring the Gothic chapel and Great Hall, with its intricately carved portico, offer some relief from the military severity of the defenses.

From the ramparts of Krak (if the weather isn't too hazy), you can see the tall white keep of Chastel Blanc, 15 miles (24 km) to the northwest. Set on a hill amid orchards and olive groves, the castle was established in 1112, but most of what survives was built by the Templars, another order of fighting monks, in the early 13th century. The outer walls have almost disappeared,

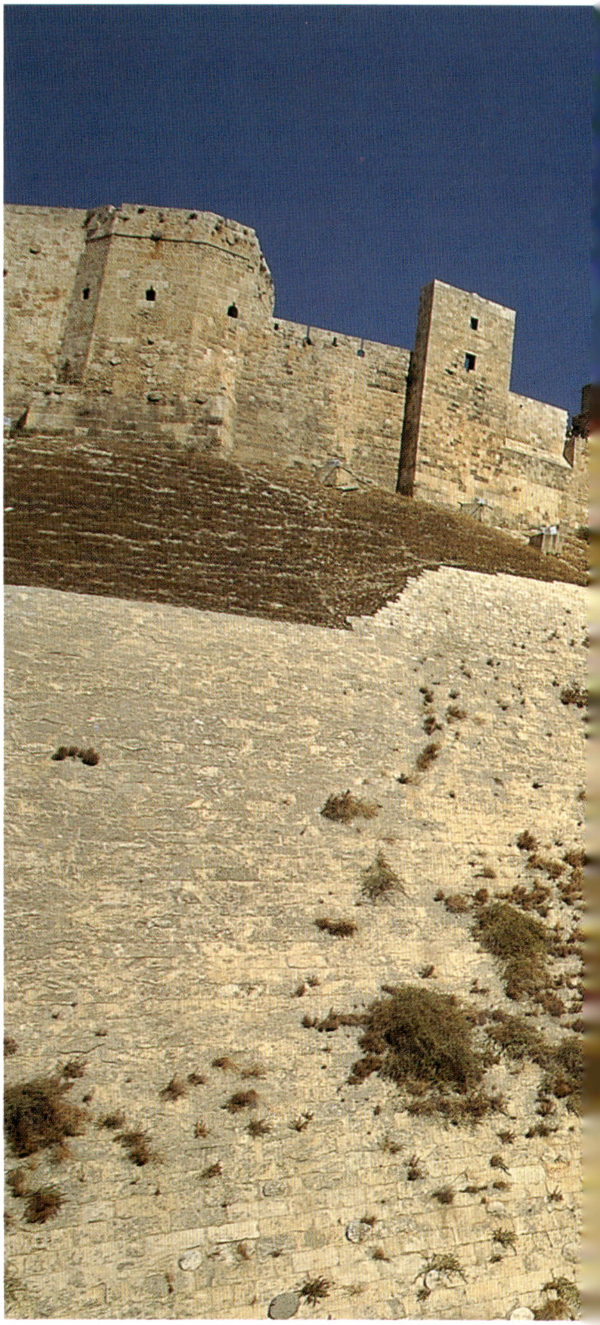

and today the village of Safita straggles right up to the keep itself. This is a pretty and relaxing place—its altitude keeps it fairly cool even in the summer—with old stone houses built around courtyard gardens.

THE CRUSADERS' LAST STAND

From Safita it is 18 miles (30 km) to Tartus, an attractive if tacky old port on the Mediterranean coast, whose streets of low stone houses have changed little since the Crusades, when it was called Tortosa. Locals stroll along the waterfront in the evening while men play backgammon and smoke *margules* (pipes) in the many coffee shops. Some comfortable hotels make Tartus a good place to spend the night.

The Crusaders' keep can still be seen on the shore, but the main relic of their era is the Cathedral of Our Lady. First built in 1123, it was restored by the Templars after Saladin sacked it. The dour, fortresslike exterior conceals a Gothic interior that might grace a French city. Just offshore is Arwad Island, the Crusaders' last outpost, where they clung on until 1302, eleven years after the mainland had fallen. There are plenty of boats making the short crossing, and amid the winding lanes full of cafés and netmenders are the remains of two citadels, one Templar, one Muslim.

About 24 miles (38 km) north of Tartus, not long before you reach the town of Baniyas, rises the grim bulk of an extinct volcano, with spectacular views across the Mediterranean. On it stands the gigantic and somber Crusader fortress of Margat (Qalaat Marqab), built from black basalt quarried from the mountain itself. The triangular curtain wall and round keep were built by the Hospitallers after they took over the castle in 1186. The Great Hall is now a ruin, though the chapel, with its graceful Gothic arches, survives intact.

The Crusaders believed passionately that they were liberating historic Christian territory—with churches like that of St. Simeon (below), near Aleppo—from the "infidel."

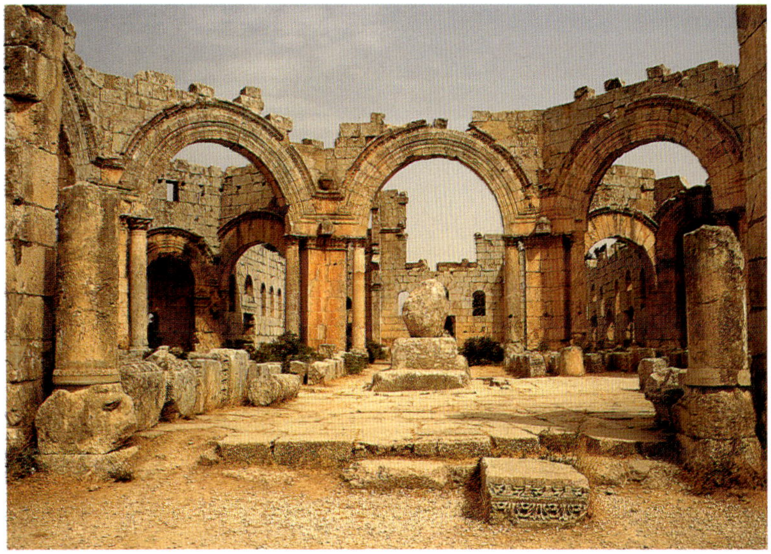

Some 35 miles (56 km) to the north, a steep road zigzags through dramatic gorges to where the Crusader castle of Saone perches atop a narrow ridge between two ravines. It has been known since 1957 as Qalaat Saladin in honor of its conqueror. Originally built by the Byzantine Greeks, whose ruins can still be seen, Saone was occupied around 1120 by the Crusaders, who vastly strengthened the fortifications. The castle is divided into two parts, a lower ward and a more fiercely defended upper ward dominated by a squat, powerful keep. The moat is cut out of solid rock; one of the castle's most remarkable features is the tall needle of stone 90 feet (28 m) high rising out of the moat to

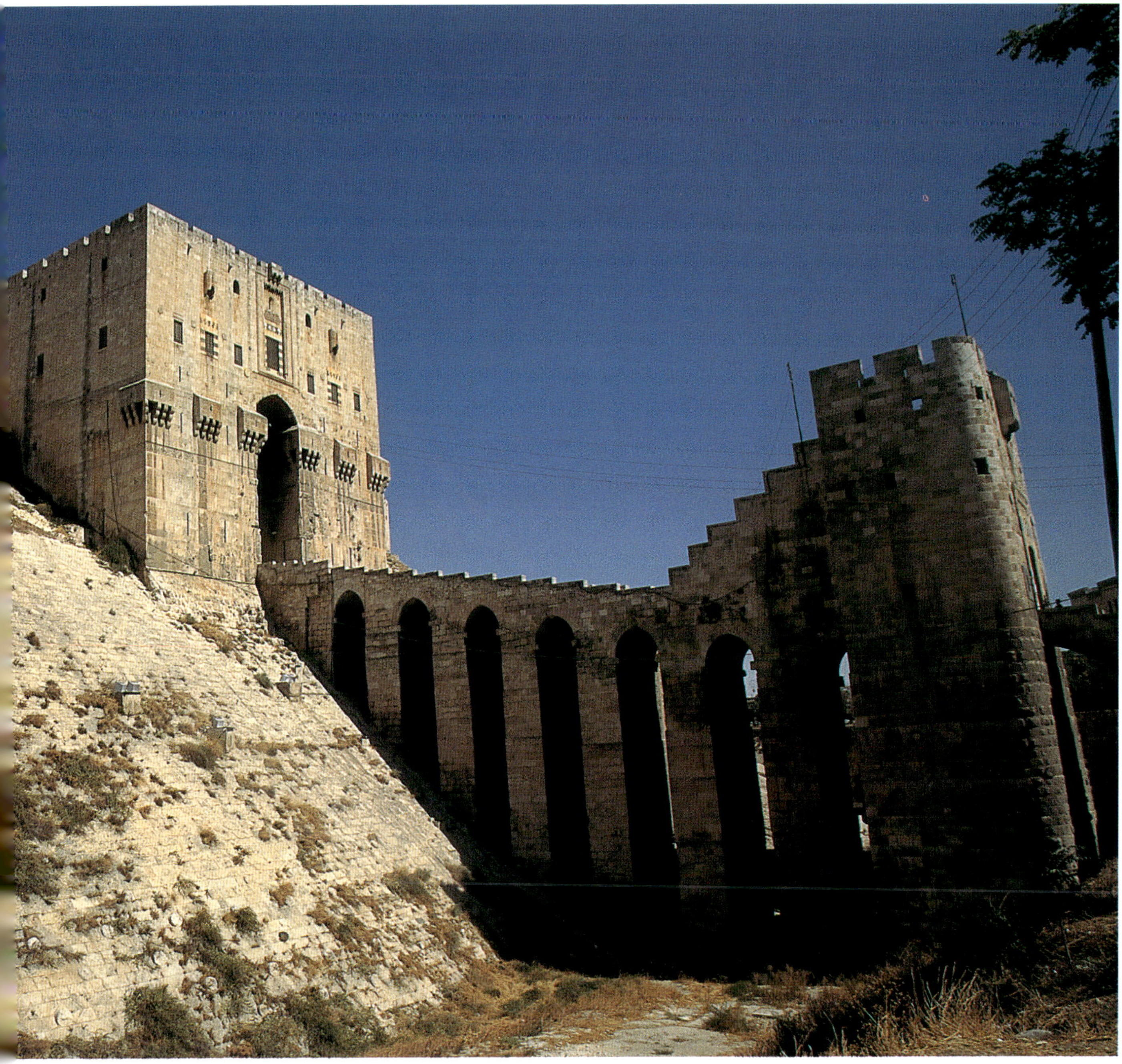

support a drawbridge. Qalaat Saladin is best reached by taxi from Latakia, Syria's main port and a major holiday resort, which makes a good base for exploring the area. In Roman times it was called Laodicea ad Mare, and a triumphal arch and a ruined Temple of Bacchus survive from that era.

To gain an idea of the power and brilliance of the Crusaders' Islamic opponents, you could finish off your trip with a stay in Aleppo (Halab), 100 miles (160km) to the north. In Crusader times it was one of the great cities of the Muslim world; today it is Syria's biggest commercial and industrial center. Its massive citadel, mostly built by Saladin's son Ghazi, is one of the most impressive examples of Islamic military architecture in Syria. The old quarter of the city contains more than enough to make a stopover worthwhile, including many historic mosques, well-preserved *hamams* (bath houses), and ancient *khans* (hostels). Most absorbing of all perhaps is the souk, some 10 miles (16 km) of narrow winding passageways lined with stalls and bustling with trade, where you can display your skills at haggling. When tired, you can try some of the tiny restaurants serving local olives and kebabs, perhaps washed down by *oud*, an aniseed-flavored liquor resembling Pernod. The local beer is also drinkable but few people praise the wine.

Aleppo's 13th-century citadel (above) is one of the most brilliant examples of Islamic military architecture, combining formidable defenses with structural elegance.

Northern Europe

"I have wandered all my life, and I have also traveled; the difference between the two being this, that we wander for distraction, but we travel for fulfilment."

HILAIRE BELLOC, FRENCH-BORN ENGLISH WRITER, 1870-1953.

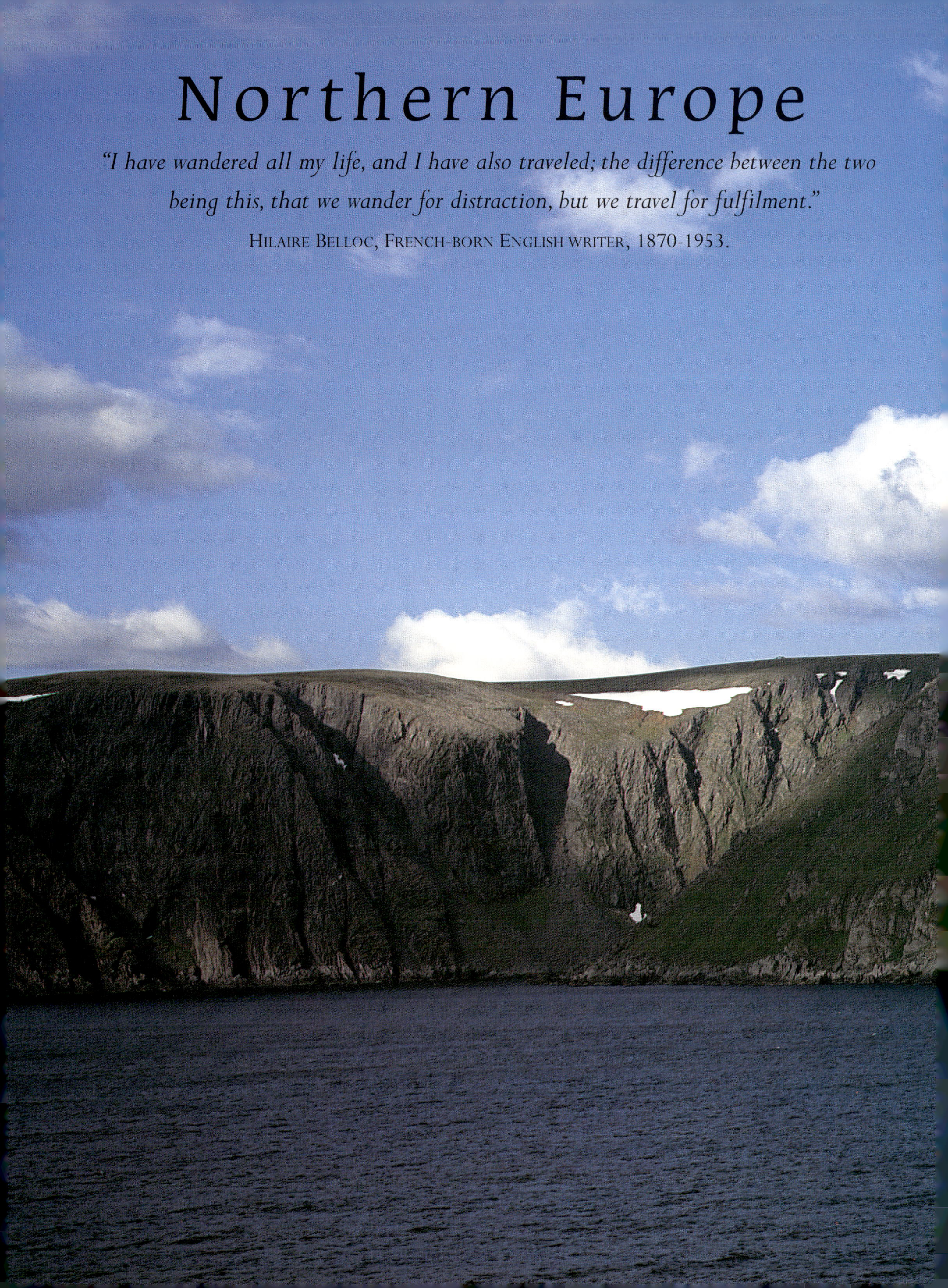

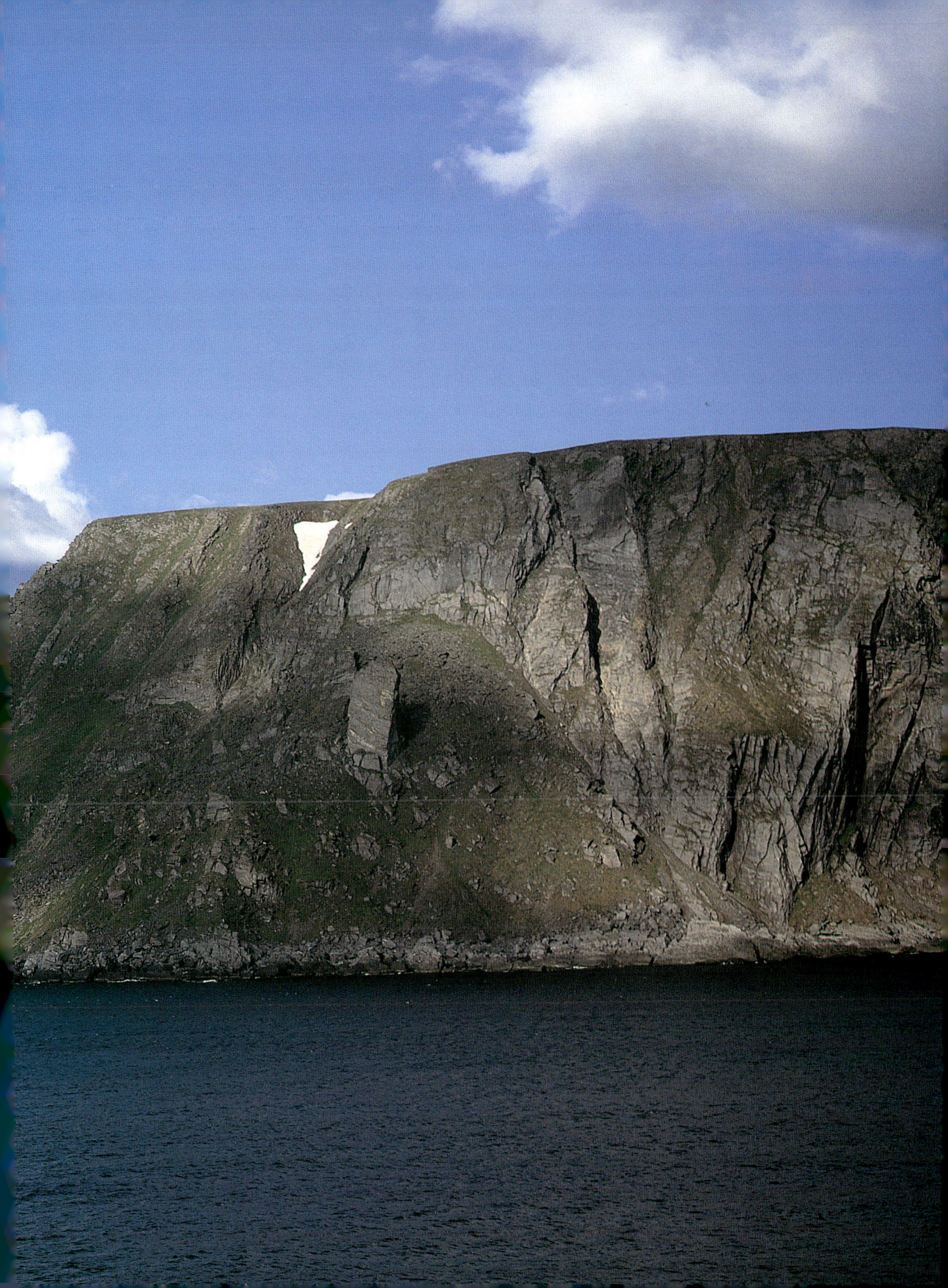

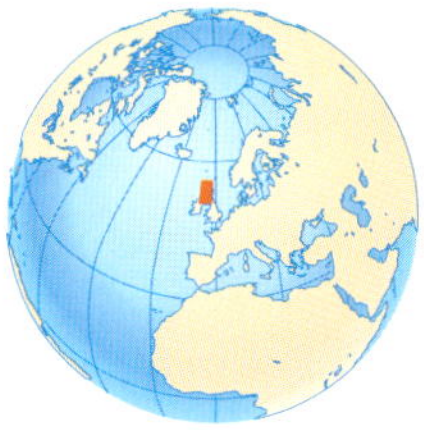

Western Isles of Scotland

Beyond the windswept shores of this wild and sparsely populated archipelago, there is nothing but the Atlantic Ocean until America.

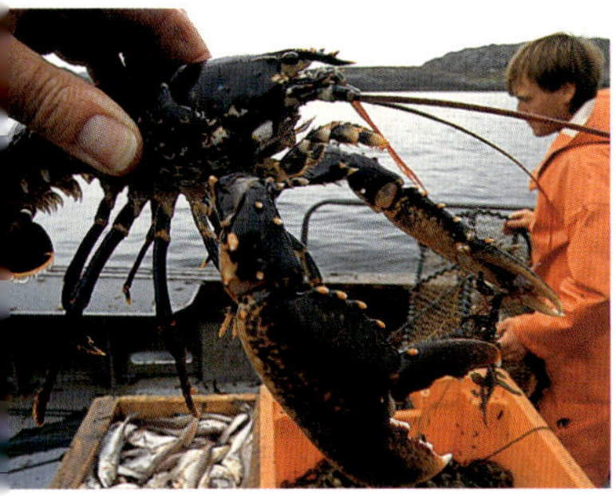

ASTONISHINGLY, EVEN A COUNTRY as densely populated as Britain contains one of the world's remotest, wildest regions. In the Outer Hebrides—a 130-mile (208 km) long arc in the North Atlantic, separated from the Scottish mainland by a turbulent channel called the Minch—you are geographically as far from London as Geneva or Frankfurt, culturally perhaps even farther, for the ancient Gaelic tongue is still spoken here..

You can stay in a remote croft (farm cottage) and experience profound solitude. Walking for miles on deserted beaches in the pellucid light of endless summer evenings, there is nothing to be heard but the cries of seabirds and the barking of seals. On a cloudy, moonless night it is so dark you can't see your hand in front of your face; when it clears, the sky blazes stars, and you may see the Northern Lights (aurora borealis) perform their ghostly dance across the heavens.

FERRY ACROSS THE MINCH

The main departure port for the Western Isles is Ullapool in Ross and Cromarty. This picturesque old fishing port, built in the 1700s, lies on an inlet called Loch Broom, ringed by heather-clad hills.

Don't be surprised if you see notices in Russian around the town—Russian factory ships come here to buy fish from local trawlermen. There are decent hotels, excellent seafood restaurants, and cheerful pubs (bars). Enjoy these while you can—the landscape of the Western Isles is stunningly beautiful, but the towns and villages are dour, functional places. The puritanical morality of the dominant Free Church of Scotland means pubs are few and everything closes on Sundays.

As the car ferry chugs out of Ullapool on the crossing to Stornoway (Steornabhagh), gulls and kittiwakes scream and wheel above the Minch. Stornoway is on

FACT FILE

Population: 30,000 in the Western Isles.

Currency: British pound sterling.

Climate: Maritime; it seldom freezes at sea level, but expect rain, fog, and very strong winds all year round.

Time to go: Spring through to autumn; autumn colors are amazing.

Nearest airports: Glasgow, Stornoway.

What to take: Insect repellent, waterproof clothing, and footwear.

What to buy: Harris tweed, island malt (Scotch) whisky.

Accommodation: "Bed and breakfasts," which offer simple but comfortable beds and very full Scottish breakfasts, including bacon, eggs, and kippers, are usually reasonably priced and comfortable.

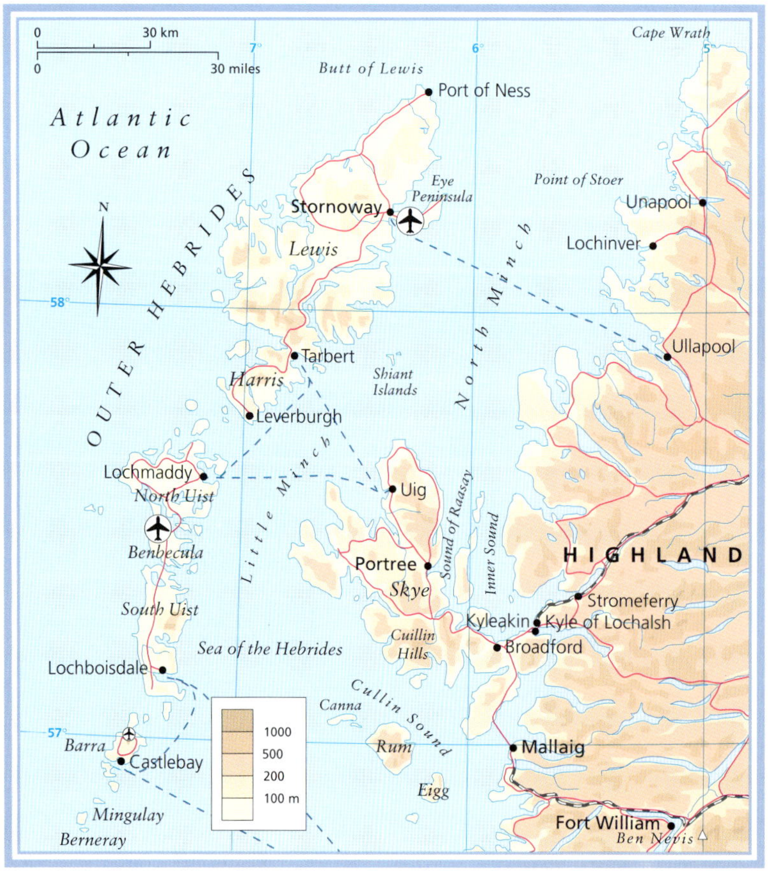

Fishing is a way of life in the Outer Hebrides; the fresh lobster (above left) may well be on its way to one of the excellent seafood restaurants in Ullapool.

Fishing port on the island of Skye (right), the largest island of the Inner Hebrides.

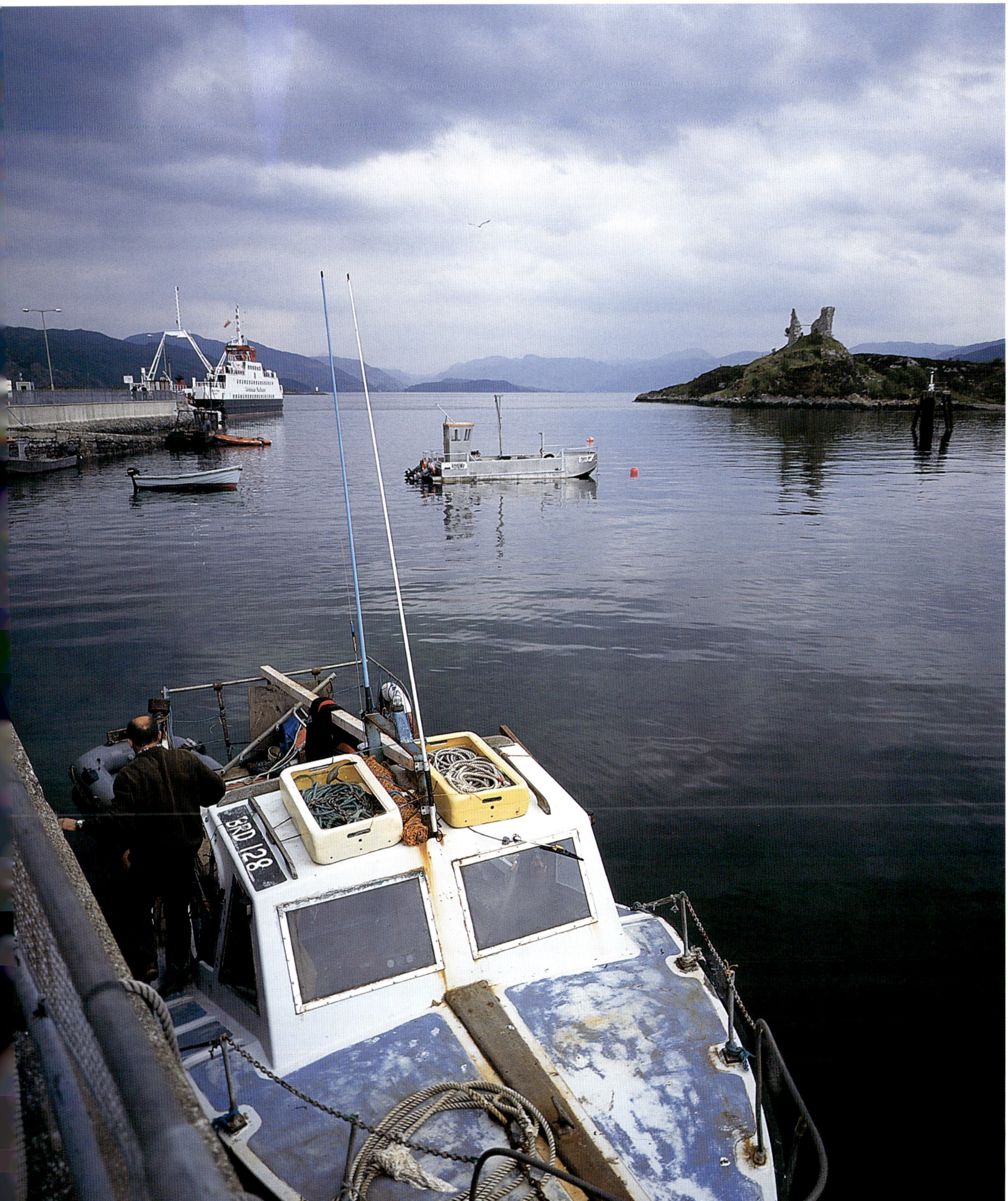
BRD 128

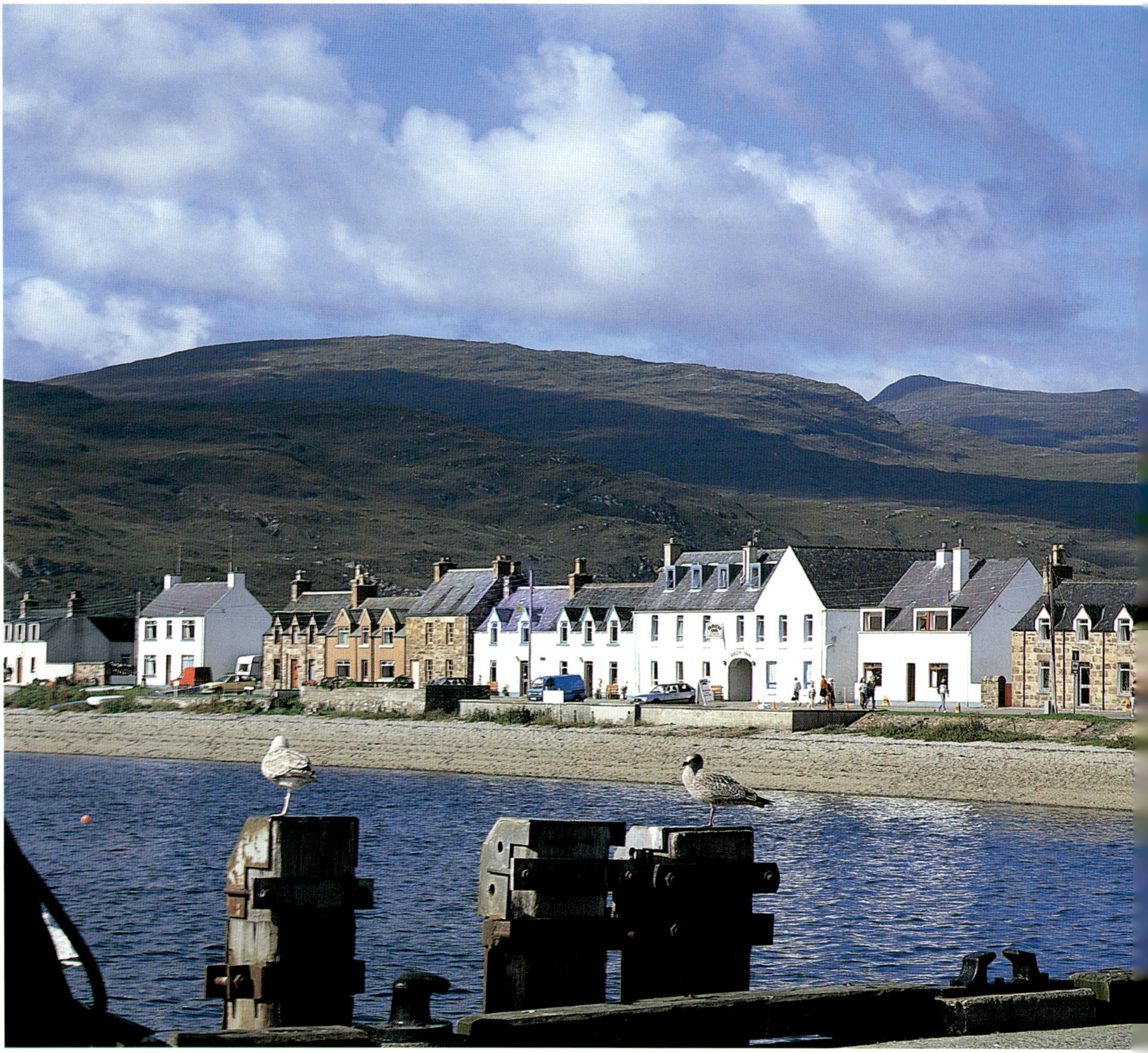

Ullapool (above) is the main starting point for a ferry tour of the Western Isles.

the east coast of the largest and northernmost Outer Hebrides, the "Long Island," which is divided into two: Lewis (Leodhas) and Harris (Na Hearadh). With a population of 8,000, it is the largest town in the Western Isles. The occasional old hotel lends a flourish of Victorian grandeur; more unexpected are Stornoway's tandoori restaurants—there's a small Gaelic-speaking Pakistani population here. Otherwise, gastronomic pleasures are restricted to seafood, usually excellent and very fresh, or the Lewis specialty: boiled gannet (seabird) with potatoes.

All of the islands are connected by causeways or short ferry crossings. Don't expect the going to be fast, though; bus services are infrequent, and even if you rent a car in Stornoway, the deeply indented coastline makes any journey a circuitous one. From Stornoway, it is about 25 miles (40 km) across barren peat moors to the island's northernmost tip—the rocky, storm-battered cliffs of Butt of Lewis, a familiar name to any who listen to BBC Radio's shipping forecasts.

South along the coast road, one of Europe's most awe-inspiring prehistoric monuments, the Ring of Callanish, overlooks a loch (lake). This neolithic circle consists of some 50 stones, erected between 3000 and 1500 B.C. for unknown religious purposes. At their center is a chambered tomb, probably added centuries—if not millennia—later by a chieftain for his own grave. Around it stand the 13 tallest stones, their gray gneiss as deeply veined and twisted as driftwood. Harris starts where Loch Seaforth—a fjord of Scandinavian grandeur—cuts deep into the island from the east. The land beyond, North Harris, is mountainous and bleak. A narrow isthmus with the main port, Tarbert, connects it to South Harris, almost another island. Its interior is boulder-strewn and uninhabited, but the east coast shelters small fishing villages such as Kyles Stockinish (Caolas Stocinis) and Ardvey (Aird Mhighe). Deep inlets make the east coast road so convoluted that you may have to stay overnight at one of these places. On the west coast of South Harris, it is possible to walk all day without meeting a soul, along sandy beaches buffeted by Atlantic winds and backed by grassy duneland known as *machair*. In summer this terrain blazes with wildflowers; their scent so strong that ships at sea used to take their bearings by it.

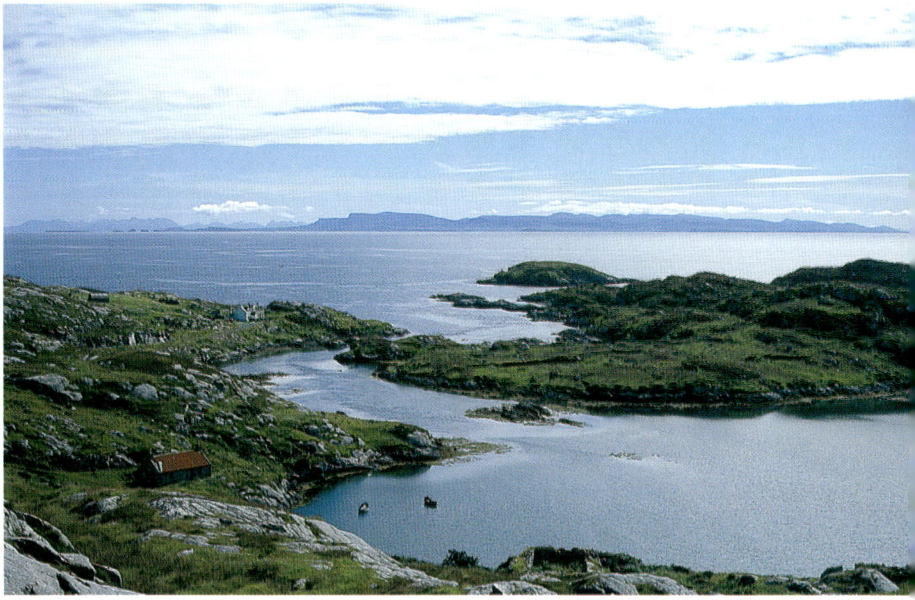

The scent of wildflowers on the island of Harris (above) is so strong in summer that ships used to take their bearings by it.

GATEWAY TO THE SOUTH

From Tarbert or Leverburgh in the south of Harris, a ferry takes you the short hop to the island of North Uist, gateway to the southern reaches of the Hebridean chain. Wildly beautiful and sparsely populated, North Uist, Benbecula, and South Uist are connected by a causeway. Between the long shell beaches on the Atlantic side and the labyrinth of rocks, cliffs, islands, and inlets of the eastern coast of these islands, rise spectacular peaks such as South Uist's Beinn Mhor.

Beyond South Uist, take the ferry again to Barra, a *machair*-covered island just 8 miles (13 km) long, its wild beauty somewhat impaired by tourism and a small airport on the beach. Adventurous travelers can go down to the waterfront at Castlebay (Bagh a Chaisteil), the old port in the south of Barra, and try to persuade one of the boatmen to take them on the hair raising trip to the archipelago's southernmost and wildest islands: Mingulay and Berneray. Uninhabited, these are mere wave pounded outcrops in the tempestuous Atlantic, where guillemots, kittiwake, and puffins wheel around the massive cliffs, nesting in every rock face crevice.

"ISLAND OF CLOUD"

There are also ferries from Tarbert in Harris or Lochmaddy on North Uist back across the Minch to Skye, largest of the Inner Hebrides. Skye—"Island of Cloud" in Old Norse—is a place of magical contrasts, veiled in mists that suddenly clear to reveal heather-clad moorland, lush green valleys, and spectacular peaks. Though the island is just 60 miles (100 km) long, its coastline is so deeply gashed by sea lochs that you would have to cover almost 1,000 miles (1,600 km) to walk around it. Porpoises, basking sharks, and killer whales swim in its waters, while sea eagles patrol the skies.

Whether you come from Tarbert or Lochmaddy, the ultimate destination is Uig, a small port ringed by dramatic cliffs on Skye's northeastern peninsula, the Trotternish. This is dominated by spectacular basalt pinnacles called the Storr—a primordial chaos of giant crystals of solidified lava that seem to have just burst through the earth's crust. The highest, the Old Man of Storr, soars 160 feet (50 m), and has only been climbed once. At the far end of the peninsula, another cluster of basalt spires, the Quiraing, looms from the mist and sea spray.

Portree, the only town of any size on Skye, shelters beneath a steep cliff where the Trotternish Peninsula joins the main body of the island. An attractive 18th-century port with a harbor full of brightly painted fishing boats, its many hotels and bed and breakfasts make it a good base for exploring the island. From here the road runs south to Broadford and the Cuillins, the mountains that dominate the south of the island. As you travel west, the Red Cuillins, a range of granite hills, give way to the higher and more spectacular Black Cuillins. These great black ramparts, their peaks often dusted with snow, rise to more than 3,000 feet (900 m), forming a massive ring around fjordlike Loch (lake) Coruisk.

From Broadford, the road continues to the village of Kyleakin, joined to the mainland of Scotland by a controversial new road bridge. If that seems an anticlimactic end to your Hebridean odyssey, you can still return by the ferry from Kylerhea, 4 miles (6 km) down the coast.

Neist Point Lighthouse (below) stands guard on high, forbidding cliffs south of Loch Dunvegan on the Island of Skye.

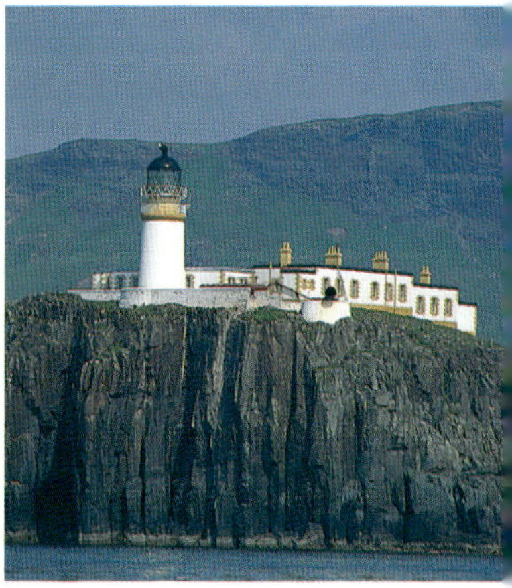

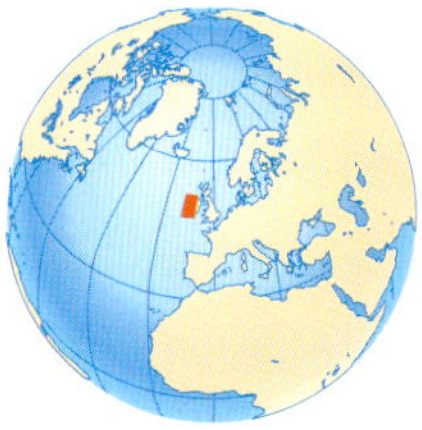

The West Coast of Ireland

The outermost edge of Europe, where the windswept fingers of Ireland's west coast harbor haunting wildernesses and an ancient culture.

FACT FILE

Population: 3.5 million (Republic of Ireland).

Currency: Irish punt.

Climate: Maritime; very wet all year, but temperatures seldom fall below 38°F (4°C).

Language: Old Irish or Gaelic is the official language, but English is universally understood.

Time to go: March — October.

Nearest airports: Cork, Galway, Shannon, Knock.

What to take: Warm, waterproof clothes, insect repellent, good shoes, good road maps, flashlight.

What to buy: Aran sweaters, Donegal tweed.

Food and drink: Guinness and Irish whiskey (with an e) are the most famous drinks in the many pubs. Irish coffee (black coffee with sugar, whiskey, and cream) is popular. Seafood, especially oysters and mussels, is excellent, as is the meat.

ON THE LAST STRETCH OF LAND before the Atlantic Ocean lies an intoxicating blend of lively towns, old fishing villages, haunting monastic remains, and wild landscapes.

When learning was eclipsed in Europe after the fall of Rome, western Ireland shone like a beacon, drawing scholars and saints to the edge of the known world, where traces of their culture survive today. Along much of this coast, Gaelic (old Irish) is still spoken, cold nights are scented with peat smoke, and impromptu music may start up in a pub at any time.

Grand country houses, built by the old Anglo-Irish gentry have adapted to the needs of the traveler, and simpler B&B (bed and breakfast) accommodation offers hearty food and a warm welcome. To travel easily, rent a car—buses are infrequent. Motoring is a joy; there are few vehicles, no congestion—and often no signposts, so a good map is essential. But the real thrill comes when you take to the sea to visit the wind-lashed islands, and join the gulls and kittiwakes screaming around the wild headlands.

At the southwestern corner of Ireland, in the counties of Cork and Kerry, four rocky peninsulas of red sandstone extend into the Atlantic. The best base for exploring them is Killarney, a small but tourist-conscious town crammed with pubs, restaurants, and B&Bs. Its setting amid lakes and mountains is glorious, but for wilderness head for the southernmost promontory, Mizen Head, whose cliffs look out to the lighthouse rock of Fastnet. The Beara peninsula, to the

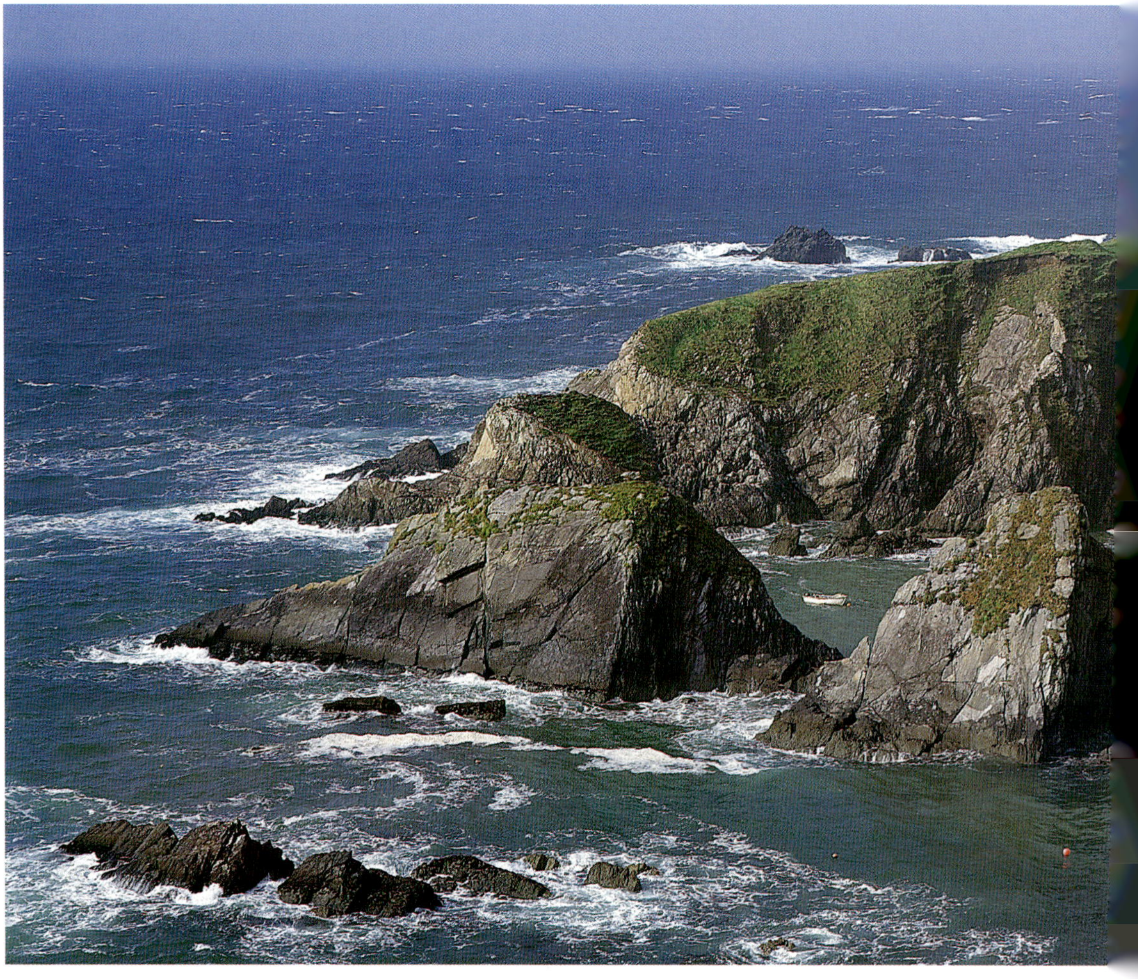

Dunquin Head takes the full force of the Atlantic waves.

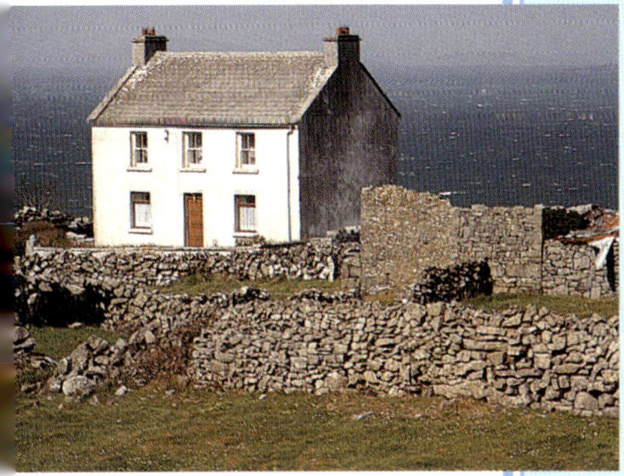

★ *Many traditional stonebuilt houses like the one above on the Aran Islands offer "Bed and Breakfast" accommodation.*

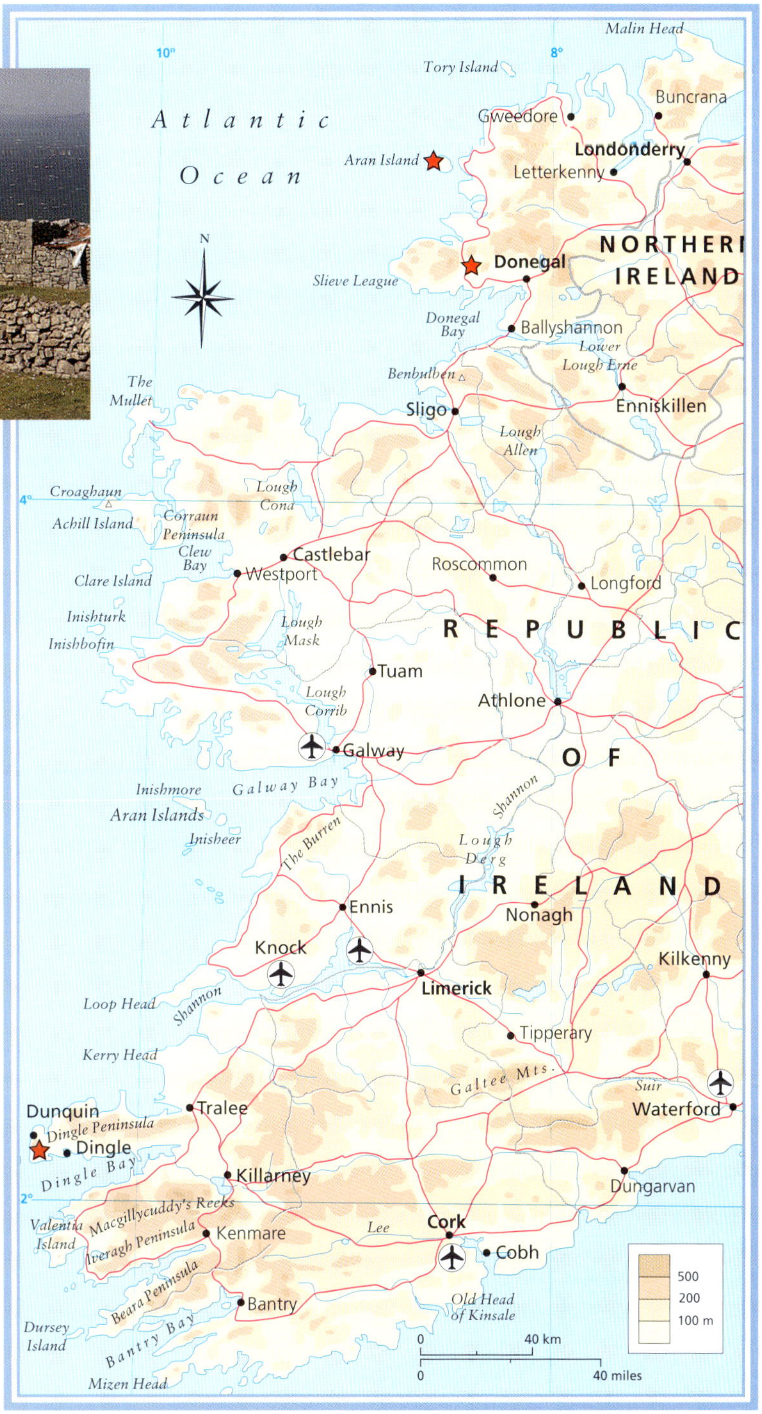

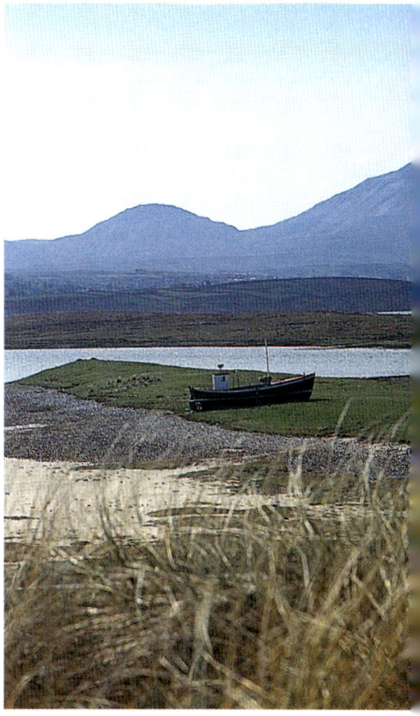

★ *County Donegal (above), has a wild coastline with some sheltered inlets,while inland are quiet lakes and dairy farms.*

★ *The medieval Gallarus Oratory (below), on the Dingle Peninsula, a retreat for monks.*

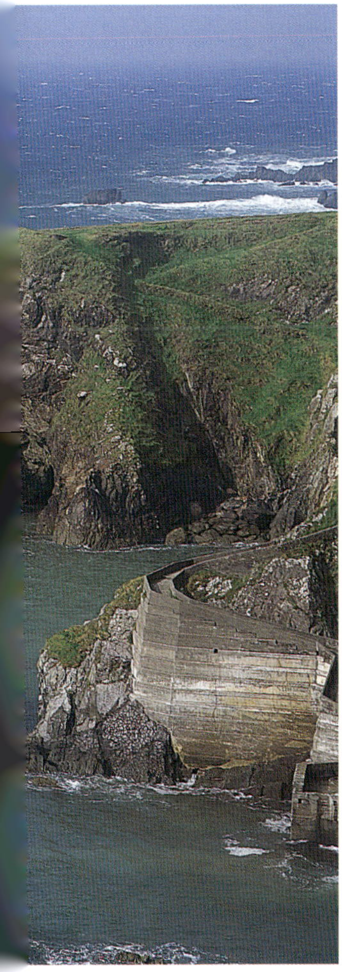

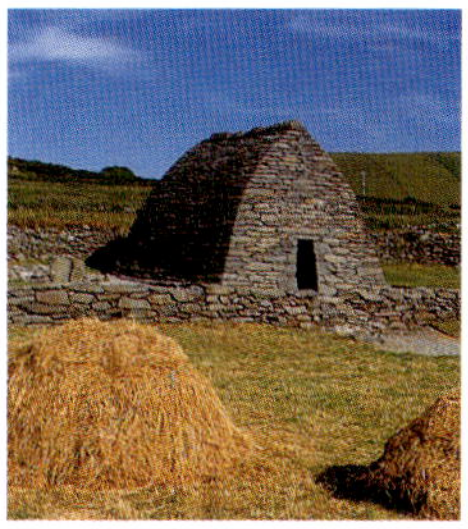

north across Bantry Bay, is a magical place. Along its spine runs the mist-shrouded ridge of the Caha and Slieve Mickish mountains, a land of boulder-strewn moorland and plummeting waterfalls. At Garinish, the peninsula's western end, take a hair-raising ride in a swinging cable car from the sheer cliffs to wind-blasted Dursey Island. The largest peninsula is Iveragh, whose mountains are the highest in Ireland, rising to almost 3,500 feet (1,066 m) in Macgillicuddy's Reeks, ringed by the Ring of Kerry, a 75-mile (120 km) circuit of roads. Beyond the peninsula's tip, the rocky island of Skellig Michael rises 700 feet (213 m) from the waves. Clustered around the ruined church of St. Michael are the beehive stone cells of the monks who lived here in the Middle Ages.

The northernmost finger, the 30-mile (48 km) long Dingle Peninsula, was also a place of retreat for early monks; the corbeled stone Gallarus Oratory, built

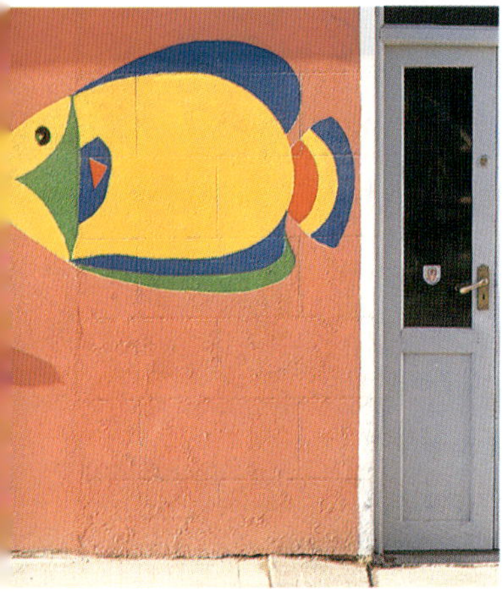

Strong colors in a misty land: a County Kerry fish restaurant advertises its wares.

between the 9th and 12th centuries, is astonishingly well preserved. From this, the westernmost point of Europe, in the 6th century, St. Brendan—whose shrine still stands on Brandon Mountain—set off on the Atlantic voyage that reputedly took him to America. Dingle is a large fishing village of brightly painted houses, with lively music in its pubs. From here, a ferry crosses to the hump-backed Blasket Islands. The ruined village on Great Blasket sadly recalls the fishing community whose last members were evacuated to the mainland in 1953.

To the north, across the Shannon estuary in County Clare, the Cliffs of Moher form a sheer wall of shale and sandstone stretching for 5 miles (8 km), and rising 660 feet (200 m) above raging seas. In the shadow of the cliffs nestles the little village of Doolin, a great center of traditional music. In summer, musicians play in the bars practically every night of the week. Inland rises the Burren, a huge, bleak limestone plateau covering 100 square miles (260 square km). But every crevice is alive with mixed alpine, arctic, and mediterranean flora. The Burren is also riddled with ancient monuments, like organic outgrowths of its strange rock formations: Stone Age tombs, Iron Age forts, round towers, medieval churches, and four fine 12th-century stone crosses.

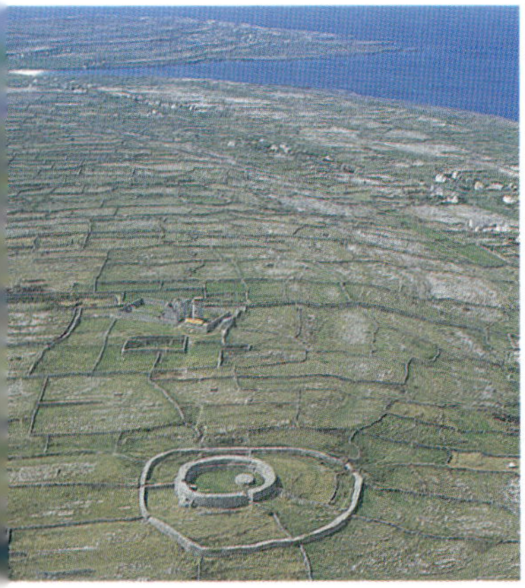

The pre-Christian fortress of Dun Aenghus at Inishmore on the Aran Islands (above) among farmland where soil is scant and limestone walls many.

ANCIENT TRADITIONS

To the north, Galway Bay cuts 30 miles (48 km) inland. On its northern shore, at the mouth of River, maritime Galway City is a splendid old town with its medieval church of St. Nicholas and a magnificent 1400s town house, Lynch's Castle, its stone facade decorated with gargoyles.

The city is nowadays renowned for its annual arts festival, held in July. From the pier a ferry makes the rough one-hour crossing to the Aran Islands, which look like fragments broken from the Burren—with limestone pavements, wild flowers, and prehistoric remains—scattered across the bay.

The largest island, Inishmore, is an 8-mile (13 km) long sliver of rock. Perched above its 300 feet (90 m) cliffs is the prehistoric fort of Dun Aenghus, three concentric semicircles of gray stone walls. The playwright J. M. Synge (1871-1909) recorded the islanders' traditions in the 1800s when they were already disappearing. Many still live by fishing, Gaelic is still widely spoken, and the old ballads of the islands are still sung in the pubs.

Beyond the graceful town of Westport in County Mayo, planned by the architect James Wyatt (1747-1813), lies mountainous Curraun Peninsula. A bridge connects it to Achill, at 14 by 12 miles (22 by 20km)

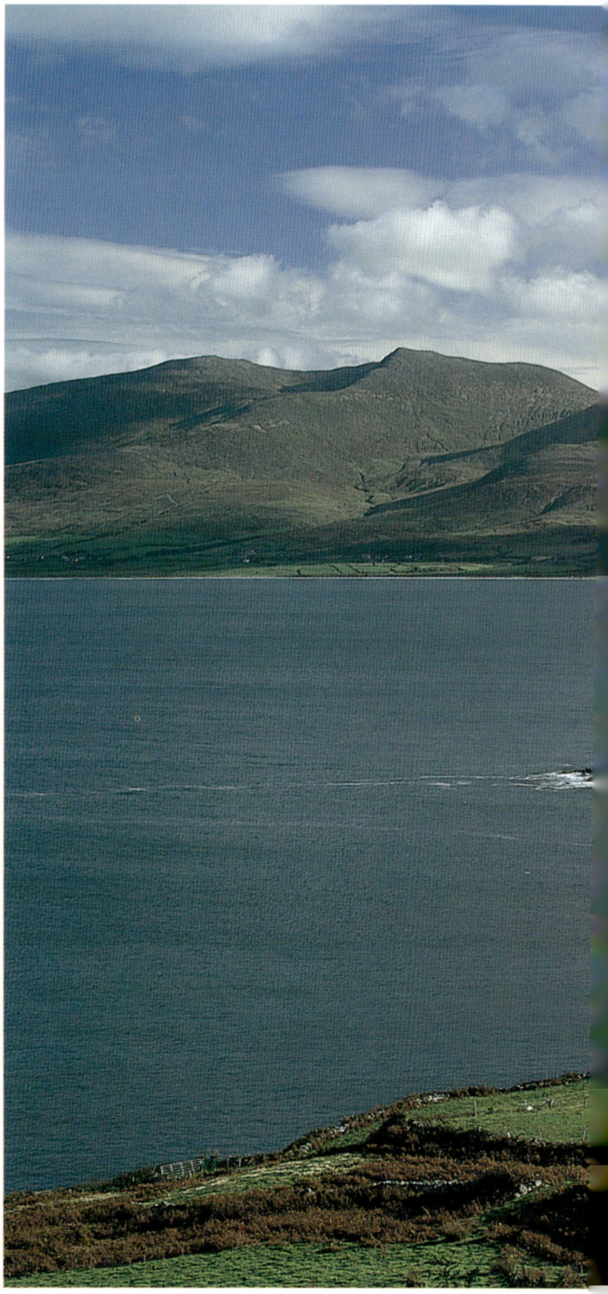

the largest island off the coast. It's a wild place, with long golden beaches, mysterious caves, and old fishing hamlets, where salmon fishermen's currachs (boats) are moored. The island rises to its western extremity, where the 2,192-foot (668 m) Croaghaun drops sheer to the sea, with cliffs sculpted by the elements.

THE NORTHERNMOST COUNTY

Sligo's subtly beautiful landscape of wild, wooded glens and glistening silver lakes has become inseparably associated with Ireland's best-known poet, W. B. Yeats (1865-1939), who spent his early years here and is buried in the churchyard at the foot of the bare stone

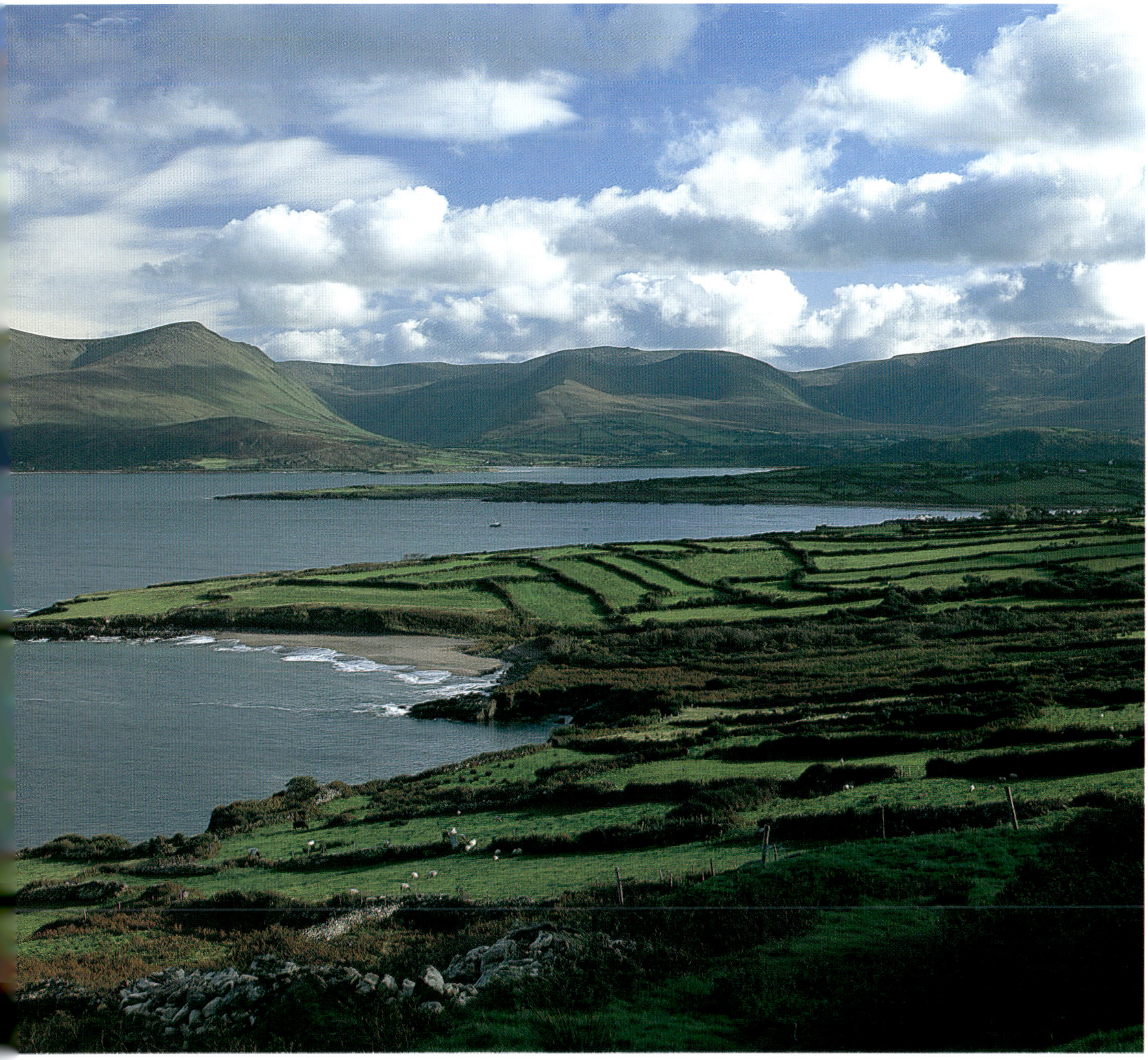

mountain of Ben Bulben. Sligo's other big peak, Locknarea, is crowned by a massive prehistoric cairn, which is said to be the last resting place of the legendary Queen Maeve.

Beyond Donegal Bay lies the Republic's northernmost county, and its most unspoiled: Donegal is a mosaic of purples, russets, greens, and blacks, of loughs (lakes), rivers and moorland with white-walled houses isolated against bare hillsides. Scattered along the 200-mile (320 km) coastline are small, uncommercialized fishing towns, little changed since the 1800s, and long sandy beaches.

Standing at the head of the bay and overlooked by a castle ruin, Donegal Town is a fine old market town where Gaelic is still spoken. Letterkenny, on the shores of Lough Swilly to the north, draws musicians from over the world to its August folk festival. At the county's westernmost point, the boiling Atlantic is framed by the mighty Slieve League cliffs, at 2,000 feet (608 m) the highest in Europe.

To the north, at Malin Head, Ireland's west coast ends as it began, in a defiant crag. A signal tower and lonely pub look out to the automated lighthouse that guides shipping through terrifying seas, where whirlpools suck at jagged teeth of rock. Cut into the rock face is a monk's tiny cell, the "Wee House of Malin," the harshest imaginable place in which to commune with God.

A quieter face of the Dingle Peninsula on a fine day (above), showing its fine sandy beaches, and verdant, unspoiled countryside.

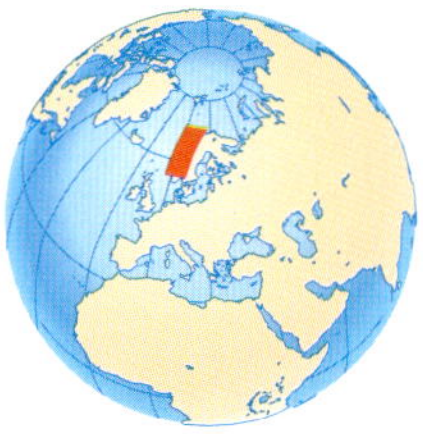

Along the Coast of Norway

Travel up the coast by ship from Bergen, see the fjords, cross the Arctic Circle to the Lofoten Islands and glimpse at last the Midnight Sun shining at the world's northmost edge.

FACT FILE

Currency: Norwegian Krone.

Climate: On the coast, surprisingly moderate. At Bodø the average July temperature is 60°F (15°C).

Time to go: May—September, but for the Midnight Sun, June—early July.

Nearest airport: Bergen.

What to take: Insect repellent, sunglasses, good boots, warm windproof clothing, binoculars.

Food and drink: Breakfasts are enormous in Norway: fish, meat, cheese, and bread are served with boiled or fried eggs. Seafood, notably salmon, herring, lobster, and shrimp, is common at other times, as is venison. Aquavit, a liquor like schnapps, is the national drink but tough restrictions on alcohol in general operate and it is expensive.

THE LAST GREAT EPIC JOURNEY in western Europe is the "north way," from which Norway gets its name. This long stretch of water between the fjord-gashed Atlantic coast of Scandinavia and the chain of islands that run alongside is warmed by the Gulf Stream which allows ice-free ports and habitable land far north of the Arctic Circle. The North Way has been a favored shipping route since the Vikings sailed it 1,000 years ago and their route can be traced today, by boats and ferries which ply the 1,450 miles (2,334 km) from Bergen to Norway's northeasternmost town, Kirkenes. They take you through ruggedly spectacular scenery to where the Midnight Sun shines in chilly splendor over an enormous subarctic wilderness, whose vastness is both daunting and exhilarating.

The starting point is Bergen, Norway's second largest (and most rainy) city. Clinging to the coast beneath steep, wooded hills, it is a proper, salty old port, reeking of fish and tar and the tang of the sea. Once the northernmost outpost of the medieval Hanseatic League, its atmospheric old warehouse quarter, known as *Bryggen*, is full of tall, steeply gabled old merchants' houses. Two excellent museums use old furniture and costumes to recreate the feel of the medieval trading port. Bergen is an enjoyable, welcoming town full of attractive shops, bars, and—as

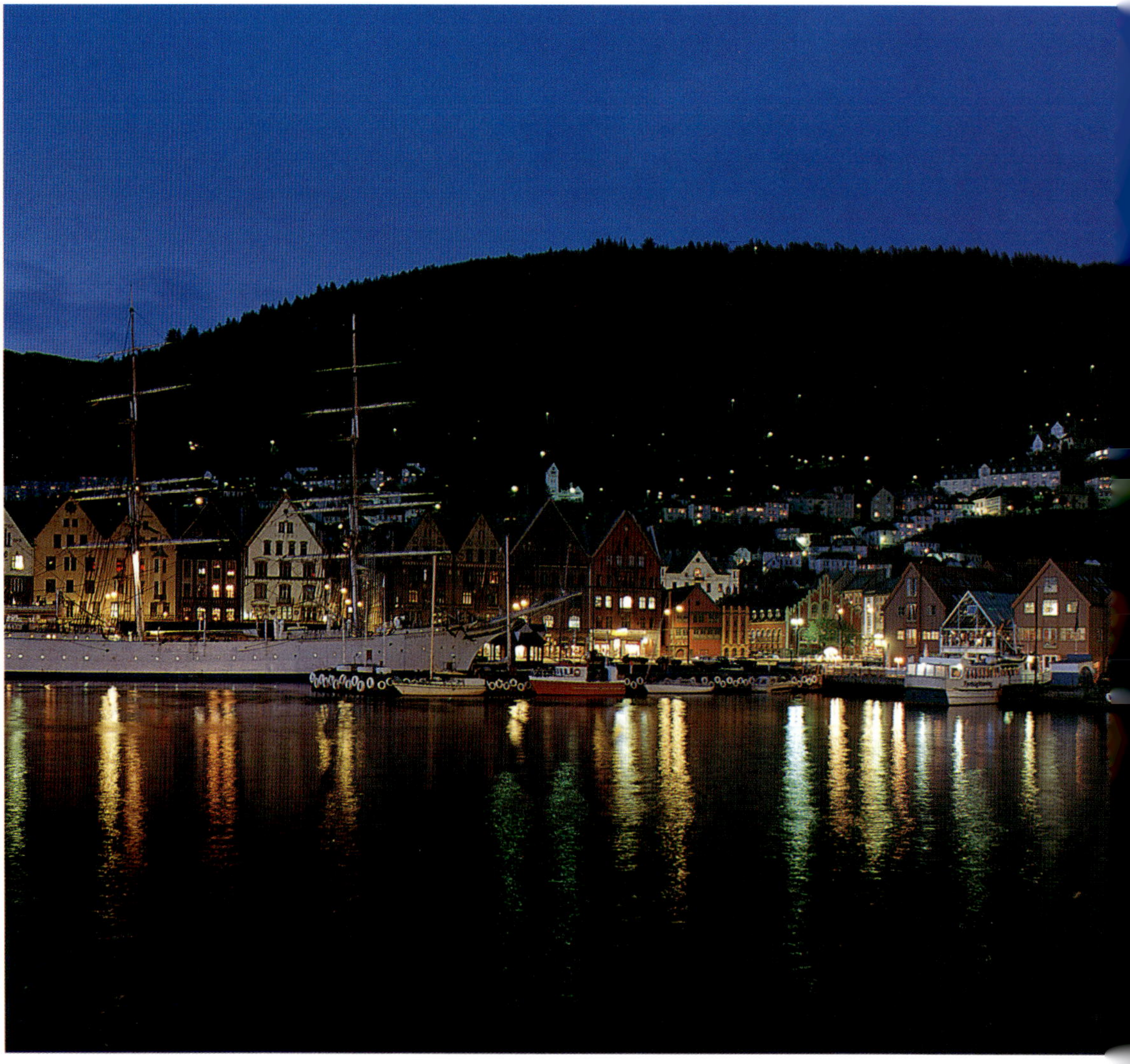

Bergen's harbor, with its tall ships and old waterfront buildings, nestles beneath steep, pine-clad hills.

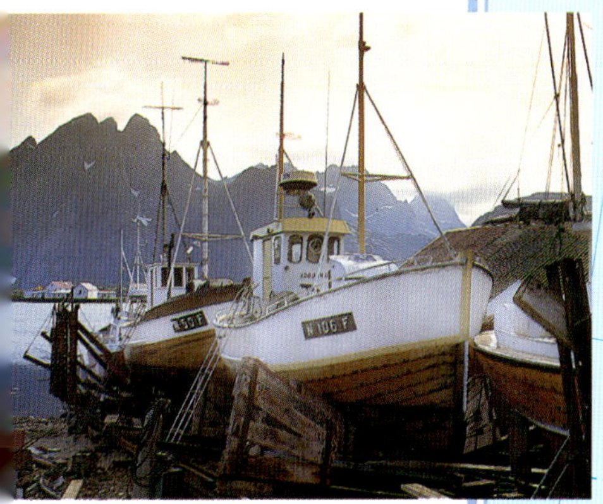

★ *A fishing boat undergoes repairs in the harbor at Flakstadøya, one of the southernmost—and most beautiful of the Lofoten Islands.*

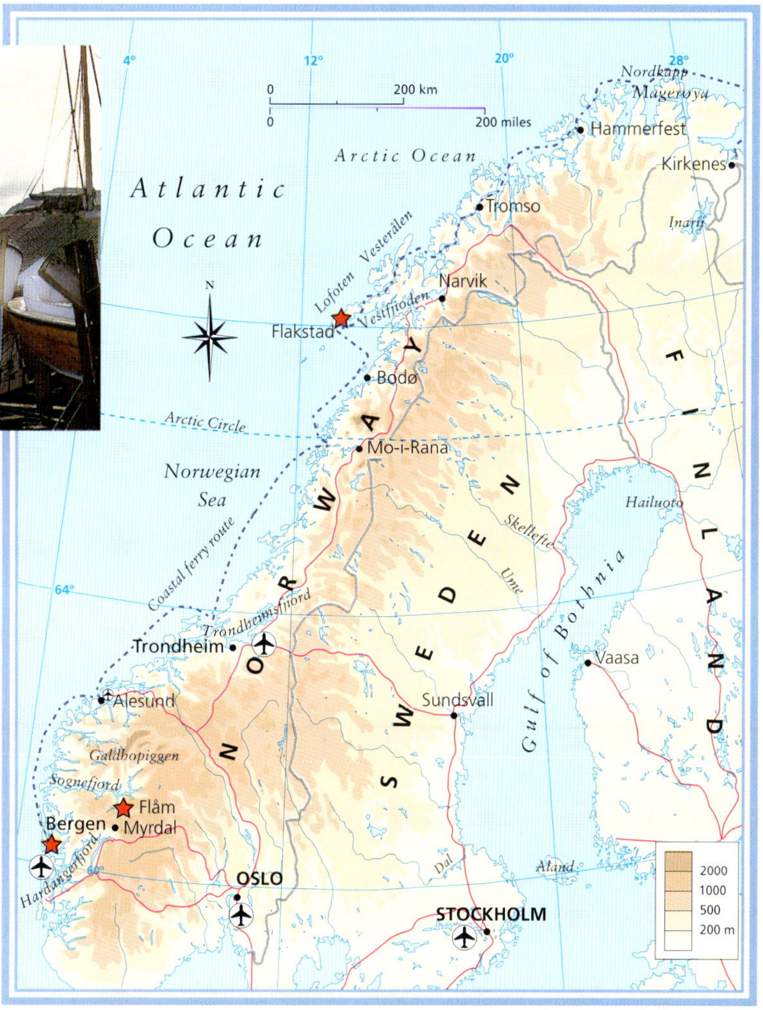

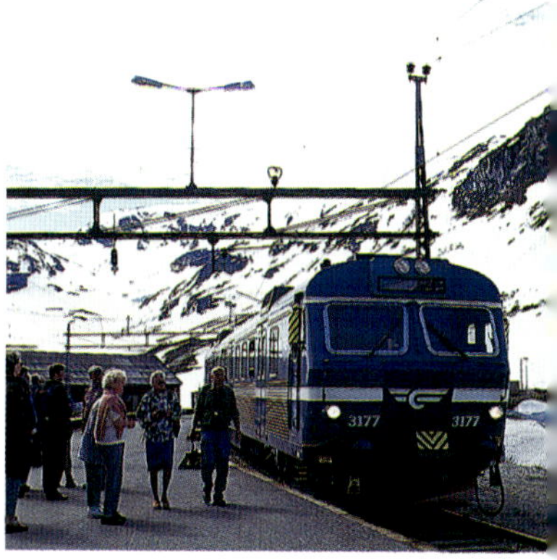

★ *The railway (above) from Myrdal to Flåm on the shore of Aurlandsfjiord, is one of the steepest and most spectacular train journeys in the world.*

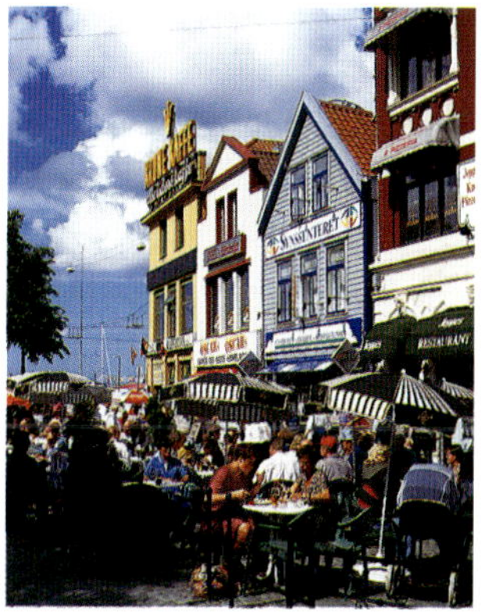

★ *Holberg Square, the center of Bergen's atmospheric merhcant quarter, the Bryggen. Many of the tall, gabled houses date back to the era when Bergen was the northern outpost of the mighty Hanseatic League of trading cities.*

might be expected—excellent fish restaurants. There's a good choice of hotels, several of them characterful places in the old quarter.

ICE-CARVED FJORDS

Before you set out for the far north, explore some of the fjords near Bergen. Although they emerge at the coast, they reach way inland—and, because of the varying cutting action of the glacial ice that formed them, their deepest and most spectacular stretches are often far from the sea.

The fjords are probably the most familiar image of Norway, but nothing prepares you for the reality of these immense gashes in the rocky, wooded landscape. From Myrdal (two hours by train from Bergen) the mountain railway descends a dizzying 3,000 feet (900 m), past waterfalls and sheer rock faces to Flåm, a pretty village amid meadows and orchards on the edge of the Aurlandsfjord. Return by ferry to Bergen along unbelievably narrow canyons whose sheer rock sides exclude the sun except at midday in summer. The effect is unsettling—the sky seems like a thin ribbon of blue far above you, as if you were looking down to a river.

You can travel north from Bergen by the coastal ship *Hurtigrute* (Rapid Route), an eleven -day round trip. These ships, which double as car ferries, stop at small fishing villages to take on local passengers and goods. Cabins are available (though you can sleep in the lounges), and there's food on board. It's possible to buy a ticket for part of the journey and then pick up a bus or train (though the latter go no farther north than Fauske), rejoining the boat later.

Two days out of Bergen, the *Hurtigrute* docks at Trondheim, one of the few towns in Norway resembling a historic European city. It was a major pilgrimage site in the Middle Ages, and in its quiet cathedral close stands the finest medieval church in Scandinavia, the Nidaros Domkirke. Its towering west front is covered in tall Gothic niches filled with statues. Above the main portal is an enormous rose window; in the morning, the sun pours through its stained glass to

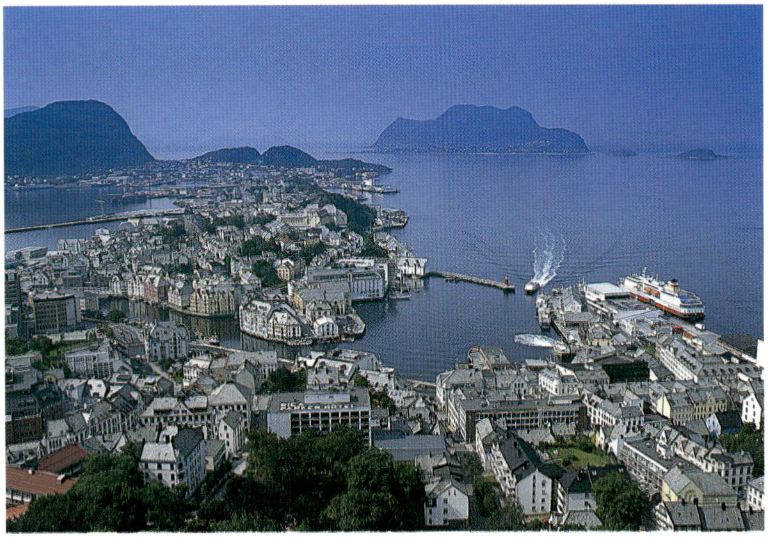

Stunningly located at the mouth of the Storfjiord, the fishing port of Alesund was rebuilt in grand Art Nouveau style after a fire in 1904.

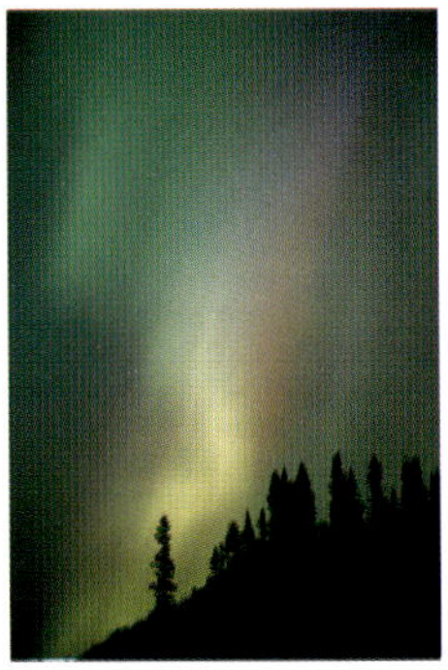

The eerie Northern Lights, or Aurora Borealis, are produced by electrons from the solar wind bombarding the Earth's atmosphere.

Aurlandsfjord (right), was carved into its steep-sided magnificence by the massive force of a glacier.

set the shadowy interior ablaze. Down by the Old Town Bridge is an area of old gabled wooden warehouses, many converted into shops and restaurants.

The morning after leaving Trondheim, you cross the Arctic Circle on the way to Bodø some 460 miles (740 km) to the north. Until now the coast, seldom out of sight, has remained remarkably green and fertile for such northerly latitudes; but now, as the boat threads its way past countless small islands, it becomes harsher and more mountainous. Inland is mostly uninhabited moorland; in clear weather you can glimpse the gleaming mass of the enormous Svartisen glacier.

A GREEN ARCHIPELAGO

If this seems chilling, there's a pleasant surprise in store. Beyond Bodø, you land at Stamsund in the Lofotens, a rocky archipelago some 70 miles (112 km) long about 40 miles (64 km) offshore. Behind their jagged, gray-green cliffs, the Lofotens are a welcoming place, where patches of gentle farmland nestle between fjords and crags. The climate is astonishingly mild for so far north. In the old fishing villages, you can stay a few days in *rorbuer*, brightly painted fishermen's huts. The islands are of particular interest to birdwatchers, with large colonies of puffin and other marine birds.

Beyond the Lofotens are the lower-lying Vesterålen Islands. The steamer passes though the narrow channel Raftsunde which separates the two groups. In summer, the boat then makes a brief scenic detour between the sheer, blank rock walls of the sinister Trollfjord. Farther north still, the *Hurtigrute* calls at Tromso, the largest town in northern Norway and the world's northernmost university. Apart from the main square, with its 19th-century wooden cathedral, it is a bland modern town. but the sight of a well-lit bar full of students is strangely reassuring after so much natural vastness. Check in to a restaurant and dig into a reindeer steak and a few beers from the world's northernmost brewery.

Almost a full day's voyage from here, around a bleak, fjord-gashed coastline is the fishing village of Honningsvåg, sheltering on the landward side of the barren island of Magerøya. A bus journeys the final 20 miles (32 km) to Nordkapp. Since this bare and wind-lashed cliff top was dubbed the North Cape in 1553 by an English sailor Richard Chancellor, it has been recognized as the northernmost point of Europe. Despite the presence of a visitors' center and the touching idealism of the big round bronze roundels with designs by children from all over the world, there is an awesome sense of being at the end of the world as you stare out at the Arctic Ocean.

By now, you have rounded the top of the Scandinavian peninsula and will be traveling not from south to north, but from west to east. The scenery—bare cliffs and tundra—is monotonous but compelling and hypnotic. As you sail up the Varanger Fjord, the sight of Kirkenes—the last port for the *Hurtigrute*—could scarcely seem more welcoming. It is just 10 miles (16 km) from the Russian border, though even in these post-Cold War days, the crossing is off limits.

THE MIDNIGHT SUN

"The northern sun, creeping at midnight along the horizon, and the immeasurable ocean in apparent contact with the skies, form the grand outlines of the sublime picture presented to the astonished spectator," wrote the Italian traveler Giuseppe Acerbi in 1802. It is precisely the midnight sun that gives any Arctic voyage in summer an air of unreality. The Arctic Circle is the line north of which the sun never dips below the horizon at the summer solstice—though you get a midnight twilight some way farther south. The farther north you go, the longer the phenomenon lasts: in Bodø, the Midnight Sun is visible from the first week of June to early July; and at Nordkapp from early May to late July. When planning when to travel, bear in mind the opposite effect, the Polar Night—in these latitudes it remains dark for months either side of the winter solstice.

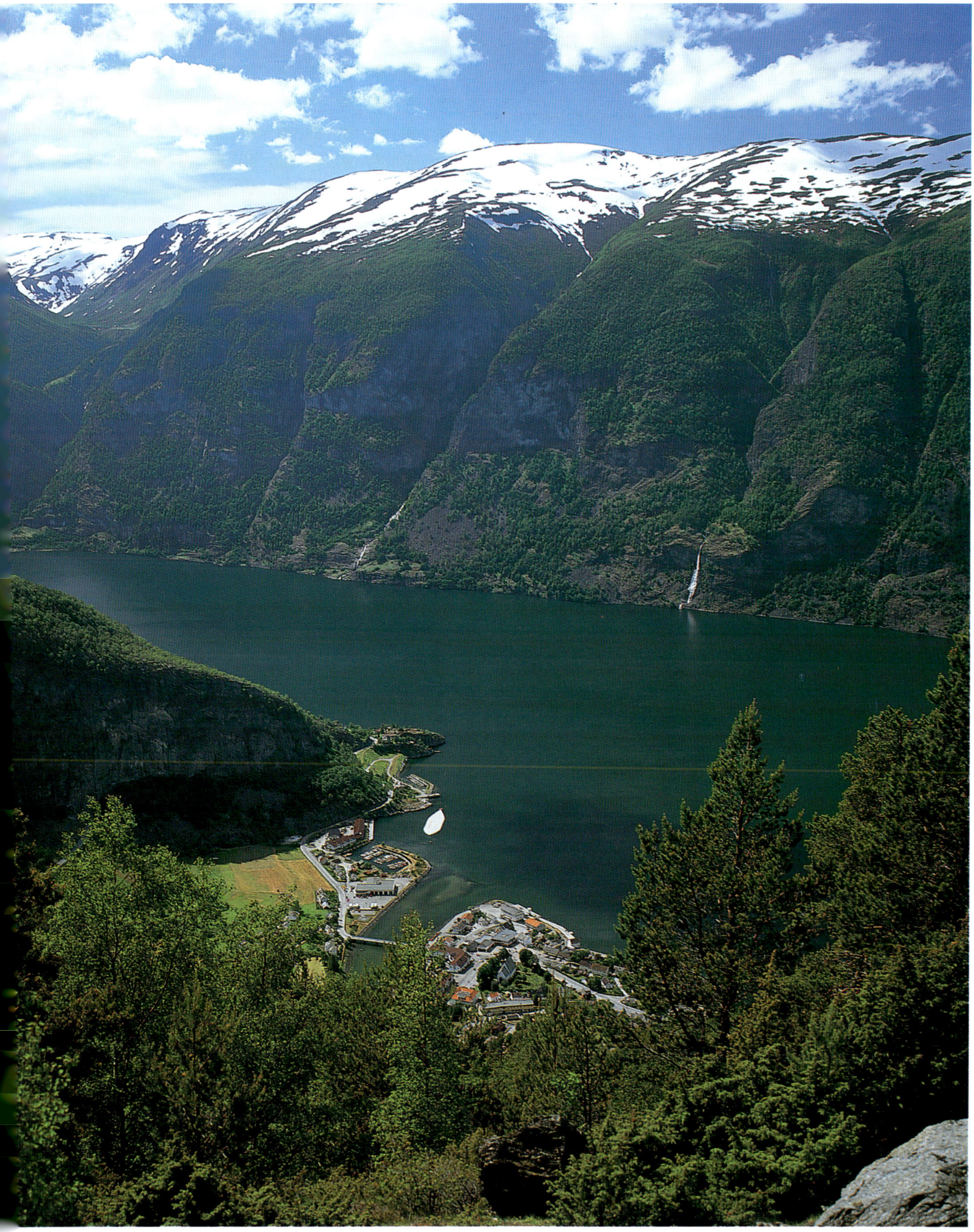

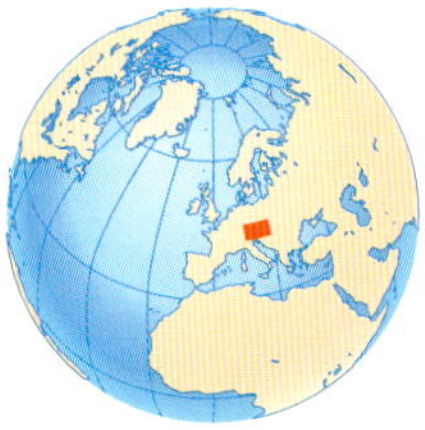

Elegant Cities of Middle Europe

Travel to the heart of the old Habsburg empire to experience the café society and high art of Vienna, and the Baroque cityscapes and lively countercultures of Prague and Krakow.

FACT FILE

Currencies: Austrian schilling; Czech crown; Polish zloty

Climate: All three cities have a fairly continental climate; warm in summer (especially noticeable because of high humidity) with temperatures in the low 80°s F (c 28°C), they can be very cold in winter and autumn,and heavy snow is common.

Time to go: Spring and autumn to avoid the crowds and extremes of weather; Christmas is a particularly good time to be in Vienna.

Airports: Vienna, Prague, Kraków.

Food and drink: In Vienna, Wiener schnitzel (veal coated in breadcrumbs) is a national institution, accompanied by some of the local Riesling wines; in Prague you should drink beer to accompany the *knedliky*, dumplings; in Kraków, sample the national Polish dish of *bigos* made with sauerkraut, fresh cabbage, onions, and leftover meat, washed down by Polish vodka, of which there are many flavored varieties.

THERE IS A LAND IN THE HEART OF EUROPE, whose borders do not appear on any map. It has been described as a lost continent sunk by the tides of history, whose peaks today break the surface as scattered islands. If you visit three of those islands today—the old Habsburg cities of Vienna, Prague, and Kraków—you will discover that Mitteleuropa (Middle Europe) still exists as a way of thinking, living, and feeling. There is something easygoing about it, always very sharp intellectually but humorously aware of life's difficulties and delights.

The region has taken almost everything this century could throw at it, but the joyously elegant architecture of these cities remains remarkably intact. Four or five days spent in each will reveal how much of their old spirit survives as well. Since the fall of the Iron Curtain, travel between these cities has become easy again. Though you can fly into Vienna or Prague, the train journey between the two makes you realize how close they are, both geographically and in spirit. The 150-mile (240 km) journey across the low wooded hills of northern Austria and the southern Czech Republic takes six hours, and from Prague to Kraków is only 240 miles (380 km) farther .

The place to start is the old imperial capital itself, Vienna. The city's historic center—the Innere Stadt—is surrounded by the Ringstrasse, a wide, sweeping boulevard flanked by grand 19th-century buildings and

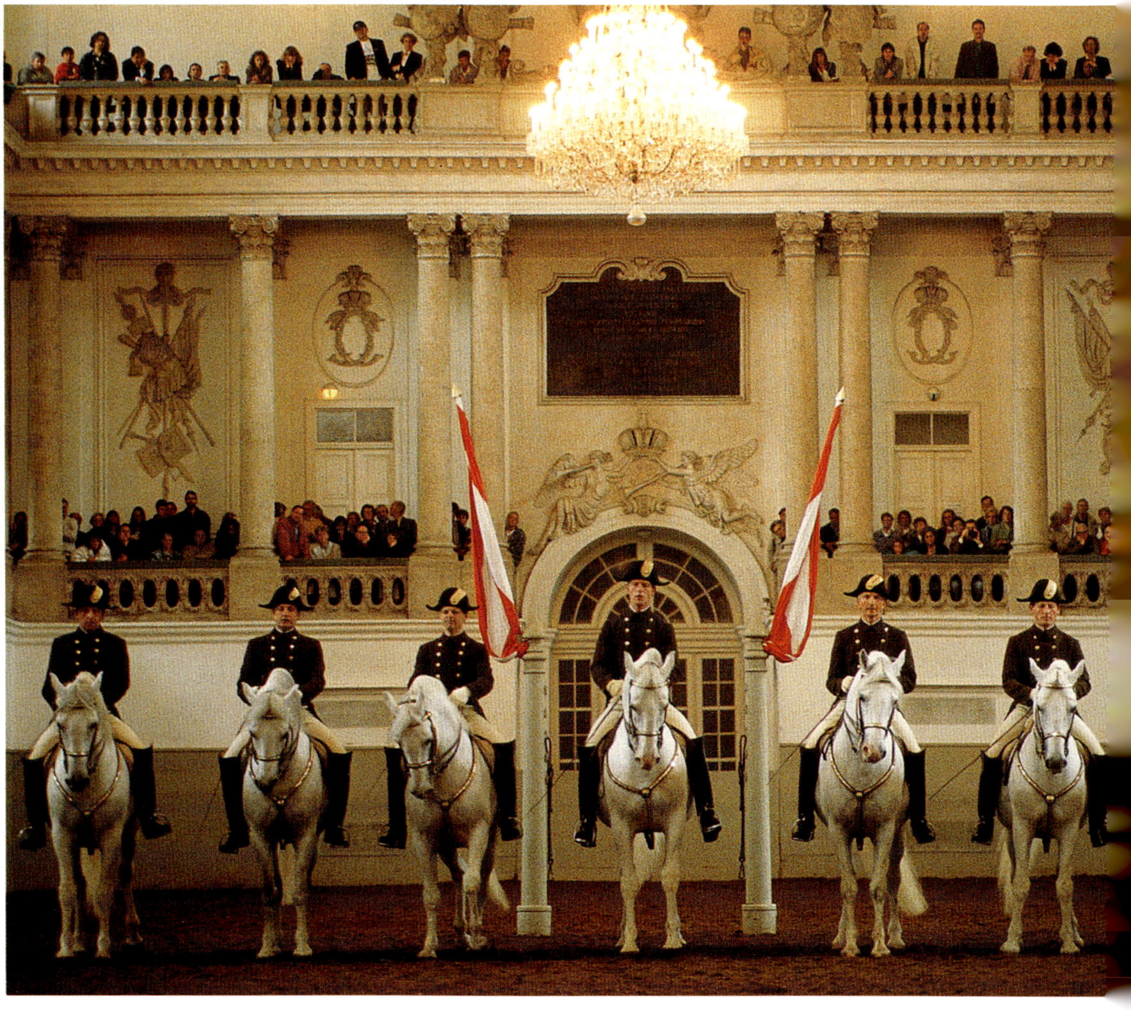

The world's best known Lipizzaner horses, a breed that specializes in high-stepping dressage, are those trained at the Spanish Riding School in Vienna (right).

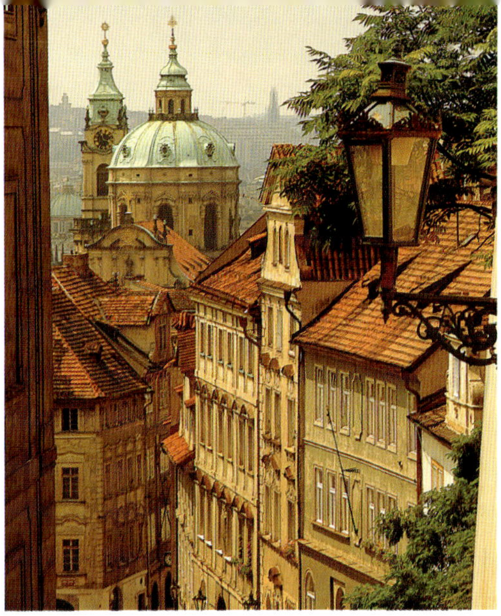

★ *Prague's picturesque Malá district (left) is dominated by the green dome of the 17th-century Baroque church of St. Nicholas.*

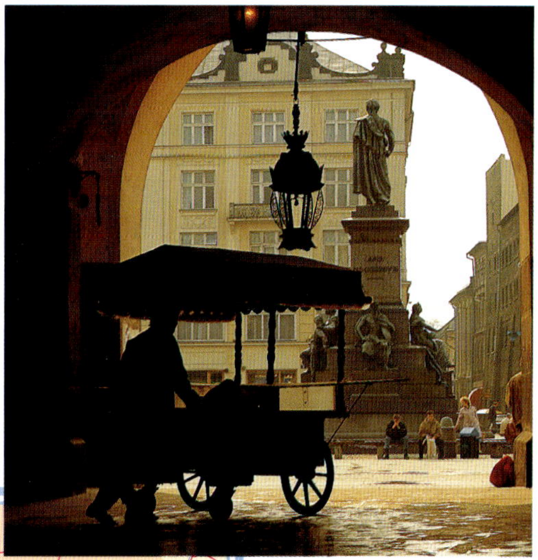

★ *Krakow market place (above) has been the scene of markets since Medieval times.*

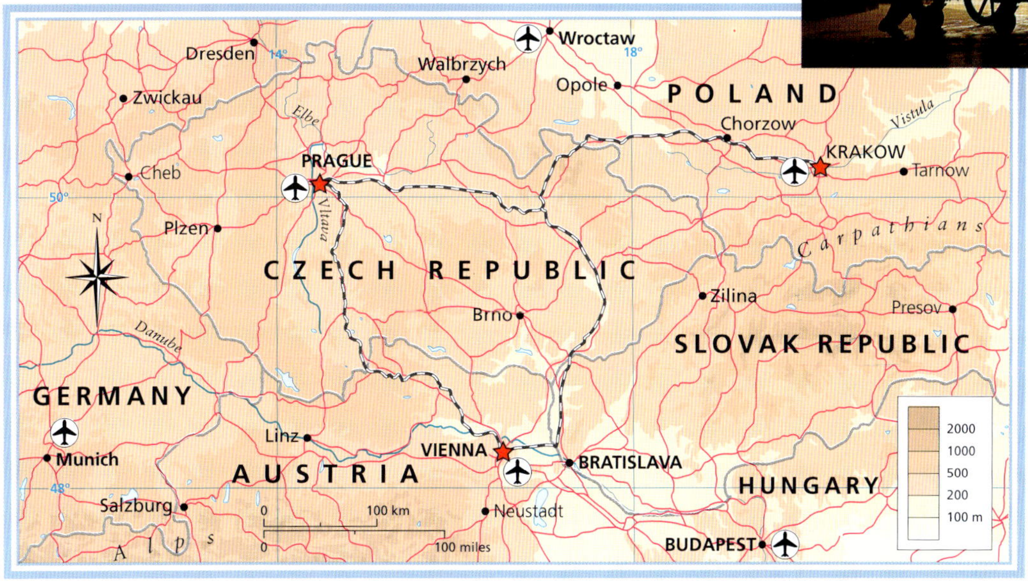

elegant coffeehouses. Bang in the center is the Stefansplatz, dominated by St. Stephen's Cathedral, whose spire—which the Viennese affectionately call Steffl (Little Stephen)—and steep roof of glazed tiles dominate the city skyline.

Southwest of the center is Schönbrunn Palace, built under Emperor Leopold I between 1696 and 1730 and extended in the mid-1700s to become Empress Maria Theresa's main palace. The long, yellow façade has a restrained Baroque elegance, but the state rooms inside are a riot of Rococo swirls in wood and plaster. North of the city center, across the Danube canal, the Prater, a big park, extends to the banks of the Danube itself. Here is the amusement park with the giant ferris wheel where Orson Welles made his memorable appearance in *The Third Man*.

As befits the former capital of a great empire, there are world-class classical concerts at the Musikverein and opera at the Vienna Staatsoper; you can watch the elaborate dressage of the Lipizzaner horses in the Spanish Riding School, or hear the Vienna Boys' Choir sing in the Hofburgkapelle. You can window-shop at the jewelers on elegant Kärntnerstrasse, or, if you're in Vienna at Christmas, buy decorations and spiced biscuits at the Christmas markets, while sipping *Glühwein* (mulled wine) against the cold.

There are many fine restaurants, as well as humbler taverns serving hearty Austrian fare. The cosmopolitan empire influenced Austria's cuisine—Hungarian goulash and Czech dumplings are on almost every menu; even Wiener schnitzel actually came from Milan. An unmissable Vienna experience is to sit in one of the city's marvelous coffeehouses and watch the world go by. They are decked out with chandeliers, gilt mirrors, and red velvet seats; old ladies take *Kaffee und Kuchen* (coffee and cakes), students play chess, and whiskered gentlemen scan the newspapers while the rich smell of coffee pervades the air.

A Fairytale City

Where Vienna is sedate, Prague is lively, irreverent—and as pretty as a city in a fairytale. The entire city center is a jumble of Gothic turrets and Baroque

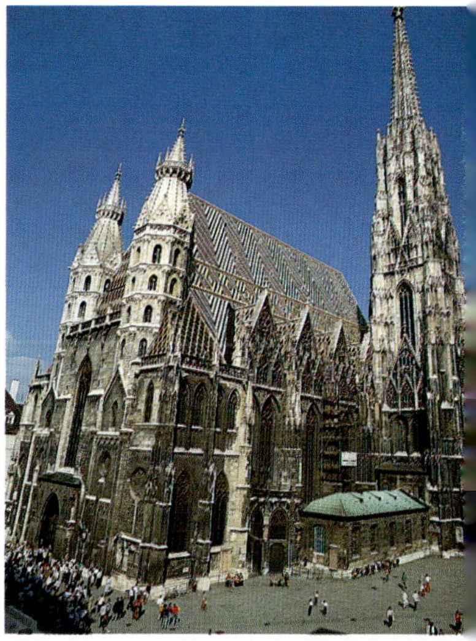

★ *In the heart of Vienna stands the Gothic cathedral of St. Stephen (above).*

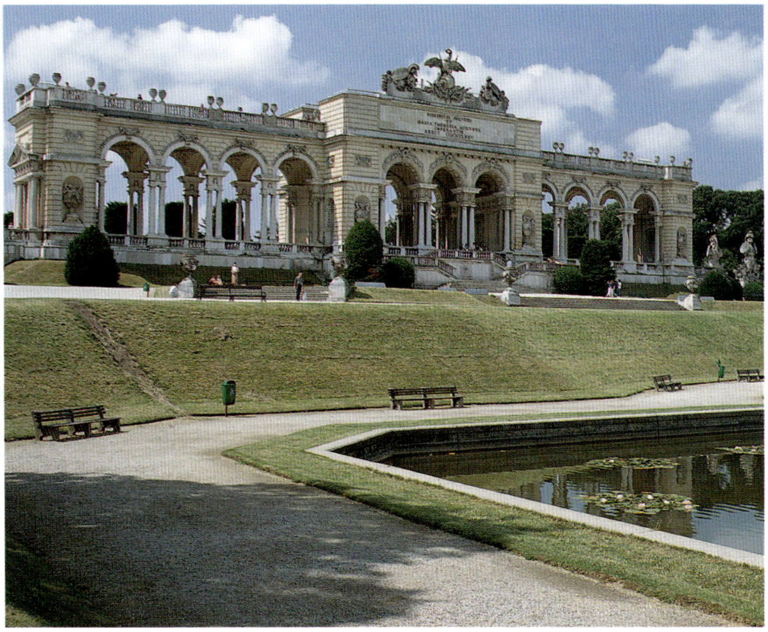

The colonnaded pavilion known as the Gloriette (above), on a hilltop in the grounds of the Schönbrunn Palace, commands splendid views across the city.

The Charles Bridge (right) that links the two halves of Prague is lined with Baroque statues added in the 17th and 18th centuries.

Viennese artists and architects were at the forefront of the Art Nouveau and Art Deco movements, and their work is evident in many of the city's buildings.

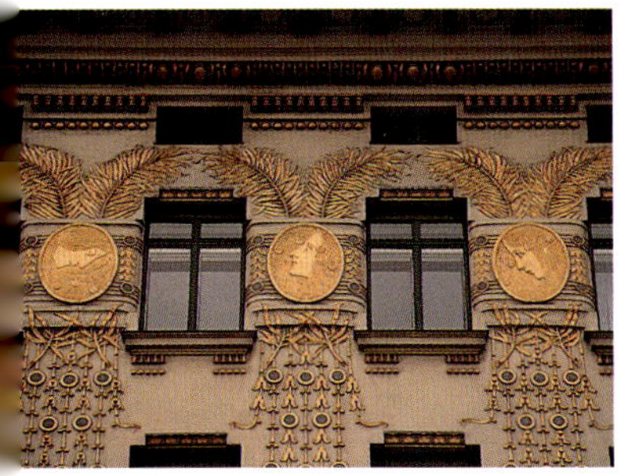

domes, winding cobbled streets, and mysterious passageways. Much of it has now been spruced up in pink, green, and ocher, but backstreets often lead to haunting old courtyards still unrestored. Every corner has its lively bar, where you can sample famous Czech beers. In summer, the place is packed with visitors; in autumn and winter it is shrouded in mists, the night air sharp with the sulfurous smell of coal fires.

Prague straddles the Vltava River. The western bank rises steeply to the Hradcany, the castle, whose forbidding walls enclose the seat of the Czech government and the cathedral of St. Vitus, with its soaring Gothic towers. Standing in one of the cobbled lanes below the castle, you sense its looming presence, and reflect that the great Prague writer Franz Kafka once lived in a tiny cottage here on Zlatá Ulicka (Golden Lane).

The neighboring district of Malá Strana is a richly atmospheric place. Its central square, Malostranské Námestí, is overshadowed by the towering walls and green dome of the Baroque church of St. Nicholas. Around the edges of the cobbled square, arcades house atmospheric bars and jazz clubs. Narrow streets wind their way past aristocratic palaces and gardens of the 1700s down to the Charles Bridge, lined with gesticulating statues and thronged in summer with crowds, street musicians, and gnats.

On the east side of the river is the traffic-free Staré Mesto. Here lies Staromestské Námesti (Old Town Square), overlooked by the twin towers of Tyn Church and surrounded by pavement cafés and bright painted houses of the 1500s with fantastic carvings. In the passageways leading off are old bookshops, and cellar restaurants. In the northern part of Staré Mesto is Josefov, the old Jewish quarter, an eloquent reminder of the rich Jewish culture of Middle Europe destroyed in the Holocaust, and a place of pilgrimage for Jewish visitors from all over the world. The Old-New Synagogue, dating from 1270, is one of the oldest surviving in Europe, while the cemetery with its richly carved tombstones leaning at all angles is a haunting memorial.

YOUTH CAPITAL

East of the Sudeten Mountains, Kraków, capital of Poland, is today coming to rival Prague as youth capital of Europe. There's a buzz about the place, with its lively student population and glorious old town packed with bars, restaurants, and cafés oozing old Middle European charm. You can dine on Polish specialities such as mountain trout in the stately surroundings of the Wierzynek Mansion, Kraków's oldest restaurant, going back to 1364 .

Miraculously, the old town survived the Second World War with little physical damage, and is now listed by UNESCO as one of the world's twelve most significant historic sites. It centers on the Rynek Glówny, a vast flagstoned square—the largest medieval square in Europe—flanked by the long arcades of the Sukiennice, the city's 1500s cloth hall, with its scrollwork parapet topped by grotesque faces. The Mariacki Church (St. Mary's) on the east side is topped by a bizarre cluster of pinnacles. Once, goes the legend, a watchman on its tower saw a Tartar raiding party approaching, and blew the alarm on his trumpet, only to be cut short by an arrow. Every hour, a lone trumpeter still plays the plaintive melody, stopping abruptly at the point the watchman was hit.

Towering above is Wawel Hill, a rocky crag overlooking the River Vistula. Right on the top is the castle, with its splendid Renaissance courtyard and red brick cathedral with Gothic turrets and Baroque cupolas. This was the traditional burial place of the kings of Poland, and their elaborate tombs—in every style from medieval to the 1700s—line the interior.

Not far south from Wawel Hill is another reminder of the rich Jewish heritage of Central Europe—the old ghetto of Kazimierz. If these narrow medieval streets, with their white painted houses with round doorways and deep-set windows, look familiar, it may be because *Schindler's List* was filmed here. The grandest of the six surviving Kazimierz synagogues is the Old Synagogue, completed in 1557. The main façade has an imposing Renaissance portico and is a museum devoted to Kraków Jewry's history. Kazimierz, however, now has a bright and lively air with restaurants and cafés.

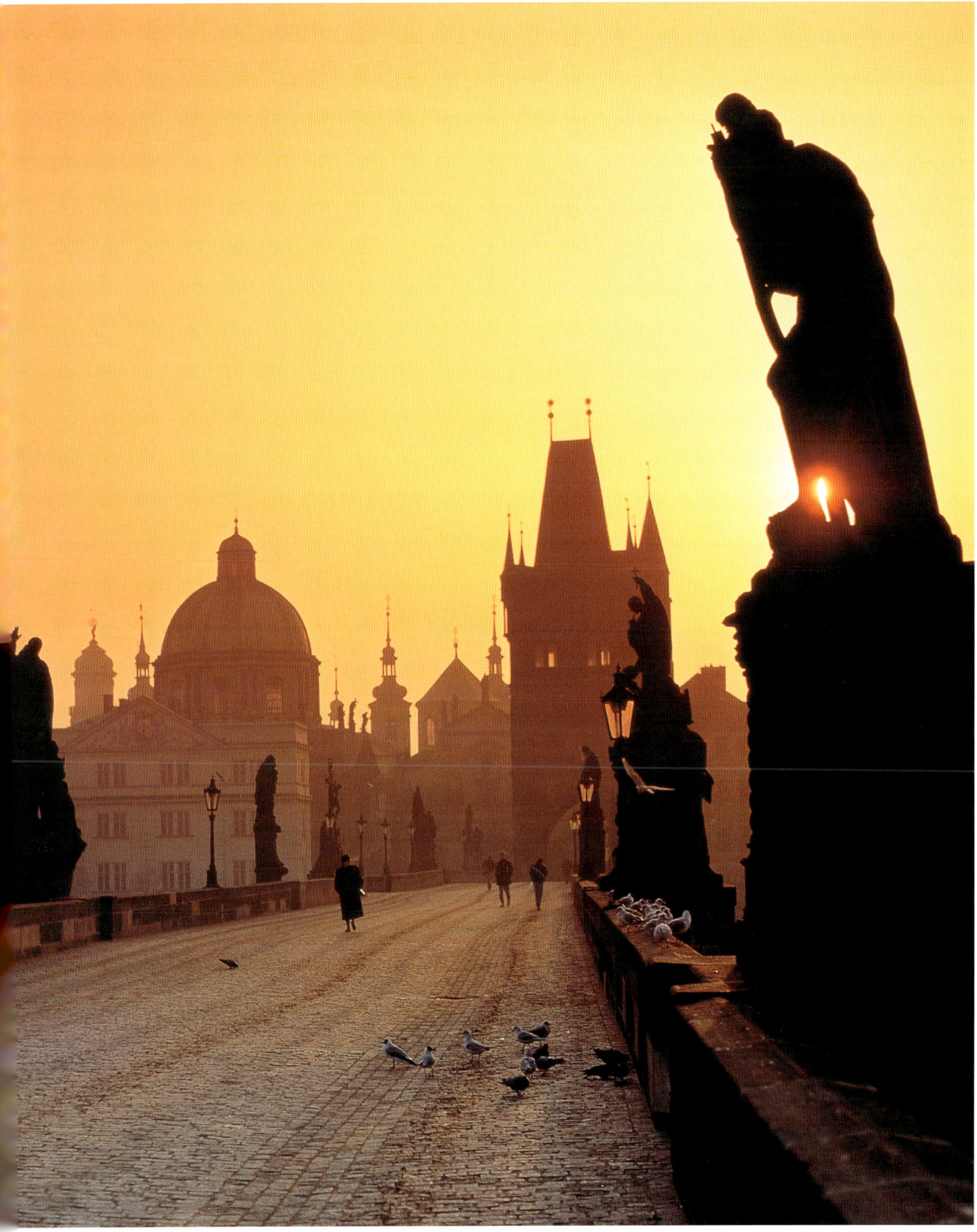

Northern Asia

"A good traveler has no fixed plans and is not intent on arriving."

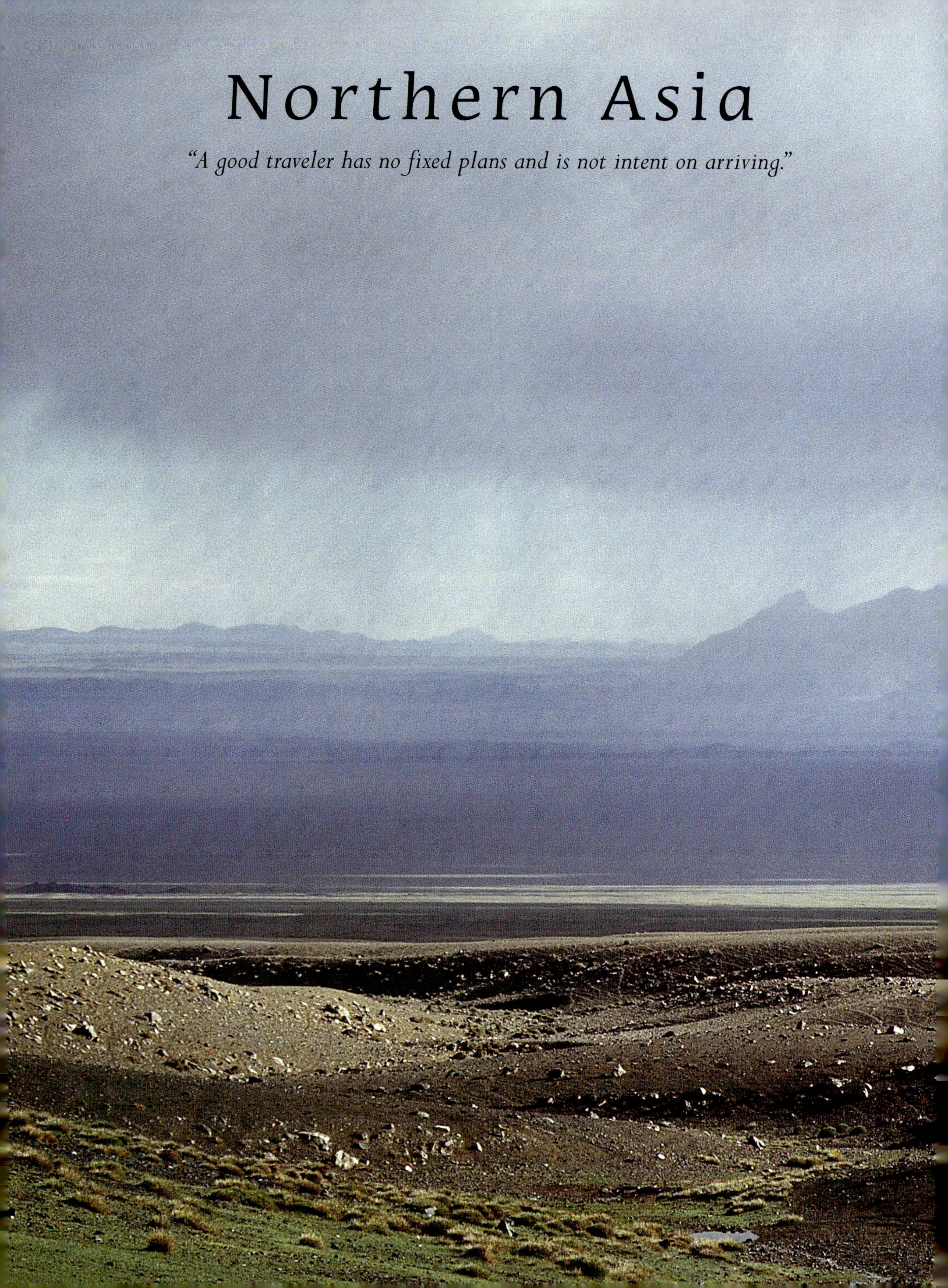

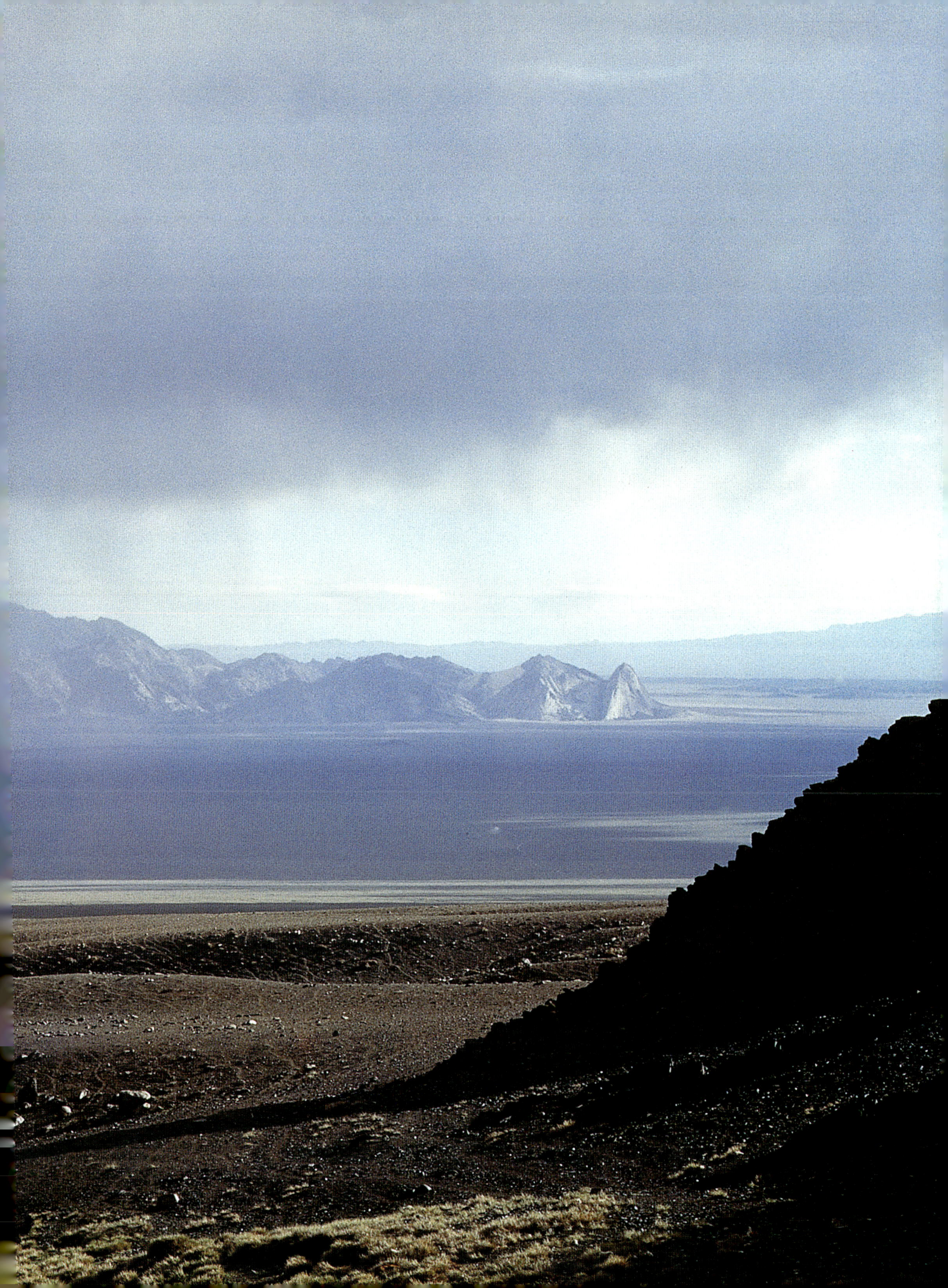

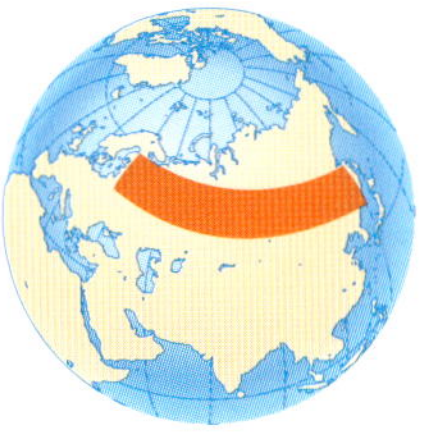

The Trans-Siberian Railroad

Crossing continents and time zones, stretching almost halfway across the planet, the Trans- Siberian Railroad remains one of the world's classic train journeys.

The 16th-century St. Basil's Cathedral in Moscow (right) is a confection of nine churches in one.

NOT ONLY TRAIN BUFFS KNOW of the Trans-Siberian Railroad, the world's longest rail journey which links the Baltic Sea to the Pacific Ocean. It runs through the heart of old Russia, tracing the route of the Russian peoples eastward in the 16th and 17th centuries—a corridor of opportunity and exploration through the lands of the middle Volga, the southern Urals mountains, between the taiga and mountains of southern Siberia, until finally reaching the Pacific Ocean at Vladivostok. The journey is a world classic, and offers a literally unique opportunity to appreciate the enormity of the Russian landscape, and the indomitable character of its people.

Under the Communists (1917-91) the rail route was changed to run from Moscow, but the true starting point is St. Petersburg, the "window on the West" founded in 1703 by Tsar Peter the Great as his new capital. Built on 100 islands and linked by 300 bridges, the "Venice of the North" glitters with gold-domed palaces, towers, and churches. At the end of Nevsky Prospect, the principal street lined with cafés, shops, and theaters, lies the Hermitage housing what not only Russians consider the world's grandest collection of western painting. The decor inside is so ornate—high ceilings inlaid with goldleaf, marble floors, and columns—that it can distract you from the pictures (by Leonardo, Rembrandt, Breughel, El Greco, Cézanne, Picasso, among many others). After a day spent trekking around the literally miles of galleries, your feet and neck will tell you it is time to go.

Leaving St. Petersburg, the journey to Moscow through fields and forests takes less than a day—the fastest part of the whole trip. Moscow, the Russian capital, concentrates its sights around Red Square: the Kremlin, St. Basil's Cathedral, and today McDonalds and Pizza Hut. You can see them in a day before boarding the train which will take you to the far ends of the earth, for Moscow lies at the epicenter of the huge Russian rail network.

Once the Trans-Siberian Express leaves Moscow, it stops only to change locomotives, take on food and

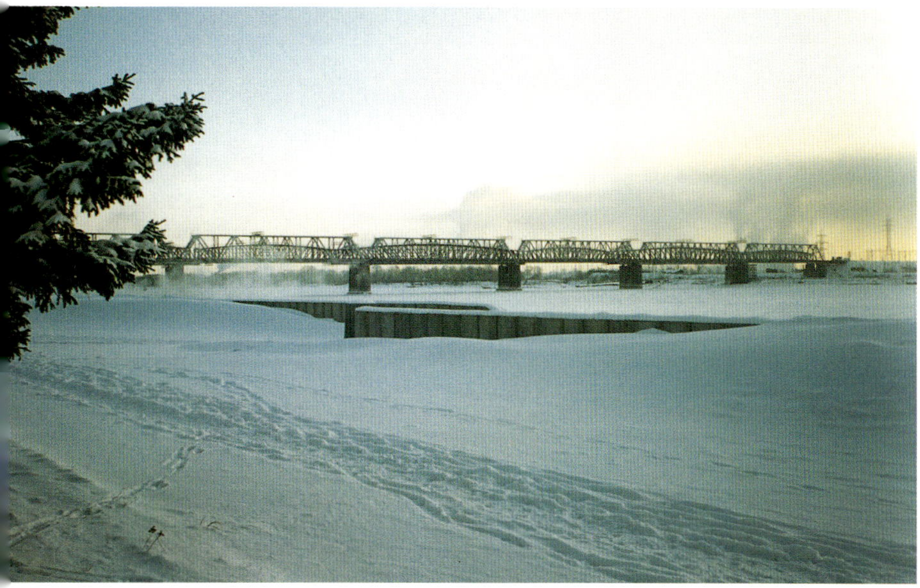

Crossing the largest and deepest river of its route—the Ob at Novosibirsk (above)—presented one of the greatest obstacles in the building of the Trans-Siberian railroad. The city is a cultural gem—the result of highly educated deportees who ended up settling there.

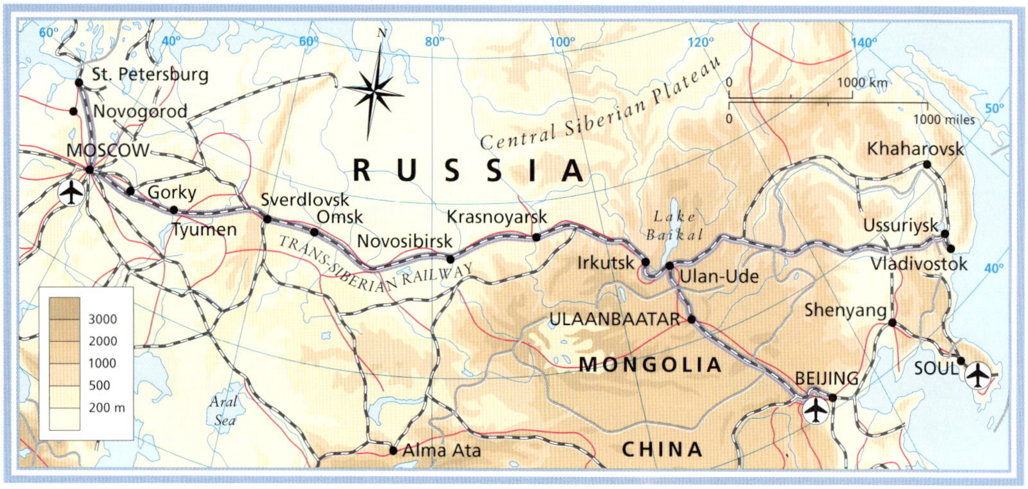

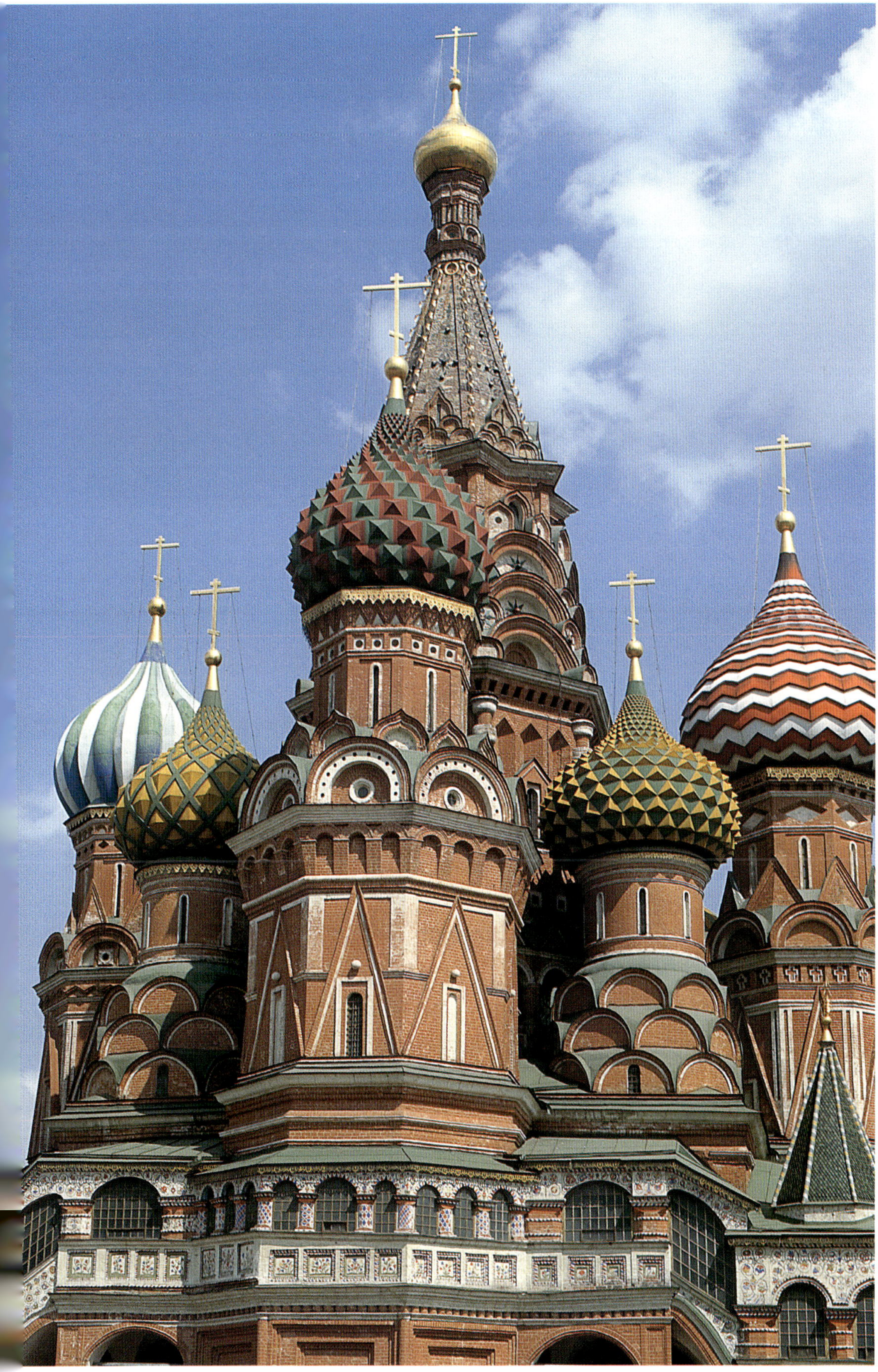

FACT FILE

Language: Russian. Very little English spoken anywhere.

Money: Roubles and (preferably) U.S. Dollars. The rouble devalues often.

Time: The Trans-Siberian crosses 8 time zones between St. Petersburg and Vladivostok, but all trains run on Moscow time. It can sometimes be confusing.

When to go: Trains run all year round, but summer and Christmas are the most popular times to go, so are best avoided. Temperatures in summer vary from 50°F to 96°F (10 °to 35°C), and in winter they go down as far as minus 40°F (minus 40°C).

Trains: The true Trans-Siberian Express is the Rossiya (Train #1 & #2), which goes all the way between Moscow and Vladivostok. The journey time is 7 nights/8 days. You need a separate train to go to/from St. Petersburg. There are numerous trains to destinations in between plus trains to Ulaanbaatar in Mongolia and Beijing in China.

Distances: Moscow - Vladivostok 5,776 miles (9,297 km); Moscow-Ulaanbaatar Beijing 4,887 miles (7,865 km); Moscow-Beijing 5,592 miles (9,001 km).

What to take: A vacuum flask (boiling water is available from the samovar at the end of each carriage), penknife, flashlight, deck of cards, tea, coffee, toilet paper, a large mug, snacks, chocolate, dried fruit.

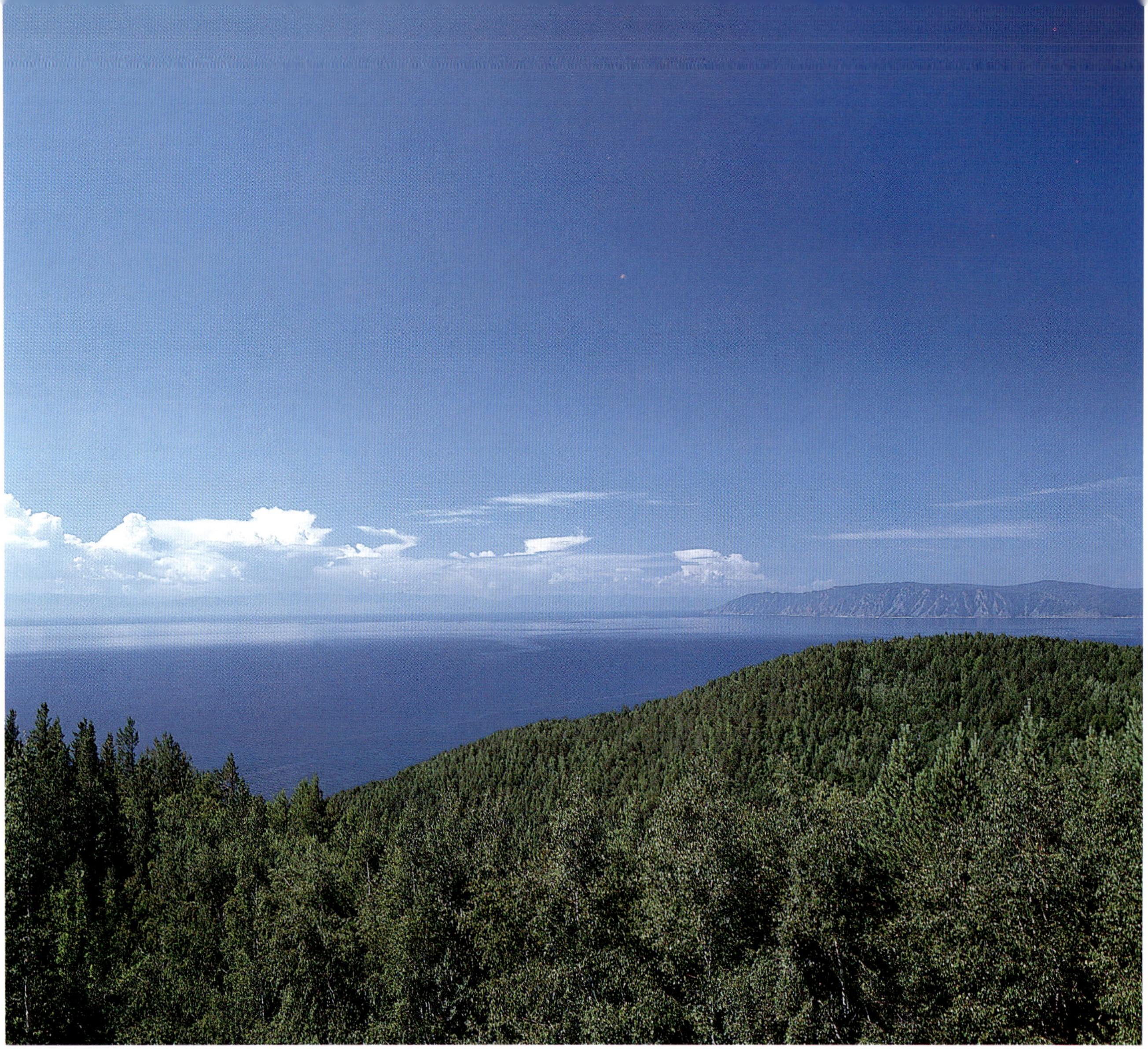

water, or take on and let off passengers. Getting off the train at these stops is no problem. You can stretch your legs, try some local food, or just try to chat with the Russians. The length of the stopovers varies from just a few minutes to more than half an hour. Your carriage conductor, called a *provodnik* (male) or *provodnitsa* (female), will tell you how long each stop is and keep an eye out for you if the train starts to leave. As most trains travel the same route, it is possible to break your journey and stay a few days in, for example, Ekaterinburg, where the last Tsar and his family were murdered by the Bolsheviks, Irkutsk on Lake Baikal, or Novosibirsk (New Siberia), the largest city in Siberia.

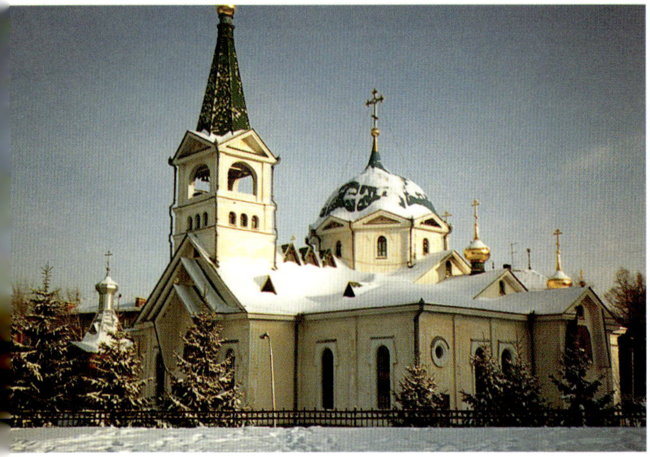

There are about 20 carriages plus a dining car on all the Trans-Siberian trains. They are comfortable if basic, with bunkbeds and bedding, though they feel a little cramped with four in a cabin in second class. First class has two berths. You'll probably have to wait your turn for the two bathrooms, particularly early in the morning. At the end of each carriage is a boiler called a samovar which provides plenty of boiling water 24 hours a day. The food in the dining car sometimes leaves a lot to be desired, being pretty tasteless, but it is not too expensive.

There are more than 800 stations between Moscow and Vladivostok, most very small and simple, but each with a personality of its own. At every station there are roving food sellers. Little old ladies (babushkas or grannies) sell home-made salami-type sausages and boiled potatoes covered with chopped salad onions. Others sell ice cream, bread, fish, cookies, beer, soft

Lake Baikal (above) holds a volume of water equivalent to that of all five of North America's Great Lakes.

The chapel at Novosibirsk (left) is reputed to be at the geographical center of the old Russian Empire.

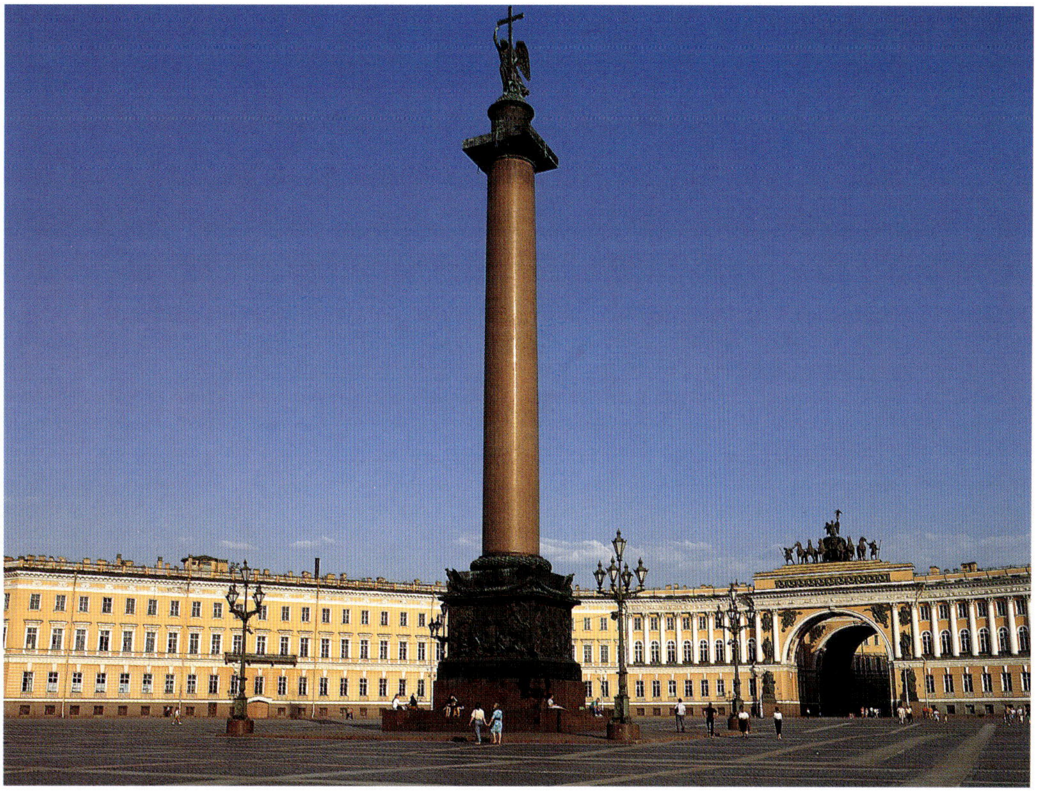

The Alexander Column towers over Palace Square, St. Petersburg (right), a top tourist spot now, and the starting point for the revolutions of 1905 and 1917.

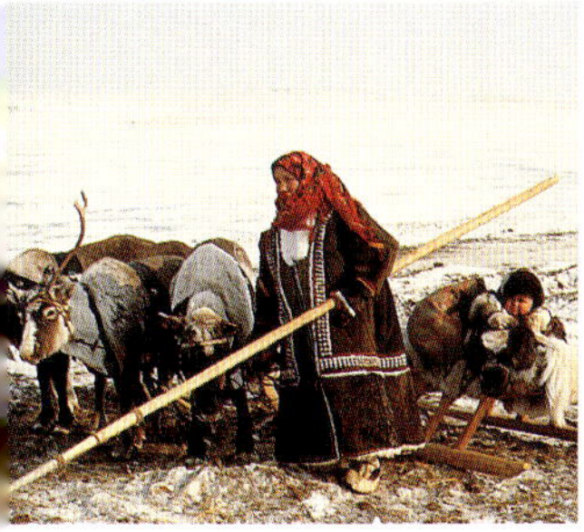

A babushka (old woman or grandmother) tends her reindeer near Tyumen in Siberia.

drinks, including the national drink, vodka. Pot noodles and other subsistence items are available from small kiosks on the platforms.

INTO SIBERIA

Siberia is generally flat and covered in taiga, but traditional houses and small villages fill gaps in the forest, and there are huge swathes of purple and blue wildflowers in spring and summer. Winter is perhaps the most atmospheric time to travel, when the land is covered in a sparkling blanket of white, and the locals travel in horse-drawn sleighs. The train at times rumbles over long bridges over the immense rivers of the Irtysh, the Ob, and the Angara.

Perhaps the high point of the journey comes when the train runs around the steep forested shores of Lake Baikal. This is the world's deepest freshwater lake at 5,372 feet (1,637 m), holding about one-fifth of the world's reserves of fresh water. The water is so clear that you can see a white 8-inch (20-cm) disk down to 130 feet (40 m). It is also the world's oldest lake, formed around 20 million years ago, and has been reckoned to have 50 species of fish, 500 species of animals, including the world's only species of freshwater seal, and 1,200 plant species, of which two thirds are endemic to the region. However, the lake has become severly polluted and is shrinking rapidly. Strangely, 338 rivers flow into Lake Baikal, but only one flows out. Before the Trans-Siberian Railroad was completed, trains and passengers were transported across the lake by ship. The British-built ship, the *Angara*, is now a floating museum in Irkutsk, Siberia's capital. Listvyanka is the main town at the southern end of the lake; its primary industry is fishing and it is a delightful base for exploring the region. You can go trekking in the nearby Baikal National Park, but in summer the mosquitoes and blackflies are a nuisance.

Siberia used to be a name of dread—the place where Russia sent her troublesome misfits, criminals, political dissenters, and often totally innocent people to work in the mines of its coldest, most desolate parts. Deportees were often sent for life and lost all civil rights. If they survived their penal term, they might be permitted to settle somewhere in Siberia, but could seldom return to European Russia. But now Siberia is more interested in travelers than deportees.

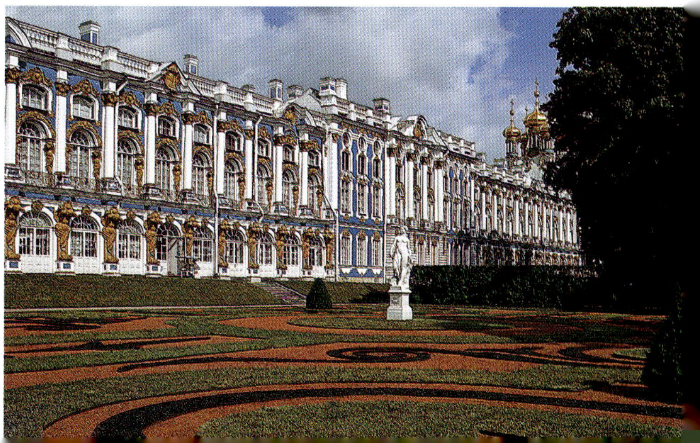

The Pushkin Palace (right) on the outskirts of St. Petersburg is named for the great Russian poet who spent his formative years in the area; it is part of the Grand Catherine Palace.

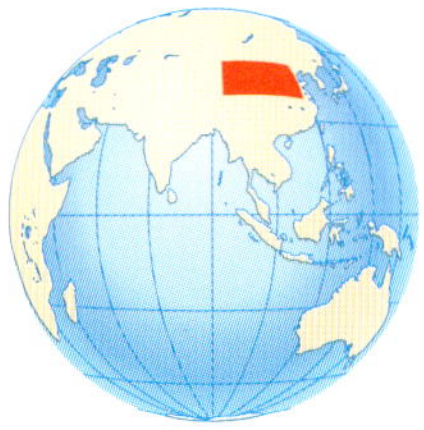

The Great Wall of China

China's Great Wall has always inspired superlatives—unsurprisingly, for it is one of the greatest building enterprises in the history of the world.

FACT FILE

Best time to visit: Spring and summer. It is very cold in winter.

Language and names: Confusion is rife. Chinese signs and names are often transliterated, but not always. Transliteration officially uses the Pinyin system; but the older Wade--Giles system may be more familiar to some Westerners. In addition, many Chinese place names have changed, and minority languages often have their own names for places—which may also be transliterated. If in doubt, ask.

Health notes: Avoid unbottled or unboiled water, salads, uncooked vegetables, and peeled fruits. Rabies is common, so avoid animals.

Visas: Compulsory, but easy to get at embassies.

Most vital accessory: Business card.

Currency: China has two, one for locals (Renminbi, or RMB); and another for foreigners (Foreign Exchange certificates, or FEC). Chinese prefer FEC. U.S. dollars are very acceptable.

THE WALL TODAY is much as it was when Lord Macartney, heading the first British embassy to China, which was also the first ever Western embassy to China, saw it in 1783—fortified walls "carried along the ridges of hills, over the tops of the highest mountains, descending into the deepest valleys, crossing upon arches over rivers." For foreigners it was then a legendary wonder and inconceivably remote. Built to mark the barrier between the highly cultivated lands of China to the south and the open steppes to the north, the Wall runs for the most part through mountainous territory, making maximum use of every cliff or precipice to increase its defenses—and also its grandeur. Its westernmost section marches out into the

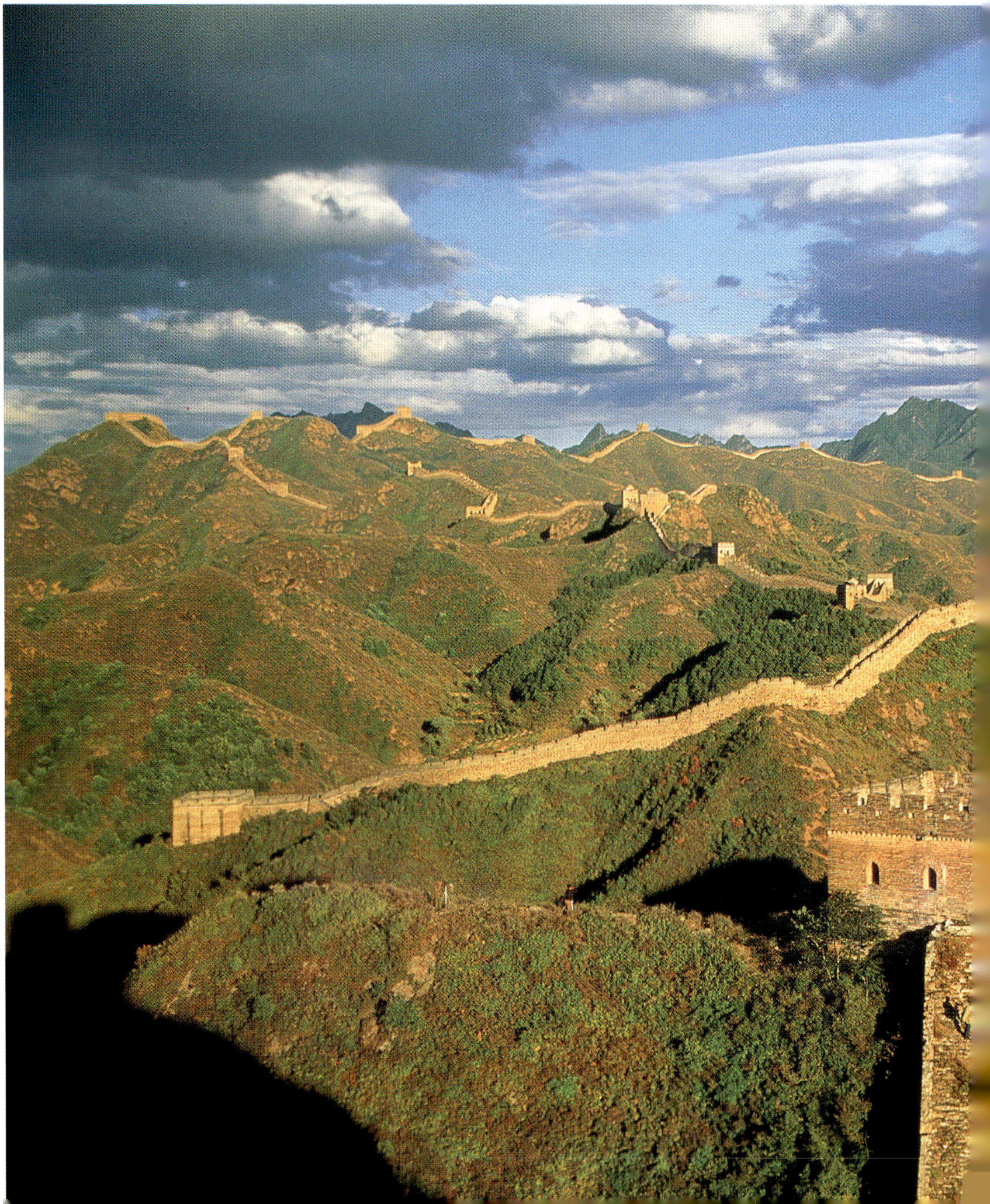

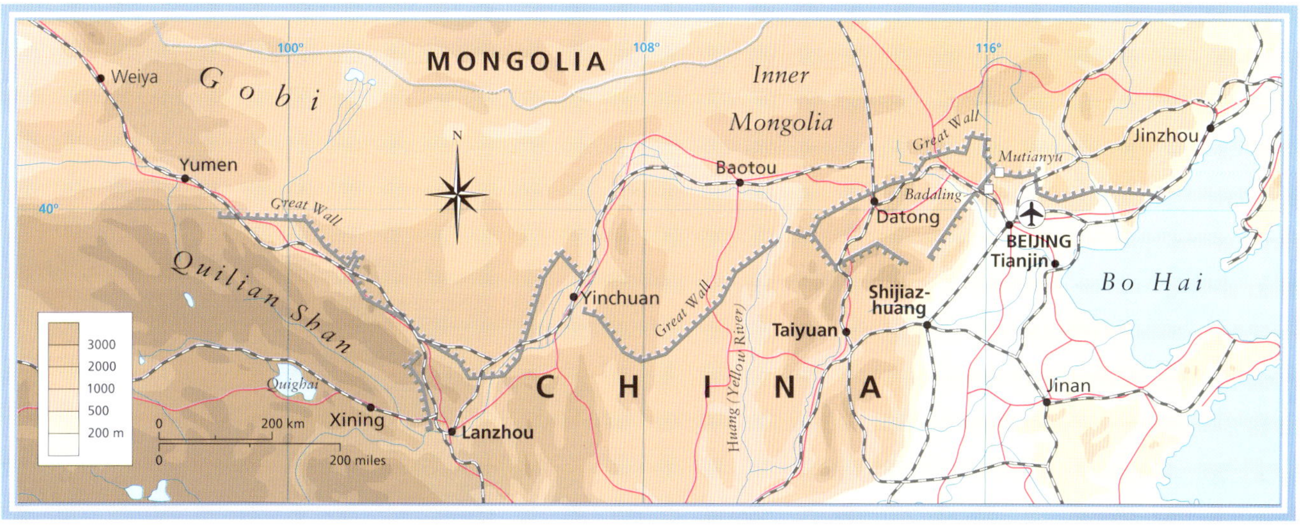

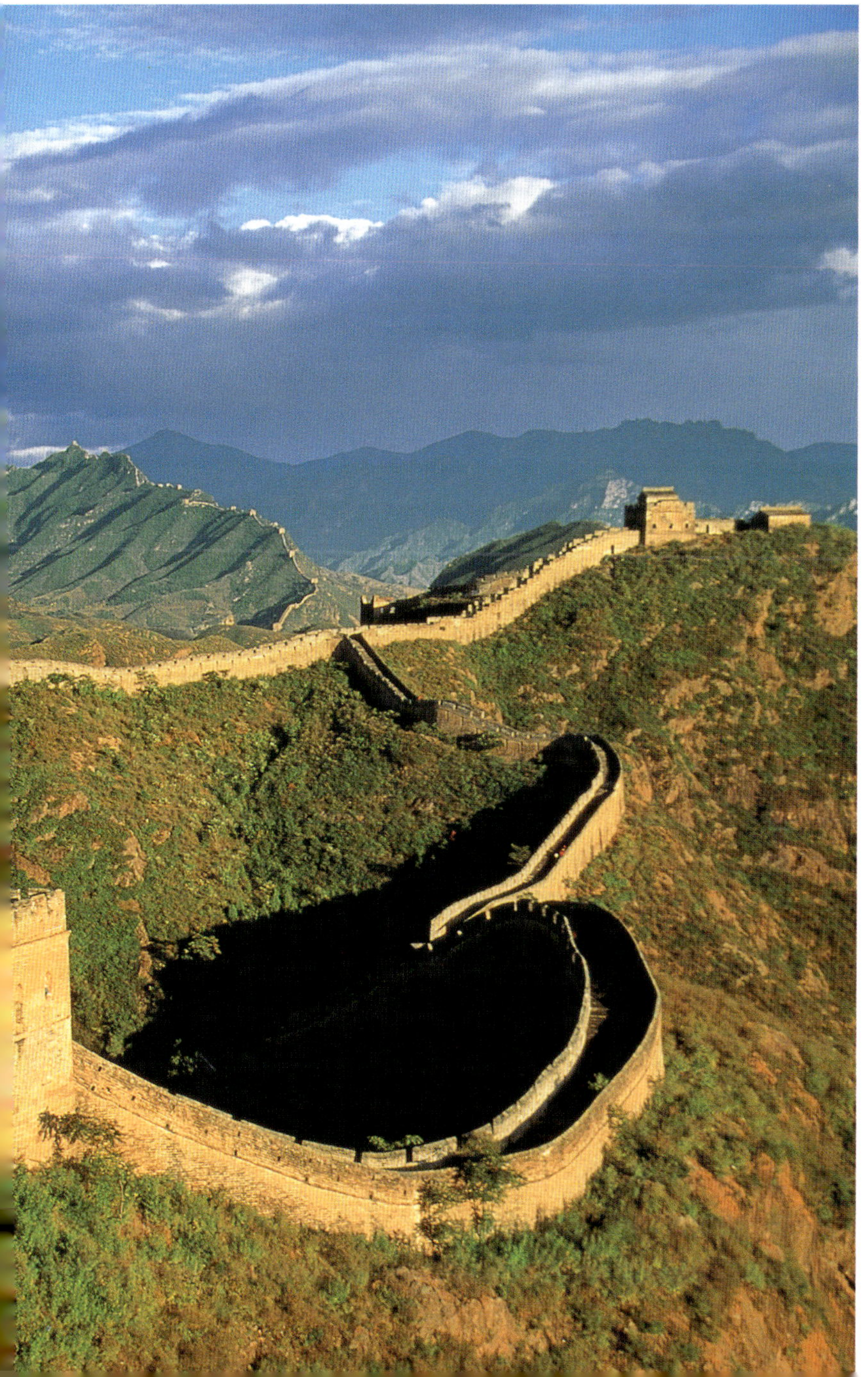

As the map shows, the Wall rambles from the far West past Beijing, where it is at its most picturesque (left). As the ancient guardian of Chinese territory, it is honored by soldiers in traditional Manchu dress (right).

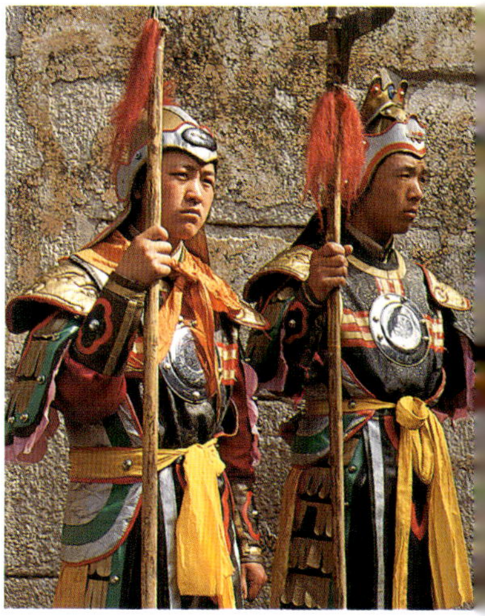

Gobi Desert, a region of sandblasted, almost lunar landscapes, feared by garrison troops more for its bitter winters and baking summers than any barbarians, while its eastern end expires amid the factories and farms of the densely populated marshy coastlands of the Yellow Sea.

Today, the Wall's great ramparts can be seen snaking like a viaduct across China's barren northern hills by any visitor to Beijing (Peking) willing to ride in a bus or a taxi for an hour. Millions do it every year, catching tour buses in Tiananmen Square—the world's larges square, covering 100 acres (40 ha) at the very center of imperial Beijing—or the rail station, or arranging trips through their hotels. In addition, trains run to the wall from Beijing's main station, on their way northwest. Most visitors see little more than the 27-foot (8 m) high section at Badaling, 40 miles (70 km) outside the capital. At this solidly restored bastion, which guarded a hilly pass to the northeast, tourists can take a cable car to the 20-fo0t (6 m) wide rampart, buy T-shirts, and take snapshots. Another popular section is Mutianyu, 55 miles (90 km) north of Beijing. On the

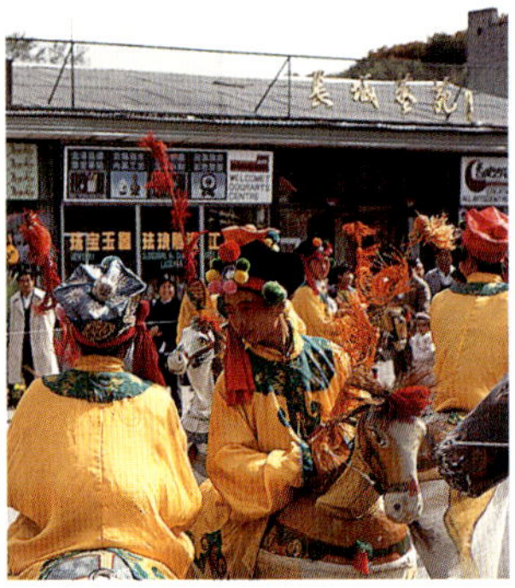

A pageant at the Great Wall exemplifies how it is used for many aspects of Chinese life, including tourism, education, commercial enterprise, and entertainment.

way back from the Wall, you can easily make a detour to visit the Valley of the Ming Tombs, where 13 of the 16 Ming emperors lie in state in impressive mausoleums.

ACROSS SWITCHBACK HILLS

Unless you are willing to venture into areas without any tourist facilities—where you really need to speak Chinese—the best place to see the Wall in pristine form, and without too many tourists, is Simatai, 70 miles (110 km) northeast. Here an 11-mile (19 km) section over switchback hills displays 135 watchtowers, which overlook stretches that climb up slopes so steep they can only be scaled on all fours. It is very easy to imagine the time when this was frontier territory, where conscripts stared down at armies of nomadic barbarians as they surged out of the endless grasslands of Mongolia or Manchuria.

Today's tide of tourism scarcely touches the Wall itself. It stretches for some 1,500 miles (2,400 km), though estimates vary, because it is not a single entity. In some places two or three walls were built, so the total length may exceed 3,000 miles (5,000 km)—no exact figure yet exists because no complete archaeological maps have been published.

MYTHS AND FACTS

Tiantan (below)—"The Temple of Heaven"—in Beijing, is set in its own park.

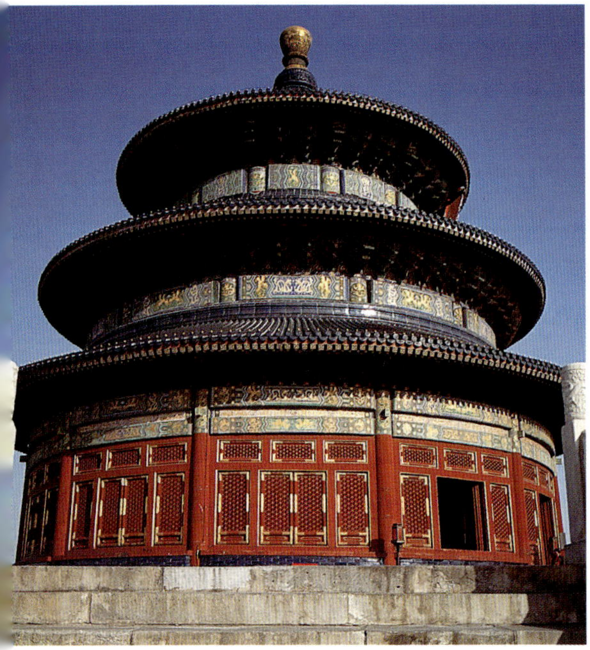

The Great Wall is as much myth as fact. Among the myths: that today's Wall is more than 2,000 years old. In fact, the Great Wall, or its surviving sections, represent the last and greatest of dozens. Wall building was a constant theme throughout Chinese history from the 3rd century B.C. onward, inspired by the constant need to keep at bay the hordes of restless and acquisitive nomads to the north. For two millennia, Chinese rulers experimented with different ways of dealing with the "nomad problem," trading, intermarrying, attacking, conquering—and only as a last resort, building walls to keep them out. Nothing worked. In the 13th century, the Mongols easily bypassed the Great Wall's early sections to establish their own Chinese dynasty.

The emperors of the Mongol's successors, the Ming (1368-1644), decided on a more lasting solution: a new Great Wall, which was mainly built in the second half of the 1400s, replacing and joining up previous walls. These earlier versions were partly built of mud, which eroded quickly. The present Great Wall was made of brick and stone, and built by forced labor. The crenellated rampart was constructed to take five horsemen riding abreast—it was always as much a military highway as barrier—and towers punctuate it every few hundred yards. These were both bases for garrisons and used for signaling, to track the mercurial nomads in their perpetual gallops in search of weak points.

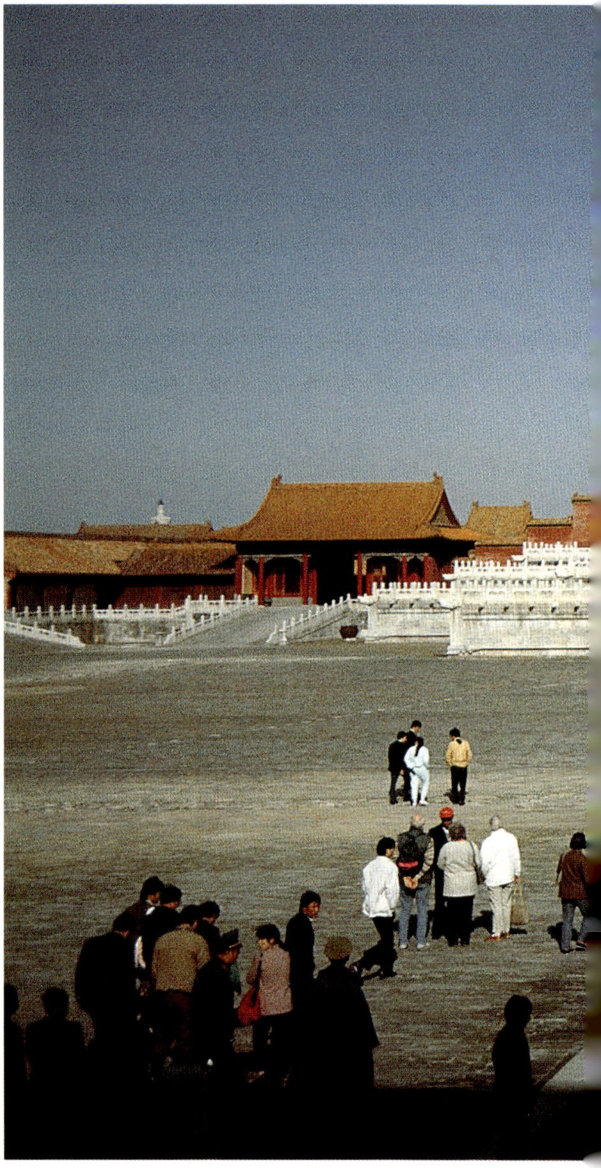

Building started in the west. Then, in response to Mongol attacks it snaked eastwards, creating barriers along the southern edge of Mongol territory, cutting north of Beijing and finally heading east to the Yellow Sea coast. Despite its grandeur, it was as useless as its predecessors—a century after it was finished, China fell to the Manchus of the northeast, and the Wall

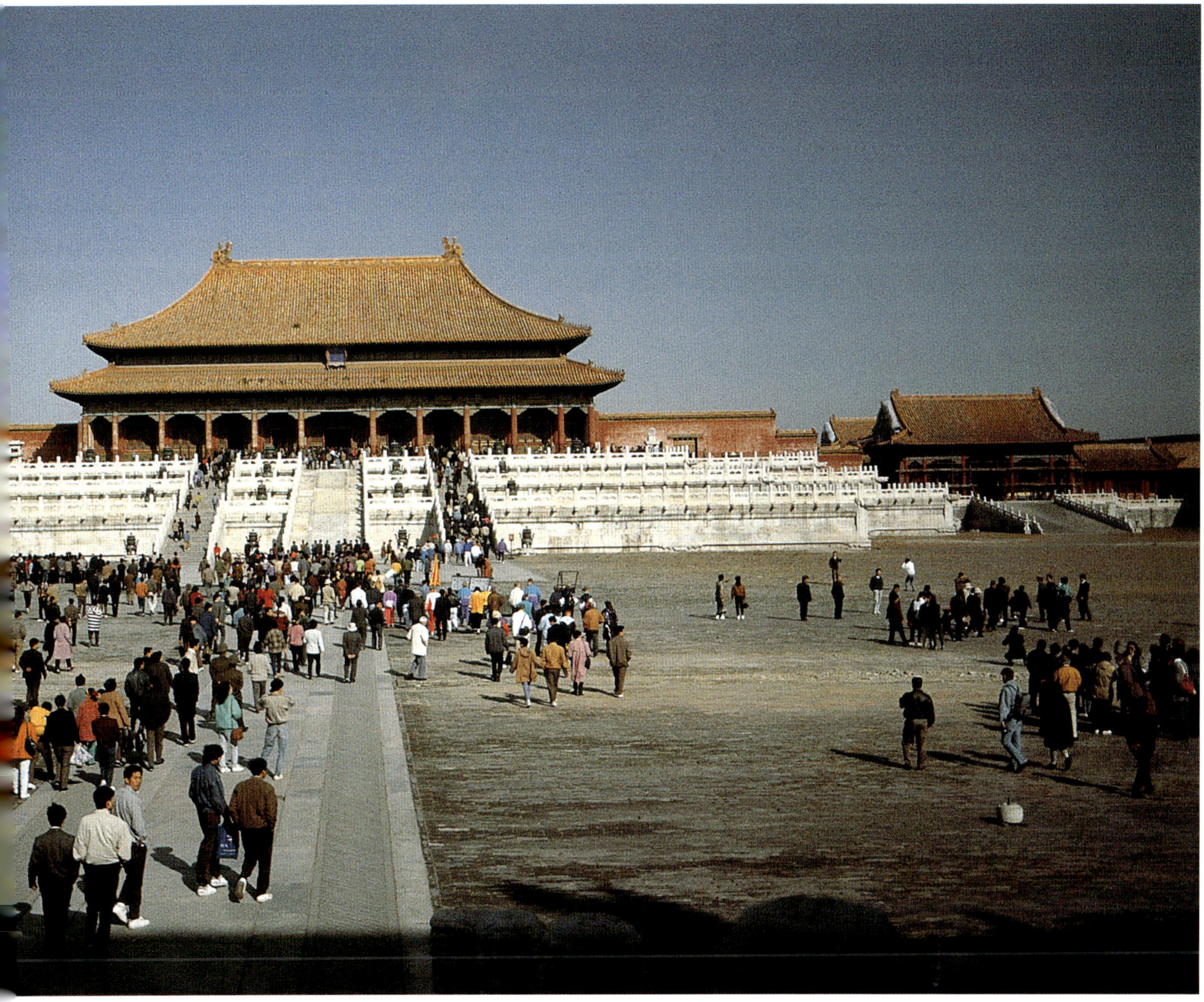

ceased to mark any frontier. The grasslands that were once regarded as barbarian borderlands soon became an integral part of China.

Though much of the Wall has crumbled and whole sections are isolated, the most visited parts have been carefully restored as the result of a policy decision in the 1980's. Premier Deng Xiaoping initiated the campaign, which had as its slogan: "Let us love our country and restore our Great Wall!" As a result, after centuries of ill treatment, the Wall has undergone a renaissance along much of its length, and so remains a symbol of China itself to the Chinese. They refer to it by the name of its most ancient predecessor—"the 10,000-li wall," a li being 0.3 mile (0.5 km). Many legends and myths, which indiscriminately mix fact and fiction, old walls and new, ensure that it remains a bastion of culture in Chinese minds and hearts—as well as in awe-inspiring fact.

BELIEVE IT OR NOT? NOT!

Once, did-you-know items in magazines used to say that the Great Wall was the only human structure visible from the moon. The notion, originating at the turn of the century, was widely believed after it appeared in Robert Ripley's Believe it or Not, *a bestseller in the 1930s. No one, of course, could check until men first walked on the moon in 1969. In fact, from there it is hard to spot China, let alone the Wall, which is hardly visible to the naked eye even from earth orbit. But, to stretch a point, something of the Great Wall became visible in orbit in the 1990s—it is the name taken by China for its satellite-launching company.*

Beijing's Forbidden City (above) is made up of a complex of gates, halls, and temples.

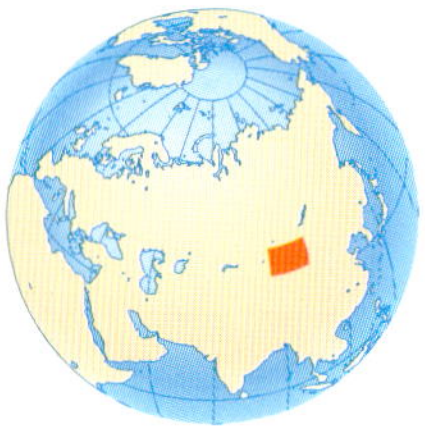

The Flaming Cliffs of the Gobi Desert

Virtually unvisited for decades, the Flaming Cliffs of Mongolia have long been renowned for dinosaur fossils. Now this scientific Mecca can be seen by anyone in search of true wilderness.

FACT FILE

Access: Flights into the Mongolian capital, Ulaanbaatar, via Beijing, Moscow, and the Kazakhstan capital of Almaty. There are several flights a week in summer to the southern Gobi town of Dalanzadgad.

Accommodation: Gobi-Juulchin Camp, or the three hotels in Dalanzadgad. Arrangements can be made through Mongolian tour operators, and/or via the Ulaanbaatar Hotel or Bayangol Hotel in Ulaanbaatar.

Summer climate: Often up to 100° F (38° C), and very dry. If you travel in a car or bus, the heat is not too unpleasant.

Time to avoid: Winter, when temperatures reach -40°F (-40°C).

When to go: June through September.

Dress: Sun hat, good shoes and sturdy jacket—winds can be vicious.

Language: Mongolian and Russian, but English is coming up fast.

"ONE GREAT SCULPTURED WALL we named the 'Flaming Cliffs,' for when seen in early morning or late afternoon sunlight it seemed to be a mass of glowing fire." So wrote the American explorer and scientist Roy Chapman Andrews on his first fossil-hunting expedition in the Gobi in 1922.

It is a sight many at the time yearned to see, but few succeeded. For the next 70 years, Mongolia's backcountry, like the country itself, was locked away in the heart of the Soviet empire. Now access is there for the asking. Outside of the southern Gobi town of Dalanzadgad, two desert camps cater for tourists (mainly Japanese, to whom the Gobi's vast open spaces have a particular appeal). Buses and cars are available for the 50-mile (80 km) run to the Flaming Cliffs. There are no proper roads—the whole country has only 1,500 miles (2,400 km) of paved road—but the

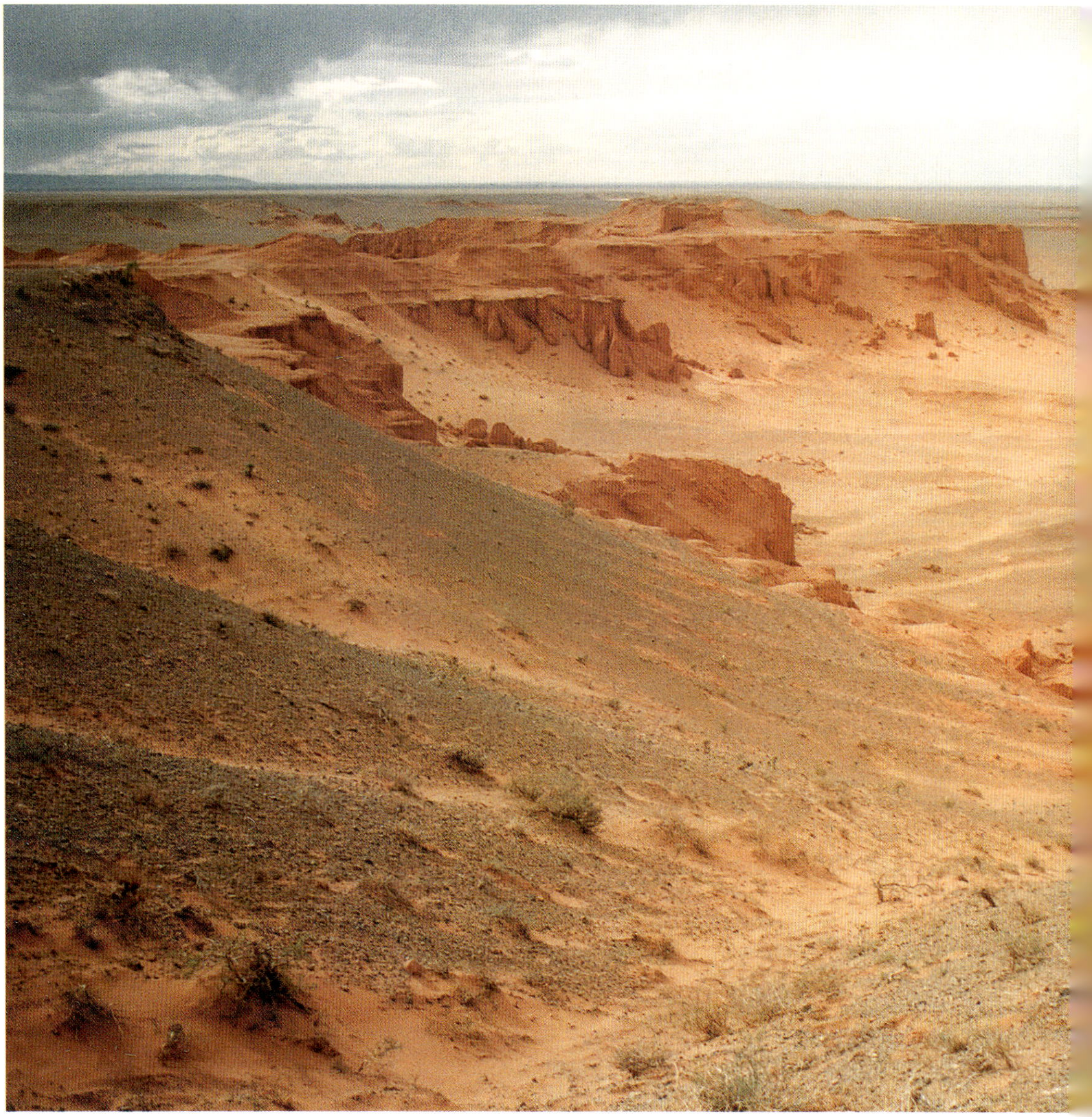

The Flaming Cliffs (right) are in a place known as Bayan Zag—"rich in Saxauls" to the Mongolians. It is still rich in dinosaur fossils, and now legally protected.

desert's gravely surface is crisscrossed with tracks which are wellknown to locals.

A trip to the red sandstone cliffs, known locally as Bayan Zag, provides a chance to see other little-known sites nearby. The cliffs lie just north of a new national park, The Three Beauties, named for the three mountain ranges it contains. This knotty oval of peaks, canyons, high pastures, sand and gravel is the most easterly of the ranges and outcrops of the Gobi Altai. Its 8,100 square miles (21,7006 sq km) ranks Three Beauties with the ten largest parks in the world. The badlands, dunes, and mountains contain a surprising range of flora and fauna—including snow leopards and wolves. There has even been a report of the very rare Gobi bear, of which a mere 30 are thought to exist.

One destination is the Vulture's Gorge. On the northern edge of the mountains, a track leads into a steep-sided gorge where ground squirrels dart away into burrows and the strong, sweet scent of juniper trees drifts down from the lower slopes. The gorge is choked by ice, dirty with mud and gravel. A marker shows the thickness of ice built up during the winter: 30 feet (9 m). This bulk, combined with the overshadowing peaks, ensures that most years the ice lasts right through the summer.

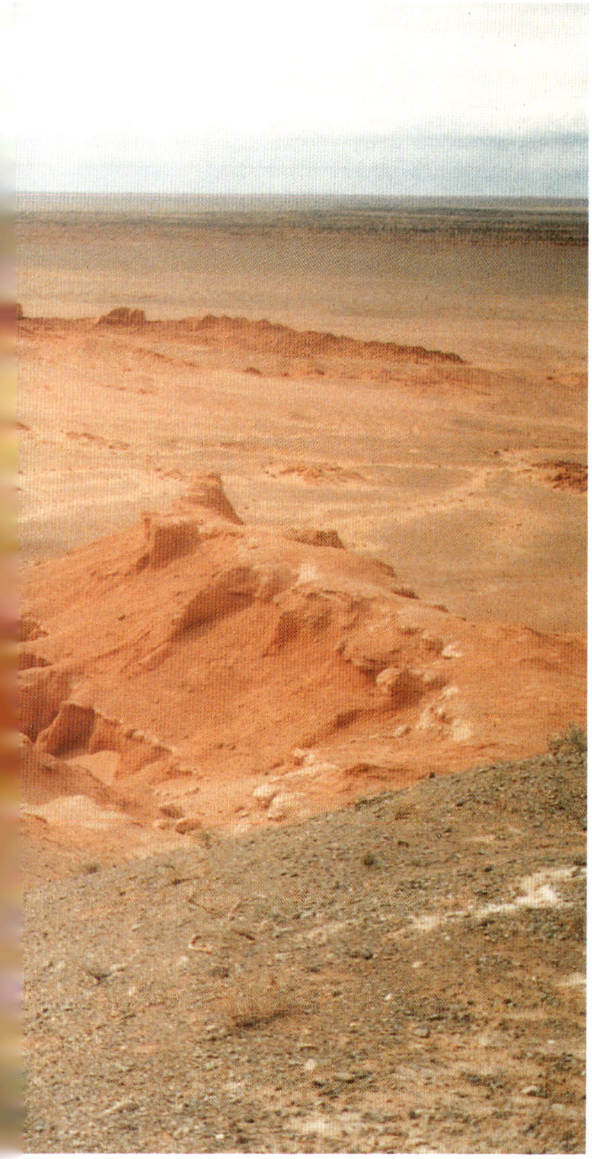

About 100 miles (160 km) west towers a narrow line of sand. Dunes are rare in the Gobi, and these are the highest—up to 800 feet (242 m). The dunes, created as the prevailing wind funnels along a corridor between two mountain chains, have a peculiarity: they "sing." This ghostly phenomenon, which supposedly used to draw travelers to their doom, is made when winds from the right direction move the silica-covered grains, creating an electrostatic charge which gives off a deep hum.

REVOLUTIONARY DISCOVERIES

But the region's greatest treasure is the Flaming Cliffs themselves. They became famous as the focal point of a great scientific enterprise, after the discoveries made there in the 1920s transformed awareness of early life on earth. The mastermind behind the discovery, Roy Chapman Andrews, on whom movie director Steven Spielberg based his character of Indiana Jones, was a genius at organizing field work. Chapman Andrews' ambitions lay in the Gobi, largely because his chief at the New York Museum of Natural History, Henry Fairfield Osborn, predicted that Asia would yield the key to human origins. Scientifically, this was almost

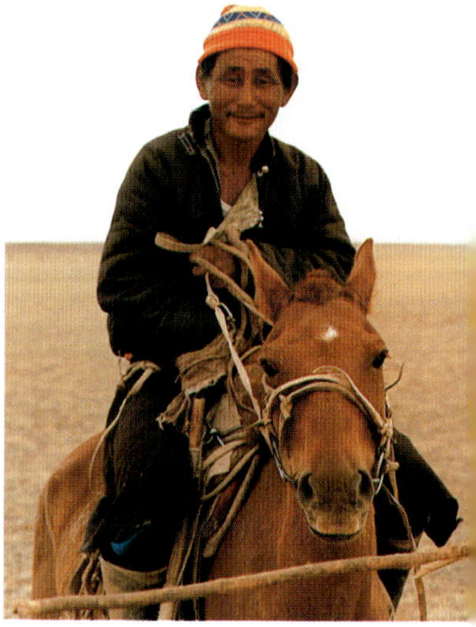

Though arid, the Gobi is home to a scattering of herdsmen. This one is part of a family group on a summer migration to mountains west of the Flaming Cliffs.

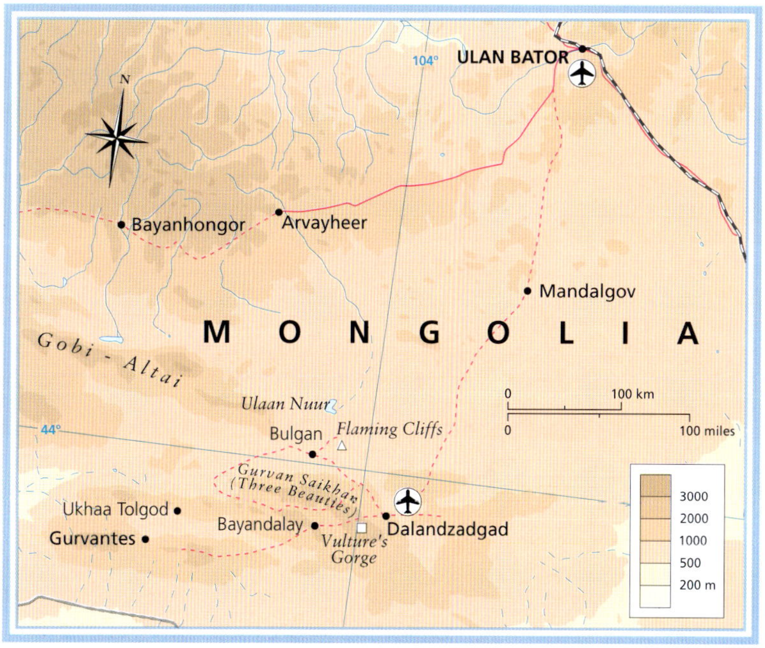

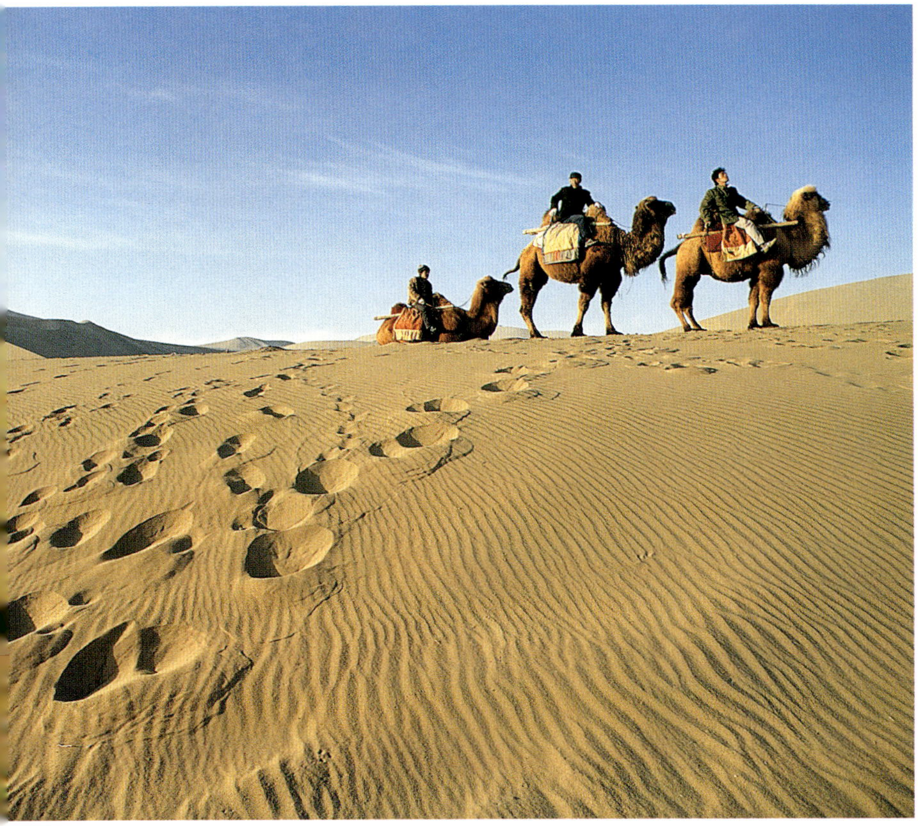

virgin territory. The major problem was one of logistics. Previous explorers had relied on camels, yaks, and horses, and expeditions were slow, small, and unable to bring back many specimens. Andrews and his team used cars, with supplies of fuel carried in advance by camels. This combination allowed the dozen scientists to compress ten years' work into five summer months. His five Central Asiatic Expeditions, between 1922 and 1930, revolutionized paleontology.

In 1922, after a generally successful but unsurprising summer's exploration, the major find came almost by chance. The expedition's photographer, J.B. Shackelford, found himself on the edge of a sandstone basin which looked ideal for fossils. He climbed down the steep slope of soft rock, and at once saw a tiny skull. Within minutes, other finds followed. That evening, as the sun spotlighted the red cliffs, Andrews christened the gullies and peaks.

The "Flaming Cliffs": the name proved a masterstroke of public relations when the expedition returned triumphant with 2,000 fossils. Moreover, Andrews had found a missing link of a sort—a reptilian one. The tiny skull provided an ancestry for a group represented by Triceratops, well known in North America. Scientists named the sheep-sized creature, with its parrot beak and neck-shield *Protoceratops*

Camel herders in the Gobi climb a dune on their way across one of the rare stretches of sand in a gravel and rock wilderness.

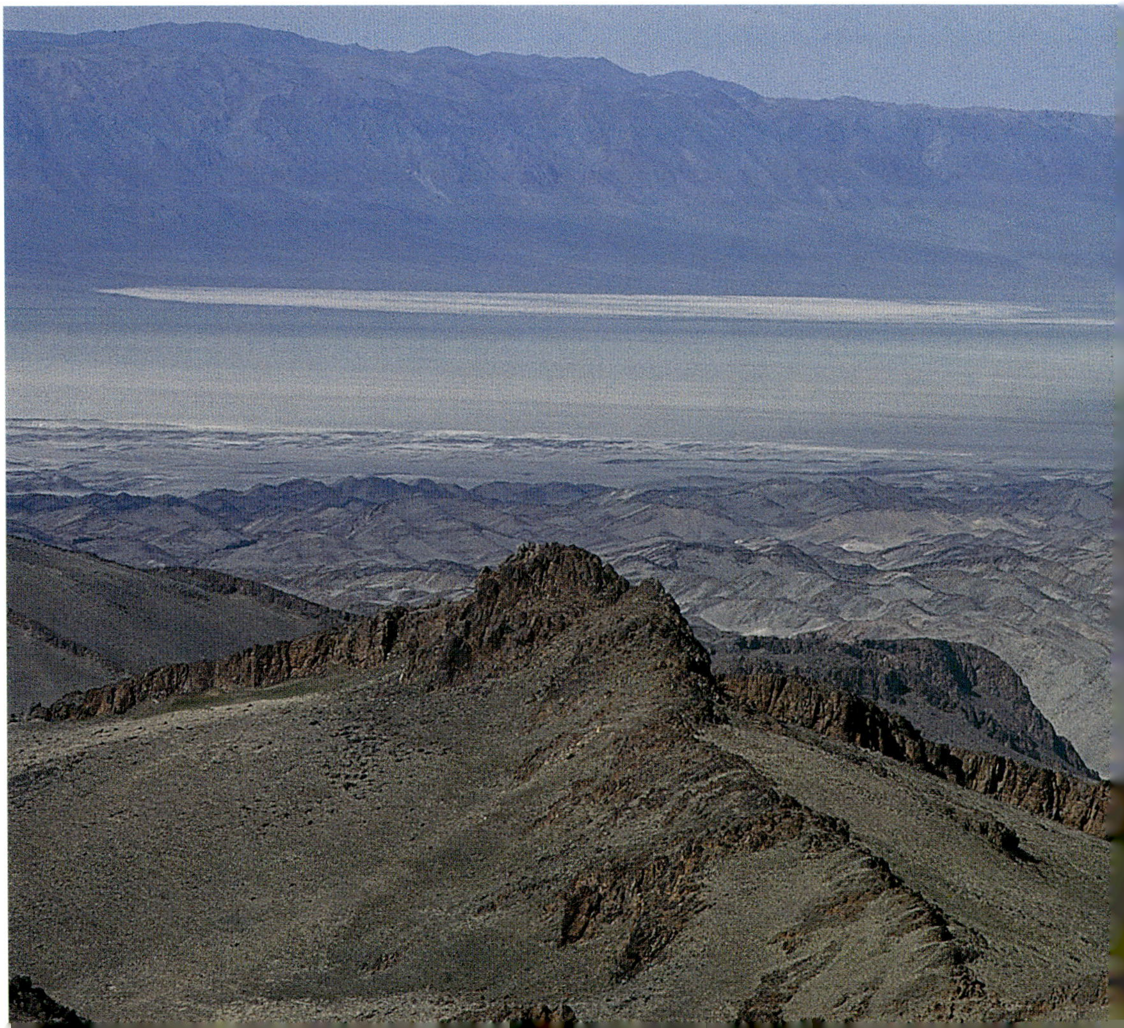

Shapes in a barren landscape recall the form of the dinosaurs which once roamed here; beyond them, plains give way to the distant Altai Mountains of the western Gobi.

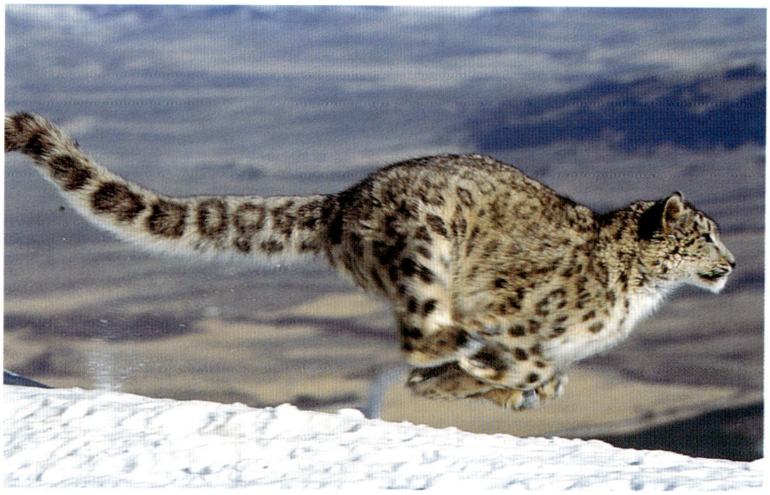

andrewsi—"Andrews' first horned face." The following year, Andrews returned to the Flaming Cliffs, with more astonishing results.

Among the new finds was a fleet-footed predator, *Velociraptor*, now famous as the smart and vengeful anti-hero of the book and film *Jurassic Park*. And finally came the find for which the expedition was best remembered: dinosaur eggs. Suddenly, dinosaurs acquired new features, appearing less the monstrous clodhopping reptiles of the popular imagination, than almost charming, maternal creatures. When Andrews arrived home, he was mobbed, and acquired the status of a Hollywood star.

The following year, the largest expedition so far set off for Mongolia: 40 men, eight vehicles, 125 camels, 4,000 gallons of fuel, many tons of food. In May, back at the Flaming Cliffs, more new discoveries emerged, this time evidence of human presence from 12,000-7,000 years ago. Finally, Andrews found fossils of 11 rat-like mammals, which showed that already in dinosaur times the mammals were well established. In the Flaming Cliffs lay some of life's deepest roots.

For the next 70 years, with Mongolia firmly inside the Soviet empire, the only scientists who could follow in Andrews' footsteps were from the Eastern Bloc. One site, the Nemegt Valley at the far western end of the Three Beauties, proved itself a second wonderland for fossils. Then, after 1990 and the end of the Soviet Union, came a series of expeditions in a direct line from Andrews' work. The Natural History Museum sent annual expeditions to the Nemegt, which produced a flood of new material, again revising ideas about the origins of mammals and birds.

Living in these harsh regions is not easy. But this and surrounding areas rank as some of the most significant and most rewarding, as well as least known, of destinations.

Mongolian snowleopards are normally mountain creatures, but commute across open desert to colonize isolated ranges; they are rarely glimpsed in the wild.

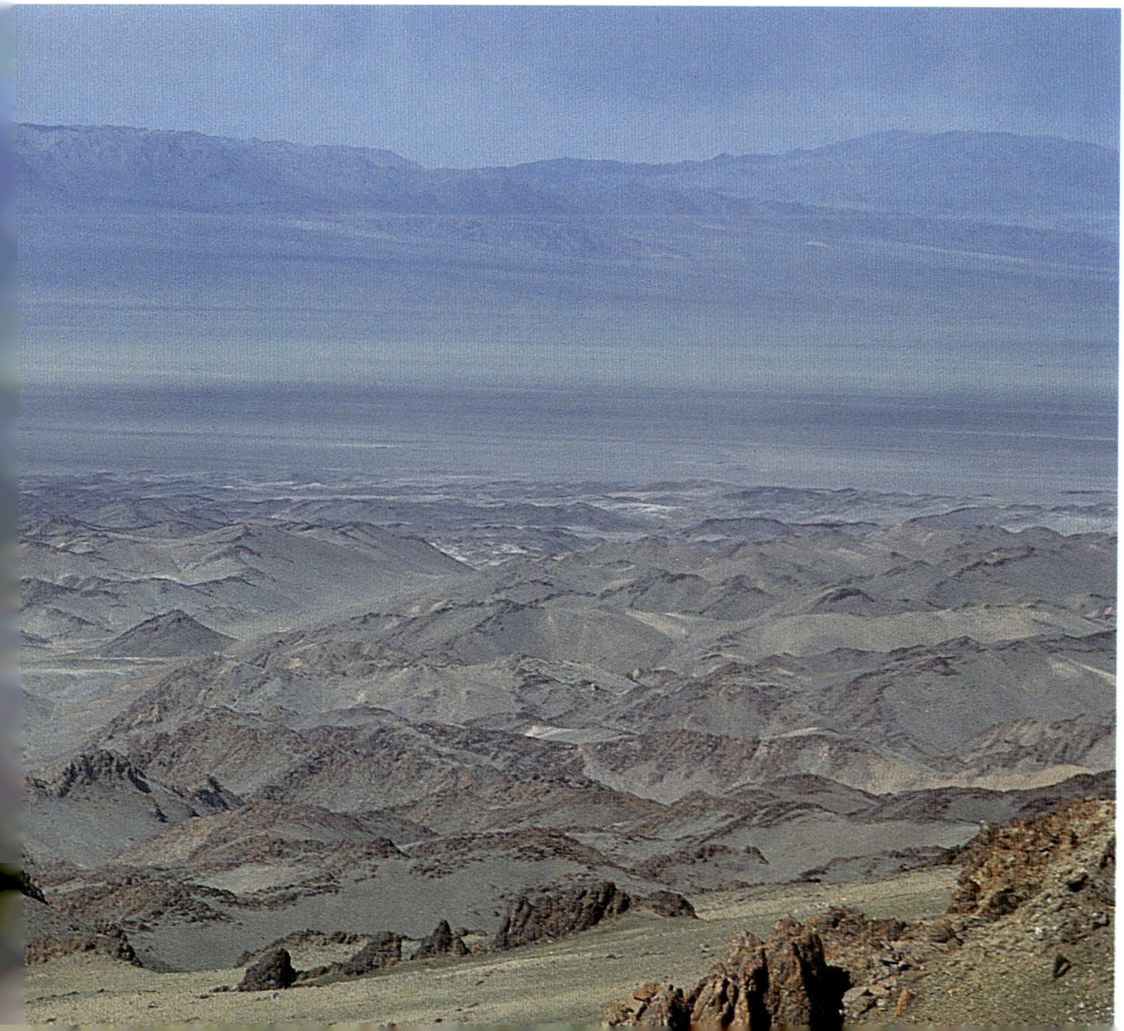

Mongolians sport national costume (below) for their National Day, whether in the capital or in distant outposts of the Gobi Desert.

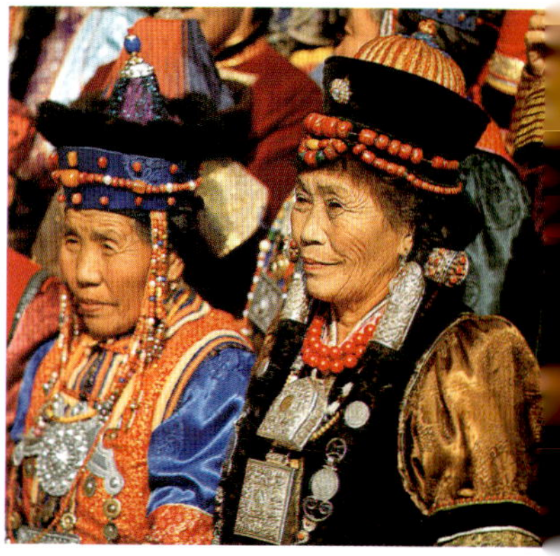

Central Asia

"A journey is a person in itself; no two are alike."

JOHN STEINBECK, AMERICAN WRITER, 1902-1968.

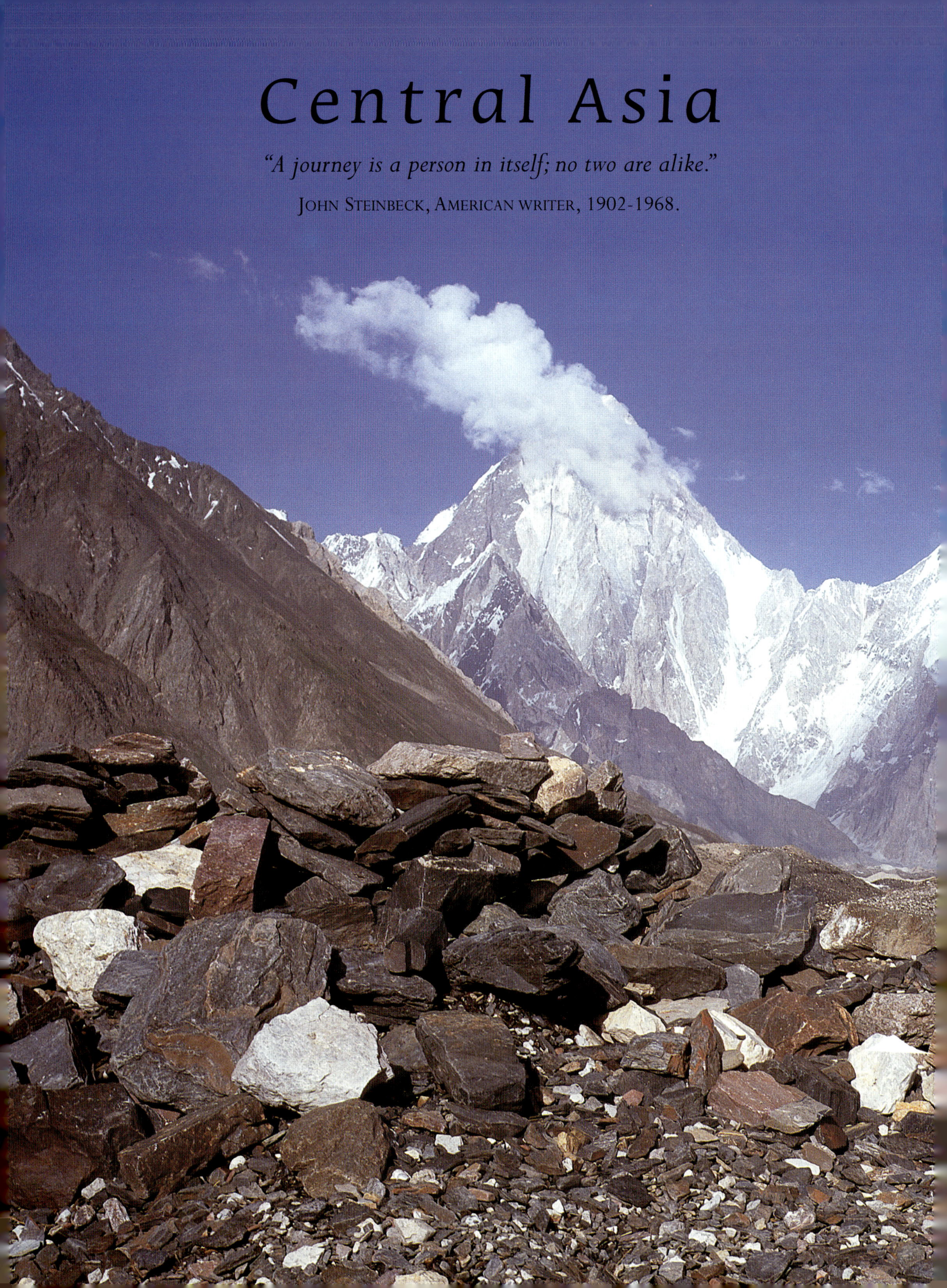

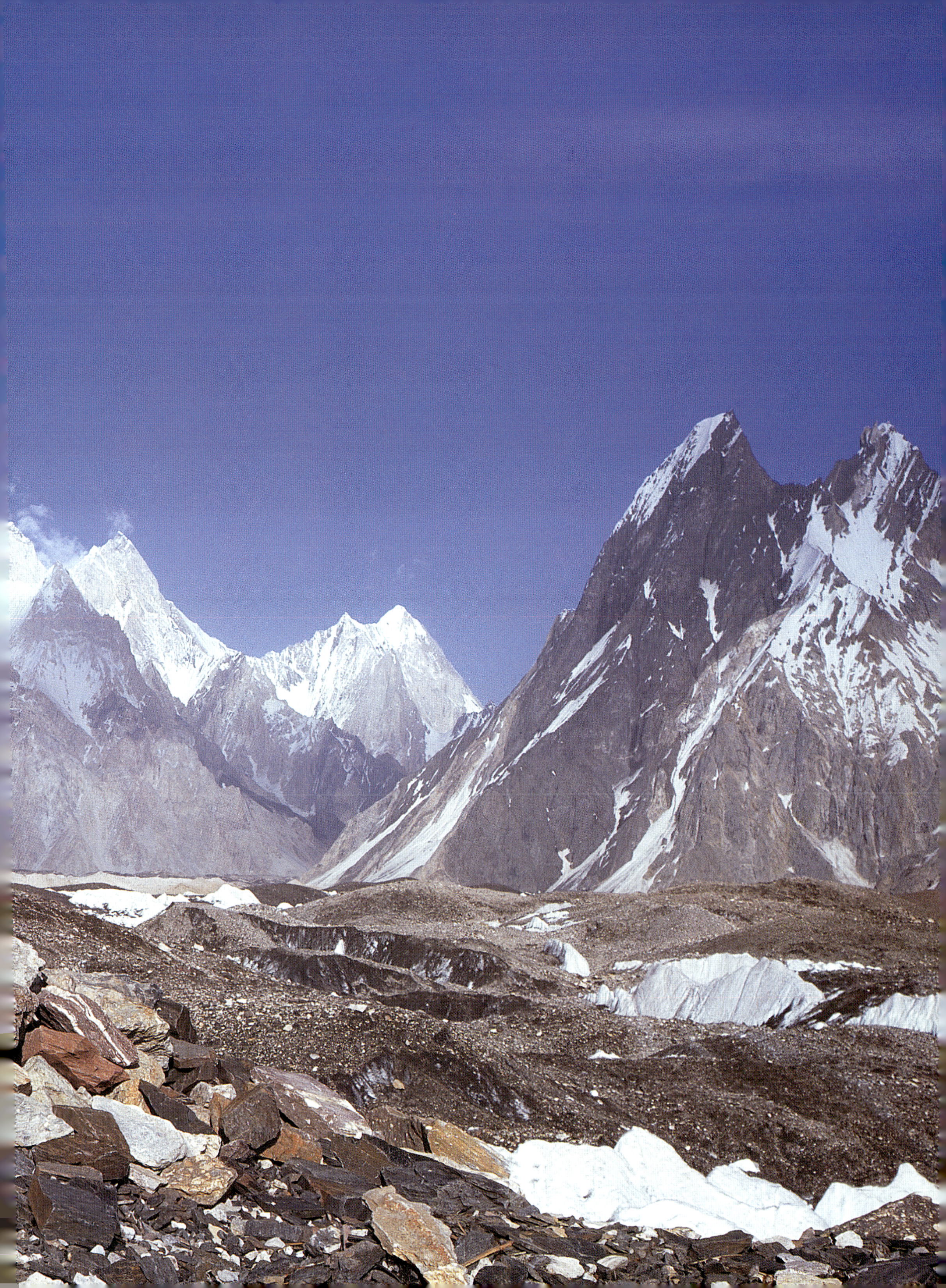

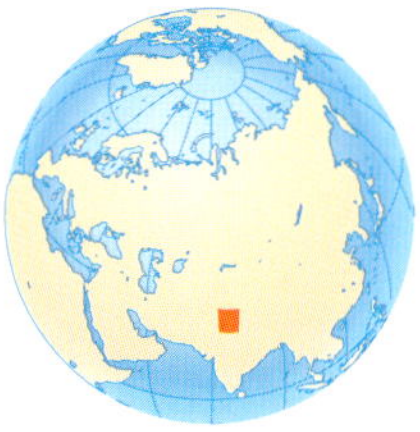

The Karakoram Highway

Threading through gorges and over passes, the Pakistan-China link through the Karakorams is as notorious for its beauty as for its challenges.

FACT FILE

Timing: Rawalpindi (or Islamabad) to Kashgar round trip can be done in six days, with side trips, two weeks.

Visas: Get them in advance in your own country. They are not available locally.

Time zones: There is a three-hour time difference between Pakistan and China.

Mode of travel: Few people drive their own vehicles. Most go by bus.

Best time to travel: May—June. The Khunjerab Pass is open May 1 to mid November.

What to take: Good walking shoes, warm clothes for nights.

THE 750-MILE (1,200 KM) HIGHWAY from Rawalpindi in Pakistan to Kashgar in China shoulders through the ruins of a continental collision that millions of years ago created one of the most awe-inspiring mountain landscapes on earth.

The restless peaks and valleys are a dream for geologists as well as travelers. The Karakorams were thrown up—are still being thrown up—by the ongoing collision between India and Central Asia. Some 50 million years ago, India's diamond-shaped rock plate, surfing northward on a plume of molten magma, slammed in slow motion into Asia. Over a period of 20 million years, a coastal plain rose 3-4 miles (c.5.6 km), forming a "crumple zone" stretching across the Tibetan plateau. India's geological "bow wave" is formed of four great ranges—the Hindu Kush, the Pamirs, the Himalayas; and in the center, dividing Pakistan from China, the Karakorams. Here tower some of the world's greatest peaks, including the world's second highest, K2 28,400 feet (8,611 m) and 50 others over 23,000 feet (7,000 m). There are five glaciers over 30 miles (48 km) long, including the longest outside the polar regions. Geology and climate combine to make this an unstable land. Fractured by subterranean forces and chiseled by rain and frost, the peaks and cliffs crumble into rivers that slice deep into the remnants of long-dead volcanoes and ancient shores.

From the official terminus, Havelian, the highway plunges on up the valley of the Indus, locally called the "Father of Rivers." After Besham in the Indus Gorge, the river tears through the mountains like a chainsaw of silt—five million tons of it every day. The road clings to cliffs up to 1,000 feet (300 m) above the torrent or winds up side valleys to avoid impossible climbs. Peaks

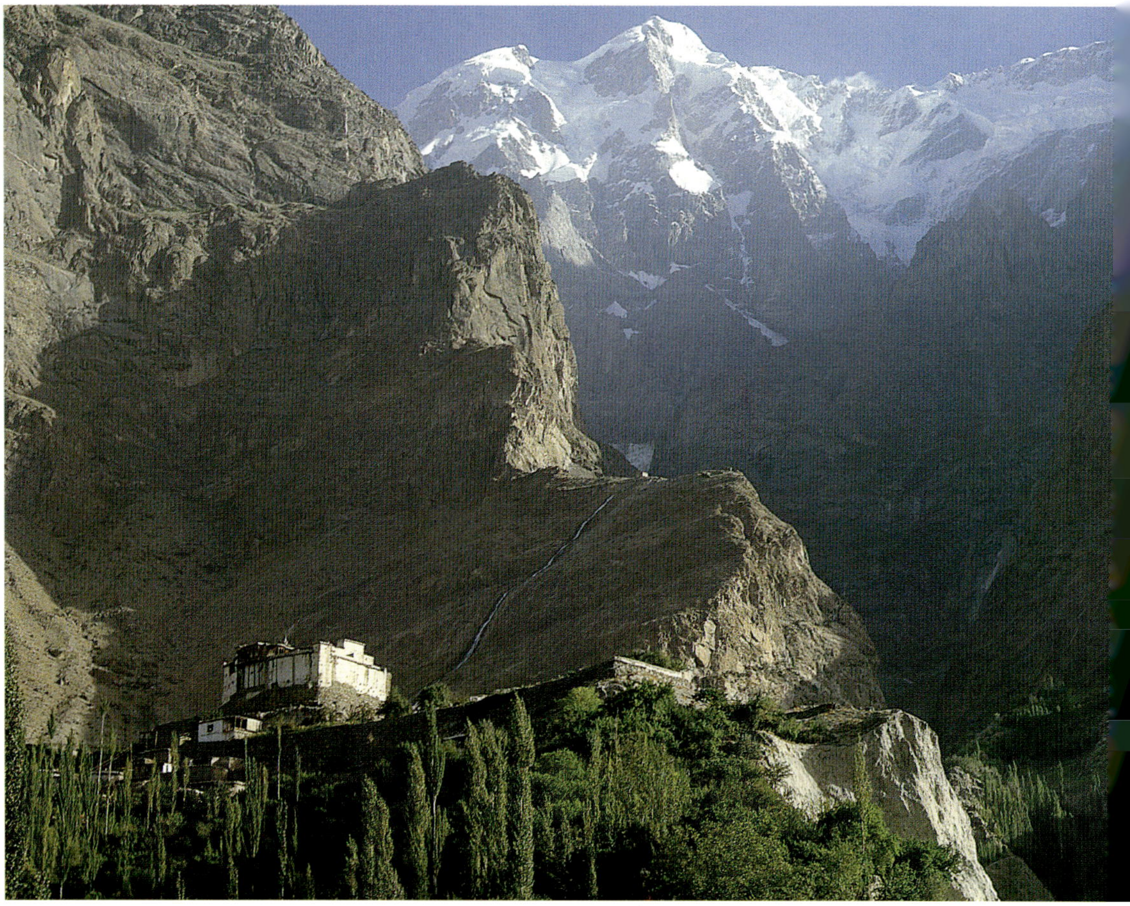

Baltit Fort, the 600-year-old home of the Mirs of Hunza, is one of the Highway's most famous landmarks. It stands guard over Karimabad.

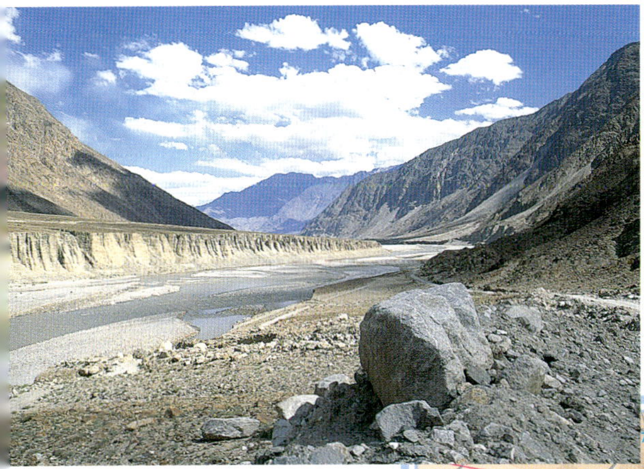

★ *Near Gilgit, the Indus (above) cuts its way between the Himalayas and the Karakorams.*

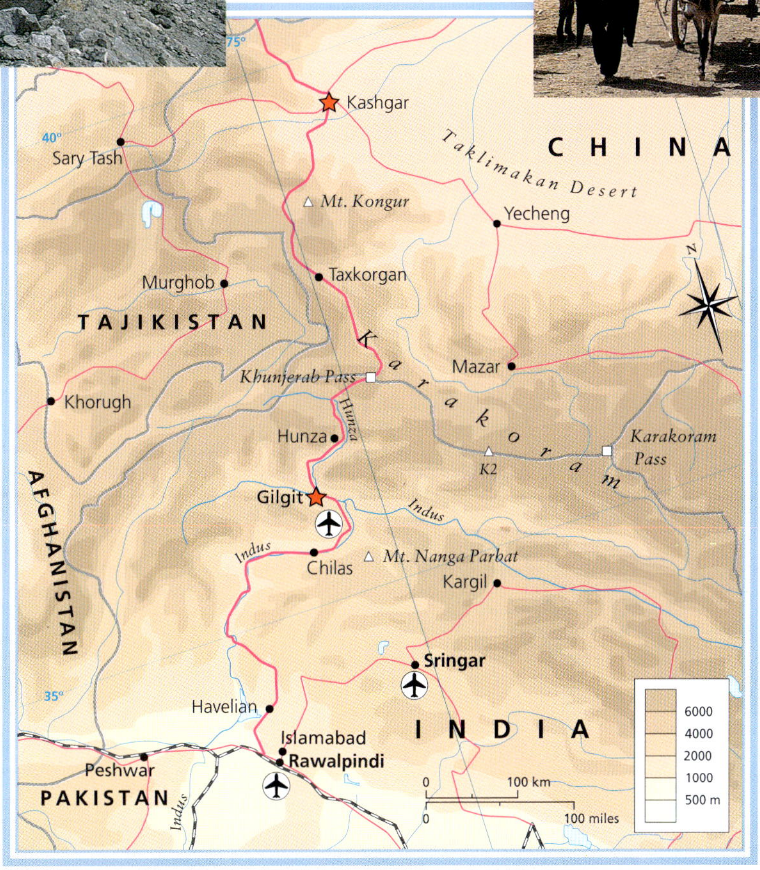

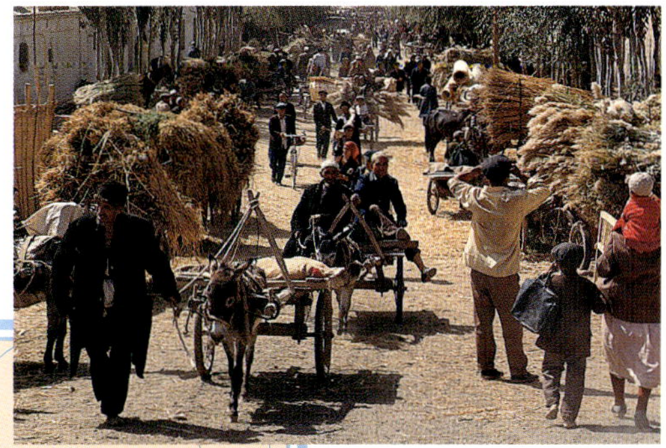

★ *Kashgar's busy market (above) lures traders from all over Central Asia.*

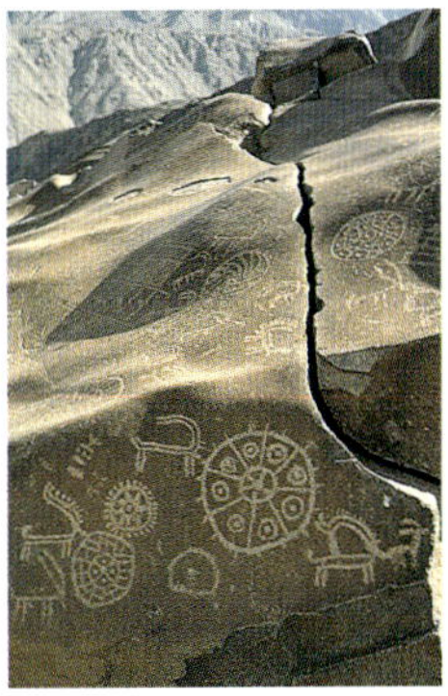

Buddhist iconography dating from the 2nd century, carved into the rocks alongside the Highway.

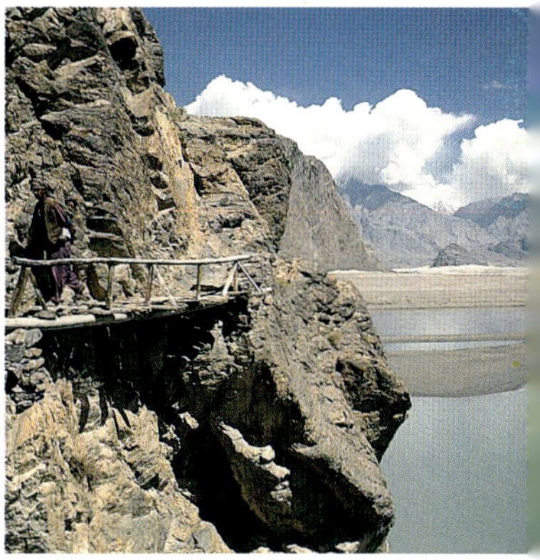

A few miles south of the Highway, a cliff trail runs perilously beside the Indus.

rise up to 16,500 feet (5,000 m) on either side, their higher slopes seldom visible above the vertiginous cliffs. At Chilas the gorge broadens and the river becomes tamer. Here for 2,000 years travelers carved names and pictures into rock. Chilas's fort reminds today's travelers that this was the center of Kohistan, one of many bandit-ridden valley kingdoms on which the British tried to impose their will in the 19th century with mixed success.

GILGIT, GATEWAY TO CHINA

The road follows the Indus eastward, providing views to the immense shoulders of Nanga Parbat 26,815 feet (8,126 m), 18 miles (29 km) from the road to the south. At this point in 1841 an earthquake threw a landslip into the river and dammed it, forming a 37-mile (60 km) lake some 1,000 feet (300 m) deep. When the dam broke, the waters swept downriver and drowned an army encamped 200 miles (320 km) away. Today the lake floor remains as a silty waste, across which the road runs north away from the Indus to Gilgit. Overlooking the confluence of the Gilgit and Hunza Rivers, the town was the gateway to China for centuries until the silk trade died in the 16th century. In the 1890s it became a pawn in the rivalry between the two empires expanding into central Asia, the British and the Russian. Gilgit was Britain's advance post in these wild regions. Near here, a British agent and explorer, George Hayward, was slain by the local maharajah after revealing a series of atrocities (his grave is in the old Christian cemetery). In 1947, when India and Pakistan divided, Gilgit went to Pakistan.

Today, the town, with its airy suspension bridges over the river, is a thriving market, crammed with buses, trucks, and cars heading to and from Afghanistan,

China, and India. Taxis abound, but the dozen hotels are all within walking distance. Given good visibility, Pakistan's PIA airline flies to and from Islamabad up to three times a day in summer. Beyond Gilgit lies the Hunza Valley, a narrow cleft along which the road clings to the cliff face. At 25,667 feet (7,823 m) Rakaposhi looms over glaciers and other 23,00 foot (7,010 m) peaks fringed by terraces of apricots. The road follows the Hunza River over sparsely cultivated scree and rock for some 50 miles (80 km) to the Chinese border, passing four glaciers, all within walking distance for trekkers. Most travelers choose to spend the night at the Pakistani border post of Sust.

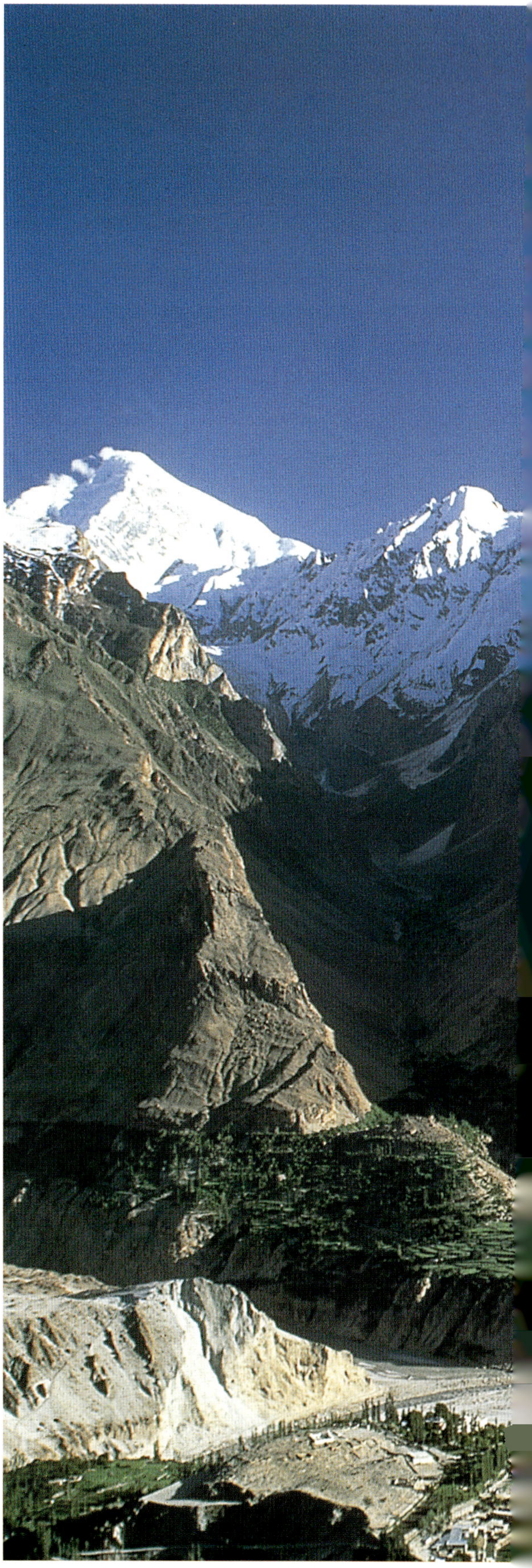

The towering Karakorams (right) were a formidable challenge to the engineers who built the Highway.

CONNECTING TO THE SILK ROAD

The route makes a long and gentle climb over the Khunjerab Pass at 16,280 feet (4,934 m). International buses make the full journey, but travelers on local buses change at the border from Pakistani to Chinese vehicles. The road descends through the outlying ranges of the Pamir mountains to the Chinese border post 60 miles (100 km) on at Tashkurgan. Hotels are basic and hot water is a rare luxury. From here, buses cover the 187 miles (300 km) to Kashgar in a day, passing two great peaks, Mustagh Ataz at 24,900 feet (7,546 m) and Kongur at 25,472 feet (7,719 m), and finally dropping on to a 50-mile (80 km) run of flat, smooth road to Kashgar, or Kashi in Chinese, once a crossroads of Silk Road routes. Since the breakup of the Soviet Union, it has again become a thriving international market. The 280,000 residents are mostly Muslim Uighurs. Besides the exotic bustle of its bazaar, Kashgar offers a link to modern civilization, with a bank, tourist information, air transportation to Urumchi, and offices for permits for travel and visa extensions. Beyond lie the oven-hot wastelands of the Taklamakan Desert.

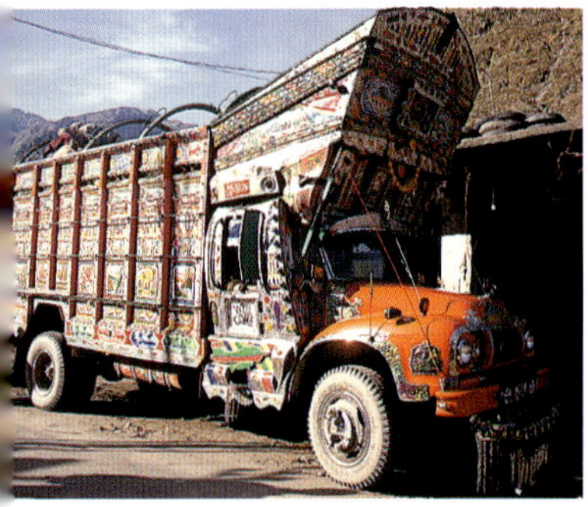

Pakistani trucks with baroque decorations ply the Highway between China and Pakistan.

BUILDING THE HIGHWAY

This extraordinary highway was the product of international politics. In the early 1960's China broke with its former Soviet ally and looked to Pakistan as an ally and a "window on the west." A frontier dispute was settled in Pakistan's favor, and the road was started in 1966. Pakistan upgraded the unpaved roads, paths, and donkey tracks almost to the border, while China undertook to build all the bridges and to tame the high and unstable section from Gulmit, 60 miles (100 km) inside Pakistan. The work demanded the removal of 700 million cubic feet (20 million cubic meters) of rock and the creation of a border pass, the Khunjerab, crossing at almost 16,500 feet (5,000 m), high enough for lowlanders to feel the need for oxygen. Of the 15,000 Pakistani workers hacking out their stretch of road, 400 died in accidents. The highway was opened in 1982, with the first tourists traveling it in 1986, but repairs and upgrading go on continually.

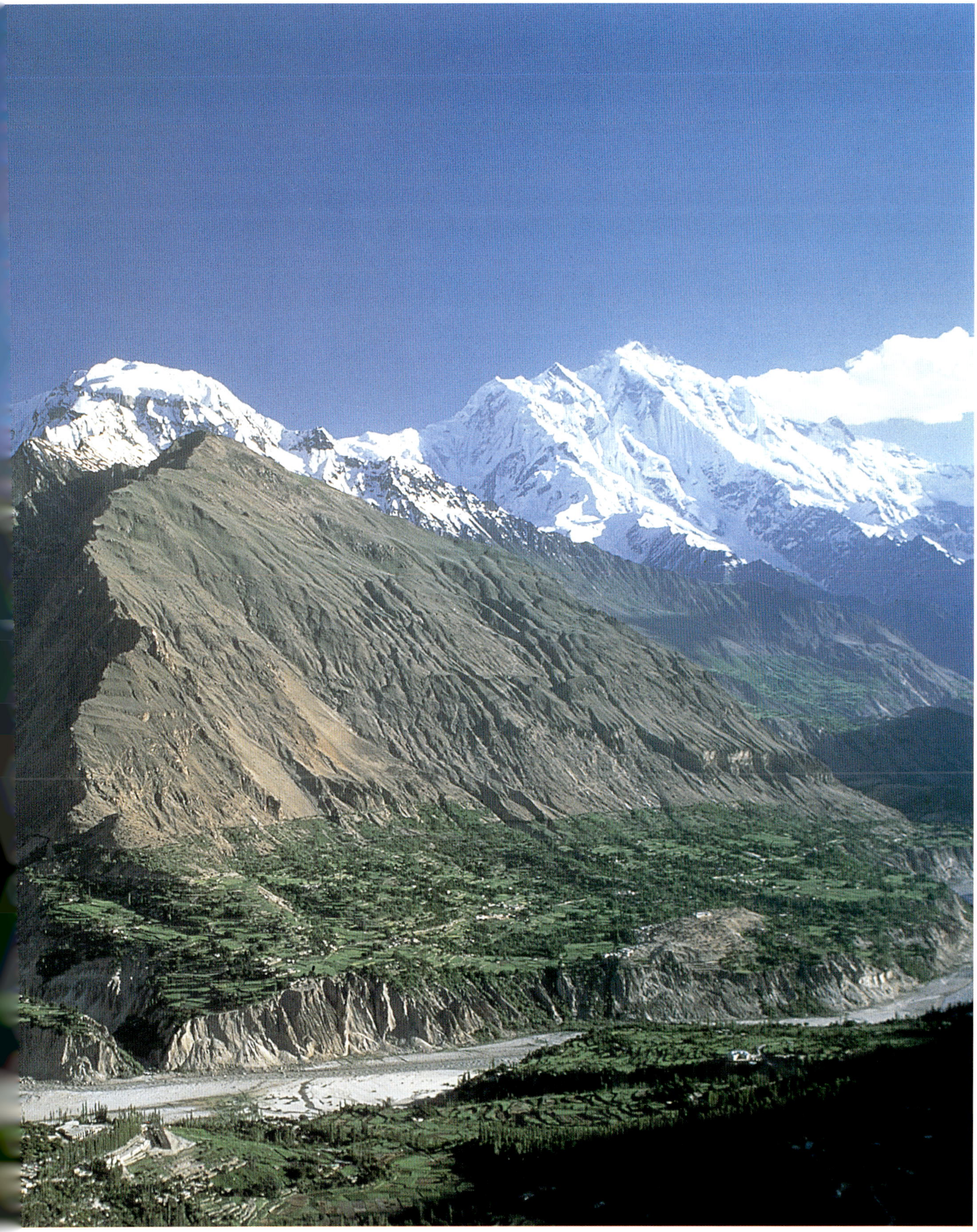

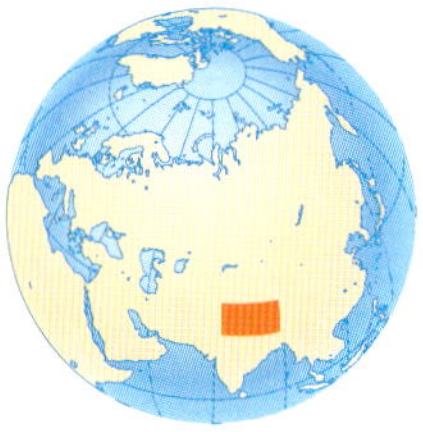

To the Roof of the World

Traveling through the valleys and passes which traverse the world's highest mountains can be tough, but the cultural and spiritual experience more than compensates for any discomfort.

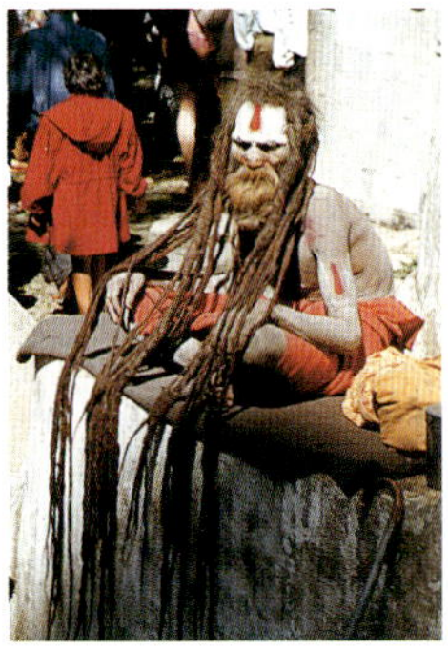

A sadhu in Kathmandu (above), with dreadlocked hair to represent the many-tributaried Ganges, and smeared with ashes to represent the god Shiva's role as destroyer.

North of the Himalayas, the vast Tibetan plateau (below) stretches, much of it uninhabited.

THE AWARENESS OF BEING in the highest part of the whole earth, and the splendor of the Himalayan Mountains on a clear, blue day is an experience that, as the Irish travel writer Devla Murphy wrote, should not be "trapped in mere words." You can walk, bus, or fly by helicopter or small plane from Kathmandu to Lukla, to join the steady stream of trekkers, sherpas, and porters on the Everest Trail—the main commercial route, but in reality no more than a yak path—to the market town of Namche Bazar and beyond to Base Camp. The flight along the rim of the Himalayas, a dazzling frieze of white peaks along the edge of the world, is a fitting overture to what lies ahead. Beneath lies rural Nepal: russet and gold foothills—though such a term seems inadequate for the giant sculpted folds and valleys dark with depth—remarkably carved into a thousand terraces, with barely a sign of modern civilization.

Or you can submit to the lure of Tibet as well, and take what must rank as one of the world's most unforgettable bus journeys, from Kathmandu to Lhasa, a return trip that takes 10 days. A word of warning: This is not for the faint-hearted or unfit. Preparation, in mind, body, and equipment, is essential.

After the riots and reprisals of 1987 and 1989, Tibet was virtually closed to foreigners. It has been the focus for three great empires' ambitions—British, Russian,

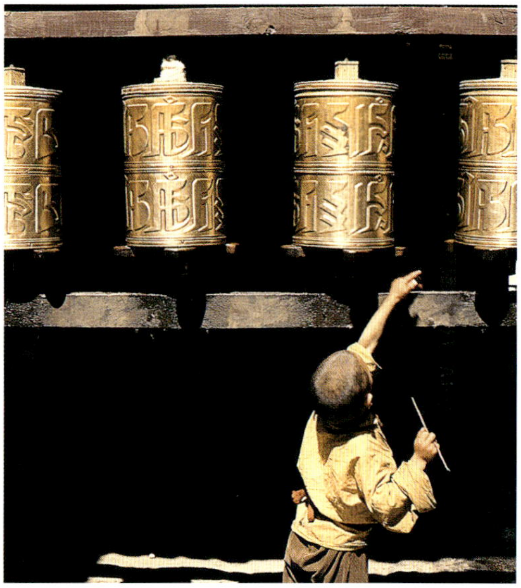

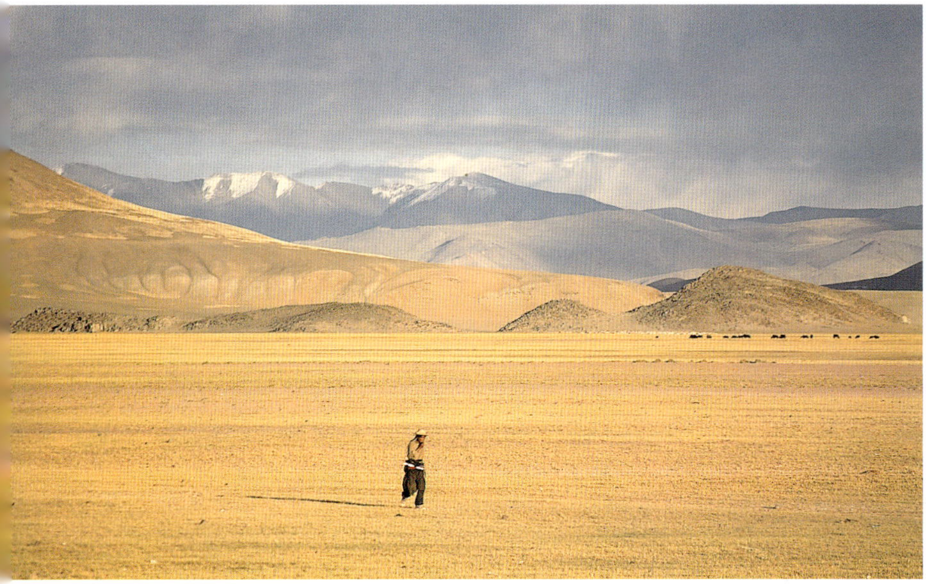

and, most recently, Chinese. Its geographical isolation behind the highest mountains, its political isolation after China's invasion in 1951 have combined with a reputation for spirituality and magic, heightened in recent years by the Dalai Lama's high profile in the West. Together, these elements give Tibet a romantic quality. Nowadays, visitors can fly in from Beijing, Chengdu, or Kathmandu, though flights to and from Nepal are subject to delay and cancellation. After tortuous negotiations, it is also possible to take private vehicles in from Nepal.

TRAVEL REALITIES

The bus journey is in the hands of two companies, one Nepalese, the other Chinese, with a transfer at the border. Though Nepalese buses are ramshackle, the journey into the high Himalayas from Kathmandu to the Chinese border is only about half a day. At the Nepalese border post of Kodari, passengers must either walk or transfer to a truck, which carries them the 6 miles (10 km) across no man's land to the Chinese border at Zhangmu. It can take up to two hours to complete the crossing formalities, before resuming the journey in a Chinese bus to the first night's hotel (which may well prove to have no running water, let alone hot water). From here the road leads over

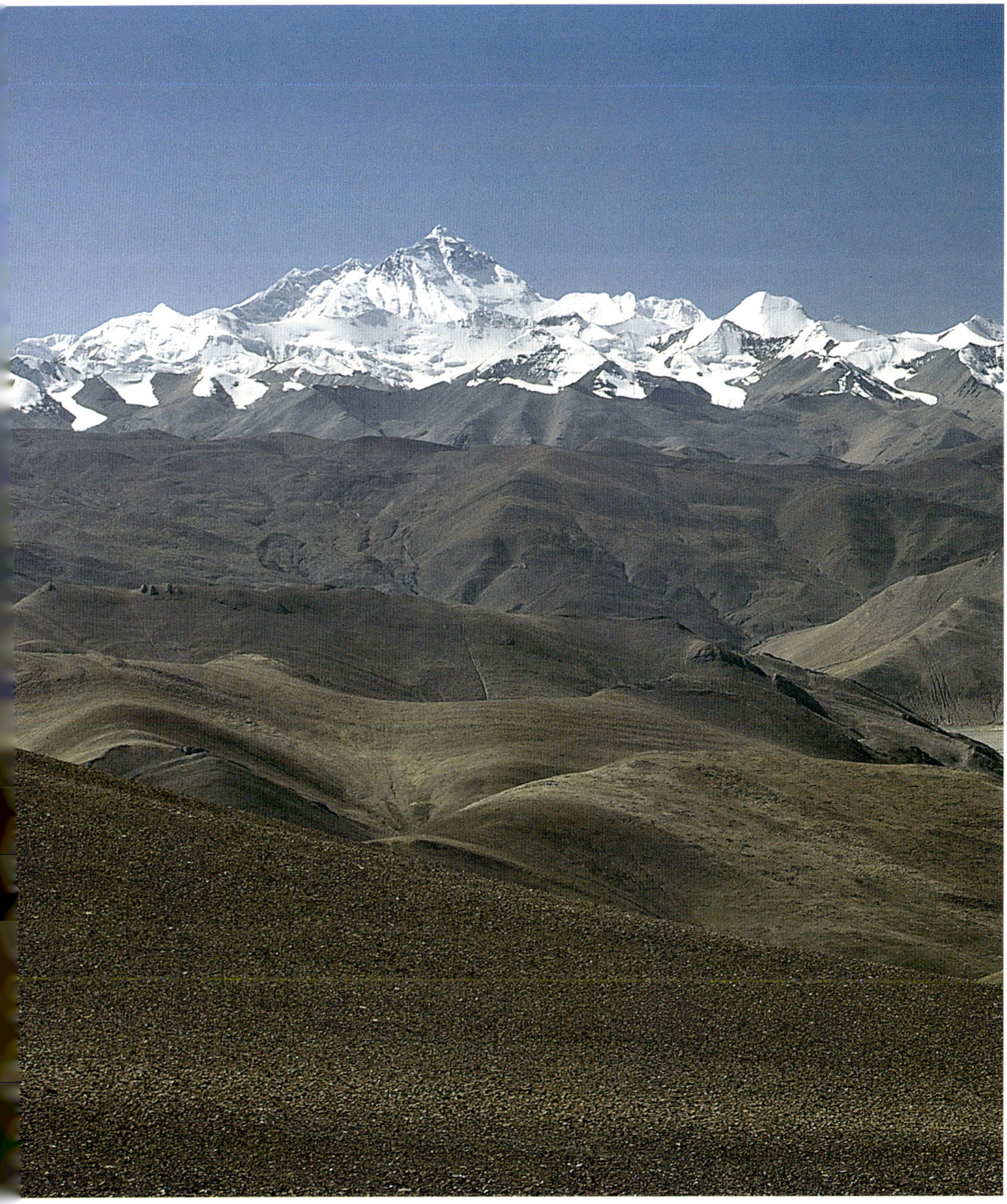

FACT FILE

Currency: Dollars in Nepal, dollars and yuan in China.

Climate: Impassable in winter. Even in summer, nights can be near freezing.

Best time to travel: The trip is only possible in summer.

Dress: Down jackets, good sleeping bags.

Airports: Kathmandu in Nepal and, less useful, Lhasa.

Four main dangers: Mountain sickness due to oxygen deficiency at altitude, stomach disorders; extreme dehydration; fierce dogs.

Medication: Consult your doctor for remedies to counter mountain sickness and intestinal infections.

Most vital piece of equipment: Water bottle(s).

Most vital "don't": Don't drink unboiled water.

A sight of Everest—or Chomo Lungma ("Mother goddess of the world")—as it is more descriptively called by the Sherpa people, brings with it an awe-inspiring awareness of being near the top of the world.

undulating barren plateaus, with occasional steep drops and climbs. The vegetation is so sparse as to seem virtually nonexistent, exposing the gritty ground. On this high desert,well protected from monsoon rains by the mountains, the going is sometimes tortuous, but mostly merely uneven.

On the second day, the road climbs up to 18,000 feet (5,500 m), over the stunningly beautiful Lublungla Pass, which is high enough to leave the unacclimatized gasping. In addition, most people new to this altitude, consuming about a gallon (4-5 l) of water a day and perhaps on altitude-sickness pills as well, find they are forced to relieve themselves frequently by the roadside. All such indignities and adversities are rewarded, however. To the southeast, blocking the horizon, is a line of mountains from which looms one glorious, familiar pyramid: Everest, 50 miles (80 km) away, a sight stirring enough to carry passengers through the 12 long hours of journey to the small, nondescript town of Lhaze.

Next stop is Tibet's second largest city, Shigatse, with better hotels and restaurants, and famous for the monastery that is the seat of the Panchen Lama, who ranks just below the Dalai Lama. His 15th-century

A Tibetan boy spins the prayer wheels that line a monastery wall (above left).

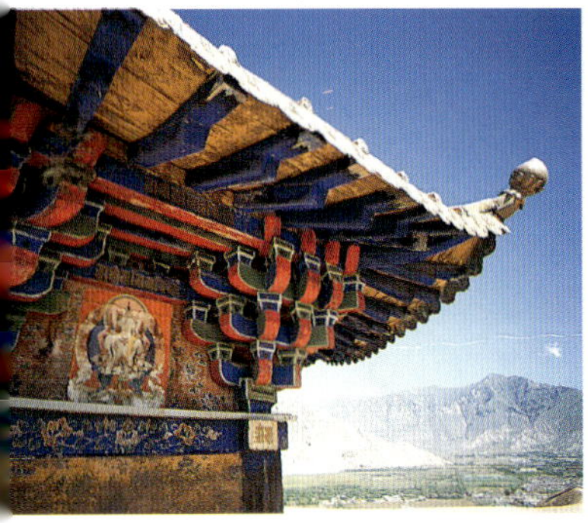

monastery, Tashilhunpo, which houses some 600 monks, has a 90 foot (27 m) statue of the Maitreya Buddha and the gold encrusted tomb of the 4th Panchen Lama. Its many dark chapels, with their gilded statues, are rank with the smell of yak-fat candles and sculptures made of butter, which are eventually fed to dogs. On a hilltop are the ruins of a fortress shattered when China occupied Tibet in 1959.

For travelers, Shigatse offers the first sight of Tibetans en masse. They are unbelievably poor by western standards, and running water is a rarity. Children commonly go barefoot, even in bitter weather, and very young children have holes cut in their clothes to allow them to relieve themselves in the street without soiling their clothes. But foreigners find that this material poverty is balanced by an open hospitality and a winning curiosity. Tibetan ways and poverty contrast starkly with the unnerving presence of Chinese troops and the relative wealth displayed by Chinese immigrants, who receive financial inducements to move to these remote and bitter parts.

Gyantse, the fourth stopover point, is only a small town, but it too has a better class of hotel, with hot showers. The 15th-century Palkhor Monastery has a pilgrim circuit covering 108 chapels and nine levels, and a hilltop fort overlooking the countryside. From here, it is one more day's ride to Lhasa, over the 16,000 foot (4,900 m) Kampala Pass. There is a superb view of Yamdrok Yumtso Lake, a vast mirror for the sky framed by snow-capped mountains. Traditionally, it was here that lamas came when they wished to receive guidance in finding new reincarnations.

Lhasa (whose name means "City of the Sun") is dominated by the sweeping wall of the Potala Palace and is divided between Chinese and Tibetan sections. Chinese apartment buildings are modern, charmless, and spartan. Since a spate of anti-Chinese violence in the late 1980s and subsequent brutal clampdowns, the Chinese military presence has been all-pervasive. The central square is often dominated by military parades. By contrast, the Tibetan section, all narrow alleys and potholed roads, at first sight appears squalid but is surging with life. For westerners, one advantage of the Chinese occupation is the presence of a few good, and many semi-decent, hotels, shops, and restaurants.

The Potala, the gleaming white palace that Tibetans simply call "the Peak" looks like a tidal wave of masonry sweeping up the side of Red Mountain. This is the Dalai Lama's winter palace, dating from the 17th century, once the seat of government and now a museum. Its two palaces form a maze of thousands of rooms and chapels, with stunning, bejeweled tombs of former Dalai Lamas, to which pilgrims shuffle slowly to admire. Many of the rooms are gloomy and lit by flickering candles, but the living quarters of the Dalai Lama at the top are full of light.

A roof detail (above left) of the Dalai Lama's winter palace, the Potala (right) shows the Tibetan's love of color in a cold and barren world.

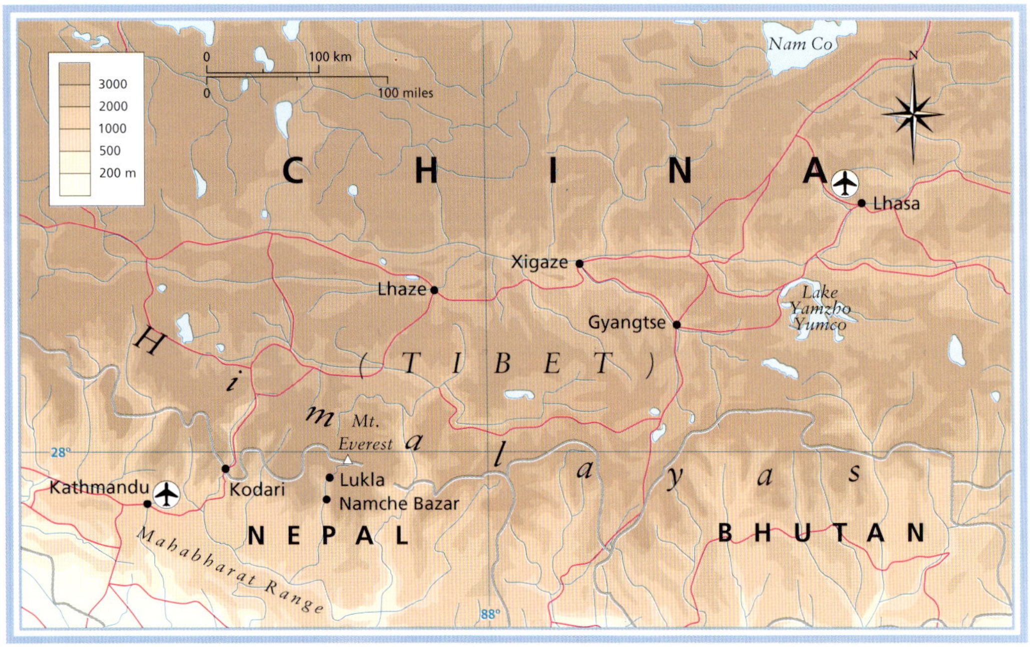

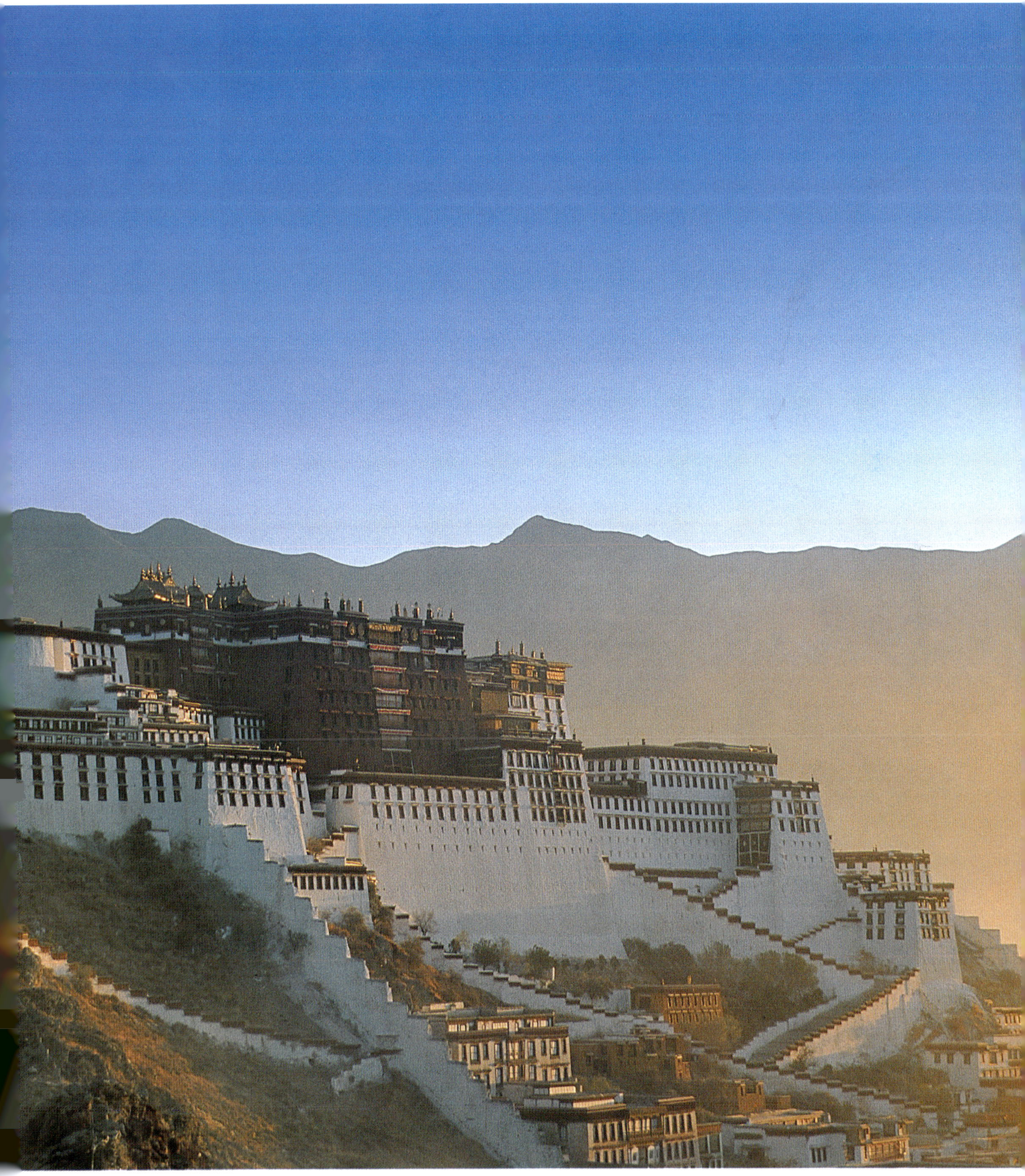

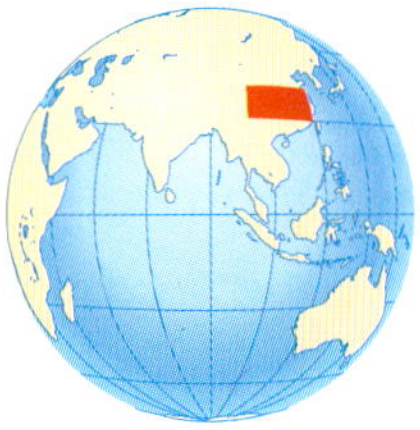

Gorges on the Yangtze River

The journey down the Yangtze River in central China, especially the passage through the Three Gorges, has inspired artists—and challenged boatmen—for more than 3,000 years.

THE GLORIOUS THREE GORGES, with their ferocious currents, mark the highpoint of any journey down the Yangtze, past tall rocky peaks capped with pines trees and ruined temples. But hurry—though the Gorges' glory will remain, their ferocity will not, once an immense dam at their lower end is completed in 2008.

The Chinese call the river simply Chang Jiang, "the Long River," Yangtze being a European name taken from a section near the mouth. Long it certainly is—the longest in China, third longest in the world—flowing 3,915 miles (6,300 km) to the sea from the Tibetan highlands. But the navigable section only starts at Chongqing (formerly Chungking).

In the Three Gorges, the river is lined by ancient and carefully tended terraces (right).

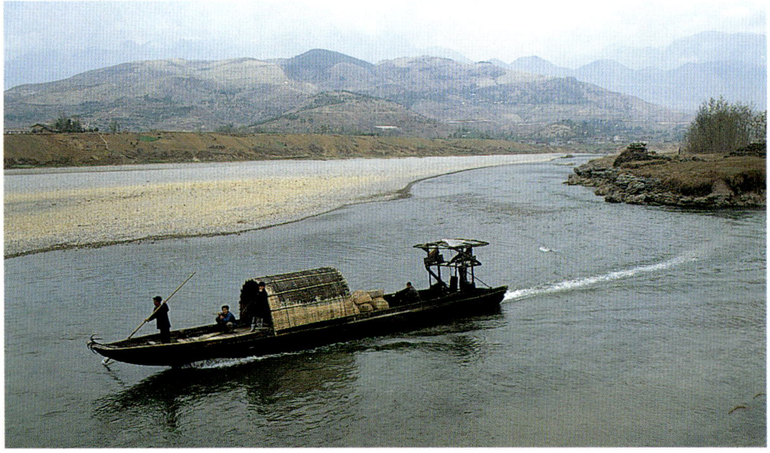

Although the chief industrial city of southwest ern China, and so filled with the usual factories, skyscrapers, and traffic, Chongqing still has its own appeal, for it is constrained by a very hilly peninsula marking the junction of the Yangtze and Jialing rivers. It is a city that, almost uniquely in China, has no bicycles—no one could cope with such hills. Here, travelers buy tickets for the two-day trip to Yichang, at the far end of the Gorges, or to Wuhan (three days), or even for the one-week, 1,500-mile (2,400-km) journey to the sea at Shanghai.

A CROSS SECTION OF LIFE

For much of the journey, the varied and noisy life of the boat itself is almost as fascinating as the scenery. Several boats leave daily to various downriver destinations. Try to get hold of second class cabins (first class does not exist), each of which has two "soft" beds—a Chinese term as opposed to "hard"—and a sink. But the pressure on space is great, and you may find yourself in a third or even fourth class cabin, in a dormitory with three-tiered bunks sharing with up to 40 other

In the upper reaches of the Yangtze , wherever the current allows, traditional rivercraft (above), provide an element of timelessness.

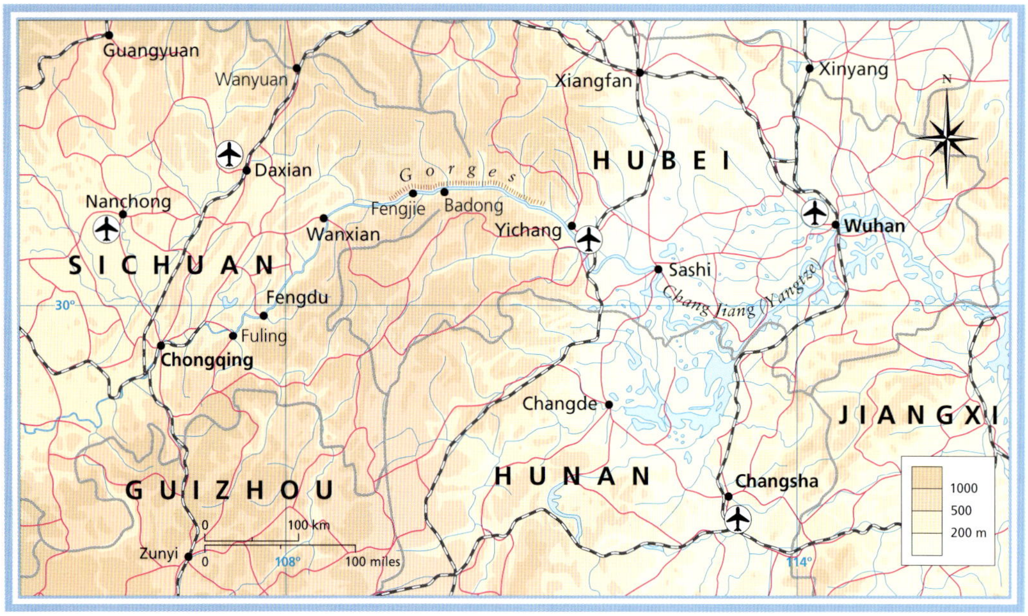

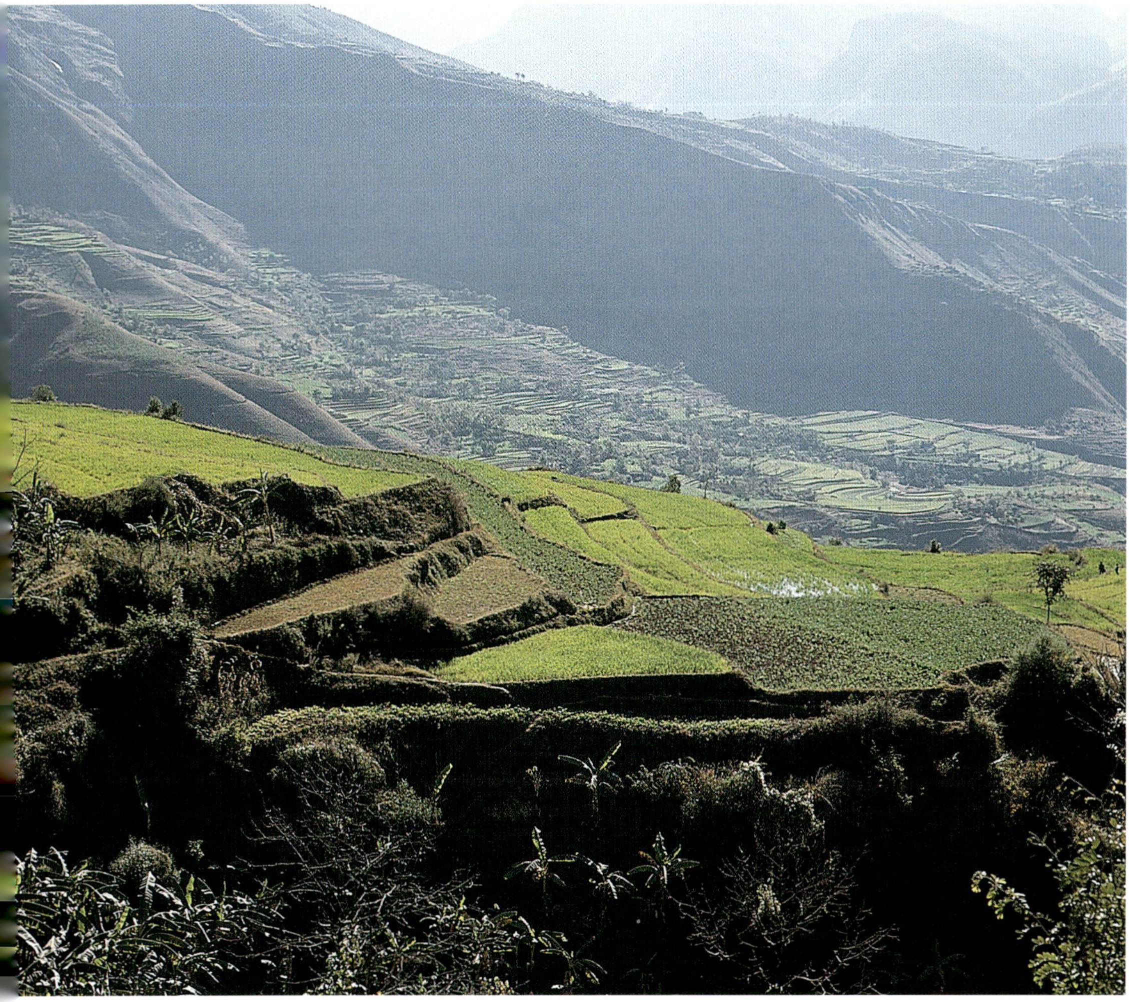

FACT FILE

Best time to visit: Spring and summer.

Language and names: Confusion is rife. Chinese signs and names are often transliterated, but don't rely on it. Transliteration officially uses the Pinyin system, but Westerners may be more familiar with spellings in the older Wade-Giles system. In addition, many Chinese place-names have changed, and minority languages often have their own names for places, which may also be transliterated.

Visas: Compulsory, but easy to get from embassies.

Most vital accessory: Business card.

Currency: China has two, one for locals (Renminbi, or RMB, and another for foreigners (Foreign Exchange certificates, or FEC). Chinese prefer FEC.

Equipment: Rainproof clothing (the gorges are subject to heavy rain).

people. There is even an unofficial fifth class for deck-passengers. Tickets allocate your beds and are exchanged for tags that must be reexchanged for your ticket at journey's end.

It is only after a day of travel, below Fengjie, that the river becomes living drama, ripping through the Three Gorges for 120 miles (192 km). The 8th-century poet Tu Fu described the entrance to the first gorge, Qutang, as the gateway where all the waters of Sichuan province battle for access. The banks close in to become a canyon up to 2,000 feet (600 m) deep, breaking up into headlands and pinnacles. With the river's width contracting down to 330 feet (100 m), the water has been known to rise by up to 170 feet (50 m). Before the days of steam, it took up to 400 men up to a month to haul a large ship upstream.

Qutang Gorge, at 5 miles (8 km), is the shortest of the three, but the fiercest. Currents become wild and unpredictable, running at up to 20 mph (32 km/h), producing swirling cauldrons. River captains treat the river as an enemy to be wrestled with and vanquished. Every rock and defile has its name: Teardrop Number 1, The Weeping Lady, Yellow Cat Gorge. Next comes Wu Gorge, 25 miles (40 km) long, dominated by the 12 Fairy Peaks. At their feet is a slab of rock with a 3rd century A.D. inscription commemorating an alliance of local states. Many of the boats moor in this gorge, at the town of Badong. Above, clinging to the precipitous slopes, are half-timbered cottages and terraces of fruit trees, some set so precariously that their owners have to rappel to them with ropes.

Xiling Gorge is the longest of the three at 50 miles (80 km). It used to be the most dangerous. One set of

As this view (below) from one of its highrise towers shows, Shanghai is a fitting destination or starting point for anyone traveling the world's third longest river.

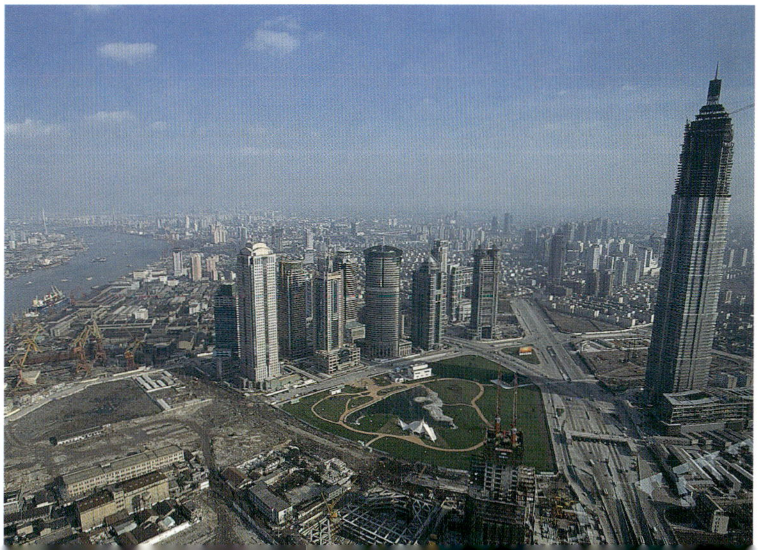

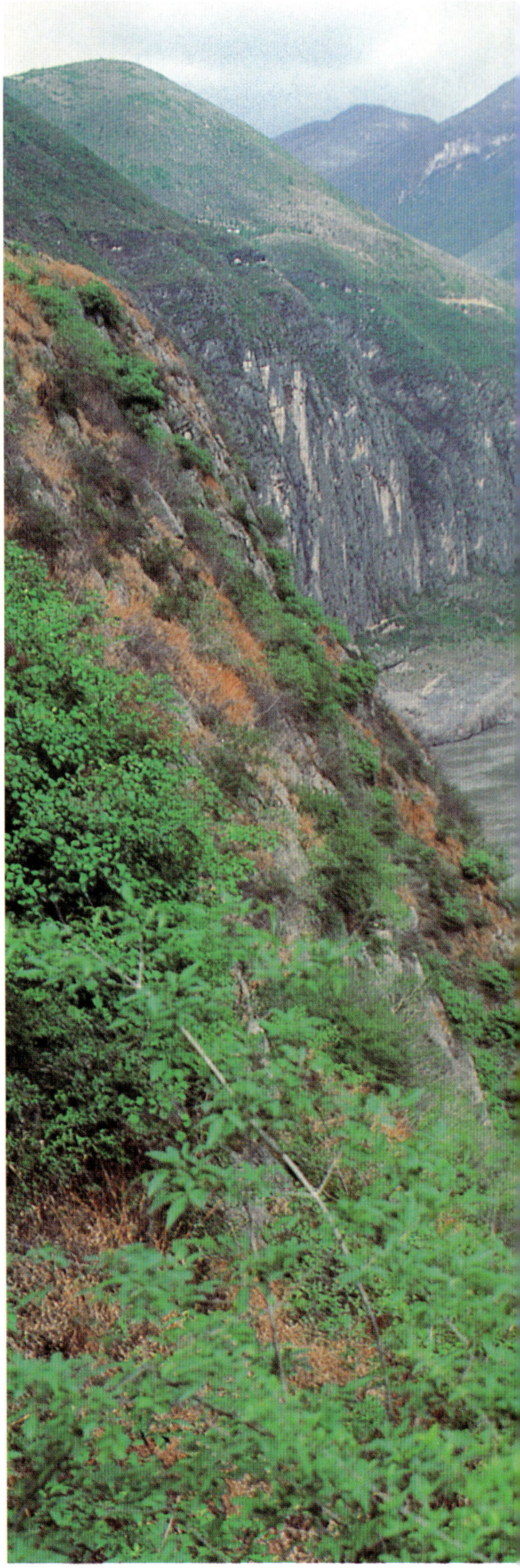

A view from the top of one of the Three Gorges reveals why they have for centuries been considered one of China's most stunning sights.

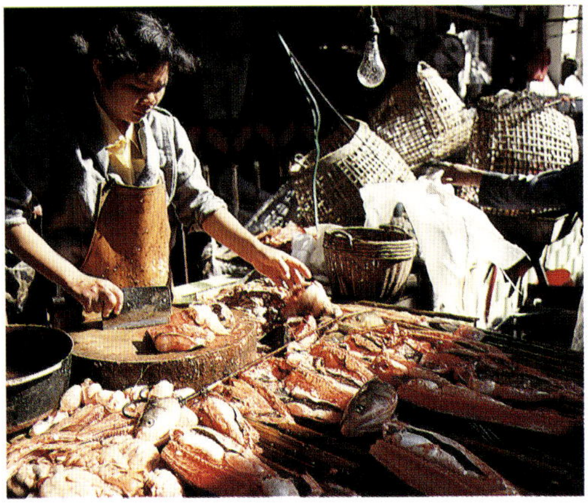

Shanghai's markets include stallholders selling fresh Yangtze fish (above) that escaped the attention of cormorants (below).

rapids claimed 17 steamships in the first half of the century, and above another stands White Bone Pagoda, so named from the human bones cast up on the river bank. But in the 1950s the worst rocks were dynamited, and boats hurrying downriver now have only the wild current to fear. Beyond the rapids everyone crowds on deck, first to see the massive construction works of the Three Gorges Dam, and then to watch as the boat passes through the locks of the huge Gezhou Dam, which will control the river's flow until it is replaced by Three Gorges.

Yichang, the next port of call, has little to offer, except a chance to escape from the boat. Many choose to stay aboard for the slow and gentle ride over downriver plains to Wuhan. This city of 3 million, the capital of Hubei province, straddles the river, its two sections being linked by an immense 1,200-yard (1,110 m) bridge, one of Communist China's first great engineering feats. Some then remain aboard to follow the broad stream across the lowlands to Shanghai, while others catch another boat for the slower, five-day return journey through the pounding waters of the Three Gorges.

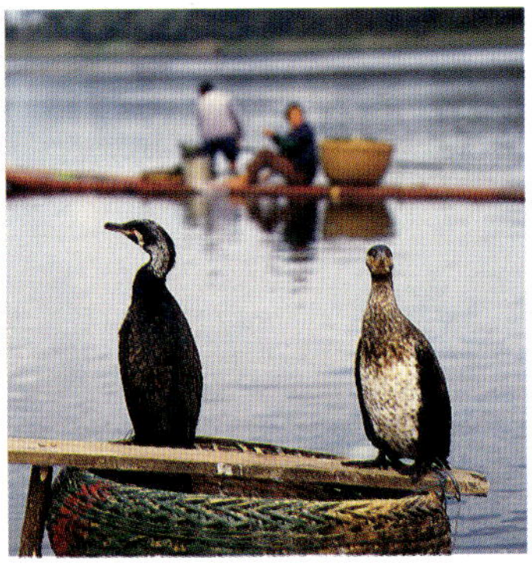

THE THREE GORGES DAM

This immense and controversial project, which will slice across the Yangtze at Sandouping 25 miles (40 km) above Yichang, is part of China's attempt to open up its hinterland by taming the Yangtze. Under discussion for years, it was started in 1992, and should be finished by 2008.

Over a mile (2 km) wide and 600 feet (185 m) high, it will create the world's largest reservoir, incorporating the Three Gorges into a lake 343 miles (550 km) long and providing almost a fifth of China's electrical needs. Two million people will have to be relocated. There should be an end to destructive floods downriver as well as to the fearsome rapids of the Three Gorges. Five locks will allow ships into the Three Gorges, and they will then proceed easily to Chongqing, which will become a lakeside port.

Only time will tell whether the environmental and social losses will be outweighed by the gains.

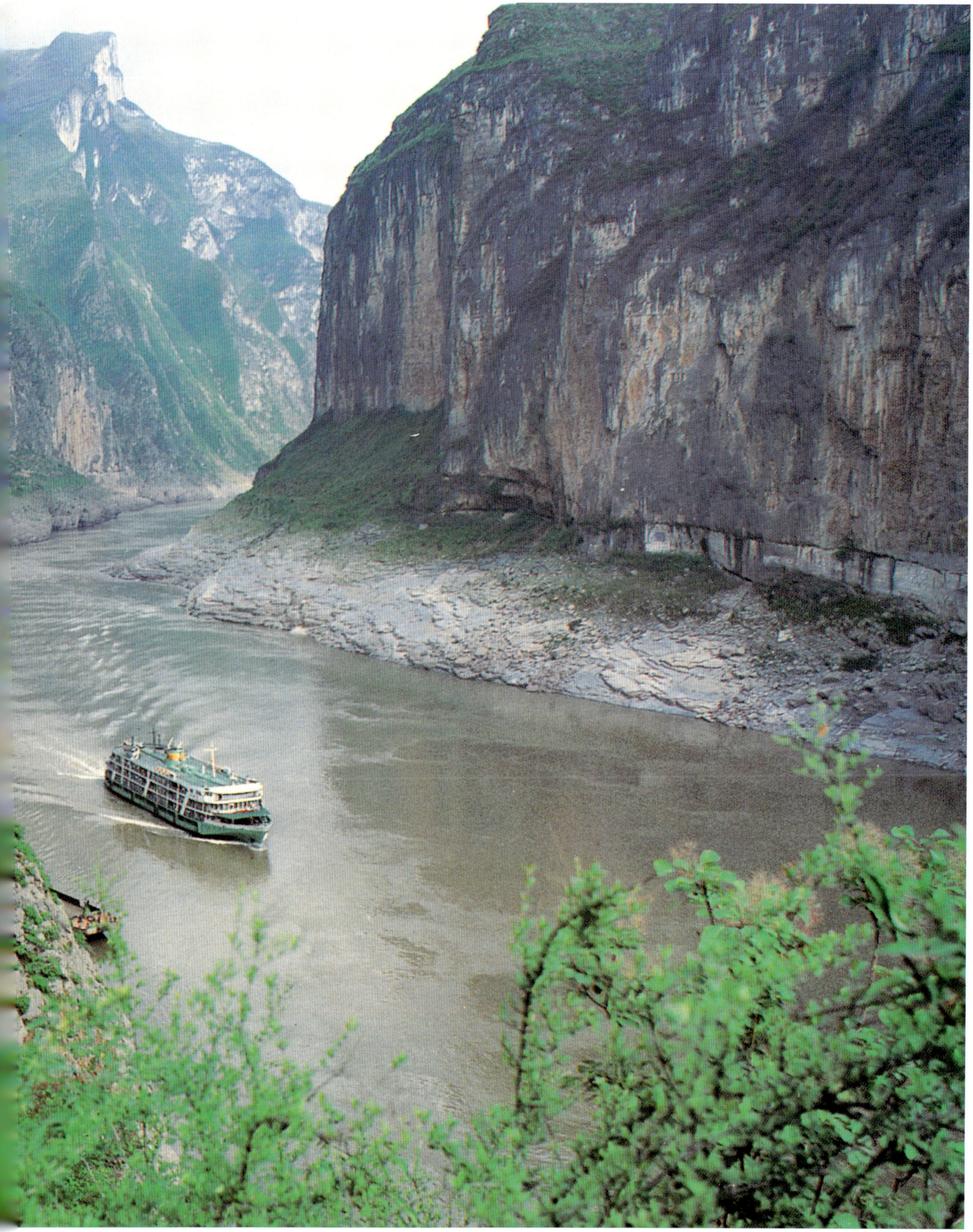

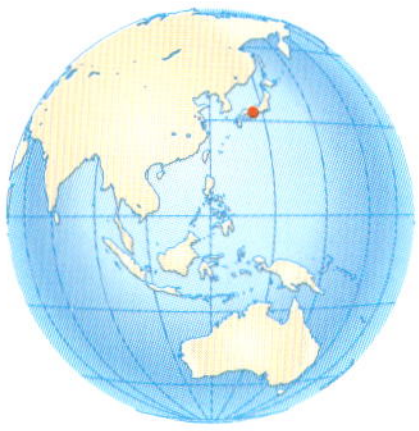

Kyoto, Heart of Japanese Culture

A modern city with a medieval heart, where abundant gardens and temples soothe the mind.

FACT FILE

Behavior: For outsiders, the subtleties of Japanese manners are a life's work. A few guidelines: a deep nod will do instead of a bow. In homes, remove outdoor shoes and put on slippers provided (there are other slippers for use in the toilet). Don't tip. Bring small presents. In dress, be very neat and clean.

Things to bring: Slip-on shoes.

Good buy before departure: Japan Rail Pass.

Addresses: Western-style house numbering does not exist. Ask, ask, and keep on asking.

Best times to visit: Spring, for the cherry blossoms; Autumn for the maples; and (for Nara) late October through early November, when Shoso-in treasures are on display in Nara National Museum.

Among Kyoto's many temples, one in particular commands veneration, and not only from Buddhists. In the 13th-century Hall of the Thirty-Three Bays, stand 1,001 gilt Buddhas, ten deep in 100 diagonal rows. They were created to save the world from disaster. They certainly helped to do so, for in 1945 Kyoto was one of the cities on which the United States considered dropping the atomic bomb. It was a Japanese-educated art historian, Langdon Warner, who vetoed the idea, arguing that Japan's old capital was its cultural treasure house. To destroy Kyoto would be to destroy not simply the country's will to resist but its essence. The essence remains, preserved not only in temples like the Hall of Thirty Three-Bays, but in its galleries, houses, gardens, and traditions.

From its foundation 1,200 years ago to the early 1600s, Kyoto was Japan's capital. It was chosen carefully, in accordance with the strict rules of geomancy, on a plain sloping south toward the sea and backed by mountains, like a seat protecting the emperor and his empire. A river flows south and west, and a mountain guards against evil spirits from the

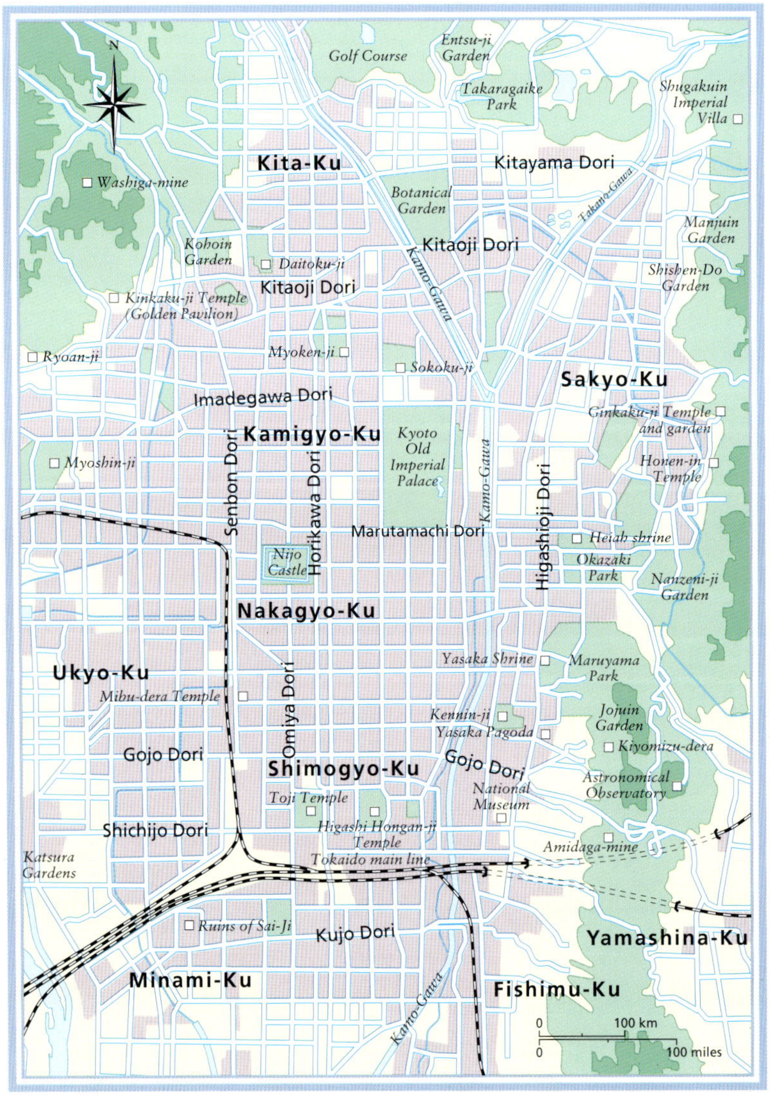

The Kinkaku-ji, or Temple of the Golden Pavilion (right) is a new version of the 14th-century original that burned down in 1950. It was regilded in 1988.

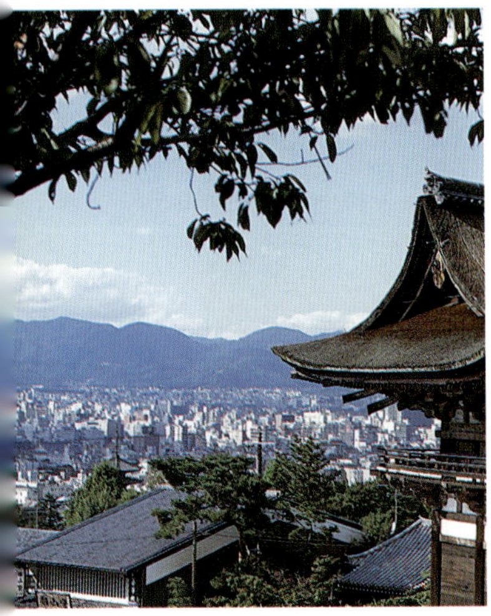

Kyoto's grid of medieval streets, which defines the modern center, is still visible in the map and looking over the city from Kiyomizu-dera temple (left).

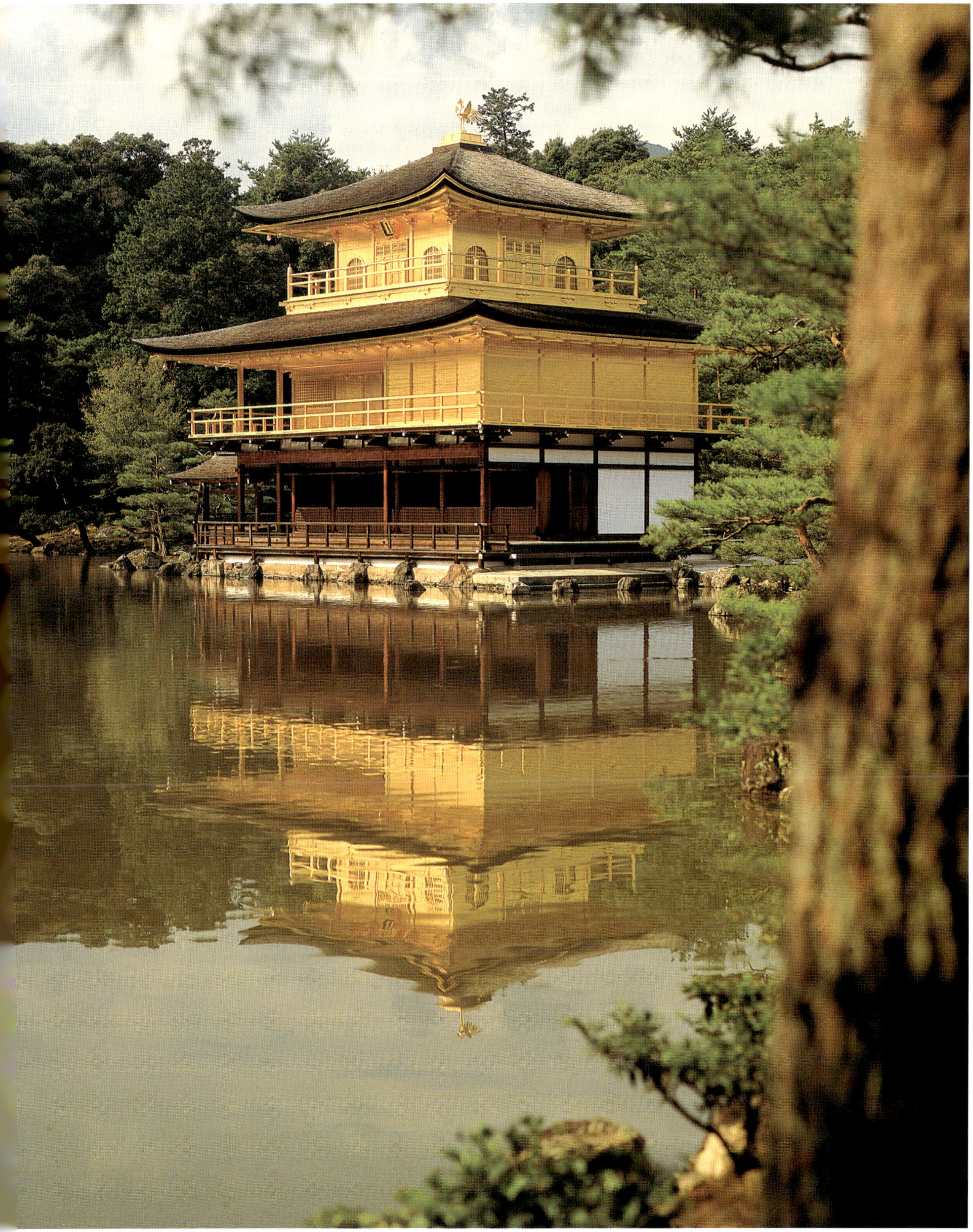

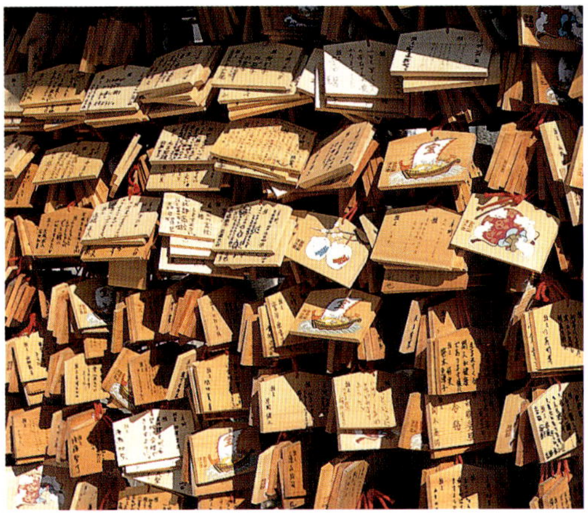

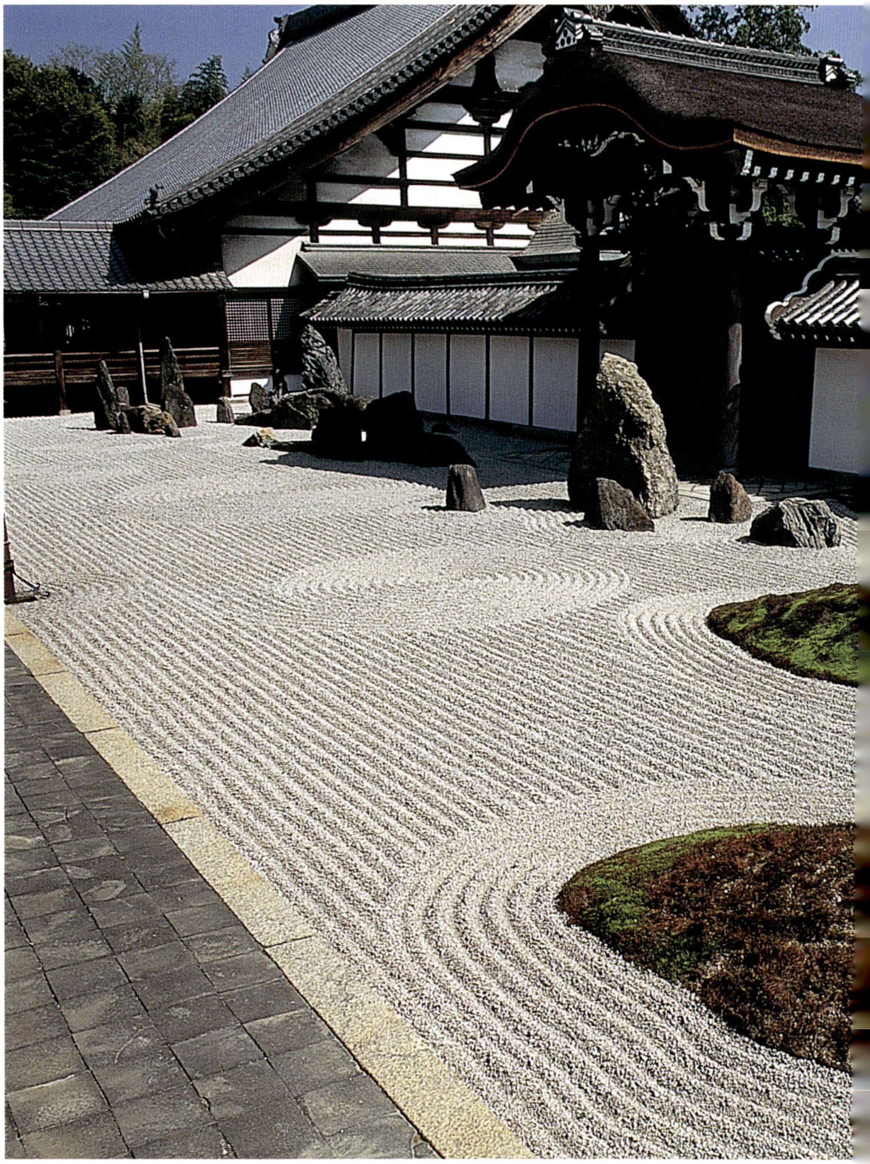

northeast. The palace compound was the city's pole, and a grid of streets divided into east-west sectors. Rebuilt several times after fires and wars, Kyoto finally developed its present graceful, peaceful air from aristocratic residents, after power had shifted permanently to Tokyo in 1868.

ZEN GARDENS AND TEA CEREMONIES

Beneath its modern concrete carapace, ancient Kyoto still exists in streets dotted with enough attractions to occupy a lifetime. Here, ancient arts and crafts—dancing, music, ceramics, woodblock printing, scroll painting, and calligraphy—thrive. The city has Japan's two most famous schools for teaching the tea ceremonies. The purpose of the ceremony, introduced in the 16th century, is to induce contemplation and harmony, and the teahouse is ideally set in a complementary garden.

Visiting Kyoto's gardens are perhaps the best way to get a feel for the city's rich and complex character. Japanese gardens owe more to human concepts than to nature. Beautiful objects—rocks, plants, trees, and ponds—are revered as homes of spirits and symbols of a wider landscape. The development of Zen Buddhism in the 1400s inspired a new asceticism in which simple elements—rock, raked sand, pebbles—were formed into patterns to assist contemplation.

In Ryoan-ji temple, Kyoto has the oldest surviving *karesansui* (rock and gravel garden). Built around 1500, it was "discovered" in the 1930s, when western architects began eulogizing about its use of space. The garden is astonishingly austere: a 102/ 50 foot (31/15 m) rectangle of raked gravel, surrounded by low stone walls, and set with 15 boulders in five groups. The only plants are the lichens and mosses on the rocks. Are the rocks mountains or dragons? Are the raked patterns waves or lines of rice in a paddy field, or do they represent the subconscious with the rocks emerging as tips of the conscious mind? There is no one way to see it—there are infinite ways.

CHERRY BLOSSOM TIME

Kyoto's open spaces are gardens of a different kind, stages on which the city's social life plays itself out. April, cherry blossom time, is a subject dear to Japanese artists and poets. As symbols of life's transient beauty, they are mentioned in countless *haiku*, the classical 17-syllable verse form, like this one:

Fallen petals rise
back to the branch—I watch:
oh... butterflies!

The blossoms signal the start of a week of drinking and celebration. One place to admire them is the courtly five-acre (2-hectare) garden of the Heian Shrine, built in 1894 to mark Kyoto's 1100th anniversary. Another is

Contemplative harmony is the purpose of this Zen garden (above) at Tofukuji Temple. Stones set in the raked quartz can be seen as islands in a quiet sea or tips of the conscious emerging from the subconscious.

Prayer plaques (above left) proclaim the power of ancient Buddhist beliefs at a Kyoto temple.

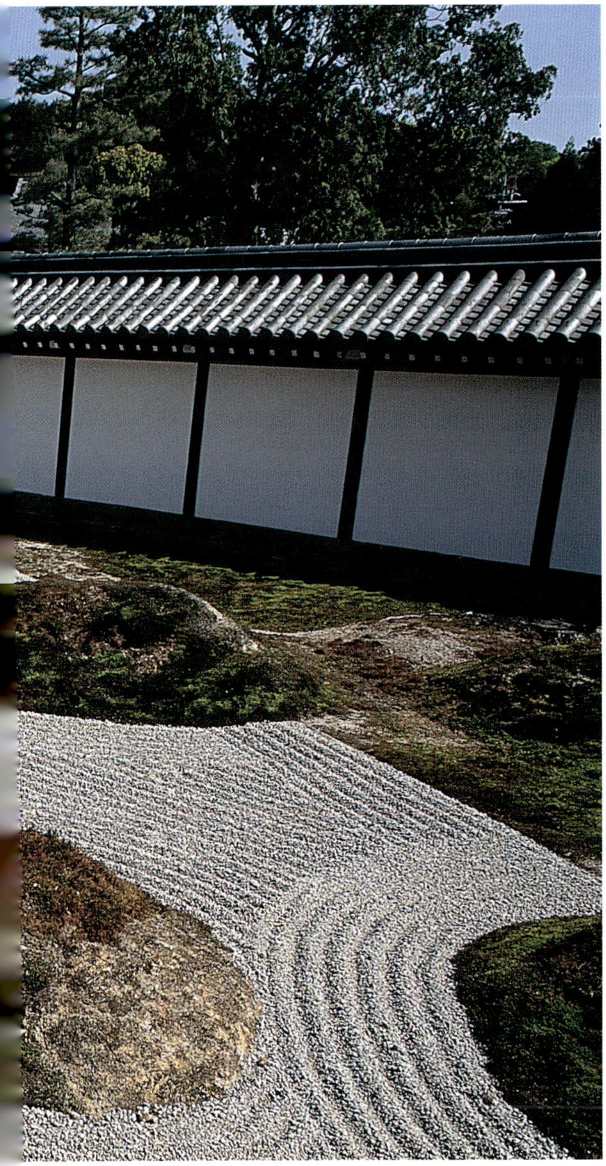

cool, and families hang out their richest possessions—kimonos, screens, scrolls ostensibly to expel the damp and mold of the rainy season. In autumn, Kyoto's residents like to head northwest to the suburbs of Arashiyama and Sagano, where maples and gingkos splash the hills with startling reds, oranges, and golds. Nearby are the informal gardens of Koryu-Ji, whose Treasure House (Reihokan) contains one of the most celebrated sculptures of Oriental art, Miroku Bosatsu. The slim and graceful boy in beatific meditation was carved in lustrous red pine, probably in the 6th century by a Korean. Winter is dominated by the New Year celebrations, when almost the entire city descends on the Yasaka Shrine in the Gion district to light tapers from a sacred fire and every temple bell is rung to drive away the evil of the year past. Then people make a point of marking the firsts of the new year—the first visit to a temple or the market, the first cup of tea—and look forward to the first blossoms of spring.

THE TREASURES OF NARA

Just 30 minutes by train from Kyoto, Nara was Japan's capital for a century in the 700s. Its parks, pagodas, and treasure houses bring the past into the present, without any industrial overlay. Its main glory is Tadai-Ji (Eastern Great Temple), which together with its subsidiary temples commemorates the introduction of Buddhism. Opened in 752, it has the world's biggest wooden structure contained by a single roof—suitably imposing for an emerging empire and its new religion. The roof of today's Daibutsu-den (Great Buddha Hall) is 18th century, but the original was even larger— 290/165 feet (88/50 m). It protects its colossal namesake, a 50-foot (15 m), 400-ton metal Buddha.

Cherry blossom season is a time for picnics in Kyoto parks. Double-flowered cultivars are sometimes planted as specimen trees in temple gardens.

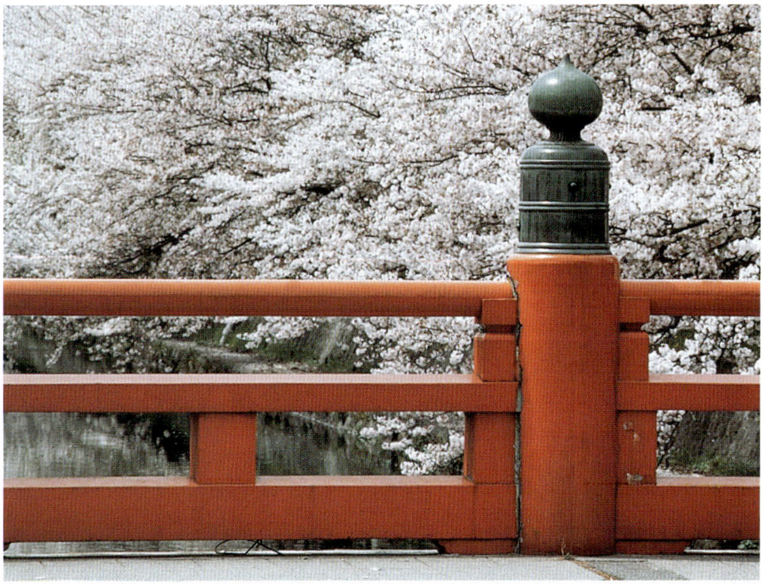

the one-mile (1.6 km) path that leads away from Nanzen-Ji, one of the greatest of Zen temples. The path is actually two paths on either side of the Shishigatani Canal, along which a university professor, Nishida Kitaro, loved to stroll. In the 50 years after his death, the Philosopher's Walk along the flanks of the hills hemming Kyoto's eastern edge has become very popular. Its lines of trees, interspersed with tearooms and craft shops, run past three temples, one with an exquisite sloping garden of raked gravel, sand, moss, and flowering trees. The path ends at Ginkaku-Ji, The Temple of the Silver Pavilion, built as an imperial retirement villa.

Summer is festival time. On July 14-17, the city stops for the Gion Matsuri parade of ancient shrine floats. Gion itself, where aging geishas are still to be seen performing in teahouses, is enlivened by food stalls. Residents spray and wash the streets to keep

India and Southeast Asia

"I travel not to go anywhere, but to go. I travel for travel's sake. The great affair is to move."

R.L. Stevenson, English writer, 1850-1894.

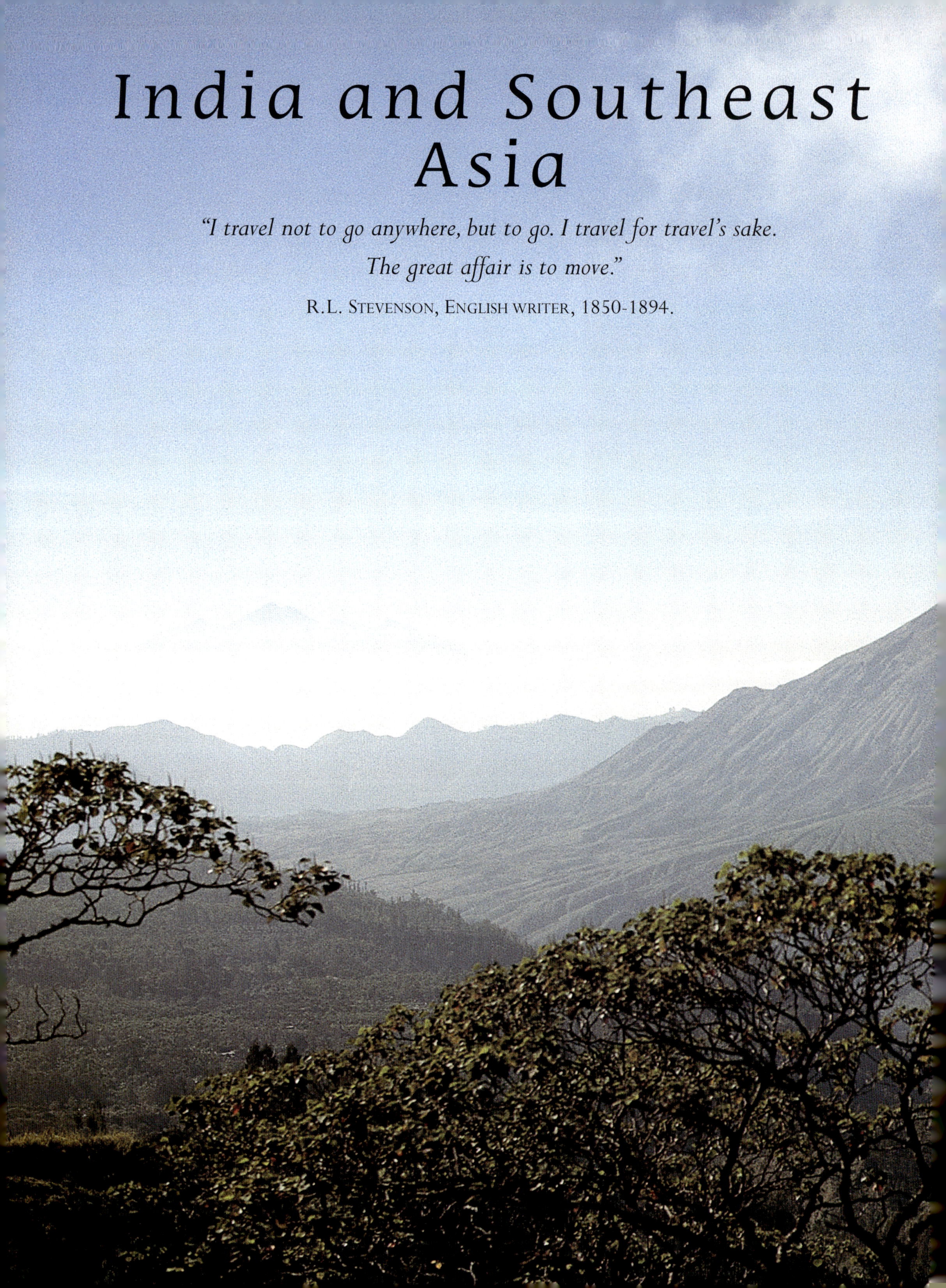

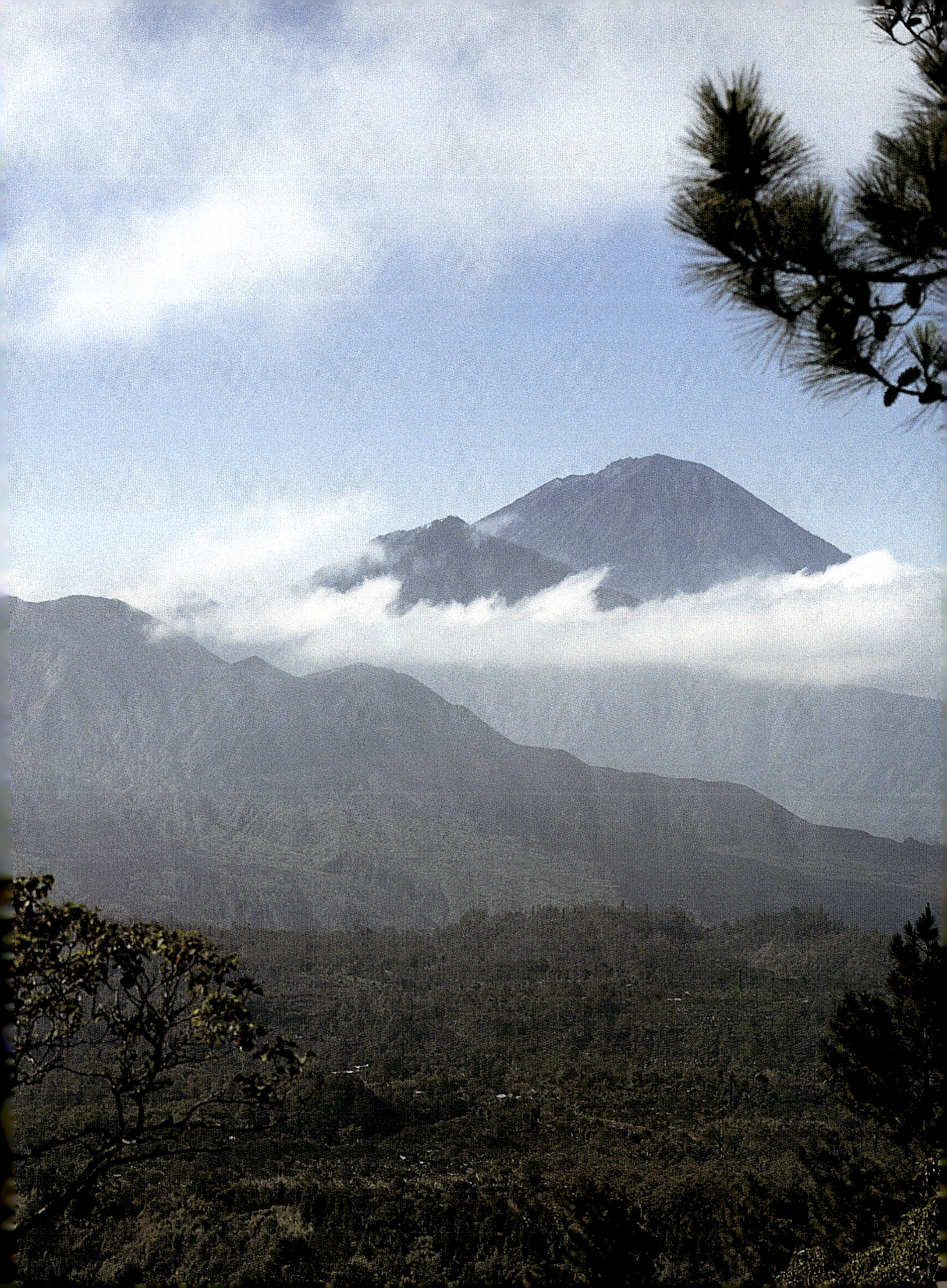

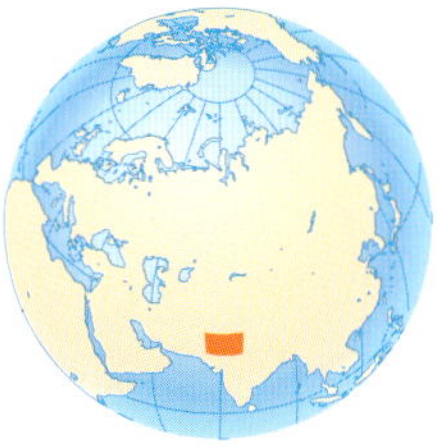

The Princely State of Rajasthan

Palaces, temples, towers, and pavilions rise from the desert in the regal cities of Rajasthan.

IT MAY SOUND UNPROMISING AT FIRST, for Rajasthan's north and west is a parched and forbidding desert, but south and east of the forested Aravalli Hills lie wonders: palaces, mosques, gardens, and temples. From these, you can approach the desert itself, and find amid its barren rocks a treasure of another kind. All this can be seen in style by traveling in the so called Palace on Wheels, a train of royal carriages with air conditioning, bedrooms, and lounges, which link the Indian capital Delhi to Rajasthan's greatest cities.

The "Land of Kings"—which is what Rajasthan means—has two chief jewels, Udaipur and Jaipur, although Jodhpur, too, is a magnicicent walled city on the edge of the Thar Desert, an equestrian center which has given its name to closefitting riding pants.

This whole area, from the shifting sandhills of the Thar Desert across the forested and craggy Aravalli Hills to the fertile valleys and fields of the southeast, once seethed with princely rivals, the rulers of 22 fiercely independent states. But all of them shared a common origin as Rajputs, members of the warrior clans whose love of war was matched by an exalted but

The honey-pot turrets of Jaisalmer (below) rear from the desert in the far west of Rajasthan; the sandstone walls conceal medieval alleys.

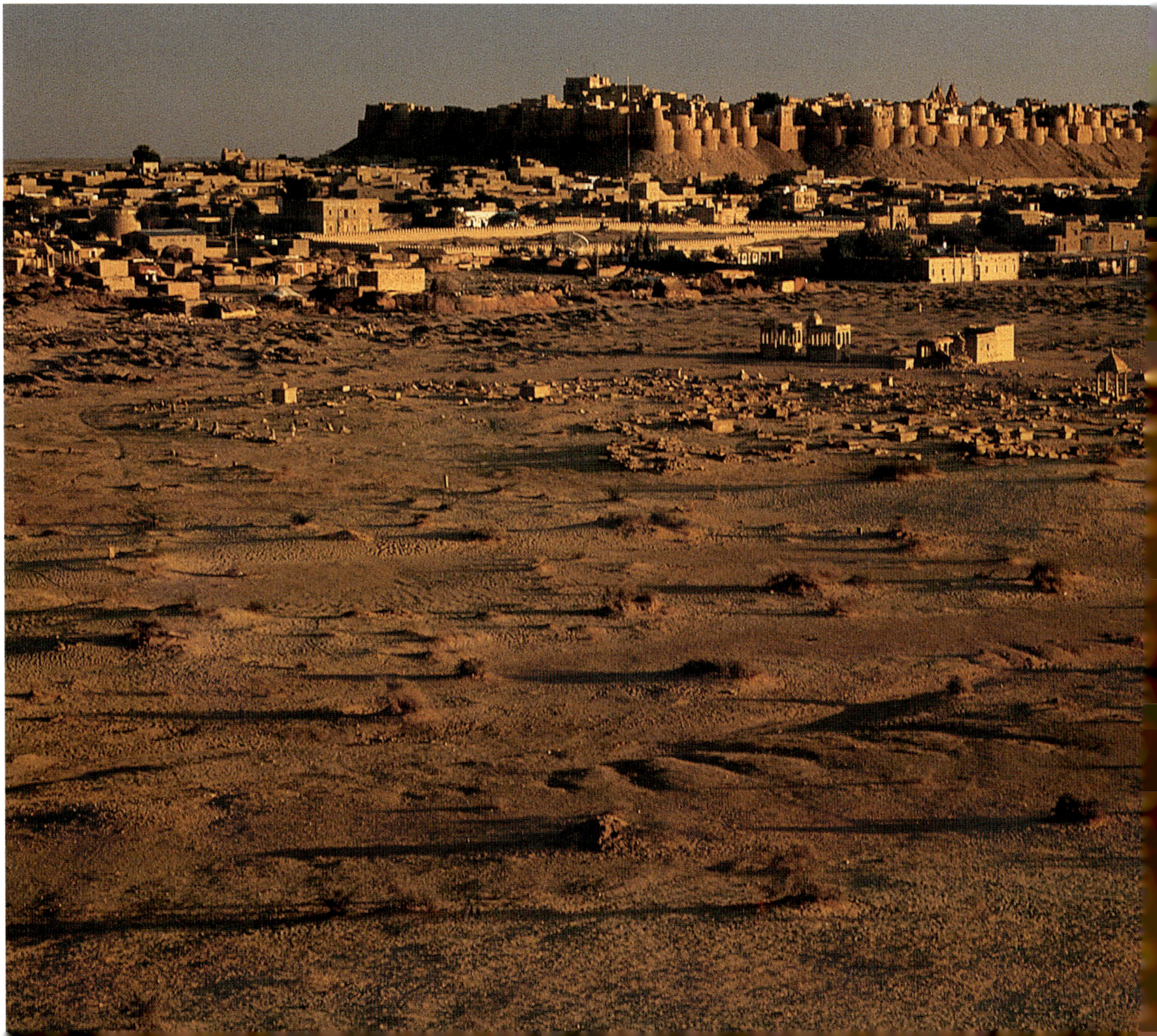

severe chivalric code. When the Muslims conquered Delhi in the 1100s, they looked enviously toward the rich lands of the Gujerat beyond Rajasthan and constantly tried to conquer the Rajput states to secure trade routes. The Rajputs fought back, retaining their independence for 350 years. When the Mughal rulers seized Delhi in the 1500s, they generally proved more accommodating to the Hindu princes, and the Rajputs coexisted profitably with them. After Indian independence in 1947, the many Rajput states were merged to form Rajasthan, but Udaipur, glistening above its lake, and Jaipur, "the Pink City," remain as emblems of the Rajputs' power and belated wealth.

The Pink City

Coming from Delhi, Jaipur, the state capital, is an easy 187 miles (300 km) from Delhi. It therefore caught the flow of wealth as soon as it was founded by the state's ruler, Jai Singh, in the early 1700s. Even as a teenager, Jai Singh proved a ruler of genius. Planning for a new era of peace and prosperity, he named his new capital for himself, and in eight years turned it into an architectural showcase, following rigorous Hindu architectural traditions. High walls with ten gates enclose the city, which is divided into seven sections by straight streets, all of the prescribed width.

Jai Singh also welcomed artists and businessmen. That ideal inspired a later ruler to dress the whole city in pink, the traditional color of welcome, for the visit of the Prince of Wales, later Edward VII, in 1876. A tradition was established. Now the state's largest city (its population is 600,000) insists on pink washes for its central buildings. Most startling of all is the five-story facade of the Hawa Mahal, the "Palace of the Winds," where court women once watched through 593 screened windows and balconies. Although today the city has spread far beyond the confines of the original "Pink City," the flamboyance endures, matched by the flow and flutter of tie-dyed saris in Jaipur's streets. Of all Jaipur's temples and palaces, the most astonishing is the City Palace, if only because it contains Jai Singh's observatory. This collection of angular stones, like some display of abstract sculpture, forms 18 instruments whose shadows track the movements of the sun and planets. A 90 foot (27 m) sundial tells the

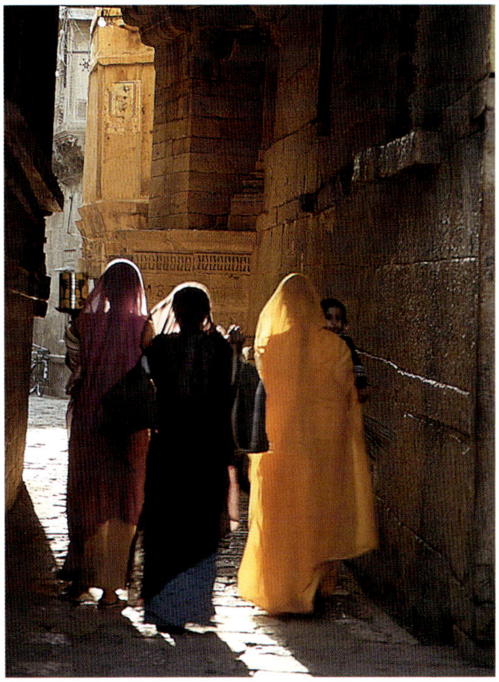

Even in a country as colorful as India, Rajput men and women are renowned for their brilliant scarlet, gold, and pink clothes, which they wear with the proud elegance of the descendants of a race of kings.

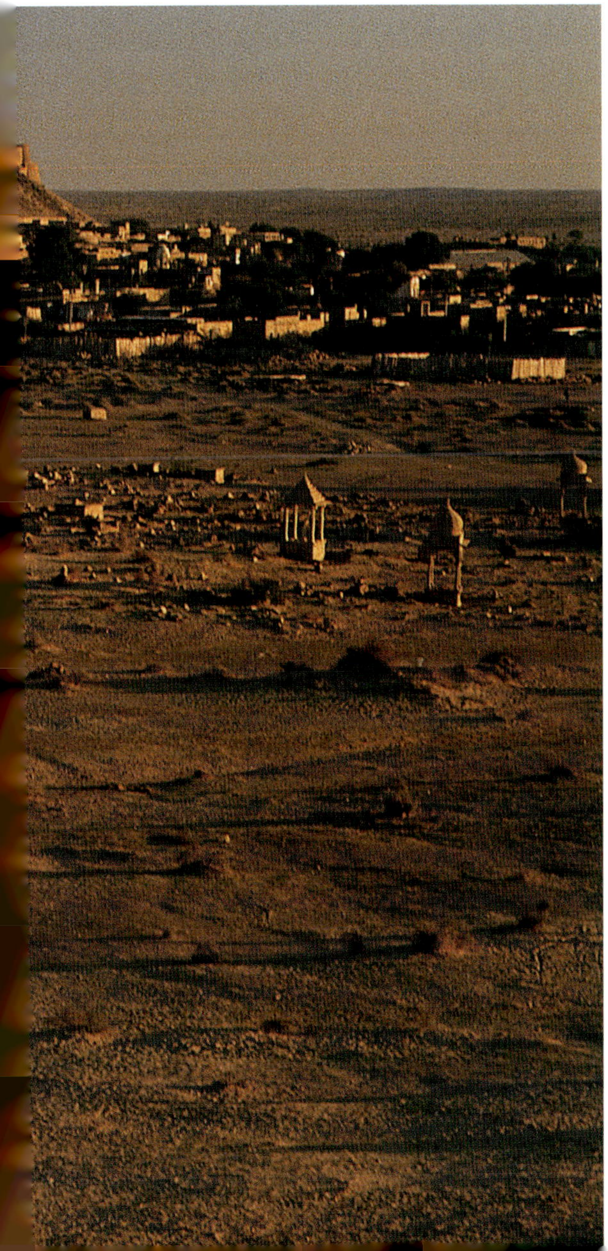

FACT FILE

Airports: International airport at New Delhi; loca flights to Jaipur.

Currency: Indian rupee.

Language: Hindi is the main language but English is widely understood.

When to go: October—April. December and January can be surprisingly cold at night. Avoid the monsoon season July—September.

Health precautions: Inoculations against Hepatitis A and B, typhoid, cholera, polio meningitis, and tetanus essential. Malaria is resistant to chloroquine-based drugs. Drink only bottled or boiled water, avoid uncooked vegetables, salads, unpeeled fruit, and unboiled milk. Take medication against diarrhea, worm pills, and antibiotics.

Tipping : Tip often but in small amounts.

What to take: Padlocks, sink plugs, mosquito net, sunblock, hats, sunglasses, tampons.

Accommodation. Book the better hotels in advance, and also the Palace on Wheels train, which leaves and returns to Delhi every Wednesday evening.

Do not: Eat food with your left hand (reserved in Asia for toilet functions); wear shoes in temples or mosques; wear shorts or go shirtless outside big hotels; swear at Indians no matter what the provocation; photograph people without asking; leave possessions unwatched.

Note to women travelers: If not accompanied by a man, especially if fair-haired, expect constant stares and mild sexual harassment.

time to within two minutes (though the time it tells is its own, up to 41 minutes behind standard Indian time).

THE JEWEL IN THE LAKE

The rulers of Mewar, the state of which Udaipur was once the capital, had more reason than most to be proud. The Sisodias could trace their lineage back 1,400 years. When their former capital, Chittor, was sacked by the Mughals in 1567—an act that inspired 13,000 women to cast themselves and their children into a funeral pyre—the young king, Udai Singh II, retreated into the fertile hills and ravines of the Aravalli. One morning, out hunting on the shore of Lake Pichola, he came across a sage meditating and asked the question that had been tormenting him: "Where, O Revered One, should I build my next capital?"

"Why, right here, of course," said the sage, "where your destiny has brought you to ask such a question."

So in 1559 the king did just that, enlarging the lake and (of course) naming the new city for himself. It now forms a sublime contrast with the original capital, today's Chittaurgarh, which is little more than a colossal fort sitting starkly on a rocky bulwark 70 miles (115 km) northeast of Udaipur. Udai's city, with its high whitewashed houses and narrow streets, seems the epitome of peace.

For visitors, the journey is made easy by plane, train, and road. In Udaipur, they explore the old city's switchback network of little streets by taxi, rickshaws, or bicycle. Many take a ferry into Lake Pichola at sunset to view the two 17th-century island palaces, and the ruler's old residence, the City Palace, which seems to rise in a sheer pale yellow stone from the eastern shore of the lake to an exuberant crest of domes, arches, cupolas, turrets, and crenellations. Reflections shimmer on the lake, backed by rolling expanses of green hills. The City Palace's southern end is now a deluxe hotel, *Shiv Nawas.* So vast is the palace—it was once a complex of 11 palaces—that it contains a museum, a maze of courtyards and rooms glittering with miniatures and mosaics, and a hill.

Udaipur's Lake Palace, now a hotel, seems to float on Lake Pichola like a luxury cruise ship.

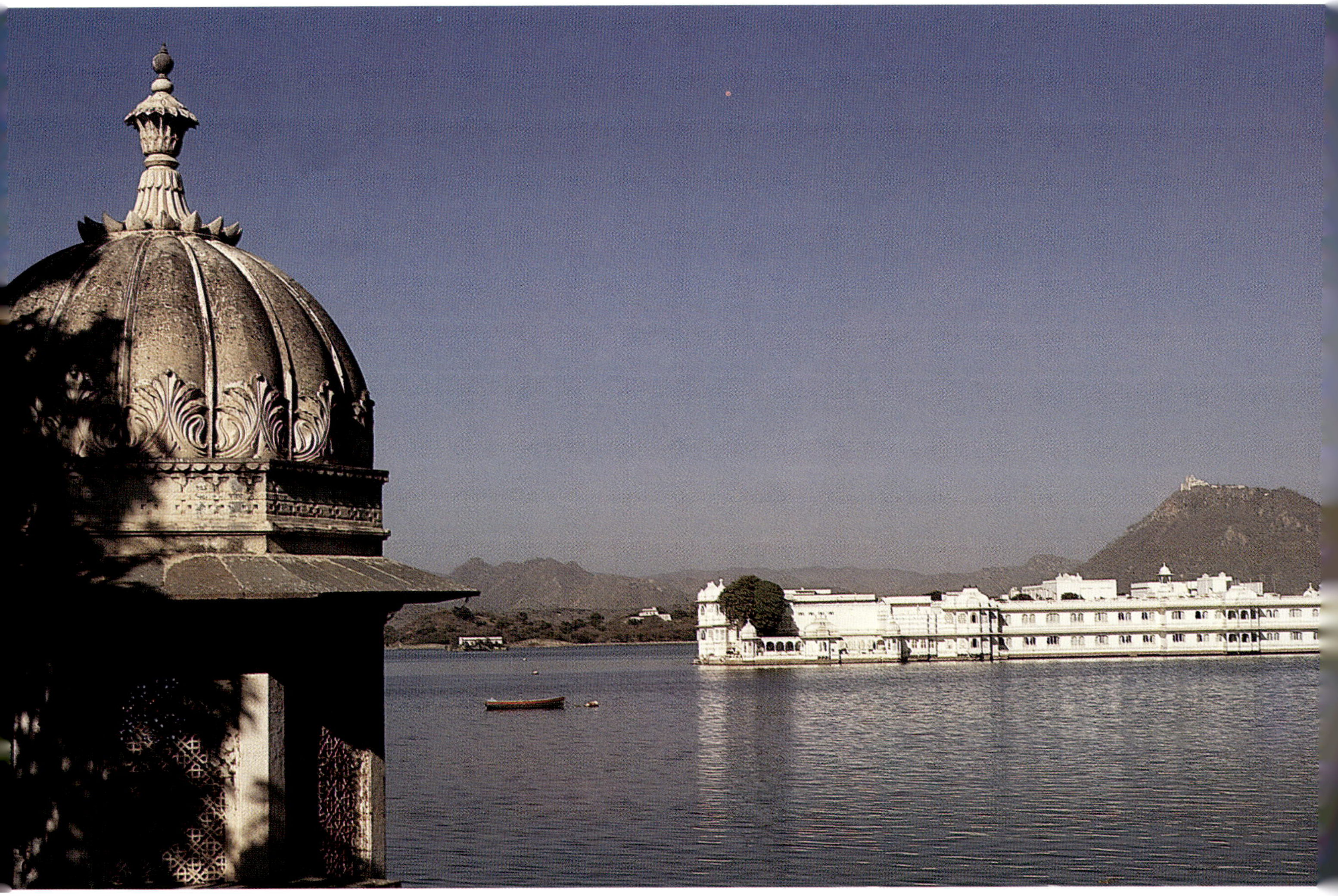

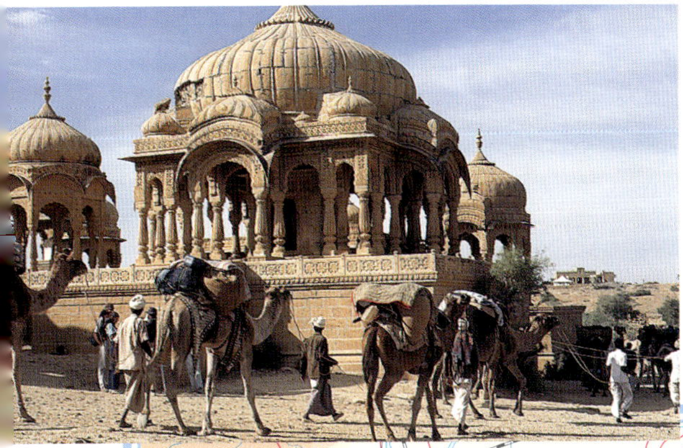

★ *Bada Bagh, 4 miles (6 km) north of Jaisalmer is an area of surprising fertility centered on cenotaphs honoring the city's rulers (left).*

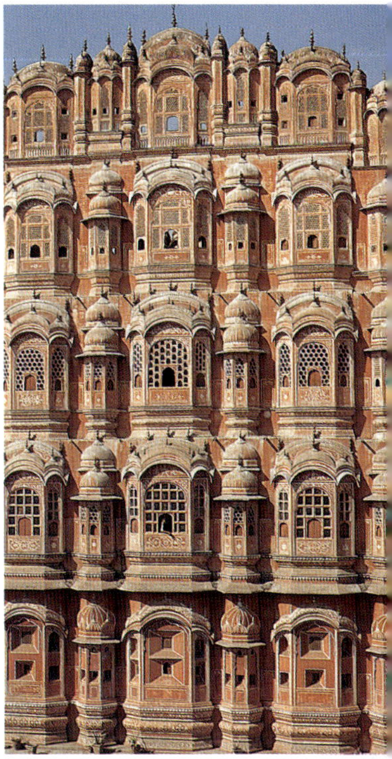

★ *The facade of Jaipur's most famous landmark, the Palace of the Winds (Hawa Mahal) is a honeycomb of windows.*

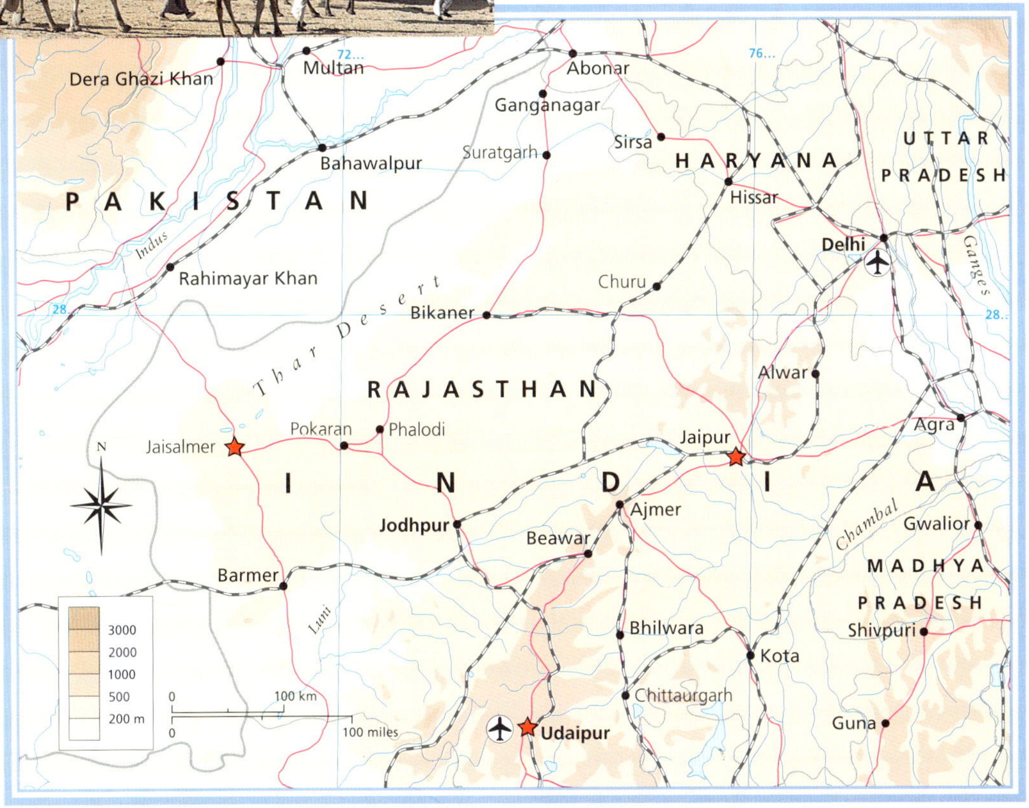

DESERT FORTRESS

Far to the west, in Rajasthan's desert hinterland, lies Jaisalmer, one of the subcontinent's most surprising places. As you approach Jaisalmer over the level plains, it looms up like a castle from *The 1,001 Nights*, its soft yellow stone bulwarks glowing golden in the sun, looking rather like a row of pawns set up for a gigantic chess game. "Jaisal's Rock," an outpost of bandit chiefs, was founded in the 1100s. War followed war, in sieges that became the subjects of epic poems, but trade between Delhi and Central Asia brought prosperity, until Bombay's growth in the 1800s sidelined the city. Now this warren of alleys and neighboring mansions is again bound to its neighbors by road, rail, and air, but it remains largely untouched, offering visitors a feel of the desert with camel safaris over the Thar's shifting dunes and gravels.

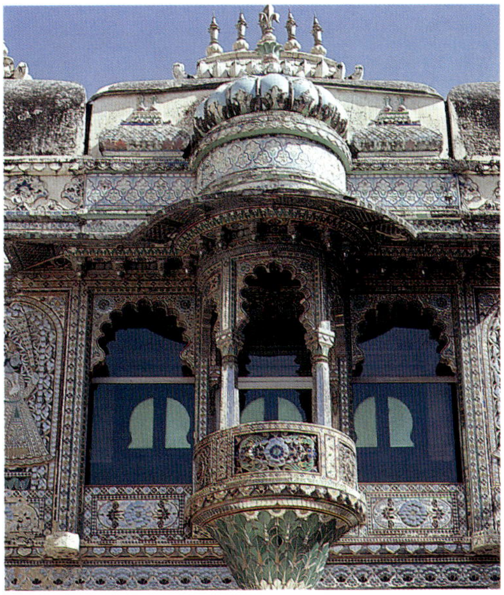

★ *The ornate stonework of the City Palace, Udaipur makes this the most imposing royal residence in Rajasthan.*

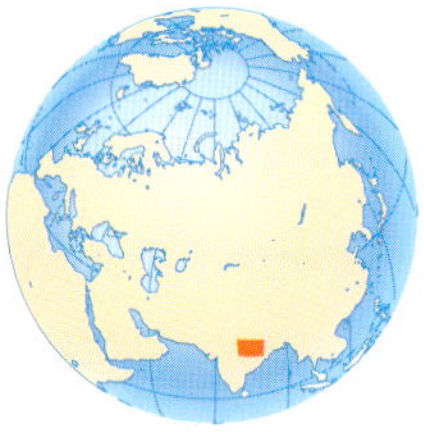

Varanasi, India's sacred city

Varanasi is one of the greatest shrines on earth. Hindu and Buddhist pilgrims by the million flock to it, seeking purification and escape from life's sufferings in its holy waters.

The old city of Varanasi—a name meaning "the city between two rivers (the Varuna and the Asi)"—stretches back from the west bank of the Ganges.

For non Hindus, the first sight of the banks of the Ganges at Varanasi is extraordinary: a 3 mile (4.8km) crescent of river, lined by long gray ghats (steps), to which very day tens of thousands crowd, seeking the blessings conferred by the sacred waters—purification in life, release from the cycles of reincarnation at death. As pilgrims wash themselves in the flowing waters, families tend funeral pyres, sending smoke drifting over the city's huddled streets and temples. In Varanasi the odor of sanctity is all pervasive.

For Hindus, the Ganges is the most sacred of their seven sacred rivers, and Varanasi—the site of the most sacred of temples devoted to Shiva, one of their chief deities—is one of the seven cities with the power to give salvation, a power it has had for millennia. Varanasi is one of the world's most ancient continuously inhabited sites—in Mark Twain's awed words, "older than history, older than tradition, older even than legend." A city has stood here for 4,000 years. From the earliest days of Hinduism, more than 3,000 years ago,

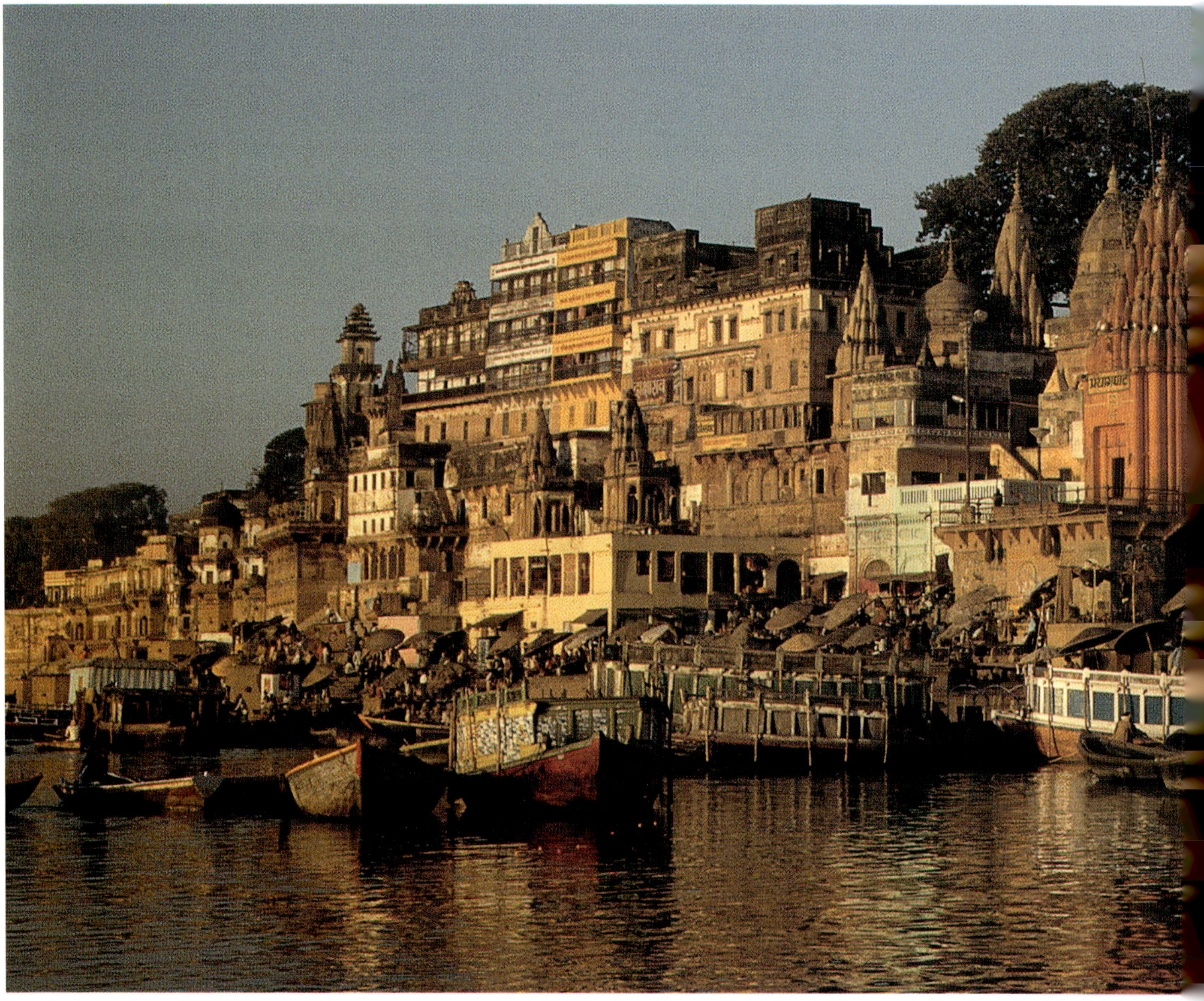

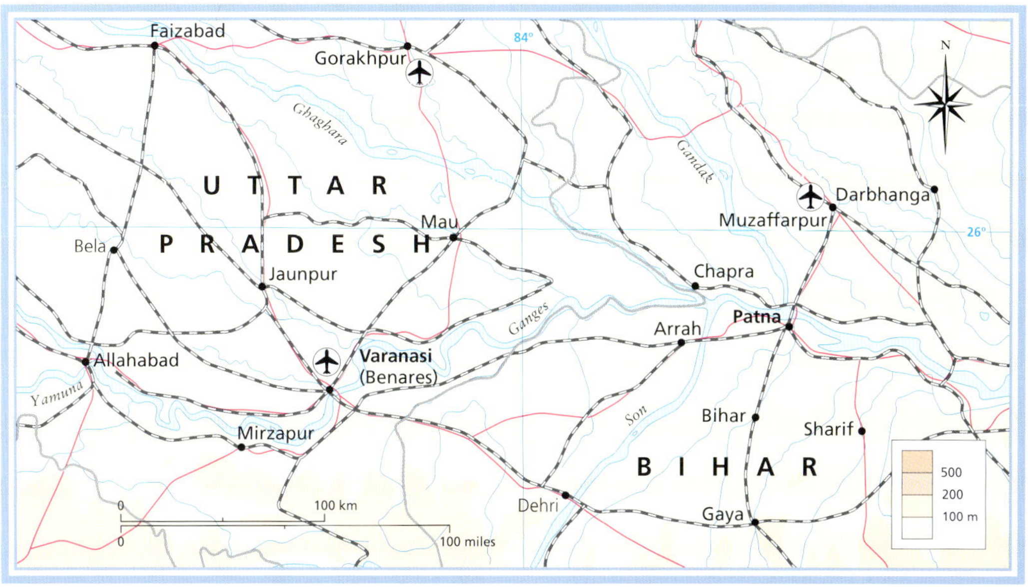

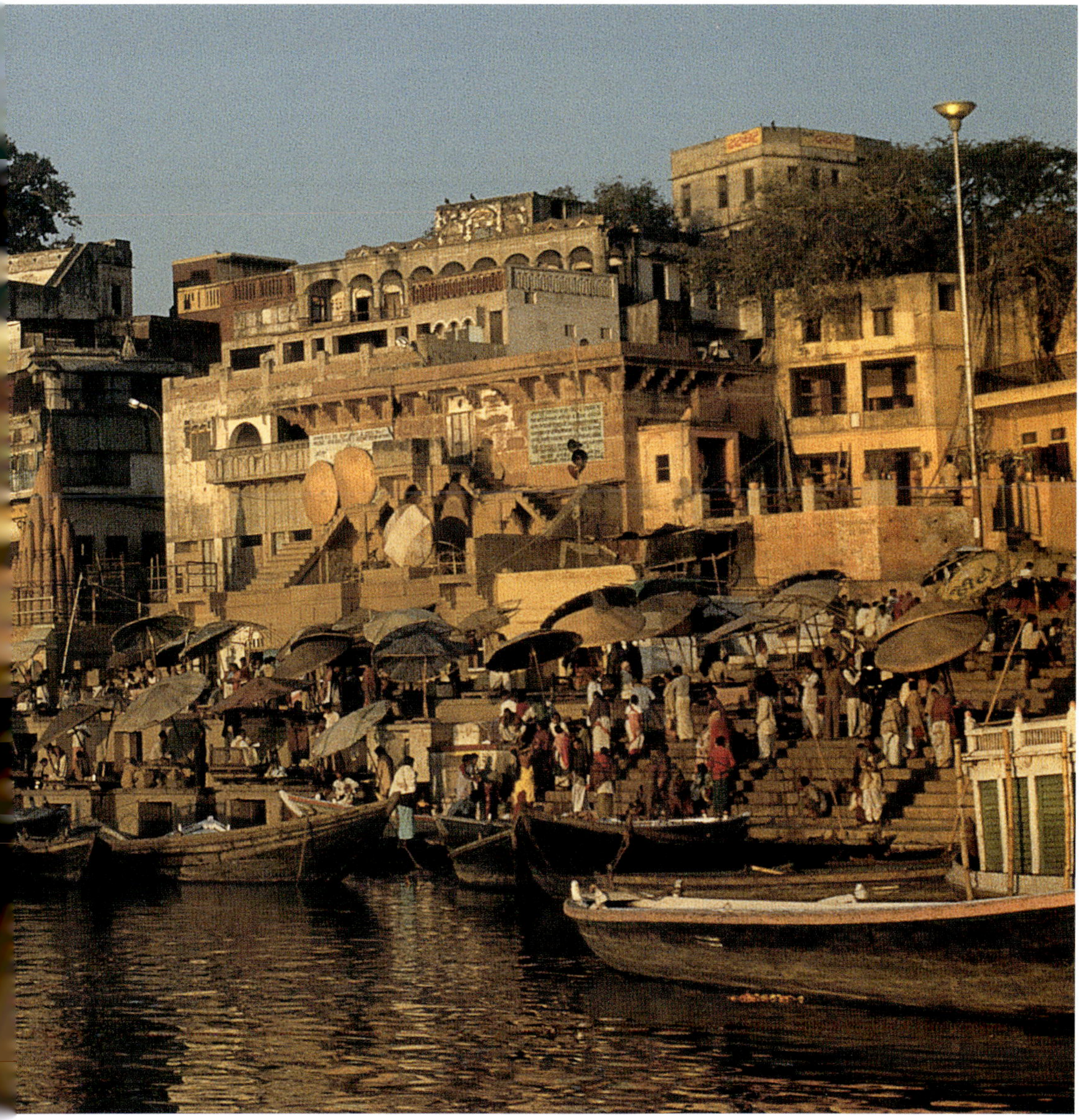

FACT FILE

Airports: New Delhi international airport, local flights to/from Varanasi.

Currency: Indian rupees. U.S. dollars accepted at banks and money exchanges.

Language: Hindi , but English is widely understood.

When to go: October—April. December and January can be cool at night; avoid the monsoon July—September.

Health Precautions: Inoculations against Hepatitis A and B, typhoid, cholera, polio, meningitis, and tetanus are essential. Malaria is resistant to chloroquine based drugs. Drink only bottled or boiled water, avoid uncooked vegetables, salads, peeled fruit and unboiled milk. Take medication against almost inevitable attacks of diarrhea., plus worm pills, antihistamine pills, and antibiotics.

Tipping: Tip hotel/restaurant staff.

What to take: Padlocks, sink plugs, mosquito repellant, sunblock, hats, sunglasses, tampons.

Accommodation: Plenty of hotels to suit most budgets.

Do not: Eat food with your left hand (reserved in Asia for toilet functions); wear shoes in temples or mosques; wear shorts or go shirtless outside big hotels; swear at Indians no matter what the provocation; assume it is okay to photograph people.

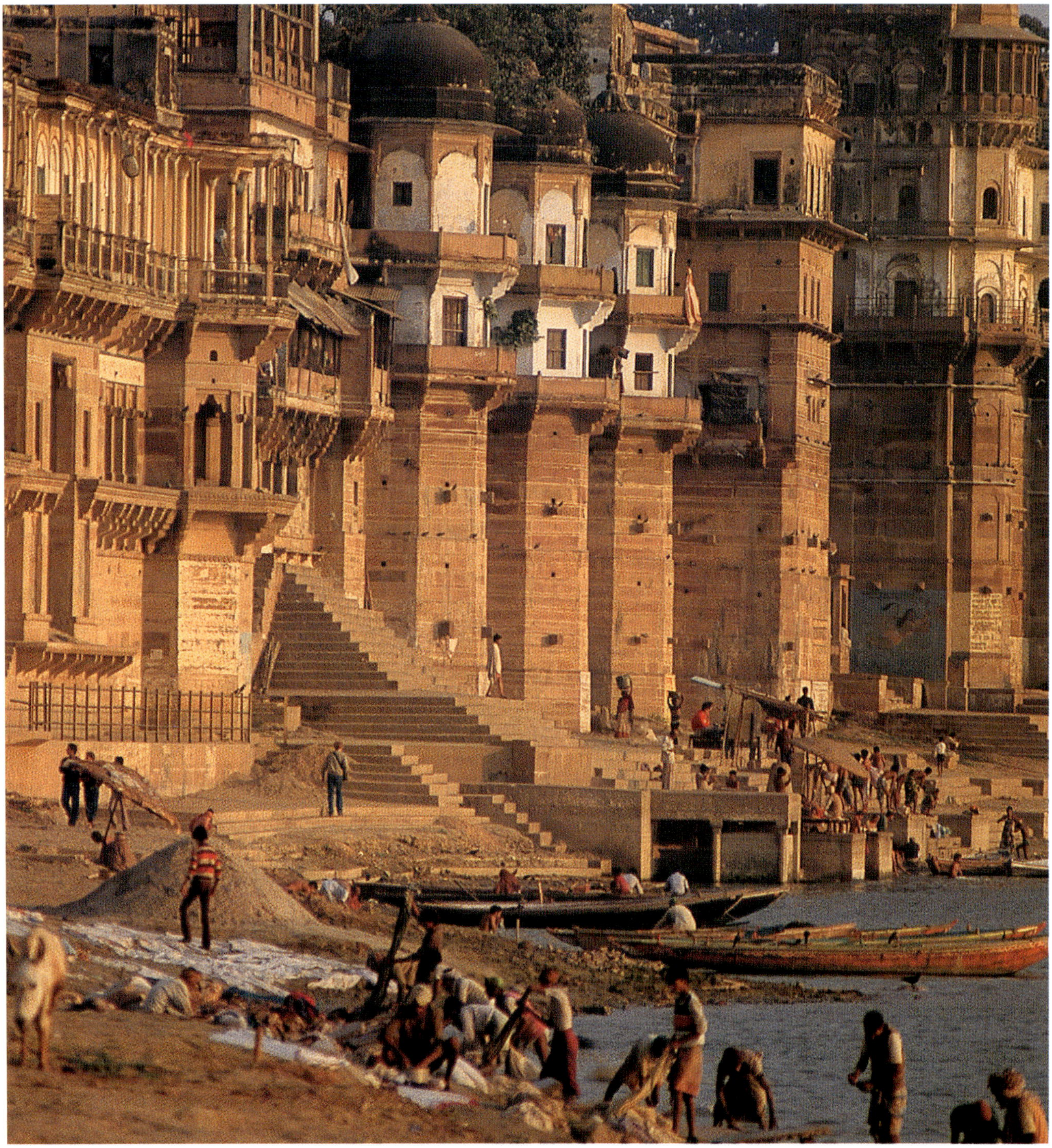

The bathing ghats on the west bank of the Ganges; the most magical time to visit them is early morning.

the devout referred to it as Kashi, "the Luminous." Known for two centuries by its anglicized form Benares, the city reverted after Indian independence in 1947 to its ancient name, derived from two Ganges tributaries: the Varuna and the Asi.

THE HOLY RIVER

Lying in the middle of the intensively cultivated and densely populated Gangetic plain, Varanasi today is a large city teeming with life. But its focal points are still the ghats, of which there are more than 100, each marked with a lingam, the universal Hindu stone phallus (usually simplified into the inoffensive shape of an inverted test tube). At sunrise, the series of steps, which are exposed and covered as the water rises and falls throughout the year, become a shifting mass of almost naked bathers, priests, yoga adepts, and mourners. Much to the astonishment of visitors arriving from the luxury hotels on the city fringes,

Hindus regard the Ganges as the "elixir of life," and immerse themselves in its muddy waters, often rather cautiously at first, despite the ashes of corpses and open sewers that turn the river into a potential health hazard. But, such is the special nature of the Ganges waters—a sign of divine blessing according to believers—this hazard seldom produces the epidemics of cholera or typhoid you might expect. Despite this, visitors are advised not to bathe in, let alone drink, its waters.

So great is Varanasi's holiness that any Hindu dying within its confines is regarded as being released from the otherwise endless round of reincarnations. The city is therefore a refuge for the aged, who often seek shelter in the temples awaiting death, a pitiable sight to nonbelievers but an inspiration to the devout. Once released from life, their corpses are cremated on the two "burning ghats." One, Jalasi, next to the most sacred of all the ghats (Manikarnika), is always crowded with funeral parties and the ghat's guardians (but note: photography is forbidden).

Each of the ghats, dividing and linking the line of 18th and 19th century temples and palaces, has its own significance and its own adherents, being the Hindu equivalents of Catholic shrines with their associated saints. The best way to see them is to get up before dawn—except in chilly midwinter this early hour makes the best viewing time anyway—and hire a rowboat with a boatman. You can then view the ghats in sequence as your boat moves silently along the river, the early morning mist on the waters mingling with the smoke from many pyres before the fierce heat of the Indian sun dissipates it.

Five of the ghats are of special significance, forming the Panchatirthi ("five crossings"), at which pilgrims should bathe in sequence, performing rituals at each. One confers particular merit: the Dashashwamedha ("ten horse sacrifice") Ghat, named for a sacrifice performed by the god Brahma. Pilgrims can benefit from his perfection simply by bathing.

Winding Hinterland

The city is more than its riverside. Ranging back from the central ghats is the Old City. Its local name, Vishwanatha ("Lord of All"), derives from its main temple complex, also known as the Golden Temple, from the gold plating on its spire. It is dedicated to Shiva in his manifestation as Lord of the Universe. Visitors find their way to it by edging through a maze of overhung alleys that are crammed with the bedlam and acrid smells of hundreds of shops and stalls. They are rewarded by the sight of a smooth black stone set in a silver plinth. It is a shivalingam, one of many worshipped at Shiva shrines across the Hindu world. Here, though, it has special import. A short walk north of the Golden Temple is Jnana Vapi ("Wisdom Well"), where Shiva is said to have cooled his lingam. The waters, considered to be a fount of knowledge, are covered to prevent a rush from the faithful.

The Buddha's Park

Varanasi is also sacred for Buddhists, for Siddhartha Gautama, the Buddha (Enlightened One) gave his first sermons here in the 6th century B.C. Gazelle Park where the Buddha "set in motion the Wheel of the Law" is at Sarnath, just 6 miles (10km) north of Varanasi, an easy cab or bus ride away. About 1,400 years ago, there were 30 Buddhist monasteries there. After Buddhism's eclipse under the impact of Islam in the 1200s, time and vandals destroyed almost everything. British archeologists reopened it in the 1800s and more restorations, amounting almost to rebuilding, followed in the 1920s, partly financed by American Buddhists. Now its immaculate if somewhat sterile ruins draw pilgrims from the world over. Temples and shrines gather as if in obeisance round two stupas—one a mere stump, the other a 100 feet (33m) tower—both of which are said to mark the exact spot of the Buddha's first sermon.

In Varanasi, the Hindu and Muslim worlds also abut, intermingle, and sometimes clash. The great 17th century Jnana Vapi mosque was built by the Mogul Emperor Aurangzeb—a fanatical Muslim—as a deliberate affront to Varanasi's sanctity as believed by his Hindu subjects. But the mosque takes its name from the Hindu Wisdom Well, which stands a stone's throw away.

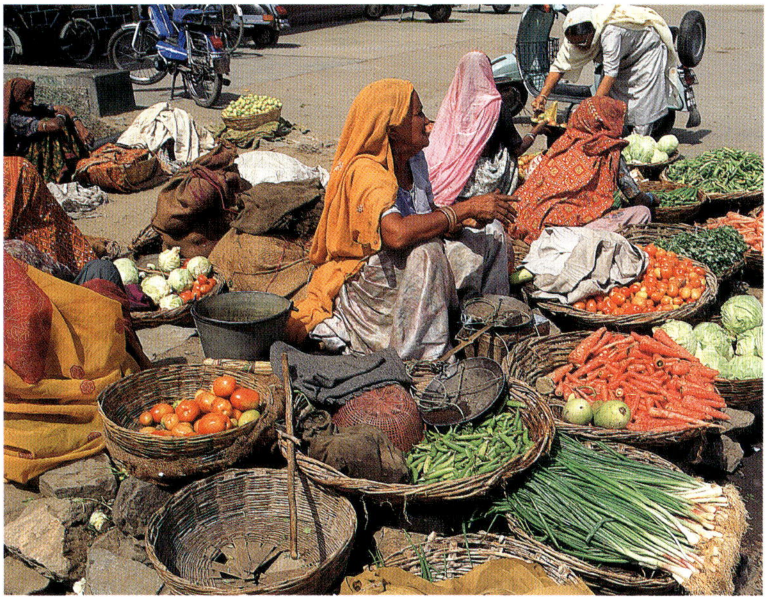

The streetsellers are colorful, their wares enticing, but if you buy fruit or vegetables, wash them in sterilized water, or peel them before eating.

A little Hindu girl sells votive offerings for pilgrims to lay at the many shrines.

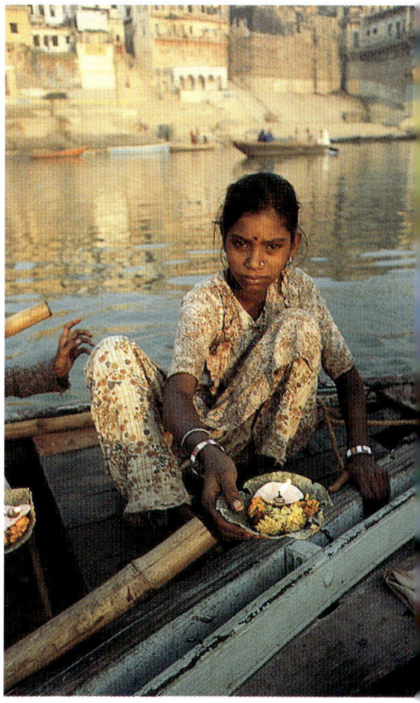

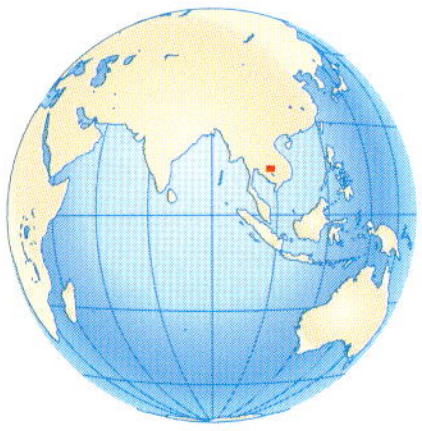

Jungle Temples of Cambodia

"An architectural creation that has never had, or ever will have, its equal in the world."—Henri Mouhot, French naturalist, 1860.

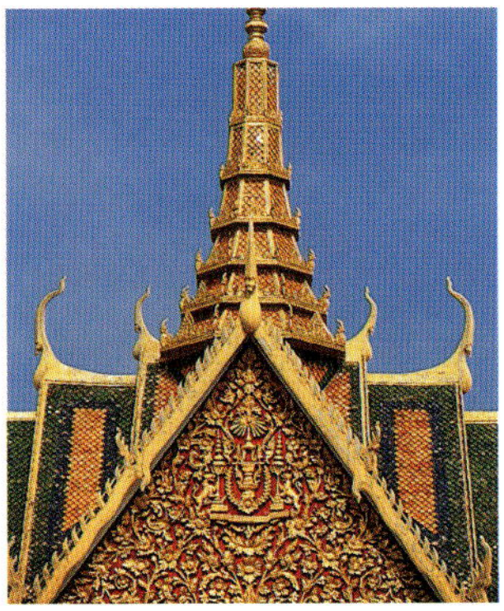

From Phnom Penh, where the royal palace's silver pagoda (above) recalls the city's 15th-century origins, visitors travel north to Siem Riep and on to Angkor.

IN 1860, HENRI MOUHOT CAME ACROSS ruins in the Cambodian jungle, a vast and mysterious archipelago of carved sandstone. For centuries the jungle had grown over it, until roots, branches, creepers, and stones had united around it and the stones were pulled apart. For Mouhot, the experience was like stumbling onto an artifact built by beings from another planet.

Mouhot's awestruck descriptions of his findings made the ruins famous, and carried them instantly into the realm of myth. At some undefined ancient time, it was said, a great civilization, the Khmers, had sprung up from nowhere and later vanished without a trace. As France began to establish its empire in Southeast Asia in the 1860s, French archaeologists stripped away the trees, and some of the romance, and began restoration. They revealed many treasures, and a context in which to place the ruins.

About A.D.800, Cambodia was united by a Khmer king, Jayavarman II, who introduced the cult of the god king. The dynasty, and the cult, endured for over 600 years. Angkor Thom, one of several capitals, was its greatest manifestation. Angkor's main temple (or *wat*) was built by Suryavarman II in the early 1100s as both a temple complex to Vishnu, one of the main gods of the Hindu pantheon, and a mausoleum. Many other such temples were built over the following century, with each new king matching his predecessor until the effort sapped the economic life of the kingdom.

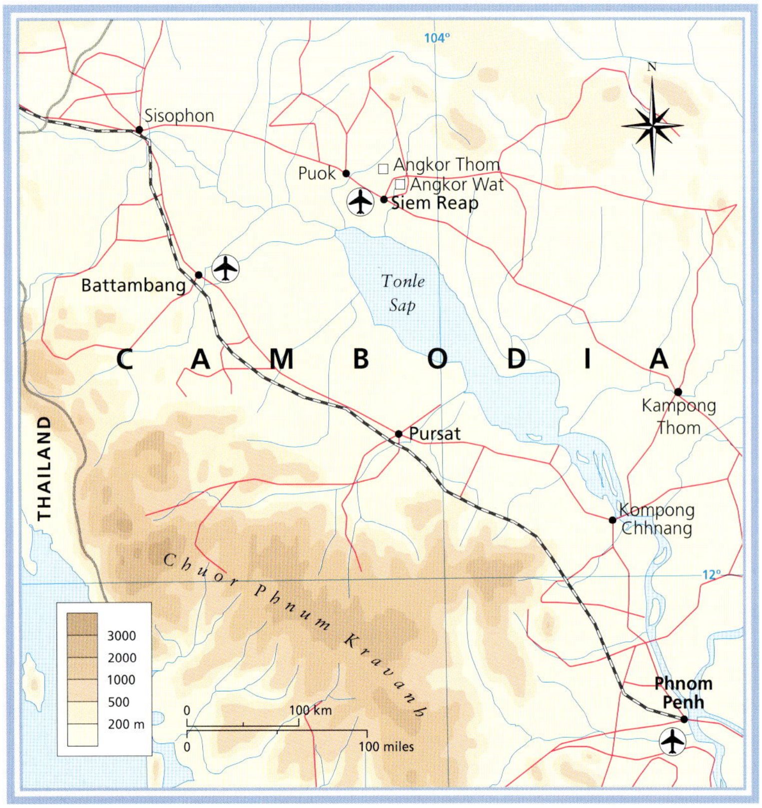

Angkor Wat is the greatest in the collection of royal temples—about 100 in all—that stand in and around the old capital of Angkor Thom. The main ones are Cambodia's prime tourist attractions, indeed for most people the only ones outside the capital, Phnom Penh. For two decades, when Cambodia was at the mercy of the Khmer Rouge and then shattered by civil war, very few visitors came here; there was heavy fighting among the temples, which the Khmer Rouge despised, and the jungle returned. Now, despite an uncertain present and future, the tourists are starting to come back, but independent travel away from the main tourist sights is still not recommended. Most visitors fly to the quiet—but fast developing—town of Siem Reap, with its growing choice of hotels and restaurants. Local food is similar to, if less spicy than Thai cooking (the freshwater fish are renowned). Visitors, usually in jeans or shorts, T-shirts, and sandals, then take group trips or hire a cab to Angkor. Ferries also run between Phnom Penh and Phnomh Krom on Tonle Sap Lake, 7 miles (11 km) south of Siem Reap.

A CORNUCOPIA OF CARVINGS

Angkor Wat's stonework is a cornucopia of symbols. Like other funerary temples, it replicates the Hindu concept of the universe: a central tower symbolic of Mount Meru, the nub of the Hindu world and Siva's dwelling place; a surrounding wall symbolizing land; and a 200-yard (190 m) moat representing the oceans. An avenue over 500 yards (475 m) long leads away from an immense gateway past a 10-foot (3 m) statue of Vishnu—as Suryavarman liked to see himself—cut from a single block of sandstone. The 0.8 square mile (2 sq km) site has half a mile (800 m) of bas-reliefs, all set in curlicued decorations, which illustrate epics, mythology, and Cambodian history. In one brilliant

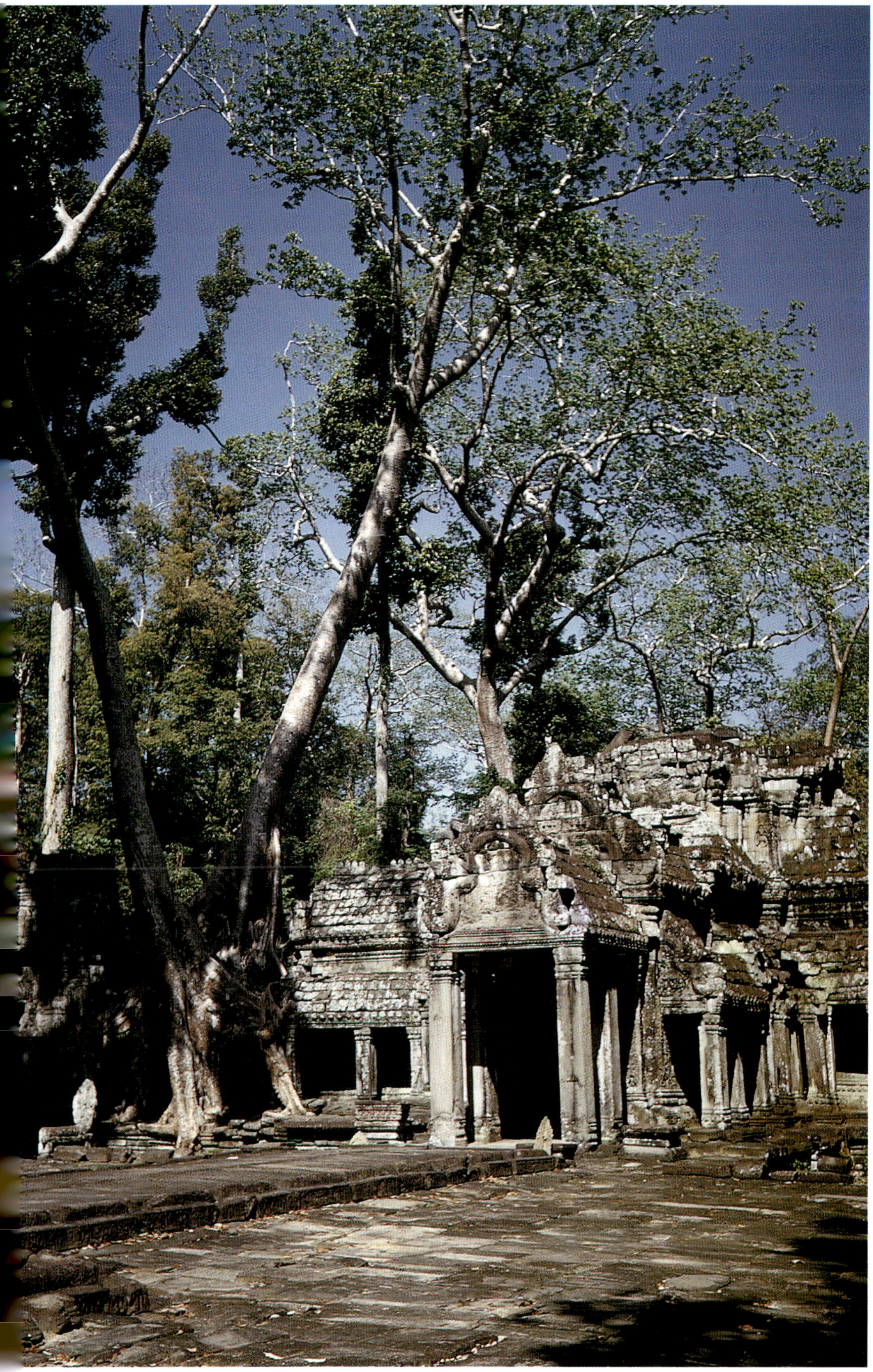

FACT FILE

Climate: Upper 60°s F (20°sC) to upper 90°s F (30°s C), year-round.

Rainy season: May—October.

Best time to visit: December —January.

Equipment: Sunscreen lotion, moneybelt, wide hat, backpack.

Currency: U.S. dollars are accepted everywhere, as well as local riels.

Visa: Obtainable on arrival in Phnom Penh.

Insurance and dangers: In many places Cambodia is still potentially dangerous due to bandits and the Khmer Rouge, and landmines are common. Keep to the main marked routes, do not travel by land more than you have to, and check that your insurance will cover you. Do no attempt the land crossing from Thailand.

Language: Khmer; but French is widely understood, and English is coming up fast.

Health: Malaria is prevalent in Cambodia, now resistant to chloroquine and sulfadoxine. Polio and bilharzia (in stagnant water) are also common. Water should never be drunk unless bottled or sterilized, salads and peeled fruits should be avoided, and care should be taken with dairy products and meat.

Angkor's ornate ruins, once enmeshed in jungle, are still embraced by tangles of roots and branches.

Canals are an important means of transport and communication in the lowlands of Cambodia.

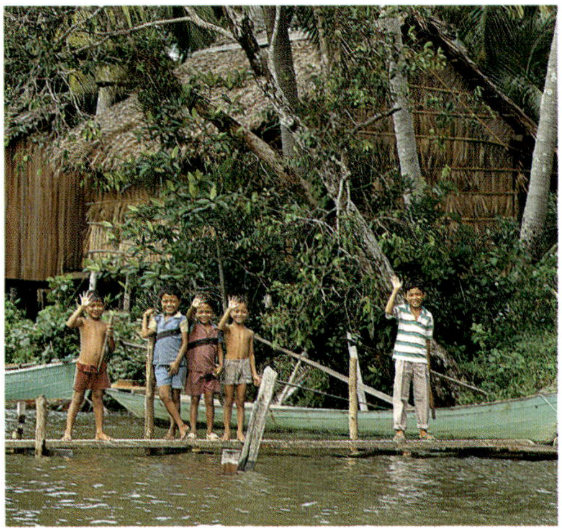

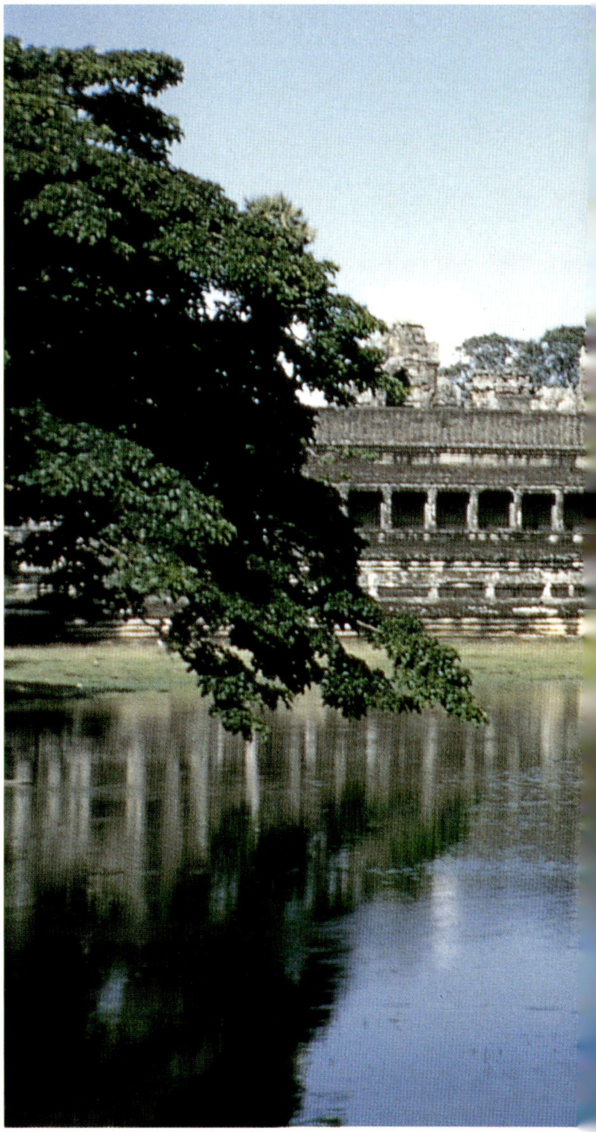

panorama, 88 devils and 92 gods churn the sea to extract the elixir of immortality. Despite the exuberance and lavishness of the architecture, the style is dense, with tight little corridors and no grand arches. Khmer architects apparently never discovered how to make wide spans. They relied on the width of their sandstone blocks, which form only four square lintels.

The statues are mainly of kings, princes, queens,and dignitaries, portrayed as gods, either Hindu or—after the coming of Buddhism in the second half of the 1100s—as the Buddha. But this is no cathedral. Here, ordinary people, if they were admitted at all, came not to worship gods, but kings.

Suryavarman's creation could easily have been the high point of Khmer architecture, for less than 20 years after his death Angkor was sacked by one of the Khmer subject peoples. But a successor king, Jayavarman VII, fought back, retook Angkor, and set about an astounding program of temple building, creating most of those that constitute the architectural gem that is Angkor Thom today. Before his death in 1201, he also built 121 pilgrim hostels along the roads leading to his capital, and 102 hospitals. Seldom in the history of the world has one man been responsible for the cutting of so much stone.

Rice paddies (below) supply the country with its main food resource; maize, bananas, rubber, and tobacco are other important crops.

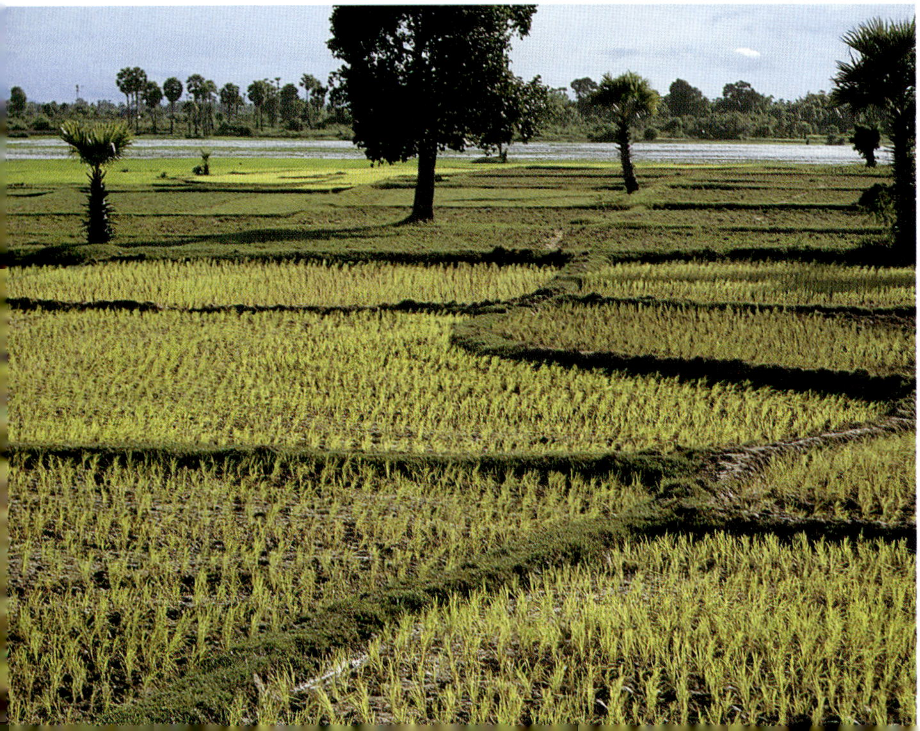

THE TERRACE OF THE ELEPHANTS

Only 2 miles (3.2 km) away from Angkor Wat is one of Jayavarman's greatest creations, a temple-pyramid known as the Bayon. The Bayon was doubly central, within its own site, and in the exact center of the royal city. The Bayon complex, taken over from an older temple, was built in three stages. Later shrines enclose earlier ones, creating damp and sinister corridors. Galleries, terraces, and passageways intermix, a maze intricately carved with 11,000 statues and capped by 54 bizarre towers, from each of which four giant human

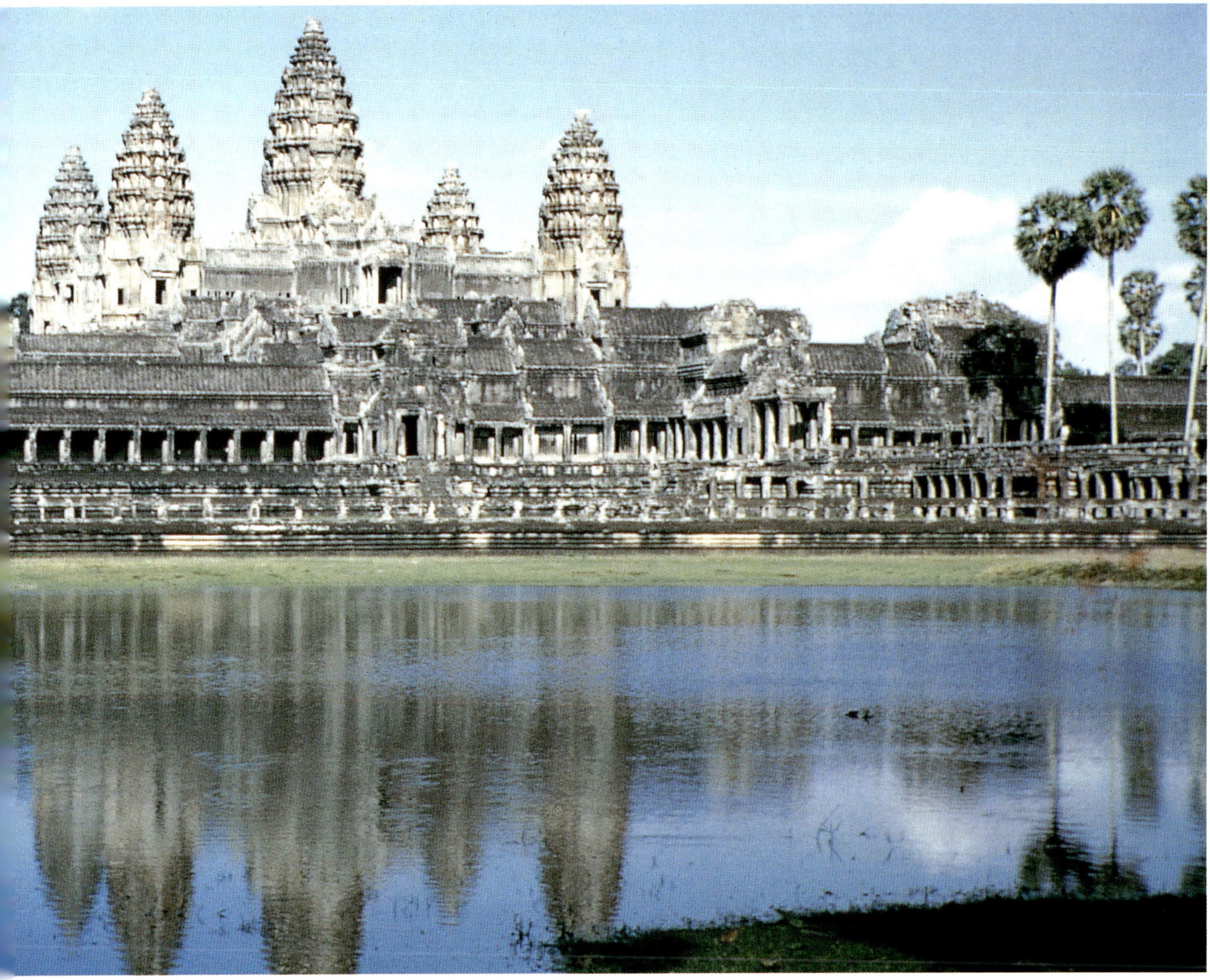

faces stare out, each with a soft Mona Lisa smile. Everything is made to serve the central sanctuary, a cavelike cell that held the very essence of the dead godking, portrayed as Buddha.

Angkor Thom's other sights include a huge reviewing stand on the central square, the Terrace of the Elephants. On the left, at the end of the square is the so-called Terrace of the Leper King, though the name is recent. It derives from the terrace's lichen-covered statue, possibly Yama, the god of death and a suitable guardian for what may have been a crematorium.

Another great temple, Ta Prohm, some 2 miles (3.2km) from the Bayon, has been left undisturbed. Its immense mass of towers and courtyards, once maintained by 80,000 people, is still locked together by roots and branches. Nothing could better exemplify the creative surge that produced these buildings, or the destructive power of the jungle that could so quickly hide them from later generations.

Angkor Wat's five towers (above) are reflected in its reservoir. The central tower rises to 200 feet (60 m). Water buffalo (below) are as much part of life now as they were when their images were carved into Angkor's Wat bas-reliefs.

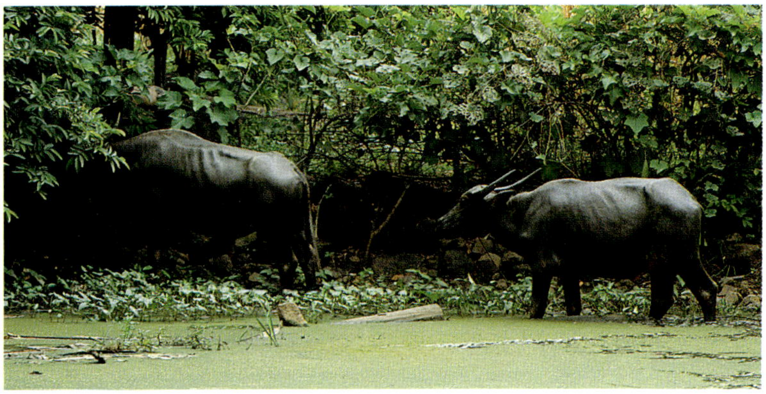

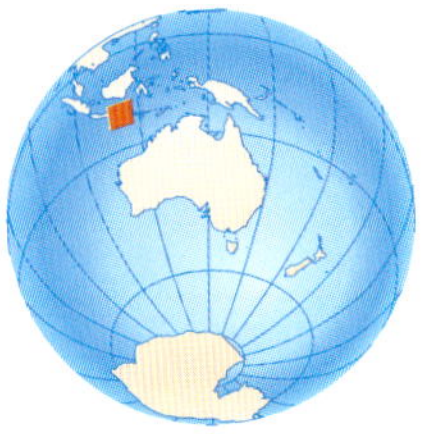

Bali, East of Java

Bali has often been considered the closest to paradise you can get on this earth. Both the people and the landscapes deserve their legendary appeal.

BALI IS SO MUCH THE EPITOME of tropical beauty that Bob Hope and Bing Crosby included it in one of their postwar "Road to ..." series of movies. The setting was a studio-made pastiche. If it had been shot on location, it would have been ravishing, for the island really does look like a movie set—rice paddies descending hillsides like giant steps, cloud capped-volcanoes, dense jungles, long sandy beaches, crashing surf, a rich culture, and people renowned for their charm. The island owes its appeal to an odd junction of geographical and historical influences. Measuring only 60 by 40 miles (100 by 64 km), it is large enough for variety, but small enough for accessibility. Volcanoes have made it very fertile, with only the occasional recent eruption to disturb the peace. Though part of the Indonesian archipelago, it

Brightly painted outrigger prahus (below) fish the abundant subtropical waters off Bali's coasts.

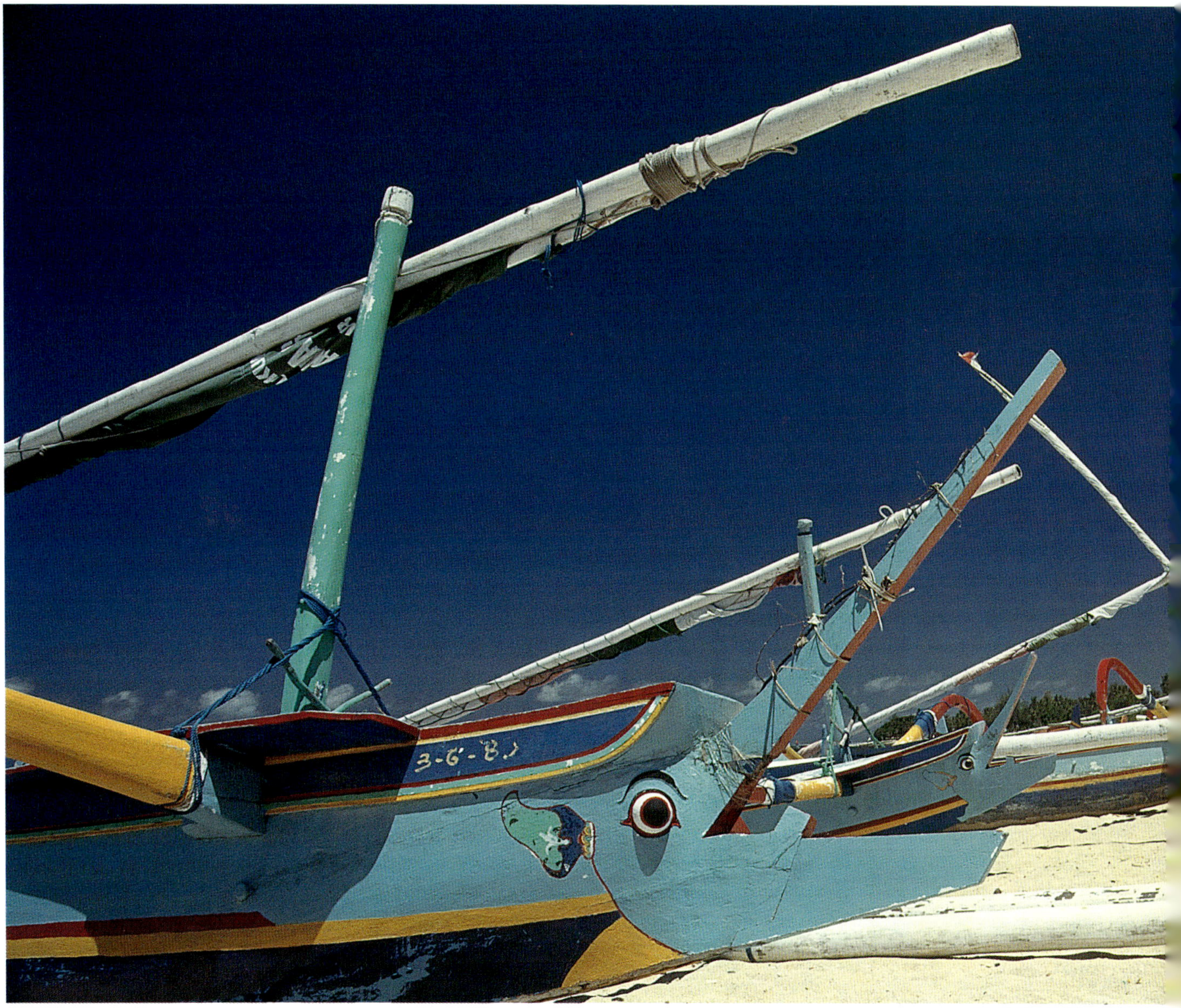

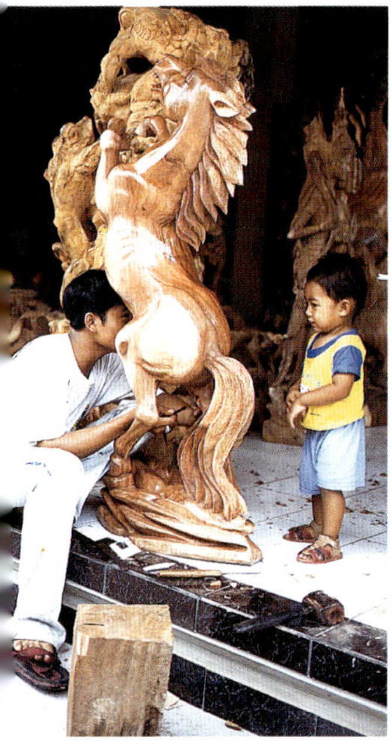

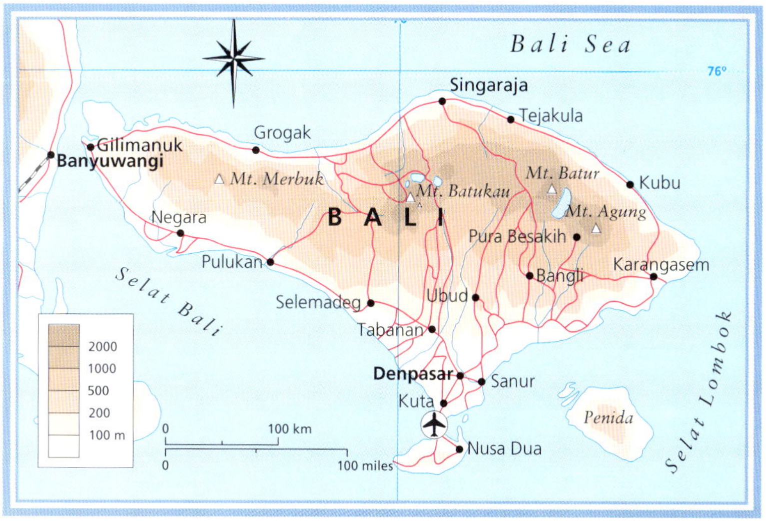

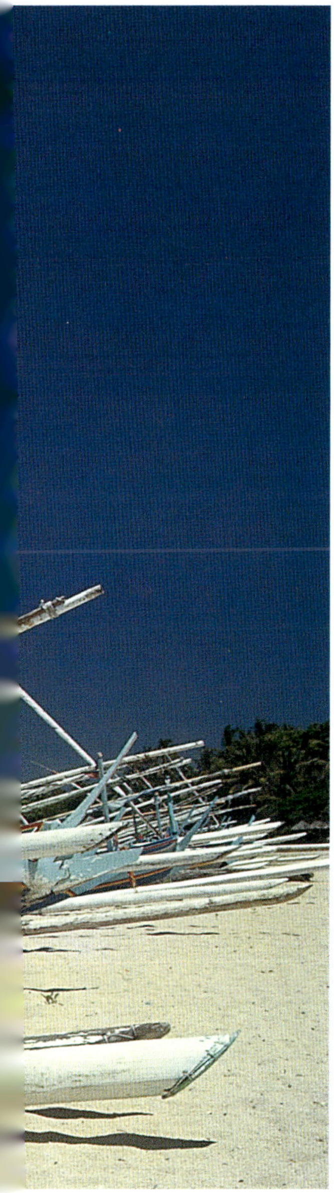

Woodcarving (above left) inspired by the characters of Balinese myth, traditionally decorated important buildings; now, freestanding sculptures and ornaments are also made, mainly for the tourist market.

Theater and dance (below) are an integral part of Balinese life, an expression of religion, and a means of entertainment for local communities.

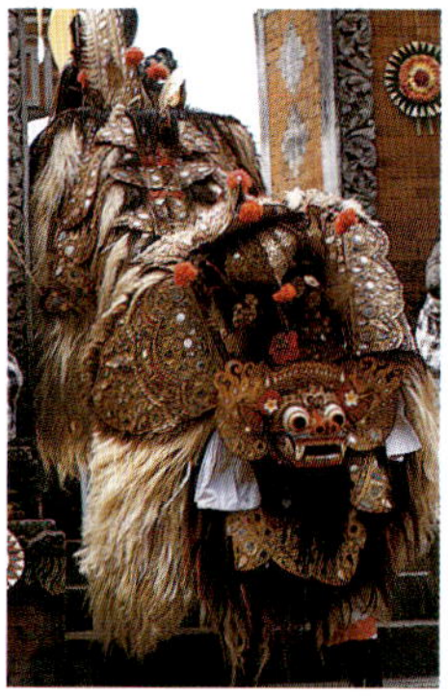

retained its special form of "Agama Hinduism" when Islam spread throughout the rest of the archipelago. The result is 2.5 million people living happily, with a wealth of religious ceremonies and festivals which underpin a strong sense of identity. The central volcanic spine preserves a sense of isolation and mystery, intensified by local beliefs in the holiness of its mountains.

Bali often strikes outsiders as a sort of paradise, though one that has been under threat from an ever-increasing number of tourists for decades. Bali's beach life is famous, the southern resorts of Kuta, Sanur, and Nusa Dua being the best known. Once little fishing villages, they are now big international beach resorts, famous for sand, surf, sunsets, and importunate sellers, who can hustle you as you try to sunbathe. Every year, hundreds of thousands arriving at the capital Denpasar's airport find this is all they need from a vacation. Surfers love it, though the breakers don't pack the punch of Hawaii's. (Note to surfers: There's little equipment available locally—bring all you may need with you.)

Traces of Eden

Lovers of the island always wonder if it has been ruined. The answer has always been: Not yet. With such a variety of landscape, some areas remain wilderness. Away from the resorts, more ambitious visitors find that Bali still offers challenges as well as more than a trace of Eden. Close to Denpasar lies Bali's cultural capital, Ubud. Set safely inland, it avoids the worst aspects of tourism and offers a chance to see contemporary examples of Balinese painting, dancing, carving and architecture, with walks that lead past rice fields and through dense but accessible forests. One of these is the sacred monkey forest at Sangoh, home to a

FACT FILE

Airport: Denpasar

Climate: Equatorial and never cold. Average temperature in the 80°s F (20°s C).

Currency: The rupiah, but this can be volatile, so take U.S. dollars.

Religion: Overwhelmingly Hindu, with a few Muslims and Christians in the North.

Best time to visit: Drier season, April—October, but rainstorms can occur all year.

Clothing: A sweater and rainwear if you're away from the beaches. In the mountains, nights are cool.

Time to avoid: Christmas, and May—August, when Bali is Australia's favorite get-away spot.

For beach lovers: T-shirts, sunblock lotion, hats, insect repellent, flashlight.

For surfers: Surfboard, wet suit booties, resin, hardener, glass, sandpaper, and first-aid kit (coral and sea urchins can cause nasty cuts).

Best surf: Ulu Watu.

Health tips: "Bali belly" can be a problem, so avoid peeled fruits, uncooked fish and vegetables, ice cubes (unless made from pure water), salads, and tap water. Cholera and hepatitis are common, so immunization is advisable. Also, take precautions against malaria if you are going outside the main tourist resorts. Rabies is widespread, so beware of animal bites.

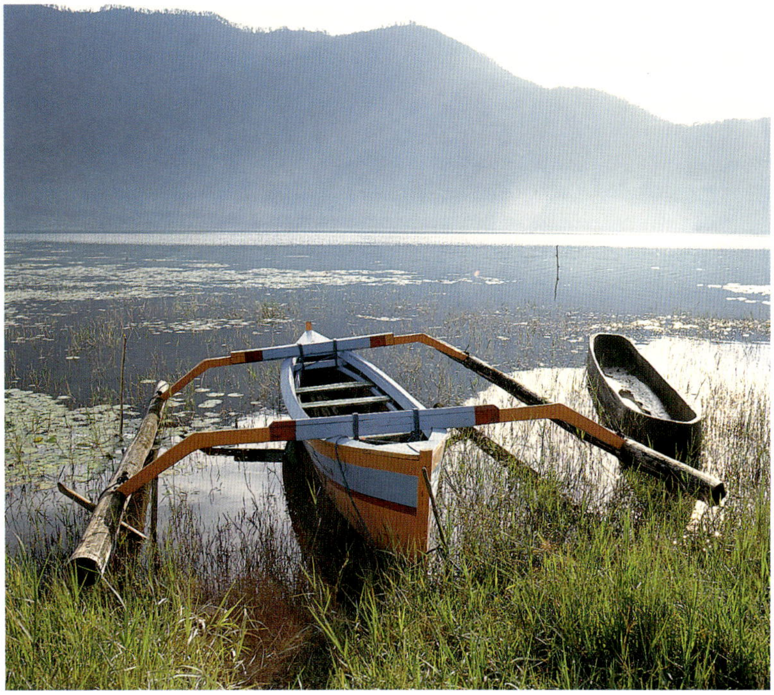

Lake Bratan (above) is in a fertile basin dotted with vegetable gardens and encircled by forested mountains—one of the delights of an interior still untouched by tourism.

variety of exotic apes that gibber loudly and can jump disconcertingly onto your shoulders. Treat them politely, however, and they soon lose interest in you. In Ubud, as elsewhere, there is no shortage of cheap but simple places to stay.

CULTURAL VITALITY

Bali's Hindu culture spread from neighboring Java in the 11th century. When Java converted to Islam in the 15th century, its priests, artists, dancers, musicians, and actors fled across the intervening straits, bringing traditions that have endured. There are temples in every village, shrines in most fields. Moreover, Balinese Hinduism is shot through with a unique sense of enjoyment.

Terraced rice fields (far right) supply Bali's staple crop.

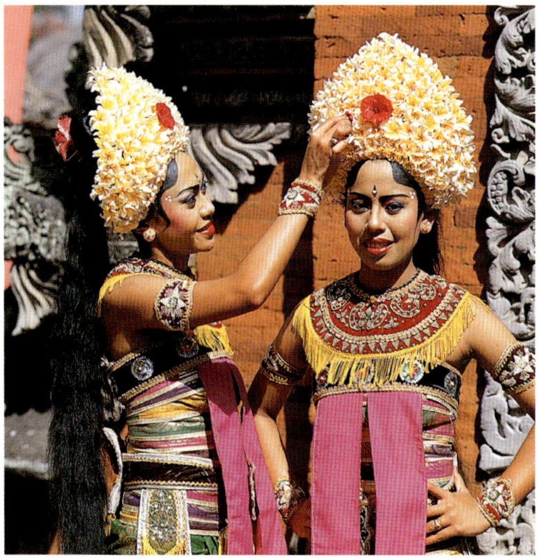

Ornate costumes and headdresses (right) are an essential part of the Balinese rituals and dance.

Festivals, dictated by two local calendars running in parallel, delight every sense and passion. They involve cockfights, offerings of beautifully arranged food, and processions, all accompanied by music from gamelans—orchestras of gongs, xylophones, voices, and flutes. Women dance the stately pendet, making offerings to the gods. The greatest festival is the annual Galungan, celebrated over 10 days. At this time, all the gods, including Bali's own supreme deity, Sanghyang Widi, are invisibly present, and barongs—men clothed as mythical lion dogs that champion the cause of good over evil—prance from village to village.

Though most Balinese temples belong to particular places, the holiest site, Pura Besakih on the slopes of Mt. Agung, is held communally. This 1,000-year-old complex, consisting of 30 separate temples, all with distinctive Balinese thatched roofs sited on seven terraces, is Bali's equivalent of a cathedral, as befits its position on the island's holiest mountain. Agung, the "navel of the world," dominates the eastern end of the island, towering 10,300 feet (3,140 m). This once perfect cone blew its top off in 1963, in an eruption that killed thousands. Whole villages were wiped out, but the temple complex, almost halfway up the mountain, survived. The Balinese New Year is celebrated with elaborate rituals here every March.

Those who relish a physical challenge can walk up to Agung's sulfurous crater from the temple or via a number of other routes. Whichever route is chosen, the stiff climb should take a long day. Newcomers are advised to hire a guide—or equip themselves with a flashlight, rainwear, a water bottle, and warm clothing in case they miss trails through the forested lower flanks, and fail to make it back before nightfall. For a relaxing change away from the surfing crowds, try the fine beaches on the north coast near Singarajah. There is no surf, for a coral reef shelters the beaches, offering wonderful diving.

One of the great delights of Bali is its variety of cuisines. Indonesian food is universal and western menus common, but it is worth searching out those restaurants that serve local dishes, like babi guling (spit roasted suckling pig), betutu bebek (duck roasted in banana leaves), roasted dragonflies, frogs' legs, and lobster. Bali has a cornucopia of fruits, like hairy red rambutans, purple-brown mangosteens, and starfruits—though newcomers usually do not relish the infamous durian, which has been likened to raspberry blancmange smelling like a filthy toilet. Indonesian beer, including Heineken brewed under license—almost the only relic of Dutch colonial rule—is widely available.

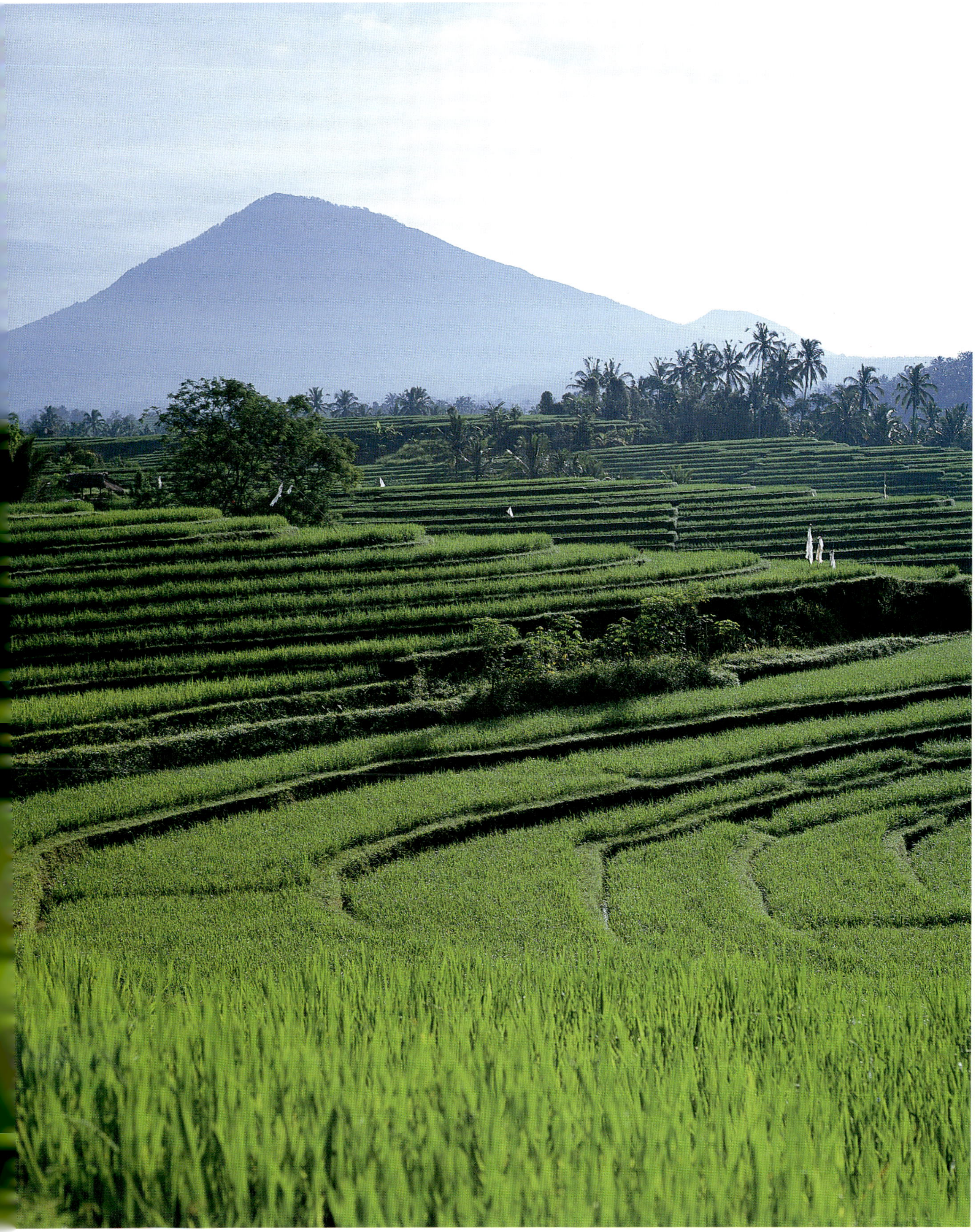

Australia and New Zealand

"Even disasters—there are always disasters when you travel—can be turned into adventures."

Marilyn French, American writer, b. 1929.

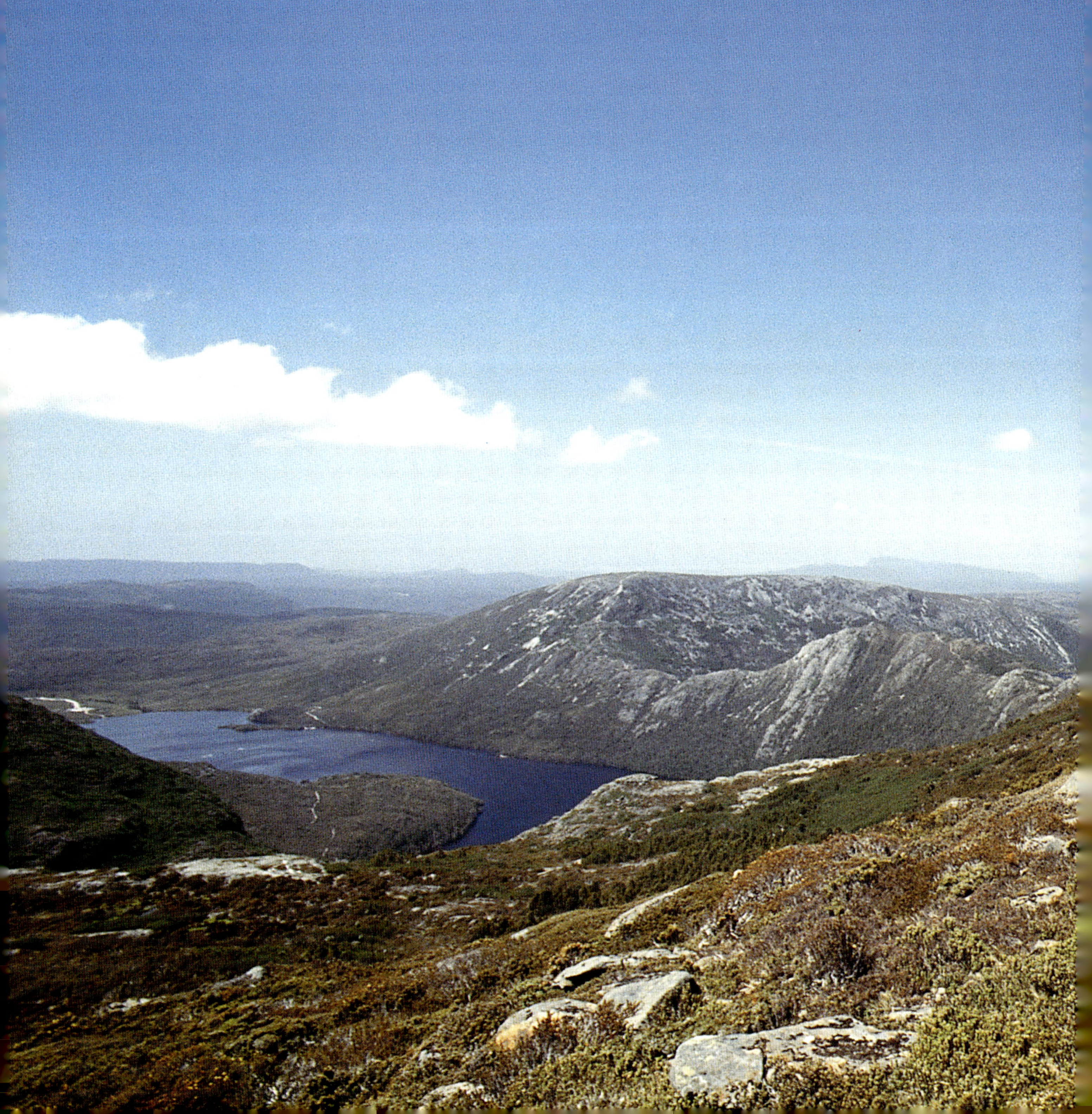

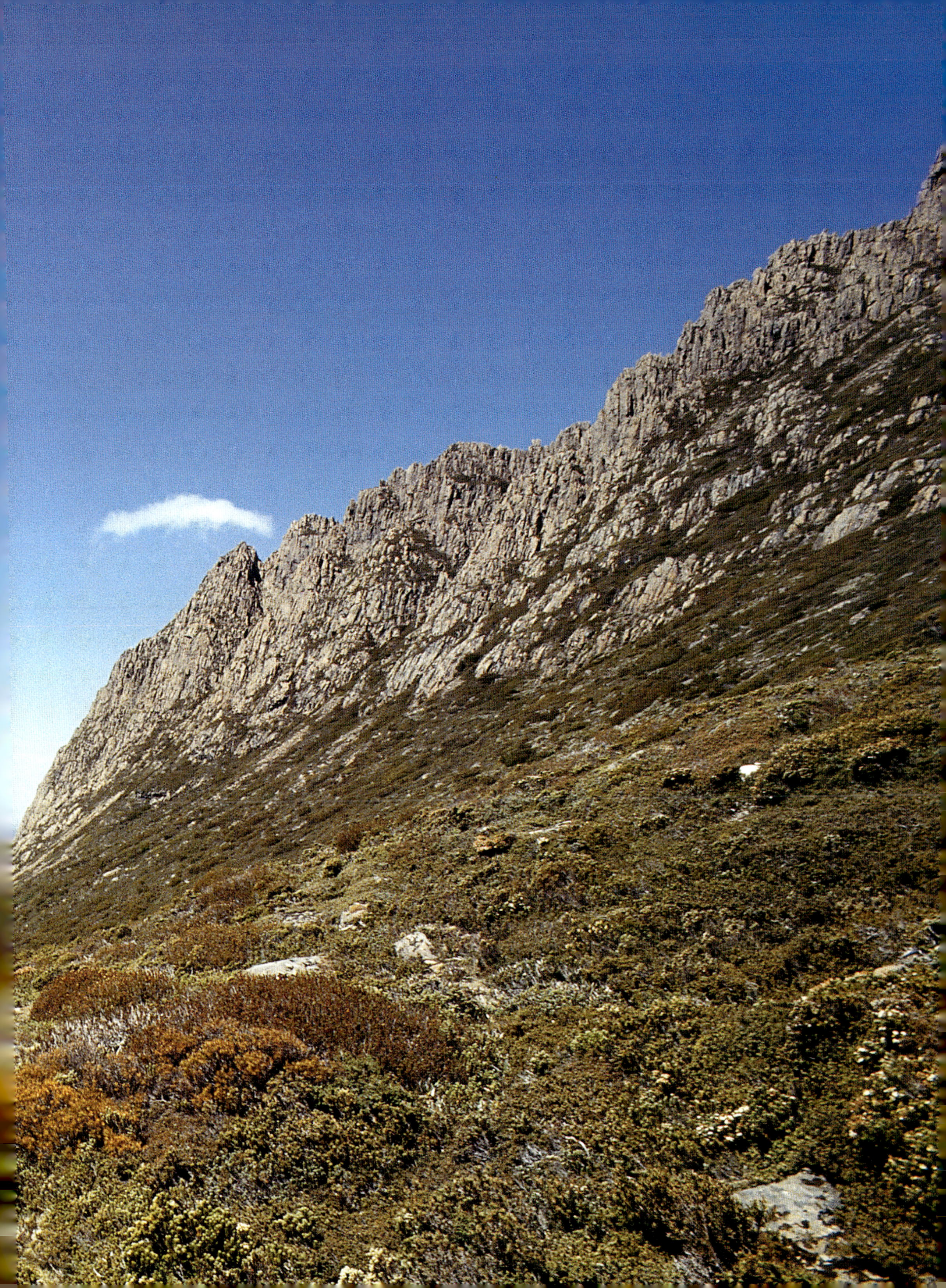

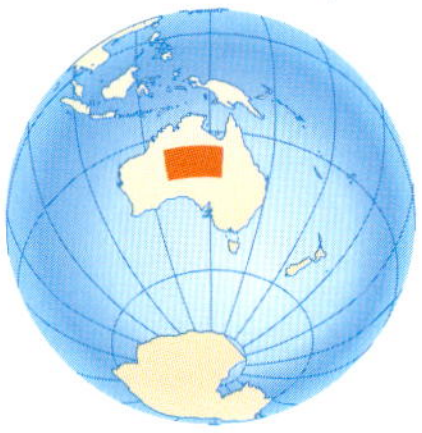

Dreamtime in the Northern Territory

A seemingly barren landscape harbors Dreamtime spirits and wind-sculpted mountain islands.

FACT FILE

How to get there: Fly to Alice Springs and drive or fly direct to the airport near Ayers Rock Resort.

Climate: Markedly continental, with hot summers—the temperature can reach 110°F (45°C) between November and March—and surprisingly cold winters, when it can fall below freezing at night, particularly if skies are clear.

When to go: April to October.

Nearest town/airport: Ayers Rock Resort, 12 miles (20 km) from the Rock, is the service village for the park. The airport is 3 miles (5 km) outside town and connects with most Australian cities and airlines.

Things to do: Scenic flights over the Rock; a night-sky show relating Anangu legends; watching the Rock change color at dawn and sunset (for cultural and safety reasons, Aborigines request that visitors do not climb the Rock), free ranger-guided tours; vist the Cultural Center. Uluru and Kata Tjuta are UNESCO World Heritage Areas.

Things to buy: Aboriginal artifacts; paintings, batiks (during special exhibitions only), and carvings.

What to take: Sunscreen, hats, water bottles, comfortable clothes.

As you drive southwest from Alice Springs along the Stuart Highway, you enter the untamed heart of Australia, an ancient, barren landscape long worn down by wind and water. The monotony of the outback scrubland is relieved by the raw umbers, startling reds, and rich golds of its rocks, by dry river beds, tortuously sculpted by rare but violent rains, and by shimmering expanses of crusty-rimmed, crystalline white salt pans where shallow lakes have evaporated. An incongruous note is struck by the Outback Camel Farm at Stuarts Well, about 55 miles (90 km) south. Australia has the world's only numerous surviving wild camel herds, about 15,000 camels in all, descendants of those imported by the early settlers in the 1800s.

Farther inland, make a detour off the Stuart Highway to the sandstone monolith of Chambers Pillar, a couple of hours southeast on the fringes of the Simpson Desert, and to Kings Canyon, some 200 miles (300 km) from Alice Springs. Don't miss the loop walk, offering breathtaking views from the canyon's 300-foot (100 m) high walls, with detours to the "lost city," a maze of weathered domes, and the "Garden of Eden," a sunken valley with permanent waterholes and lush vegetation.

But nothing in the generally arid immensity compares with your first sight of Uluru/Ayers Rock (285 miles/460 km from Alice) as it appears massively above the horizon. It grows until it appears as large as a mountain amid the low-lying bushland. This is no mountain, but your eyes are not deceiving you, for the Rock is huge, the world's largest sandstone monolith, rising abruptly, pitted with caves and gullies, 1,145 feet

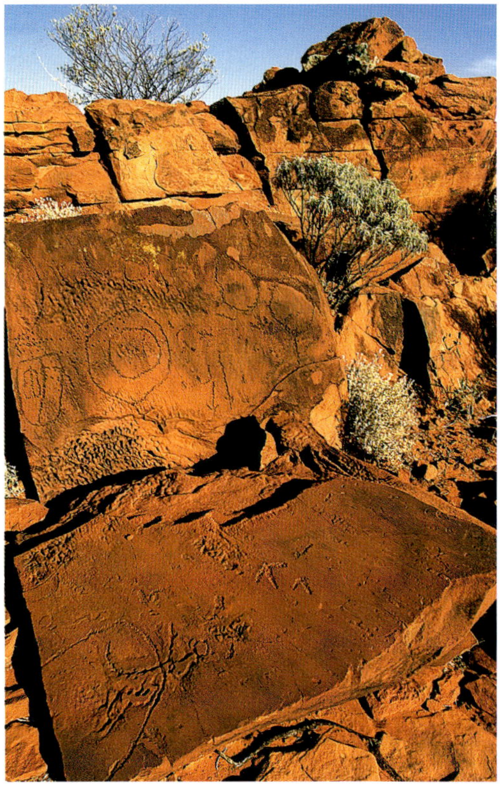

(348 m) above the surrounding flatness of the scrub. The first European to report seeing the Rock was a surveyor named Ernest Giles, in 1872. A year later it was climbed by William Gosse, who described it as "certainly the most wonderful natural feature I have ever seen" and named it for Henry Ayers, then Premier of the colony of South Australia. The Rock is now

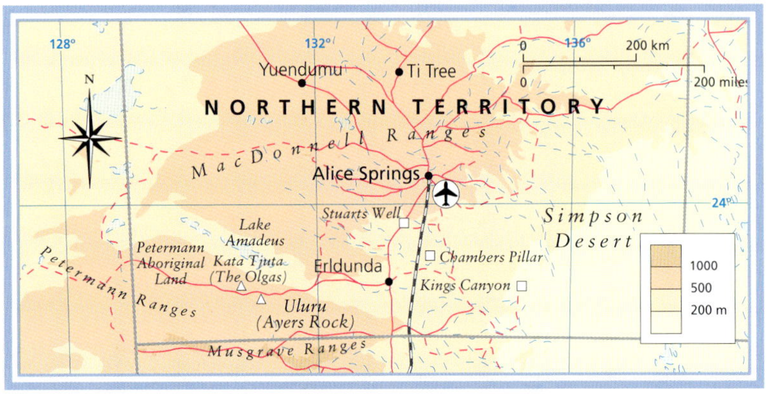

Aboriginal rock carvings (above) near Alice Springs. Uluru, or Ayers Rock, is a key site associated with the law and culture of the local Aborigines. Much of this immense sandstone rock is submerged beneath the ground.

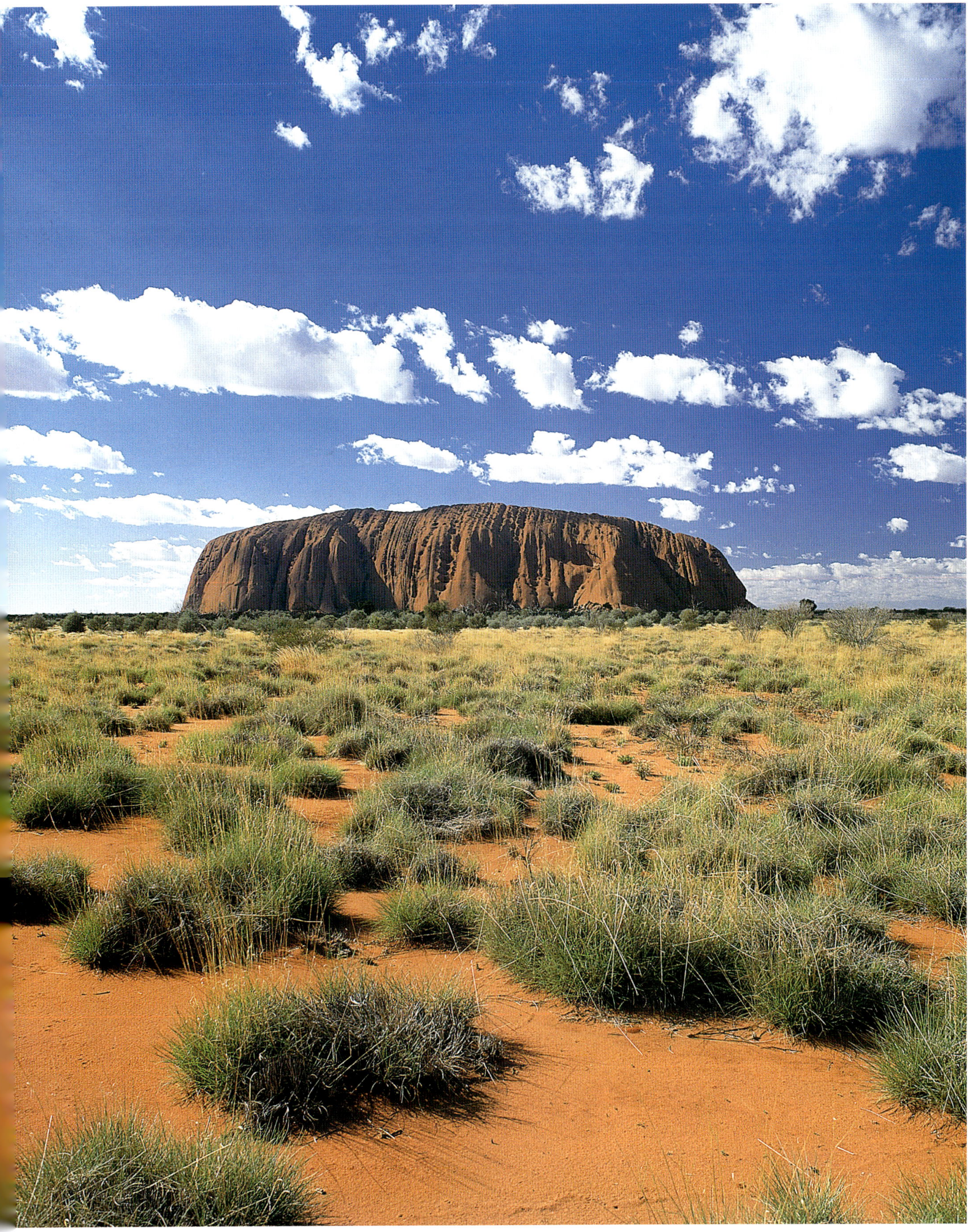

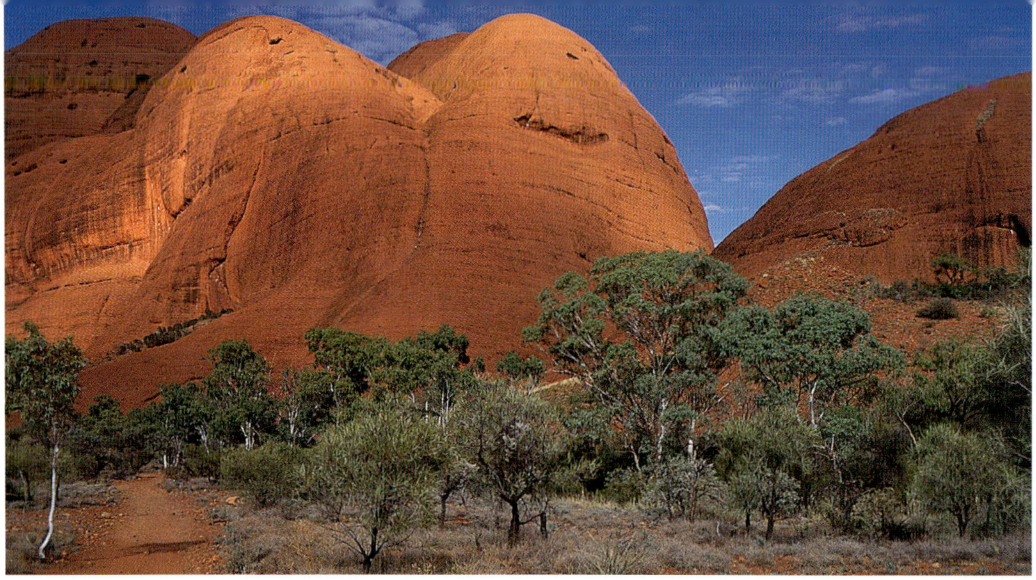

The monstrous bald heads of Kata Tjuta/the Olgas in Uluru-Kata Tjuta National Park, west of Uluru/Ayers Rock, conceal the eerie Valley of the Winds (left).

known by its Aboriginal name, Uluru, which is the name the local Aborigines gave to a rock hole high up on the monolith. There are many sacred sites round the oddly deserted base of Uluru, and though they are normally fenced off, the park rangers can explain their significance.

Ownership of the Rock was returned to the Aborigines in 1985, but, reluctantly accepting the inevitability of tourism, they leased it back to the federal government. It is now administered jointly by its traditional owners and Environment Australia.

The sunset color show

Until the end of the Second World War, only a few intrepid travelers visited Uluru on camels, guided by local cattle drovers; then in 1948 an asphalt road was built. The Ayers Rock Resort has sprung up 12 miles (20 km) away, at the edge of Uluru-Kata Tjuta National Park, to cater for travelers, and is connected by air to Alice Springs.

No photographs or verbal descriptions can fully capture the allure and weird beauty of the Rock. The closer you approach, the more beautiful it grows—grander, rounder, steeper, even softer, as if it were half alive, a prehistoric monster. It has a circumference of 6 miles (9.4 km), and it is thought that some 8,000 feet (2,500 m) of rock lie under the sand, beneath the visible monolith, like a desert iceberg. It is, in fact, an island mountain, technically called an inselberg, which was pushed up by Earth movements around 500 million years ago.

The 1-mile (1.6 km) climb takes about two hours. There is a chain along the steepest section at the beginning but no fence. The Rock is closed to climbers after 8 AM in summer, when temperatures can soar above 100° F (38°C), and also in wet or windy weather. It can be very cold in winter. The climb is not

The Dreamtime

Australian Aborigines believe that the ancestral beings moved about the land in the creation time (sometimes known as the Dreamtime), forming its physical features and leaving their mark on the landscape. Many ancestral Dreamtime spirits are connected with the formation of Uluru and Kata Tjuta. Uluru is also an important meeting point of the mythical and sacred pathways that crisscross this area, marking the journeys the ancestors made as they molded Australia's harsh landscape. The Aborigines fear that their laws will be broken and their sacred sites violated if tourists are allowed to intrude into sensitive areas.

Desiccated desert oaks in the Australian outback near Kata Tjuta, west of Uluru. The rare rainfall is the trigger that causes otherwise dormant flowers to bloom.

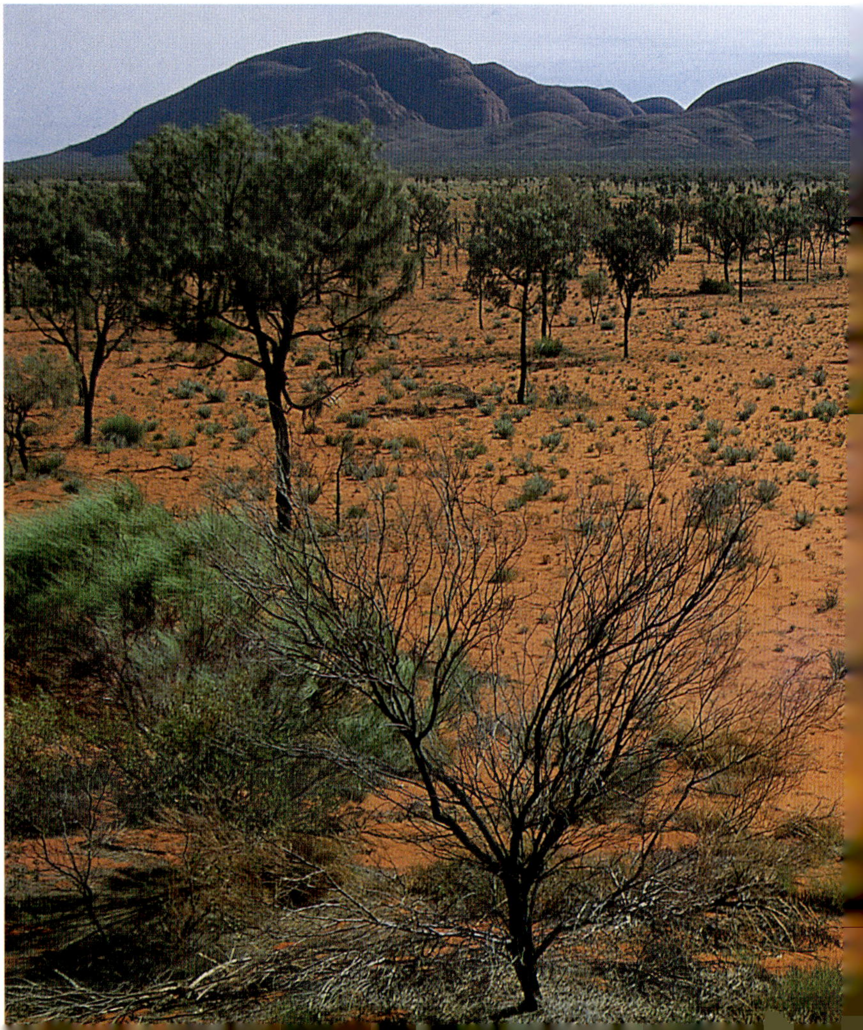

recommended for anyone with heart problems or who suffer from vertigo. Several people have died from falls or heart attacks while climbing the Rock.

For a short but sensational experience, take your car (you will need a car) to the prominently marked Sunset Viewing Spot to the west. The Rock rapidly changes color from yellow to orange to red to purple, and finally flares scarlet, as if giving off heat from deep within it. The color show lasts for only a few minutes before the Rock fades to dull brown and then is lost in the swiftly falling night. On the rare occasions when it rains, Uluru takes on an ominous black metallic sheen.

MANY HEADS AND WINDY VALLEYS

The Uluru-Kata Tjuta National Park covers an area of 327,584 acres (132,566 ha). It is a very arid region, with only about 8 inches (200 mm) of rain annually, so the vegetation is mostly sparse bushes. But the sudden showers that occur in summer produce an explosion of wild flowers, including Stuart's Desert Rose, which is the Northern Territory's floral emblem.

Some 20 miles (30 km) west of Uluru rise the Olgas, a clutch of 36 egg-like mountain fragments once submerged in a long-vanished sea. The largest, Mount Olga, was named for a German Queen by Ernest Giles, who described the rocks as like "enormous pink haystacks, all leaning against each other."

The Olgas are now known by the name the Anangu Aboriginal people gave them: Kata Tjuta, meaning "many heads." It is obvious from a distance how the rocks earned this name; they have been worn down over aeons into giant, deeply creviced bald domes of composite granite and basalt, cemented together with mud and sand. The highest, at 1,790 feet (546 m) above the plain, is some 600 feet (200 m) higher than Uluru. They are an important site in Aboriginal men's law.

A memorable 4-mile (6 km) trail from the northern parking lot leads through the Valley of the Winds and it can be a haunting experience. The shadows play among the rocks, and the winds whistle uncannily even in almost calm weather, though it is also a green oasis amid the outback, where daisies, mint bushes, and acacias grow. Look out, too, for rock crevices deep in shade, where rare rainfall may linger just long enough to germinate an extraordinary range of plants, such as the peach-like quandong, which has waxy, blue-green leaves and edible red fruits.

The Rock is an important meeting point of the "dreaming tracks," the crisscrossing mythical and sacred tracks that mark the journeys the ancestors made as they molded Australia's harsh landscape.

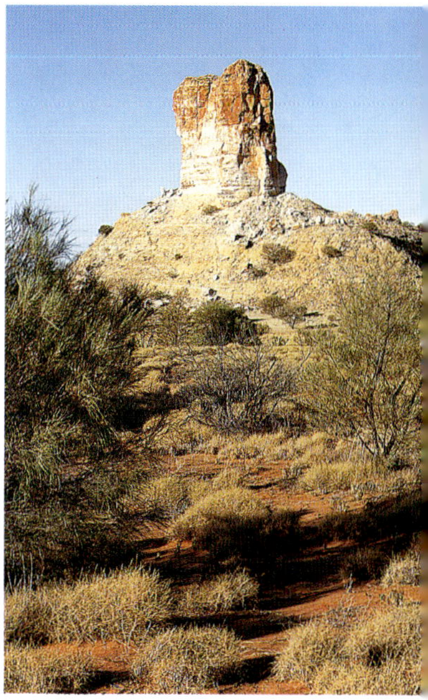

Chambers Pillar, on the northern edge of the Simpson Desert, is a couple of hours' drive southeast of Alice Springs. Iron oxide gives the sandstone its red coloration.

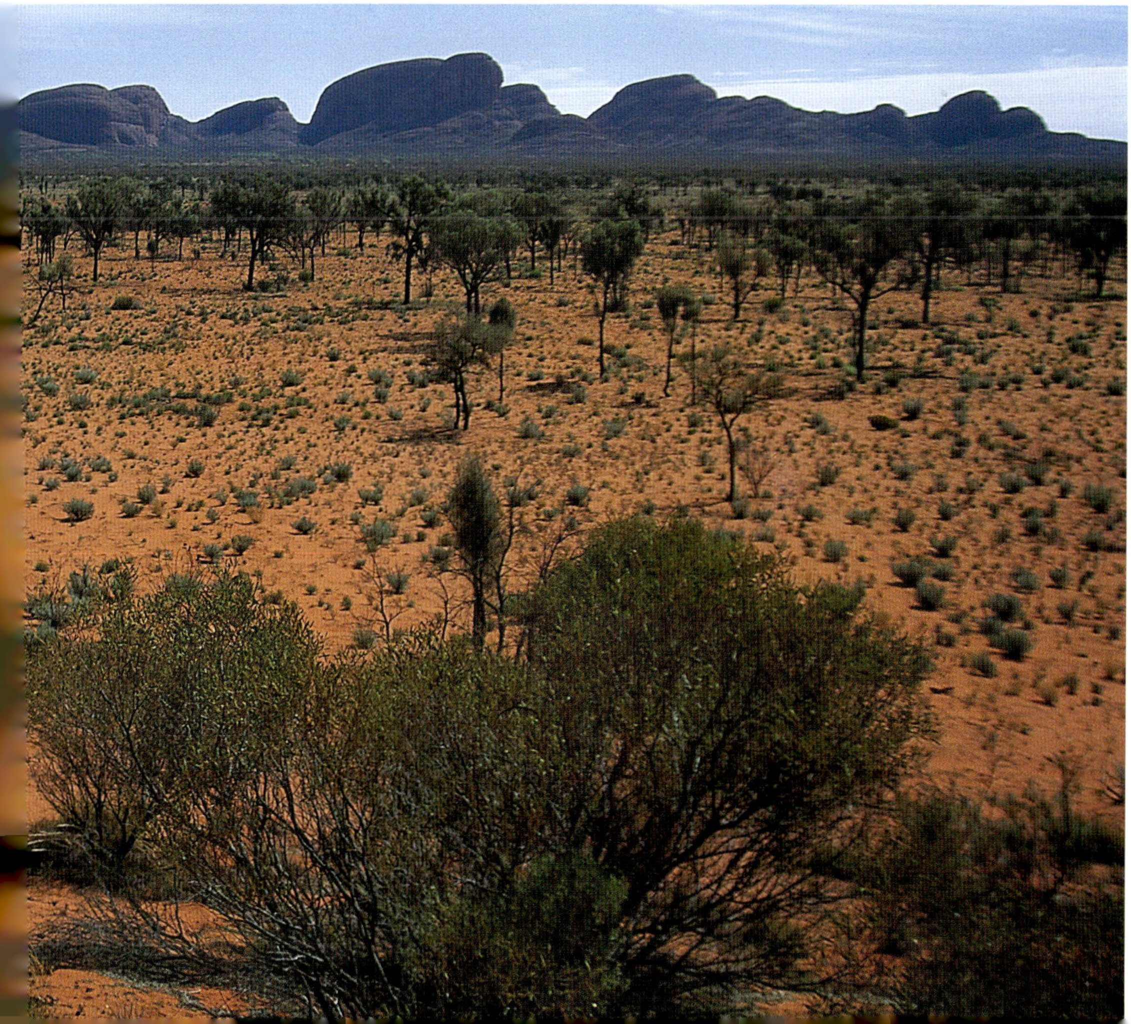

A detour on the way to or from Uluru brings you to the scenic Kings Canyon, the highlight of Watarrka National Park.

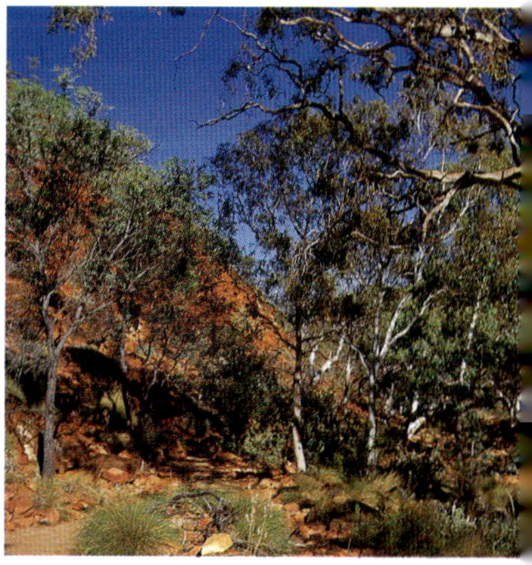

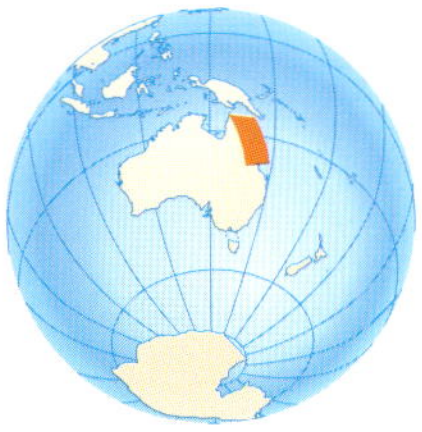

The Great Barrier Reef

To stand on the world's greatest coral reef off the northeastern edge of Australia is like walking on water; all around is ocean as far as the eye can see.

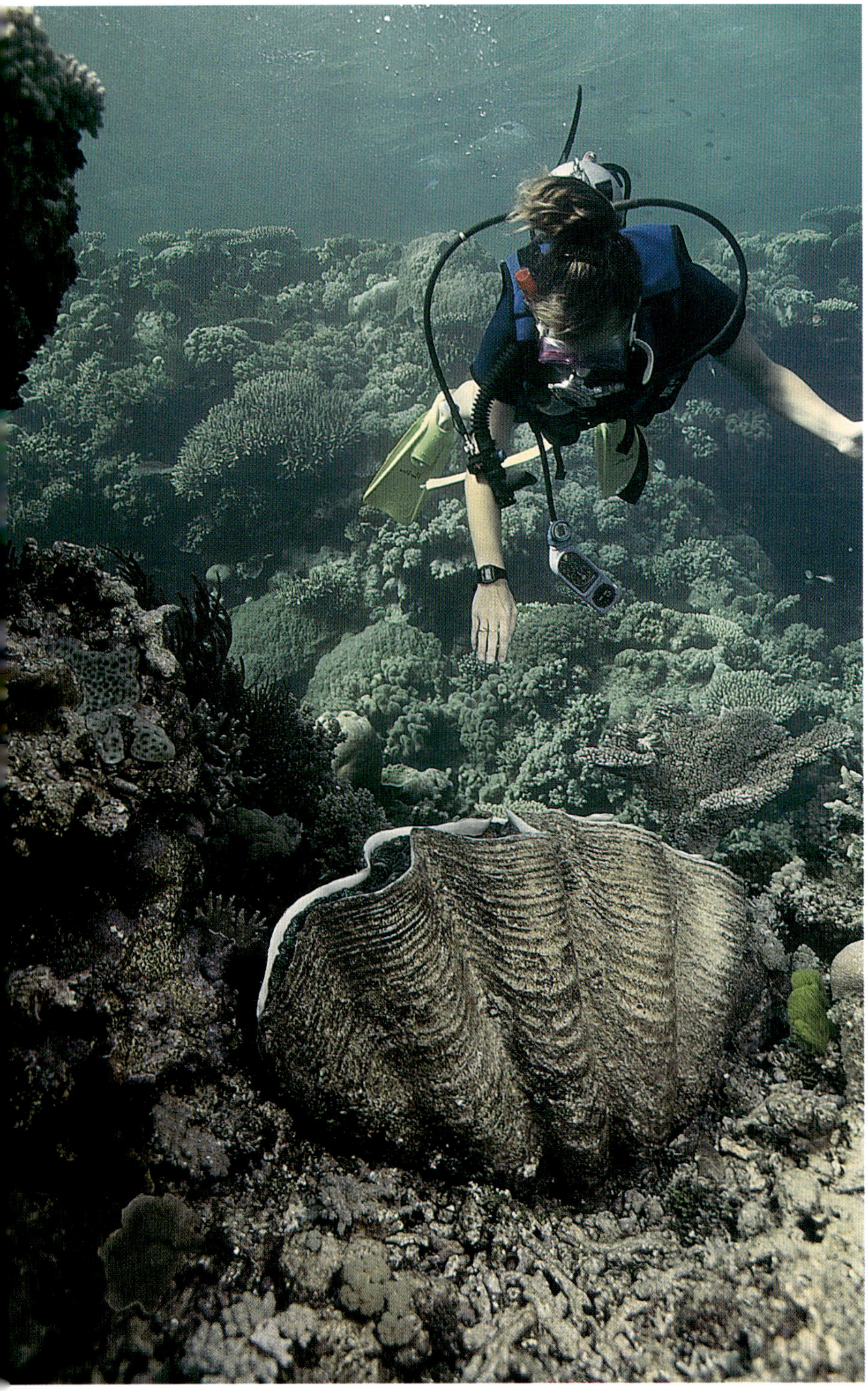

THE GREAT BARRIER REEF, a chain of coral reefs fringing the coast of northeastern Australia, dwarfs every other coral reef on the planet and has the richest submarine ecology in the world.

Rise early to take a tour boat out from the Queensland coast. Dawn breaks to reveal a line of white breakers on the horizon, and you can feel the sea change in mood as it moves over shallower waters approaching the coral shelf. Where the water is shallowest of all, it is possible to stand on the reef (wearing shoes as a guard against the razor-sharp coral). Above the waterline you are surrounded by ocean; look below, where the reef falls away, to see a kaleidoscope of marine life through crystal-clear water. Corals like petrified plants in hues of peach, pink, and white are home for a richness of marine life that competes for space in the warm, sunlit, oxygenated waters of the reef. You can find sea lilies, sponges, urchins, anemones, sea squirts, clams and fishes, often so brightly colored they look artificially painted, as if each species is trying to outdo the others in brilliance of design to make its mark among the crowds.

VITAL STATISTICS

The Great Barrier Reef, now 8,000 years old, is the world's largest structure made by living organisms and is a UNESCO World Heritage site. It is a chain of more than 2,900 individual reefs and some 700 islands stretching 1,200 miles (2,000 km) near Fraser Island, just south of the Tropic of Capricorn, to Cape York and Torres Strait, south of Papua New Guinea. At its southern end the reef is about 200 miles (320 km) from the mainland, but in the north it is much closer to the coast and less broken.

Coral reefs are delicate structures built up from the skeletal deposits of living creatures, marine polyps. New generations of polyps attach themselves to the remains of their predecessors, and in their turn die, and so a reef builds up, generation upon generation, at a rate of an inch (2.5 cm) or so a year. The skeletons are white, but it is the pinkish, still living, top layer of

Divers may encounter a giant clam (left), which can be over 3 feet long and weigh up to 440 lb (200 kg). On spawning, clams release over a billion eggs.

FACT FILE

Airports: Cairns, Brisbane, many smaller airports.

When to go: Best avoided during the rainy, hot months of January through March. Temperatures never drop below 68°F (20° C) on the coast.

What to take: Sunproof lotion, wide-brimmed hats, flashlight, shoes for walking on coral.

What to do: Snorkeling, scuba diving, swimming, sightseeing by boat, hiking on Great Keppel and other islands, white water rafting.

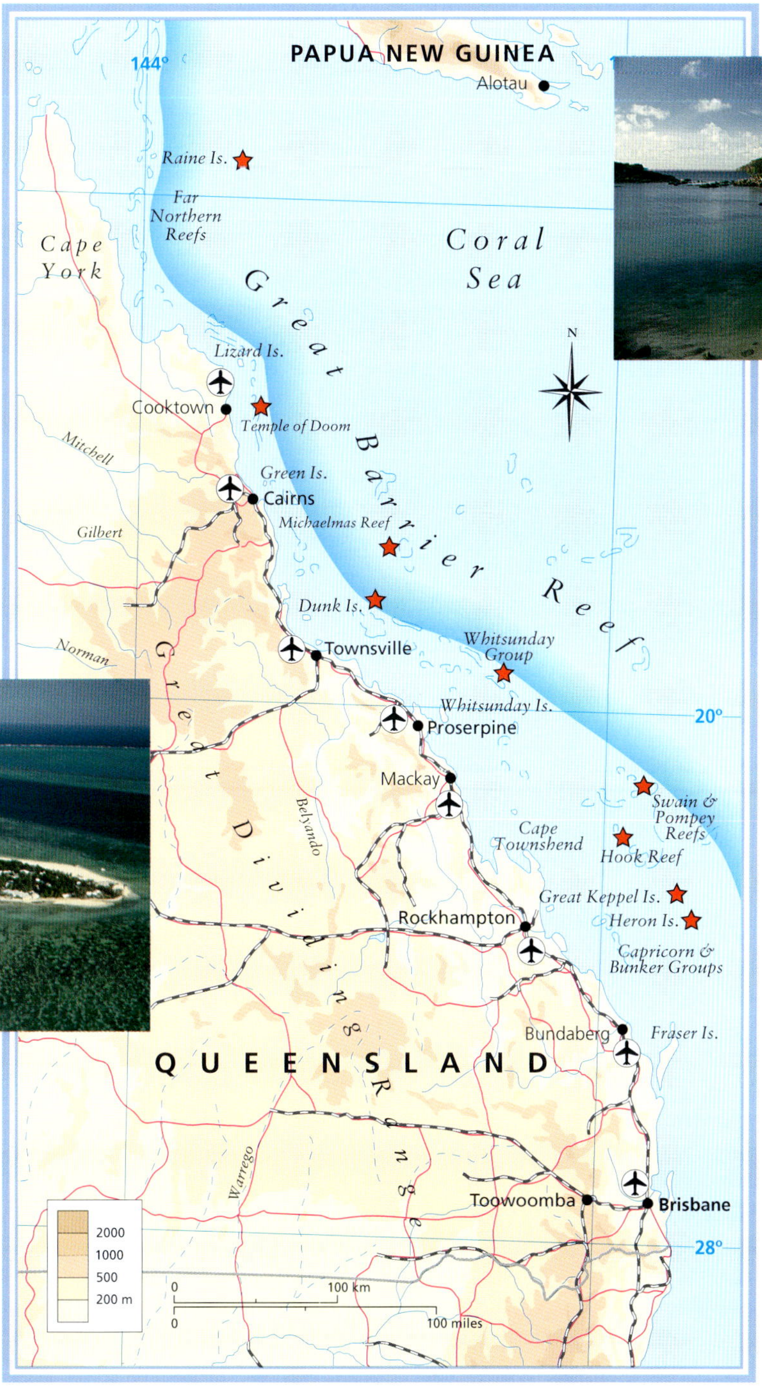

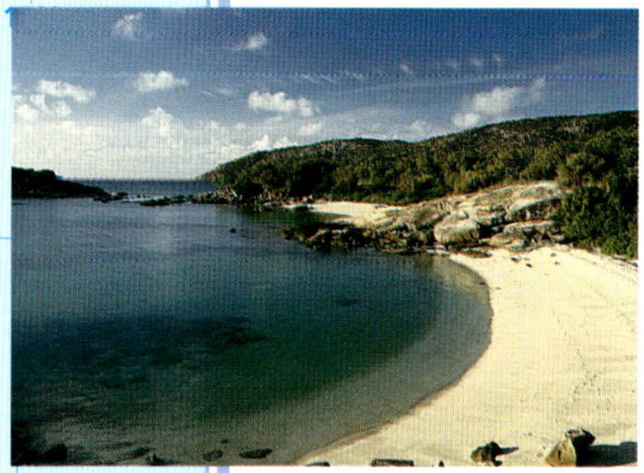

★ *The starred locations on the map are the top diving spots along the reef. Lizard Island (above) is one of the most northerly.*

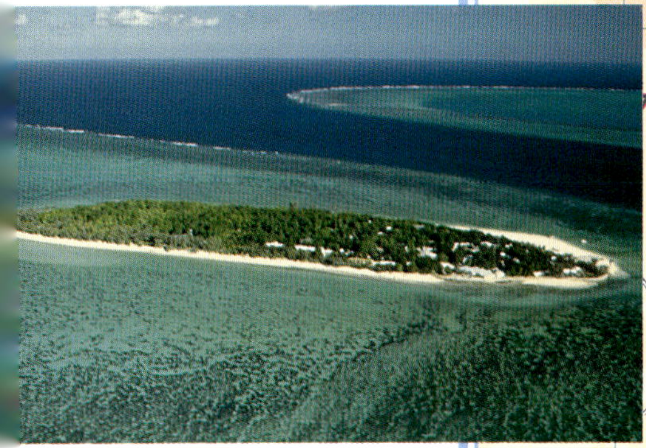

Heron Island (above) is a cay, or coral, island, one of the 71 cays that constitute the reef. They are known to be havens for a myriad seabirds.

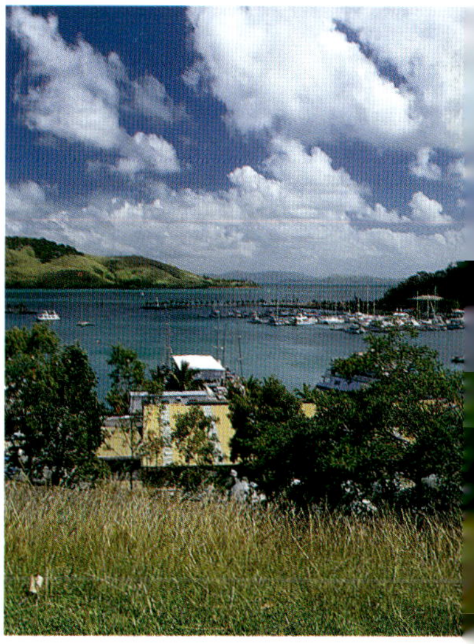

Whitsunday Island is a continental island—once a mainland mountain—and renowned for its splendid hillwalking.

polyps that give the reef its rosy hue.

Coral polyps are fussy creatures, not tolerating water much below 68°F (20°C), which explains the reef's southern limit, nor muddy waters like the Fly River estuary in Papua, which accounts for its northern limit. Nor will coral grow beneath a depth of 100 feet (30 m), because it needs sunlight.

The coral itself is a dense, submarine jungle of shape and color, with some 400 different species, brain and staghorn coral among them. Near Orpheus Island, for a few nights following a full moon in late spring, you can see the different species of coral spawn simultaneously. The normally crystal-clear waters turn into a gigantic underwater snowstorm, as a myriad tiny bundles of sperm and eggs shoot upward from the reef and burst.

A BALANCED ECOLOGY

There are about 1,500 species of fish and 4,000 species of mollusks, and, on a larger scale, the gentle dugong (the sea cow thought to be the origins of the mermaid myth, which is endemic to the reef), green turtles, and

There are 25 island resorts along the coast; Hinchinbrook Island (right) here viewed from Goold Island, is particularly unspoiled.

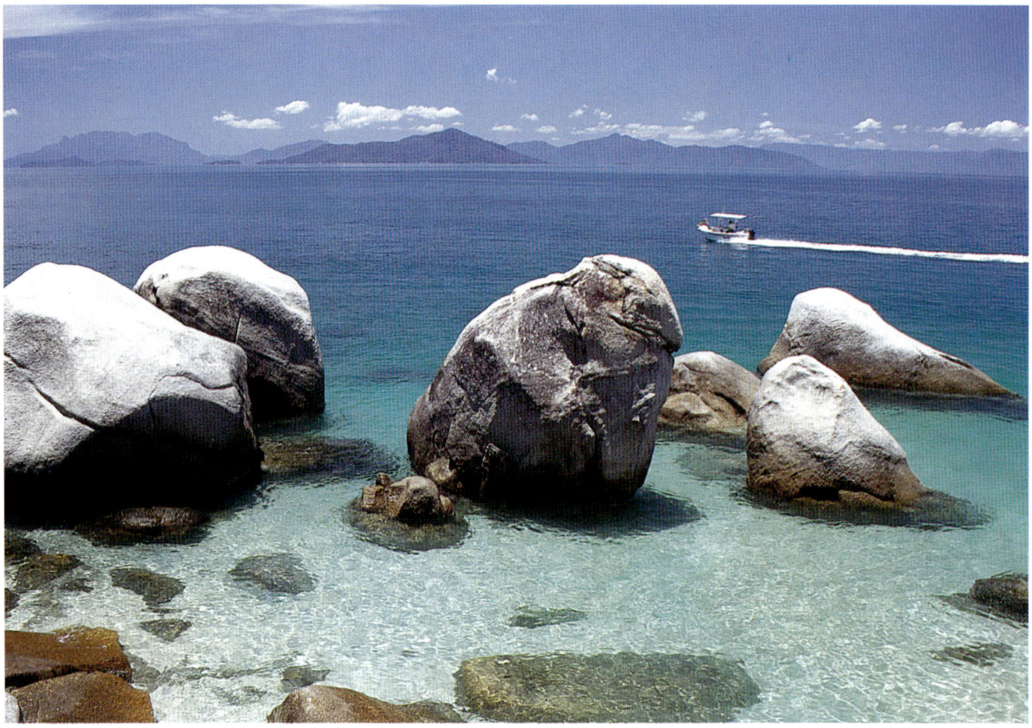

The Gold Coast claims to have the best surfing in Australia. Inland from Surfers Paradise (right) there is subtropical rainforest.

In summer, loggerhead turtles (below) haul themselves ashore to lay their eggs in the sand. The young emerge 4–8 weeks later and make a desperate bid to reach the sea without being eaten by predators.

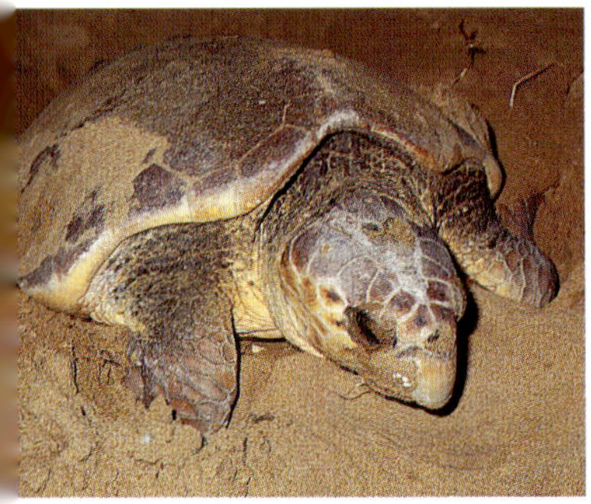

humpback whales, which migrate north every winter from Antarctica. There are less welcome inhabitants, too; in the warmer months (November through April), deadly box jellyfish lurk off the reef's north-facing beaches, hard to detect except in the clearest waters, so don't swim unless locals have given the okay. Great Keppel Island is normally fine for swimming all year round, but still ask. Saltwater crocodiles may also be a hazard, but more common problems are scorpionfish, with their beautiful but highly poisonous spines, and stonefish, which lie on the bottom looking exactly like a stone. Sea snakes can be a problem, but oddly the much-feared shark is not. Despite the area's wealth of marine life, this is a delicately balanced ecology. Some years ago, crown-of-thorns starfish were devouring the reef; the threat seems to have abated for now, but the hordes of human visitors have not. The basic rule for starfish is: look, but don't touch!

View the reef through the base of a glass-bottomed boat, don snorkel and goggles, or take a diving course. For here you can find not only the most rewarding scuba diving in the world, but the cheapest as well, and much of your learning is "on-reef." You can dive from most of the coral reef islands, or cays, which are connected to the mainland by fast catamaran or helicopter. The three mainland bases are Airlie Beach, Townsville, and Cairns. From Cairns—a town of 68,000 people—the reef is only a few miles offshore. A quieter alternative is Great Keppel Island, at the southern end of the reef.

BACK ON DRY LAND

Great Keppel is a continental island, the remnent of a mainland mountain, submerged thousands of years ago when the sea level rose. On islands like this and the Whitsunday group you can find relief from the overabundance of sea life in hill-walking and exploring the bush and its native wildlife. Or you can head inland through a coastal region lush with sugarcane to one of Queensland's 211 national parks, such as Endeavour River National Park, near Cooktown, where there are superb examples of Aboriginal rock art.

The Tully and North Johnstone Rivers, in the mountains between Cairns and Townsville, make for great whitewater rafting. The Tully River, though reduced in volume because of the hydroelectric dam on it, has in the past carved out a spectacular gorge, now a national park, through a rainforest-covered plateau that makes a good day's hiking.

A scenic railroad snakes 19 tortuous miles (30 km) from Cairns up to Kuranda. It was built in 1888 at vast expense, and has dozens of bridges and tunnels through the mountains. The railroad passes the Barron Gorge, with its waterfall, at its most impressive after the rainy season, before reaching the tiny town (population 750) of Kuranda, a popular resort almost overgrown with palm trees. Here there is a Wildlife Noctarium, where you can see native animals in a simulated night, and you can also make other expeditions into the surrounding rainforests.

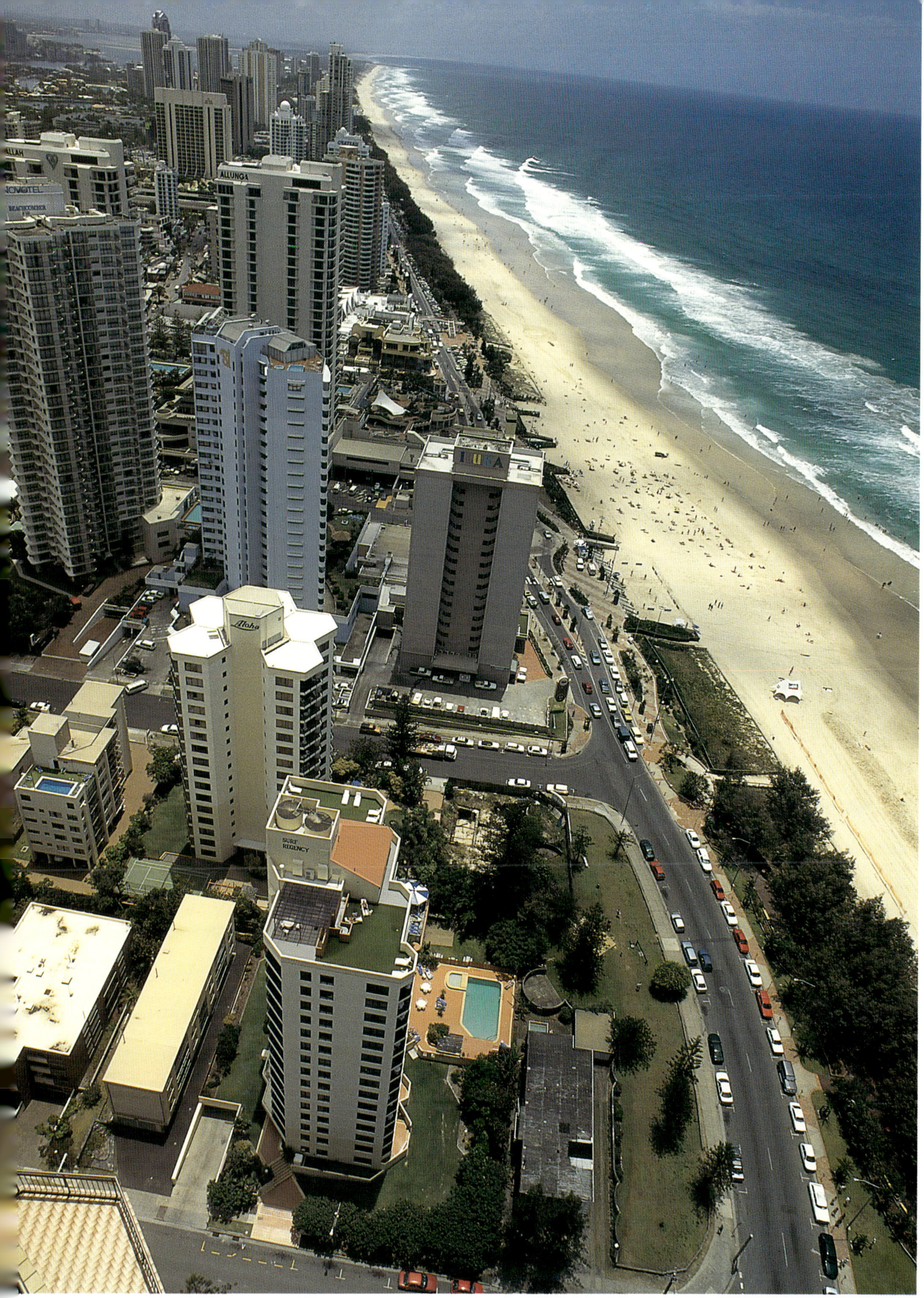
ALLUNGA
NOVOTEL
Aloha
SURF REGENCY

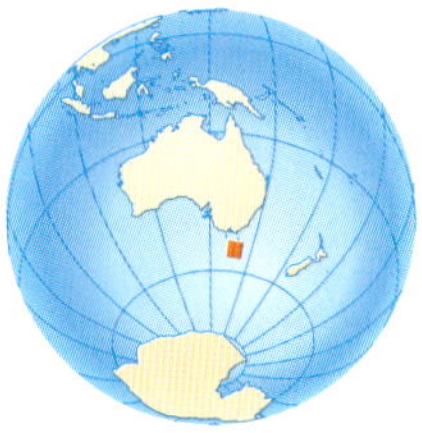

Cradle Mountain, Tasmania

Spectacular peaks, deep gorges, jewel-like lakes, and wild open moorlands combine to make Cradle Mountain-Lake St. Clair National Park one of the finest walking areas in the world. But its wildness is for serious walkers; it is no place for a casual stroll.

FACT FILE

Airports: Burnie, Devonport, Launceston, Hobart.

Transportation: The Park and Overland Track are accessible from Launceston in the north and Hobart in the south by regular bus services.

Distance: The Overland Track itself is 50 miles (85 km) and takes 5–7 days to walk depending on pace.

When to go: November—April, when the weather is most stable. March and April are particularly good for walking.

Permits: Range from one-day permits to a permit valid for entry to all Tasmania's national parks for two months. Rangers check for permits; defaulters incur on-the-spot fines.

Special equipment: Be prepared for extremes in weather conditions; sleeping mat and good four-season sleeping bag; solid footwear essential.

Accommodation and supplies: Huts throughout the park; campsites, lodges, and some cabins at each end of the track. All trekkers must carry a tent since the huts are often full. The park is a "no fire" zone so you must carry a portable stove. Limited supplies are available at either end.

"THIS MUST BE A NATIONAL PARK FOR ALL TIME. It is magnificent. Everyone should know about it, and come and enjoy it," declared Gustav Weindorfer, an Austrian immigrant scientist who fell headlong in love with Cradle Mountain in Tasmania on first seeing it in 1910. His simple but impassioned words echo the sentiments that have led to the preservation of the entire wilderness around it, including Mt. Ossa, Tasmania's highest mountain at 5,300 feet (1,617 m), and Lake St. Clair, Australia's deepest lake. Cradle Mountain-Lake St. Clair National Park is part of a UNESCO World Heritage area.

Tasmania, Australia's southernmost and only island state, is extremely rich in rugged scenery, and has a markedly cooler, wetter, windier climate than most of Australia. High cliffs along the southern and southwestern coasts look out toward the not-so-distant Antarctic, and empty moors stretch for miles.

The most impressive location of all is the 325,845-acre (131,921 ha) Cradle Mountain-Lake St. Clair National Park, with its precipitous, jagged peaks, deep, ice-scoured valleys, lakes and tarns, expanses of wild moorland, and abundant wildlife. Thin soils and scrub and dramatic, shattered rockfaces bear witness to the glaciers' swift retreat at the end of the last ice age; for this is one of Australia's most heavily glaciated areas. But in spring and early summer, the wild flowers are legion, and autumn leaf colors are enhanced by those of Tasmania's only native deciduous species, the tanglefoot beech, with leaves that turn from bright green to gold and red. Despite the park's popularity—in high season more than 100 people set out on the trails every day—the pristine wildness of the area has been kept remarkably intact.

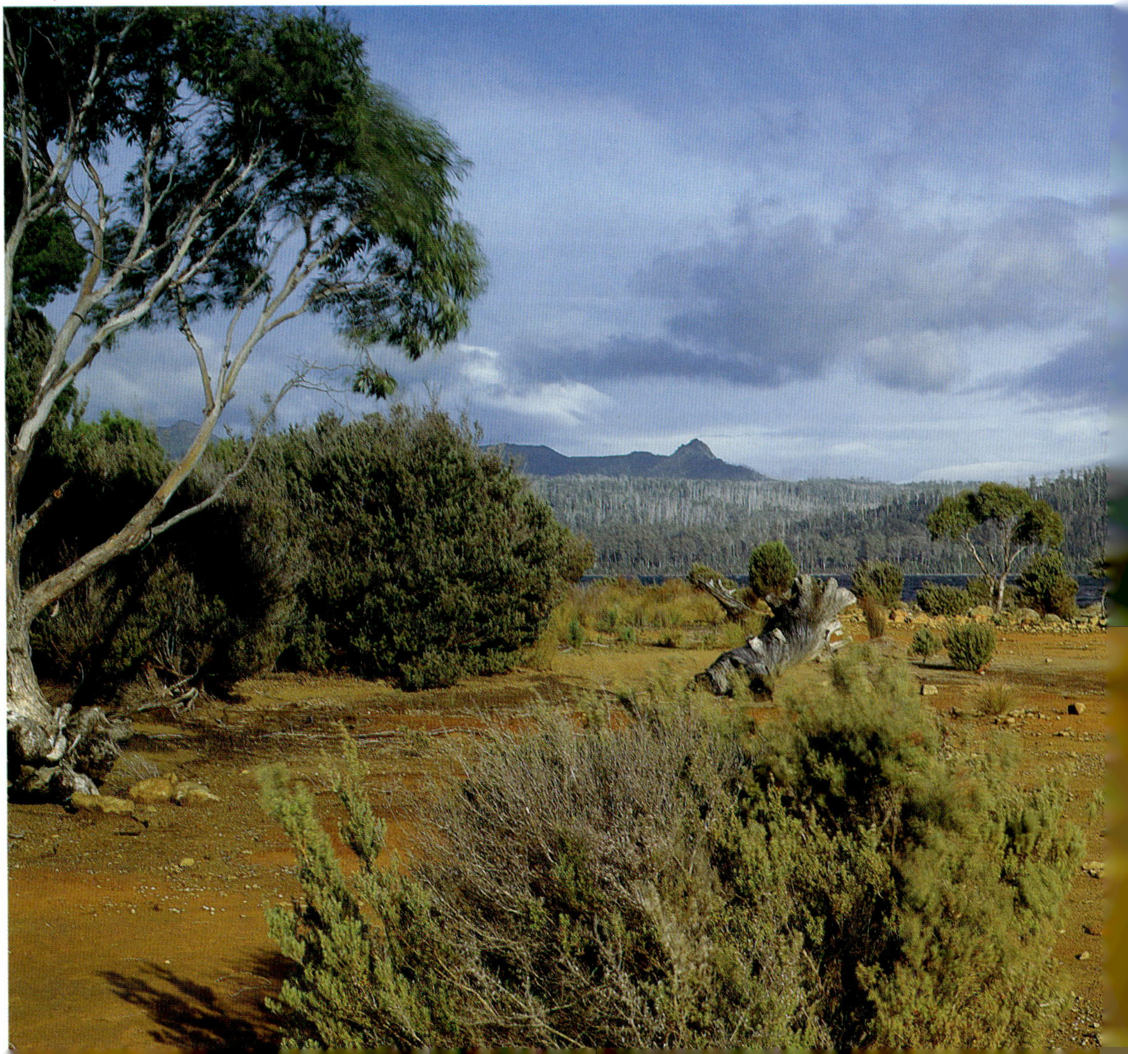

Walking the Wilderness

There are numerous day walks in the area, but the 50-mile (85 km) Overland Track from Cradle Valley to Cynthia Bay at the foot of Lake St. Clair attracts most visitors. The track can be walked in either direction, but most travel north to south, beginning at the Cradle Mountain ranger station and finishing at the ranger station near Derwent Bridge. The track can be walked at an easy pace in five to seven days, but a fuller exploration of the region including an ascent of Mt. Ossa, would require eight to ten days. Walkers should sign the logbook at Waldheim Chalet before setting out and on completing their walk. They should also check at the park ranger station before setting out and be sure family or friends know of their whereabouts, so that a search will be triggered if they go missing.

November to April is the best time to walk, though experienced walkers sometimes like to do the track in winter, to see the snow-covered moors and peaks flashing white against a brilliantly deep blue sky, hundreds of miles from any pollution. Even in summer the weather can be unpredictable, with sudden rainstorms and days of dramatic cloud. The track is well marked for its entire length, and there are

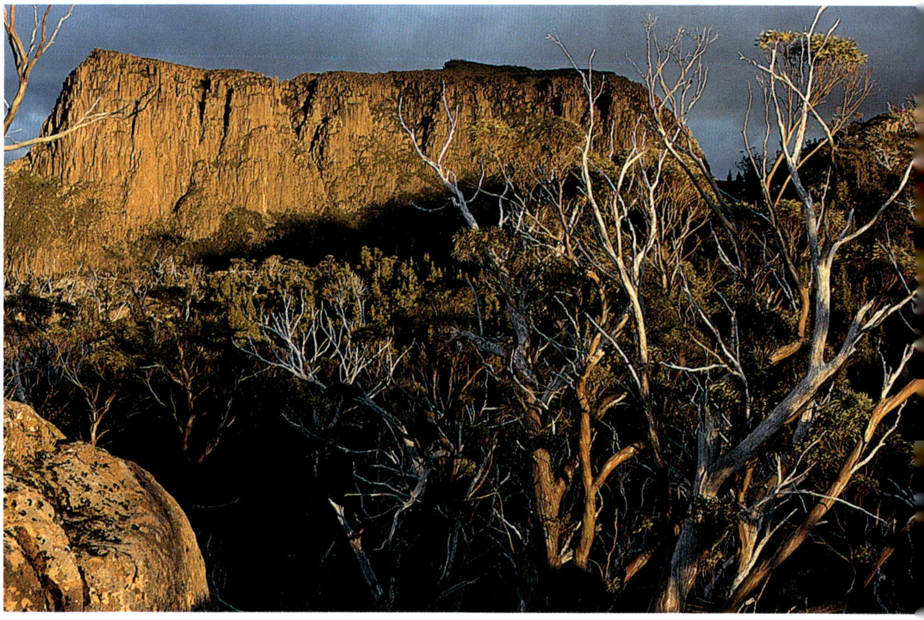

Bushland forms the runup to Lake St. Clair (below), the deepest lake in Australia seen here in the distance.

The Acropolis (above), one of the views from the Overland Track, is aptly named.

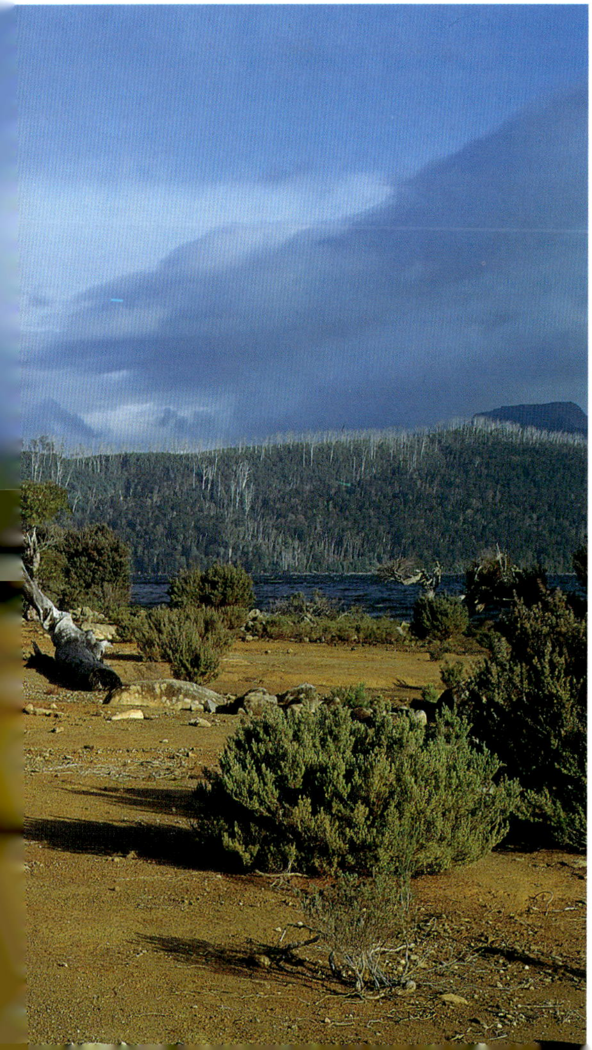

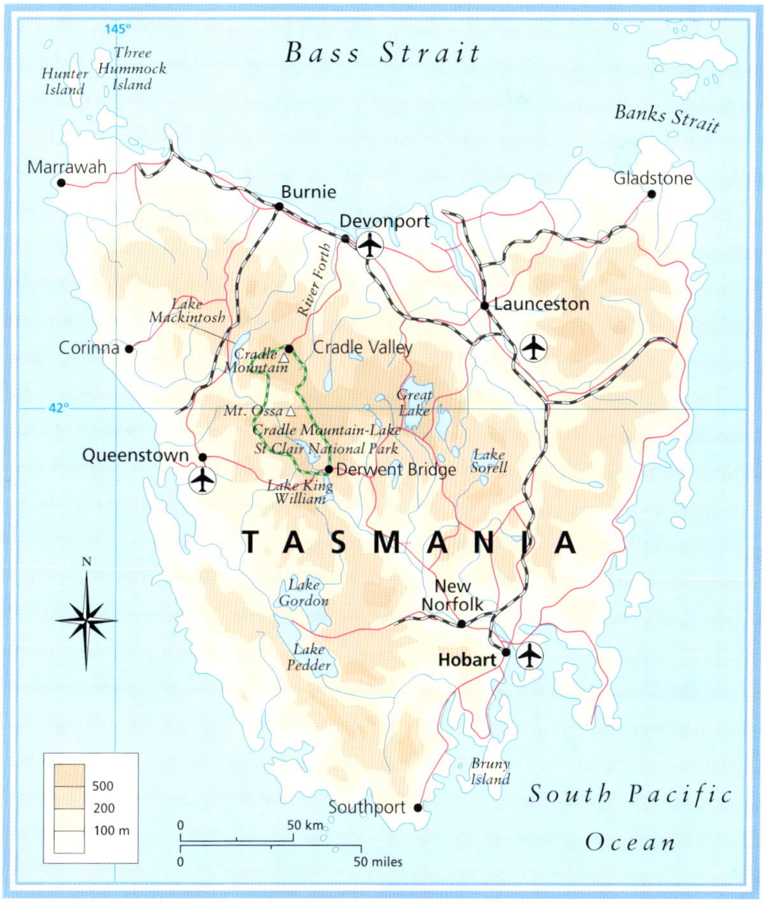

12 unsupervised huts along the route that walkers can use for overnight accommodation. Try to start walking early; these huts are often full, being taken on a "first there, first in" basis. The easiest way to walk the Overland Track is in stages of five to six hours, allowing time to explore some of the other tracks.

Beginning in Cradle Valley, which is scattered with eucalyptus trees—look out for the snow gum—a journey of some 8 miles (13 km) to the Waterfall Valley huts takes a comfortable five to six hours. From Marions Lookout, the reflections of Cradle Mountain on the surface of the lake give a perfect vista of the sharp peak in calm, clear weather. Just past Kitchen Hut is a signposted track to Cradle Mountain summit, an extremely steep, rocky track which takes an hour each way. The panoramic views from its top are splendid, and a bronze plaque indicates all the surrounding mountains, including Legges Tor, the highest peak of Ben Lomond, at 5,160 feet (1,572 m) Tasmania's second highest mountain, almost 100 miles (160 km) distant. There are a number of superb waterfalls within a few hundred yards of the Overland Track.

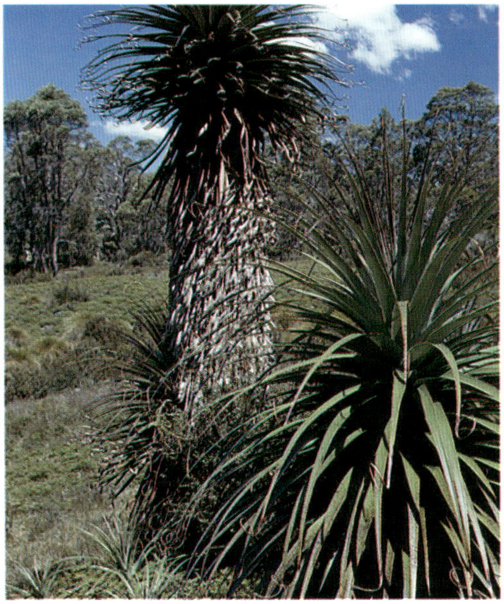

The giant grass tree (left) lends a subtropical air to some parts of the Tasmanian bush.

From Waterfall Valley to Lake Windemere is another 8 miles (13 km) over a sharp ridge, with extensive views in fine weather, and then across open moor and forest, remarkably similar to parts of the Scottish Highlands, to the shores of Lake Windemere. There is a modern, heated hut that sleeps 28 people. By the end of the first day, everyone is usually discussing walkers' favorite topic—food.

The track runs on, always well signposted, through a terrain which varies from eucalyptus forest to marshy plains of buttongrass and finally reaches Cynthia Bay on Lake St. Clair. Gentler alternatives for the less energetic, there are several shorter, one-day walks from Cradle Valley. Call in at the Visitors Center for advice on those best-suited to the weather. The 4-mile Dove Lake circuit takes two hours and offers magnificent views.

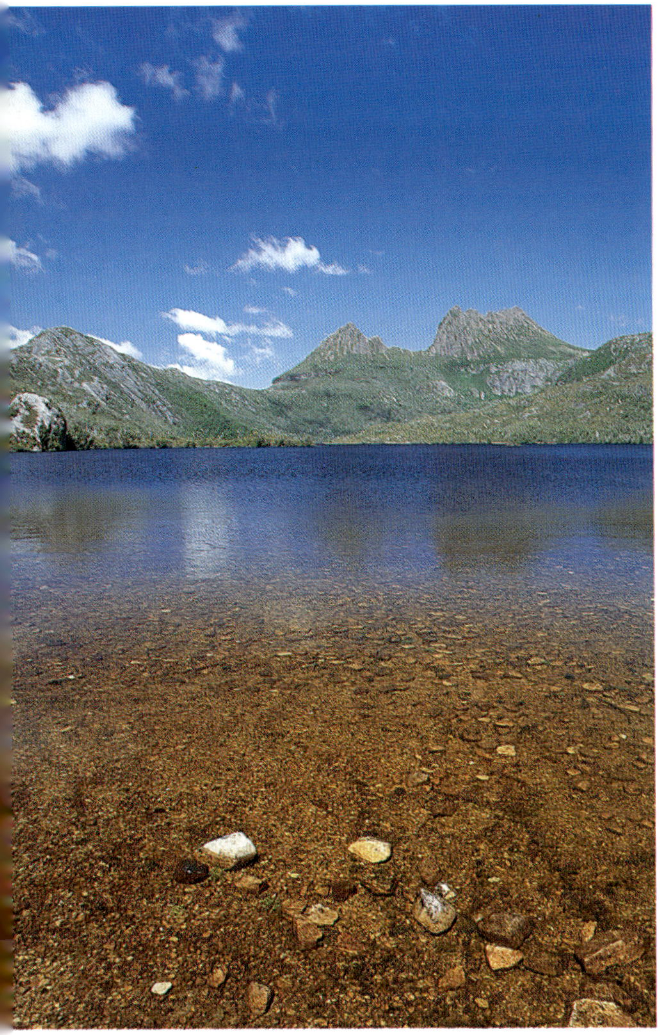

Many trails start from Dove Lake (left), but one of the most delightful is the two-hour lake circuit.

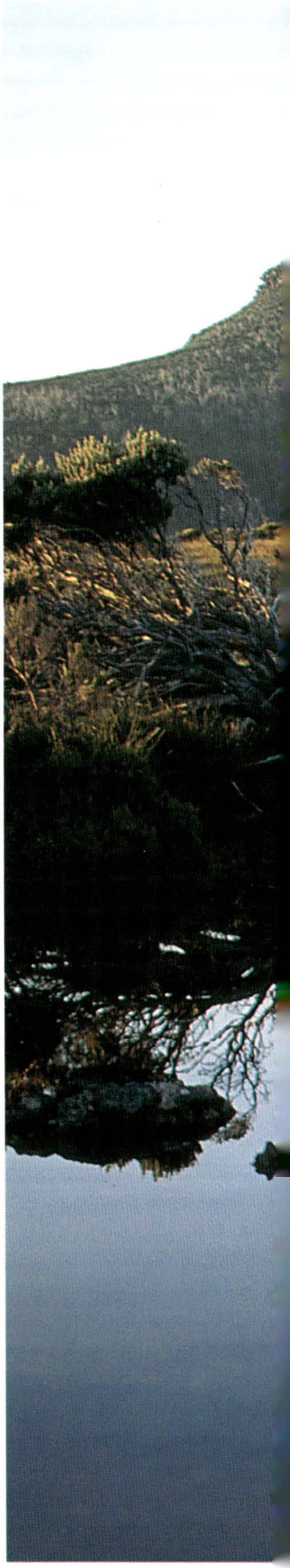

The ice-scoured cliffs of Mount Pelion West are mirrored in the calm waters of Lake Ayr (right).

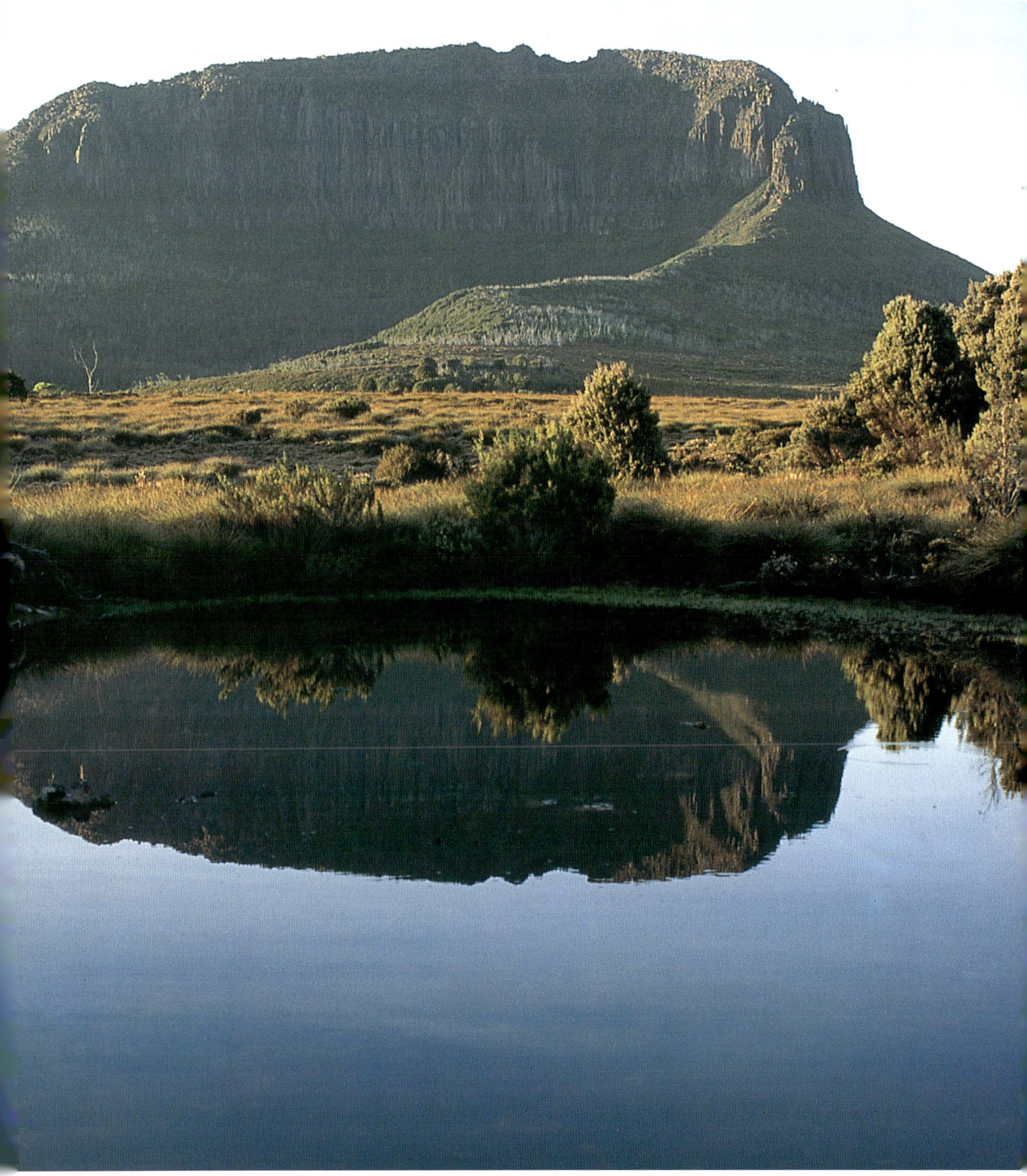

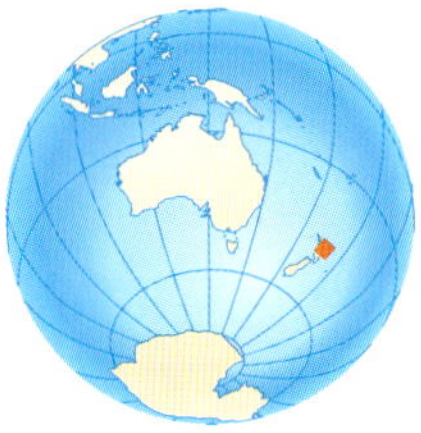

Rotorua, Geothermal Hotspot

Mountains ring a land of steaming volcanic spectacle, lakes of plenty, and lush, virgin forest.

FACT FILE

Best time to visit: Summer (December—March), avoiding the high vacation season on either side of the New Year.

Fishing season: October—June.

Climate: Subtropical, all year, with temperatures seldom falling much below 68°F (20°C) or rising much above 82°F (28°C). Rain throughout the year.

What to take: Sunblock, sunglasses, sun hat, a sweater for cool evenings, waterproof clothing.

Currency: New Zealand dollar.

What to buy: Maori craft works and textiles.

Accommodation: Plentiful in Rotorua, except in peak season.

Special note: Tipping is not generally expected in New Zealand.

THE TOWN AND LAKE OF ROTORUA lie on a hotline of geothermal activity between the great volcanic plateau and crater of Taupo 50 miles (80 km) to the south, and White Island in the Bay of Plenty. Here are places where the Earth's crust is so thin that boiling mud bubbles to the surface and high-pressure spouts of steam and boiling water explode through the ground.

The closer you are to "Rottenrua," as the town and lake are fondly known, the more powerful the smell of rotten eggs, or hydrogen sulfide, from the geothermal activity. But after half an hour or so, it is hardly noticeable. As you explore the lakeside and the surrounding area, you are constantly surprised by continuous columns of steam rising from the ground, in the middle of the town park, or in a burnt-out forest clearing. Visibility can suddenly drop as steam appears, like a hot fog. There are gurgling hot springs; thermal pools edged with mineral deposits of pink, red, and green; and mud pools with a vocal range from deep ponderous plops to high-pitched blips.

It is worth renting a car rather than taking a tour so that you can find the natural treasures beyond the main attractions. New Zealand gets about 1 million tourists a year, and most of them go to Rotorua, but it is not difficult to escape the hordes. Drive south from Auckland for a splendid cross section of North Island landscapes, past rolling, white-fenced stud farms and horseracing "gallops," the pastoral city of Hamilton, and a great tract of virgin forest, or from the delightful seaside city and port of Tauranga (Maori for "resting place for canoes") at the heart of the country's kiwi fruit region, in the Bay of Plenty.

The most visited and most spectacular geysers are in

Whakarewarewa spouts (right) do justice to Rotorua's status as one of the top three geyser regions of the world.

Pools of boiling mud (below) heave and bubble in slow motion, in a range of different rhythms and tones.

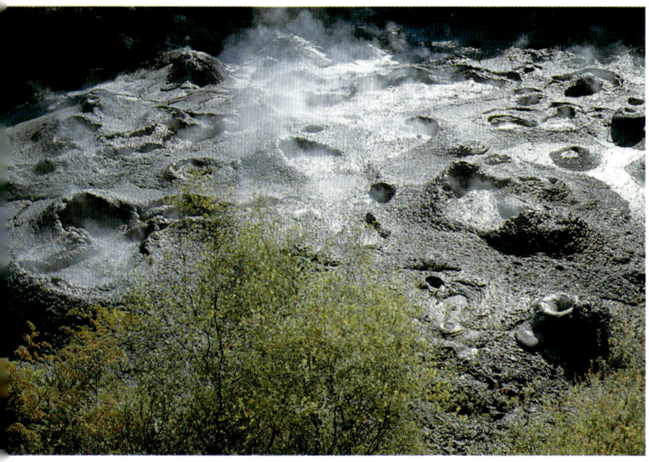

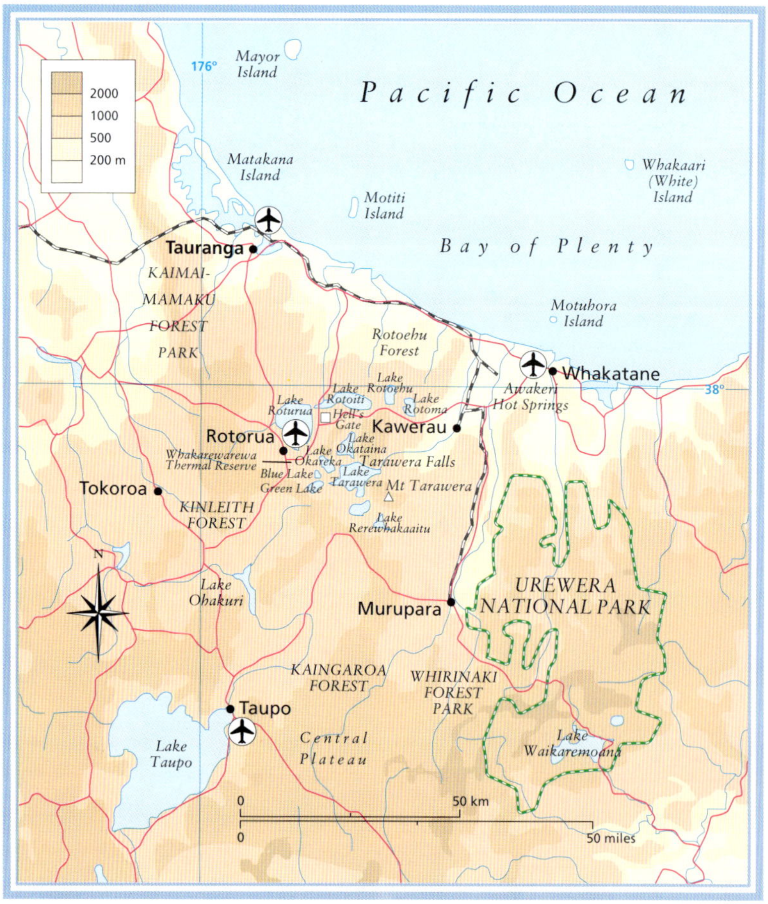

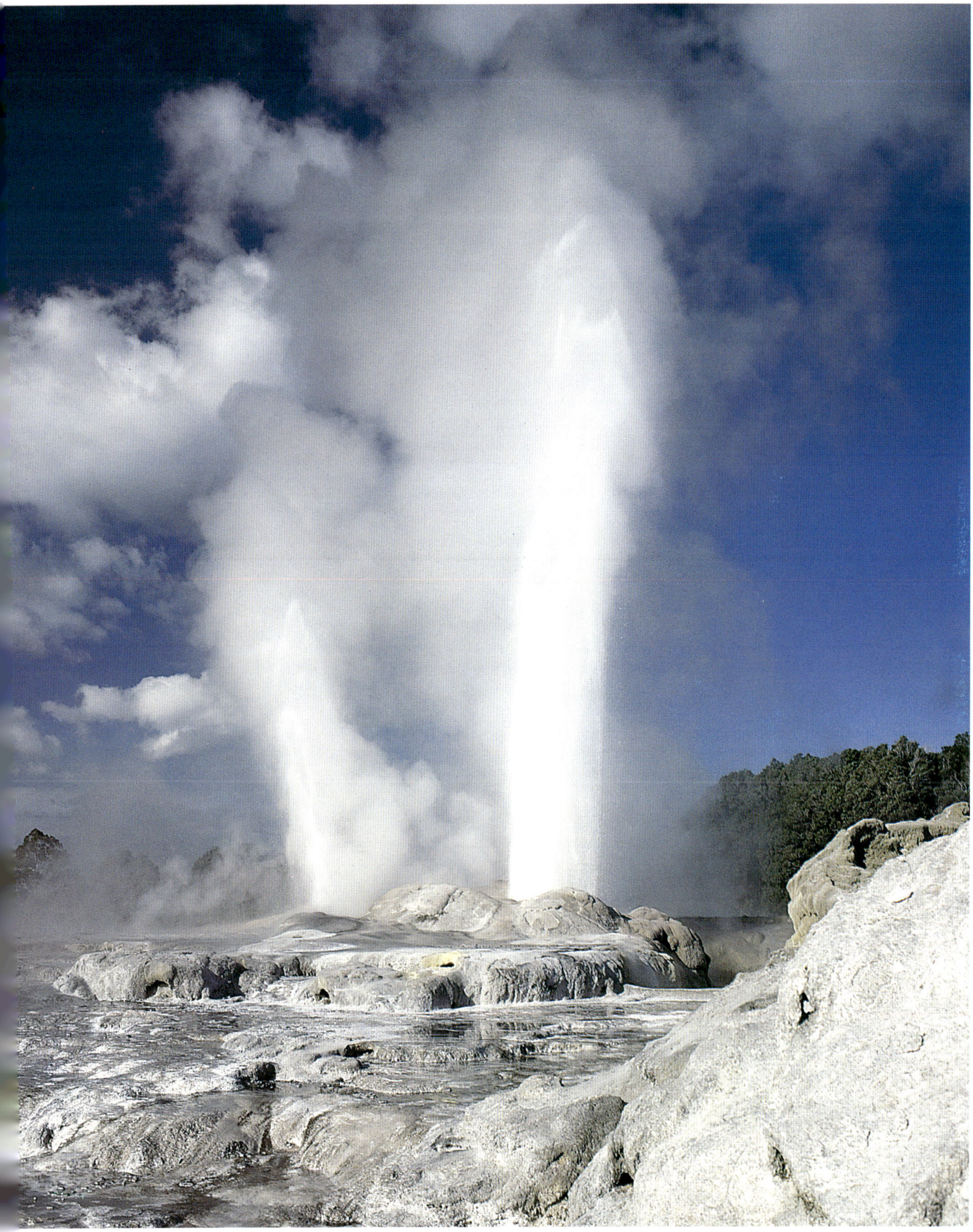

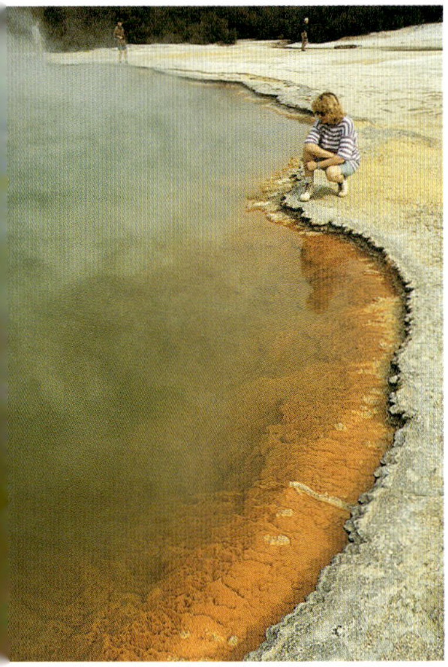

Whakarewarewa Thermal Reserve, south of the lake, where Pohutu (Maori for "big splash") can spout plumes of boiling hot water 100 feet (30 m) into the air for several minutes at a time. Its eruption is always preceded by the nearby Prince of Wales' Feathers. There are admission charges to walk around these geysers—where you are strongly advised to stick to the marked paths, or a sudden spout could scald you. There are no geysers at Hell's Gate, 10 miles (16 km) east, but there is plenty of steam, and viciously hot water jetting from crevices (again, stick to the paths), the largest hot thermal waterfall in the southern hemisphere, far fewer tourists, and it is considerably cheaper.

LONGSTANDING TRADITIONS

The Maoris have used the natural resources of Rotorua for washing, cooking, and bathing since they first settled there, probably in the 1300s. The hot earth, for example, is utilized to create New Zealand's only authentic native cuisine. Food is placed in baskets and covered with wet cloths and effectively steamed in the earth ovens. Specialties are smoky-flavored pork and sweet potatoes. It is possible to have a precooked dish warmed up in a microwave, but this is not the way to do it, as the real thing takes several hours. An alternative is to go via a local tourist office to an arranged event that may also feature Maori music and dancing, including the exuberant hongi (nose to nose contact).

The Maori culture is still very much alive, and its traditions can be explored at the Museum of Art and History in Rotorua and 2 miles (3 km) down the road at Whakarewarewa, or "Whaka," a replica Maori village. At the lakeside Maori village of Ohinemutu, now virtually absorbed into the suburbs of Rotorua town, little vents of steam bubble up from the ground beside the Anglican St. Faith's Church. Inside are beautiful Maori carvings, painted scrollwork, and a modern stained glass window depicting Christ in a feathered Maori cloak, looking as though he is walking on the real lake outside, just beyond the window.

Mineral deposits lace the edge of the ever-bubbly Champagne Pool (above) in the Waiotapu area, 19 miles (31 km) south of Rotorua.

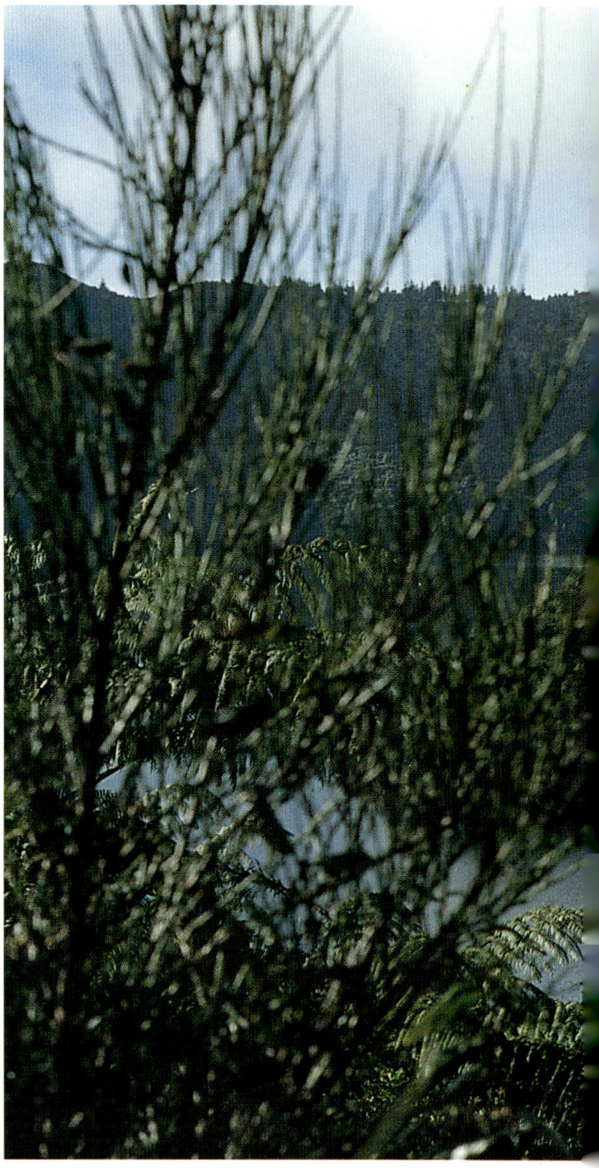

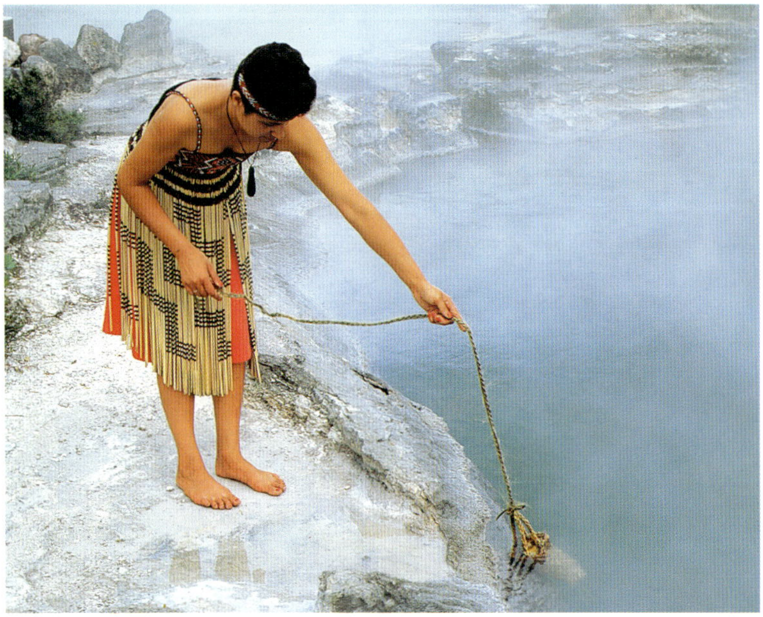

The Arawa group of Maori's—who came to New Zealand from Polynesia in the 1300s—were drawn to the natural cooking facilities in Rotorua.

WATER POWER

The Maoris have long appreciated the medicinal properties of Rotorua's waters; the town did not begin to develop as a more widely known health resort until the late 1800s, when Europeans began to visit in the hope of finding cures for a range of complaints and diseases by drinking or bathing in the mineral-rich waters, and established a tourist industry.

You can take the waters today, both in Rotorua,

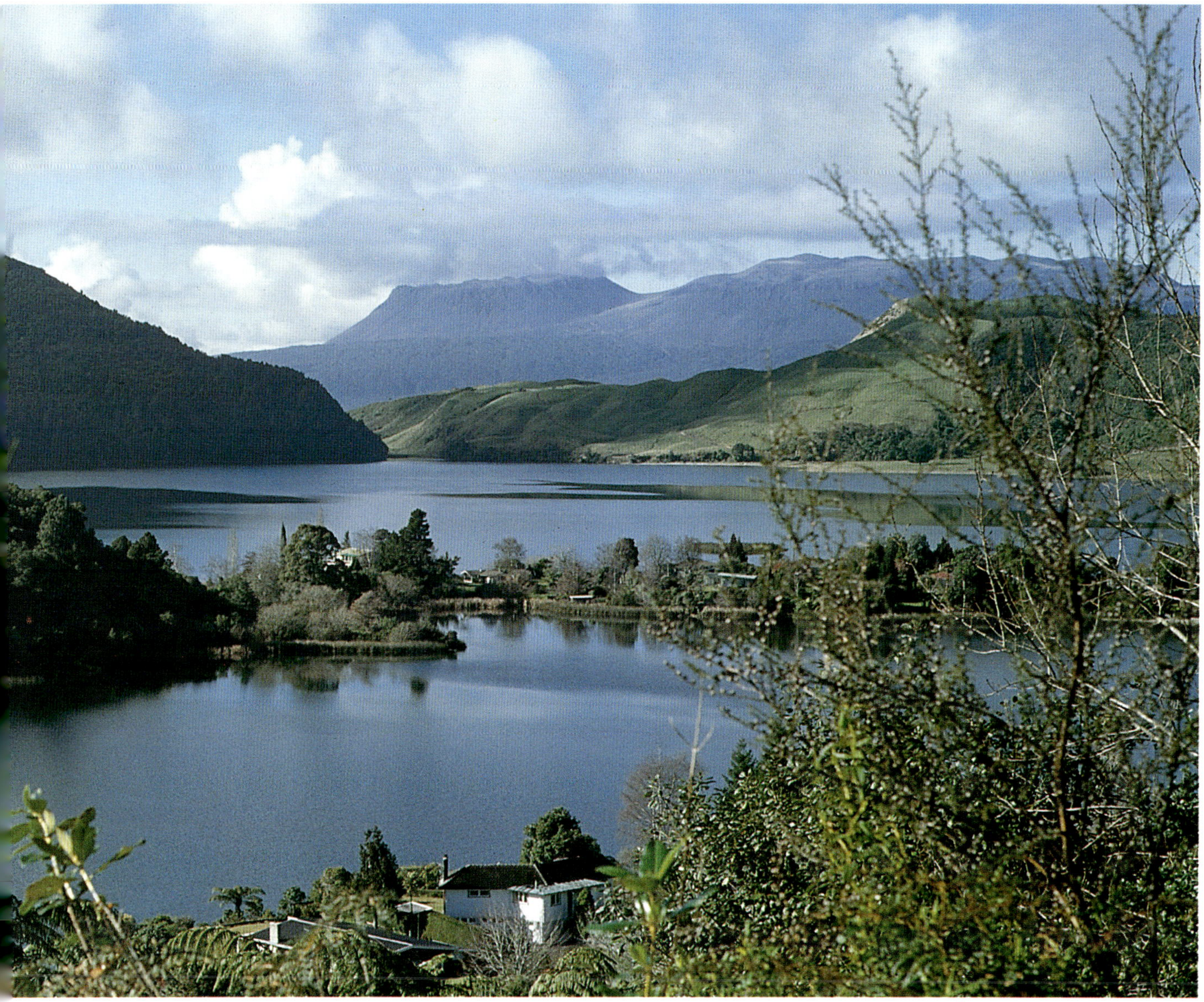

where there are bath houses at the lake's edge, and at Walkite Thermal Mineral Baths, 19 miles (30 km) away, an open air mineral pool whose waters remain a steady 102°F (39°C) all year.

More active ways of appreciating Rotorua's waters include watersports and cruises on the lake itself, and farther afield, in the surrounding hills, for whitewater rafting in the gorges of the Kaituna and Rangitaiki rivers. But such frenzied activities risk missing out on another of the area's assets: its incredible abundance of trout. Brown trout were introduced in the late 1800s and have so thrived in the clear waters that today Lake Rotorua claims to have the best trout fishing in the world. Whatever the truth, locals all but guarantee that you will catch a fish, but you need a license. You can rent a small fishing boat and drift out into the lake or just fish from the waterfront. Many trout streams feed the lake, the best known being the Rainbow Springs Trout and Wildlife Sanctuary, where the trout amass in feeding frenzies.

The Pink and White Terraces, formed by silica deposits from the volcanic activities of Mount Tarawera to the southeast were a fabled 19th-century tourist attraction—until they were destroyed by a mighty eruption in 1886. The village of Te Wairoa was buried beneath volcanic ash—its excavated remains can be visited today—and 150 people were killed. A tourist flight over the volcano reveals the sheer force of the eruption that split the mountain open. Tarawera is the largest peak of the region, at 3,667 feet (1,111 m), with its native podocarp forests descended from an ancient plant family that evolved before flowering plants. Here, too, are sink holes, a disappearing river, waterfalls, and thermal areas. The road from Rotorua is astonishingly scenic, passing by the Blue and Green Lakes, which spectacularly live up to their names.

Mount Tarawera, on the horizon, is around 9 miles (15 km) southwest of Rotorua; the area is rich in opportunities for bushwalking, boat trips, and hotwater swimming in the waterholes in the surrounding forest.

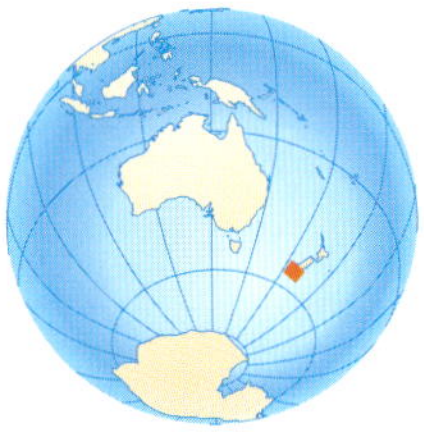

Queenstown, adventure capital

A holistic experience, where ley lines and natural wonders meet adventure sports and a cosmopolitan lifestyle.

Kawarau Bridge, Arthurtown (right), Queenstown, where you can take the plunge in the home of bungee jumping—or just watch others do it from a viewing platform. Alternatively take a jet-boat ride through the rapids of the Shotover River (far right).

YOU DON'T HAVE TO BE SPORTY to appreciate Queenstown, but it helps. It is the ultimate adventure resort, the reputed home of bungee jumping, and a mecca for antipodean skiers. But in a country that has an excess of sights of outstanding, unpolluted natural beauty, Queenstown is supreme in its combination of natural and human facilities. Quite apart from the carefully cultivated adventure scene, it combines a stunning position between lake and the aptly named Remarkable Mountains, with accessibility (not to be taken for granted in this deeply dissected landscape) and an equable climate. To the west is wet, densely forested, forbidding coastline, where cliffs drop sheer into the sea; south are chill marshlands. But Queenstown is a haven, a "rainshadow zone" sheltered from the heaviest rains and not far from the spot which scores one of the country's highest number of sunny days a year. Though the resident population is only around 2,500, there's a cosmopolitan buzz, with international eateries from pizzerias to Japanese teahouses, and a great line in New Zealand seafood specialties such as Bluff oysters, crayfish, South Island whitebait, and Nelson scallops, all brought in fresh daily from the ocean less than 100 miles (160 km) distant.

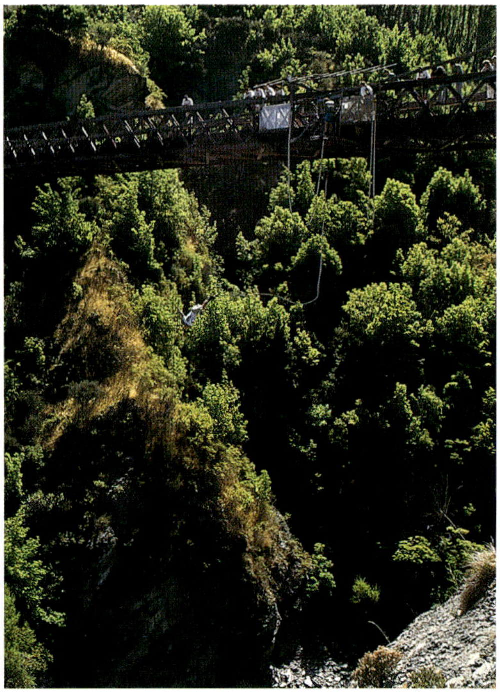

Queenstown was once a Maori settlement, but the area was deserted when the first westerners arrived in the 1850s. Then in 1862, two sheep shearers discovered gold on the banks of the Shotover River, and within a few year, a classic goldrush town was born. The streets were laid out and impressive buildings erected to accommodate the thousands of people pouring in to make or spend their fortunes. But the gold ran out, and by 1900 Queenstown was almost a ghost town, the population having dwindled to a couple of hundred.

Paragliding offers perhaps the most remarkable overview of the Remarkables.

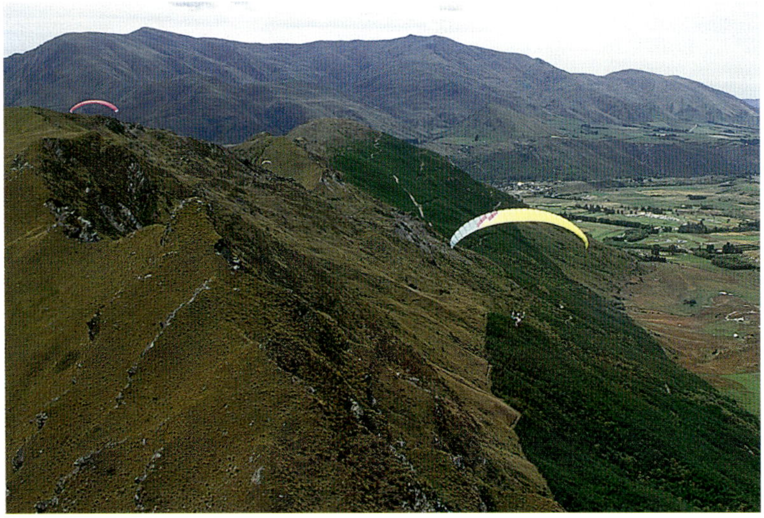

NATURAL ADVANTAGES

The Remarkables and the Eyre Mountains are, by geological standards mere youngsters, which explains their vigorous upsurge to almost 10,000 feet (3,000 m) and the gorge-cutting power of the rivers. But you don't need to be a bungee jumper, a hangglider, a hot-air balloonist, or a heli-glider (though there are opportunities for all four activities) to appreciate the stunning mountain, lake, and river panoramas. There are leisurely cruises on Lake Wakatipu, South Island's second largest lake, which elbows its way 100 miles (160 km) through the island's mountainous spine. One's on a coal-burning steamship that was once the region's chief means of transportation and communication with the outside world. Or you can walk above the town to Queenstown Hill, at 3,000 feet (900 m) or take a trip on the Skyline Gondola (cable car). The town is at its prettiest, say the winter sports

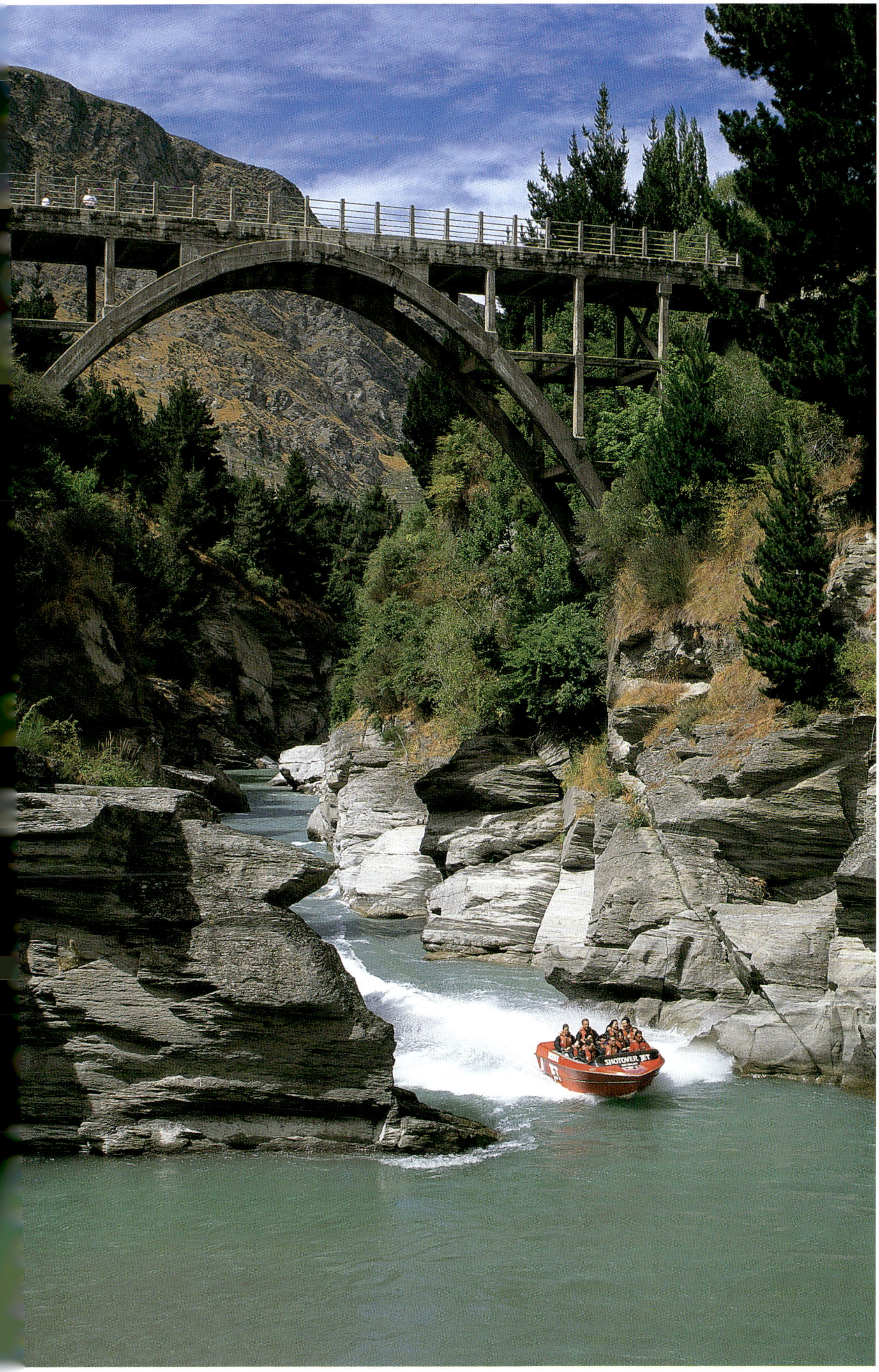

FACT FILE

Getting there: By air from Auckland, Christchurch, and various local connecting flights; by bus from Christchurch, Dunedin, and Invercargill.

Currency: New Zealand dollars. No exchange problems.

When to go: November—April, lower rainfall, although it rains a lot and sudden storms are common year round. In winter snow can be heavy. Temperatures depend on altitude. New Zealand's vacation season, December—January, is best avoided.

Accommodation: Queenstown has many hotels but they fill up in season, so book in advance.

What to take: Sunglasses and sunblock. The hole in the ozone layer is directly above New Zealand in November. A raincoat and sweater are advisable, and heavy clothing in winter.

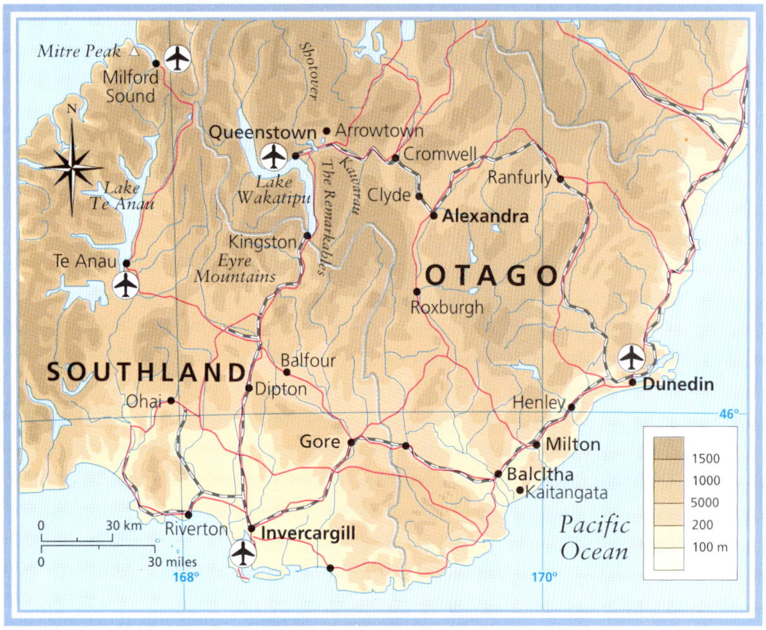

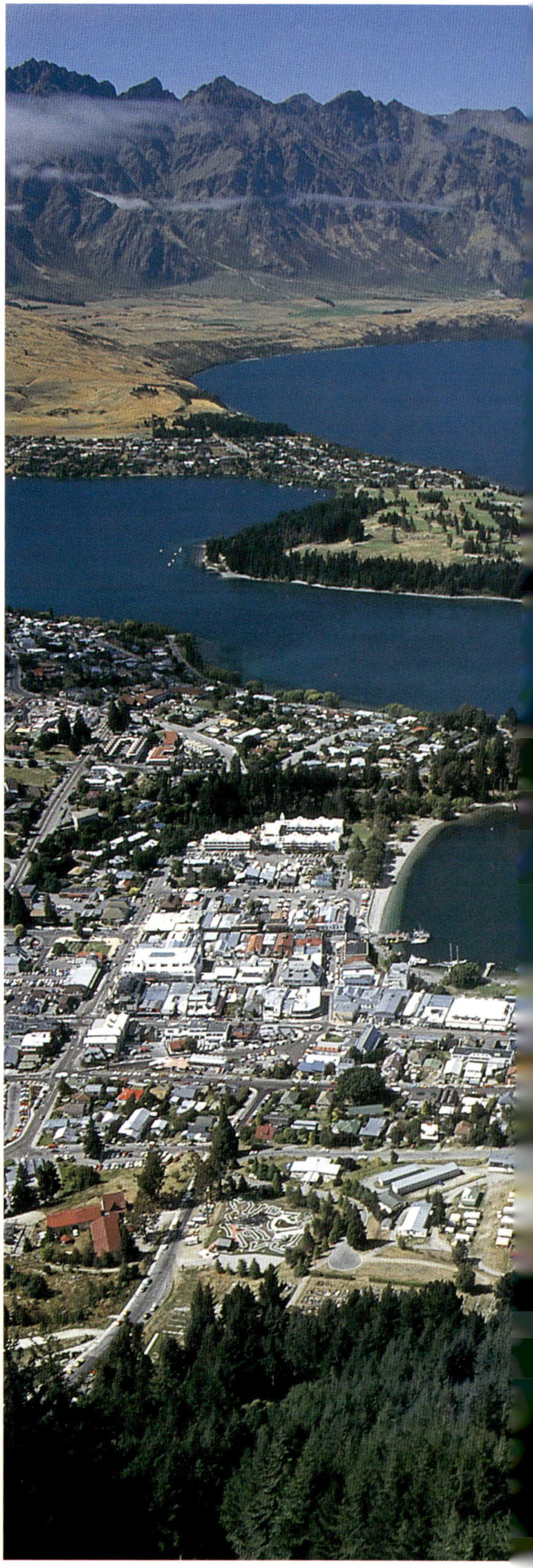

enthusiasts, in winter, when the locals sometimes have to ski to work, and the "après ski" life is reputedly among the best in New Zealand. The slopes are just snow-covered rock above the low tree line, not at all like the forested runs of Europe. But autumn is a mosaic of golds and russets among the southern beech forests on the lower mountain slopes; this is the time to explore the trails around Arrowtown, which still retains some old gold rush charm.

Take a good look at the trees and flowers: New Zealand's flora developed in isolation from the rest of the world, and more than 75 percent of it is found nowhere else. The bird life is similarly distinctive: the kea is a notorious resident of these parts and one of the world's biggest parrots. What it lacks in color—a drab brownish-green with a flash of red on the underwing—it makes up for in sassiness. Kea have been seen sliding down rooftops, legs in the air, and are notorious for stealing moldings and windshield wipers from cars to play with.

THRILLS WITH A VIEW

Summer is the time to go upriver for some serious action. This is the area that introduced the world to bungee jumping and the jet boat. Pipeline, on the site of a former water pipeline for gold sluicing, claims to be the highest bungee jump in the world. The drop is 340 feet (102 m), and those who take the plunge are rewarded with a commemorative T-shirt. At Kawarau Suspension Bridge 10 miles (16 km) from the town there are observation platforms for vicarious thrills overlooking the 142-foot (43 m) drop from the bungee

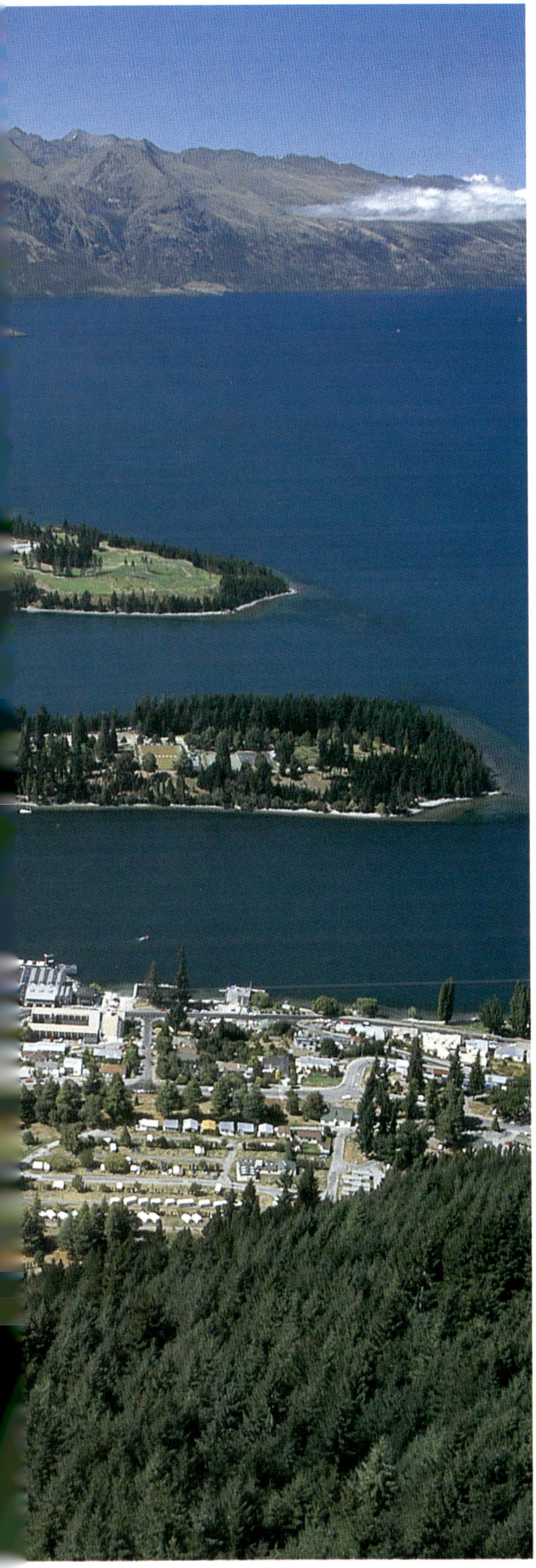

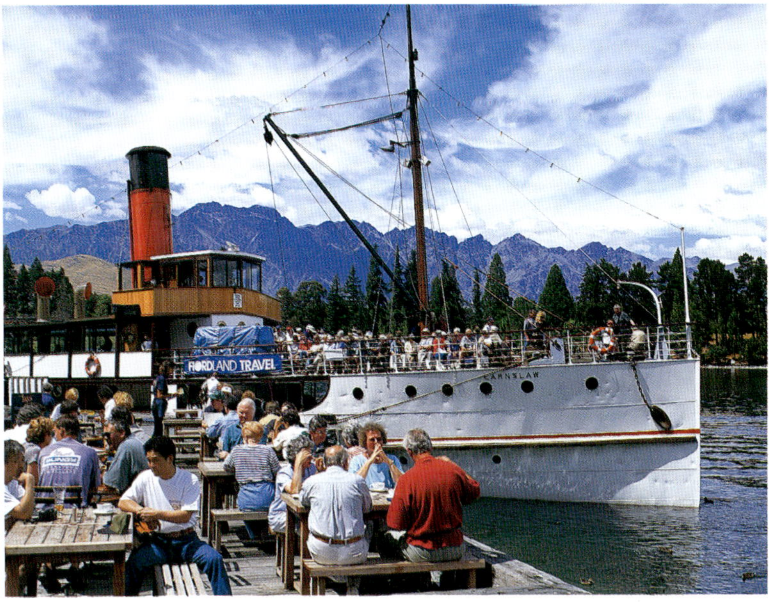

takeoff point to just above the river below. Hair-raising jet boat trips hurtle down through the turbulent Shotover and Kawarau Rivers, shooting rapids, and dodging rocks and right-angle bends in the steep-cliffed gorges. There's pure whitewater rafting as well as the local variant on plastic sleds. The rivers are graded from 1 to 6, 6 being unnegotiable; most of the Shotover Canyon is 3-5.

Mountain biking among such mountains is for the seriously fit, although it is possible to have your bike ridden up to the highest point, and you just follow the route down. There is unrestricted access across hill tracks. The ultimate experience for trekkers is the three-day trip to Milford Sound via the 24-mile (39 km) Routeburn Track, with hostels along the way.

More leisurely activities are possible including cruises on Lake Wakatipu, New Zealand's second largest lake (above).

EIGHTH WONDER OF THE WORLD

From Queenstown's small airfield it is only a short flight to what the English writer Rudyard Kipling (1865-1936) described as "the eighth Wonder of the World": Milford Sound on the west coast. The sound is only 9 miles (15 km) long but it is surrounded by mountain cliffs rising 4,000 feet (1,200 m) vertically and laced with giant waterfalls dropping directly into the sea. A cruise on one of the many ships on the Sound should be missed by no visitor to South Island, for it allows you to come right up to the spectacular Bowen Falls, the Stirling Falls, and Mitre Peak, rising 5,558 feet (1,694 m) like a pyramid out of the sea. Back on dry land, you can spend the night at Milford Sound, with its rather limited accommodation, or take the road 100 miles (160 km) south to Te Anau on Lake Te Anau, another mountain-encircled lake.

The Pacific

"The earth belongs to anyone who stops for a moment, gazes and goes on his way."

COLETTE, FRENCH WRITER, 1873-1954.

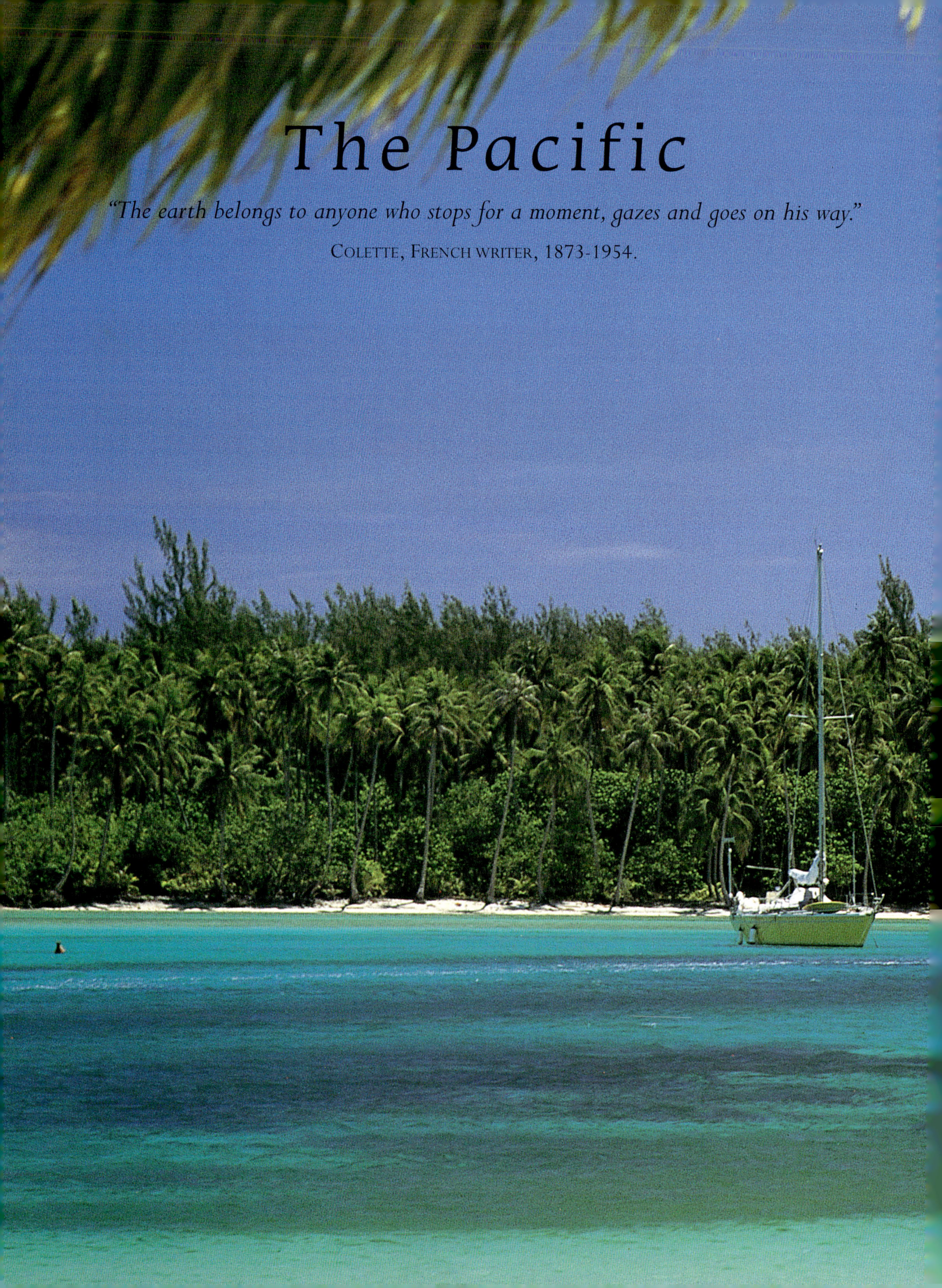

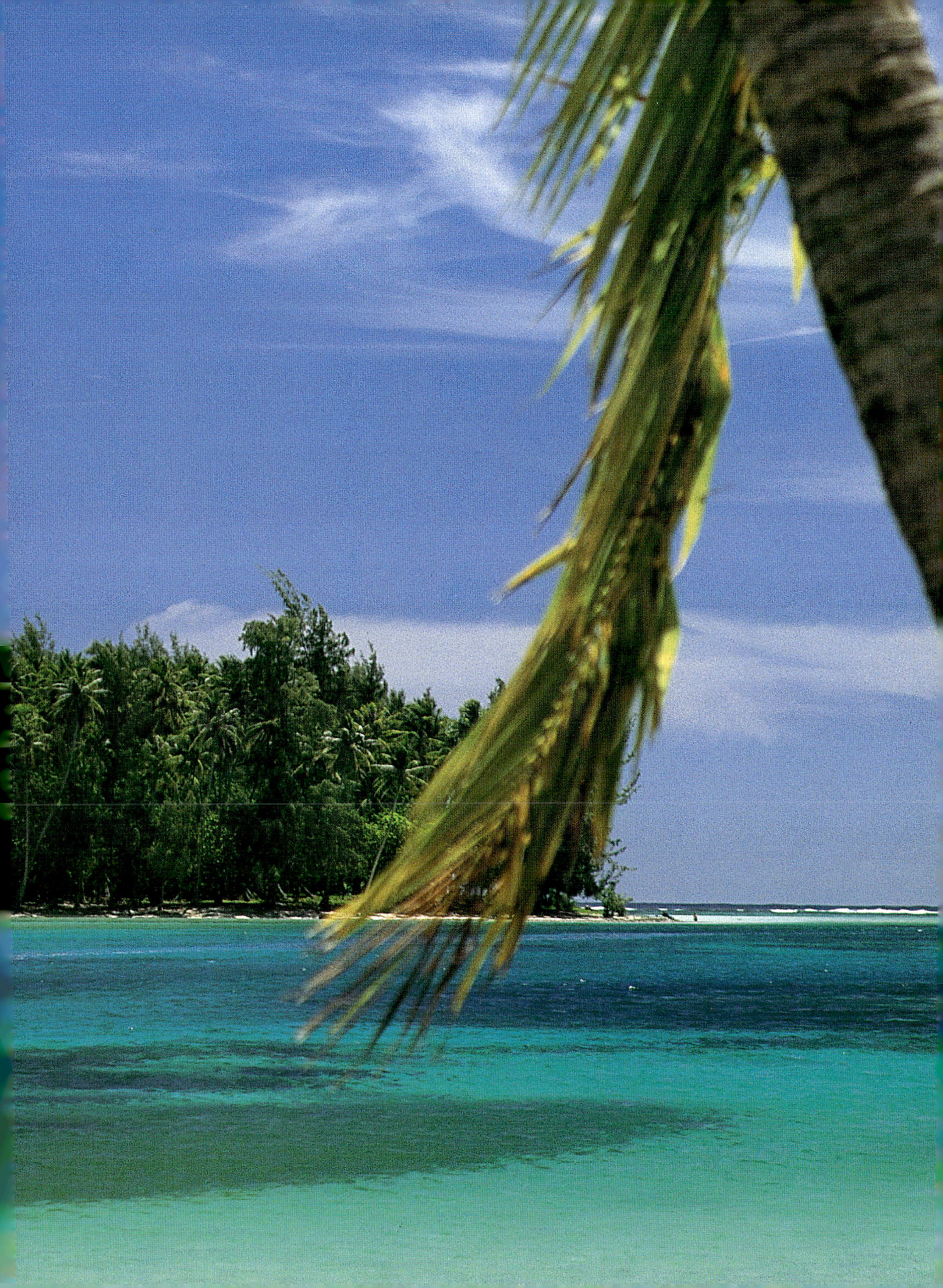

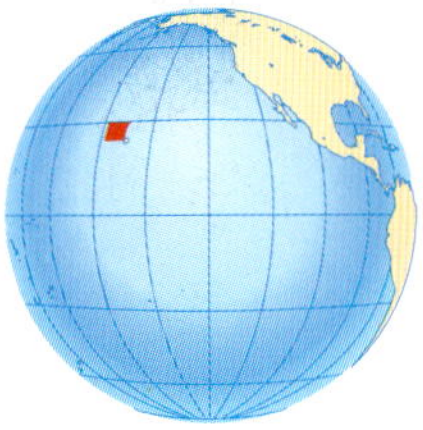

Hawaiian Contrasts

Forged by volcanic fire, molded by the winds and the ocean, the Hawaiian islands are one of the most beautiful archipelagos in the whole Pacific, and among the most varied in the world.

FACT FILE

Climate: Warm all year round, into the high 80ºs F (low 30ºsC) most days. The mountains have heavy rains December—February, but other parts remain mostly dry.

Tourist season: December—March: best avoided.

Surf season: October—April.

Significant Hawaiian words: *Aloha*: love, welcome. *Hula*: dance. *Lei*: flower garland. *Mana*: spiritual power. *Mu'umu'u*: long loose dress. *Taro*: food plant. *Tsunami*: tidal wave.

Food and drink: Oriental influences on what is basically American cooking. Special Hawaiian dishes include Chicken luau, chicken pieces cooked with taro tops and coconut cream Pineapple also figures prominently.

HAWAII'S EIGHT MAIN ISLANDS mean many things to its many visitors: tropical playground, wildlife paradise, geological wonder—the archipelago is a positive geological conveyor belt of volcanoes—and an exotic fusion of many different cultures. "*Aloha*," the pilot says as the planes come in to land, "welcome to Hawaii," with the authentic catch between the two i's. Hawaii is not only varied, it is a land of extremes—Mount Waialleale on Kauai is the wettest place in the world, with a rainfall of 450 inches (1.143 m), yet the Kau Desert on Hawaii Island is one of earth's driest spots. But generally, the archipelago has just about the balmiest climate on the planet, thanks to perpetual trade winds which keep it temperate. There is no bad season in Hawaii, which explains its year-round popularity—although there is a peak tourist season from December through March. Tourism brings in $20 billion annually.

As you arrive in Honolulu, on the island of Oahu after a long flight—Hawaii is 2,400 miles (3,860 km) from the U.S. mainland—you drop down into the valley that gives the island its butterfly shape. Here you could have a simply terrific vacation without moving from the capital's resort, Waikiki, with its 2 miles (3 km) of sand, skyscrapers, and exuberant beach- and nightlife. The old harbor area has recently been turned into an appealing waterfront development, with shopping plazas, restaurants, and sidewalk entertainers. But Honolulu offers more than just these; it is living history. Downtown, the statue of King Kamehameha

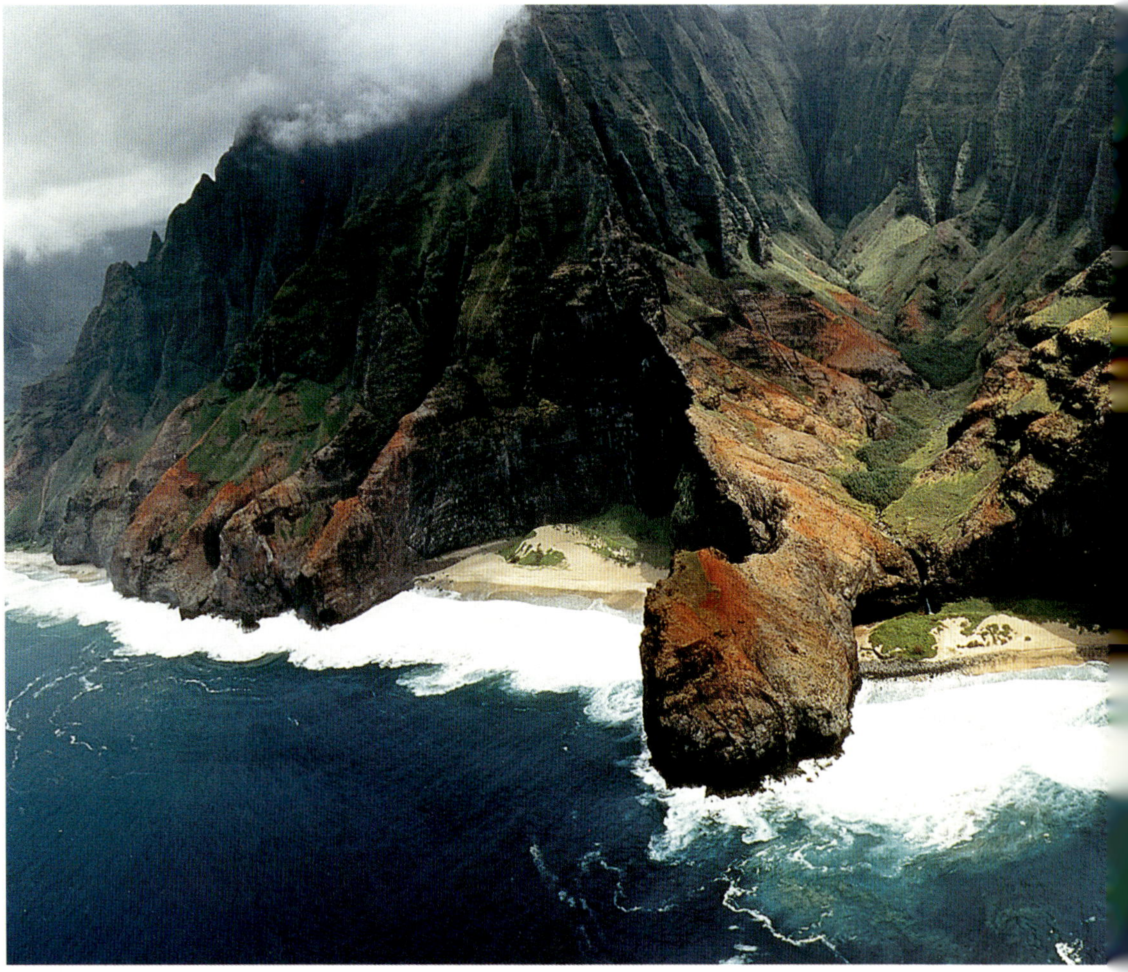

Deeply wave-cut coves and lush valleys—the one in the photograph is the lost tribe valley of Honopu—make Kauai a prime film location, as well as a destination for off-the-beaten-track travelers.

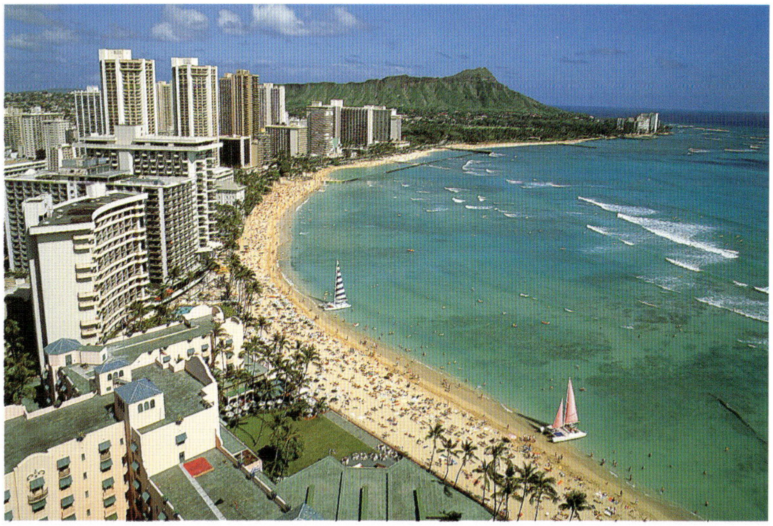

★ *Waikiki Beach, Honolulu's waterfront (left), is Hawaii at its most exuberant, and most expensive.*

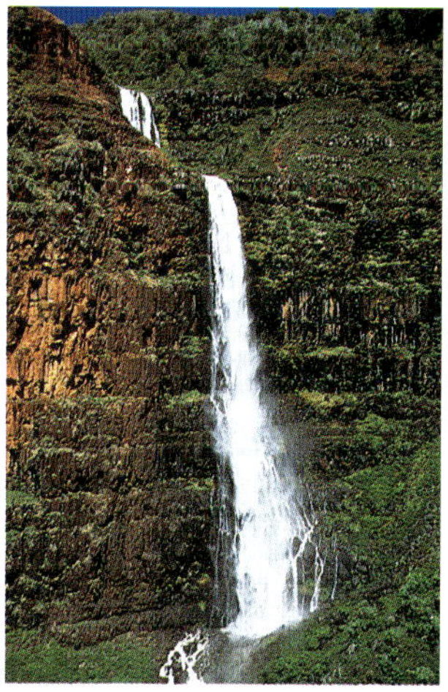

★ *Waimea Canyon's waterfall (above) is in a State park on Kauai's beautiful and remote west coast.*

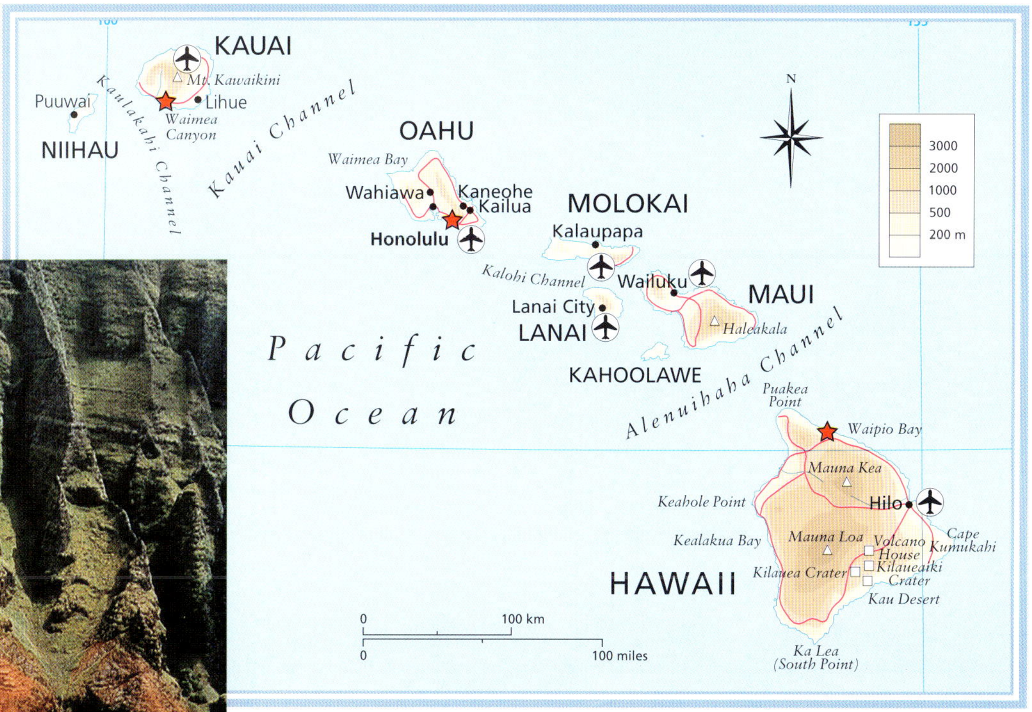

★ *Subtropical vegetation and dramatic cliffs plunge down to sandy Waipio Bay on Hawaii island (below).*

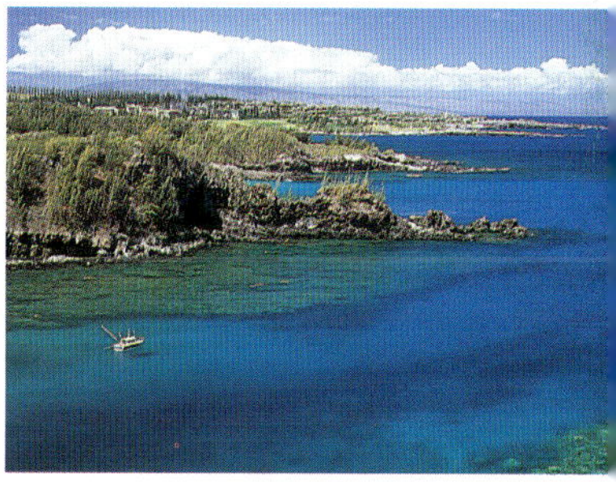

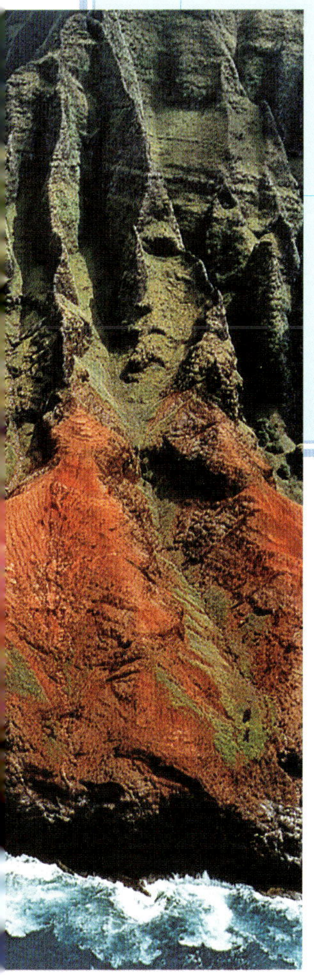

(pronounced "ka mia mia") recalls the man who unified Hawaii in 1795. Opposite stands the Iolani palace, seat of the later monarchs until the last was deposed in 1893, five years before the U.S. annexed the kingdom. (Hawaii finally became the 50th State in 1959). These are historical fossils embedded among modern buildings, with a population of Caucasians, Japanese, Hawaiians, Chinese, and Koreans making Honolulu probably more cosmopolitan than any other U.S. city.

LAND OF EXTREMES

Take a plane trip and the pattern of more than 100 islands, with eight main ones strung out over 400 miles (640 km), will open up before you. To the west lies Pearl Harbor. The U.S. first set up base there in 1908 and still mounts guard with 20 nuclear submarines. It was here, on the morning of December 7 1941, that the Japanese attacked, an event still recalled by the Arizona Memorial.

On Oahu, giant waves—up to 30 feet (9 m) high—roll into Waimea Bay on the north shore to create what some claim is the best, though also some of the riskiest, surfing on earth. Waimea, too, has its historical reminders. One is a *heiau*, or temple of human sacrifice, where fearsome tattooed warriors slew and ate three members of a British expedition in 1792.

A stay on Hawaii itself—the "Big Island"—for which the whole state is named, provides an insight into the archipelago's origins and a unique experience. The

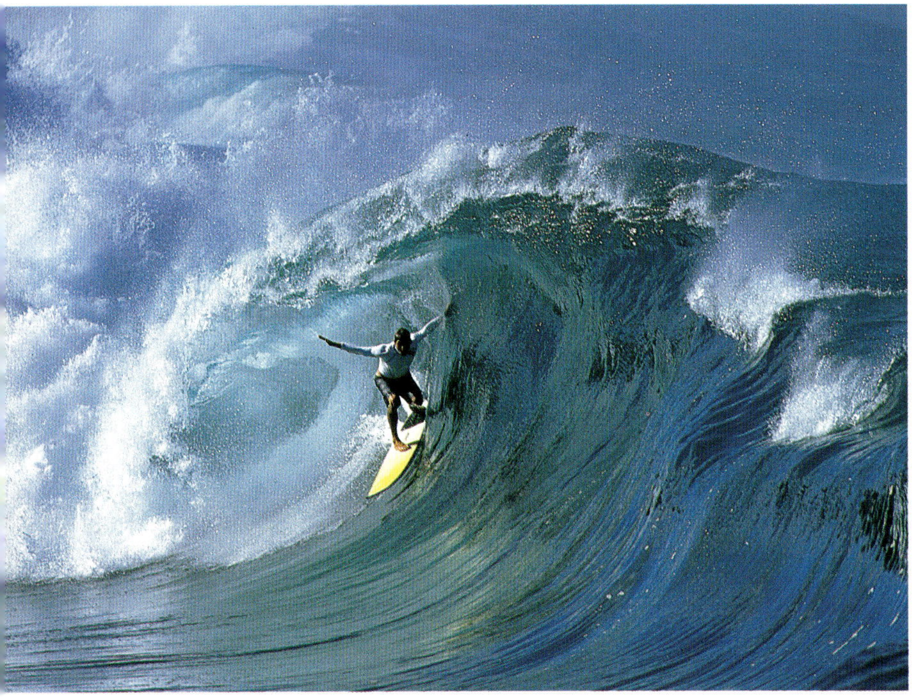

Breakers like this give Waimea on Oahu's north coast its reputation as the best surfing beach in the world—and one of the most dangerous.

entire chain owes its existence to a "hot spot" in the earth's crust, which continually vents lava, building new land on the Pacific bedrock, almost 3 miles (5 km) below. But that bedrock, driven by subterranean currents that power continental drift, is moving steadily northwest. No sooner was an island formed than it was cut off from its volcanic source, allowing another island to form. The process has been going on for 70 million years. Indeed, extinct volcanoes or "seamounts" make a line stretching 3,000 miles (4,800 km) toward the Siberian coast. The only active one is over the "hot spot" itself, on the Big Island, which is a mere 6 million years old. Contrasting with Honolulu's throngs, the Big Island is sparse and wild—130,000 people in 4,000 square miles (10,000 sq km). The contrast appears at its starkest on a drive along the bleak Saddle Road from Hilo to the extinct volcano of Mauna Kea, climbing through mists over rusty red volcanic rocks to the observatory on the summit.

But another contrast awaits to the south, in Hawaii Volcanoes National Park. Its heart, Kilauea, is still very much alive. This active caldera is merely an outlet on the flanks of the much larger Mauna Loa, at 13,677 feet (4,103m) the largest volcano in the world. Kilauea is not explosive: it seeps molten rock that oozes slowly down to the ocean. Here roads and trails cross scenes of lunar desolation, where recent flows have left undulating pillows and fields of lava. Access is monitored, but visitors can often approach steaming, newly formed flows of this easy flowing, pasty lava, known by its Hawaiian name, *a'a*.

The Big Island has its own more recent history. On the west coast is Kealakekua Bay, where Captain James Cook met his death in 1779. He had returned to the islands after a grueling journey up America's northwest coast, and been received in style. Too much style, as it turned out. When his ship was forced back into the bay by a storm, the Hawaiians turned resentful. A boat was stolen; there was a scuffle. Cook lost his temper, and fired. The crowd hacked him and four marines to death. A 27-foot (9 m) obelisk, raised in 1884, marks where he died, but only the adventurous see it close up. The road leads to the edge of the bay, but to reach the shore, and the memorial, demands a four-hour round hike down the 500-foot (150 m) cliff that shelters the bay and gives it its name, which means "pathway of the god." A good supply of water should be taken.

PEARL HARBOR REVISITED

Though most of the base is off limits, the battleship Arizona still lies where she sank, preserved as a memorial to the 900 men who died on her. At the time, the attack was thought infamous. Now, since many Japanese tourists are drawn here, the commentary on the attack emphasizes its military brilliance.

In the vast harbor that Sunday morning, all was quiet: Attended by over 100 cruisers, seven of the fleet's eight battleships lay at their jetties along "Battleship Row" (the eighth was in dry dock across the harbor). The attack caused fearful destruction: four battleships sunk, 188 planes destroyed, some 2,400 men killed. It seemed a masterstroke. In fact, historians agree, the attack was less damaging than it seemed—the dockyard installations and the oil supplies were largely untouched, and two carriers were safely at sea. Even much of the damage done was repairable—six of the eight battleships took part in the war later. More to the point, the attack instantly turned the United States from a nation struggling to stay at peace into a determined belligerent. Pearl Harbor united the nation as no other act could have done. The following day President Roosevelt, announcing war, told a cheering Congress that December 7 was "a date that will live in infamy." Britain declared war on Japan the same day. There would be no rest until the Japanese threat had been removed.

A silversword fern (right) colonizes new volcanic rock spewed out by Haeleakala on the island of Maui.

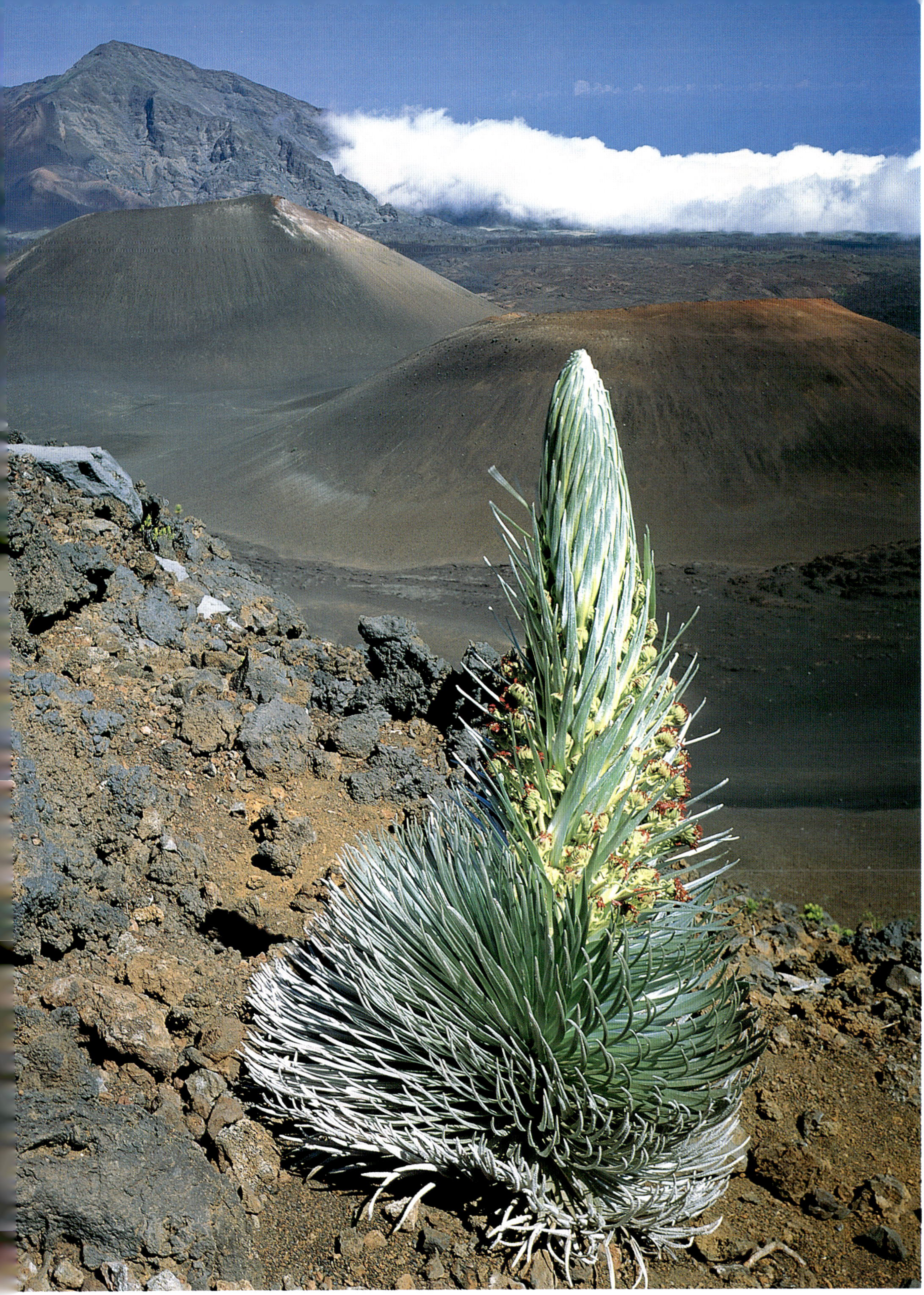

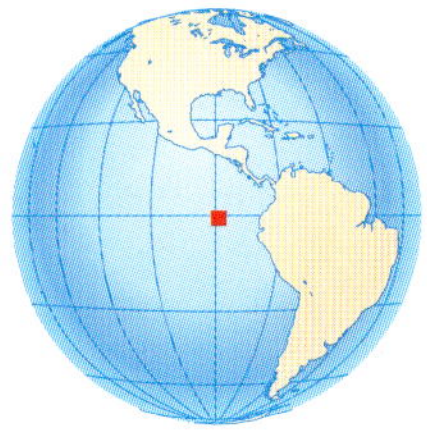

Cruising the Galapagos

Neither palm trees nor beaches lure visitors to the Galapagos Islands, but the unique chance to see close up the species that helped inspire Darwin's theory of evolution.

FACT FILE

Equipment: Good walking shoes, flashlight.

Recommended: Suncream, brimmed hat, lightweight raincoat.

Time to travel: Year-round, but May—June offers the best balance of climate, and preempts the summer rush.

Currency: Ecuadorean sucres, but take U.S. dollars, for the sucre is a very weak currency.

Mainland airports for flights: Quito, Guyaquil.

Accommodation: Limited and not cheap, so book in advance.

Food and drink: Avoid peeled fruit and salads as well as the water. Ecuador's national dish is baked guinea pig washed down by its good beer.

THE GALAPAGOS ISLANDS ARE MOSTLY rather ugly, even weird-looking islands of black volcanic rock thinly covered with scrub. They do not have many good beaches, nor particularly marvelous swimming or surfing, and certainly no great food or wine. But they do not need to enter any beauty contest, for they have one tremendous asset:they are in effect natural laboratories, where you can see evolution in action. Unique species have evolved here, which the 19th-century naturalist Charles Darwin described and publicized, and the islands have become one of the world's finest ecotourist sites. Visitors who arrive by plane or boat on the main island of Santa Cruz 500 miles (800 km) from the mainland can still see the famous Galapagos tortoises being reared at the Darwin Research Center just outside the main town Puerto Ayora. The wildlife freely visible elsewhere is even more astounding. Ferries run once or twice a week from Santa Cruz to the other main islands, San Cristobal, Floreana, and Isabela, while private boats take in smaller islands as well and an air service links Santa Cruz, San Cristobal, and Isabela.

The most rewarding, as well as the largest, island is Isabela. Although forming over half the group's total area, it is remarkably undeveloped. Its main town, Puerto Villamil, offers little to tourists, but for the adventurous there are rewards. The island has six volcanoes. In sea channels a few minutes' walk from the port, schools of white-tipped sharks swim in and out. The island's own breed of giant tortoises are on view at a Rearing Center. More live in the wild and en masse on Volcan Alcedo, a 4.5-mile (7 km) caldera. But feral goats thrived on the volcano's scrubby slopes, unbalancing the fragile ecosystem, and the site is closed to casual visitors until the goats are eradicated.

Every island—many of which still bear alternative English names, recalling the time when British and American whalers and sailors made casual use of

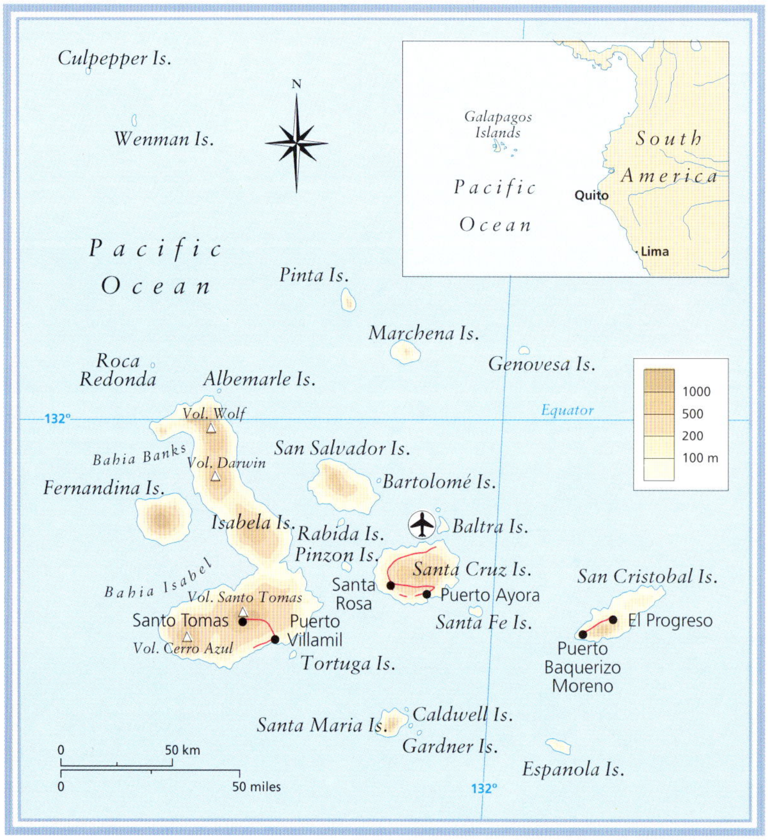

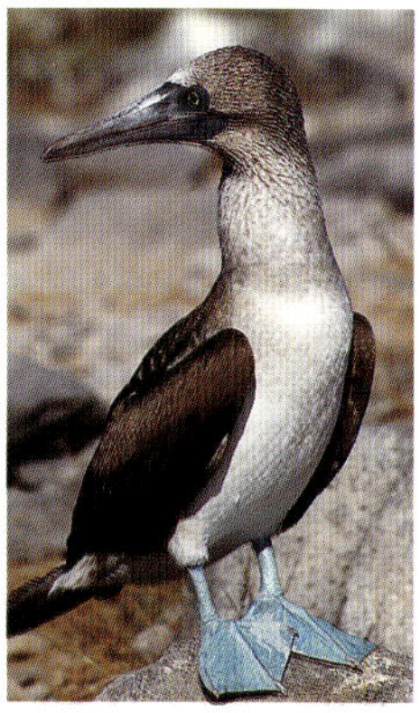

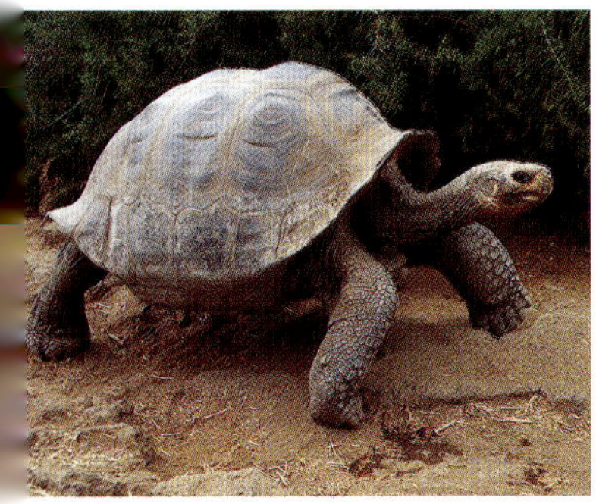

The endemic creatures of the Galapagos archipelago include giant tortoises (left), which gave the islands their name, and the blue-footed booby (above), which nests on the ground.

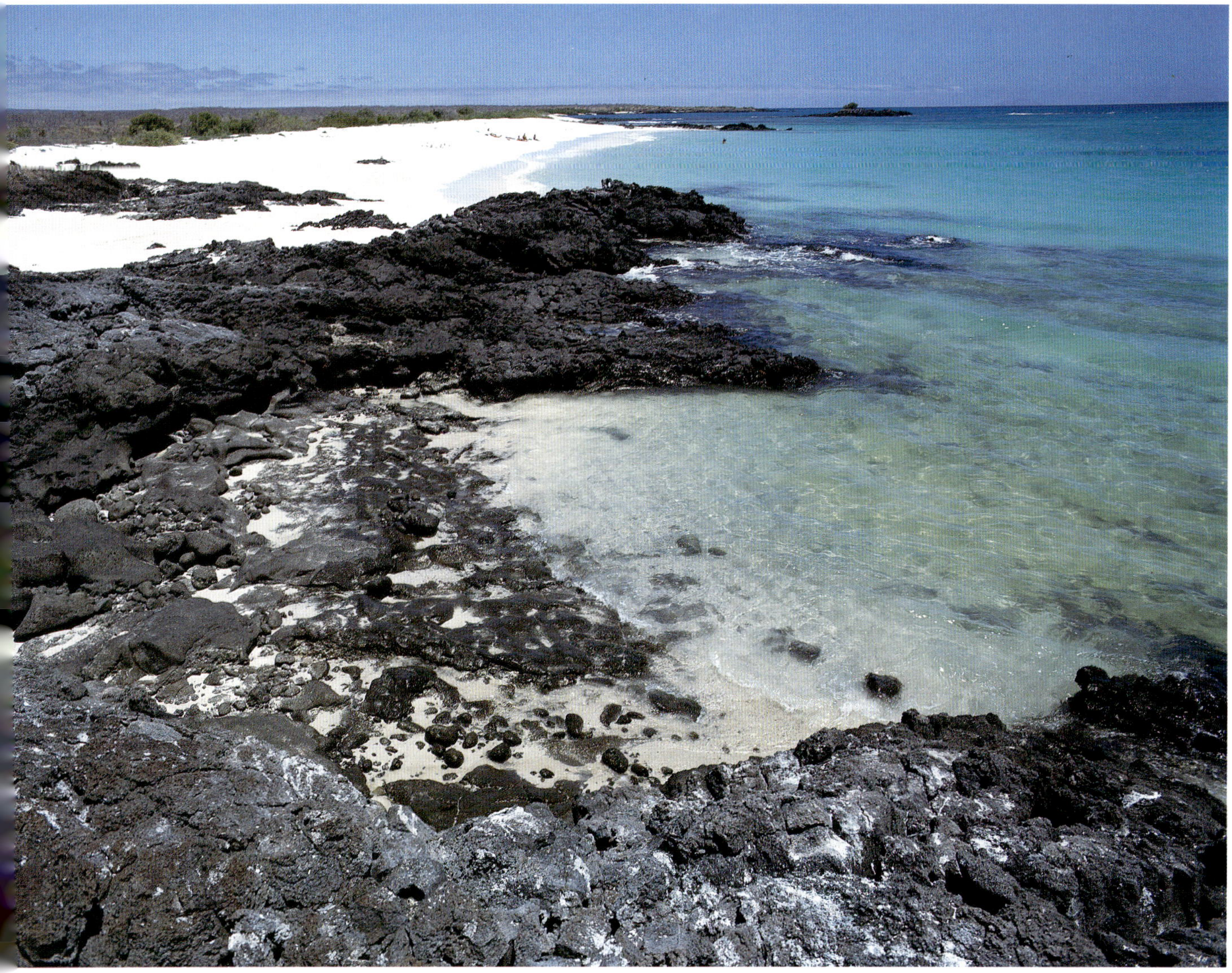

them—has its own character: Bartolomé is a kaleidoscope of red, blue, and black lava fringing shimmering beaches; Espanola has remarkably tame mockingbirds; Santa Cruz possesses one perfect beach of white sand, where you can swim, snorkel, and even swim with marine iguanas and turtles that give the bay its name, Tortuga Bay; Santiago, though assailed by voracious goats inland, has a wealth of marine creatures on its beaches; and Floreana is famous for the tempestuous life and death of three eccentric Germans in the 1930s.

VIRGIN ISOLATION

Some 4.5 million years ago, all these islands emerged as lava from a volcanic vent some 500 miles (800 km) off the coast of what is now Ecuador, forming 14 main islands and numerous pinpricks. As the rock cooled, seeds blew in from the mainland, birds blown far from home landed, and animals arrived on driftwood. In this virgin isolation, they evolved into separate species: birds minutely adapted to their own niches, giant tortoises, the world's only seagoing lizards, a local penguin,and masses of sea lions.

Many species became adapted to their own island—a flightless cormorant is found only on Isabela and Fernandina Islands—for the main islands are too far apart for easy travel between them. When Darwin saw them in September 1835, three years after they were claimed by Ecuador, his mind began to nurture a new vision of life on earth. Most famously, he was struck by the 13 endemic types of finch, still referred to as "Darwin's finches," including one that uses cactus spines to probe for food. Here, he wrote later, "we seem to be brought somewhat near to that great fact—that mystery of mysteries—the first appearance of living beings on this earth."

The result was *The Origin of Species* in 1859, with its premise that species owed their existence to natural processes—changing through time as the "fittest"

Though the main base for tourism, Santa Cruz island has a rich variety of wilderness areas, like this bay (above), which can only be reached by boat.

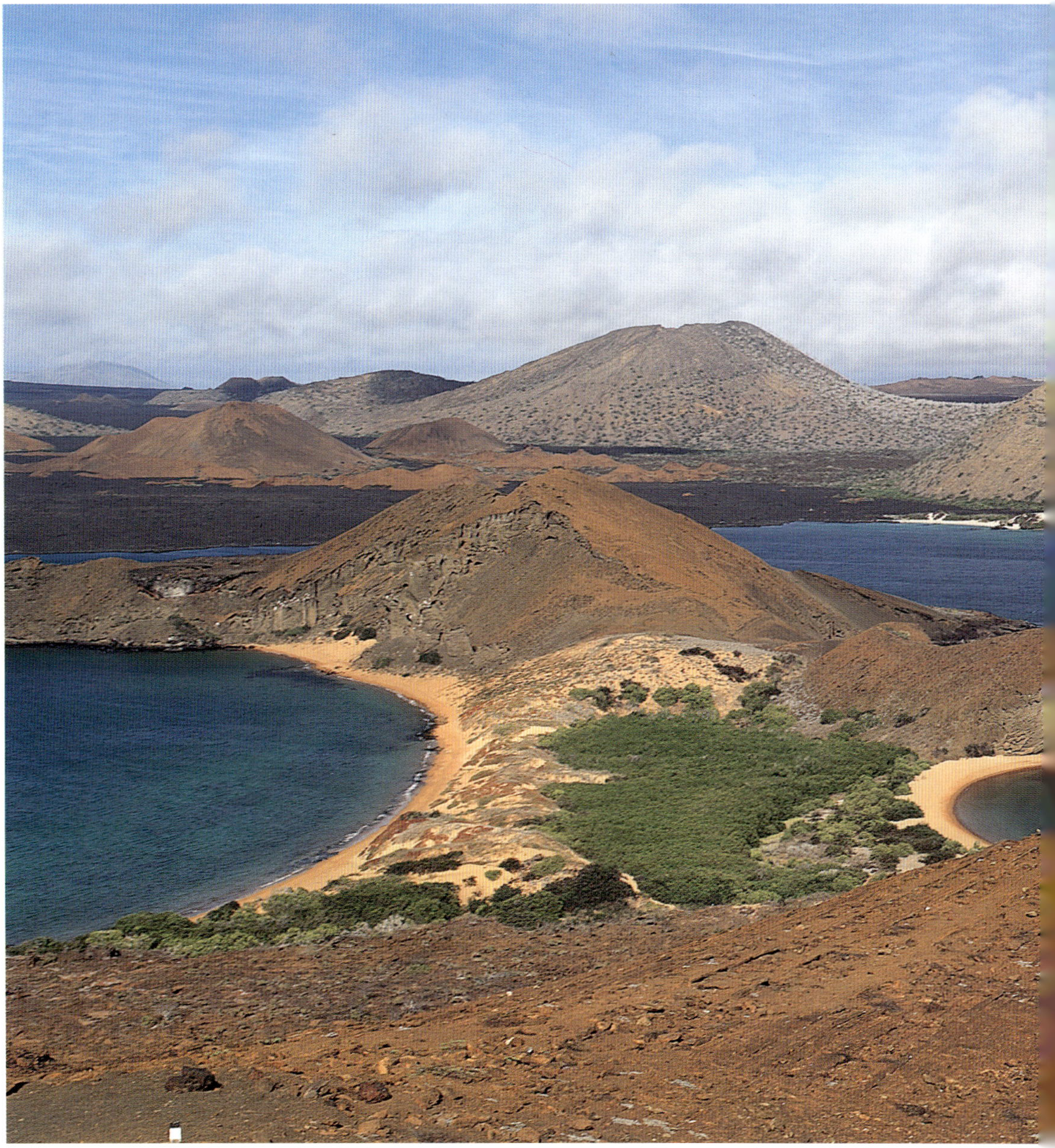

The bizarre marine iguana (below), unique to the islands, feeds on green algae and can stay underwater for up to an hour.

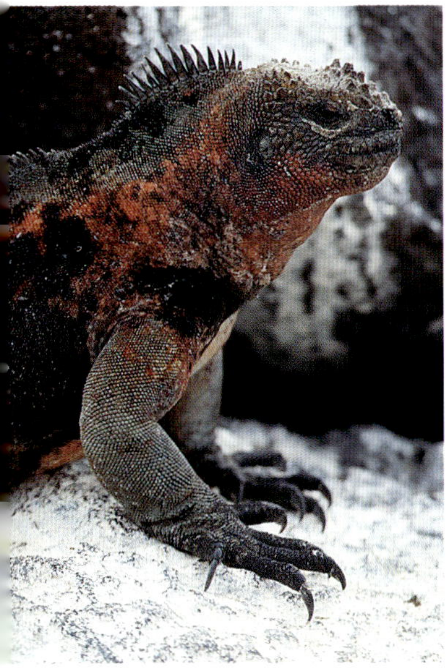

THE GALAPAGOS SEA DRAGON

The marine iguana, the world's only sea-going lizard, "is a hideous looking creature," wrote Darwin, "of a dirty black color, stupid and sluggish in its movements." Today, most people would be more guarded in their judgments, though no less amazed than Darwin at how the creatures have adapted. They live on shallow-water algae, dive to over 60 feet (20 m), and can hold their breath for an hour.

They are best seen on Fernandina, where a coastal trail leads through their colonies. Hundreds at a time can be seen scrabbling from the waves to bask on the rough lava, absorbing the heat of the sun into their spiny bodies to regain heat lost during underwater feeding, and comically sneezing out salt in powerful little water jets. Though herons and hawks snatch their young, they thrive here because of the lack of predators from outside.

survived to reproduce—rather than divine creation. The idea of evolution was not new, but never before had it been presented with such overwhelming evidence, or with such persuasive power. It unleashed a furore that has never truly subsided.

Even when Darwin was there, pressures on the wildlife were growing. The giant tortoises, which grow up to 550 pounds (250 kg) and last for weeks without water, had long been used for meat by passing sailors. Indeed, the islands themselves, originally called Las Encantadas, the Enchanted Islands, were renamed after the tortoises—Islas de los Galapagos: the Tortoise Islands. Some boats would lift several hundred on board and eat them one by one. Over time, rats and dogs from the ships destroyed their eggs. Goats ate their food plants. Three of the original 14 subspecies are now

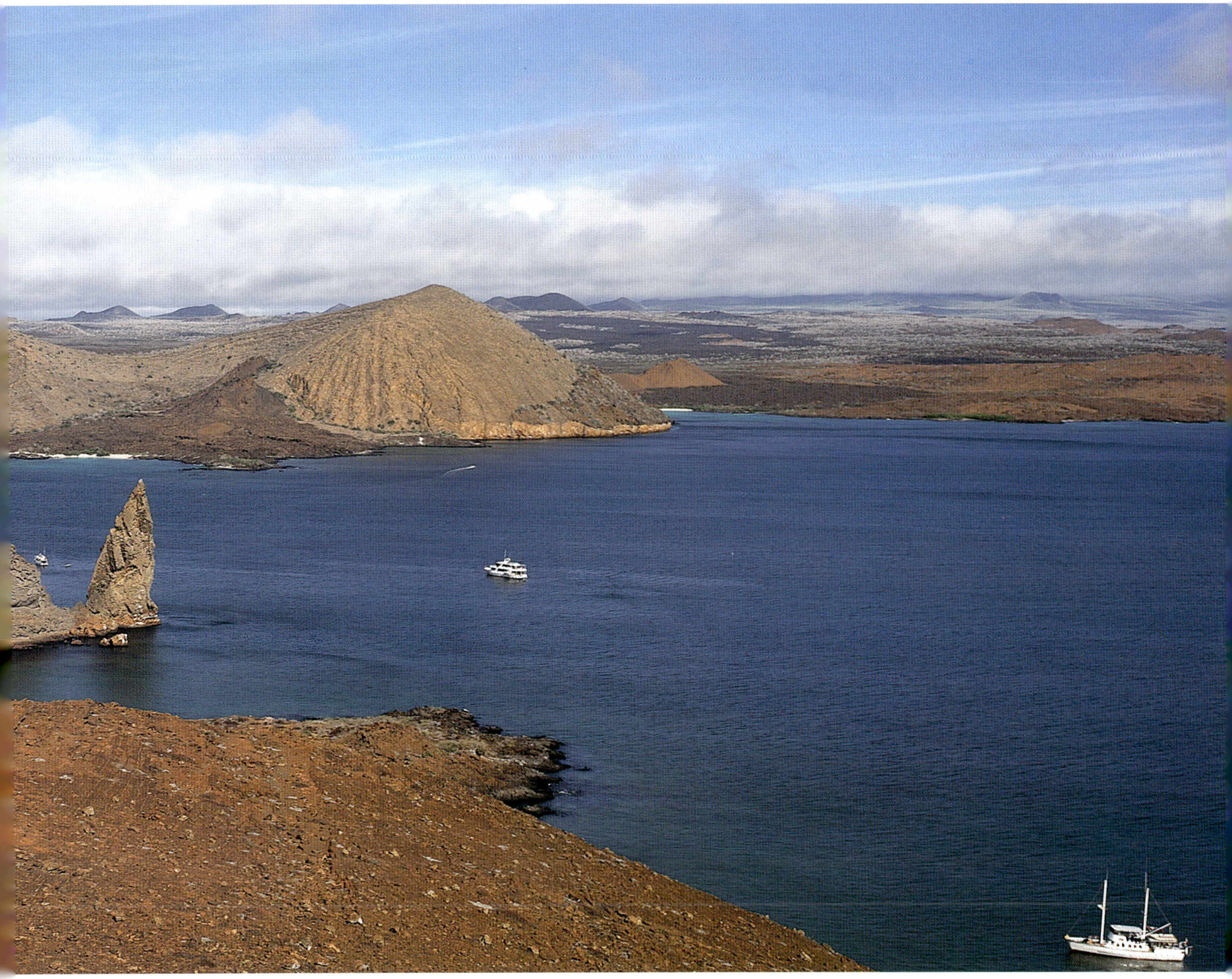

extinct, and five others endangered. But the species as a whole should survive, guaranteed by its scientific importance and its popularity.

A NATIONAL PARK

It was these human pressures, and their imported animals, that persuaded Ecuador to declare the islands a national park in 1959. Because the islands are a very popular cruise destination, with a few good hotels, access is strictly controlled, and there is a limit on numbers as well as an $80 entrance fee. Most people come in groups, often in cruise ships which originate in the U.S., but some people fly in from the capital Quito, high in the Andes. Today tourists provide most of the vital funds that allows scientists to preserve the creatures and their environments. Many local guides are wildlife experts.

Other trips can be made to misty, bird-rich forests,, to odd tunnels of rock lava—tubes—through which lava once flowed, and to mangrove inlets where turtles swim. Offshore, South Plaza Island has a beach of vociferous sea lions and a desert landscape dominated by prickly pear cacti—the local equivalent of trees.

Many of the smaller islands are hard to reach,but Fernandina, just off Isabela, is worth the effort. It is the most westerly island, the newest, and the most volcanically active (the most recent eruption was in 1995). It is also pristine: rats, goats, and dogs never made it across the narrow straits from Isabela. Visitors are required to keep it that way, in particular so that the hordes of marine iguanas can be left in peace.

Behind Bartolemé's two beaches, its volcano has produced a barren, cactus-strewn landscape that is a kaleidoscope of red, blue, and black rocks.

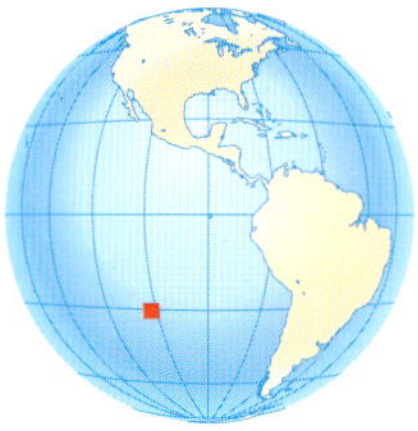

From Tahiti to Easter Island

From the lush, outgoing islands of French Polynesia to the isolated, and enigmatic Easter Island: the two are separated by a vast expanse of ocean, but linked by a common people—and by air.

A DOT IN A MAP OF THE SOUTH PACIFIC marks the world's loneliest inhabited island and a spectacular and extraordinary archaeological sight. On the 10-mile (16 km) long Easter Island—or *Rapa Nui* (big Rapa), over 800 vast stone *moai* (statues) stare inland over grassy, treeless landscapes, their backs to precipitous cliffs and shark-infested seas.

Easter Island is a volcanic pimple in the ocean, well over 2,000 miles (3,500 km) from the South American coast, and the Polynesian island of Pitcairn, 2,250 miles (3,622 km) miles to the northwest.

The mysterious Stone Age moai, carved from the island's dark volcanic rock, are up to 30 feet (10 m) tall, angular of nose, chin, and brow. They hail from a time when the island was covered with rainforests dominated by giant palm trees and settled by a thriving community. The first inhabitants, arriving from Polynesia in the early centuries A.D., made clearings in

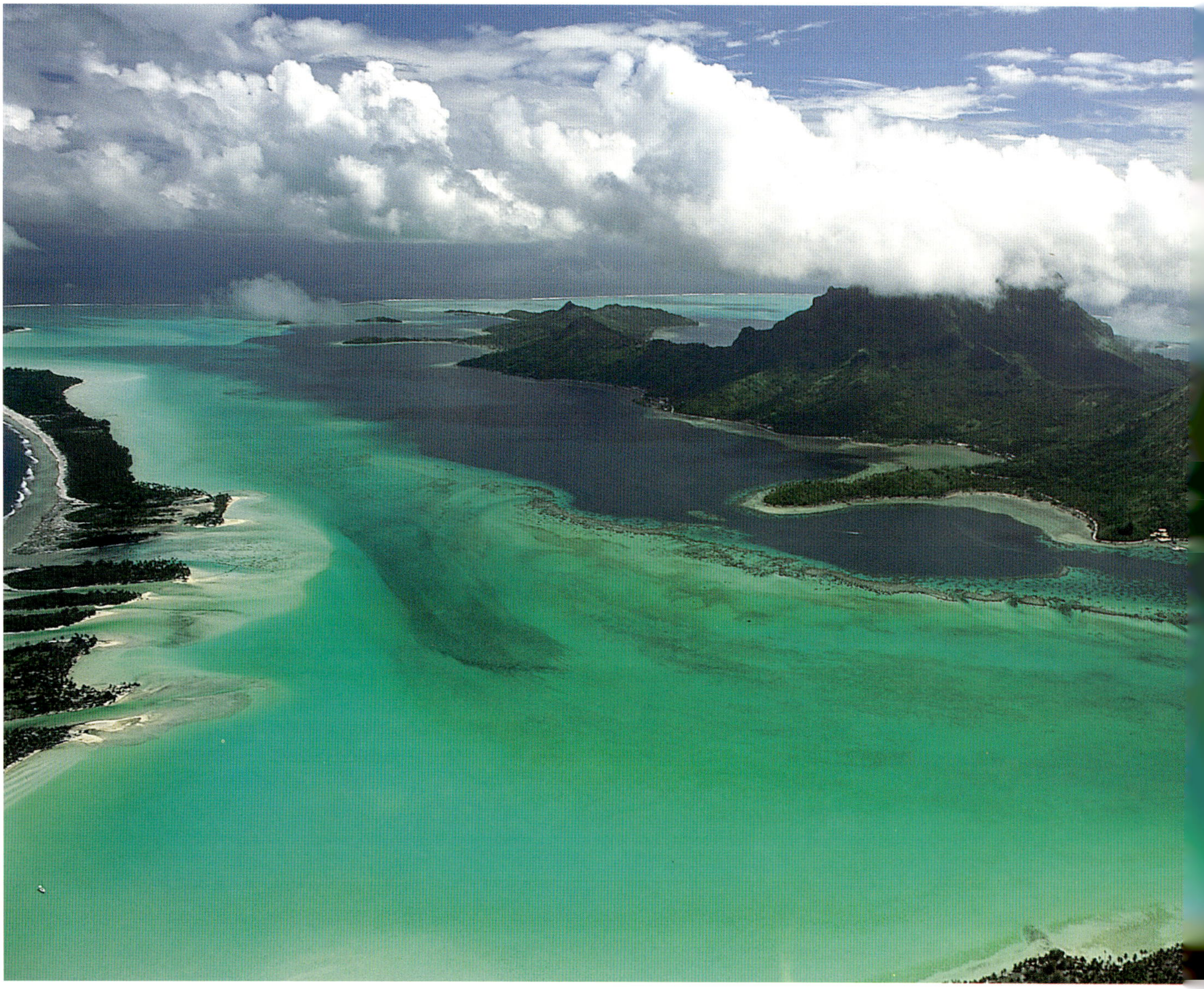

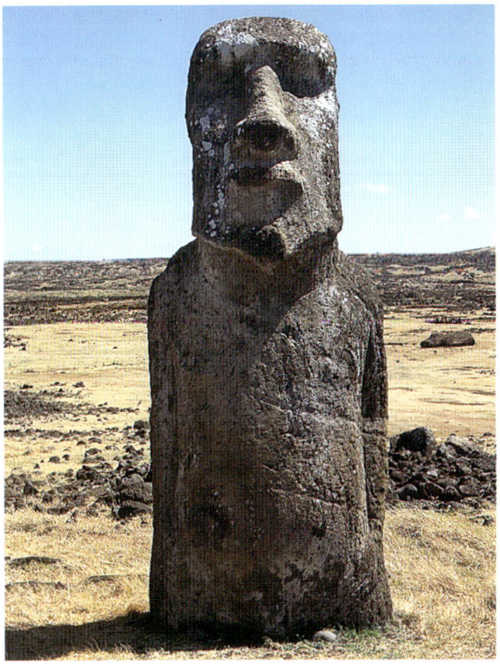

the forest, planted crops, and developed a distinctive culture and religion which peaked around the beginning of the 16th century. Though the trees—there is only one species left on the island today—the crops, and all bar 1,000 or so inhabitants, have long gone, the tutelary gods built by the Polynesian settlers remain, stark against a barren land.

The island's decline perhaps has alarming lessons for all of humankind. The demands of the population—by A.D. 1500 reaching around 20,000—consumed what was left of the forest. Without trees, there were no more canoes; fishing became impossible; soil erosion set in, and harvests failed. The starving people fought over what remained. The whole culture collapsed and many people died. When the first Europeans arrived in 1722, a mere 2,000 were left, who could provide the merest inkling of their past, leaving many mysteries that still remain to be solved.

Enigmatic statues on Easter Island (above) are evidence of a culture that was in its death throes when Europeans arrived.

SCULPTURAL AND OTHER CHALLENGES

The statues were hewn in the vast Rano Raraku quarry in the crater and some 400 part-finished statues, including the 66-foot (20 m) tall El Gigante, still lie there today. The completed figures were hauled to the edges of the island, and erected on platforms 7-33 feet (2-10 m) high, most facing inward to watch over the settlements.

Today's visitors can rent horses or four-wheel drive vehicles to search for shards of volcanic glass (once used as spearheads) among the windswept grass, explore the ceremonial village of Orongo, with its wealth of rock art, perched high on a cliff between the volcanic crater and the coast, and the 1,764-foot (536 m) Rano Kao volcano, with its quarries and crater swamps. And you can trace the awesome route of the young men who each year negotiated a sheer 1,000-foot (300 m) cliff face and swam across shark-infested

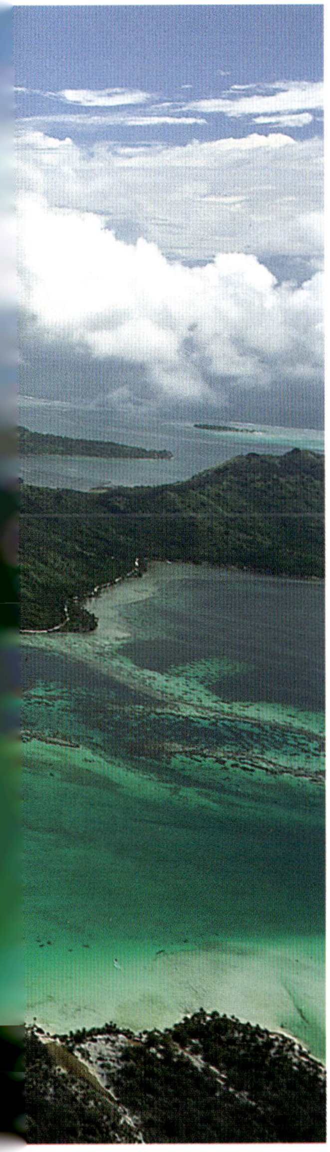

Bora Bora (left) has claim to be the most beautiful island in French Polynesia, a romantic stopover for anyone visiting Easter Island (below).

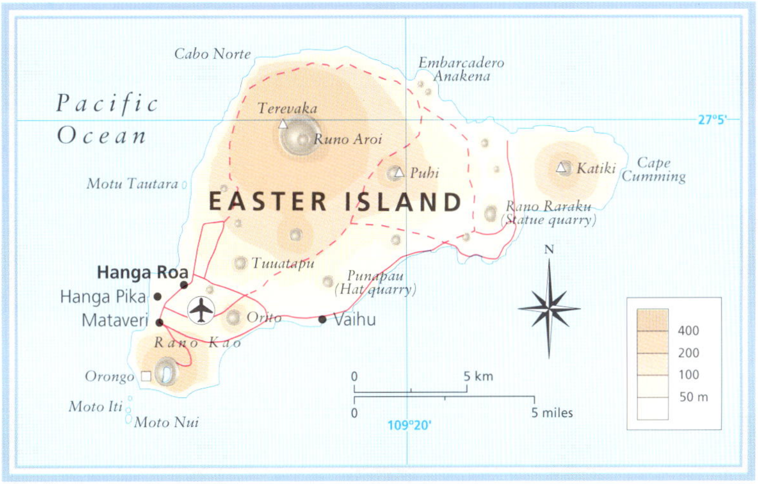

FACT FILE

How to get there: Easter Island by air twice weekly from Tahiti, November-February; once a week the rest of the year. Tahiti has flight connections to Los Angeles and Sydney.

Status: Chile administers Easter Island as a conservation site; Tahiti is an autonomous French territory.

Languages: On Easter Island, Spanish or English; on Tahiti, Tahitian, French, with English widely understood.

Best time to visit: May through October (dry season).

Water temperature: About 82°F (2° C) year round at Tahiti.

Currency: On Easter Island: Chilean Pesos. On Tahiti French Pacific Francs (CFP), fixed to the French Franc.

Health: Care should be taken with drinking water in both places but there are no major health risks.

What to bring: Sunscreen, a hat, sunglasses, insect repellent .

Food and drink: Rather limited on Easter Island. On Tahiti French, Chinese, Italian, and Vietnamese restaurants compete. Popular local dishes include smoked bread fruit, mountain bananas, fafa (spinach) with young sucking pig, varied seafood.

waters to the islet of Motu Nui to collect the egg of the sooty tern. The master of the first one back became the chief or "birdman."

THE POLYNESIAN TRIANGLE

The historically logical and most rewarding setting-off point for Easter Island is five hours' flight away, in French Polynesia. It was from here, 1,000 years ago, that the Polynesians, taking animals and plants in hardy double-hulled canoes, spread to Easter Island and north to Hawaii.

The first time Westerners saw Tahiti, they thought they had found a paradise. Palm-fringed beaches, good food, a lush climate, beautiful people, and sex for the asking—no wonder it drew artists (most notably Paul Gauguin) and writers like Herman Melville, Robert Louis Stevenson, and Somerset Maugham. South Pacific became the stuff of dreams, a musical waiting to be written.

Captain James Cook put Tahiti and its islands on the map in 1767. Westerners changed Tahiti's history forever, for they brought weapons and new diseases, and opened the way for missionaries, whalers, and traders. Paradise was quickly lost, and never rediscovered. Tahiti, though the biggest island of French

From the crater of Rano-raraku (below), Easter Islanders mined the soft volcanic rock which they made into statues.

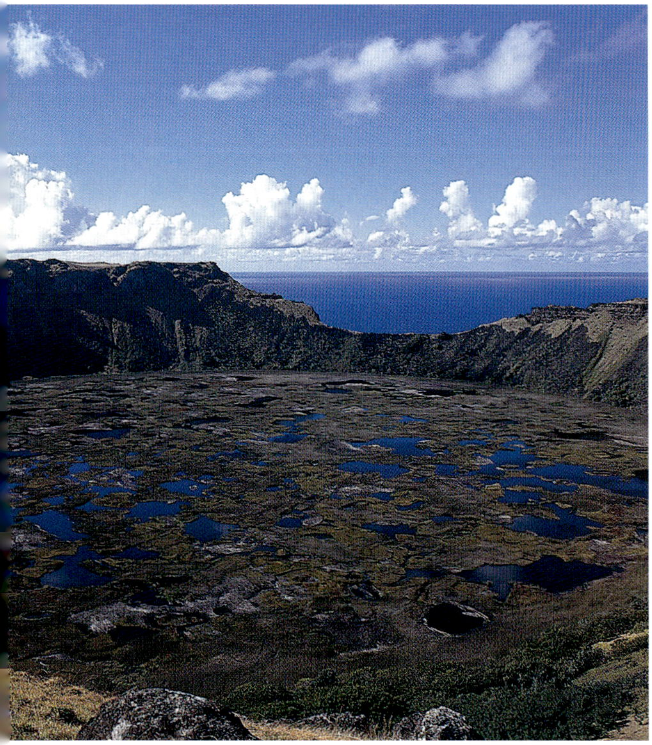

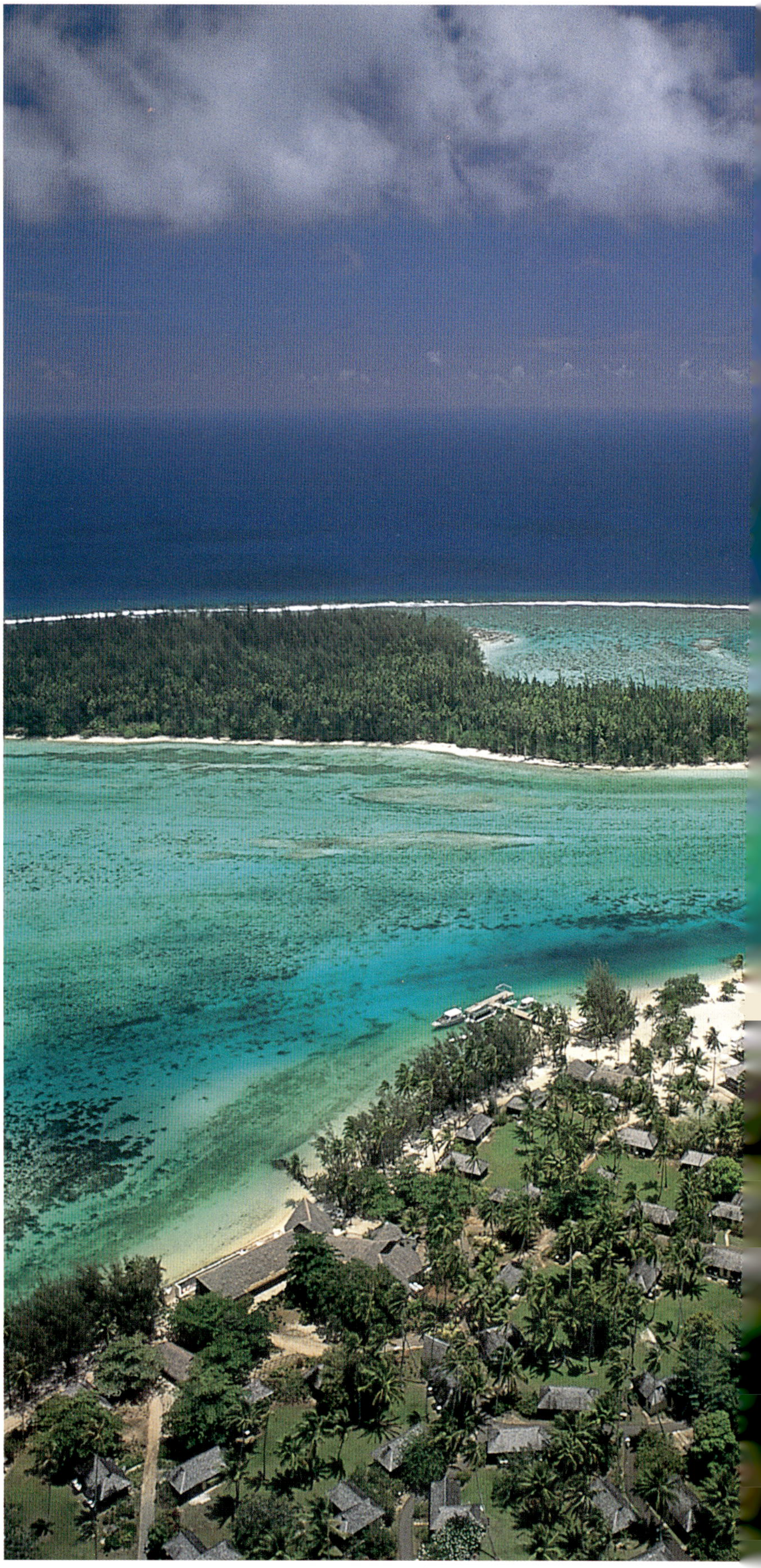

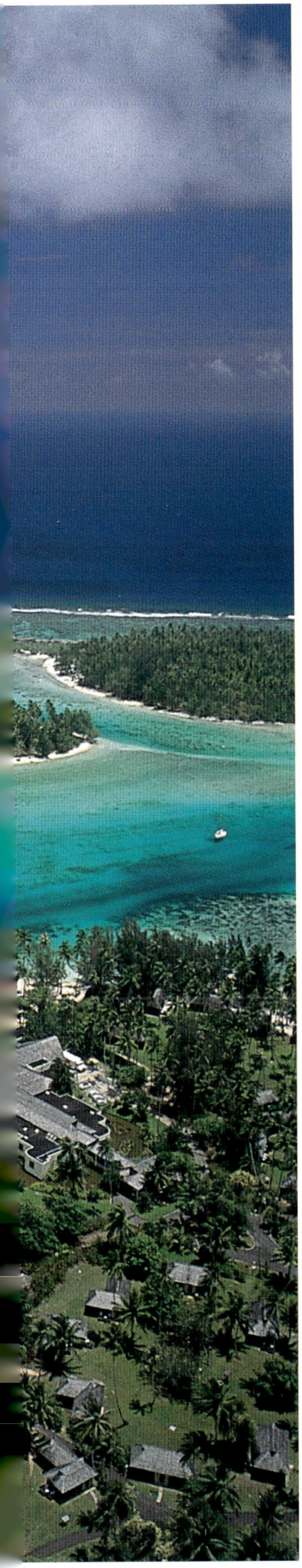

The dazzling white beaches of Moorea (left), a 7 minute flight or 45-minute ferry journey from Tahiti, lie beneath volcanic peaks.

Polynesia, is not typical of the Territory's 118 islands. Scattered over 1.5 million square miles (almost 4 million sq km) of ocean, these are extinct volcanoes, circled by coral reefs. In some, the central cone remains; in most it has eroded away, leaving a halo of coral, an atoll. The 200,000 inhabitants, mostly living on Tahiti, depend on coconuts, pearls, tourists, and, until recently, the salaries of those working on France's nuclear testing program.

PEARL OF THE PACIFIC

Of all the Polynesian islands, Bora Bora is still the one to die for. This spectacular half-drowned volcano, with its soaring green cliffs and turquoise coral seas, consists of a main island which juts up like a tropical Gibraltar, though about twice the size, and a surrounding reef. There is only one navigable channel, and Bora Bora is a natural harbor, something which has defined most of the island's recent history. It was the model for James Michener's Bali-h'ai in his *Tales of the South Pacific*,and under this name achieved further fame in the Rodgers and Hammerstein musical *South Pacific*. It only achieved such fame, of course, because Michener was there with 6,000 other U.S. servicemen who arrived in 1942 to build a stepping stone toward Japan. When they departed in 1946, they left behind a huge runway that was Tahiti's international airport until 1961. Coastal guns and an old radar station are still in place.

Planes arrive several times a day from Papeete and other islands, and two ferries make the journey three times a week. Whether they transfer by catamaran from the airport to the main town of Vaitape or arrive by sea, most visitors come for the scuba diving, cruising, and beach life. After a three-day diving course a new arrival can swim alongside giant manta rays in the lagoon, or encounter moray eels which guard the lagoon's entrance. One excitement for those out picnicking on the dazzling white reef sands is shark feeding. It won't cost you an arm and a leg—the lagoon's sharks are used to free meals and are quite safe.It is also possible to rent four-wheel drive vehicles to explore old Second World

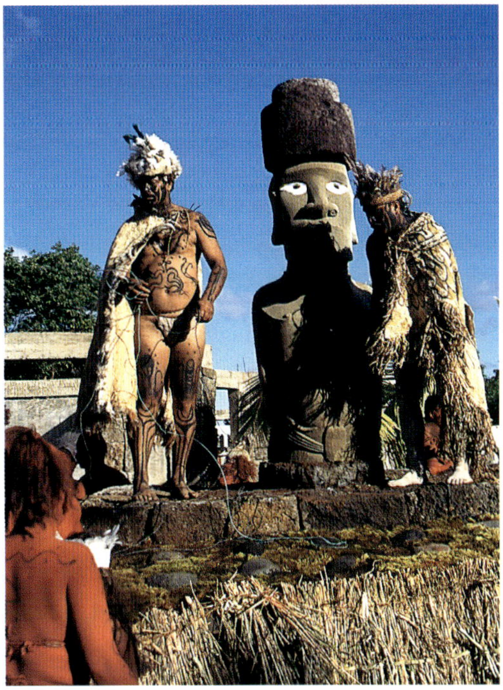

Easter Islanders recall their ancestral culture in an annual festival.

War tracks, trips that allow visitors to see ancient *maraes*, coral bases for temples in use before the missionaries came in the 1800s. Game fishers can charter boats of up to 60 feet (18 m). In mid November, there's the final leg of a three-day, 72-mile (116 km) canoe race, when 60 or so six-man pirogues pound between four islands, arriving after a 32- mile (52 km) crossing in Bora Bora to the beat of drums and wild yells from the thousands lining the shallows.

Bora Bora, like Tahiti, is no pristine wilderness. Even ignoring the scars left by the Second World War, present-day pressures have left their marks: a Club Med abandoned after a cyclone, a hotel site abandoned when the cash ran out. But those volcanic peaks, the cloak of lush green, the dazzling beaches, the iridescent lagoon—they are the stuff of reality, as well as dreams.

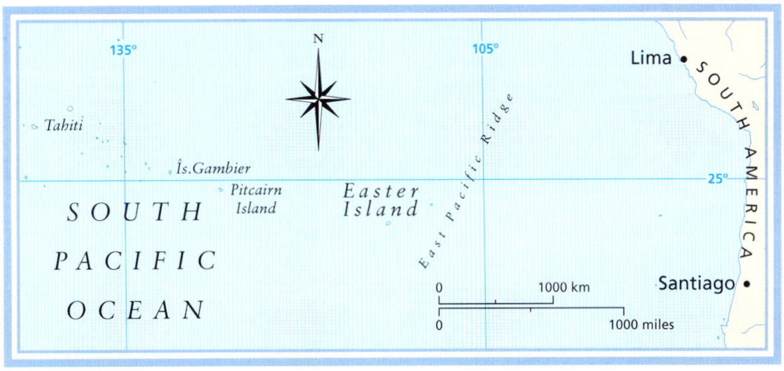

Easter Island belongs to Chile, over 2,000 miles (3,500 km) east.

Directory of useful addresses

NORTH AMERICA

Banff
Alberta Tourism, PO Box 2500, Edmonton, Alberta T5J2Z4
Tel: +1 (403) 427 4321 / (1-800) 661 8888

Yosemite
Visitors' Center, Yosemite Village
Tel: +1 (916) 372-229
Wilderness Center, PO Box 577, Yosemite National Park, 95389
California Office of Tourism, 801 K St, Suite 1600, Sacramento, CA 95814-3520
Tel: +1 (916) 322 2881/(1-800) 862 2543

Grand Canyon
Grand Canyon National Park Visitor Center
Tel: +1 (516) 638-7888

Florida
Everglades National Park, 40001 State Road, 9336, Homestead, FL 33034-6733
Tel: +1 (305) 242-7700
Walt Disney World
Tel: +1 (407) 824-4500

CENTRAL AND SOUTH AMERICA

Heart of Mexico
Tourist Office, Amberes 54, Mexico City
Tel: + 52 5 525 9380

La Ruta Maya
Tourist Office, Amberes 54, Mexico City
Tel: + 52 5 525 9380
Inguat, 7 Avenida 1-17, Centro Civico, Zona 4, Guatemala City, Guatemala
Tel: + 502 331 1333
Belize Tourist Board, 83 N. Front Street, Belize City, Belize, Tel: + 502 02 77213

Costa Rica
Costa Rican Institute of Tourism (Instituto Costarricense de Turismo), Plaza de la Cultura, Avenida Central, C3/5, San José, Costa Rica, Tel: + 506 222 1090

The Amazon
EMAMTUR, Av. Sete de Setembro 1546, Manaus, Brazil
Tel: + 55 (0)92 633 983 / 633 2850

Inca Trail
Municipal Tourist Office, Portal Mantas 188, Plaza de Armas, Cuzco, Peru
Tel: +51 (0) 84 263 176

AFRICA

Egypt and the Nile
Tourist Information Office, Adly Street, Cairo, Egypt, Tel: + 202 391 3454

Timbuktu and the Mali
No official tourist offices but American Express Offices also house:
The Africa Transervices, Avenue du Fleuve, BP 2917, Barnako, Mali
Tel: + 223 22 24 81

Marrakesh and the Atlas Mountains
170 Avenue Mohammed V.
Tel + (212) 04 432097
Ouarzazate
Boulevard Mohammed V.
Tel + (212) 04 882485

Victoria Falls/Okavango
Tourist Center, Mosi O Tunuya Road, PO Box 60343, Livingstone (Maramba), Zambia, Tel: + 2603 3214040415
Zimbabwe Tourist Board, 7th Floor, 3 Anchor House, 54 Jason Moyo Avenue, PO Box 3Y286, Harare, Zimbabwe
Tel: + 0758 73014
Tourist Information, BAG 0047, Gaborone, Botswana
Tel: + 267353024

Rift Valley
Kenya National Tourist Board, PO Box 54666, Nairobi, Kenya, Tel: + 3310130
Tanzanian Tourist Board, PO Box 2485, Dar es Salaam, Tanzania
Tel: + 255 51 111 244

MEDITERRANEAN AND THE NEAR EAST

Crusader Castles
Ministry of Tourism, rue Victoria, Damascus, Syria, Tel: + (11) 223 7940;
Fax: + (11) 224 2636
Middle East Tourism, PO Box 201, rue Fardoss, Damascus, Syria
Tel: + 963 (11) 221 1876;
Fax + 963 (11) 224 6545

Istanbul
Touring and Automobile Club of Turkey, I. Oto Sanayi Sitesi Yani Seyrantepe, 4. Levent, Istanbul
Tel: + 90 212 282 7874-75;
Fax: + 90 212 282 8042

The Meteora, Greece
National Tourist Office of Greece (EOT), Sindagma, Athens, Greece,
Tel: + 30 1 322 3545.
Trekking Hellas, Filellinon 7, 105 57 Athens, Greece
Tel: + 30 1 325 0853 / 325 1958
Fax: + 30 1 323 4548
Email: trekking@compulink.gr

Venice
Italian State Tourist Office (ENIT), Piazza San Marco, Venice, Italy
Tel: + 39 41 (0)522 6356

Renaissance Italy
Florence - Via Cavour 1r, Firenze, Italy, Tel: + 39 (0)55 290 832
Siena - Via di Citte 43, Siena, Italy
Tel: + 39 (0)577 42 209

Moorish Spain
Andalucian Tourist Board (Junta de Andalucia Turismo), Plaza Mariana de Pineda 10 bajo, Granada, Spain
Tel: + 34 58 22 66 88

NORTHERN EUROPE

Provence
Parc National Regional du Luberon, 1 place Jean-Jaures 84400 APT
Tel: + 33 490 74 08 55
Comité Departemental de Tourisme de Vaucluse, La Balance, Place Campana B.P. 147, 84008 Avignon
Tel: +33 490 86 43 42;
Fax: + 33 490 86 86 08

Chamonix, France
Office de Tourisme - Place du Triangle de l'Amitié - BP25 - 74400 Chamonix.
Tel: + 33 (0)4 50 53 00 24;
Fax + 33 (0)4 50 53 58 90
Email: info@chamonix.com

Cities of Middle Europe
Vienna Tourist Board (Wiener Tourismusverband), Kärntnerstrasse 38, Wien
Tel: + 43 (0)1 513 8892
Prague Information Service (Prazske informacni sluzba), Na prikope 20, Nove Mesto, Prague 1
Tel: + 4202 54 44 44
Krakow Tourist Office, ul. Pawia 8, Krakow, Poland
Tel: + 48 (0)12 221 921

Norway
Norway Information Centre (Norges Informasjonssenter), Vestbaneplassen 1, Oslo, Norway
Tel: + 47 22 83 00 50

The Western Isles, Scotland
Scottish Tourist Board, 23 Ravelston Terrace, Edinburgh EH4 3EU
Tel: + 44 (0)131 332 2433

The West Coast of Ireland
Irish Tourist Board (Bord Filte), Information Service, PO Box 273 IRL-Dublin 8
Tel: + 353 1 602 4000;
Fax +353 1 602 4100

NORTHERN ASIA

General
Steppes East, Castle Eaton, Cricklade, Wiltshire, England SN6 6JU
Tel: (01285) 810267

Gobi Desert
No official tourist offices abroad. Contact local embassies and specialist tour operators. In Ulaan Baatar: Bizinfo, 4th Floor, Ulaan Baatar Hotel
Tel: + 324 237

Transiberia
Intourist Office, 7 Pereulok Boitsova, St Petersburg, Tel: + 812 321 1356
Intourist Office, Milivitinsky Pereulok, Moscow, Tel: + 7095 924 3050

CENTRAL ASIA

Karakoram Highway
CITS (see China)
Pakistan Tourism Development Corporation (PTDC), House No 2, Street 61, F7/4, PO Box 1465, Islamabad-44000
Tel: + 92 51 811011

Kathmandu-Lhasa
Officially tours are discouraged. Contact private tour agencies.

INDIA AND SOUTHEAST ASIA

Angkor Wat
Cambodia has virtually no official tourist information. Use guide books and travel agencies.

China
Both the China International Travel Service (CITS) and the China Travel Service (CTS) have offices in major capitals. CITS in Beijing: CITS, Beijing Tourist Building, 28 Jianguomenwai Dajie, Tel: +86 411 515 8570

India
The Indian government has tourist offices in Sydney, Ontario, Kuala Lumpur, Amsterdam, Singapore, Bangkok, London, Los Angeles and New York. Government of India Tourist Office, 88 Janpath, Delhi (332-0005). Major cities have RTDC (state tourist) offices. Main office: RTDC, Platform 1, Railway Station, Jaipur
Tel: + 91 141315 714

AUSTRALIA AND NEW ZEALAND

Cradle Mountain
Tasmanian Travel and Information Center, 20F Davey Street, Hobart
Tel: + 61 (0)3 6230 8233
Visitors Center, Cradle Mountain Lodge (at entrance to park)
Tel: + 61 (0)3 6492 1110

Barrier Reef
Queensland Government Travel Center, corner Adelaide and Edward Street, Brisbane
Tel: +61 (0)7 13 1801
Far North Queensland Promotion Bureau, corner Grafton and Hartley Street, Cairns
Tel: + 61 (0)7 4051 3588

Uluru/Ayers Rock
Ayers Rock Resort Tourist Information Center, Ayers Rock
Tel: + 61 (0)8 8956 2240

Central Australia
Central Australian Tourism Industry Association, Gregory Terrace, Alice Springs
Tel: +61 (0)8 8952 5800

New Zealand
New Zealand Tourism Board , 89 The Terrace, PO Box 95, Wellington
Tel: + 64 4 472 8860

THE PACIFIC

Tahiti
Tahiti Tourist Board (GIE), Fare Manihini, Blvd Pomare, Papeete, Tahiti
Tel: + (689) 50 57 00

Galapagos
Corporacion Ecuatoriana de Turismo (CETUR), Eloy Alfaro 1214 and Pasaje Carlos Tobar, Quito
Tel: + (02) 229 330

Index

Credits

Quarto would like to thank and acknowledge the following sources for the use of pictures on the following pages in this book

Key
t = *top*
b = *bottom*
r = *right*
l = *left*
c = *centre*

Alternative Travel Group, Oxford: 106 tl; Axiom Photographic Agency: 49 tl, 50 tl, 51, 69 tr, 70 tl, 70 bl, 105 l, 105 r, 106-7, 151 tl, bl & br; 152 l, 154 tr, 154 bl, 158, 159 br, 160 tl, 164-5, 186 t, 186-7, 187 br; Mark Azavedo: 58, 90 bl (David Forman); 204 tr (David Forman), 206-7 (David Forman), 220 bl, 221 r; Clark/Clinch: 20 t, 28 bl, 69 tr, 91b, 102 t, 104 bl, 120, 132 bl, 142-3; 219; Sylvia Cordaiy: 6-7, 14, 24 tl, 60-1, 62 t, 81 br, 172-3, 179 t & b, 177-8, 178 tl & bl, 181 tl, 190, 191 br, 192 t, 193,196 bl; Cameron-Cooper: 104, 154 tl; Ecoscene: 15, 20 b, 23 rr, 27 r, 54t, 74-5, 76, 93, 150, 152-3, 174, 192 b; ffotograff: 112-3, 113 tl, tr, & br, 114-5; Lesley Garland: 121 tl & tr; 122 tl; Nick Hanna: 27 bl, 180-1, 191 tr & bl, 200; Robert Harding: 42 br; Image Bank: 38-9; 139 l, 146 tl, 155, 165 br, 184, 208-9; 209 tr & br; 214-5; Image Select: 198, 200-1; Sally Jenkins:10 bl, 54 bl; Joel Photo Library: 3, 32, 33 tl & bl, 91 tr, 94, 108-9, 123 br, 124 tl, 137, 141 r, 142 tl, 175 b, 185, 199; Geoffrey Roy/Kaa: 67 tl, 68 tl, 75 tr, 77 tr 7 br; John Man: 6 l, 134-5, 144-5, 145 tr, 146 7; John Miles: 156 tl, 184-5; David Noble: 18-9, 21 r, 24-5, 82-3; 88-9, 90-1, 131 br, 132 tl; Papilio: 48 l & r; 53; 54 tl, 66-7, 67 tr, 68 - 9, 76 b, 78 tr, 80, 81 tr, 94 tl, 122 bl, 166-7, 181 br; Pictor: 130; Pictures Colour Library: 10-11, 40-1, 42 tl, 43 l & r, 52 l, 55 t, 63, 68-9, 89 t, 160 cl, 209 tl; C. Schuller: 111 l & r; Skyscan: 204 bl, 124 bl, 119, 121; The Stock Market: 31; Tony Stone: 21 l, 32 t & b, 33, 56, 64 -5, 140-1, 147 tr, 156-7, 200 bl, 210 tl, 211; Travel Ink: 16 l, 16-7; 17 br, 26, 34 tl, 47 tr, 49 bl, 57, 59, 92, 114 tl, 118, 121 br & b, 123 tl & tr- 148-9, 162 bl, 164 tl, 176, 195 tr, 196-7; The Travel Library: 22-3, 27 t, 28 r & tl, 33 tr, 34 r & bl, 44-5, 46-7, 47 br, 70 tr, 78 bl, 79, 95 tl, bl & br, 96t & b, 97, 103 l & r, 104-5, 104 tl, 109r, 110 l & r, 120, 123, 131 tl & tr; 133, 139 tr & br, 151 tr, 163, 175 t, 182 t & b, 183, 205, 207 r, 208-9; 212 l & r, 214, 218-9, 220 r, 122-3, 124-5; Walter: 136, 138 b;World Pictures: 30, 55b 65 tl & br, 94-5, 138 t, 147 br, 187 br, 194-5, 213.

Special thaks to: Sandy Abbot, New Zealand consultant: Robert Mckay, India and Australia consultant; Richard Trillo, Marketing Director, Rough Guides Ltd.; STA Travel, 85 Shaftesbury Avenue, London W1.